# California Central Coast Pioneer Families

Originally published in the *Santa Maria Valley Genealogical Society & Library Quarterly*, 1980-2003

## Volume II

Genealogical Research by

## Barbara Bruce Cole

Santa Maria, California
**Janaway Publishing, Inc.**
2009

*California Central Coast Pioneer Families. Two Volumes*

Copyright © 2009 by Santa Maria Valley Genealogical Society

ALL RIGHTS RESERVED. Written permission must be secured from the
Santa Maria Valley Genealogical Society or the publisher to use or reproduce any part of this book,
in any form or by any means, including electronic reproduction,
except for brief quotations in critical reviews or articles.

Published by
Janaway Publishing, Inc.
732 Kelsey Ct.
Santa Maria, California 93454
(805) 925-1038
www.JanawayPublishing.com

2009, 2018

ISBN: 978-1-59641-186-9 (Two-Volume Set)
ISBN: 978-1-59641-418-1 (Volume One)
ISBN: 978-1-59641-419-8 Volume Two)

Second Printing: September 2018

Cover photograph courtesy of the Santa Maria Valley Historical Society.

*Made in the United States of America*

# JENKINS
## PIONEER PROFILES -- SANTA MARIA VALLEY AREA
## EARLY DAY GUADALUPE RANCHER

John Jenkins was the owner of a well developed ranch in the Guadalupe area which he successfully farmed. He was a native of Santa Barbara County, being born at Guadalupe on May 21, 1900. He was the son of John Jenkins, Sr. and Mary (Perrinoni) Jenkins. His father, John Sr. was born in County Cork, Ireland, in 1840 and died in Guadalupe in 1908. As a young man he had done some mining in Australia and later worked at building trades in San Francisco. He also raised hogs in Guadalupe where he moved with a team of horses from San Francisco in 1873.

Mary (Perrinoni) Jenkins was born in Canton Ticino, Switzerland and came to the United States in 1887, locating in Santa Barbara Co. She became the wife of John Jenkins in 1898. By a former marriage she reared three daughters: Mrs Henry Filliponini, of Santa Maria; Mrs Marion Ellis, of Santa Maria, and Mrs Minnie Rianda of Lompoc.

John Jenkins graduated from the Santa Maria High School in 1919. His first employment was with the E. D. Rubel Company, at the old Crescent Garage in Santa Maria where he remained until 1921. At that time he moved back to Guadalupe, having moved from Guadalupe to Santa Maria in 1915. He then gave his full attention to operating the ranch which his father had originally purchased on coming to Guadalupe. Since he owned and operated the ranch vegetables were produced exclusively. The Jenkins ranch had produced one of the first acreages of lettuce to be commercially packed from the Santa Maria Valley, and in 1935 the first extensive planting of artichokes.

John Jenkins jr was married to Miss Ramona Evangeline Fitzgibbons on Sept 20, 1921, in Santa Barbara. She was born in Aromas, Monterey County, CA Aug. 16, 1900. She attended public schools at Paso Robles. She is the daughter of Michael F and Maggie (Waiters) Fitzgibbons, Maggie being a native of Georgia. Her father was native of Ireland, located in San Francisco and was a hotel man. John Jenkins jr and Ramona had two children, Eugene Michael, born in Guadalupe on March 14, 1927, and John Lee, born in Santa Maria, Aug. 20, 1936.

*Note*: the information above was taken out of the *History of Santa Barbara County, Its People and Its Resources*, Harold McLean Meier, Publisher, 1939 Santa Barbara, CA; Biographical Editor: James Clement Reid, Ph.D. Santa Maria Public Library.

Obituary from the *Santa Maria Times*, September 5, 1908: John Jenkins passes away. John Jenkins died in Guadalupe on Tuesday last, aged 68 years and 3 months. Mr Jenkins had been in ill health for several weeks and although everything possible was done to prolong his life, the end was inevitable. The funeral took place on Wednesday afternoon in the Guadalupe Cemetery.
The above obituary was taken from the Santa Maria Valley Gen. Society's quarterly for Fall/Winter of 1987…excerpts from early weekly newspaper…*Santa Maria Times*.

In the *Santa Maria Times* of Wednesday, Feb. 1, 1984 appeared a "Notice of Sale of Real Property" – in The Matter of the Estate of John Jenkins, Deceased…(John Jenkins, Jr.), John Jenkins, Jr. died in 1978. So the ranch passed out of the hands of the Jenkins family after three generations, having been worked by Grandson, Eugene Michael Jenkins for sometime also.

Eugene Michael (Mike) Jenkins also passed away in February 1985, burial in the Santa Maria Cemetery. Obituary in *Santa Maria Times*, of Tuesday, February 19, 1985.

Submitted by Kathryn Brown

# JENSEN
## DANISH PIONEERS OF THE CENTRAL COAST

Jens Peder Jensen     b. Adsbol DK 19 June 1840
   1910 cen: Mesa Rd., Nipomo     d. Nipomo 4 Oct 1913 @73/3/15; SM cem
   imm. 1884     notice Local Paragraphs Oct 11
     F: Thomas Jensen
     M: Sinnet Marie Jessen
     GF: Jens Pedersen; GM: Maren Thomasdatter
    m. Loite-Kirkeby, Ensted Parish, Schleswig-Holstein 13 Jan 1866
Mette Helene Holdt     b. Loite-Kirkeby 27 June 1843
   1910 cen: imm. 1898; 8 births 6 living     d. at home of dau Mrs Laura Abeloe, Careaga
   1929: 4 sons 2 daughters     27 Nov 1929 @85/7/9; SM cem
     obit Fri Nov 29 p.5. 32 yrs SMv

   Mette and the six children immigrated to Nipomo between 1884 and 1888, according to family history; Jens came in the late '90's – (compare with census date). All the children were born in Loite-Kirkeby. Through the centuries this area was Danish, then German, then Danish, then Prussian, and again German. The "Schleswig-Holstein question" was finally settled in 1920 with a democratic vote by the local inhabitants. Its history is complex, but this family is not; it is Danish.

1. Maria Jensen     b. Loite 17 Nov 1867
     d. Nipomo 20 June 1937 @69/7/3; SM cem
     obit Mon June 21 p.1; to SM 50 yrs ago
    m. San Luis Obispo 6 July 1891 by Wm M Hersman, D28
     wit: Mary H Hersman, Hugh S Hersman
   Hans Mehlschau     b. Apenrade DK 21 Jan 1866
    Mehlschau ranch, Nipomo     (Apenrade = Aabenraa)
    1910 cen: Nipomo, imm. 1880     d. Nipomo 29 Nov 1950 @84/10/8; SM cem
    1892 GR: 26 5'11¾ lt blu auburn     one of five brothers
    farmer DK Nipomo; nat 25 Nov 1887     F: Peter Hansen Mehlschau
    SLO Sup Ct; wit: John C May, Joseph     M: Cathrine Dorathea Lorenzen
    Wear, 1st V P Santa Maria Guarantee Building-Loan Assn.
    a. Mattie Catrina 1892-1977 SM cem; single
    b. Flora Helen 1894-1910 SM cem; single
    c. Hans Christian jr 1902-1976 SM cem; m.1 Lillian Freeman 1905-1960 SM cem; 2 ch
       m.2 Alma Anna (Peterson) Mead 1903-1993
2. Thomas Jensen 1868-1958    See his chart
3. Laura Jensen 1871-1936    See Michael Abeloe jr chart
4. Lawrence H Jensen     b. Loite 18 April 1877
    1910 cen: Nipomo-SM Rd     d. Nipomo 23 Sep 1931 @54/4/8; SM cem
     m. San Luis Obispo Co 4 Oct 1901; wit: Hans Lorentzen, Nipomo; Emma Hansen, SLO
   Johanna Abeloe     b. SLO co 24 Sep 1883
    1900 cen: w/Uncle Mike     d. Nipomo 17 Feb 1940 @56/5/14; SM cem
    1910 cen: 3 births 3 living     F: Peter Andreas Abeloe 1853-1930
     M: Ingeborg Beck 1861-1896
    a. Albert Ingward 1903-1952 SM cem
      m.1 1922 (div 1930) Luella Alice Schofield b. c1908
         she m.2 Abino Francis Chiesa 1900-1959 IOOF cem SLO
         m.3 - - Mason, in Long Beach 1944
      m.2 (div 1945) Maybelle Lucille Clayton 1900-1960
         she m.1 1922 (div 1932) Warren Otheo Knotts

  b. Inga (Ingeborg) Elizabeth 1905-1988 SM cem
    m. Carl Christian Marinus Nielsen 1901-1981 SM cem; 2 ch
  c. Lawrence Peter 1907-1958 m. Emma Evelyn Adams 1907-1971; 4 ch
  d. Ida Martha 1911-1994  m.1 James Frank Draper 1902-1989 div; 2 ch
            m.2 Clifford "Logan" Roach 1905-1992
  e. Johanna Amalia b. 1918  m.1 Harold Fobes Brown div; 2 ch
            m.2 Wesley Brkovich, 1 ch

5. Jens Laurtz Jensen      b. Loite 20 May 1881
  1910 cen: w/parents, single    d. Arroyo Grande 6 Aug 1945, bur Watsonville
  imm. 1896; in Arroyo Grande 1937 (Verde Canyon)
    m. Alameda co 20 Mar 1914
  Hanna Christina Hansen    b. Watsonville 6 Apr 1886
    Lived w/daughter after Jens' death  d. Watsonville 4 Aug 1969; bur Watsonville
    No issue          F: Hans Hansen
              M: Cathrina Margareta Nissen
                m.1 Andrew Alex'r McGlashan 1869-1912
                dau Myrtle Georgina 1910-1993; m.1
                  Laurence Royal McIntyre 1901-72, 1 dau
                  m.2 Eugene Field Jensen b. 1906
                son Ralph Harly 1912-1912

*Note*: Many Jens Jensens lived in the local area. Some of them acquired nicknames. Jens Laurtz Jensen was "Little Jim", James Hans Jensen, husband of Maria (Abeloe-Paulson) Jensen, was "Big Jim", and Jens Jacob Senus (J.J.S.) Jensen (no relation) was "Smiling Jim". As recently as 1995 there were still people in the area that needed to identify the different Jim Jensens by using their nicknames of "Little, Big, & Smiling".

6. Miland Jensen        b. Loite 18 Nov 1883
  nat. 15 June 1915; wit: George Kohler,  d. Oceano CA 13 July 1948 @64/7/25; SM cem
    SLO; Peter Andrew Abeloe, SLO; in Berros 1937
  1940-1 Dir: wood bus 1633 N Bwy
    m. at home of bride's sister Gertrude Porter Cook, Santa Barbara 16 Feb 1921
      wit: Mr and Mrs Frank B Southwick. Thirty guests, incl: Hans Mehlschau jr, Nipomo;
      Mr and Mrs Studley, Nipomo; Percy Porter, Orcutt; Mr and Mrs Mike Abeloe, Orby;
      Ward J Mead, Bicknell
  Frances Mignonette Porter    b. Concordia KS 7 Apr 1872
    "Minnie"         d. Santa Maria 1 July 1938 @66/2/24; SM cem
    to Nipomo 1903; station agent PCRR;  F: Abel G Porter; M: Sarah Jane Baker
    artist; see display, board room    m.1 Daniel Brown Mead 1869-1920
    Mid-State Bank, Nipomo      son Ward John 1901-1978;
    No issue          m. 1921 Elsie L Sans (div)

Thomas ("J") Jensen       b. Loite, DK 12 Dec 1868
  1910 cen: Nipomo Mesa     d. Whittier CA 18 Feb 1958 @89/2/6 (cem)
    (imm. 1884) farmer      or @87 (obit); SM cem. 7gch 5ggch
  1920 cen: Nipomo (imm. 1889)    obit Thu Feb 20 p.9 imm. @12 (obit)
  1922 Dir: T J (Margt) floorman Bwy Gar h 406 E Mill
  1930 Dir: T J 406 E Mill
    nat 11 May 1891 San Luis Obispo; wit: Louis Hertz, C H Jasperson
    m. San Luis Obispo 26 Sep 1895; wit: Hans Mehlschau, Maria Mehlschau, Nipomo
Karen Margrethe Hansen     b. Aastrup DK 11 Sep 1871
  "Maggie"          d. at home of dau Catherine, Oakland CA

1910 cen: imm. 1888  30 Oct 1951 @80/1/19; SM cem
   7 births 6 living  obit Thu Nov 1 p.6. r SM 64 yrs
   1951: 4 dau 1 son  F: (Hans M Hansen); M: (Lena Marie Jensen)
   1951 pall bearers: Herman Abeloe, Hans  Bros: Jacob "Jack" Peter Hansen 1869-1957
      Mehlschau, Marinus Nielsen, Herman  Peter Hansen d. SMv 1896 @34
      Peterson, Russell Jenkins, Lawrence Abeloe

1. Helena Mette  b. Nipomo 31 July 1896
   later Helen Elizabeth  d. Whittier 31 Dec 1979 @83/5/0; SM cem
      m. Presbyterian manse, San Luis Obispo 11 Oct 1920; div c1940
   Ralph Hilton  b. Paso Robles 26 June 1898
      d. Santa Maria 17 Apr 1973 @74/9/12; SM cem
      F: Nathan Marshall Hilton
      M: Ann Maude Knaus
         1892 GR: N M Hilton 42 … NC r Estrella
   a. Ralph Elmore Hilton  b. Orcutt 3 Jan 1922; r Orange CA
      m. (3ch)
   Dorothy Edith Bell  b. Pasadena 25 Feb 1924
2. James Peter (I)  b. Nipomo 26 Jan 1898
   d. Nipomo 25 Apr 1898 @3 mos; SM cem
3. James Peter (II)  b. Nipomo 28 May 1899
   1922 Dir: Jas mech  d. Santa Maria 14 May 1942 @42/11/16;
      Crescent Gar r 406 E Mill  SM cem
   1930 Dir: r 111 Palm Court
   1940-1 Dir: slsmn Frank D Roemer h 600 N Lincoln (Buick & GMC trucks)
      m. Los Angeles 26 July 1923
   Bertha Patricia Lieber  b. Los Angeles 29 June 1900
      1940-1 Dir: slsldy Ames & Harris  d. Santa Maria 14 Apr 1962 @61/9/15; SM cem
      r 600 N Lincoln  F: Alfonso Lieber; M: Elisabeth Hanrahan
      1955-6 Dir: clk City SM  m.2 1955 Henry Baxter Ames (Ames&Harris)
      r 111 Palm Court Dr  (1879-1967)
      1st wife Nettie Hansen 1879-1953, son Oliver
   a. Patricia Dawn  b. Santa Maria 28 May 1926; rS Maria
      m.1 (3 ch, div)
   John Russell Jenkins  b. Maricopa CA 8 Apr 1924
      m.2
   Francis Whitten  b. Medford MA 4 Apr 1924
4. Matilda Eleanor  b. Nipomo 11 Oct 1901
   "Tillie"  d. Whittier 8 Sep 1962 @60/10/17; SM cem
   1922 Dir: Matilda opr SB Tel Co. h 406 E Mill
      m.1 Santa Barbara 4 Oct 1924; wit: Helen Day Burns, Geo Burns, Santa Barbara
        div. 1926, no issue
   Fred Oliver Hanson  b. Paris TX c1898
      mgr oil co store, Bicknell
      m.2 San Luis Obispo co 17 Oct 1931; wit: O L Larsen, SLO; div, no ch
   Harvey Eugene Blumberg  b. Delta CO 24 Feb 1906
      "Monk", sheet metal wkr  d. Delta CO 18 Mar 1948
      1940-1 Dir: H E (Tillie)  F: Frederick Blumberg; M: Elizabeth Barkley
        mech h 729 E Orange
   Helen and Tillie living in Norwalk 1951, Whittier 1958
5. Katrina/Catherine Dorothy  b. Nipomo 8 Jan 1905
   1922 Dir: Catherine opr SB Tel co  d. Claremont CA 5 Jan 1996; bur Hayward CA

  r 406 E Mill
 living in Oakland 1951, 1956
  m. St Joseph's Ch, San Jose 14 Oct 1927
   wit: Mary Elizabeth Kerr, Berkeley; D E Alvin, Hollywood, (groom's 2d marriage)
John William Goodfellow        b. Brookings SD 25 Feb 1894
 "Jack", physician          d. Claremont CA 23 Feb 1978; bur Hayward
              F: Shepherd Herbert Goodfellow
              M: Elise Dora Richter
              his dau: Dorothy
 a. Janet Elise            b. Oakland 20 Mar 1935
  m. (2 ch)
  John Ernest Shelley         b. Oakland 20 Mar 1933
 b. John Wm (Jack)          b. Berkeley 10 Feb 1936
  m. (3 ch)
  Jane Spencer Howard        b. San Francisco 15 Oct 1938
6. Mary Elena             b. Nipomo 16 Mar 1906
 1922 Dir: Mary stu h 406 E Mill; single   d. Los Angeles 18 July 1933 @27/4/0; SM cem
7. Harold Thomas           b. Nipomo 4 Apr 1909
              d. Nipomo 12 Sep 1910 @1/5/8; SM cem
8. Margaret Harriet          b. Nipomo 23 July 1912
 living in Sierra Madre 1951, Pasadena 1958, Solvang 1996
  m.1 Santa Maria Inn 2 Dec 1936 by Rev W F S Nelson; wit: Tom J Jensen,
   R C Smith, Santa Maria; div 1942, no issue
 Jack Wilder Duncan          b. Helena MT 28 Jan 1900
              d. 6 Nov 1947 @47/9/8; SM cem
              inf: Jack W Duncan jr
  m.2 St. Peter's Ch, Santa Maria 21 June 1947; wit: Phillip M Daniel, Patricia D
   Jensen, Santa Maria
 Arthur Edwin Mann          b. Glasgow, Scotland 18 July 1911
  architect
 a. Margaret Karen          b. Manhattan Beach CA 17 Oct 1948
  m. (div, no issue)
  Scott Letterman
 b. Elisabeth Carol ("Lisa")        b. Manhattan Beach CA 20 Jan 1951
  m. (5 ch)
  James Todd Dirkes         b. Long Island NY 1 Oct 1952
9. Thomas Harold           b. Nipomo 9 Jan 1915
 1940-1 Dir: plantman SM Milk Co r 726 S Bwy
 1955-6 Dir: Thos H (Kath) emp City SM h 500 W Mill
  living in Santa Maria 1996
  m. St. Mary's Ch, Santa Maria 9 Mar 1946; wit: Joseph G Alexander, Santa Maria;
   Patricia Dawn Jensen, Santa Maria
 Catherine Ann Brumana         b. Santa Maria 17 Feb 1923
              d. Santa Maria 23 Feb 1996
              F: John Batista Brumana 1889-1969
              M: Rosalia Ybarra 1889-1977
              m.1 Carrol Cramer, Lt, USAF; d. WWII
 a. Kathleen Margaret         b. Santa Maria 22 Dec 1956
  m.1 (div, 1 son)
  Harold Owen Thompson III       b. Pasadena 4 May 1958
  m.2 (2 sons)

| | |
|---|---|
| Joseph John Wade | b. San Luis Obispo 2 Feb 1961 |
| b. Timothy James | b. Santa Maria 21 Feb 1960 |
| c. Thomas Harold jr | b. Santa Maria 14 May 1961 |

## Notes on the T "J" Jensen Family
### by Laura Abeloe

Tom was a farmer and for a time he was also the engineer of the "Nipomo Creamery Company" which operated from 1894 to 1910. Some of the creamery stock-holders were members of the Dana, Runels, Paulson, Mehlschau, Abeloe, and Callender families. Tom retired in 1918 and the family moved to Santa Maria in 1921.

Around 1951 they moved to Whittier to be with their daughters Helen and Tillie. Maggie was at the home of her daughter, Catherine, when she died. Tom died in Whittier, six years later.

Tom used the fictitious middle initial "J" to distinguish himself from the other Thomas Jensen of the area; the "J" appears on records in the 1920's and 1930's only.

(Like the two Thomas Browns, covered in this publication who were brothers-in-law, these two Thomas Jensens were related by marriage, although less closely; the other Thomas came to Nipomo in 1890 to work for his cousin Jacob "Jack" Hansen, brother-in-law of Thomas "J". Several of their children bore the same names, (as did Browns') so a chart of the "other" Thomas Jensen is also included here. – Ed.)

### Helen & Ralph

Helen was working at the telephone company and Ralph with Union Oil Company. They lived south of Orcutt on Union Oil's "Orcutt Hill" where Ralph was employed. Around 1932, Ralph was transferred to the Compton-Norwalk area in Southern California. Around 1940 they were divorced. Helen and her sister, Tillie, who was also divorced, lived together and remained in the Norwalk-Whittier area. Helen worked as a salesclerk. Their parents, in their later years also lived with Helen and Tillie.

Ralph continued working for Union Oil Company and retired with 35 years of service. He moved back to Santa Maria after his retirement.

### James & Bertha

Bertha's birth name was Gertrude Elizabeth Lieber, but was changed when she was baptized. James attended the Nipomo Grammar School and Santa Maria High School. He attended the State Mechanical School in Los Angeles until 1916. Upon returning to Santa Maria he worked as a mechanic for local car dealers, then went into partnership with Henry L. Tilley as co-proprietor of the Automotive Garage from 1927 to 1931. He later went into business for himself. In 1937 he joined the Frank L. Roemer car dealership company and was the manager of the used car lot. James belonged to the Santa Maria Redmen Lodge and was an avid hunter. He died at the age of 43 of a heart ailment.

### Tillie

Tillie attended the Nipomo Elementary School and later the Santa Maria High School. She had been working in Santa Barbara for 18 months when she and Fred were married. Fred was also working in Santa Barbara at the time. Shortly after their marriage they moved to the Bicknell Oil Fields, south of Orcutt, where Fred was employed as manager of the store on the oil lease. Tillie would attend to the store during Fred's absence. They were married briefly and were divorced in 1926. They had no children.

Tillie's second marriage was to "Monk" Blumberg (pronounced Bloomberg). He is the son of Frederick Blumberg, born in Wisconsin, and Elizabeth "Bessie" (Barkley) Blumberg, born in Kansas. Tillie was then living in Santa Maria and working as a telephone operator. Monk was also living in Santa Maria and was a sheet metal worker. They moved to Delta, CO, where they lived for a time. Tillie and Monk were later divorced. They had no children.

Tillie returned to California to live with her three sisters. She would stay with Margaret, Helen or Catherine, for different periods of time. In 1947 she moved permanently to live with her sister Helen, in Southern California.

### Catherine & Jack

Catherine was enrolled in a fashion design class in Los Angeles when a photograph of her attracted the attention of the Hollywood film industry. She appeared in several movies in the 1920's while still continuing her classes in design school. Her first job designing clothes was for a firm in Seattle, Washington. She returned to California after a year or so and enrolled in the Armstrong Secretarial School located in Berkeley. In 1927, she was living in Berkeley and working as a secretary for a large company in San Francisco, on Montgomery Street.

Jack was a physician in Los Angeles and came to Santa Maria in 1921 to work in the office of Dr George C. Bell, while Dr Bell was on vacation. He returned to his practice in Los Angeles but later relocated to Santa Maria. He then moved his practice to the Oakland area and this is where he and Catherine were married. They later moved to Southern California.

### Mary

Mary was the sixth child born to Tom and Maggie in Nipomo. The family lived and worked on a farm located one-quarter mile south of the historic Dana Adobe at the end of South Oak Glen Ave. Mary attended the Nipomo Elementary School and the Santa Maria High School. When she was fifteen, the family moved from Nipomo to East Mill Street, in Santa Maria.

At the age of thirteen, Mary began to have epilepsy attacks. Through the years her condition continued to worsen. In 1929, further complications required her to be hospitalized near Los Angeles. The family moved to Compton for a time to be near her and to also be near their daughter, Helen. Tom and Maggie later moved back to Santa Maria, to East Orange Street.

Mary remained hospitalized near Los Angeles for the last four years of her life. She was 27 years old when she died. Rev William F.S. Nelson officiated at her funeral service in Santa Maria.

### Margaret & Jack

Jack came to Santa Maria in 1929 and worked for the City of Santa Maria. Margaret attended the Berkeley College and later enrolled in the Business School at Berkeley. They had no children and were divorced in 1942.

### Margaret & Arthur

Arthur Edwin Mann immigrated from Scotland to Los Angeles in 1925. In 1947, he and a friend, Phillip M. Daniel, started an architectural firm in Santa Maria. One of their projects is the Santa Barbara County Courthouse Complex on East Cook Street in Santa Maria. Their firm later became the Daniel, Mann, Johnson & Mendenhall Corporation headquartered in Los Angeles. The company is now part of the AECOM Technology Corporation, engaged in international design projects throughout the world.

Margaret & Arthur lived and worked in Southern California for many years. One of their lovely homes was located in San Marino and it was featured in the Architectural Digest magazine in the 1970's. They retired in 1979 to the Alisal Ranch in Solvang, into a new home designed by Arthur.

### Tom & Katie

Tom was working for the Knudsen Creamery Company as a plant man when they married. Prior to their marriage Katie had served in the U.S. Air Force during World War II and had been married to Lt. Carroll Cramer. Lt. Cramer died on Attu Island, in the Aleutian Islands, southwest of Alaska. After the war Katie returned to Santa Maria.

Tom continued to work for Knudsen Creamery Company for several years and then went to work for the City of Santa Maria as a meter reader. He retired from the City of Santa Maria in 1978, after 32 years of service.

Katie worked at Sister's Hospital, the Santa Maria Post Office, and was working in the Civil Engineer's office on Vandenberg AFB when she retired. Katie was a member of the Eagles Lodge, the St. Mary of the Assumption Catholic Church, and she volunteered for the A.L.S. Society (Amyotrophic Lateral Sclerosis) a disease known as the Lou Gehrig Disease.

Vol. XXIX, No. 1, Spring 1997, p.19


**Corrections and Additions**     [Page numbers refer to those in Quarterly]

p.15.    Jens Laurtz Jensen Naturalized 1902; 1920 cen: Los Berros

1927. Nipomo Nov 29 – Jas Jensen of Arroyo Grande and Myrtle McGlashan of Santa Cruz called on Mrs Metta Jensen. –MTrib

1910 cen: Nipomo. Daniel B Mead 40 m.10 IA OH IL telegraph opr Frances M 37 1 birth 1 living KS C/E ME artist; Ward J 9 IA IA KS Gertrude Porter sis/law 27 S IA C/E ME slswm dry gds store.

1910 Nipomo Notes. Tom Jensen has moved his family from the Hourihan ranch to his brother's cottage. –Oct 1

## The Other THOMAS JENSEN
### LOS ALAMOS PIONEERS

Thomas Jensen     b. Orra DK 30 May 1861; imm. 1889 alone
- bio M/H 955, to SF 1990,     imm. again 1894 w/family
- then Nipomo, cousin Jacob Hansen     d. Edie res Newlove Acres 8 May 1945
- 1898 to Careaga ranch     @83/11/8; SM cem. inf: Neils Jensen
- 1906 Dir: f 6½ m SE; Mrs; Tesana Miss     obit Tue May 8 p.6. 7 ch 14 gch, 3 ggch
- 1910 cen: tp6, Los Alamos tp Orcutt Rd     Moose, Neighbors of Woodcraft, Danish
- 1922 Dir: Careaga Dist Sch Bd,     Lodge, SM Pioneers
  - res Los Alamos     F: Jens Hanson; M: Anna Maria Thompson
- 1940-1 Dir: rancher Los Alamos     brother Hans in DK
- m. Orra Denmark 1888

Dorthea Maria Nielsen     b. Yesta or Varda DK 4 Dec 1859; imm. 1894
- 1910 cen: 7 births 7 living     d. at home 4 mi NW of Los Alamos 20 March
- 1902: 482a ranch Los Alamos,     1931 @70/3/16; SM cem; obit Sat Mar 21 p.3
  - supervised by Jas Jensen, Mrs Mary Serpa     in Los Alamos 35 yrs; 8 gch, 2 sisters in DK
- 1931 pall bearers: Hans Wybrandt, SLO; Hans Mehlschau, Nipomo; Jack Hansen, SM;
  - Michael Abeloe, Harriston-Careaga; Thomas J Jensen, SM; James Hans Jensen, Nipomo

1. Anna Maria Jensen     b. Riba DK 8 Aug 1890; imm. 1894
   - 1966 phbk: Annie Los Olivos     d. Los Olivos 18 Sep 1973; Ballard cem
   - m. San Luis Obispo co 22 Oct 1913; wit: Nels and Mattie Jensen
   - Frederick Christian Lang(e)     b. San Luis Obispo 10 Feb 1879
     -     d. Los Olivos 4 Oct 1950; Ballard cem
     - fireman, eng PCRR     F: Andreas Hansen Lang
     -     M: Ellen Christina Jespersen
       - 1842-1879 IOOF cem SLO
       - m. 1901 Lillie Sophronia Phillips 1881-1958
       - See end of chart
   - a. Alfred Andrew     b. Solvang 11 July 1914
     - m.1 Donna June Clarke
     - m.2 Anna Theresa (Ruggera) Rapp
   - b. Margaret Dorothy     b. Los Olivos 25 Nov 1918
     - m.1 Wallace Edward Kaeding
     - m.2 George Michael Vernor 1912-1975
2. Nels/Niels Peter Jensen     b. Riba DK 23 Aug 1891
   - wrangler     d. Santa Barbara 22 Oct 1953; Ballard cem
   - m. San Luis Obispo 10 Nov 1919; wit: Mrs Fred Lang, Los Olivos;
     - Mario Guidotti, Los Alamos
   - Olivia Mary Guidotti     b. Sudden ranch, Lompoc 20 July 1897
     - cook, Nielsen ranch     d. Solvang 18 Nov 1989
     - S Ynez HS & Mattei's Tavern     F: Pietro Luigi "Louis" Guidotti (1878-1959)?
     - No issue     M: Celestina Morisoli 1877-1939
3. James Jensen     b. Nipomo 11 Jan 1896
   - 1940-1 Dir: Jas (Mattie M) f Los Alamos     d. San Fernando Vets Hosp 3 Aug 1966
   - 1955-6 Dir: same     @70/6/22; SM cem; obit Aug 5 lived w/step
     -     dau Mrs Wm Edwards, 2 step-gch
   - m. c1936?
   - Mattie Mabelle Kindle     b. Graysville OH 1 Apr 1890
     -     d. SM 18 Jan 1963 @72/9/17; SM cem obit Sat
     -     Jan 19 p.2 r 390 St Joseph St, Los Alamos.
     -     8 gch

    her children:                                            m.1 Charles Mathews
- Charles E Mathews in OH 1963
- Jake Mathews in Prescott AZ 1963
- Grace Mathews (Wm A Edwards) in Los Alamos 1963

1963: brothers: Homer Kindle, OH; Clyde Kindle, Los Angeles; Howard, Beve, Wm Kindle, Mindina (Medina?) OH; sisters Mrs Mary Craig, Woodsville OH; Mrs Anne Berger, Long Beach

4. Matilda Madeline Jensen            b. Nipomo 23 Feb 1897; m. of Los Alamos
    "Mattie"                               d. Santa Maria 5 Oct 1970 @73/7/12; SM cem
      1922 Dir: Mattie Jensen housekeeper Careaga Dist
          m. Santa Barbara 23 Dec 1926; wit: Julius Luis, Christina Luis, Los Alamos
    Lawrence Kansas Edie            b. Middleburg dist, nr Pawnee City NE
     to Solvang 1928, in Solvang 1931      10 June 1889 or 8 June; m. of Los Alamos
     1940-1 Dir: janitor SM Sch Dist        d. Santa Maria 19 Sep 1980 @91/3/9, SM cem
       r Newlove Acres RR2              F: Isaac Edie     M: Nellie Kaserman
     1955-6 Dir: Parks Supt City of SM h 205 Newlove Dr Rt2
    a. Donna Lee b. 1929 (Billy Joe Adams 1927-1979) r Ventura; 3 ch
    b. Richard Dean b. 1933 (Carol Anne Dryden); 4 ch

5. Christina Margaret Jensen           b. 13 July 1899 Los Alamos
    "Patch"; in Turlock 1945               d. Riverbank 10 Nov 1989; SM cem
        m. Santa Barbara co 26 June 1922; wit: Mattie Jensen
    Julius Ignacio Luis                 b. Azores 28 Feb 1900; imm. @7
     dairy, barber; in Los Alamos 1931     d. Riverbank 27 July 1956
     1939 to Hilmar (etc)                 F: Manuel Ignacio Luis
                                           M: Maria Palamira Lopes
    a. Gloria Marilyn 1922-1981 (Claude Kenneth Sanders II) 3 ch
    b. Harry Gordon b. 1926 (Katherin Dolores Heitkotter) 5 ch
    c. David Donald 1929-1985 (Elaine Kacenta) 5 ch
    d. Stanley Dale 1931-1931
    e. Dennis Dale b. 1934 (Margaret Louise Wyrsch) 2 ch
    f. Noma Jean b. 1937 (Jack Leon Watters) div, 2 ch
    g. Ronald Dean b. 1940 m.1 Constance Jean Parker 3 ch m.2 Judith Annette Dyer 1 ch
                     m.3 Barbara Ann Seymour (no ch)

(5)      m.2 c1959
    Theodore "Bud" Riley               b. San Francisco 8 Jan 1885
     in Riverbank 1966                   d. Riverbank CA 1 Dec 1971 (or Oct?)

6. Carl Hans Jensen                    b. Los Alamos 14 May 1901 (Careaga ranch)
    "Charles"                               d. Santa Maria 13 Oct 1984; cremated
        m. Lompoc 12 Sep 1925; wit: Julius Luis, Mattie Jensen, Los Alamos
    Laila Bethra McCollum              b. Hutchinson KS 28 Aug 1909; m. of Lompoc
     1929: truck driver (Knights of Pythias)   d. Santa Maria 8 Aug 1992; cremated
     1940-1 Dir: Chas (Laila) truck driver,    F: Frank McCollum; M: Iva Mae Stephens
       h 309 E Church
     1955-6 Dir: Chas H (Laila) emp Knudsen's, 510 W Park (501?)
    a. Robert Hans 1926-1979 m.1 Jean Beatrice Dobell 2ch; m.2 Shirley Ann (Dappen) Belk
                  m.3 Juanita (Walden) Aldrich 1939-1993
    b. Earl Thomas b. 1929 m.1 Rita Laverne Allen m.2 Dianne Louise Burritt 1937-1985 3 ch
    c. Dorothy Mae 1931-1989 single
    d. Carl Hans 1936-1986 m.1 Shirley Diane Douglas 5 ch; m.2 Janet Sue Ulmer

7. Mary Henrietta Jensen               b. Los Alamos 29 June 1903
    1931: Miss, Los Alamos               d. Los Alamos 6 Aug 1970

Vol. XXIX, No. 1, Spring 1997, pp. 20, 21

| | |
|---|---|
| | m. Dania Hall, Solvang 25 Aug 1934; wit: Charles Jensen, SM; Nels Jensen, S Ynez |
| Antone Lawrence Serpa | b. Kings co CA 4 July 1903 |
|   1940-1 Dir: Antone L (Mary) |   to Los Alamos c1930 |
|     farmer Los Alamos; 1955-6 Dir: same | d: Hanford CA at home of sister Ollie |
|   No issue |     Evangelho, 18 May 1978; Los Alamos cem |
| | F: Frank Lawrence Serpa; M: Anna Lawrence |

Tom emigrated by himself, and after earning enough money working in Nipomo for his cousin Jack Hansen, went back for his wife and two children, according to M/H, or sent for them, as otherwise thought. Before quitting Nipomo for the Careaga ranch near Los Alamos, he also worked at the Nipomo Nursery, owned by Samuel A Dana, and Lauritz/Lawrence Holdt, uncle of the first Tom Jensen.

Frederick Christian Lang 1879-1950
See first page of this chart

His father, Andrew Lange, came from Vedsted near Schleswig, in 1873, settling in San Luis Obispo in 1874. He registered to vote in 1892, age 56, 5'5, fair complexion, grey eyes, brown hair, farmer; born Denmark, residence SLO precinct Corral de Piedra, PO SLO, and was naturalized on 6 Nov 1876 in SLO Sup Ct. His wife died shortly after Fred was born.

| | |
|---|---|
| Fred   m.1 1901 | |
| Lillie Sophronia Phillips | b. Silver City NM 11 June 1881 |
|   in Los Angeles 1928 | d. Paso Robles 7 June 1958; IOOF cem SLO obit *SLO* |
|   1910 cen: tp4 Los Olivos |    *Telegram-Tribune* Sat June 7 p.2; to SLO 1930 |
|   2 births 2 living | F: General Marion Phillips 1855-1943 |
| | M: Anna Margaret Sorenson 1857-1928 |
| |   Anna immigrated 1870 from Denmark with |
| |   mother and step-father (?) Christ Markham |
| 1.  Lillian I (Remschner) | b. 20 Feb 1901; SSDI |
|     in SLO 1958 | d. SLO 17 Oct 1991 |
| 2.  Dorothy E (Mankins) | b. 18 Mar 1905; SSDI |
|     in Lansing IL 1958 | d. June 1982 (Fort Worth TX) |
| Lillie  m.2  Harry L Rice | b. Oct 1877 |
| 3.  Harry Laurie | b. 1 Mar 1914 (322 100 OR SLO) |
| | d. 11 Mar 1974; IOOF cem SLO |
|     Lillie's step-dau: Mrs Cora Lane, King City 1958 | |

*Note:* Ye Ed. submitted an article on the family of General Marion Phillips to the *Bulletin* of the San Luis Obispo Genealogical Society which was published in Vol 23 No 4 Winter 1990. Another Phillips daughter, Anna Margaret, born in 1891, married first, 1909, Thomas Sawyer, son of Thomas Sawyer and Guilma Grace _____ 1857-1910, whose second husband was Lyman L. Potter of SLO and Rinconada; Annie's second husband, whom she married in Santa Barbara in 1919, was William W. Knapp, 1869-1934, uncle of Ye Ed's mother-in-law. She was divorced again and married, third, a man surnamed Gordon. We would like to track her down, living in Paramount CA in 1971 but deceased by 1982

# JESSEE
## SANTA MARIA VALLEY PIONEERS

Archer Catron Jessee      b. Russell co VA 25 Dec 1821
  bio M/H p. 250      d. Florence AZ 19 Aug 1877
  to CA 1846
  1860 cen: Solano Co, Green Valley, PO Rockville
    m. (Atchison co MO) 1842
Mary A Harbin      b. TN Jan 1822 (cen)
     d. Santa Maria 17 Nov 1901 @79/10/16 (*Times*)
     F: James Harbin
  1880 cen: SM, wid, w/Willard, Mat, Jennie, Perry, Frank, Henry
  1900 cen: same w/Virginia, Perry, Frank, Henry
    *Note*: the ages are not consistent on the censuses
1. Anna E      b. (MO) c1845
     d. (Yolo co 5/3/1912 @60)?
    m. (Sebastopol) CA c1861 or Solano co 13 Oct 1861 (IGI)
  F M Grady      b.
     d. (Frank Grady d. SLO co 1/26/1916 @85)?*
  (1890 GR: Frank Grady 56 GA policeman SM #1. Reg Sep 1)?
  (1902 GR: Grady Frank 71 Corral de Piedra PO SLO)
    Issue: 1 known
2. James Lee      b. (Sacramento)? May 1847
     d. (St Helena) Napa co 5/25/1930 @83
       spouse initials H A
  1880 cen: Huasna, cattle herder (w/ Easton Mills in 1900)
  1892 GR: 45 5'7 light complexion grey eyes light brown hair rancher CA Huasna
  1902 GR: 55 La Panza SLO co; reg. Sep 14
  1900 cen: SLO co, Salinas tp, svt on farm of Easton Mills
    m. c1875 (cen)
  Ellen A      b. VT Nov 1856 (cen)
     d. Napa co CA 3/14/1928 @71
    Issue: 5 births, 3 living 1900
3. Ellen Parlee      b. (Napa valley) CA 1849
    m. c1872      d. (Long Beach CA c1940)
  James Roy Wilkinson      b. MO July 1848 (cen)
    1877 GR: 30 MO S Maria      d. (Long Beach) 1/17/1923 @58 (?)
    1880 cen: Arroyo Grande      1884 GR: 36 MO S Maria
    1900 cen: Riverside co, Hemet; 1902 GR: 53 Huasna
      Issue: 10 children
4. John Victor      b. Woodland CA June 1852 (cen)
     d. Santa Maria 26 April 1937 @84/9/29
    1890 GR: 34 CA surveyor SM #2 Reg. Aug 4
    1900 cen: SM
    1906 Dir: Lincoln st SM
    1909 Dir: 408 S Lincoln, C Eng
      m. S Maria 16 Feb 1888 by Morton, 3484 (*Times*)
  Mary Elizabeth McHenry      b. CA 1869 (cen)
     d. (Santa Rosa) 14 Jan 1965 @95; SM cem
     F: Wm Spencer McHenry c1834-1904
    Issue: 3 children      M: Amanda M Hamby c1841-1909

5. Archer Catron                         d. @5

6. Willard                                   b. (Napa) CA Jan 1856 (cen)
                                          d. San Luis Obispo 10 Dec 1931 @74; AG cem
      1892 GR: 36 5'10 light complexion grey eyes light brown hair; scar under chin
         farmer CA Arroyo Grande. Reg Aug 25
      1900 cen: Arroyo Grande tp     1912 Dir: AG rancher
      1920 cen: Branch city (AG?)      1902 GR: 45 Arroyo Grande #1
        m.
   Kate A Meacham                       b. CA July 1866 (cen)
                                          d. San Francisco 20 Sep 1946
                                          F: James B Meacham 1818-1894
                                             (AG cem stone read as "Amos")
              Issue: 3 children         M: Hannah 1825-1905

7. Aurelia                                 b. Middletown CA c1859
                                          d. Santa Maria 11 May 1928 @68; SM cem
            m. 1 March 1880
     Charles Bennett Dutcher          b. Sag Harbor LI, NY 1 Jan 1850
                                          d. Santa Maria 1 June 1938 @88
        1896 GR: 45 NY Sisquoc carpenter
        1906 Dir: Garey
              Issue: 5 children

8. Virginia Jennie                      b. (Napa) Mar 1862 (cen)
                                          d.
        lived w/brothers up to 1930 or later
            m. by 1937
   Largo/Larco

9. Perry Davis                            b. (Lake) co CA Sep 1866/5
                                          d. Santa Maria 11 Nov 1919 @53/1/21
        1890 GR: 23 CA lab SM #1 Reg. Aug 9 single

10. Francis Marion                     b. (Lake co ) CA Dec 1867/6
                                         d. Santa Maria 11 June 1928 @61/8/20
        1890 GR: 22 CA lab SM #1 Reg. Aug 9
        1909 Dir: Saloon, Jessee Bros r 112 N Lincoln
        1920 cen: 112 N Lincoln; also Virginia and Madison

11. Henry Haight                         b. Lake co CA Apr 1870
                                         d. Santa Maria 15 Jan 1925 @54/9/5
        1890 GR: 21 painter CA SM #1 Reg. Aug 4
        1896 GR: @27 6' light complexion brown eyes brown hair
           CA Santa Maria Deputy Sheriff
        1906 Dir: Liquor Dealer, Jessee Bros, r Main st; Mrs
            m. after 1900
    Harriett Hart                            b. England 1868; imm. 1881 or 1880
    No issue                                   d. Los Angeles 2 Oct 1932 @64/5/50; SM cem
                                          F: John Hart d. Guadalupe 27 Feb 1905 @66/10/10
                                             1890 GR: 53 painter Guadalupe; nat. Dec 20 1887
                                             SLO Sup Ct. Reg Sep 10;
                                             b. Dale Abbey, Derbyshire, Eng
                                             bro of Thomas and Reuben Hart

**Corrections and Additions**   [Page numbers refer to those in Quarterly]

Ye Ed. had Mat Jessee so firmly ensconced in the Earl family that he was left out of the Jessee chart. He should be #7 and others changed accordingly.

These San Luis Obispo marriages were located after the *Quarterly* was printed.

1. Anna E Jessee
    Frank M Grady                               b. GA; res SLO co 50 y
        1890 GR: 56 GA SM #1            d. San Luis Obispo 6 Jan 1916 @85
        policeman                                obit *SLO Daily Telegram* Jan 28
        1899: Frank Grady hurt plowing on Schiefferly place near Edna ... well known here.
                                                    -*SLO Tribune* quoted in *SM Graphic* Mar 17
        1902 GR: 71 res Corral de Piedra* PO SLO   *near Edna
        1916: marshall, SLO; brother in GA; no immediate relatives in CA except in-laws
            in Arroyo Grande and Santa Maria.

2. James Lee Jessee                          m. @20 (probably 26) of SLO
        m. San Luis Obispo 14 Oct 1873 by W W Glover MG, A170.
            wit: A C Jessee, Mary Jessee, SLO co
    Ellen Edda Meacham               m. @18 of SLO; probably sis of Willard's wife

7. Madison Jessee                           m. @29 of Santa Maria
        m. San Luis Obispo 17 Oct 1883 by W D King, A574
            wit: Frank Grady, SLO; Mary Winters, Santa Maria.  Divorced by 1920
    Lizzie Earl             m. @19 of Santa Maria

8. Aurelia Jessee                            m. @20 of Central City
        m. San Luis Obispo 8 March 1880 by G W Barnes JP, A371
            wit: W T Mills, SLO; Frank Grady, SLO
    Charles P (sic) Dutcher             m. @ 28 of Los Angeles


Vol. XXVI, No. 1, Spring 1994, p. 5


3.b. Clarence Leonard Jessee 1886-1943, thought to have been single, as no wife or children were mentioned in obituary.  However, Clarence, age 26, of Santa Maria, was married in San Luis Obispo 20 July 1912 by H. H. Hocker, I444
        wit: Margaret Campbell, SLO; Mrs Hocker, SLO.

    Bernice Doak          b. WA          m. @24 of Santa Maria

It may be fairly assumed that they were divorced.

p.19. James L Jessee's wife was Ellen Edda Meacham, sister of his brother Willard's wife Kate. Their father, James Burritt Meacham, was a pioneer of Arroyo Grande. See In Memoriam, by P J Black, *Santa Maria Times* Jan 20 1894

Parlee Jessee Wilkinson died in Long Beach 22 Aug 1940. Her husband was a son of James Wilkinson who died before 1870 and Martha who died near Old Creek, SLO Co in 1872 @47. Their eldest daughter, Maud, married in 1898 Walter Lathrop, son of A A Lathrop and Mary Meacham, the oldest Meacham sister.

The divorce suit of John V and Mary L Jessee was brought April 15 1916; handled by Preisker & Preisker. –See *Santa Maria Times*

John Victor Jessee was survived by children Vera A Fletcher, San Quentin; Mrs Elma J Crakes, Santa Maria; Author (sic) E Jessee, Martinez; sisters Virginia Largey (sic), Los Angeles and Parlee Wilkinson, Long Beach. –Mon Apr 26 1937 p.1

p.20. Mrs John Jessee and family have moved to San Francisco. –Personals June 26 1909

Negro Attacks Mrs Jessee. Man in Uniform Sought by Police. Mrs Mary Jessee, 74, 211 W Orange, victim of attempted attack by a Negro soldier in front of her home shortly before 11 o'clock as she returned home from Pocahontas Lodge meeting ... he grabbed her by the throat and dragged her six feet. She stuck him with a hat pin 2-3 inches long before he was frightened away by her screams. Dr Conser said the fingerprints were still noticeable on her neck ... The Santa Maria Army Air Field is holding a suspect. –Jan 10 1945 p.1

Marriage: Willard Jessee @30 of Huasna m. Arroyo Grande 21 March 1887 by R W Bailey, B200p; wit: Matt Jessee, AG; Lizzie Jessee, AG.   Kate A Meacham m. @20 of Huasna.

Willard Jessee was survived by wife, 2 daughters, a son, sisters Virginia Jessee, Santa Maria, and Mrs Parlee Wilkinson, Santa Paula; brothers Madison and John, Santa Maria.
–Dec 11 1931 p.1

Aurelia Jessee Dutcher was survived by husband, sons Elmer W, San Francisco, and Eugene, Sisquoc; 3 daughters: Jessee Webber, Sisquoc; Beulah Fischer, Sisquoc; Daisy Simas, Moro; brothers: James Jessee, Petaluma; Willard, Arroyo Grande; Pardee (sic), Long Beach; John, Mathew (sic) and Frank, Santa Maria; sister Jennie of Santa Maria; 5 gch. –Fri May 11 1928 p.1
Charles B Dutcher lived with his daughter Beulah Fischer, Sisquoc. Survived by 2 sons, 3 daughters: E W Dutcher, San Francisco; Eugene H Dutcher, Santa Maria; Jessie Webber, Pine Canyon; Daisy Simas, Morro Bay; Mrs Fischer.                        –Wed June 1 1938 p.1

#7 Madison Jessee was omitted on the chart; he is shown on the Earl Chart, p.14

p.21. The last four Jessees had no issue

Uniform Adopted. The Star Base Ball Club of this place have adopted a uniform to be worn by members while practicing. It consists of white shirt, blue knee pants, red belt, red stockings, and canvass shoes. The club is composed of some fine looking athletes and will undoubtedly present a splendid appearance when uniformed.                               –Apr 22 1882

Star Baseball Club: James Wilkinson, Matt Jessee, Jeff Grady, Henry Morris, Will Tunnell, Perry Jessee, Dennis Wilkinson, Tom Welch, C B Dutcher, J V Jessee.          –May 6 1882
*Note*: seven of these men are related.

Mattie Norris Luis died 1956; see Norris chart.

# LOGAN
## SANTA MARIA VALLEY PIONEERS

Samuel Hays Hulet Logan     b. MO 1839; m. 2 @46 of SM
  1870: MEN co Calpella tp     d. Los Angeles 16 Dec 1914 @75
  1880: MEN co Little Lake pct     obit Dec 19 p.1; 5 dau 2 sons
  1890 GR: 51 MO f SM     (F: Hulet Logan m. Boone Co MO 1833
           Zerelda West)?
  1892 GR: 53 6¼ light complexion hazel eyes brown hair MO SM #1; reg Aug 8
  1896 GR: lab 57 6¼ lt haz br MO SM #1
  1900: wid, father-in-law w/Ed Norris
  1900-1905: nightwatch, Santa Maria (*Times*)
  1906 Dir: SM retired
        m. 1 Healdsburg CA 4 Feb 1858 by J T Barnes, A116; Divorced
Sarah Jane Hopper 1840-1925; see Hopper chart
        m. 2 at res of bride Santa Maria 2 Sep 1885 by Rev Chas Leach, C247
          wit: Miss Emma Logan, Darla S Leach; Div, Mar 1887 (*Times*)
Margaret Ann Lewis Mrs     b. Louisville KY 30 May 1846
  1880: SM widow     d. Lompoc 5 July 1915; SM cem
  1900: Lompoc widow w/son-     obit July 10 p. 1
     in-law J W Hobson     m.1 1860 Joseph M Lewis 1826-1909
  1910: Lompoc widow w/son     obit *Lompoc Record* Fri Apr 16 p. 1
     Walter Lewis     1870; SM. divorced SLO Co 1883; see *SLO Tribune*
           Jan 18 1884 p. 3

Children (by first wife) 8 births 7 living 1910
1. John Hulet (Hugh)     b. Ukiah CA 29 Aug 1859; m.1 @24; m.3 @65
    to SM 1878     contractor of SLO
    1884 GR: SM     d. SLO 14 Aug 1933 @72/11/15; SM cem; obit
    1890 GR: 30 stockraiser SM     Aug 15 p. 6; *SLO Daily Telegram* Aug 14 p. 8
    1892 GR: 33 5'10¾ lt blu lt CA stockraiser Alamo/Huasna PO SM
    1896 GR: 36 5'11 lt gry lt CA La Graciosa
    1900: wid w/Martha Garrett;     1906 Dir: horse dealer, r Broadway SM
    1914 Dir: Housemover 301 E Mill SM (Nettie)
    1920: 301 E Mill SM
    1923: sold construction business to A A Patterson, m. to SLO
        m. 1 SM 25 Nov 1883 by Wm Shaw ME ch; C89; wit: J Wm Shaw, George Hopper
   Emily J Garrett 1863-1897; see Garrett chart
     1897: Delinquent Tax List. Emily J Logan, Washington dist 8.58-Jun 12
        m. 2 Santa Barbara Co 23 June 1902
   Nettie O Howe Mrs     b. IL Oct 1852 (1900 cen) or 1855 (1920 cen)
    1900: 961 Folsom, SF     d. 340 Pismo st SLO 23 Oct 1926 @71/11/26
     w/Ben T Shell     SM cem obit *MTrib* Tue Oct 26 p. 4
          F: SCT; M: IL 6 births, 5 living 1900
          known Howe children: Venia (Ben T Shell),
          Ernest, Laura (Chas I White)
        m. 3 SLO 16 July 1928 by H C Taylor ME ch; Q24; wit: Frank Hopkins, Los Angeles:
          Irvin York, SLO     -*SLO Daily Telegram* July 17 p. 3
   Josephine Dover Cass     b. Templeton 8 Dec 1872; m.1 @16; m.3 @54
     1900: Morro tp SLO Co     of SLO
          d. SM May 1946 (IOOF cem SLO?)
    3 births 2 living     obit Thu May 23

Albert York 1889-1964
Irvin York 1897-1971

F: James Madison Dover 1836-1913
M: Margaret Elizabeth Hynes 1844-1931
m. 1 1887 James York 1861-1918
m. 2 c1919 Chas Albert Cass 1857-1927
m. 4 Thomas Bell Rice 1869-1956

Children (by first wife)
a. Dora
    b. (SM) 14 Oct 1884
    d. (SM) 23 Sep 1979 @94/10/29; SM cem; no obit found

  m. 1 SM 5 Apr 1903 (*Times*), apparently divorced c1926
  Frederick E Strong
    1910: Mariposa Co
      Indian Pk tp
    1914 Dir: housemover 301 E Mill (w/Logan)
    1920: 601 W Mill SM
    1926: Not responsible for debts…F E Strong-Oct 20
    4 births, 4 living 1910
    b. CA 1880
    d. (living in Redwood City 1950)
    parents IL

=Emily J b. 6 Nov 1904 (*Times*)
=Emery H b. 21 Aug 1906 (*Times*); d. Santa Cruz Co 8-26-1987; SSDI
    Came to Hugh Logan's wedding 1928
=Mona G/J b. 1908
=Frederick E b. 4 Mar 1910; d. (Prunedale) 21 Aug 1993; SSDI
=Dorothea E b. 1913

a.   m.2 _____ Edmands; living in Watsonville 1933
b. Gracie Lee
    b. 4 June 1886 (*Times*)
    d. 3 Oct 1887 @1/4; SM cem
    Card of Thanks Oct 8

c. Garrett Hulet
    1906 Dir: apprentice
    b. 12 Oct 1888 (cen) or 1886 (cem)
    d. 4 Aug 1911 @22/8/23; SM cem
  1905: Garrett Logan foreman for C L Davis harnessmaker has gone to SF to be foreman for Main & Winchester Harnessmakers. -*Times* Sep 9

d. Aymee J
    b. 5 Oct 1890 (*Times*)
    d.
  1891: Fair Premiums—Prettiest baby, Annie Logan –Sep 12
  1906 Dir: Amy Miss stu
  m.
  Frank Hopkins
    1922: SM
    1926: Los Angeles
    1933: SLO
    b. (23 Dec 1887; SSDI)
    d. (Apr 1965)
    F: Samuel Louis Hopkins 1849-1911
    M: Martha Jane Stubblefield 1860-1907

e. Lillian Clare
    d. Washington district 1 Apr 1897 @1 mo whooping cough; SM cem (*T*)

2. Zerelda J (Rilla)
    b. Mendocino Co Apr 1862; m.2 @45 of Orcutt
    d. (Los Angeles 1-28-1945 spouse J E)
  m.1 1879
  Caleb Pancoast Lownes Jr
    1880: MEN Co Calpella tp
    1884-5 McK: 160a Potter Valley sheepraiser
    1890 GR: 34 CA lab SM #1
    1896 GR: liv stab 40 5'9 lt blu br MO* SM #1   (*my error?)
    1897: Cale Lownes, asphalt mines…-1 Aug 28
    b. CA Sep 1855
    d. SM 16 July 1906 @49/10/9 (cem) or 49/10/30 (funeral card); SM cem; no obit (paper n/a)
    F: Caleb Pancoast Lownes 1803-1891
    M: Sophronia Applegate 1828-1883

1900: 8th tp sta eng      1906 Dir: Church st SM
  m.2 SLO 19 Nov 1908 by H E Smith JP; H295
    wit: C W Carpenter, Orcutt; Laura Lownes, Orcutt

James E Harvey            b. PA/MI c1867; m. @41 of Orcutt
  1910: SB            d. Los Angeles 6-22-1946 spouse ZJ
  1920: 867 Wall st Los Angeles; 1925, 1940: Los Angeles
    household included Geo B Geddes 21 MA boarder w/3 others

Children (by first husband) 5 births 5 living 1900

a. Carrie Emma            b. Calpella tp Jan 1880
    1898: visitor Sisquoc sch            d. Los Angeles 7-18-1921 spouse EA
      of Asphaltea/Sisquoc Mines (ONT)            @41
        m.1 Santa Barbara 22 July 1900
    Charles Clinton Higbee            b. IA Dec 1873
      1900: tp 3 blksm w/mother            d. (Los Angeles 4-6-1946 spouse CH??)
      1906 Dir: lab Church st            F: Chas Jas Higbee 1834-1920
      1910: Bicknell foreman oil well            M: Catherine M 1836-1907
      1922 Dir: Casmalia district oil wkr
      1920: Orcutt, Pan-American Petroleum co Lease, alone
a.     m.2 before 1920
    Ernest A Hilburg/Hilberg            b. IL 1862
      1920: 523 S Crocker, LA            d. (Los Angeles 2-3-1955 spouse JH??)
    Children (by first husband) 3 births, 2 living 1910
    =Eldrid Leland b. 20 Sep 1901: d. Guadalupe 8 Nov 1901 @6 wks; SM cem
    =Mildred H b. SM 18 Aug 1902 (*Times*); 1920: w/Ernest A Hilburg
    =William b. Oil Wells 28 Oct 1905 (*Times*); 1920: w/Ernest A Hilburg called Willena, s/dau

b. Albert            b. Ukiah 30 May 1881 (cen) 1880 (obit)
    1906 Dir: w/parents            m. @23 of SM
    1910: SB w/Harveys, no wf            d. SLO 29 May 1959 @78/11/29; SM
                                               cem obit T-T May 30 p.2;25ySM Oil Co
      m.1 SLO 7 Aug 1909 by H E Smith JP; H442
        wit: Jas G (sic) Harvey, Careaga; Zeralda (sic) Harvey, Careaga
    Ethel M Dunton            b. KS m. @24 of Los Angeles
      m.2
    Martha Rose Kwasigroch            b. Iron River MI 9 May 1887
      to Los Angeles @ 2            d. SLO 16 Aug 1958; SM cem obit *SLO*
    =Carl            *Telegram-Tribune* Mon Aug 18 p. 2

c. Lauretta            b. Aug 1883
d. Leroy            b. Jan 1886
      1906 Dir: w/parents; 1910: SB w/Harveys            d. (Los Angeles 2-10-1952 spouse HC)?
    (Hazel C            b. 2 Jan 1899; SSDI
                                               d. Los Angeles 4-24-1981)?

e. Laura            b. Nov 1891; m. @18 of Orcutt
    1910: SB w/Harveys; no husband
      m. SLO 18 Nov 1908 by H E Smith JP; H294
        wit: Jas E Harvey, Orcutt; Zarilla (sic) Harvey, Orcutt
    Carl W Carpenter            b. IA m. @24 of Orcutt (10 Aug 1888)?
                                               d. (SB June 1972; SSDI)?

f. Charlie            b. SM 18 Feb 1890 (*Times*)
                                               d. (before 1900)?

    Sisquoc school 1898: Charlie 1st gr; Laura 1st gr: Albert 5th
    Sisquoc school Fall 1899: Laura 1st; Loretta 9th; Roy 3d (ONT)

3. Greenberry Madison (Matt)   b. Mendocino Co, Nov 1863; m. @22
   1890 GR: 26 CA f SM #1   d. Bakersfield 15 July 1935 @73; obit
   1892 GR: 28 5'11½ lt gry br     *Bakersfield Californian* July 16;
     rh small CA Sisquoc PO SM; reg Aug 8     *SM Times* July 20; lion hunter; Tehachapi
   1900: Butte Co Humboldt tp     Cattle Co; Miller & Lux
   1910: Mariposa Co, Indian Pk tp
   1914: Taft
       m. SM 13 April 1886 by M C McCann ME ch; C301
          wit: Mrs S E McQuire, Mrs Anna McCann
  Elzina Jane Scott   b. Santa Rosa Sep 1866; m. @19
     d. Bakersfield 3 Sep 1946; Greenlawn Mem Pk
      obit *Bakersfield Californian* Wed Sep 4 p. 5
     F: Benjamin Welcome Scott 1830-1909
  6 births, 6 living 1910   M: Eliza Jane Freshour 1838-1909
  a. Minnie (Thatcher)   b. SM 3 Jan 1887
     d. Mariposa May 1993; SSDI
  b. Benjamin H   b. Sisquoc Mar 1892
     d. (9-1-1961 spouse L; SSDI)?
  c. Alma J   b. Jan 1898
    m.   d. Kern Co 6-24-1968; SSDI
    Albert B Hunt   b.
      1948 Dir: orthopedic mech Kern Gen   d. Kern Co 12-22-1967; SSDI
        Hosp r2127 Potomac, Bakersfield
      1952 Dir: fire observer CF&FD h1400 Lake Bakersfield
  d. Lena P (Melton)   b. (2 June 1900; SSDI)
     d. (14 Nov 1991)?
  e. Harry H/M   b. 1901
    1927 Dir: clk r1822 L, Bakersfield
  f. Ora M   b. 22 May 1909; SSDI
    m.   d. Kern Co 24 Jan 1980 (Kernville)
    Kenneth A Stubblefield   b. Kern Co 14 Feb 1908; SSDI
      1948 Dir: oilwkr   d. Bodfish/Kern 6 Nov 1969
        h1313 26th Bakersfld   F: Robert A Stubblefield 1862-1913
     M: Kate Estella Ramey 1871-

4. Emma Josephine   b. Mendocino Co Sep 1865; m.2 @24
     d. Santa Cruz Co 1-19-1933 @63 spouse HS
       m.1 Sisquoc 4 Oct 1885 by L K Morton JP; wit: Mrs Effie Stanley
  Edwin/Edward J Colby   b. ME 1848
    blacksmith   d. SM 12 Feb 1888 @39/5/17 (*T*); obit Feb 18
  a. Edna   b. Oct 1886
  b. Elsie   b. SM 19 Apr 1888 (*Times*)
      m. 2 SM 7 Aug 1889 by H W Baker JP; D41; apparently divorced
  Huston Phillips   b. TN June 1845
    1890 GR: 39 TN livry SM   d. Bakersfield 27 Jan 1922 @75; obit
      reg Aug 4     *Californian* Sat Jan 28 p.2 Jan 30
    1892 GR: 45 5'10½ dk blu   F: Reuben Phillips 1821-1892
      blk TN Santa Rita   M: Julianna (Bunch?) 1820-
      P O Stuart; reg Sep 20     m.1 1871 Georgianna Music 1854-
    1900: Arroyo Grande tp SLO Co     1937; (div)
  c. Sadie B   b. SM 26 July 1890 (*Times*)
     d. Santa Rosa 5 June 1978 @87

       m.                                            obit *SR Press-Democrat* June 9 p.15A  
        Joseph T Remington                  b. Providence RI 1882  
                                               d. Hayward CA 8 Dec 1960 @78  
                                                   obit *Hayward Review* Dec 10 p. 7  
                                               F: Henry L Remington 1859-1939  
                                             M: Martha B   1871-1938  
     =Garna (Campodonico)              b. 7 Jan 1907; SSDI  
                                             d. Santa Rosa Sep 1982  
     =Velva Nadyne (Quinliven) (Boxley)  
4.      m.3 by 1914  
   Harry S Crosby                         b. WI Aug 1880; adopted by Andrew B Crosby  
     (Harold?)                            d. (Santa Clara Co 5-18-1946; SSDI)?  
     d. Elden                             b. 1907  
       1920: 3172 23rd San Francisco  
5. Mary Frances (Frankie) 1867-1952; see Norris chart  
        m.1 at Washington schoolhouse by Rev Amon 31 May 1885; C221  
            wit: H Baker, Elizabeth Baker, also (*Times*); apparently divorced  
   Edward Thomas Norris 1866-1918  
        m.2 after 1914  
   Joseph E Geddes                    b. MA 1880 (cen) 1884 (death record)  
     1920: 867 Wall St LA              d. Los Angeles 3-2-1924 @40  
6. Georgia A                            b. Mendocino Co 1872; m. of SM  
                                             d. 1950  
        m. 1 on the Alamo 28 Feb 1892 by Rev Amon (*Times*); divorced  
   Stonewall Jackson Garrett 1858-1928; see Garrett chart  
   a. Nellie A                              b. April 1893; m. @18 of Orcutt  
                                           d. (living in Ventura 1928)  
         m. SLO 20 June 1911 by Geo Willett, Congl, I235  
            wit: F J Rodriguez, SLO; S J Garrett, Orcutt  
    Charles R Cline                     b. KS c1891; m. @21 of Orcutt  
      1920: Los Alamos                  d. (Los Angeles 1-14-1951)?  
     =Henrietta I       b. 1913  
     =(Elizabeth d. 11-3-1915 @11 hrs)  
     =Charlotte E      b. 1915  
     =Neville M (dau)   b. 1916  
     =Genevieve V     b. 1919  
   b. Eva C                                b. Jan 1895; m. @18 of Orcutt  
                                           d. (living in Ventura 1928)  
        m. SLO 28 Aug 1913 by Wm Mallagh JP: J25  
            wit: Mrs James Trujillo, SM; W M Duff, SLO  
          *Note*: Jas A Trujillo m. SLO 2 June 1913 Matilda H Bonetti  
    Benjamin Bonetti                  b. CA; m. @21 of Orcutt  
   c. Inez B (Brown)                   b. May 1897  
       m. 2 by 1914                    d. (living in Los Angeles 1928)  
   W J Bryan   (in Stockton 1914, Mayfield 1925, Palo Alto 1935, Los Altos 1940)  
7. Marcia L                              b. Mendocino Co Nov 1875  
  1914: Mrs Lownes in Lompoc (*Times*)    d. at home Orcutt 1 Oct 1940 @66/2/0; SM cem  
  1940 Dir: 836 (rear) Union, Orcutt       obit Oct 1 p. 1  
       m. SLO 18 Apr 1895 by V A Gregg, Judge D533  
            wit: E P Unangst, SLO; Maud Scott, SLO; Interlocutory decree of divorce  
               Isaac R Lownes vs. Marcia L Lownes,         -*Times* Nov 3 1915

Isaac Richard Lownes (Dick)    b. Mendocino Co May 1870
  1896 GR: lab 26 5'10½ lt    d. at home of son Neill, Atascadero, Sat
    blu br CA SM #2      June 1 1935 @60/0/25; SM cem; obit
  1900: tp 8 asphalt mine      Mon June 3 p. 6
  1906 Dir: W Cypress & Curryer, eng    F: Caleb Pancoast Lownes 1803-1891
  1910 __ eng pumping plant    M: Sophronia Applegate 1828-1883
  1922 Dir: Bicknell, engineer
    3 births, 3 living 1900; 4 births, 3 living 1910
  a. Annette    b. May 1896
       d. Arroyo Grande 16 May 1901 @7 (*T*)
        or @5/0/10 (cem); SM cem
  b. Carl Dewey    b. May 1898
    1910: w/parents    d. 11 Sep 1920 @22/4/1; SM cem
    1919: aviator, home from      obit Sep 13 p. 1; auto acc nr Whittier
      Ellington Field, Houston—Mar 22
      m. (March 1919?)
    Hazel Virginia Slater    b. WV 1 July 1899; m. 2 @24
       d. 5 Apr 1982 @82/9/5; SM cem
        obit Wed Apr 7 p. 23
       F: Stephen A Slater 1876-1961
       M: Erla A Kelly 1878-1932
       m. 2 SLO 17 July 1923; M470
      Wm Albert Gardner b. CA m. @39 of Bicknell
       d. SB Co 11-3-1971; SSDI
    =Pauline (Albert Novo)    b. 1920
  c. Audell V    b. nr Los Olivos Apr 1900
       d. SLO 19 Dec 1994
        obit Sat Dec 24
    m. 1919
    Dorothy I Slater    b. (WV) 10 Mar 1901
       d. San Jose 20 Aug 1979
        obit the *Cambrian* Aug 23 p. 10
       F: Stephen A Slater 1876-1961
       M: Erla A Kelly 1878-1932
    =Doris Lucille d. 30 Sep 1921 @1/9/3; SM cem
    =Betty Jane (Smalley) living in Cambria 1995
  d. Neill Wade    b. 11 Aug 1905 (*T*); m. @26 of Orcutt
    1940 Dir: oilwkr Orcutt    d. Santa Rosa 29 Jan 1982
      m. St James Episcopal ch Paso Robles 20 Feb 1932 by Rev C L Thackrey S109
        wit: Marcia L Lownes, SM; Myrle C Bridge, Paso Robles
    Dorothea Myrle Bridge    b. CA m. @21 of San Miguel rte, Paso
      1940 Dir: opr Dalessi Beauty Shop     Robles
        624 S Bwy, r836 (rear) Union, Orcut
       F: Marcus A Bridge 1879-1965
       M: Myrle C Reese 1886-1970

# LOGAN

    Sam Logan married into the Hopper clan in 1859; after eight children and more than twenty years he and Sarah parted company and Sam came to Santa Maria. In 1885 he married Maggie Lewis; in 1900 he told the census-taker he was a widower. He may have lived for some time in the vicinity of King City, as his son, Hugh, having come from there, reported him "hale and hearty" in January 1910.

Some of Logan's adventures were reported in the *Santa Maria Times*: Sam Logan returned on Thursday evening from Chicago-having gone thither with Mr Merritt's horses, sold to Graves of that city. Sam made the round trip without coming in contact with any cyclones or hurricanes so common east of the Rockies. -Nov 22 1890. Says the *Peoples Journal*, "Samuel Logan, of Santa Maria, visited Lompoc this week. About eight years ago he visited his old friend G W Moore our popular merchant. He expresses great surprise at our metropolitan appearance. Such wonderful growth seldom seen in an agricultural community." -Dec 6 1890. Cook and Sam Logan of Santa Maria passed through here last week. They were on some trading expedition. -Pine Grove Items, Dec 28 1896. Sam Logan is now watching after the nighthawks and fire bugs, and other little affairs that may drop in town while honest folks sleep. -Aug 18. 1900. Sam Logan has resigned nightwatchman in favor of Bud Cheney. Chas Lewelling officiates as his deputy when necessary.
-Mar 25 1905

Pioneer Passes Away

Sam Logan, one of Santa Maria's pioneer residents and for many years the nightwatchman of this city, died suddenly on Wednesday in Los Angeles. He was almost 76 years of age. He leaves five daughters and two sons, being Mrs Morris (sic)* at Taft, Mrs Harvey at Los Angeles, Mrs Bryan at Stockton, Mrs Crosby at San Jose, Mrs M. Lownes at Lompoc, Hugh Logan of this city and Matt Logan of Taft. Remains will be brought to this city and buried here...
*Norris                                                                                                              -Dec 19 1914 p.1

Maggie Lewis is an example of a difficult research subject. The 1885 marriage record for her and Sam shows them both divorced, the first and last time, apparently, that they admitted to it. She, with her first husband, Joseph M Lewis, children and step-children, had come to Santa Maria before the 1870 census, on which they appear; on the 1880 census she is shown as head of the household, "widowed" though separated may be more accurate, as Joseph didn't divorce her until 1883, as listed in the report of divorces granted in the Superior Court of San Luis Obispo County for 1883 in the *San Luis Obispo Tribune*, Jan 18 1884. Her union with Logan was terminated by her in March 1887-*Santa Maria Times* Apr 2 1887.

Sam's claim to widowerhood instigated an unsuccessful search for a death date for Maggie Logan. To make a long story short, various clues pointed to Maggie's having resumed the Lewis name, and so it proved to be. The 1900 and 1910 census-takers found her in Lompoc, <u>widow</u> Lewis. There is a space on the census form for D for divorced, but, as is so evident to researchers, honesty does not always, or often, prevail.

For the record, Joseph Lewis was survived by sons J F, W A and Charles Lewis and daughter Mrs H McDaniels of the Lompoc valley, and George Lewis of Los Angeles. Six years later Maggie was survived by Walter and Charles of Lompoc, Frank in Arizona, and step-children Lizzie and George Lewis. Other children deceased, were Ada, 1869-(1884); William, 1875-1903; and Mattie, 1862-1890, wife of J W Hobson, whose children, Frank L Hobson, Marguerite (McKay), and Grace (Saunders) were reared by their grandmother Lewis.

Hugh Logan    In his early years Hugh ran stock on a ranch on the Huasna, north of the Santa Maria river. He moved into the Santa Maria valley, and in 1887 "L Forrester moved Logan's dwelling from his ranch south of town and attached the same to his restaurant on the north side of Main St." -Oct 29. This may have been in connection with the Crosby House, established by brothers J A and A B Crosby as the first hotel in Santa Maria. It burned down in 1884, but was rebuilt. The restaurant, the Crosby Dining Palace, apparently was separately operated, William F Dutton, Hugh's step-father taking charge in 1888. In 1890 Mr and Mrs Henry Roberts (Adeline Wheat, related to the Forresters and Twitchells) became proprietors. Skipping to 1905, we find "Mrs Lena Osborne, daughter of L Hopper, leased the Crosby House" -Sep 9, but in 1906 "Baths every Tuesday, Thursday, Saturday and Sunday at the Crosby Lodging House" were being advertised by Mrs J W Clark, proprietor. One last connection to this family is the marriage of Harry Crosby, son of A B Crosby, to Emma Logan, Hugh's sister, as her third husband.

In 1907 the *Santa Maria Times* reported that Hugh Logan, "who has lived in the valley ever since he has been knee high to a grasshopper, removed to Peach Tree in Monterey County" and would be sorely missed. "His handsome residence on Pinal avenue has been purchased by Cash Glines the well known stock rancher." -Dec 28. Hugh returned to Santa Maria early in 1910, and took over where the Forrester Bros had left off in the housemoving and construction business. His ad in the 1922-23 Directory sums up his work: Logan the Housemover. House Mover, Wrecker, Building Materials, Lumber. Houses Bought and Sold. Santa Maria, San Luis Obispo, Paso Robles. 519 W. Orange Street, Santa Maria. In 1916 he "completed the razing of the old brick school house on east Main St. When the cornerstone was removed, Hugh found the original receptacle with contents in a fine state of preservation." -Jan 22. (The school was built in 1887)

The second Mrs Logan, Nettie Howe, had five living children in 1900; her obituary, obviously garbled, names, besides Hugh's daughters, Richard E (no surname) and Mrs J H Morrisey, and a sister in San Francisco. Another of her sisters, Mrs Ella Armstrong, wife of Mark Armstrong, had died at the Logan residence in 1916, survived by five daughters: Mrs A Parker, Portland; Mrs M Halivin of San Francisco; Mrs Phillips, Roseburg, OR; Mrs B F Lucas; Mrs J A Horn of Bisbee, AZ; and son Roy. Besides Mrs Logan, Mrs Armstrong was survived by a sister, Mrs Hines, of Bakersfield.

The third Mrs Logan, Josie Cass, became such in a "quiet ceremony" at the home of the bride in San Luis Obispo, 232 Higuera st. "The bride was attired prettily in blue crepe and carried Cecil Brunner roses. The couple was unattended. Following the ceremony a collation was served…." Present were Mr and Mrs Irving York and daughter Vivian; Mr and Mrs Henry Cass and children Betty June and Buddie; Mrs Frances Vaudoit; Mr and Mrs Frank Hopkins; William Bailey and Emory Strong.       -*SLO Daily Telegram* July 17 1928 p. 3
For additional details, see chart.

Greenberry "Matt" Logan     Greenberry Madison Logan, twenty years younger than his uncle, Greenberry Barton Hopper, lived in the valley for a few years but moved away before the turn of the century. When Fred Strong, Hugh Logan's son-in-law, bought a ranch in Indian Peak township, Mariposa county, in 1909 (T Apr 17 or 24) there were already several relatives in that scenic area. John Hopper had acquired a 160-acre parcel of government land and wrote his son Ken, in Hawaii, to come on back for an adjoining parcel. Ken, whose two children were Hawaiian-born, acceded so as to have at least one of his children born in his own natal state. Thelma, the oldest child, wrote and published an account of the life there before their return to Hawaii in 1910. She mentions "Uncle" Matt Logan and Newt Phillips; other related families, living in close proximity, according to the 1910 census, were Fred Strong and George Foster, neither of whom stayed long, as Fred came back to Santa Maria to work with Hugh Logan, and George, a long-time Santa Maria valley resident, moved back to the coast, establishing his residence in Arroyo Grande. (See Foster chart). Newt Phillips was the oldest son of the second husband of Emma Logan, and was married to Nettie Scott, daughter of B W Scott of Sonoma, San Luis Obispo and Santa Barbara counties. Matt Logan and George Foster also were sons-in-law of B W Scott, whose story we hope to feature in this publication before the year is out.

Matt's obituary in the *Bakersfield Californian* was headed "Former Lion Hunter Summoned by Death." "In his younger days a lion hunter in the mountains of Kern county where he had made his home for the past 40 years... He had lived intermittently in the county old peoples' home for the past four years, before that making his home with Mrs Ora Stubblefield, a sister (sic)*....Besides his hunting vocation, Mr Logan was long in the employ of the Tehachapi Cattle Company and of Miller & Lux....Survivors....four sisters: Rilla Harvey, Los Angeles; Frankie Geddes, Bellflower; Georgie Bryan, Palo Alto; Marcia Lownes, Orcutt... 11 grandchildren, 2 great-grandchildren..." When his wife died eleven years later, there were 12 grandchildren. *Ora is a daughter.

Logan Girls   Of the girls it is hard to write, what with multiple marriages and geographic scattering. Of Marcia Lownes, who spent her life in the valley we can say that she sang the Star Spangled Banner for the dedication of the flagpole in the intersection of Main and Broadway in 1918, according to the obituary of her son, Dell Lownes, who died recently. The Lownes family is included in *From Acorns to Oaks*, the history of Potter Valley 1855-1985.

Vol. XXVII, No. 1, Spring 1995, p. 21

**Corrections and Additions**     [Page numbers refer to those in Quarterly]

p.14.   Hugh Logan made a real estate trade with Cook...                              -Oct 15 1887
    Hugh Logan has rented the building bought from R D Cook and moved to the north side of Main St, to a gentleman to be fitted up for a chop and oyster house.        –Oct 22 1887

p.15.   Bert Lownes had a finger badly smashed at the Tepesquet (ranch) last Saturday while working.                                                                  –June 22 1912
    Aymee Logan's first husband was Earl W Bailey; their children were Jack and William, who died @18/3/15, listed in the Santa Maria cemetery record as Earl Logan Bailey. William Bailey was named with his mother and step-father as a guest at the third marriage of his grandfather, Hugh Logan, in 1928. Aymee G was listed with Frank Hopkins, batteryman "Exide Batteries" res 618 S Broadway, in the 1922-3 Directory, also as Mrs Frank Hopkins, clerk, Northman's, res same.
    Mrs Earl Bailey, daughter of Hugh Logan, came from Taft with two children to visit friends & relatives. (also) Mrs Earl Bailey arrived Monday from Whittier.          –Jan 10 1916
    Cousin of Luther Hopper is Killed. Billie Bailey, 18, Polytechnic student, was instantly killed yesterday morning when his car crashed off the highway near Pismo Beach ... broken neck. Nearby farmers who heard the impact rushed to his aid, but Billie was dead ... son of Mrs Amy Hopkins of San Luis Obispo and E W Bailey of Bakersfield, 2d cousin of Luther Hopper of Santa Maria. Jack Bailey, a brother, and J H Logan, grandfather, survive.        –Mon Aug 19 1929 p.8

p.17    MARRIAGE:   Carl Dewey Lownes m. @21 ME ch Santa Barbara 5 Aug 1919
        Hazel Virginia Slater @20 (Anc West, op cit)
    Guests of the Al Gardner home were Mr & Mrs Russell Cook and two children of Shandon; Mr & Mrs Everett Brickey and children and Steve Slater of the Rice ranch, and Miss Frances Slater of Santa Paula.                                                                  –Wed Dec 2 1936
    The Norris-Logan wedding at the Washington school house five miles south of town, with reception at S Logan's got a lengthy write-up in the *Santa Maria Times* by H W Baker, June 6 1885.

Vol. XXX, No. 1, Spring 1998, pp.5, 6

# LOWNES
## CALIFORNIA PIONEERS

Caleb and Sophronia Lownes came west from Indiana in 1850, settling first in Benecia, where he was judge for some time, and where she had a hand in making the first U S flag flown in California. From there they moved to Mendocino County, settling first in Cold Creek, going to Potter Valley in 1877. See *From Acorns to Oaks (Potter Valley 1855-1985)* by Delight Corbett Shelton, p. 263.

Caleb Pancoast Lownes                b. Philadelphia PA 9 Dec 1803
    1860: Vacaville                         d. 1891
    1880: MEN co. Calpella tp
    1884-5 McK: Potter Valley, FP&CP Lownes sheep raising
    1890 GR: 87 PA f Santa Maria #1; reg Sep 1
Sophronia Applegate                  b. IN 3 March 1828
      6 boys 3 girls                    d. 1883; parents KY
1. John Edward                        b. CA 1852; d. MEN co 10-6-1924 @72
2. Franklin Pierce                     b. CA 14 Apr 1853; d. MEN co 2-22-1926 @72
    1900: Inmate, St Prison San Quentin
        m.1 1887 Luzernia Viola Scott
        m.2 Elizabeth Shelton Dickey
3. Elizabeth 1854-1955 m. William Brown Hopper   See Hopper chart
4. Caleb Pancoast Jr. 1855-1906 m. Zerelda J Logan   See Logan chart
5. Ann                                  b. CA 1856; died young
6. Ellen (Hurd)                        b. 1858; living in Witter Springs, Lake Co 1935
7. Charles H                           b. Solano Co 1859; living in Ukiah 1935
8. Robert S                             b. June 1861; d. (Orange Co 9-9-1933 @72)
    1890 GR: 28 CA f Santa Maria #1: reg Sep 22
    1900: Calpella tp
    1910: Potter Valley
        m. after 1880 Nancy Ann Pickle
9. Emma (Cannon)                  b. 1868; living in Ukiah 1935
10. Isaac Richard 1870-1935   m. Marcia L Logan   See Logan chart

# McBANE
## GUADALUPE PIONEERS

Samuel McBane     b. Tuscaroras co OH 8 Apr 1834
    1850 cen: Tuscaroras co OH     d. at home of son-in-law & dau B Knotts
       Oxford tp       Nipomo 24 Oct 1901. AG cem "Father"
    to Oso Flaco 1883       obit T Nov 2; *SLO Breeze* Oct 28 p.1
    1892 GR: 58 5'9¼ fair com-     F: Nathaniel McBane
      plexion blue eyes grey hair     M: Charlotte
       dairyman OH r Oso Flaco PO Guadalupe
    1900 cen: Lompoc
    1890. On The Oso Flaco. Mr McBane has 400 acres of Pat More's place.     -July 19
    1901. County News. Samuel McBane, brother-in-law of supervisor Moore,
       died Friday, Nipomo…*Tribune*.     –*Santa Maria Times* Nov 2
      m. 1865
Mary Magdalena Moore     b. (Co Cavan) IRE 15 June 1834
    d. at home Pismo* st nr     d. Pismo* 17 Sep 1913 @79; AG cem "Mother"
      Toro, SLO; in SLO 8y       obit DT Thu Sep 18. sister Mrs Thomas
      in CA 30y       Shipman. (Eliza Shipman 1847-1923;
       Thomas Shipman 1843-1934, IOOF cem SLO)

      Her son M Fitzpatrick (obit)
       Michael Fitzpatrick       b. GA m. @22 of Oso Flaco farmer parents IRE
         m. Oso Flaco 10 Sep 1880 by M Lynch, B68
           wit: Wm Young, Lompoc; Kate McBane, Oso Flaco
      Finis Hand       b. IL m. @22 of Oso Flaco, parents IN
    Her brother "Pat" Moore died in the Halcyon Sanitarium (the old Coffee Rice
      house), Oceano 18 June 1905 @73 (obit) or 72 (cem). Born Co Cavan IRE;
      to US in youth, lived in Ohio, naturalized 16 Feb 1868 Wyandotte OH Probate
      Ct (1892 GR). To CA 1854. 1st wife Sarah J (1841-1902 AG cem); 2nd wife
      Mollie O'Connor. No issue. Obit *SLO Morning Tribune* Tue June 20 1905. cancer.
      3 terms SLO County Supervisor
6 births, 5 living 1900; "5 grown children" 1901
1. John Nathan     b. OH 1867
    1892 GR: 25 5'11½ lt blu     d. (living in Santa Maria 1901)
    lt lab OH Oso Flaco PO Guad
       m. Santa Barbara 26 Aug 1900 (Co Marriage rec)
    Winifred Deguan
2. Katherine     b. m. of Oso Flaco
               d. (living in SLO 1901, Los Angeles 1950)
      m. San Luis Obispo 18 June 1894, D427 (by RA Loomis JP)
         wit: Hernando Fernandez, SLO; Mary Alice Fernandez, SLO
    Fidel A Rodriguez     b. (SLO) 1870; m. of Corral de Piedra
    1900 GR: 30 Corral de     d.
      Piedra PO Edna     F: Desidero Rodriguez 1822-1908 OM cem SLO
                widower 1880 SLO tp
      (Katherine Rodriguez     d. Riverside co 9-25-1959)?
      (Fidel R Rodriguez     d. Riverside co 3-28-1957)?
3. Anna <u>Dora</u>     b. CA 1873
    Confirmed St Isidore's     d. (Kern co 1-18-1960) living in Bakersfield 1901,1950
    Ch Guad 1 Apr 1886 @ 12, sponsor Mary Hourihane
      m. Santa Barbara 9 Feb 1896 (Co Marriage rec)

    Lyman C Ross
4.  Mary Ellen (Mamie)               b.  IL June 1875; m.2 @25 of Lompoc
    Confirmed St Isidore's           d.  Nipomo 28 May 1904 @28; AG cem (@28/11)
     Ch Guad 1 Apr 1886 @11;           obit T June 3; Semi-wkly *Breeze* June 3
     sponsor Kate McBane             d. at mother's home of blood poisoning
  1891. Guadalupe Notes: Mr Miles and Miss McBane have the same birthday-June 20.
  1900 cen: Lompoc, w/parents, divorced
       m.1 Lompoc 9 Feb 1896 (Co Marriage rec)
  Joseph A Terry (Terra)            b.  CA/POR
  a. May F                               b.  (Lompoc) Dec 1896
       m.2 Nipomo 7 Mar 1901 by S M Dana JP, F210
         wit: B Adams, Los Alamos; Minnie (Knotts) Adams, Los Alamos
  Burnett Knotts                 b.  Elwood IN Mar 1870; m.2 @30 of Nipomo
    to Nipomo 1887             d.  at home Nipomo 19 May 1944 @74
    liquor merchant                obit Sat May 20 p.2
    Jocko's restaurant            F:  Emery Knotts 1842-1912
                            M: Lenora 1849-before 1910
                            m.1 Sallie Wood; div (later Sadie West of SM)
                            m.3 1906 Pearl L Drumm of Orcutt; div.
                            m.4 1915 May Josephine Corwin 1880-1930 AG cem
                            m.5 Teena ___; div 1938, SLO U 342
5.  George A                      b.  Springfield IL 18 Mar 1882
    to Oso Flaco @1             d.  Guadalupe 18 Jan 1950 @67; Guad cem
    Lompoc High School           obit Thu Jan 19 p.1 Druid
    Confirmed St Pat's Ch AG       S P Milling co Guad 35y
     3 June 1894 @12; sponsor James Adam
      m. 1
  Elena Feliz                     b.  San Luis Obispo 16 Mar 1878
                            d.  at home Guadalupe (16) Feb 1939; Guad cem
                               @60, obit Sat Feb 18 p.2
                          F:  Vincente Feliz 1841-1921 OM cem SLO
                          M: Bersabe Vasquez 1848-1923 OM cem SLO
  a. Irene                        b.
     m.                           d.  (living in Guad 1950, SM 1962)
    Earl W Leach                b.  18 Dec 1903; SSDI
                            d.  (Santa Maria) Mar 1980
   No issue
  b. George Samuel/Sammy        b.  Guadalupe 22 Dec 1908 (*Times*)
     1940-1 Dir: trkdrvr SB Co      d.  Santa Maria 22 Apr 1962 @53/4/0; SM cem
      5th Rd Dist                  obit Mon Apr 23 p.2; no wife/ch
      r210 S Curryer               Supt Co Rd Dept. WWII
     1947-8 Dir: Geo Sam (Elva) emp SB Co h400 W Tunnell
      =Brian Michael buried 3 Sep 1948 @2 days, first child of Mr and Mrs
       G S McBane. –*Times*   SM cem
  c. Mary/Marie                b.  (Guadalupe)
       m.1 Frank Dennis            living in Philippines 1939
       m.2    Galindo              living in San Francisco 1950
5.     m.2
  Marie Antoinette Delnotaro      b.  (Guadalupe) 30 Oct 1904
    1947-8 Dir: clk Pete's         d.  Guadalupe 7 Dec 1986; Guad cem
    Food Mkt Guad               obit Tue Dec 9 p.5

```
                    F:  Desidero Delnotaro 1868-
                    M.  Mary Bontadelli 1874-
                        m.1 Albert P Castro (Living in SF 1943; his
                        mother Mrs C Thine in Berkeley 1943)
                        (Carmela Thine d. Alameda co 12-17-1952)
                        Her dau: Estelle Maxine Castro,
                        b. SF 27 Aug 1929; d. Guad 20 Feb 1943
                        Second Death of Meningitis in Guadalupe
                        Girl Follows Matron (Mrs Lois Faye Mabray @19)
                                                      –Sat Feb 20 1943 p.1
```

1939:   Elena McBane's family: brothers: Dick Feliz, Los Angeles; Vicente Feliz, Jr., San Luis Obispo; sisters: Mrs Martha Feliz, San Luis Obispo; Mrs Delia Martensen, San Francisco

1986:   Marie McBane's family: Julia A Caligari, Guadalupe; Lydia Antognazzi, died 1977; Emilio Delnotaro, died 1977; Milton Delnotaro, died 1979. Nieces: Mavis Hartzell, Templeton; Eleanor Hartzell, Cayucos; Arlene Murray, Covina; nephew Milton Caligari, died 1977.

Vol. XXVIII, No. 2, Summer 1996, pp. 13, 14

**Corrections and Additions**   [Page numbers refer to those in Quarterly]

p.12.   Mr & Mrs Pat More (sic) of Arroyo Grande attended the funeral of Sterling Tyler. More is guardian of his heirs.                                            –Mar 4 1893

# McCARTNEY
## SANTA MARIA VALLEY PIONEERS

George McCartney      b. IL c1846; parents IRE
  1884 GR: 36 IL f La Graciosa      d. Long Beach 30 Oct 1941
  1890 GR: 40 IL f Sisquoc      F: Arthur McCartney d. IL 1882
     M: Mary McGill 1801-1886
  1910 cen: Arroyo Grande-Nipomo rd 13 births 12 living
  1912 Dir: farmer Arroyo Grande
         m. 1878
Ida E Coon      b. IL 10 Apr 1861; F: C/E; M: PA
     d. Long Beach 11 Apr 1942 @81
     mother's maiden name Bowman

  1886. Burned to Death. On Saturday last a terrible catastrophe happened about twelve miles southeast of this place, in the vicinity of Cat Canyon, resulting in the fatal burning of Mrs McCartney, a lady 80 years of age. Mr McCartney and family and his aged mother were camping out and on the day of the tragedy he and his wife left the children in camp with their grandmother and went a short distance to where he was chopping wood. What transpired after they left the camp as told by the children was the fire went out and the old lady scraped together the dry limbs and leaves and started another, and in the operation her clothing took fire. The little children did what they could to extinguish the flames by throwing water upon her and finally ran for the nearest neighbors, but when they arrived the old woman was burned beyond recovery and expired shortly after. She was buried in the Catholic burying ground at the mouth of Foxen canyon on Sunday last.      –Sep 25

1. Mary McCartney (Stewart)      b. c1879 (1 Feb 1879; SSDI)
     in Redondo Beach 1931      d. (Los Angeles co 8 Nov 1962)?
2. Sarah Catherine McCartney      b. TX 26 Oct 1880; m. @26 of Arroyo Grande
     "Kate" in Ventura 1931      d. 28 Nov 1976; Calvary cem SB
     in Oxnard 1974
         m. Arroyo Grande Cath ch 23 Jan 1907 by Fr F M Lack, G456
           wit: John McCartney, Arroyo Grande; Annie Foxen, Los Alamos
     Gerald E Foxen      b. Tinaquaic ranch 11 March 1879; m. @27 of
       1906 Dir: Gerald painter      Los Alamos
       r suburban Los Alamos      d. (Ventura) 19 Dec 1962; Calvary cem SB
       for Foxen see ONT 17-42      F: Francisco Thomas Foxen 1852-1925
         M: Adelaida Botiller 1855-1933
     a. Mary Helen Foxen 1907-1908 (died at 6 weeks); San Ramon cem
     b. Joseph Francis Foxen 1909-1985 (Anne J Sierra 1919-living 2000)
     c. Cecilia Gertrude Foxen 1911-1999 (Carlos Howard Getman 1910-1999)
     d. Margaret Ursula Foxen 1913-1999 (Frank Umbro 1912-living 2000)
     e. Ida Foxen 1916-1991 (Wallace A Taylor 1907-1987)
     f. Thomas Anthony Foxen 1918-2000; Fr Bertin, OFM
     g. Josephine Edna Foxen 1922-  (Robert Davison Neville)
     *Note*: Of the six siblings, only Josephine Neville is said to be still alive, in Bozeman, Montana.      -*Times* Mar 4 2000
3. Elizabeth McCartney      b. IL c1882
     Single in New Orleans 1931      d.
4. John C McCartney      b. IL c1883 (cen); (12 Feb 1883; SSDI)
     1910 cen: w/parents;      d. (Orange co 4-11-1965)
     also head of household Los Alamos; in Long Beach 1931

5.    Hannah E McCartney     b. CA c1885
      1910 cen: w/parents     d. (before 1931?)

6.    Joseph Edward McCartney     b. ranch nr Santa Maria 6 Apr 1889; (twin)
      1910 cen: w/parents; also             bap San Ramon chapel
        w/John in Ventura 1931     d. Santa Barbara co 11 Feb 1974; Calvary cem SB
      ret Shell Oil co 1952; worked      obit *SB News-Press* Wed Feb 13 E4; 8 gch 12 ggch
        15 y in construction for            1 bro 2 sis
        Sisters of Immaculate Heart
        of Mary, Montecito
      1974. Pall bearers: Geo Daut, Carlos Getman, Milton Hayes, Robert Neville, Gerald Seim,
        Eugene Stewart
        m. St Anthony's ch, Los Alamos 28 June 1911 (the first wedding in that church)
     Maria Anna Catherine Foxen     b. Tinaquaic ranch 30 Dec 1882
       "Annie"     d. Santa Barbara co 18 May 1982; Calvary cem SB
            F: Francisco Thomas Foxen 1852-1925
            M: Adelaide Botiller 1855-1933
      a.   Phyllis Agatha McCartney 1917-    (Rbt J Ulery 1915-1970)
           Phyllis Ulery in Ojai 1974    (Robert Craun)
      b.   Richard Edward McCartney 1919-2000   Single in SB 1974
      c.   Leonora <u>Clara</u> McCartney 1920-    (Thomas Dutton Welch) in SB 1974

7.    Josephine Edna McCartney     b. Santa Maria 6 Apr 1889 (twin); bap San Ramon ch
      Catholic nun     d. St Louis MO 6 Nov 1973; Calvary cem St Louis

8.    Paul Francis McCartney     b. Sisquoc 3 Nov 1891; bap Santa Ynez mission
      1910 cen: Los Alamos     d. at home Berros Sat Dec 19 1931 @40/1/16; SM cem
        lab w/Moritz Irefeldt      obit Mon Dec 21; 5 bro 6 sis
      1922-3 Dir: Los Alamos tool dresser
      m.
     Mila More Gragg; see More chart

9.    Peter McCartney     b. CA c1892
      1910 cen: w/John      not in Paul's obit; George A, Lompoc, in Paul's obit;
            also of Westwood in Joe's obit. See note at end of
            chart

10.   Charles A McCartney     b. CA c1896
      in Ventura 1931     d. (before 1974)

11.   Ida <u>Edith</u> McCartney     b. CA c1897 (29 Oct 1896; SSDI)
      Single; in Long Beach 1931;     d. (Cypress 23 Nov 1979 SS; or d. Imperial co –CDL)
        Cypress 1974

12.   Lawrence E McCartney     b. c1900
      in Fairfax 1931     d. (before 1974)

13.   Alice G McCartney (McGee)     b.
      in Long Beach 1931     d. (before 1974)

*Note:* The chronological listing of Paul's brothers in his obituary places George A McCartney of Lompoc between John C and Joseph E. There is room for a birth in 1887. Is this he? George Andrew McCartney b. 27 Mar 1887/8; SSDI; d. Los Angeles 3 Feb 1978?

*Compiler's Comment:* Interest in the McCartney family was geanerated by a query from Mildred D Browning (Mrs George A) of Montgomery, Alabama, in 1995. She is descended from a brother of George McCartney who was the only one of the clan to come to California. The account of the tragic death of her ancestress, Mary McGill McCartney, was a sad but necessary addition to her family history.

# McNEIL
## PIONEERS OF THE CALIFORNIA CENTRAL COAST

Willard McNeil      b. OH Oct 1840; parents IRE (NY?) m.2 @44 of San Jose valley
- 1870 cen: Santa Barbara co
- tp #3 PO Santa Maria
- 1880 cen: SLO co San Jose tp
- 1884-5 McKenney Dir: W McNeil, Poso (sic)
- 1890 GR: 47 OH f San Jose reg Oct 25 1887
- 1892 GR: 51 5'8 light complexion blue eyes blond hair farmer OH Pilitas Pilitas Pozo reg Aug 19
- 1896. Former AG resident who lived in Pozo, now back in AG. —(attribution lost)
- 1900 cen: Arroyo Grande landlord parents NY
- 1902 GR: 61 AG #2
- 1910 cen: Bridge st AG; also Charles Ballagh, 50 S NY bro/law
- 1912 Dir: farmer Arroyo Grande
- 1920 cen: AG pct #2

d. died at home Arroyo Grande 10 Nov 1920 @80; Price cem AG; notice (*T*) Thu Nov 11; *SLO Daily Telegram* Sat Nov 13; funeral from home of son John

    m.1 Sutter Creek Amador co CA

Margaret A Wilson (Maggie)
- b. Lockport IL 1850
- d. 8 Nov 1880 @30/7/17; OM cem SLO
- F: Thomas Benjamin Wilson 1822-1912; bio T/W SB co 314
- M: Anna Maria Quinlon 1825-1884

    m.2 San Luis Obispo 17 Feb 1885; B42
      wit: James Wilson, SLO; Adelaide Wilson, SLO; he before married to Maggie Wilson

Ambrosina Ballagh "Amby"
- 1900 cen: 2 births 1 living
- 1901 Confirmed St Pat's ch AG 7 Oct @53; sponsor Maria E Black
- 1910 cen: 2 births 2 living (?)

b. NY Feb 1849; m. @30
d. 28 Apr 1920 @71; Price cem AG
F: Robert Ballagh d. 14 June 1903 @85; Pozo cem
M: Ellen Shelly

1. Francis Willard McNeil    b. "Center" Creek (Sutter Ck?) CA 13 July 1867
   - 1890 GR: 21 CA f San Jose reg Aug 21 1888
   - 1892 GR: 25 5'9 lt blu lt f CA Pilitas Pilitas Pozo reg Sep 10
   - 1902 GR: F W 35 Pozo

   d. Pozo 26 Mar 1926 @59; Carroll-McGovern cem obit *SLO Morning Tribune* Sat Mar 27 p.4; Pozo Postmaster 12 yr mcht Pozo 1900-    3 sons, 6 dau, 5 bro

   - 1909 Pozo Notes. Pozo Dec 20. Mr F W McNeil has been very sick the past week with a severe attack of grippe, but is now convalescent.
     G Philbrick, who visited Pozo a few weeks ago is now back, he having leased McNeil's little ranch of 80 acres near Pozo, and will in the future run the blacksmith shop at this place along with his ranching. He is a son-in-law of E Nohl. Pozo people are glad to welcome such people as Mr Philbrick and family.    —*SLO Daily Telegram* Mon Dec 20
   - 1910 cen: San Jose tp, Pozo mcht genl
   - 1916 GR: Pozo McNeil; Francis W merchant, Mrs Isabel E housewife, Miss Margaret clerk, Willard E rancher; all Republicans
   - 1918 GR: Pozo McNeil; Francis J farmer, Progressive; Francis W merchant, Republican; Mrs Isabel E housewife, Rep; Miss Margaret none, Rep; Willard E farmer, Prog
   - 1920 cen: Pozo
   - 1920-21 VR: 5'9 CA Pozo

          m. SLO co 27 Oct 1891

| Isabel E Nohl | b. Quincy (LaSalle?) IL 28 Mar 1871 |
|---|---|
| "Pet" | d. at home of son Frank 416 E Church st Santa Maria |
| 1900 cen: 5 births 5 living | 19 May 1935 @64; Carroll-McGovern cem; obit |
| 1910 cen: 9 births 9 living | *SM Times* May 21 p.5; May 23 p.6; 54y CA, 8y SM |
| 1920-21 VR: 5'4 IL Pozo | F: Eugene William Nohl 1839-1911 dep co assr SLO co |
| to SM after death of hus | M: Margaret J/A Jackson 1849-1918 |
| 1930 Dir: 214 E Cypress SM | |
| 1935: nc Miss Neva Wilson, SLO | |

a. Willard Eugene McNeil        b. (Pozo) 21 Aug 1892
    bio Phillips II 151            d. Ventura 12 Nov 1964
    1910 cen: Pozo w/parents clk genl store
    WWI. 1920-1 VR: 5'9 CA Pozo; to SM c1922
    1920 cen: w/parents
    1920 Pozo Apr 26. W E McNeil brought a truckload of calves from SLO Fri.
                                                                        –*SLO Daily Telegram*
    1924 Valley Service Station sold; on S Bwy cor Gary rd (now Stowell); (Fred) May
       and (W E) McNeil to L R Clark of Lompoc.          –*SM Times* March
    1925 Dir: W E (Marian) prop Valley Oil co r317 W Mill SM
      McNeil Brothers Service Station Personal Service New Penn, Red
      Crown, Richfield and Associated Gasoline. Free Crankcase Service
      Expert Chassis Lubrication. Broadway at Fesler Santa Maria, Calif.
      F J (Louise) prop Valley Oil Co r420 B S Lincoln
    1928 Dir: McNeil 310 W Fesler; Isabel wid; Gladys bkpr; Leonora bkpr; Jack stu
      W E (Marian) prop McNeil Bros ser sta r214 E Tunnell
      F J (Louise) prop McNeil Bros ser sta r213 S Lincoln
      full page photo McNeil Bros Complete Auto Service 400 N Broadway
    1930 Dir: McNeil Bros Inc serv sta 400 N Bdwy ½ page ad *SM Vidette*
    June 27 1930 photo McNeil Bros bldg
    McNeil F J r213 S Lincoln
    Isabel E Mrs r214 E Cypress
      Auto Service Stations, McNeil Bros, Inc. "One Stop Auto Service" Richfield
        Gasoline And Oils  Auto Brake Service  Firestone
      Products   400 N Broadway   Phone 485
    1935 in Ventura
        m. on the Alamo (ranch) at the house of M/M J A Oakley 22 Dec 1922
                                                                           -(*Times*) Dec 23 p.6

| Marian Oakley | b. on the Alamo 1 Sep 1897; SSDI |
|---|---|
| 1919: tchr Agricola sch | d. 10 May 1990 no place given |
| (w of SM) | F: William C Oakley 1866-1935 |
| 1922-3 Dir: tchr Mill st sch | M: Bertha Belle Rice 1869-1919 |
| r317 W Mill | |
| 1972 Dir: Marian O wid Willard ret 913 S McClelland     1982 Dir: Same | |

b. Margaret Mary McNeil       b. Pozo (1 of 10 ch born on McNeil ranch)
    Single                                 19 Jan 1894
                                    d. Atascadero 2 May 1980; rSLO obit *SLO*
                                       *Telegram-Tribune* May 5?; photo; bro, 2 sis
"liberated woman from the moment she left the family farm in Pozo, when she was in her 20s, until her death Friday." To SLO to live with sister, worked in a dress shop on Higuera st. Mamie Motz trained her to be a buyer in San Francisco and Los Angeles; she inherited Motz Style Shop 1940s, ran it 30 years until retirement in 1970s. First woman

on SLO City Council, served one term 1962. SLO Woman of the Year 1967. Political and charitable organizations, Soroptimists, Childern's Home Society, etc.
    1914 Dir: Motz Geo L (Mayme) mgr A Sauer Co 1303 Garden SLO
      Sauer A Co, Geo L Motz mgr grocers 848-850 Monterey SLO
    1920 cen: w/parents Pozo
    1920-21 VR: Miss 5'9 CA Pozo
    1938 phbk: McNeil Margaret r954 Pismo SLO
        Motz Style Shop 856 Higuera SLO
    1926, 1935, 1970 in SLO. Single.

c. Francis Jesse McNeil — b. Pozo 28 Mar 1896
   "Frank" — d. on the ranch Pozo 16 Nov 1970 @74; IOOF
   Dir: see above — cem SLO; obit Wed Nov 18 p.2; cattle
   1920 cen: Pozo — rancher 35y; wife, son, 1 bro, 4 sis, 7 gch
   1920-21 VR: F J 5'6 CA Pozo
   bio *Who's Who in SM*: to SM 1923; 2 bro 6 sis
   K of Pythias 1929; sta owner
   1932 in SM
     m. Inglewood 21 June 1923
  Louise Stickney — b. (24 Aug 1895; SSDI)
                                   d. Pozo/Santa Margarita 22 Dec 1979
                                   no obit found
   1938 Locals. Mrs Frank McNeil and two sons returned Wednesday from Glendale where they visited with her parents. Mrs Leona (sic) McNeil accompanied them, and will visit her daughter Mrs Wm Gaydos of El Segundo.
                                                   –*Arroyo Grande Herald-Recorder* Fri May 20
   1936 Los Angeles Extended Area phbk: Stickney A B 903 N Eucalyptus av, Inglewood; Stickney Chas A 815 N Palm, Burbank; Stickney R K 47 N Grand Oaks av, Pasadena (5 others)
  = (Helen Louise McNeil) — bur SM cem 8 Apr 1926 @0/0) ?
  = Leonard McNeil — b. (SM) 21 Dec 1927
                                     d. (before 1970)
  = Robert McNeil — b. (SM) 27 Mar 1930
   1970 in Pozo — d.

d. Belle E McNeil — b. Pozo Dec 1897
   1920 cen: w/parents — d.
   1920-21 VR: Miss 5'7 Pozo
   1926 in SM Single
   1935 in Los Olivos
   1970, 1980 in Ojai
     m.
  Stanley Slebeska
   1932. Mrs I McNeil visited dau and hus Stanley Slebeska and family, Buellton, with dau Margaret McNeil.         –Apr

e. Grace M McNeil — b. (Pozo) Sep 1899
   1920 cen: w/parents single — d. before 1970
     m.
  James Davis
   1926, 1935 in Templeton

f. Gladys E McNeil — b. (Pozo) 1903
   1920 cen: w/parents single — d. before 1970 ?
   1926 in Pozo single

m. San Diego 27 Aug 1930
- Kenneth Eugene Wilson  
  bio *Who's Who in SM*  
  1929 to SM; asst mgr McN Bros; r141 Palm Ct Dr  
  1929 K of Pythias; salesmn  
  1935 in Ventura  
  b. Phoenix AZ 2 Mar 1902; SSDI  
  d. Fremont co WY Feb 1976  
  F: James Wilson  
  M: Elizabeth

g. Leonora Adele McNeil  
   1920 cen: w/parents  
   1926 in SM single  
   Dir: see above  
   1932 Leonora Adele McNeil grad Knapp College of Nursing, SB; mother Isabel r214 E Cypress.  —Sep? 15  
   1935 in SB single; Rogers in Escondido 1970  
   b. 18 July 1905; SSDI  
   d. May 1996 Escondido  surname Rogers

h. Leita M McNeil  
   1920 cen: w/parents  
   1926 in Pozo single  
   Soper: 1935 in SB, 1970 Lakeside OR  
   1938 phbk: E H Soper r1739 Clearview rd SB  
   Harold Soper, Associated Service 1835 State SB  
   Harold Soper r115 W Junipero SB  
   b. 7 June 1907; SSDI  
   d. Dec 1977 Lakeside OR  surname Soper

   m.  
   (Harold Soper  
   b. 14 June 1903; SSDI  
   d. Lakeside OR Feb 1985)

i. Leonard N McNeil  
   1920 cen: w/parents  
   b. 28 Jan 1909  
   d. 15 Sep 1922; Carroll-McGovern cem Pozo

j. Jack Clyde Gilbert McNeil  
   1929 SMUHS  
   1929 K of Pythias slsmn  
   1932, 1935 in SM  
   1940-41 Dir: J C (Adelaide) mgr Union Ser Sta #820 (cor Bwy & Stowell) h214 N Pine  
   1970, 1980 in Ventura  
   b. 18 Sep 1911; SSDI  
   d. Ventura 2 Mar 1987 @75

   m.  
   (Adelaide Hilford  
   b. Utah 15 Nov 1914  
   d. Ventura 10 May 1995 @80  
   M: Kunkle)

*Note*: Willard's wife and Fred May's wife were Oakley sisters; Fred died in 1960, and the sisters lived together, apparently, in the May house on S McClelland.

2. John Thomas McNeil  
   1890 GR: 21 CA f Pilitas reg Sep 10 1890  
   1892 GR: 23 5'10½ lt blu blond, warts on both hands f CA Pozo Pilitas Pozo reg Sep 14  
   1900 cen: Arroyo Grande 1 birth 1 living  
   1902 GR: 33 AG #2  
   1910 cen: Arroyo Grande 3 births 3 living  
   1912 Dir: lab AG  
   b. Santa Maria CA June 1869; m. of Pozo  
   d. on outing w/son Leo 13 Nov 1932 @63; AG cem obit (*T*) Mon Nov 14 p.1; former res SM; caretaker AG cem many yrs, wid, 3 ch, 3 bro; sis/law Mrs Isabel McNeil, nephews Frank & Jack, SM

1920 cen: Allen st AG
1926, 1927 in AG
    m. Eldorado (school dist 4 mi N of Pozo) 18 Nov 1891, D94;
      wit: J P Williams, American dist SLO co; Frank McNeil, Eldorado

| Leonie Charlotte Schwab | b. Virginia City NV 8 Mar 1872; m. of Pozo; parents GER |
|---|---|
| 1938 phbk: Leona Mrs r130 Allen AG | d. San Luis Obispo 19 Jan 1960 @98; AG cem obit *SLO Telegram-Tribune* Jan 20; rPozo, then AG 34 (?) yrs; son dau bro Erwin Schwab, Alameda; 4 gsons, 13 ggch |
| 1938. Locals…Mrs Leona (sic) McNeil…will visit her daughter Mrs Wm Gaydos of El Segundo. | F: |
| | M: Hildebran(d) |

  –*Arroyo Grande Herald-Recorder* Fri May 20

a. Herbert George McNeil     b. Pozo 6 June 1893
   "Bert"                 d. SLO 26 Apr 1939 @45; spouse LW; AG cem
                                obit *T-T* Thu Apr 27 p.4; 40y AG; eldest son
   1914 Dir: Bert AG       of John & Leona, wid, 2 sons, mother, bro all
   1938 phbk: AG H G r    of AG; sis El Segundo
    AG Herbert G barber 104 W Branch

> Independent Laundry
> DELIVERS THREE TIMES WEEKLY—WILL CALL FOR
> AND DELIVER
> —SUITS CLEANED AND PRESSED—
> M c N E I L ' S   B A R B E R   S H O P
> Arroyo Grande, Cal.         Phone 51-J

                      –*Yesterday Today Tomorrow* Vol. 5 p 61 (undated)
  m. SLO co 6 June 1916

| Lyda May Clevenger | b. Saratoga CA (obit), more likely AG 15 Aug 1891 |
|---|---|
| "May" | |
| 1900, 1910 cen: w/parents AG | d. at home 30 Jan 1981 @89/5/15; SM cem obit Mon Feb 2 p.10; 2 sons, 9 gch, 6 ggch |
| 1922-3 Dir: Herbert G (Lydia M) hskpr Bicknell | F: William Thomas Clevenger 1830-1920 (reg to vote Arroyo Grande 1888) |
| 1938 Mrs May McNeil of Arroyo Grande a surviving | M: Louisiana Jane Jarboe 1851-1938 |

   daughter of Mrs Clevenger. M/M Bert McNeil lived with Mrs Clevenger after the
   death of her oldest son, Archie, in 1936.    –*Arroyo Grande Herald-Recorder*
  Fri May 17 p.1
   Locals. Mrs Nellie Kifer of Mountain View came to mother's funeral, is guest of
     sister Mrs H O (sic) McNeil.            –Ibid. inside page
  1940 to SM
  1947-8 Dir: Lyda M opr Assoc Tel Co h314 N Miller Santa Maria
  1955-6 Dir: Lydia emp Alvin av sch r129 E El Camino SM
    May wid Herb G tel opr h129 E El Camino SM
  1972 Dir: Lyda M (wid Herbert) ret h129 E El Camino

= Alton Thomas McNeil     b. AG 7 Dec 1919
   1939 in AG                d. at home SM 1 Mar 1993 @73; SM
                               cem; obit Wed Mar 3 A7; 3 dau,
                               3 sons, 9gch, 1ggch

  m.

        Helen
            1976 Dir: A T & Helen emp Union Oil h322 W Mill SM
            1972, 1982 Same
            2001 phbk: A Tom McNeil 322 W Mill
        + Elizabeth McNeil (Wilcox) Akron IA 1993
        + Patricia McNeil (Lail) SM 1993
            1982 Dir: Lail Larry & Patricia mgr Kelly-Moore Home Improvement Center
                h1038 W Cypress
            2001 phbk: Lail Joshua 322 W Mill SM
        + Gail McNeil (Doug Speer) SM 1993
            2001 phbk: Doug & Gail SM
        + Richard McNeil SM 1993
            1982 Dir: Rchd & Cynthia h815 Soares st Orcutt
        + Lloyd McNeil (Terri) SM 1993
            2001 phbk: Teri SM
        + David McNeil (Lisa) SM 1993
            2001 phbk: Lisa & David 304 W Mill SM
     = Louis Herbert McNeil                     b. (AG) 4 June 1922
         1939 in AG                             d. Sacramento co 3 Mar 1994
         1981 in Alameda
  b. Margaret C McNeil                          b. 23 Mar 1902
        1960 in Los Angeles                     d. Los Angeles co 20 Nov 1992; surname
        m.1                                        Seitrich
     William Gaydos                             (b. PA 2 Feb 1903
        1938, 1939 in El Segundo                 d. Los Angeles 4 Sep 1946
                                                 M: Stiranka)
        1960 in Los Angeles surname Seitrich
  c. Leo John McNeil                            b. Arroyo Grande 16 Mar 1905
        1928 Dir: Leo (Florence)                d. SLO 10 Aug 1960 @55; heart attack obit *SLO*
           ser sta opr r304 E Tunnell              *Telegram-Tribune* Thu Aug 11 p.2 r200 Nelson
           Santa Maria                             st AG family to AG from Pozo 1897 27y
        1939 M/M Leo McNeil, sons                  mntnc and transportation supt; wife, 2 sons,
           Harry and Baird of AG                   sis, 6gch, AGUHS          -(attribution lost)
        m.
     Florence Baird                             b. (Florence Helen b. KS 23 Feb 1905
        1960, 1969 in AG                        d. Napa co 26 Aug 1979)?
     = Harry McNeil                                b. (AG)?
        (or is this Gary?)
     = Baird Douglas McNeil                     b. Santa Maria 19 June 1929
        1960 in AG                              d. at Huasna rd home AG 10 Sep 1969
                                                   obit Thu Sep 11 p.2; real estate,
        m.                                         Fissori & McNeil
     Kathleen
        2001 phbk: K D McNeil 2061 Huasna rd AG
     + Ann McNeil
     + Mark McNeil
        2001 phbk: Mark & Linda McNeil AG
     + Rexall McNeil
     = Gary McNeil
        1960 in AG
        1969 in Concord CA

3. James William McNeil     b. Santa Maria 15 May 1871
    1892 GR: 21 5'10 fr blu     d. San Luis Obispo 8 Jan 1948 @76; res Paso Robles
      blond thumb lh bkn f CA     73y (?); obit *SLO Telegram-Tribune* Fri Jan 9 p.10; 4
      Pilitas Pilitas Pozo reg Sep 14     sons, 4 dau, 26 gch
    1900 cen: w/brother Frank, Pozo
    1902 GR: James W 30 Pozo
    1914 Dir: Jas W pumper Santa Margarita
    1920 cen: Pozo
    1920-21 VR: 5'9½ CA Union pct SLO co
    1927, 1932 in Pozo
    1938 phbk: J W rPozo
        m. SLO co 14 Dec 1905
Mary Beck     b. San Luis Obispo 6 July 1884
    1920-21 VR: Mrs Mary B 5'4½     d. Atascadero 24 Jan 1944; res Pozo; obit *SLO Telegram*
      Simmler, also Union pct     *Tribune* Mon Jan 24 p.3; hus, 4sons, 4dau, 16gch,
    1934 Pozo Dec 7. M/M James     2 bro: Nels Beck (1889-1970), Carrisa Plains; Peter
      W McNeil…Thanksgiving…     Beck (1892-1952), Oceano; sis Mrs Margaret
      most of the family present:     McGinnis (1887-1958), SLO
      M/M Harry McNeil, with     F: Hans Peter Beck 1853-1919
      Jennie and Merle of Simmler;     M: Marie Heisel 1863-1916
    M/M Wm Pierce and son Ernest of Taft; Katherine, Dick, Joe and Charlotte of Pozo
    and Miss Heisel McNeil of Long Beach.     *–SLO Daily Telegram*
   a. Harry Dutton McNeil     b. 22 Dec 1906
      1944 in Atascadero     d. Fresno 8 May 1988
      1948 in Solvang
      1974 in Atascadero
        m. SLO co 9 Sep 1929 Q388
     Ruth Myrtle Kester     b. 10 Dec 1907
      1960, 1968 in Delano     d. Fresno 26 Nov 1993
                         F: Francis Marion Kester 1838-1920
                         M: Mary R Mathews 1863-1935

     = Jennie McNeil
     = Merle McNeil
   b. Lewis J McNeil     b. c1908
      1944, 1948 in Atascadero     d. (before 1974)
   c. Heisel M McNeil     b. 9 Nov 1910; SSDI FL
      1944 in Pensacola FL     d. Winter Park FL Sep 1986
      1948 in Great Mills MD
      1974 in Winter Park FL
     (H G Carter)
   d. Allan A McNeil     b. 1912
                         d. SLO co 26 May 1923 @11; IOOF cem SLO
   e. Doris Marie McNeil     b. c1915
      1944 in Sunset Beach     d. (before 1974)
      1948 in Lost Hills
        m. SLO co 22 May 1932
     William Eugene Pierce     (b. CA 3 Mar 1907
                         d. Bakersfield 30 Jan 1976 @68)?
                         (F: Walter Wm Pierce 1874-1953
                         M: Annie E (sic) (A) Kester 1884-1968, sis of
                           Ruth Kester McNeil; son Wm in Shandon
                           1953, Morro Bay 1968)?

```
            = Ernest Pierce
                1934 in Taft
    f.  Katherine Louise McNeil             b. c1917
            1944 in Richmond CA
            1948, 1974 in San Francisco
                m. SLO co 9 June 1935
            Orval Alvin Lund                b. 18 Aug 1914
                                            d. San Francisco 26 June 1964 @77
                                            M: Greene

    g.  Richard B McNeil                    b. Santa Margarita 24 Oct 1917
                                            d. SLO 5 Oct 1974 @56; bur Atascadero obit
                                               SLO Telegram-Tribune Tue Oct 8 p.2; WWII;
                                               17y Langendorf Co; 3 dau, 2 bro, 3 sis, 8gch

            = Marilyn McNeil (Herring)
                1974 in Wausau WI
            = Barbara McNeil (Tuso)
                1974 in Torrance
            = Lodeen McNeil (Hall)
                1974 in Ontario
    h.  Charlotte Ann McNeil
            1944 in Santa Clara
            1948 in Paso Robles
            1974 in Astoria OR surname Davis
                m.1 SLO co 24 May 1941
            William Joseph Fennell
                Note: Wm James Fennell 1914-1993; d. Paso Robles
                    m. c1953
                    Margaret Mary – d. 2001
                        son Pat, in OR 1993; Pat in Paso Robles 2001—see phbk
                        dau Janet Land in Paso Robles 1993
    i.  Joseph William McNeil               b. 23 May 1921
            1944 in USN                     d. Napa co 24 Nov 1995
            1948 in Brooklyn NY
            1974 in Napa
4.  Frederick Charles McNeil                b. c1874; m. @27 of Pozo
        "Fred"                              d. San Luis Obispo 6 Sep 1927 @52; AG cem; res Pozo
        1902 GR: F C 26 Las Pilitas             obit SLO Daily Telegram Sep 8 wife 4 dau 2 sons 4 bro
          PO Pozo
        1910 cen: Branch or Pizmo st AG 3 births 3 living
        1912 Dir: lab AG
        1920 cen: AG #2 Oceano rd
        1922-23 Dir: Fred McNeil farmer south city limits state hwy PO Santa Maria (?)
        1926 in AG (?)
                m. San Luis Obispo 11 Sep 1901 by N M Ferrer, Cath, F259
                    wit: Francis McNeil, Pozo; Mary Morgante, Pozo
        Angeline Custodia Smith             b. CA 2 Oct 1884; m. @18 of Pozo; parents CA
            "Angela"                        d. SLO 8 Aug 1970 @85; AG cem
            1927 in Pozo                    m.2 6 July 1949 James Alonzo Brown
                                               1889-1975
    a.  Alice Mabel McNeil                  (b. 20 Mar 1902; SSDI
                                             d. San Jose Dec 1988)?
```

        m.1 SLO co 28 Feb 1922
   Henry Anderson Fryer                 b. CA 29 Aug 1898
    (Henry C Fryer)                    d. Sonoma co CA 10 Nov 1976
     1927 in Betteravia
     1928 Dir: Henry A Fryer, farmer, Betteravia
     1959 in SLO surname Carlson

b. Frederick Charles McNeil            b. 21 Jan 1904
   "Fred"                             d. Placer co 2 Jan 1952
   m.
   Jeanette Ludema Taylor             b. AG 18 Nov 1910
     1952 in SLO,                    d. SLO 18 Oct 1997 @86; AG cem; surname
       surname Caile                   Caile; obit (*T*) Tue Oct 21 A5; Cal Poly
     1972 in AG, surname Caile         Retiree; son, dau, 3 sis, 10 gch, 14 ggch, sis:
                                            Mary Zanoli (Jesse D Zanoli), AG (1912-
                                            1999); Helen Dana (Geo J Dana), Nipomo;
                                            Barbara Nelson (Edwin F Nelson), AG
                                        F: Oliver Taylor 1875-1952
                                        M: Lucia G Haven 1879-1972
                                       see: *Yesterday Today Tomorrow* Vol 5 p.51-54

   = Fred C McNeil
     1997 in SM
     2001 phbk: 444 Chaparral SM
   = Mary Jean McNeil
       m. SLO co 29 Feb 1948
     Alexander Wilkie Munro
     1997 in Atascadero
     2001 phbk: Munro Alexander & Mary Jean 6505 Country Club dr Atascadero
   = Dennis Taylor McNeil             b. 22 July 1938
                                        d. 25 Nov 1946; AG cem

c. George Willard McNeil               b. 1906
                                        d. 17 Aug 1916 @10; Price cem AG

d. Chester Francis McNeil              b. AG 25 June 1910
     1927 in Pozo                       d. SLO co 22 June 1959 @48; OM cem obit *SLO*
     WWII; trucking                   *Telegram-Tribune* June 23 p.2; lifelong res AG
                                        mother, 4 sis, 11 neph, 8 nc

e. Ruby Amelia McNeil                 b. 1 Mar 1912
     1927 in SLO                       d. SLO 5 July 1979 @67; AG cem surname
     1959 in SLO surname Pinnick       Pinnick
       m.1 SLO co 5 Aug 1933
   Gary Lacy

f. Dorothy Isabelle McNeil             b. 1920 cen: 6 mos old
     1927 in Pozo
     1959 in SLO
       m. SLO co 2 July 1938
   Clarence Clifford Kelley              b. CA 11 Dec 1915
                                        d. SLO co 30 Dec 1976

g. Geraldine Patricia McNeil
     1927 in Pozo
     1959 in Santa Margarita
       m. SLO co 24 Dec 1939
   William Jerome Kendall

5.  Mary E McNeil       b. 1876
             d. 14 Aug 1882 @5/7/23; OM cem SLO

6.  Edward L McNeil      b. 7 June 1878
  1900 cen: San Jose tp    d. (Culver City) 21 Aug 1963
   svt w/Cavanagh
  1902 GR: E L McNeil 24 Simmler
  1914 Dir: Edward L farmer Santa Margarita
  1918 Cambria July 16—Mrs Ed McNeil has been visiting relatives for several days. Mr
   McNeil came Saturday and they will return Tuesday to the Carrisa Plains.
                              *–SLO Daily Telegram*

  1926 in Long Beach
  1927 in Oceano (?)
  1932 in Long Beach

By Second Wife

7. Harry Wilson McNeil    b. 26 March 1891
   1926 in AG        d. Ventura co 18 Apr 1953
   1927 in Oceano
   1928 Dir: Harry W oil wkr Sisquoc; Mrs Margaret hswf
   1932 in San Fernando
  (Margaret Ann McNeil    b. IN 4 Apr 1895
              d. Ventura co 7 July 1955)?

*Note*: Clevenger, McNeil, and Taylor are treated in *According to Madge, Early Times in South San Luis Obispo County and the Arroyo Grande Valley,* Madge C Ditmas, South County Historical Society, Arroyo Grande, 1983.
  See also: *Yesterday Today Tomorrow, The Pozo Diary Et Cetera,* Special Edition 1983, p.97-99, and Vol 5, 1981-1989, South County Historical Society.

*Note*: The most recent collection of marriage dates "SLO co" with no book and page came from the recorder's office computer.

# McPHAUL
## GUADALUPE PIONEERS

William McPhaul was an early resident of the Santa Maria Valley, having come to Guadalupe in 1871 where he, though a carpenter by trade, took up sheep raising, and "soon accumulated considerable wealth" (obit). He owned some of the early buildings in Guadalupe, and, indeed, McPhaul's Hall was the scene of numerous social activities, even after his death. His name graced the Steamer McPhaul, that mythical steamboat created to ply the dry Santa Maria River from Garey to Guadalupe for the Fourth of July celebration of 1888 – a joke no doubt well understood at the time, but taken seriously last year by a writer for the Santa Maria Valley Historical Society. His occupation listed on voter registrations was Gentleman, which at the time meant Retired; although only in his early sixties, he had enough wherewithal, apparently, to cease business activities.

The IGI lists several McPhauls in Robeson County, North Carolina; theirs is the only group not using the McFall spelling.

Aside from Jennie Doane, whose family was presented in the Doane chart, nothing has been gathered on the daughters; however, the only son of the family made headlines: "Husband Kills Wife, Suicides in San Luis. Wm. McPhaul & Wife, Former SM Residents, Found Dead in Northern City" (*SM Times* Mon., Nov. 5, 1923). *The San Luis Obispo Morning Tribune*, Tue., Nov. 6, had a longer story:

### DOUBLE TRAGEDY IN SANTA ROSA ST. HOUSE

A double tragedy occurred about 7 o'clock Sunday evening at 605 Santa Rosa Street, when Mrs Mamie McPhaul, 31 was shot twice with a 12 gauge shotgun and killed, and her husband, William McPhaul, 43, after shooting his wife, shot himself through the head with an automatic pistol.

The shooting evidently occurred after Mrs McPhaul had retired for the night. From the position of the body, which was found lying beside the bed, it is believed that she attempted to rise after the first shot from the shotgun had struck her in the left arm and shoulder. The second shot, which struck her in the side just below the heart, killed her, and she fell to the floor.

The body of McPhaul was found where it had fallen. He was fully dressed. It was indicated that he had stood in front of a mirror, placed the automatic to his forehead, and fired the fatal shot.

The exact cause of the tragedy is unknown, but it is believed that the couple had quarreled. As they were alone in the house it is probable the exact cause of the double tragedy will never be known. It is supposed that they may have been drinking, as officers state a pint bottle of moonshine (prohibition was in effect) was found in the house.

The police were notified by neighbors who heard the three shots. On arriving there they found both of the McPhauls dead.

Mrs Jennie Escobar of 670 Chorro Street, mother of Mrs McPhaul, stated that she knew of no trouble between the couple. McPhaul is understood to have been working in Santa Maria as a carpenter, and to have come home to spend the weekend with his wife.

Mrs McPhaul is survived by her mother, six brothers and a sister. Mr McPhaul is survived by his mother, Mrs Alice McPhaul of Santa Barbara, and the following sisters: Mrs Warren Furman of Santa Barbara, Mrs Ed Morrell of Redondo Beach, Mrs A. (sic) C. Grisingher of Concord and Mrs Jennie Doane of Santa Maria.

The inquest will be held this afternoon by Coroner R. F. Richardson.

Mrs Alice McPhaul, mother of the dead man, was located yesterday, and will be here today, it is expected. (end)

It is only appropriate that their funerals were held on different days, and their interment in separate cemeteries (see chart).

William McPhaul                b. Robeson co NC 9 Dec 1828
   to CA 1853                       d. Guadalupe 6 June 1893 @64/5/26 (*Times*)
                                  Guadalupe cem; obit June 12
   to SBco 1871; 132a Guadalupe Rancho; Patron T/W
   1879 GR: 51 NC ranchero Guad
   1886 GR: 55 NC Gent Guad; Reg Aug 17 1882
   1890 GR: 64 NC Gent Guad
      m. Guadalupe 15 Nov 1871

Alice Lucina Battles              b. Elk Ck, Erie co PA 5 Sep 1849
   1906 Dir: A L McPhaul          d. Long Beach CA 30 Nov 1933 @84; Guad cem
      farmer Guad                       obit *SM Times*
   1900, 1910: Guad                F: Geo Washington Battles 1816-1905
   1920: 120 W Ortega St, SB       M: Freelove Crouch Bartlet 1816-1855
   1923: Santa Barbara
      5 births, 5 living;             1933: 11 grandchildren, 6 great-grandchildren

1.    Jennie Freelove               b. Guadalupe Mar 1874; m. @18
                                   d. SM 13 Jan 1943 @68/9/11; SM cem
                                      obit Thu Jan 14 p.1; r 217 N Vine SM
      m. at home of Wm McPhaul, Guad, 3 Aug 1892 by Jos W Smith (*Times*)
   George Marion Doane 1871-1920; see Doane chart

2.    Katherine E                     b. Guadalupe Oct 1875; m. of Guadalupe
     (Kate, Kitty)                   d. Sonoma co 12-23-1950
     1906 Dir: Mrs Guad, postmaster; in Concord 1923, 1933; in Petaluma 1953 (1943)
        m. Guadalupe at home of bride's mother 5 Dec 1895 by Rev J M Smith (*Times*)
     Henry C Grisingher              b. CA Aug 1873; m of Guadalupe
       1900: mcht, Guad               d.
       1906 Dir: same                  F: Acquilino Grisingher 1842-1917
       1910: Santa Cruz                M: Matilda A            1847-1921
       1920: Concord
         1 birth, 0 living 1900
     a.                                    b. & d. before 1900
     b. Vivian A                       b. 1903
     c. Carroll H                      b. 1904

3.     Alice May          b. Guadalupe Dec 1878
       (Allie)           d.
      1900: Guad w/ mother; in Redondo 1923, 1933, 1943
          m. Guadalupe 19 Dec 1901 (*Times*)
      J. Edwards Morrell

4.     George <u>William</u>          b. Guadalupe Oct 1880
      1900: Guad w/mother, painter      d. San Luis Obispo 4 Nov 1923 @43/0/18
      1906 Dir: bartender, r Main st SM          suicide, Guad cem. See article
      1920: 214 E Church, SM, carpenter
          m.
      Mamie Escobar          b. CA June 1891
        1900: Los Alamos w/fam        d. San Luis Obispo 4 Nov 1923 @31; homicide
        1906 Dir: Los Alamos w/mother          IOOF cem SLO
        1909 Dir: W Chapel SM w/mother     F: Antonio F Escobar
        No issue         M: Jennie (Silva?) 1870-1933

5.     Lulu Agnes          b. Guadalupe 16 Sep 1886 (*Times*); m. @19
      1900: Guad w/mother          d. (Santa Barbara) 2-15-1963
      1906 Dir: Miss, stu, Guad
          m. SLO at Methodist parsonage by James Blackledge; 28 Feb 1906, G281
            wit: H C Grisingher, Guadalupe; H R Rice, Arroyo Grande
      George Warren Furman         b. CA 1881; m. @25
        1906 Dir: bkpr Guad          d. (Santa Barbara) 12-18-1957
        1920: 502 E Sola, SB;           F: (Warren Furman; 1906 Dir; Guad, no occ)
          same 1923, 1933, 1943
        a. Harold          b. c1908
        b. Alice          b. c1912
        c. June          b. c1916
        d. Doris          b. 1920

Vol. XXVI, No. 2, Summer 1994, pp.12, 13

**Corrections and Additions**     [Page numbers refer to those in Quarterly]

p.12.    McPhaul-Battles marriage at residence of Thomas Dickerson near Santa Maria.
–SLO Trib

Katherine McPhaul Grisingher was living in Petaluma 1943, NOT 1953.

Vol. XXX, No. 1, Spring 1998, p.9

# MILLER
## PIONEERS OF THE CALIFORNIA CENTRAL COAST

Isaac Miller     b. VA (PA?) 1794
  1850 cen: Miller co MO     d. Santa Maria valley 14 Jan 1874 @79/9/2
    dist 13; to CA 1853        Thornburgh cem; removed to SM cem 22 Jan 1884
  1860 cen: Sonoma co Russian River tp
  1870 cen: Santa Maria
  m.
Rebecca Parker     b. VA 1795
     d. Santa Maria valley 8 Jan 1873 @77/11/12; SM cem

1.   Joel Miller     b. VA 1820; d. SMv 1880
    m. Santa Rosa 1859
    Charlotte Hinton Miller     b. IN 1830; d. Goleta 1902
     See below
2.   Elizabeth T. Miller     b. VA 1823; d. SM 1907
    m. Russian River tp Sonoma co 1858
    James Handy Harris     b. TN 1820; d. SM 1894
     See below
3.   Mary Miller     b. VA c1826
    1850 cen: w/parents
4.   Isaac Miller     b. VA 1828; d. SLO 1919
    m. NV 1864
    Anna Robrecht     b. Prussia 1858; d. (SM) 1917
     See below
5.   Sarah F Miller     b. VA c1831
    1850 cen: w/parents     d.
      m. Russian River tp Sonoma co 13 Dec 1855 by Horace Richardson, Baptist, A61
    Adam Shane     b. OH c1825
    1860 cen: Santa Rosa     d.
    a.   Mary M Shane     b. 1856
    b.   Martha E Shane     b. 1858
6.   James Sproul Miller     b. VA June 1834
    1850 cen: w/parents     d. (Sacramento 12-8-1905 @71?)
    1860 cen: Santa Rosa, sch tchr, single;     1879 GR: 44 physician SM
    1880 cen: 46 SM; 1882: (ad) Dr J S Miller Physician & Surgeon Office in
      Kallmeyers Drug Store Main St     -May 6
    1883-4 McKenney Dir: J S Miller physician Santa Maria
    1886 GR: 48 physician Central City reg Aug 16 1882
    1900 cen: physician, wid, w/Huxtable
      m. (Jas S, Sonoma co 30 Nov 1865 by McCorkle, JP, Elizabeth Patton) ?
    Susan E     b. MO Sept 1848; parents KY
    1900 cen: 1800 Howard, SF     d. San Francisco 26 Jan 1922 @73
    1910 cen: roomer w/Victor P Maynard, SF
    Susan m.2 Santa Maria 4 Jan 1885 by Chas Leach, ME ch, B185
      wit: Mrs Darla S Leach, Kitty E Miller; 1st husband still living
    Captain Elliott More 1822-1898; See More chart
    a.   Virginia L Miller     b. c1867
    b.   Kitty P Miller     b. July 1871
      m. 1893

       Henry Huxtable         b. Australia Sep 1861; imm 1872; parents ENG
          1900 cen: 342 Prospect Av SF motorman
          2 births 2 living (Harry J Huxtable d. Alameda co 4-12-1939 @74 spouse initial K)?
       = Charles H Huxtable        b. Jan 1896
  c.   James S Miller             b. Dec 1873; 1900 cen: w/mother
  d.   Mary E Miller              b. c1877
  e.   Georgia Miller             b. June 1880; 1900 cen: w/mother

1.   Joel Miller                  b. VA 1820
    1853: to CA                d. SMv 1880; reinterred SM cem 16 Jan 1884
    1858: Feb, Accts allowed Sonoma co Bd of Sups: Joel Miller's recorder's fees and blank
        warrants.                                     –*Sonoma Searcher* 17:4
    1860 cen: Santa Rosa, clerk. Joel & Charlotte's homestead recorded Somona co
        14 Dec 1860.                         –*Sonoma Searcher* 23:1
    1862: Mr Joel Miller will open a private school in the Christian Church at Santa Rosa on
        Monday. Tuition $2.50 per month.     –*Sonoma County Democrat* Jan 21
        in *Sonoma Searcher* 23:1
    1868: to Santa Maria valley
    1870 cen: Santa Maria; justice of the peace
    1879 GR: 59 59 VA farmer Sisquoc
    1880 cen: Santa Maria valley. Photo of house and family in *This Is Our Valley* p.250
    1883: Summons. Superior Court SB co: Henry J Laughlin, plntf, vs Milton D Miller,
        Admin of estate of Joel Miller, dec, and Charlotte Miller, Emma More, Everett
        Miller, a minor, Jennie Miller, a minor, and Thomas H Miller, a minor . . .
        Mortgage $4,411.50 SE4 S11 T10N R34W, SB Patent Book 234.     -*Times* April 28
      m. Santa Rosa 20 March 1859 by W W Stevenson, Min, Disciples of Christ, reg. A-4
  Charlotte Hinton Miller        b. Fort Wayne IN 15 Apr 1830
    1900 cen: tp #8 Sisquoc         d. Goleta 5 Dec 1902 @72/7/19; SM cem; obit Dec 13
    9 births 6 living              F: James Hinton
                                   M: Tress Davis   See Sleath 264
                                   m.1 Milton Davis Miller 1825-1858
                                   F: Miles Miller 1806-1874
                                   M: Rebecca Wolfe (Walsh?) 1805-1874   See Sleath 267
  a.   Emma Miller               b. (Santa Rosa) Jan 1860
      m. 1892                   d. (Santz Cruz) 11 May 1948
    Charles Owen More 1854-1932; See More chart
  b.   Everett Miller              b. (Santa Rosa) Feb 1863
      in SM Band 1881;           d.
      photo *This Is Our Valley* p.252
      1900 cen: 230 N Hill st Los Angeles, cook
        1 birth 1 living
        m. 1889
     Inez Rich                  b. OH May 1864; parents OH
     = Melville Miller 29 Apr 1896; SSDI; Aug 1967 Sunnyvale
  c.   Jennie Miller               b. (Santa Rosa) Oct 1866; m. @26 of Garey
                                  d.
      1888. Hames Valley Jottings. A party of young people, composed of J L and Nannie
        Bedwell, Chas and May Gandaubert of San Jose, Jennie Miller of Santa Maria,
        and Geo and Al Ernest, lately returned from a trip to the coast and report
        having had such a splendid time that everyone is "coast struck".
                                                                    -*Salinas Valley Index* Aug 23

*Note*: Jennie's half-brother, Milton D Miller, moved from Santa Maria to
Hames Valley (west of Bradley) about 1883.
   m. at home of bride's mother, Garey, 30 July 1893 by JW Kelsey;
     SB co marriage bk D, also *SM Times*

    Clement C Tinker                      b. MI Sep 1864; m. @28 of Goleta
      1860 GR: 26 MI f Hope             d.
      1900 cen: tp #3 (Goleta)          F: Chauncy Tinker 1817-1911
        3 births 3 living
      1911: Chauncy Tinker d. at home 630 W Mission st, SB. Pioneer to SB 1873.
        Widow, dau Miss Minnie; 2 sons, CC, Goleta; Kelly (J), SB.
                                                       -*SB Morning Press* Wed Jan 12
   = Verva Tinker b. Goleta 28 Oct 1894 (*Times*); d. Goleta 29 Aug 1990; SSDI
      m. "Frank Heinrick, orthodontist, Santa Barbara"         –Sleath 269
      1939 Goleta Dir: Dr A F Heimlich, Via Hierba, Hope Ranch
      1940 phbk: Heimlich A F Dr orthodontist 1824 State St SB; rVia Hierba
   = Dorothy Tinker b. (Goleta) 2 Apr 1896; May 1986 Goleta; SSDI
      m. Fred McCloskey 23 Mar 1896; June 1982 Goleta; SSDI
      1939 Goleta Dir: McCloskey Fred G (Dorothy L) f RFD Santa Barbara
      1940 phbk: Fred G McCloskey rHollister (Goleta)
   = Virginia Tinker b. (Goleta) July 1899
      m. David Van Reese
      1940 phbk: David Dewey Van Reese rGrove Lane Santa Barbara
   = son ( - - Sleath)
   = Chadwick Tinker killed WWII

  d.   Thomas Handy Miller               b. SMv 17 May 1869
      1890 GR: 21 CA f Sisquoc         d. (Goleta) 24 Nov 1923 @54; Goleta cem
      1900 cen: w/mother, single           obit *SB Morning Press* Sat Nov 24
      1910 cen: tp #3 (Goleta)
        Hollister av; 2 births 2 living
      m. 1904
    Mary M Sutton                         b. CA (6 Sep 1877; SSDI)
      1880 cen: Carpinteria              d. (Mar 1971 Long Beach)?
      1890 GR: Benj S Sutton 61 NY f   F: Benjamin S Sutton 1828-  ; bio Storke 293
        Carpinteria                        M: Mary Barnard c1838
                                        m.2  Albert Johnston(e) Holloway 1876-1951
                                              photo Sleath 197
                                             F: John James Holloway 1839-1918
                                             M: Rebecca Tress Miller 1853-1883
                                             See Sleath 164
   = Dorian H Miller (11 July 1905; SSDI; Dec 1979 Salt Lake City)?
   = Marian C Miller (18 Dec 1908; SSDI; Nov 1967 Corona)?
     1923. Yeast Spores Kill Pioneer. Strange Affliction Fatal to Early Resident of Santa
        Maria Valley…first white boy born Santa Maria valley; 21 years Goleta. Yeast
        spores from alfalfa…Widow Mary, son Dorian, daughter Marian, sister Mrs
        C O More, Los Alamos.                        –*SB Morning Press* Nov 24
      1939 Goleta Dir:   Albert J Holloway (Mary M) f POB 365 Goleta
                           Mrs Mary M Holloway tchr Goleta Union sch
                           Miss Marian C Miller tchr Box 365 Goleta

2.    Elizabeth T Miller                 b. VA 1823
     in SMv 30y                          d. Santa Maria valley 14 May 1907 @83/6/17
                                       SM cem. death notice May 18; obit not available

m. Russian River tp Sonoma co 10 Mar 1858 by Rev W W Stevenson, A111

James Handy Harris      b. Bedford co TN 15 Mar 1820
  to AL 1823, 12y; to MS      d. Santa Maria 7 Jan 1894 @73/9/23; SM cem
  to CA 1849; Sonoma co 1857      obit Jan 13; wife, 3 dau 1 son
  to SB co 1867, SMv 1869      Card of Thanks by members of the family - Ibid
  1860 cen: Sonoma co Russian River tp
  1870 cen: SMv next to Isaac Miller
  1879 GR: 59 TN SM
  1880 cen: SM nr Joel & Isaac Miller jr
  1882 GR: 62 TN f SM
  1890 GR: 70 TN f SM #1

a.      Sarah Frances Harris      b. Mark West, Sonoma co 3 Dec 1858
    in SB 1940      d. at home of dau 321 E Church st SM
      1945-6 Dir: hmkr r321 E Church      16 Apr 1951 @92. obit Mon Apr 16 p.1
      Estelle L Hicks hmkr      5gch, 12ggch, 2gggch. Photo
      h321 E Church

      m. Central City 5$^{th}$ tp SB co 5 Oct 1876, by M Thornburg B229
    Charles A Lewis      b. MO 1851; F: MD; M: MO
      1880 cen: SM nr Harris      d. Manvel, 21 Apr 1900 @49 (*Times*)
      1890 GR: 39 MO carp SM #2      obit/notice Apr 28
      1900: Charley Lewis, father of our former foreman Fred E Lewis died Saturday
        Apr 21 at Manvel, San Bernardino co, @49/0/25.

= Frederick Emile Lewis      b. SM 16 Aug 1877
    1906 Dir: F E bartender      d. at home 321 E Church (20) Nov 1940
      rE Church; Mrs      @63/3/4 long illness; SM cem obit Wed Nov 20 p.1
    1909 Dir: clk r309 E Church; Mrs      "former owner of *Santa Maria Times*"
    1910 cen: E Church retail liquor dealer employee
    1916: City Happenings. Miss Adele Hicks of Santa Barbara visiting Uncle Fred
      Lewis . . . M/M Fred Lewis visited relatives in Santa Barbara. –Jan 1
    1922-3 Dir: mgr San Luis Bottling Co r321 E Church
    1925 Dir: same; 1928 Dir: clk r same
    1940-1 Dir: bartender Black Bros res same
      m. San Luis Obispo 5 May 1903
  Alyce Bradley      b. (SMv) 9 Jan 1877
      d. SM 31 Oct 1939 @62/9/22; SM cem
        obit Tue Oct 31 p.1; photo p.2
      F: Charles Bradley 1840-1913
      M: Elizabeth Booth 1840-1903
    1939. sisters Mary Tunnell, Agnes Forbes, Rachel Niverth, Sadie Kelley, SM;
      Ellen Elliott, Los Angeles; Elizabeth Howerton, Santa Barbara.
      See ONT 213ff
  No issue
    July 26, 1922. Funeral of Lucile Rachel Hinds dau of M/M Matt Hinds, held
      321 E Church, home of Mrs F E Lewis. Remains sent from Sonoma State Home.

= (Clara) Estelle Lewis      b. SM 28 Feb 1879
    1947-8 Dir: hmkr h321 E Church      d. Petaluma 6 Oct 1968 @89/7/8; SM cem
    1922. Mrs Hicks of SB and 2 ch      obit Mon Oct 7 p.2; r321 E Church
      visit brother Fred Lewis      3 sons 2 dau 12 gch 15 ggch
      m.
  Thomas Beverly Hicks      b. Goleta 29 Aug 1872 (LDS Anc File)

            d. Los Angeles 2 April 1953
            F: Thomas Henry Hicks 1850-1926
            GF: Beverly Alsop Hicks
            M: Fanny P Sawyers   See Phillips II 41
  + Lewis A Hicks 1904-1985; in Petaluma 1968, d. Petaluma
  + Charles A Hicks, in Petaluma 1968
      (Charles Albert Hicks 1912-1991 SM cem; inf Joyce Rogers, niece) ?
  + Thomas H Hicks, in No Hollywood 1968
      1940-1 Dir: Tom Hicks emp Standard Oil Co r630 Union, Orcutt 1938-9 same
      1947: inf son of Thomas Henry Hicks of Guadalupe bur Sep 2 SM cem
  + Adele Carr, in Los Angeles 1968
  + Lylabelle Burke, in Burbank 1968
  = Claude Leon Lewis       b. SM 1880
                            d. 5 Dec 1895 @15/1/29; SM cem
                              lengthy story Dec 7
Hauling for Pacific Asphalt Co with a four-horse freight wagon; wood, sand, gravel, asphalt, etc. Fell from seat, caught under wheel, found some time later by Mr Righetti; died of injuries. Pall bearers: Bertie Coblentz, Wesley Ward, Ward Jones, E Pezzoni, Roscoe Jones, Lee Lucas. Resolution from schoolmates by Orrin Treat, Lillian Fleischer, Edmond Coblentz, Committee on Resolutions, Dec 6 1895. Survived by mother, brother, sister.

  b.   Isaac Harris                      b. CA 1860; died young
  c.   Mary Harris                      b. CA 1862
      (Mary E Harris m. SB co 4 Dec 1870 George Dent)?
  d.   Eliza J Harris                  b. CA 1864
  e.   Joel Miller Harris           b. CA 1869; m. of SM
                                  d.
    m. Nipomo 28 Oct 1900 by Rev S S Sampson (*Times*)
    Mary Johnson, Mrs          b. OR Nov 1860
      1900 cen: Nipomo            d. (Los Angeles 12-6-32@72 AG cem)?
                                  m.1 - Calvert
                                  m.2 (Thomas Kearney Johnson 1852-1893)?
          Her children:   Wm B Calvert b. OR 1880
                          George C (Chester G?) Calvert b. CA 1883; (Anita L Flores
                             1884-1966) See Sturgeon chart
                        Erma M Calvert b. CA 1886
                        Nellie A Johnson b. CA 1892

4.   Isaac Miller (Jr)             b. Scott co VA 25 May 1828
   to MO 1844?                d. San Luis Obispo 8 Jan 1919 @90; SM cem
   to Sonoma co 1853        obit Jan 11 (from SLO Trib); Jan 18; bio T/W 316
   1860 cen: Sonoma co Russian R tp
   to NV 1860/1; founded Star City, Humboldt co
   to Santa Maria/Central City 1872/3
   1875 Paulson Dir: Miller & Lovett gen mdse Main, Central City
   c1879 Miller & Lovett's store NE corner Main/Bwy sold to Sam Kreidel and Jonas
     Cassner.      –Harris, *Where Pioneers Dwell*
   1879 GR: 51 VA f SM;      1880 cen: SM;      1882 GR: 53 VA f CC
   1886: Yesterday we received a sample of the fruit grown in Mr Miller's orchard near
     town and without exaggeration we believe no better is grown in the state. The peaches
     weighed half-a-pound and the apricots were sweet and juicy and of fair average size.
     No one can doubt that this is good fruit country after going through his orchard. –Aug 21

1887: *San Francisco Journal of Commerce*, Santa Maria Valley Edition, April 14 1887.
. . . Isaac Miller rancher 1 mi E of Santa Maria 160 a; apricots, prunes, peaches.
1890 GR: 63 VA f SM #1
1894: Isaac Miller was in town today, first time in three weeks, on account of sickness.
We are glad to see him out again. —Jan 13
1898: Isaac Miller and son George returned from northern California goldfields last
Monday . . . with beautiful specimens of yellow gold from claims on Feather River.
—Sep 17

    1900 cen: SM; 6 births 5 living;        1909 Dir: ret rMillers' div; Mrs
    1910 cen: E Mill st 6 births 5 living
       m. (Winnemucca) NV 29 May 1864
Anna Robrecht                      b. Prussia Nov 1838; imm. 1863
                                    d. 27 Mar 1917 @78; SM cem
                                    obit Mar 31 p.1; 3 sons 1 dau; bro in Oakland

a.    - - -
b.    Isaac Miller (Jr #2)              b. Winnemucca NV 19 June 1868; m. of SM
     1890 GR: 21 NV f SM #1          d. Sacramento 29 May 1946 @77/11/-; SM cem
     1900 cen: SM slsmn groc          obit May 31 p.1. bio Phillips II 176
       1 birth 1 living
     1906 Dir: clk cor Mill & Vine; Mrs; 1909 Dir: clk rW (sic) Mill; Mrs; Miss Herminia
     1915: City Happenings. Isaac Miller jr returned Monday from a visit to San
       Francisco and the Fair.                                     —Nov 24
     1920 cen: 224? E Mill       1940-1 Dir: 225 E Mill
      *Note*: Plenio and Sylvia (Ruiz) Tomasini lived at 218 E Mill; their daughter
         Yvonne remembers "Old Mr Miller" being annoyed at the noise her roller
         skates made on the sidewalk. For Ruiz see Sturgeon chart.
       m. San Francisco 27 Nov 1890 (*Times*)
         2y SF w/street rr; returned to SM 17y clk w/Coblentz & Schwabacher
         1912 to Bryant & Trott for 20y.
     Edith L Hamann                 b. CA Dec 1868; m. of SF; parents GER
     (Eda)                               d. Sacramento 15 July 1953 @85; SM cem
                                      obit Mon July 20 p.6; 5y Sacramento
      = Hermine Louise Miller          b. SM 22 July 1894 (*Times*)
        1920 cen: w/parents, bkpr        d. 4 Aug 1944 @50/0/15; SM cem
        Single
c.    James Herschel Miller            b. NV Sep 1871; m. of SM
     1906 Dir: Hershel clk            d. at home 26 Oct 1918 @47/1/25; SM cem
       rMillers' div; Mrs                obit Nov 2 wife and children not mentioned
       or (J H emp U Sugar r Church st; Mrs)?
     1910 cen: E Mill w/father; 2 births 2 living
       m. at home of Thomas Barrett, Garden st, SLO 1 Nov 1905 by Rev Geo Willett (*T*)
     Emma May Harper               b. c1877
                                      d. (Santa Clara co 3-14-1915 @38)?
     = Harry H Miller                     b. 24 Sep 1906 (*T*); 22 Sep 1906;
                                      SSDI Dec 1943)?
     = Cecilia B Miller                   b. c1909
        1920 cen: adopted dau           d.
          w/Chas E Chaffin, Barrett st. See Chaffin chart
        1922-3 Dir: stu rFairlawn dist
        1940: in SLO
        Son Donald C Miller in Los Altos 1971

d.     Minna Miller                        b. 21 Oct 1873; m. @20 of SM
        1920-1 VR: 5'4 CA SLO #7           d. at home of dau SLO 14 Jan 1933 @59
                                                  obit Sat Jan 14 p.1; dau, 3 bro, 2 gch,
                                                  38y SLO; also *SLO Daily Telegram* Jan 14
                                                  p.6; 542 Islay st SLO
           m. Santa Maria 30 Apr 1894 by V Aguilera, Cath; wit: MW Thea, Minna Smith
      Thomas Barrett jr                      b. Suisun CA June 1868; m. @24
        to San Carpojo @1                   d. at home 542 Islay st SLO 17 Oct 1927 @58
        1892 GR: 23 5'5¼ fair complexion       Old Mission cem. obit *SLO Morning Tribune*
          brown eyes brown hair scar on          Tue Oct 18 p.8; Thu Oct 20 p.8
          left cheek, clerk; CA; SLO             F: Thomas Barrett 1840-1915
        1900 cen: w/father SLO;                M: N M Johnson 1847-1896
          2 births 2 liv
        1902 GR: 33 SLO #2
        1910 cen: Garden str SLO; RE agt 2 births 2 living
        1912 Dir: Thos Sr & Jr Real Estate 1116 Garden st SLO; res same
        1920-1 VR: 5'8 CA SLO #7
        1927: pall bearers; Mayor L G Sinsheimer, Albert Nelson, H W Sandercock,
           M Marshall, Alex Galewsky, H H Carpenter
        *Note*: Barrett & Russell (Thomas Barrett Sr and Charles J Russell) were developers
           of the Fairlawn tract in Santa Maria, hence Barrett street and Russell street.
           See Barrett chart.
      = Elza M Barrett                        b. SLO 25 June 1895 (*Times*)
         (Hugh "Tex" Wilson)                d. Napa Jan 1986; SSDI
         + Kathleen Wilson
         + Helen Wilson
      = Frederick A Barrett                 b. c1897; no further data
                                                 d. (WWI)?
        1898: Mrs Thomas Barrett, of San Luis, with babies is visiting relatives in Santa
           Maria this week. –Mar 19. . . . returned to SLO Wed . . .          –Mar 26

e.     George C Miller                      b. Dec 1874
                                                  d.    (in Gonzales 1917, 1933, 1946)
        1890: A surprise party . . . tendered George and Willie Miller last Thursday evening
           at the residence of Mr and Mrs Isaac Miller . . . present: Lena Tognin, Bell
           Phillips, Mary Arellanes, Grace May, Pearl Marshall, Ida Merritt, Grace
           Holloway, Alfie Phillips, Matilda Arellanes, Frank May, Joe Fauntleroy, John
           Arellanes, Clarence Whaley, Bert Blosser, Willie Johnson, Clyde Hall, Fred
           Smith, Roscoe Jones, Bert Jones, Louis Tognini, George Merritt, George Miller,
           Willie Miller. –Nov 15
        1894: Another surprise party, most of the same guests.             –April 28
        1900: Geo Miller has been looking after the wants of Geo Black's customers this
           week, while Geo is looking out for the Native Sons in San Francisco.      –Sep 15
           (Black seems to have run a cigar store.)
        1919: Geo C Miller of Gonzales is here to attend the funeral of his father Isaac.

f.     William I(saac) Miller               b. Santa Maria 18 (or 10) June 1878; m. of SM
        1902 GR: (Wm 24 SLO #4)?          d. San Luis Obispo 4 Apr 1945 @66/9/24 obit
        1909 Dir: (Wm blksm r Miller st)?      *SLO Telegram-Tribune* Wed Apr 4 p.1; also
        1910 cen: SM @31 m.4, no wife        Apr 5 p.102 bro, nc Mrs Hugh Wilson SLO; to
        1922-3 Dir: (Wm clk                   SLO after death of father
          r E Church SM)?

        1933 in SLO
                m. at home of Thomas Barrett 10 June 1905 by Rev Blackledge (*Times*)
    M Agnes Plumm                       b.
                                        d. "several years" before William

Vol. XXXI, No. 4, Winter 1999, p.11

**Corrections and Additions**      [Page numbers refer to those in Quarterly]

Isaac and Rebecca Miller, presented as parents of Joel Miller and his siblings are the uncle and aunt of that family of children. Beverley Davis of Orcutt, a descendant, tells us that the father was Abraham Miller, who, apparently, did not make the trek from Virginia to Missouri with the family; his fate has not yet been discovered.

Vol. XXXII, No. 1, Spring 2000, p.13

# MILLER
## PIONEERS OF THE CALIFORNIA CENTRAL COAST

Milton David Miller                 b. OH 11 Mar 1825
  1850 cen: Huntington co IN        d. nr Healdsburg 2 Oct 1858 (see Sleath 267-9)
                                    F: Miles Miller 1806-1874
                                    M: Rebecca Wolfe (Walsh?) 1805-1874
    1874. Died in San Francisco Mr Miller in 68th year...numerous grandchildren...foot
        amputated.                                              –*SLO Tribune* Sat May 23
    1874. Died Oso Flaco of pneumonia Mrs M Miller @70; 20y CA; large family of sons.
                                                                -*SLO Tribune* Aug 22
            m. Allen co IN 23 Dec 1847
Charlotte Hinton                    b. Fort Wayne IN 16 Apr 1830
                                    d. Goleta 5 Dec 1902 @72/7/19; SM cem obit Dec 13
                                    F: James Hinton (1850 cen: Allen co IN, Indian Lake tp)
                                    M: Tress Davis (see Sleath)
                                    m.2. Santa Rosa 1859 Joel Miller 1820-1880
1.    Milton Davis Miller           b. (Huntington co)? IN Nov 1848
                                    d. (Hames valley) 1901; buried Hames
        1875 Paulson dir: SMVFU cor Main/Bwy J M McElhaney, slsmn; M D Miller sec
        1879 GR: 30 IN f Sisquoc
        1880 cen: Sisquoc IN
        1881 Santa Maria Band, photo...Milton D Miller, Everett Miller –Valley 252
        1882 GR: 33 IN f SM
        1883 Administrator of estate of Joel Miller
        1884 GR: 33 IN carpenter SM crossed off (moved to Hames Valley?)
        1886 60a Hames Valley                           –*Salinas Valley Index* Apr 22
            Christmas Ball, Pleyto...music by James Betts, Miss Visa Betts, Miss Sadie Betts,
            Mrs C C Saylor, Miss Viola Saylor, Mr Miller & Mr Fancher. –ibid. Jan 6 1887
        1887 Literary entertainment Hames Valley schoolhouse...song of welcome...(6 women
            and) Messrs Miller and Bowden...-                           ibid.
            Hames Valley Items. M D Miller has lately returned from a trip to Santa Maria.
                                                                        -ibid. Nov 10
        1888 Hames Valley. Mr Miller and family are expected home from a visit to Santa Maria.
                                                                        -ibid. Aug 23

Vol. XXXII, No. 1, Spring 2000, p.11

1900 cen: Monterey co Bradley tp (=Hames valley)
    m.1 Santa Maria 4 Dec 1874 by Rev J W McElhaney, B88; divorce: Superior Court. M D Miller vs Mary S Miller, desertion. –*Salinas Weekly Index* Oct 22 1887

| | | |
|---|---|---|
| Mary Samantha Cook | | b. Sonoma co Sep 1857 |
|   1900 cen: gdau w/Rachel Lamb | | d. (remarried) |
|   SM: Div. 5 births | | F: Rudolph Derias Cook 1832-1904 |
|   1 living m. 8y (!) | | M: Jenetta Nelson 1838-1896 |
|   1910 cen: 300 E Church SM | | R D Cook patron T/W: Central City livery & f |
|   Div. 5 births 1 living | | b. OH; to CA 1851; to county 1869; 160a |

    a.  William R? Miller    b. June 1875
        (Albert W)
          1900 cen: w/father
        (1910 cen: San Joaquin 102-114-59)?
          (m.
        (Genevieve O    b. CA c1887)
          (= Edith M)
          (= Doris G)
    b.  Son    b. May 1880
    c.  Leo Lillian Miller    b. (1883)
    others unknown    d. @14/5/9 bur Mar 18 1898; SM cem

1.  m.2 1887
    Clara    b. CA Feb 1858; F: MO; M: AR
      1900 cen: 4 births, 4 living    d.
    f.  Jasper Miller    b. Oct 1888
          d.
    g.  Myrtle Miller    b. Aug 1890
    Clara's children, father b. TN:
    a.  Grace    b. Sep 1879
    b.  William    b. June 1882

2.  Sarah Elizabeth Miller    b. Fort Wayne IN 26 Aug 1850
    1880 cen: next to Joel    d. Los Alamos 31 Jan 1899 @48/5/5; SM cem;
      Miller SM    tuberculosis
        m.1 San Luis Obispo 17 May 1870 by J J Simmler, A112
    James Basil Linebaugh    b. IL 1845
      1870 cen: tp #3 next to    d. before 1880
        J H Harris (Eliz. Miller)
    a.  Eva Linebaugh    b. 31 Mar 1871
          d. Los Alamos 21 Dec 1897 @26 (*T*); measles
    b.  Milton (Dee or David) Linebaugh    b. 1873/4
          d. Cat Canyon 21 Apr 1887 @13 (*Times*)
    c.  James Everett Linebaugh    b. 1876; SSDI
          d. Los Angeles co 12-2-1949 spouse LL
        m.
    Elizabeth Foster Mirley/Mirely    b. IL 22 Apr 1875
          d. Los Angeles co 2 Sep 1952 @77 "Lizzie"
          mother's maiden name McCartney
    *Note*: Lizzie's first husband was half-brother of J B Linebaugh –Sleath

2.    m.2 Guadalupe 10 Sep 1884 by McCorkle, C150
      wit: Jane A Harris, J H Thornburg

John James Holloway      b. Benton co MO 26 Jan 1839

    1879 GR: 41 MO f Sisquoc patron    m.2 @45 of Oakvale dist (the Oakvale school was in his house –ONT)
    T/W: Cañada Gato f MO;
    to CA 1850    d. 3 Sep 1918 @79; SM cem
    to co 1868 326a    F: John Holloway 1809-c1852
       M: Nancy Kemp Foster 1810-1885

    bios History of SB, SLO, Ventura cos, Gidney, 1917, 546; History of So Cal, Guinn, 1907, 670; M/H 219, see also Sleath, Holloway Gen

    d. Charlotte Hinton Holloway 1885-1970 (Homer Lindsey Sturgeon 1884-1964) see Sturgeon chart
    e. Carlisle Regan Holloway 1888-1958 (Mildred Sarah Wilson 1893-1990)
    f. Cornell Diggs Holloway 1891-1903
    g. Francis Walter Holloway 1893-1984 (Marguerite Alma McLaughlin 1885-1979?)

3. Rebecca Tress Miller      b. IN 16 Apr 1853
       d. Los Alamos 13 June 1883; SM cem
    m. Santa Maria 22 Dec 1870 by Joel Miller, JP, A201

   John James Holloway see above
   1906 Dir: 1 mi E Los Alamos, Los Olivos rd: JJ, John, James, Miss Charlotte
    a. Lucy Emma Holloway 1871-1965 (Wm David McCroskey 1869-1946)
    b. Dora Beatrice Holloway 1873-1957 (John Thomas Glines 1875-1949)
    c. Nancy Estella Holloway 1874-1875
    d. Albert Johnston(e) Holloway 1876-1951 (Mary M Sutton Miller 1877-1971?)
    e. Everett Price Holloway 1878-1905
    f. James Weaver Holloway 1880-1963 (Lena J McCabe 1887-1988)
    g. Nance Holloway "son (sic) of JJ, bur Thornburgh Cem" 1883-1884

4. William Hinton Miller MD      b. c1858; m. @22 of SM
    1879 GR: 21 stu SM      d.
    in Dakota Territory 1882
        m.1 14 Sep 1880 by J W Webb, MG, B481
          wit: Madison Thornburg, Wm J E Crow
   Ellen R Crow      b. c1857; m. @23 of SM
       d.
   (other wives unknown –Sleath)

5. James C Miller      b. 17 Jan 1856
       d. at residence of Mr Geo Anderson, Big Valley, Sonoma co 5 Feb 1859 @3/0/19
       *-Sonoma Co Democrat*
       in *Sonoma Searcher* 20:3


Vol. XXXII, No. 1, Spring 2000, pp.12, 13


**Corrections and Additions**      [Page numbers refer to those in Quarterly]

p.12      Milton's second wife was Clara Hensley. 1887. Hames Valley Items. Mrs Henseley (sic) is yet away visiting friends.      –*Salinas Valley Index* Nov 10


Vol. XXXII, No. 2, Summer 2000, p.12

# DIARY OF M. L. MOORE
## A TRIP FROM VENTURA TO EL PASO DE ROBLES 1878

This excerpt from the diary of M L Moore interests us for more than one reason. It shows us that land ownership was a goal not easily reached by the farmers who flocked to this part of California in the 1860's and '70's; this is evident in the changes of address on censuses and voter registrations.

It describes for us the road and travel conditions—not in great detail, but enough to stir to thought those of us well acquainted with local terrain who are accustomed to buzzing along concrete highways reaching in hours places formerly days away. It is a lesson in appreciation; we do have something to show for our tax monies.

The trip started near Ventura and proceeded to Santa Barbara via the under-construction Casitas Pass road; the beach route was not only difficult but also risky. From Santa Barbara they traveled along the coast, the current 101 route, through Gaviota Pass to Los Alamos, thence westish, and north to La Graciosa; this was a principal road until 101 was built in 1932. The right hand road from La Graciosa led to Central City (Santa Maria), and on into San Luis Obispo county. Apparently they chose one of the canyon roads out of Arroyo Grande to San Luis Obispo, then to El Paso de Robles by Hobson's choice, the Cuesta grade, of which he makes no mention. The return trip varied by taking the beach from, probably, Avila to Guadalupe, a regrettable choice; from Guadalupe the road took them to La Graciosa. They crossed their tracks south of Los Alamos and went through the Santa Ynez valley, over the San Marcos Pass road, a toll road, and from Santa Barbara, back the way they came, finding the Casitas Pass road completed, a fact corroborated by contemporary newspapers.

Moore was a married man with two sons, recently arrived from mid-continent when he started his diary in October 1877; he came to the end of the volume on August 31, 1879, the purpose of his trip not having been fulfilled. He was a literate man; he mentions having brought his library of 100 books with him from the east. His handwriting and unusually good spelling and syntax bespeak some education. By modern standards, his punctuation is poor—but then, this is a private diary.

This diary is from the collection of Mrs George H Finley, a long-time resident of Hope Ranch and member of the Santa Barbara Genealogical Society; it is excerpted by permission of David L Cole (no relation to Moore's companion).

1878                          Monday 19th                          August

Foggy, was up quite early and made preparations for our trip Mr Cole and I go. was after 8 AM before we had all things in readiness to start, but soon reached Ventura Mr Cole drew his money and paid $80.00 cash for the Wyman horses that I have had all season. Cole put the horses in Websters barley field. Mr Cole loned me $20.00 gold. was 10:40 when we left here, went through the new road to Santa Barbara, we found the road good as far as finished but not finished, crops through Carpenteria look well, reached Bro. Foster's at supper time and drove in for the night.

### Tuesday 20th

Foggy. I mailed a postal home, was 8:15 when we started from here bound for <u>El Paso De Robles</u>. We followed the Gaviota road found it very good going, load light, is up hill and down a great part of the time, but few houses along the route. lunched some 16 miles out. find the people differ as to distance. we stoped 4:30 PM had a nice place, water not so plenty but wood plenty and feed plenty. did not reach Gaviota.

### Wednesday 21st

Foggy, was up early, slept well soon had our frugal repast ready and hooked up, our "Dick" horse stoped but induced him to go, soon reached Gaviota and turned up the pass, is some nice scenery through the pass. passed through some nice little valleys, nice running water. Crossed the Santa Ynez river and passed the old misson which has been abandoned quite a long time. found some nice wheat growing but all rusted stands 5 to 7 feet high will not be cut. took our lunch and rested one hour then moved on this afternoon met Rev S Bowers and wife returning from a two weeks trip they live near Santa Barbara. We stoped and conversed 1 hour, then moved on pased Los Alamos station and encamped, water scarce. otherwise good camping went 1 mile up a canyon to camp, Cole went in a field for some rostenears got about 1 dozen. the man saw him & charged $1.00 for it. we though it valued "high".

### Thursday 22nd

Foggy here we had a good start and moved along at a good rate killed a quail. I wrote a postal as we drove along did not write any yesterday. mailed my card at La Graciosa. here two roads we take the right hand and go by Central City the road is heavy sand the most of the way across the Santa Maria valley. we took lunch after crossing over to the hills. here we found two roads one appeared to be a private one though the best, so we kept the other, but found it the worst sand we had encountered after going about 2 miles we left it, and went to ther one and did much better good hard road. got to within 8 miles of San Luis Obispo and camped had a very good place bough(t) hay here and a roll of butter, crops poor wheat all rusted but little cut where we went through, we found a great many quail this afternoon killed 5 or 6 and had a nice stew, has been cool all day but little dust.

### Friday 23rd

Foggy some. we got a very early start this morning and after some little distance had a good road. reached San Luis Obispo at 8 AM bought some bread 25 c mailed a card home and started on our way and made good time took our lunch 2½ miles West of San Margrita Post Office. our time is one hour for lunch. we then moved along, found many opinions as to distance some say 10 miles. drive about 3 or 4 then may be one would say 14 miles yet, but we reached the Springs at 5:15 PM. I then wrote a card home from here and then made inquiry for Rev H E Adams and rec'd direction and started for his place, found it before sun down. they were not expecting us until tomorrow. found all well and we much fatigued for we traveled near 40 miles to day. it is near 175 miles from here home, quite pleasant day.

### Saturday 24th

Some fog but not enough to injure the wheat. the wheat here was good no rust straw bright grain nice. after we had breakfast and prayers, we then started on horseback to look at the country. we got samples of wheat, and found it good, when out I found some corn much better than I expected of course nothing like such corn as grows in the low coast valleys. the lay of the country is good the character of the soil here is sand coarse, underlaid with a hardpan, deep to water but good when found. fowls appear to do well here of all kinds. was very warm to day.

I wrote a letter home, then went to Misson San Miguel (107 years old) an old structure. quail plenty through this section.

### Sunday 25th

Clear not any fog. Bro Adams was up early he goes 22 miles to preach to day. the family did not rise very early I thought of going to church, but felt so drowsy could not keep awake, then had to go alone so did not go. did not do any thing but read had Sabbath School for May. the wind blew strong from South, was cool all day. was quite late when Bro Adams returned home.

### Monday 26th

Clear we mad(e) a tour on foot this AM looking at some particular tracts Bro Adams wants I should locate on a quarter section joining him on the North, but I will not be in a hurry. after noon we hitched up and drove some 6 miles East to Dry Creek found a pretty Country there all Adobe land no settlers on it all unclaimed not so much timber as on the sand, all come here to cut hay hundreds of acres cut over, think would be 130 to 160 feet to water here, I will not locate any thing now but wait and if I move up will then select a location to suit must consult the wife first. we must both be united on this point to succeed. Bro Adams is anxious we should move at once.

### Tuesday 27th

Foggy some, we was up quite early and after we had our breakfast then we made preparations to start and at 7 AM bid our friends adieu and turned our faces homeward. I mailed a card at the Springs to wife that we had started and would reach home on Saturday. nothing of any note transpired to day was quite warm did not travel so fast as when we came up. lunched at noon. reached San Luis Obispo at 5 PM bought sack barley 90c, potatoes 25c, bread 50c, can roast beef 50c. Bro Adams advised us to take right hand road here and go down on the beach. we bought the best hay this eve. we camped along road side water plenty, wood enough, my birth day 40 years old, and without a home yet, but will soon have one if I go on goverment land.

### Wednesday 28th

Foggy almost rain. got up early started in the fog did not have any sun shine until afternoon. had good going until we reached the beach. tide was low, but the sand was soft and was heavy pulling all the time we lost nearly ½ day by going this way. we passed through Guadalupe at 2 ½ PM I got some turpentine I have a sore hand. we reached La Graciosa at Sun down and camped not a good place but no water for 8 miles. had a better road this afternoon.

### Thursday 29th

Clear though some foggy. we was up early as we could see well. slept by a hay rick had a good place to camp in that respect, saw quail by the thousand Cole killed 7 at one shot, 4 at another thought that sufficient. was hot to day made the teem tire some. I stoped at Ballards Station and made inquiry about Wm Lunceford that left Ill. in April 1852. I learned that he died two years ago. one daughter and son live in San Luis Obispo, one daughter in Central City. we left here at 4 PM went the left hand road and camped near Santa Ynez river have a good place to camp plenty of wood.

### Friday 30th

Foggy had a nice start road good all the time to the grade killed 7 quail, had a nice place to lunch was warm to day the grade is long and not good road narrow, but we finally gained the Summit paid $1.50 toll and moved down grade Killed a large black rattlesnake with 12 rattles. we reached Santa Barbara at 6 PM bought box apples 1.25, bacon 1.75, dress 1.00, pulled up at Bro Fosters found all well looking for us.

### Saturday 31st

Foggy some was up quite early. we slept out doors last night I had the tooth-ache for quite awhile after first retire-ing for the night. we started quite early and traveled along as fast as possible. did not meet any old friends. we came through the pass, picked up stove wood along the road that teamsters had lost. we lunched after passing the stage station. found the road finished and a very good grade. was quite warm we did not get along as fast as I had hoped. about 5 PM we turned into the Ventura Canyon road and drove about 50 rods and we discovered that we had lost our valise containing our clothes we turned back some 3½ or 4 miles but could not find it as we had met several persons, we then came on told several persons we met. was 8 PM when we reached Ventura. I bought me pair drawers & undershirt. Cole bought him a suit of clothes as he lost the best he had. will be about $18.00 for me and $30.00 for him if we dont recover it. I bought some grapes 15c, candy 25c, melon 20c, we came on home was near 11 PM when we reached home, folks tolerable well Sade has a cold had almost given us out for this time.

*Note:* Valise returned Sep. 13

# MORE
## SANTA MARIA VALLEY PIONEERS

Captain Elliott More  b. NY 19 July 1822; parents NY
　　d. at home on the ranch nr Garey; T33 S10 R9
　　　Sat 3 Sep 1898 @76/1/15; SM cem. See Funeral
　　　Notice Card SMV Historical Society

　1860 cen: Yolo co Cache ck tp P O Prairie
　Patron T/W: res Cañada Gato farmer  b. NY to CA 1859; to SB co 1870; 920 acres
　1870 cen: SMv sheepraiser
　1879 GR: 51 NY Sisquoc farmer
　1880 cen: Sisquoc
　1882 GR: 59 NY farmer Sisquoc
　1890 GR: 68 NY farmer Santa Maria #2
　1892. Capt More of Orange Vale was in town Thursday; his daughter took the morning train to
　　San Luis where she expects to visit for a few days.　　　　　　　　　　–Dec 17
　1893. Christmas Eve Party. On Christmas Eve, M/M Wm Forrester gave their neighbors a
　　pleasant reception at their home in Orange Vale. The evening was one long to be
　　remembered by all present. Music, dancing and popping corn was the order of entertainment
　　until one o'clock in the morning. The favored ones were M/M Chas More, M/M Forrester,
　　Miss Adkins, Misses Maud More, Madge More, Hopel (?) Adkins, Eva Forrester, Mr Fred
　　Baker, M Beeson, Mr Adkins, Wells, Liston, Perry Moore　　　　　　–Dec 30
　　*Note:* for Forrester see chart; Adkins and Wells same, also with Twitchell.
　1893. South Side Items. C O More proposes to increase his dairy this season as he has local
　　demand for all the butter he can make. Ed More is studying fruit culture under Prof
　　Diamond of Olive Hill. Capt More was here to buy seed wheat one day this week.　–Jan 7
　1897. "Cap" More, who has in several hundred acres of grain near Garey, was in town
　　yesterday. Although 74 years of age, Mr More will go into the field and handle a
　　pitchfork with many a young man who is 40 years his junior.
　　　　　　　　　　–Fifty Years Ago *Santa Maria Times* 1947
　　　m.1 Family tradition has it that Captain's first wife was very young; they
　　　　separated and divorced because of her homesickness.
　　　m.2
Mary Anne Hines　　b.
　　d. (St Charles IL)? 31 Jan 1857
　　*Note*: Edwin's records are unanimous in Iowa's being
　　　his birthplace.

1.　Charles Owen More　　b. IL 1853, see below
2.　Edwin Oliver More　　b. IA 17 Jan 1857
　　1879 GR: 22 IA f SM　　d. possibly early 1930's
　　1880 cen: w/father
　　1882 GR: 25 IA f Carpinteria
　　1887. Ed More bought 4 lots in Fesler's division of J Barry, paying for the same $500.
　　　　　　　　　　　　　-50 Years Ago 13 Dec 1937
　　1890 GR: 33 IA clk SM
　　1894. South Side Items. Ed More has purchased 180 acres of the Garey-Bradley tract
　　　which he proposes to improve by fencing, planting orchard, etc. Ed has lived here
　　　the greater part of his life and is satisfied that he can pay for a farm with what it will
　　　produce. M/M C O More gave a Christmas dinner for a few of their friends
　　　Christmas. As a host and hostess, M/M More have few equals.　　–Jan 6

1894. South Side Items. Ed More is pulling beans for C R Drumm. Ed's bees and chickens do not require all his time now so he puts in his spare time on the outside.  –Sep 29

1898. South Side Short Stops. Ed More visited at the home of B F Wiley Sunday.  –Sep 3

1900 cen: tp8 (Sisquoc) apiarist, single

1900. South Side. Perry More in partnership with E O More . . . first apiary on Thornburg ranch near head of Tepesquet.  –Feb 24

South Side Short Stops. Ed More came down from his Tepesquet bee ranch Tuesday, says his bees are going to make plenty of honey to live on until next year's honey season begins again.  –Apr 28

South Side Squibs. Ed More returned to the sugar mill Sunday where he has secured employment.  –Sep 1

1906 Dir: More E O grocer Main st SM

1922-3 Dir: lab Los Alamos

1926: in Oceano

    Single

Capt. m.3               divorced before 1870

Hannah D               b. NY c1832

                              d.

3.     Emma O More          b. IA c1859

                              d.

Capt. m.4  c1870

Elizabeth E              b. NY c1849; F: IRE; M: SCT

                              d. Santa Maria valley 15 June 1881 @32/2/11; removed from Thornburg cem to SM cem 22 March 1884

4.     Mary Eliza(beth) More     b. Garey 24 May 1872; m.2 @27 of SM

                              d. Pismo 23 Nov 1955 @83/9/29; SM cem

    m.1 San Luis Obispo 15 Dec 1892 by M Egan JP, D233; wit: Mrs Kate McHenry, SLO; Francis McEntee, SLO; see also *SM Times*. Divorced

Lewis Frederick Williams     b. WI 3 Jan 1867; m. of Garey

                              d. Santa Barbara 14 Nov 1947 @80

                                (spouse initials MM)

                                obit *SB News-Press* Sun Nov 16 A3;

                                cousin Percy R Harris, Ventura; no other relatives.

                                Rancher Sisquoc 60 years; retired 1937, to SB

1895. Cat Canyon Up to Date. Fred Williams has purchased the Burleson ranch, and is preparing to move his house nearer the road and water. He has a good crop of hay, which he has well taken care of.  –July 13

1900 cen: tp8 (Garey) divorced, alone

1906 Dir: L F Williams & Mrs, Sisquoc; Brenton, John & Mrs, Garey

1910 cen: tp8 Bradley tract wid; sister Nannie/Nancy Brenton and children w/

1914 Dir: L F Williams RR #1 Santa Maria

1940-1 Dir: Lewis F Williams serv sta opr Sisquoc

    Lewis Williams farmer Garey Rd.

*Note*: Jacob Williams of Sisquoc had a son named Lewis, born in 1883, who married Annie Hansen about 1910; it is difficult to distinguish their records.

1939 SB phbk: Brenton Eva S r409 E Arrellaga SB

1940 SB phbk: Brenton Eva S r714 E Victoria SB

    Harris P R r716 De la Vina; 1939 phbk: same

4. m.2 San Luis Obispo 23 Nov 1899 by M Egan JP, F63
    wit: Wm Mallagh, SLO; Wm N Ent, SLO; also *SM Times*

| | |
|---|---|
| Henry Clinton Mallory jr | b. KS 16 Feb 1874; m. @26 of SM |
|   "Clint" | d. at home Lower Orcutt Rd 9 Apr 1931 |
|   1900 cen: tp #8 well borer; |   @57/1/24 |
|     no wife |   obit Fri Apr 10 p.1, retired businessman, |
|   1910 cen: Main st Pismo |   3y SM "Drops Dead in Garden of Home" |
|     cook restaurant | F: (Henry C Mallory 1841-1913) |
|     own account; Mary E | M: Mary A 1852-1905 |

    1914 Dir: Clinton Mallory, Pismo Beach
    1916. Clint Mallory's restaurant at Pizmo opened Sunday, management of Dining room
        to brother-in-law F C Harrington.                                                  –date lost
    1920 cen: landlord rooming house, Pismo; Mary E; owns house
    1920-1 VR: Henry Clinton Mallory KS; Mary E Mallory CA, Pismo
    1927. Clint Mallory, Pismo Beach . . .                   -*SLO Morning Tribune* Oct 19
    *Note*: Though the Pizmo spelling was official for the hotel and resort only, it came to be
        used interchangeably with Pismo.
    No issue. Mary survived by nieces and nephews Doris Mallory, Helen Parrish, Cethil
        Mallory of Arroyo Grande, and Frank Mallory of Santa Maria, children of
        John Franklin Mallory 1875-1944 and Iva J Gingrich 1881-1947

5.    Laura W More                   b. Santa Maria valley Jan 1878; m.1 @16
                                     d. Pismo Nov 1926; bur 4 Nov SM cem @48
                                        obit Tue Nov 2 p.5; 10y Pismo. "Father Captain
                                        E More one of the first of the four families that
                                        settled this valley."

    1900 cen: SM w/Rbt L Jones
      hotel chambermaid; m.7, 1 birth 0 living; F: IL; M: KS (!)
    m.1 Santa Maria 4 Nov 1893 by H W Baker JP (*Times*)

| | |
|---|---|
| George R Stevenson | b. CA; m. @31 |
| | d. |

  a.   Elliott More Stephenson (sic) d. nr Garey Jan 1898 @3/4/12; infant son of
        Mrs S Hutt. – *Santa Maria Times* Jan 22. Card of Thanks M/M S Hutt     -*Times* Jan 29
        m.2 Santa Barbara 27 Aug 1895

| | |
|---|---|
| Samuel Silas Hutt | b. MO c1858 |
|   1890 GR: 32 MO f Los Alamos | d. |

    (m.1   1887 Mary Caledonia McCroskey; F: James Madison McCroskey 1835-1905,
        M: Minerva Jane Dryden 1840-1919; divorced)
    Hutt inf son d. Los Alamos 25 July 1890
    Hutt inf dau d. nr Garey 17 Aug 1892 @6mos; SM Cem
  1898. Sam Hutt has sold his effects and will depart for other parts in a short time. –Sep 17
    m.3

| | |
|---|---|
| Frank Clarke Harrington | b. OR 1885 |
|   1920 cen: Pismo, restaurant | d. (Pismo Beach) 3 July 1933 @57/11/29; SM cem; |
|     own acct rents house |   obit Fri July 7; m.2 Florence |

  1926. Laura survived by half-brother and half-sister (sic) Mrs Edwin More, Oceano, and
      Clarles More, Santa Cruz
  1933. Pismo Beach July 5. Frank Harrington, well known retired restaurant man and real
      estate operator found dead at beach cabin Monday morning . . . heart attack Sunday
      night . . . found on floor near kitchen sink where he had evidently gone for a drink
      of water when death overtook him. The water was found running by friends who
      discovered him . . . wife Florence is in Los Angeles.

Services for Frank Chatterton Harrington of Pismo Beach held yesterday . . .
Rev Thomas C Moffett, Pismo Beach Community Pres. Ch . . .       –Fri July 7
Note difference of opinion – cem vs. obit – on middle name.

Capt. m.5    Santa Maria 4 Jan 1885 by Chas Leach ME ch, B185
    wit: Mrs Darla S Leach; Kitty E Miller. "Married 4 times, 2 living 2 dead"

Susan E (Miller)     b. MO Sep 1848; m.2 @36; 1st husband still liv
    d. San Francisco 26 Jan 1922 @73
    m.1 James S Miller MD; see Isaac Miller chart

*Note*: They went to San Francisco on their honeymoon; she wanted to stay . . . he left her there. They were divorced.

Capt. m.6    San Luis Obispo 10 Feb 1892 by R A Loomis JP, D129
    wit: Carrie Oaks, SLO; Jennie Trimble, SLO. Both before married.

Clara E (Ramey)     b. ME Mar 1855; m.2 @44 of Santa Barbara
  "Clarry"     d. Casmalia 24 Apr 1904 @49/0/5     –*Times* Apr 29
    F: ME: M: ME/NY
    m.3 1899 Mattison Howerton 1863-1941
    see Hobbs chart; Howerton chart ONT 245ff

1.   Charles Owen More     b. St Charles IL 9 Sep 1853/4; m. @23 of Santa Maria
    Patron T/W: res Cañada Gato     d. at home of dau, Santa Cruz, 27 Apr 1932 @77;
    farmer b. IL to CA 1859;     Soquel cem; obit Sat Apr 30 p.1; 7 yrs SCz; wid,
    to SB co 1870; 800a     5ch, 9gch, 2ggch
    1879 GR: 25 IL Sisquoc
    1880 cen: w/father
    1882 GR: 28 IL farmer Sisquoc
    1886. Fair Play Items. Wild hogs have done considerable damage to the crops of Messrs McPherson, More, Marcum and Williams. Quite a number of the hogs have been killed. Mrs Miller and a number of her young friends have gone to the beach.
        -Aug 21
    1890 GR: 36 IL farmer Sisquoc
    1893. South Side Again. Chas O More has been laid up with a sore hand for some time but is better, now. Ed has officiated in the cow corral during Chas' sickness.
        -Oct 17
    1894. South Side Items. Apr 6. Ed. *SM Times*: The stockholders of the Alliance Milling Co of Los Alamos met Tuesday Apr 3 for the election of a new board of directors . . . J H Stewart, Pres; A H Davis, Sec-Treas; C W Martin, Mgr; C H Glines, D Spaulding, Wm Forrester, C O More, J H Winters, C R Drumm.
    South Side. C O More . . . dairy . . .     –Dec 29

*Note*: For Alvis H Davis 1858-1937 see Davis chart
    David Spaulding 1836-1916 see Davis chart
    Cassius H Glines 1850-1928 see Glines chart
    Forrester Family see Forrester chart
    John Hugh Winters 1853-1908 see Earl chart
    Calvin R Drumm 1848-1926 see Drumm chart

    1898. South Side Items. Mrs Emma More who has been staying with her daughter Madge during her recent illness has returned home to take up again the burdens of a farmer's wife.     –Sep 3
    South Side News. C O More was taking lessons in bicycle riding last Sunday. Chas thinks he can do anything that Uncle Rufus can.     –Oct 1
    1900 cen: tp8 (Sisquoc/Garey) 4 births 4 living
    1906 Dir: farmer Garey PO (Harold Gillilan says he sold the ranch for $42,000 and moved to Los Alamos.)

1910 cen: tp6 Los Alamos promoter oil stock 5 births 5 living
1919. Mrs C O Moore (sic) of Los Alamos is visiting her daughter, Mrs Geo Stewart of South Broadway. She has just returned from Santa Cruz, where she was called by the illness of her daughter, Mrs Margaret Oliver. —From Saturday's *Daily* 22 Feb
1920 cen: Los Alamos
1922-3 Dir: carpenter Los Alamos
    m. Santa Maria 4 April 1877 by M Thornburg, B271
        wit: H C Stowell, J J Holloway

Emma Miller          b. (Santa Rosa) Jan 1860; m. @17
  1922-3 Dir: hskpr Los Alamos      d. Santa Cruz 11 May 1948 @88/4; Soquel cem
                                      obit *Santa Cruz Sentinel-News* Wed May 12 p.14
                                       F: Joel Miller 1820-1880
                                       M: Charlotte Hinton 1830-1902

a.    Perry Harmon More           b. (SMv) 26 June 1878; SSDI
       1900. South Side                  d. (Santa Cruz) 27 Nov 1965; Soquel cem
       . . . w/E O More, see above
       1910 cen: 322 W Canon Perdido, SB; carpenter; 2 births 2 living
       1922-3 Dir: Perry H More (Nolan & More) contr r226 W Jones SM
              D A Nolan contr bldr
   Perry and Melvin built the Temple of the People at Halcyon for the Theosophists.
       1948. In SM, per mother's obit
       m.
       Helen Anna Thomas           b. Tranmere, Birkenhead ENG 25 May 1878
       "Lena"                               d. Santa Barbara 10 Apr 1959 @80; SB cem
       To US @7; to Lansing MI        (next to son)
         to SB 1900                      obit *SB News-Press* Sun Apr 12 A10;
                                           Mon Apr 13 B2
                                           r w/dau Bernice Osterman 222 W Haley, SB
                                           bro John Thomas, Alberta, CAN; sis Mrs
                                           Maud Carpenter, Lansing; 3gch, 5ggch
                                           F: George Thomas
                                           M: Annie Thompson
       1959. Pall bearers: Harvey Osterman, Harold Gillilan, Allan Gillilan, Elmer Kluth, Ten Naccarati
      = Melvin T More c1904-1943 single
      = Dorothy Bernice More (Gillilan) (Osterman) 1908-1992
         1938 phbk: A R Gillilan r424 W Cota SB; 1939-1940: same
         1947 phbk: A R Gillilan r222 W Haley (Artie Gillilan 1903-1980)
              Harvey W Osterman, San Marcos Trout Club
         1957 phbk: Harvey W Osterman 222 W Haley (1897-1979)
           Thanks to Harold Gillilan of Carpinteria (SBHS '48) for his help

b.    Maud Ella More               b. SMv 14 May 1880
                                           d. (Santa Cruz) 9 Nov 1962
       1901. South Side Squibs. Perry and Madge More are now in Berkeley, visiting their sister, Miss Maude, who is attending the University.    –Jan 5
       1906 Dir: Miss Maud prin Los Alamos Sch
       1910 cen: tchr Cat Cnyn, single; also w/parents, tchr, public sch
       School histories: Maud taught at Manzana school; Olive school 1908-9. Suey school organized 1879, early students . . . Maude, Madge, Perry More. Chas More trustee 1906, resided east side of Dominion Rd south of Clark Rd. Chas and Emma gave

land for Highland school.     –*San Ramon Chapel Pioneers*, Ontiveros, 1990
in Irvington 1948
m. June 1910

George I Stewart     b. KS c1880
1920 cen: 623 S Bwy SM     d. at home of sister-in-law Mrs W H Oliver
1922-3 Dir: auto dealer r423 S Bwy     Santa Cruz 13 Sep 1949; Santa Cruz cem
worked for Bethlehem Ship     obit *SM Times* Mon Sep 19 p.7, 2 sons 4gch
Bldg Co WWII

1912. Local Paragraphs. Geo Stewart, Supt of the Palmer Union Oil Co returned Monday from the city with a new 6 cylinder car.     –Dec 7?

1913. George I Stewart and F L Brown, well known operators of the oil fields, were among the Andrews hotel arrivals in San Luis Obispo last week for a few days.     –Aug 16

1915. Mrs Emma More of Los Alamos registered at the Fair; also Mrs Maude Stewart and Geo I Stewart.     –Oct 16

1917. City Briefs. Geo Stewart, popular sales manager for the Hudson Super Six started with a fine new car from Los Angeles on Monday and when he reached Goleta, a rancher took such a fancy to the machine that he sold it then and there. A part of the transaction was the trading of a Ford, in which George hoped to drive home, but before he could get started he sold the Ford also, and finally had to go home on the train.     –July 28

1922. New Rubel Building. (Special section in the *SM Times* March 10) . . . Rubel bought the Crescent Garage from A L Smith in 1913; in 1915 the Crescent garage took the Dodge agency, associated with George Stewart and Buick. The Dodge Bros policy of exclusive representation (since 1920) caused Rubel and Stewart to sever connections.

Buick Agency Shows Rapid Advancement . . . with the formal opening of the magnificent new Rubel Bldg in this community Saturday evening, it is both fitting and proper . . . to call the attention of the public to the tenant occupying the southern half of the lower floor, George I Stewart, Buick distributor . . . came to oil field in 1908 from mid-west, was superintendent Palmer-Union Oil Co five years. In August 1916 secured the Buick agency with headquarters in the old Crescent garage. Sold only 15 cars the first year . . .

1925 Dir: (Harry Neel jr Mgr/Prop Valley Motor Co, Buick, Rubel Bldg)
= Harold Allan Stewart b. Santa Maria 1916
= Donald Fairbairn Stewart b. Santa Maria 1919-1993

c. Margaret Elna More     b. SMv 28 July 1882; SSDI
"Madge"; SMHS 1901     d. Soquel 1 Dec 1978 @96
UC Berkeley 1905; MA 1907     obit Sleath 274-5; 1 sis 1 son 3gch
tchr Highland sch 1901 (ONT); also Sonoma, Santa Ana, Soquel, Aptos, Felton
in Santa Cruz 1948
m.
William Henry Oliver     b. CA 30 July 1882
"Pat"; surveyor SCz co     d. Santa Cruz 28 Apr 1947 @64
1920 cen: Soquel     F: (Wm Oliver 1830-1914)
    M: Hannah P 1840-1926

1919. Mrs P Oliver of Santa Cruz is visiting parents M/M More, Los Alamos, and sister, Miss Muriel. (date lost)
= Bernard M Oliver 1916-1995; living in Los Altos Hills 1978

d. Mila B More     b. SMv 7 Mar 1888 (*Times*); m.1 @23 of SM
1910 cen: w/parents, single     d. 28 Jan 1988; SM cem

        1920 cen: w/parents                                  obit Fri Jan 29 p.19; dau, 3 gch
                                                               5 step-gch, 10 ggch, 4gggch
                m.1 Santa Barbara 17 Feb 1912 (*Times*)
        James Irvin Gragg                               b. Benton co KY 15 May 1875; m. of Lompoc
                                                            d. San Francisco 30 Sep 1927 @52
            see Gragg chart                                 F: James Armenius Gragg 1839-1911
                                                              M: Mary Elizabeth Hudson Payne 1848-1929
        = Charles Robley Gragg b. Los Alamos 27 Oct 1912; d. Nov 1912
        = Margaret <u>Beverley</u> Gragg b. Los Alamos 13 Nov 1914; grad Santa Cruz High Sch
            m.1 1934 Jay O'Dell Womack
            m.2         Raymond Leo Davis 1916-1986; F: Bennie Ray Davis 1895-1968
  d.   m.2 after 1920
        Paul Francis McCartney                   b. Sisquoc 3 Nov 1891
                                                                  d. Los Berros 19 Dec 1931
            see McCartney chart                      F: George McCartney 1847-1941
                                                             M: Ida E Coon 1861-1942
  d.   m.3
        Raymond Nendel                               b. 6 Aug 1898
            1922-3 Dir: Ray, pumper, Orcutt;      d. 28 Oct 1970 @72; SM cem
            1925 Dir: same                                F: Frederick Nendel 1866-1948
            1928 Dir: Ray (Zelma) will (well) puller UO co
            1940-1 Dir: Raymond (Mila) trk drvr UO co rClark av Orcutt
        = his daughter Leona Nendel (Paige); SMUHS 1941; CSF Sealbearer
  e.   Muriel Hinton More                        b. nr Pine Grove 18 May 1901 (*Times*)
                                                       or (b. 17 Apr 1901; SSDI)
            1910 cen: w/parents                        d. Mountain View 31 July 1974 @73;
            in Decoto 1948                                  private interment
                                                                     obit *San Jose Mercury* Sat Aug 3 p.45;
                                                                     dau 2 sons 5gch 1ggch 2 sis
                                                                     (res Custer co CO, per SS)
            m. 11 Sep 1924
        Russell Belden Waldron                   b. CT 2 Feb 1904; SSDI
            1920 cen: sailor US Sub Base        d. Glendale 7 Jan 1973; SS benefits to Arcadia
               Los Angeles                                 F: Belden V K Waldron
            1928 Dir: R B (Muriel) oil clk           M: Lulu Ellen Gilbert
               Casmalia                                      m.2 Dodie Dow
        = Daniel Hinton Waldron 1926-1981; in Sierra Madre 1974
        = Richard Belden Waldron 1927-    ; in Pasadena 1974
        = Laetitia Meredith Waldron (Fitzgerald) (Simmons) 1929-1998
            in Los Gatos 1974

# MORRISON
## SANTA MARIA VALLEY PIONEERS

Erza Morrison came to the Santa Maria valley from Gridley in 1884; thus he was not among the very earliest of settlers, but in his twenty years' residence here he became well known and influential, and accumulated upwards of 1060 acres, scattered among ten ranches, the last of which was sold in 1981 and is already built up.

His descendants are imbued with the tradition that the land on which Buena Vista park sits was a generous donation from the holdings of Ezra and Amanda Morrison. It **was** part of their acreage in that neighborhood, and Morrison Avenue memorializes that fact; their house is said to have been located where the high school tennis courts are, south of the park. As to the need for a park, such a project was envisioned as early as 1887, when a meeting of citizens was held at the office of Jos. Kaiser in March. (It was in the same office, the same year, that M P Nicholson and others had concocted their plans to dig an artesian well in the intersection of Main and Broadway – see Nicholson chart). The park meeting was "to take steps to secure a park for the municipality of Santa Maria." Chairman S Clevenger "stated that he had reason to believe one of the citizens would take hold of the matter and improve the grounds, that H J Laughlin, Esq. would donate a tract for that purpose." –*SM Times* March 19 1987. What became of that effort has not been discovered, but it is certain that the Morrisons deeded four acres to trustees J F Goodwin, P W Jones, and Walter Elliott "until such time as the municipality be incorporated." – *This Is Our Valley* p.179. The original deed was recently donated to the Santa Maria Valley Historical Society from the collection of S J Jones in the estate of Gaylord Jones.

The donation rumor must have originated at an early date, for on April 17, 1897, this notice appeared in the *SM Times*: "Mr Morrison wishes it stated that the Real Estate transfer reporting his having donated a piece of land to the town of Santa Maria for a park was incorrect. He sold the land for cash to private parties." His obituary, eight years later, corroborated that statement: "Several years ago the site of Buena Vista park was purchased from him, and as the spirit of the park movement caught his fancy he made the trustees a very liberal offer, which was accepted and the beautiful enclosure today exists as a mark to his generosity." -Sat. October 15 1905 p.2

Annie Swain Morrison was interested in renaming Buena Vista Park in honor of Ezra and Amanda Morrison. The files of the Santa Maria Valley Historical Society contain correspondence dated November and December 1964 between Mrs Morrison and the City on the subject. The City's statement was that the deed shows a sum of $300 having been paid for the property, and that there was no knowledge of the park's ever having borne the Morrison name in the past, but, rather, always Buena Vista.

Morrison's first home was farther south of town than the park site, and his dedication to beauty was commended in the *SM Times*: "A Beautiful Place. A few days since we paid a visit to Mr E Morrison's place, at about one mile south of town. The tract has been divided into convenient fields all enclosed with substantial board fences. The grounds around his beautiful residence have been laid off in walks and flower beds and the latter already show the effect of good attention. We plucked a 26 pound cabbage head from his vegetable patch (not the largest by any means) and sat down with him to devour the best melons that it has been our good pleasure to attack this season. Mr Morrison is thoroughly in earnest on the water question and if all our farmers were like him the irrigation scheme would soon take tangible shape" – Sep 5 1885. An earlier edition of the *SM Times* published the Petition for Reclamation District, with many names, including Morrison.

Morrison's peregrinations to and from California are chronicled in the biography of his son Joseph in Guinn's book, and epitomized on the chart below. If we may be so bold as to postulate, it would appear that he and his first wife were divorced, although Guinn waffles on that issue. Divorce on grounds of desertion was not uncommon in the 19th century when there was a disparity of opinion between spouses on the advantages of moving west. Joseph, who had come to California on his father's second trip, went back to Ohio about the time his father married "a much younger woman," and didn't rejoin his father in California until twenty years had elapsed, and he was a mature family man himself, having spent 14 years in Kansas, where his mother is said to have died. By that time the offending second wife was gone, and Ezra had taken unto himself a third, going to Oregon to do it.

That presents an interesting problem: how did he become acquainted with Amanda? The obituary of Amanda's sister, Ruth Monwell, states that she and Amanda came to California together in 1873, and Ruth lived in San Luis Obispo county for seven years, then four months in Santa Maria before moving to Klamath county, Oregon. Ruth and her first husband, R W Ramsey, along with her brother, Wm P Carman and wife, Hattie, are enumerated in Arroyo Grande in the 1880 census, which must have been shortly before she left for Santa Maria and Oregon. This was several years before Ezra Morrison appeared on this scene. A connection could be their brother, Wm Carman, who was a druggist in Arroyo Grande as late as 1892, in Santa Maria on the 1900 census, and later moving to Santa Barbara, where he lived the rest of his life, which ended in 1930. There was a third sister, Mary, a maiden lady living with the Ramseys in 1880; it appears that none of these siblings had offspring, so their secrets died with them.

The Riley County (KS) Genealogical Society is one of our exchanges; in their offerings is the *Portrait and Biographical Album of Washington County*, where Joseph A Morrison lived for some years. A request was made to search for any mention of Joe, and, although there were three Morrisons, there does not appear to be a connection. Libby Wolffing, their Genealogist, suggested that the Washington County Historical Society might find something in their library/archives. The address is 208 Ballard, P.O. Box 31, Washington, KS 66968, for anyone who might wish to pursue this family.

Ezra Morrison     b. OH 30 Oct 1816
   1850 cen: Hamilton co OH     d. at home 6 Oct 1905 @88/11/6; SM cem
     Sycamore tp     obit Oct 15 p.2, 6 ch surviving
   1852: to CA; ret to OH 1860     F: (NY); M: (VT)
   1861: to CA; Sacramento
   1862-68: Trinity co, sawmill & farm
   1870 cen: Butte co, Hamilton tp w/2nd wife; in Butte 16y
   1880 cen: Butte co Hamilton tp w/2 boys, 2 Chinese, no wife
   1884: to Santa Maria
   1890 GR: 73 OH f SM #1; reg Aug 9
   1892 GR: 75 5' 7½ lt complexion blue eyes grey hair OH; SM. Lower part of rt eye torn away;
     reg Aug 2
   1900 cen: SM. also Ruth E Monwell (1847-1907) sis-in-law; divorced
     m.1 c1840
Martha Jane Van Horn     b. OH c1819
   1860 cen: Hamilton co OH     d. Kansas @60 (Guinn)
     Sycamore tp @40
     m.2 c1870 (before census)

Anna E Osborn                          b. IL c1849
                                             d. (not on 1880 census) (died during an epidemic)
                                             F: (Douglas Osborn 1815-   ) b. KY
                                             M: (Jane 1818-   ) b. KY
      m.3 Linkville, Klamath co OR 24 Feb 1886 (*Times*)
Amanda Melvina Carman           b. OH 2 Mar 1839
  1906 Dir: Ezra Mrs 1½ m SE        d. at home of dau-in-law Mrs Joe Morrison
  1909 Dir: Mrs A M same           s Pine st 26 Dec 1918 @79/9/24; SM cem
  1910 cen: same                  obit Sat Dec 28 p.7
  1914 SLO Dir: Mrs A M            bro W H (sic) Carman, Santa Barbara
      723 S. Pine, SM
    1919: Estate of Amanda M Morrison, dec …W P Carman, ex.          –Feb 7
By first wife:
1. William H Morrison             b. OH 1841
    1860 cen: w/mother            d.
      "aprentis plaster"
    1880 cen: (Wm Morrison 38 OH 1337 Washington av, St Louis
      Cornelia 36 IL, Holme 11 MO Wm 7 MO) ???
    1905: living in MO
  a. Charles Morrison              b. OH July 1869
     1900 cen: Montrose IA         d.
    m.
    Emma G                       b. MO Jan 1873
    = Edith F b. MO Oct 1893
     1900: Chas Morrison of Mont Rose (sic) IA is in the valley visiting his grandfather
       Ezra…                                                     -Aug 18
    date lost: Chas Morrison, nephew of John & Joseph Morrison is here on a visit from
       St Louis MO; member of auditing dept of MO Central RR…
2. Joseph Andrew Morrison         b. Warren co OH 28 June 1843
    1860 cen: w/mother            d. Santa Maria 1 Aug 1916 @73/1/4; SM cem
    1861: to CA w/father, teaming   obit Aug 5, bio Guinn 1743, also photo of Ezra & Joe
      in Sacramento 1861-2
    1870 cen: Trinity co, farm wkr, single, no read/write
    1870: back to OH, married      1877: to Washington co KS
    1880 cen: Washington co KS Sherman tp
    1890: J A Morrison, son of Ezra has gone back to Kansas on a business trip.   –Oct 4
     Joseph Morrison returned this week from his trip to Kansas.  He says crops were
     quite a failure in that State this past season . . . says that he was in quite a smash
     upon his train but no one was hurt.                                –Nov 8
    1891: to Santa Maria valley (Guinn)
    1892 GR: 49 5' 7½ lt blu br OH SM #1; reg Aug 8
    1900 cen: SM widower
    1901: to Klondike
    1906 Dir: J A f 2½ m SE; Mrs
    1908: Jos Morrison Has Broken Rib. May 30, 1908, Milford, Lassen co … arrived in the
     midst of a snow storm May 14 from San Francisco … 75 miles north of Reno …
     Honey Lake … I am done up in bandages so tight I can hardly breathe. I can
     walk around but it is tough when it comes to lying down … Regards to Santa
     Maria Friends.                                                   –June 20
    1909 Dir: Joe ranching 1½ m SE
    1910 cen: SM 6 years 2$^{nd}$ marriage

1912: Jas Treat and Jos Morrison are in southern Arizona near the Mexican line with
Gold Canyon Mining Corp interests (a local corp) —Dec 28
1914 SLO Dir: Jos A (Jane) 723 S Pine SM
    m.1 OH c1870
Alice B. Apgar (Apger)          b. OH 1853
                                    d. nr SM 13 Mar 1896 @43/3/8; SM cem; parents NJ
                                    Card of Thanks. J A Morrison          - Mar 14

a.    Alice Estella Morrison           b. OH May 1874
     "Stella"                                d. Nipomo 6 Mar 1912 @37/9/22; SM cem
                                           obit Mar 9; pneumonia; 3 ch
      1893: Miss Stella Morrison who has been visiting friends and relatives in this
          valley for some time returned to Santa Barbara on Monday last.     —Dec 30
      1900 cen: 2 births 2 living
      1910 cen: 4 births 4 living
      1912: Card of Thanks: P S Runels and family; J A Morrison; Mrs A F Ramirez;
          J A Morrison jr
        m. 1895
   Philip Stephen Runels 1869-1944; see Runels chart
     "Steve"

b.    Rollin P Morrison                b. OH Feb 1876
      1900 cen: Nipomo w/E H        d.
          Nicholson, svt
      1906 Dir: R f 4½ m S; Mrs
      1910 cen: SM 3 births 3 living
      1936: living in Arizona
         m. SLO co 22 Oct 1902
   Pearl Bellamy                     b. TX May 1882 (cen)
                                   (1 May 1882; SSDI;
                                   d. Phoenix Aug 1979) ?
                                   F: R A Bellamy 1856-
                                   M: Rachel M 1857-1902
   = Donald D 1904 (cen) (1903-1986)?
   = Lea R 1907-
   = baby 1910

c.    Blanche Morrison               b. Washington co KS 1878 (@2 in 1880-
                                   @29 in 1910!)
                                   d.
         m.1 Bakersfield 3 July 1898 (*Times*)
   Abel F Ramirez                  b. CA 1863 (cen)
     1910 cen: Los Angeles        d. (Los Angeles 4-22-1920 @50) ?
   = Abel F jr 1900
   = Joseph A 1905 (9 Aug 1905; SSDI; Oct 1972 SF) ?
   Blanche m.2 Campbell living in SM 1936

d.    Frank Morrison                   b. Washington co KS
     electrician SF (Guinn)          d. (Frank 5 Apr 1882; SSDI;
     1936: living in Tacoma WA        May 1977 Ruston WA) ?
        m.
   Sadie McCaw                     b. (Sadie 28 Jul 1893; SSDI;
                                   Oct 1979 rMarysvl WA; ben to Everett)?

|   |   |   |
|---|---|---|
| | e. Joseph A Morrison jr | b. Washington co KS Aug 1889 (cen) |
| |    1920 cen: Jos A 34 KS | d. (8 Aug 1890; SSDI |
| |    lodger, Los Angeles (?) |    Mar 1982 Los Angeles)? |
| 2. |        m.2 Jan 1904 | |
| | Jane D H O'Leary Shea | b. VT 1852 |
| |    1910 cen: 1 birth 1 living | d. at home 731 S Pine 30 Oct 1936 @85/10/5; SM cem |
| |    1910 Personals: Miss O'Leary, |    obit Sat Oct 31 p.3 |
| |    sis of Mrs Joe Morrison, |    her son, Wm J Shea, SM 1936; gson Paul K Shea, |
| |    returned to home in NYC. |    La Jolla, 1936; sis Joanna McDermott, Berkeley, |
| |        -Aug 27 |    1936; Elizabeth O'Leary, Pacific Grove, 1936; neph |
| |    1916: Morrison Will Filed |    Allen P Lindsey, San Jose; nc Catherine Lindsey, |
| |    Petition of Jane Morrison. |    Berkeley |

      Farmland in T10 to son Rollie subject to life estate of Amanda Morrison, rest to Jane.
      $20,000.                                                                          –Aug 12
      1917: Sale of property of Jos A Morrison by Jane, exec        –*Vidette* June 12
      1920 cen: 723 S Pine; also Nora Ayers 79 Ire, sister. She was in Joe's household 1910,
      also =Honora Ayers (Mrs S F) 26 Mar 1839-11 Jan 1929; Morrison-Runels plot SM cem
      1920: Susan E Lincoln 66 MA also w/Jane
      1920: Wm Shay (sic) arr yesterday from Pittsburgh to visit mother Mrs Morrison
      S Pine st                                                                        -*Vidette* Wed Dec 22
      1922-3 Dir: Mrs Jane wd r723 S Pine; 1930 Dir: same

|   |   |   |
|---|---|---|
| 3. | John Morrison | b. OH 1846 |
| | | d. (before 1860) ? |
| 4. | Mary E Morrison | b. OH Nov 1848 |
| |    1860 cen: w/mother | d. |
| |    1900 cen: Washington co KS | |
| |    Sherman pct no husband | |
| |    1905: living in KS | |
| |        m. 1870 | |
| | Alpheus Wing Boynton | b. Portland? ME 1833 (IGI) |
| |    1870 cen: Trinity co CA | d. |
| |      next to Joe Morrison | F: Alpheus Wing Boynton (IGI) |
| |    1880 cen: Washington co | M: Sarah Stockbridge (IGI) |
| |      KS Sherman pct | |
| |   a. Alma E Boynton | b. CA 1869 |
| |   b. George P Boynton | b. KS 1873 |
| |   c. Clara E/Clarice Boynton | b. KS June 1875 |
| |   d. Alice Belle Boynton | b. KS Jan 1878 |
| |   e. Alpheus Boynton | b. KS Jan 1884 |
| 5. | Charles Morrison | b. OH 1856 |
| |    1905: living in Tacoma | d. |

By second wife:

|   |   |   |
|---|---|---|
| 6. | John Henry Morrison | b. Gridley CA 22 Sep 1871; m. of SM |
| |    1880 cen: w/father | d. San Jose 12 July 1962 @90/9/20; SM cem |
| |    1892 GR: 21 5' 5½ lt blu br |    obit Fri July 13 p.2, 2 gsons 5 ggch |
| |    CA SM #1; reg Sep 24 | |

      1894: John Morrison rr foreman, construction.        –*SLO Morning Tribune* Feb
      1896: Johnny Morrison rides a new '96 Victor Bicycle.        –Mar 14
      1900 cen: SM clk flour mill; 1 birth 1 living;   1906 Dir: clk w/W F Kelley; Mrs
      1909 Dir: Asst rr office, rPine & Morrison; Mrs Anna
      1910 cen: S Pine, bkpr oil co; 4 births 4 living

1914 SLO Dir: John H (Anna) acct Pinal-Dome Refining Co r Garey rd at city limits, SM
1927: to San Jose, Bank of America; retired 1930. Worked as depot agt for PCRR;
   for Pinal-Dome Oil Co; for old Bank of SM.
     m. San Luis Obispo 22 June 1895 by W W Madge, Congl, D554
       wit: Mrs Thomas Dawson, SLO; Mrs W W Madge, SLO

| | |
|---|---|
| Annie Sarah Swain | b. Cayucos CA 17 Feb 1870; m. of SLO |
|   1927: living in San Jose | d. Santa Maria 28 May 1968 @98; Cayucos cem |
|   1930: built house S Bwy |   obit Thu May 30; 3 gch, 4 ggch |
|     (2445 in later yrs) where | F: Robert Corlin Swain 1815-1910 |
|     she continued to live | M: Elizabeth A Mansfield (Tripp) 1828-1872 |

  1968 pall bearers: Rob Morrison, Densil Glines, Andrew Howard, Dorian Davis,
    Manfred Sander, Winston Wickenden

| | |
|---|---|
| a. Charity Morrison (Herz) | b. SM 11 Apr 1897 (*Times*) (Apr 10, SS) |
|   Dec 1914: Honor Roll, SMHS, | d. (Nevada co 1-12-1983; ben to Alta Hill, |
|     junior class |   Nevada co) |

  1918: From Saturday's Daily: Mrs John Morrison and daughter, Miss Charity, left
    this morning for a week's visit in Los Angeles.     –Sat Dec 28
  1919: Mrs John H Morrison and daughter, Miss Charity, are registered at the
    Barbara in Santa Barbara.     –Jan 11
  1962: Living in San Jose; 1980: Living in Citrus Heights

| | |
|---|---|
| b. Grace Malvina Morrison | b. SM 9 Dec 1900 (*Times*) |
| | d. SM 22 Nov 1987 @87; SM cem |
| |   obit Tue Nov 24 p.10; res Palo Alto |
| |   1920-1973 |

  1918: 18th birthday, music, dancing…Misses Veda Tunnell, Marguerite Walker, Edna
    Jessee, Elzina Gillespie, Beth Donovan, Viola Martin, Charity and Grace
    Morrison; Messrs Geo and Alec Dalessi, Elwood Triplett, Geo Fanny, Neal
    Donovan, Romaldo Tomasini.     –Sat Dec 14
  1919: Farewell party for Mrs Elizabeth Jessee at home of Mr And Mrs Henry Strong,
    610 S Lincoln…going to San Jose.     –July 30
  1920 cen: w/Lizzie Jessee, San Jose
  1980 Dir: r2445 S Bwy SM
    m.1 SLO co 26 March 1938

| | |
|---|---|
| Lawrence Oakley Cook | b. SM 13 Aug 1895 |
| | d. Palo Alto 6 Jan 1941 @45/4/18; SM cem |
| | F: Geo Lawrence Cook 1867-1944 |
| | M: Minnie Belle Oakley 1875-1941 |

    m.2 (divorced after 20 years)

| | |
|---|---|
| Robert Schmitt | (Robert J. Schmitt d. San Francisco 6 Aug 1979)? |
| = No issue | |
| c. Marion M Morrison | b. SM 26 June 1905 |
|   SMUHS 1923 | d. SM 17 Oct 1996 @91; SM cem |
|   1962: Living in San Jose |   obit Sat Oct 19 A-5; 2 gch 3 ggch 1 neph |
|   1980 Dir: ret h4361 Heather Ct SM | |
|     m.1 | |
| John David Payne | b. MO 12 Nov 1898 |
|   to SM 1918 | d. SM 5 Dec 1972 @74/0/23; SM cem |
|   1925 Dir: John D (Marrion) slsmn; |   obit Thu Dec 7 p.2, 1 bro 4 sis 2 gch. |
|     r431 S Pine |   r624 E Sunset; Cattle rancher & Assoc Oil Co. |

  1928 Dir: John (Marian) prop Asso Oil sta, as above
  1930 Dir: Payne Svc Sta Cook & Bwy; r same

      1940-1 Dir: RR #2; Payne & McIntosh ser sta 320 S Bwy
      1955-6 Dir: drvr Tassoc (sic) Oil r2445 S Bwy Rt #2
      1960 Dir: drvr Tidewater Oil r2445 S Bwy
      1972 pall bearers: John Davenport, Burt Pereira, Rbt Thompson, Bob Rivers, Doc Dias, Rbt Jones

= John Dale b. SM 24 June 1924; d. at home 11 Jan 1989 @64; SM Cem.
   obit Thu Jan 12 p.12
     1930: Kidnapping Warrant Issued for Local Man. Six-Year-Old Baby Stolen, Father Says. John D Payne Asks Police to Find Jess Shoup…Mother Missing, Child Also Gone. Disappeared Last Monday; Reward Offered for Arrest. ($250)…taken from home at 431 S Pine by Shoup and his own mother…Payne service station owner-operator Cook & Broadway…grandfather John Morrison following meager clue in bay region…Mrs Annie Morrison here from San Jose residing with Payne.
     …Shoup a San Quentin graduate –Mon Nov 17. Masquerading as J D Payne…about 40 years old, dresses well; about 5' tall, talks out of corner of his mouth…gray eyes...      –Nov 20
    SMUHS 1942; Army Air Corps; USC Sch of Aeronautics (Hancock), 34½ years General Telephone, retired 1982. NRA.
   son Mark Payne, dau Leslie Overby, both Santa Maria
   step-son Vern Campbell, step-dau Carol Campbell, both Santa Maria
   1955-6 Dir: John D (Ruth) emp Gen Tel h817 S Barbara
   1962 Dir: John D (Ruth) foreman Gen Tel h1304 Yale Pl
   1975 Dir: John (Rena) emp Genl Tel h624 E Sunset av
   1980 dir: Dale (Rena) USAF h2845 Monte Verde Dr

c.      m.2
   Donald A Gagliardo      b. 27 Mar 1908; SSDI
                                      d. (San Jose) 6 June 1974

d. Robert Carey Morrison      b. SM 12 Mar 1907
   1940-1 Dir: RR2 ret      d. at home 15 June 1980 @73 Foxen/San Ramon
   1947-8 Dir: Cary h309 W Orange      Cem. obit suicide Mon June 16 p.2, obit
   1955-6 Dir: Rbt C rancher      Wed June 18 p. 18
     r2445 S Bwy      6 neph, 1 nc (great neph, probably)
   1970 Dir: Carey f r2445 S Bwy
   1980 Dir: same, retired
   1981: Morrison Ranch Up for Sale.      –Thu July 30 p.12
   1992: Petition to administer estate of Robert Carey Morrison. Carole Hurst, Judith Chinello, Stan Mandell, personal representatives to administer estate. Hearing July 16.
        m. (?)
   =John M(arion)? Living in Sacramento 1962, Berkeley 1980, Grass Valley 1989

7. George Washington Morrison      b. (Gridley?) Butte co CA 9 Oct 1875
   1900 cen: w/father      d. Downey CA 12 Jan 1929 @54/3/0; SM cem
     m. Santa Maria 29 Sep 1900 by O H Derry (*Times*)
   Julia Rowe      b. (28 May 1884; SSDI)
   1906 Dir: f 1m S; Mrs      d. (Pasadena CA June 1972) ?
                                     F: (Elias Rowe 1849-1915) ?
                                   M: (Florence Knapp 1848-1924) ?
   a. son      b. SM 15 Aug 1906, 12# (*Times*)

No issue by third wife.

# NICHOLSON
## SANTA MARIA VALLEY PIONEERS

Melford P Nicholson came to California from Winneshiek County, Iowa, in 1868 via Oregon, as indicated by the birthplace of his daughter on the 1870 census. It wasn't until 1880 that others of his family came from the same county to Santa Maria; his brother-in-law, Samuel Conner, and nephew, Ellis H. Nicholson. A younger nephew, Abraham L. Nicholson, came out in 1887, working for a time with his brother on the Suey Ranch. Also coming to Santa Maria in 1880, possibly influenced by the Nicholsons, was George M. Doane. The Doanes had lived in Elgin, Iowa, which although in Fayette County is only about 20 miles from Ossian, where Nicholsons received their mail. Shortly after their arrival Doanes were blessed by the birth of a son whom they named Melford; the middle name of another son was Murray, a name found in the Nicholson family as well as in Mrs Doane's Hatfields.

Still another family from Elgin, Iowa, was Andrew A Howard's. He came in 1891 to work for E H Nicholson on the Suey Ranch, and later sent for his parents, Elias and Esther Howard, according to Morrison & Haydon, although Elias Howard is mentioned in the *SM Times* in 1889, an obituary gives 1888 as arrival date. Melford Nicholson's wife was the former Samantha Howard, born in New York in 1826; Elias Howard was born in Pennsylvania in 1848. Both claimed Vermont birthplaces for their fathers. It is not within the purview of this article to define these relationships, but we would receive gladly any information on these families.

For the Doane family see Doane chart.

## NICHOLSON SCRAPBOOK

1882    M P Nicholson has on Suey Ranch 300 acres of wheat, 300 acres of barley, 200 acres of oats in fine condition. Mr Nicholson has acreage in Ventura County where he also plans to grow corn and other vegetables.                                -Apr 22

1889    E H Nicholson returned from San Francisco on last Saturday evening. While there he ordered a new threshing outfit and proposes to do some excellent work in the way of cleaning grain this season.                                -May 4

1889    E H Nicholson went to San Francisco Monday last. He went to get a new threshing outfit for the coming harvest; believing that there will be some heavy threshing to do in this valley this summer and fall. Therefore he proposes to rig up in first class order and run nothing but a No. 1 machine.                                -May 19

1898    E H Nicholson, wife and daughter are visiting Eastern friends. They expect to be absent about 30 days.                                -June 4

1898    George Nicholson is hauling corn from Guadalupe to the Suey where he will farm the coming season.
Mrs Davisson went to the Tepesquet Thursday to visit with her sister Mrs P O Tietzen.
                                -June 18

1899    Died. A C Scull, age 86 years 11 months, Feb 7, 1899 in Goleta. Mr Scull was the father of Mrs M Clemons of Martin District.                                -Feb 18

*Note*:  Abel C. Scull came to Santa Barbara county in 1863.                                -T/W

1901 South Side Squibs. Mrs Clemons has been sick for several days at the home of her daughter, Mrs Geo Nicholson.

 At this writing the infant child of Geo Nicholson is very sick. It (sic) recovery is thought to be doubtful.                  Country Cousin -Feb 16

1915 Mrs Geo Nicholson Dies Of Grief At Goleta

 Mrs Aurilla Mae Nicholson, beloved wife of Geo Nicholson of this city passed away Wednesday at the home of her brother, Edward Clemons at Goleta. Her death was due to a physical breakdown occasioned by the loss of her little son a few days prior to her own death. Mr and Mrs Nicholson had gone to Goleta to spend Christmas and expected to have a visit, when their joy was turned to sorrow by the loss of their little boy. Mrs Nicholson was too overcome to return to Santa Maria with the body of her beloved one, so Mr Nicholson came home to arrange the funeral. During his absence his wife passed away. This is one of the most pathetic instances of the kind ever recorded here, and the surviving husband and daughter have the sympathy of the entire community in their sad bereavement.

 Mrs Nicholson was 42 years of age. She was a kind and lovable woman and her death comes as a distinct shock to her many friends. The funeral took place yesterday afternoon, interment being made in the Santa Maria cemetery. Rev C L Kennedy, pastor of the Christian Church presided at the funeral service and paid a splendid tribute to the noble wife and mother who had gone to her reward.                  -Jan 2 1915-front page

 Death Claims Geo Nicholson's Little Boy

 Philip S (sic) Nicholson, the son of Mr and Mrs George Nicholson died Monday at the home of his uncle, S (sic) Clemons, of Goleta, just ten days after he celebrated his 9$^{th}$ birthday, Dec 18$^{th}$.

 The little boy had been ill for some time with diabetes, and was taken to Santa Barbara for treatment a few months ago. He had caught a severe cold and this developed into pneumonia, causing his death.

 The little fellow was a patient sufferer and was a most lovable child.

 The funeral took place Wednesday Dec 30, at 2:30 o'clock from Dudley's chapel, services being conducted at the cemetery by Rev C L Kennedy.    -Jan 22 1915-front page

 An oft-repeated historical incident is the quadruple wedding in the Methodist church, Santa Maria, April 26, 1882, by Rev Holdridge, of three Bryant siblings, two Connors, and enough other people to make up four couples: Emmett Trott Bryant and Laura W Sharp, Henry A Bryant and Addie A Connor, Etta (Esther) Bryant and Isaac Dover Rice, and Delos M Connor and Ella M Cheadle.

| | |
|---|---|
| Harry/Henry Nicholson | b. VT; d. PA |
| | F: John Nicholson (AF) |
| | M: (Abbygal, Cornwall VT)? |
| m. Dorset, Bennington co VT 16 Feb 1819 (AF) | |
| Mercy Martindale | b. Dorset VT 19 July 1797 (AF) |
| | d. Central City, NE April 1889; obit Apr 20 |
| | F: Gershom Martindale (AF) |
| | M: Ruth Gray (AF) 1762-1807 Dorset vitals |
| | m.2 before 1850 Richard E Thorne 1785-1883 |
| |  1850: Conneaut, Erie co PA |
| |  1860: Winneshiek co IA Military tp #552 |
| |  1880: Santa Maria w/Conners |

Death of Grandma Thorne

A few weeks since in company with her daughter and son in law, Mr and Mrs Samuel Conner, Grandma Thorne left this city for Central City, Nebraska; her intended future home. Five days after her arrival, it is said that she placed her head in her hands and passed peacefully away. Grandma was 92 years old and the trip was too great for such an aged body. Had she remained in California it is quite probable that she would have lived to the great age of 100 years. Mrs Thorne was the mother of Mrs Curtis of Santa Maria. She was born in Vermont in 1797. At the age of 20 years she was married to Harry Nicholson and shortly afterward moved to Pennsylvania, where they lived for many years, rearing a family of five children. While there Mr Nicholson died and a few years later she married Richard Thorne and shortly…(illegible)…1880 to California where she resided until a few weeks since and where she was a second time left a widow.

-*Santa Maria Times* April 20 1889

Richard Thorne was buried in the Santa Maria cemetery June 188*3*. Born Long Island NY 29 Feb 1786, died California 20 June 188*4*; Father: Philip Thorne; Mother: Elizabeth Cheeseman; m.1 Clinton NY 6 Sep 1806 Mary Ann Armstrong (AF). See also *Genealogies of Long Island Families*, NYG&B, Vol. II p. 223.

1. Henry Nelson — b. Dorset VT 23 Jan 1821 (AF)
   1860: Winneshiek co IA Military tp PO Ossian #547
   m.
   Mary Jane Fisher (AF) — b. PA c1818 (cen)
   a. Mary — b. PA c1845
   b. Henry George — b. PA 25 Apr 1846 (AF)
      1900: Webster City IA — d. Aug 1919 (AF)
      m.
      Almira Cecil Carver (AF) — b. IN July 1848
      =her dau: Frances Story — b. IA Aug 1887
   c. Olive — b. PA c1854
   d. Samuel — b. IA Mar 1857
      1900: Hamilton co IA; 7 children
      Laura E — b. OH May 1866
2. Marilla — b. PA May 1826
   1900: 3rd St Central City — d. (Nebraska)
   m. Feb 1852 (T/W)
   Samuel Conner — b. Meigs co OH 5 May 1819
   1860: Fayette co IA — d. (Nebraska) before 1900
      Pleasant Valley tp — F: PA   M: KY
      PO Elgin; hotel kpr — bio T/W 307: to CA 1880
   1880: Santa Maria
   a. Sally H — b. PA c1852
   b. Delos M — b. IA July 1855
      1900: Baxter-Metcalf Addn, Central City NE
         m. ME ch Santa Maria 26 Apr 1882 by Rev Holdridge (*Times*)
      Ella M Cheadle — b. CA Oct 1864
         F: Geo Lafayette Cheadle 1844-1922
            bio M/H 419
         M: Sarah Jane Ramage 1848-1923
      =Mabel — b. (SM) Sep 1883 (SB co birth record)
   c. Harry W — b. IA 1859; died young
   d. Addie A/M — b. IA Apr 1866

1900: Addie Conner w/mother Central City NE
  m.1 ME ch Santa Maria 26 Apr 1882 by Rev Holdridge (*Times*)
Henry A Bryant    b. MN Sep 1861
 1900: Kittitas co WA    d. Parkfield CA 7 Dec 1923 @63/5/4; SM cem
  alone    F: Francis Marion Bryant d. 1872
     M: Abigail Trott 1840-1924
      m.2 Benj Taylor Wiley 1825-1902

  m.2?
Joseph Ramage    b. CA Jan 1865
 1900: w/Mrs Connor Central City NE son-in-law
 =Beulah?    b. CA June 1889
 =Sara    b. CA July 1890

  m.3? (*Valley*)
George M Bryant  brother of above, living in Watsonville 1924

3. Howell Powell    b. Springboro, Crawford co PA 18 Jan 1831 (IGI)
 1860: Winneshiek co IA Military    d. Ossian IA 4 May 1921 (AF)
  tp #548
 1880: Winneshiek co Military tp #45
 1900: Winneshiek co
 1920: w/Howell P Jr
  m. Crawford co PA 11 Sep 1853 (IGI)
Caroline Woodard    b. Springboro PA 31 Aug 1828 (AF)
   d. Ossian IA 9 Apr 1920 (AF)
   F: John Woodard;  M: Mary Foster (AF)

a. Elsie    b. Springboro PA 9 July 1854 (AF)
  m. 1876
 John Matheson (AF)    b. IA Jan 1847
  1910: Cerro Gordo co IA Owen tp
  1920: Cerro Gordo co w/son Lyle
 =Floyd A    b. IA Apr 1877
 =Richard H    b. IA Feb 1881
 =Archie J    b. IA Dec 1890
 =Lyle W    b. IA Aug 1892  1920: wife Hazel

b. Ellis Harry    b. IA 1 Apr 1856 (AF)
  1880: Winneshiek co IA Springfield tp    d. Sacramento CA 23 June 1937 @81/2/23
  1890 GR: 34 IA f Santa Maria #1     SM cem, obit Thu June 24 p. 1
  1900: Nipomo tp SLO co 2 births 2 living
  1906 Dir: farm supt Betteravia; Mrs; Edith Miss
  1908: resigned Betteravia ranch (*Times*)
  1909 Dir: supt Suey ranch; rBradley Hotel; Mrs A
  1916: to Sacramento, mgr Natomas Land co
   m. Ossian IA 1876
 Agnes Elizabeth Hall    b. IA Oct 1858
   d. Chico CA 30 Oct 1912 @54/0/9; SM cem
   F: SCT   M: SCT or CAN

 =Harry Roland    b. IA Apr 1877
  SMHS 1897    d. Long Beach CA 15 May 1969
  1899: to Newhall to relieve father…     @92/0/29; SM cem; obit Tue
   -*Times* Apr 24      May 20, p.2
  1906 Dir: 2½ m SE; Mrs
  1909 Dir: rancher SM; Mrs

1910: Vine st SM foreman oil co; 2 births, 2 living
1922 Dir: 201 E Cook st SM foremn oil co; Jas, stu; Dorothy, stu
  m. at home of bride's mother Mrs H Davidson (sic) 23 Jan 1904
   by Rev Wm Clague (*Times*)

Margie M Davisson          b. Madison, Yolo co CA 31 Aug 1881
                 d. Long Beach CA 16 Sep 1970
                  @89/1/15; SM cem
                 F: Charles Obediah Davisson 1849-1912
                 M: Almeda Marmora McHenry
                       1862-1936

 + James R      b. Suey ranch 21 Mar 1905 (*Times*)
            d. El Monte CA 25 Nov 1972 @67/8/3; SM cem
              obit Mon Nov 27 p. 2.  bus driver PacGreyhnd
  m. SLO 9 Sep 1924, N335
 Ariel Roberta Glines    b.
            d. Orcutt 26 Sep 1975 @69/11/17; SM cem
              obit Sat Sep 17 (27?) p. 2; in Orcutt 3y frm El Monte
 No issue        F: Rbt Cassius Glines 1877-1933
            M: Cora Victoria McCroskey 1876-1974

 + Dorothy       b. 9 June 1908
            d. Long Beach 2 Nov 1990 @82; SM cem
              obit Nov 27; 4gch; 3ggch
  m. 30 Aug 1927
 Lemuel Elza Glines   b. Orcutt 23 Nov 1902
            d. Long Beach 16 Dec 1962 @60/9/23; SM cem
  Issue:       F: R C Glines   M: C V McCroskey as above
  -Margie    b. 1930 (Lee Eldred) (Chas Smith) rHollywood
  -Robert Rolland   b. 1931; in Bakersfield 1990

= Edith                   b. Dec 1882; living in Sacramento 1937
 SMHS 1900: UCal 1904 w/high honors; teacher Betteravia
  m. c1909
 Walter H Duncan            b. MA 1885; lived in Loyalton
  Issue: Robert               1910-1915
     Mrs Horace Johnson

c. Murray J              b. Ossian IA 3 Dec 1857 (AF)
 1900: Winneshiek co Springfield tp     d. March 1927 (AF)
 1880: Winneshiek co Military tp #46
 1920: 602 N 9th Fort Dodge IA
  m. 16 Nov 1879 (AF)
 May Madina McMillan         b. IA Nov 1859
  No issue?

d. Elva/Elvie              b. Ossian IA 17 Sep 1859 (AF)
  m. 13 Mar 1881 (AF)         d. 3 Apr 1940 (AF)
 John Harmon Logsdon

e. Elma/Elmie             b. IA Mar 1862; m. of Cuyama, tchr
                   d. (Living 1937)
  m. Bakersfield CA 10 Oct 1891 (*Times*)
 Henry C Emerson          b. CA Jan 1862; m. of Cuyama
  1900: Kern co tp #12
  1920: Kern co
 =Eunice                b. Paleta (Kern co) 26 Feb 1893 (*Times*)

| | |
|---|---|
| =Vida | b. Feb 1895 |
| =Ralph Waldo | b. Mar 1898 |
| =Zulo (dau) | b. Jan 1900 |
| =Zoe | b. c1903 |

 f. Abraham Lincoln   b. Ossian IA 30 Oct 1864; m. @27 of
  1890 GR: 25 IA f SM #1   South Side (SMv)
  1900: Santa Maria   d. 21 Apr 1946 @81/5/20; SM cem
  1906 Dir: 10 m SE f; Mrs   bio M/H 922; to SM 1887
  1922 Dir: E Main st at city limits   obit Tue Apr 23 p. 2: bros Geo & H P
   f; Mrs ME (now Nicholson av)
   m. at house of Caleb Sherman 21 Sep 1892 by Jas M Smith (*Times*)
  Mary Elizabeth Snyder   b. Hollister CA 1 Jan 1870; m. @22 of SM
   survived by 14 nieces   d. 27 May 1963 @94/4/26; SM cem
   & nephews   obit May 28
    F: John Vinton Snyder 1822-

 g. George Woodard   b. Ossian IA 15 Aug 1867; m. of San Miguel
  1906 Dir: f Garey   d. SM 20 Nov 1949 @82/3/5; SM cem
  1909: trustee SMUHS   obit Mon Nov 21 p. 1; in valley 60y
   co-mgr Suey ranch; rBradley Cyn; 11gch
   m.1 San Luis Obispo 24 Sep 1894 by Rev Geo Willett, D461.
    wit: Jas A Ford, SLO; Eva Clemons, San Miguel
  Aurilla May E Clemons   b. CA 31 Aug 1872; m. of San Miguel
    d. at home of bro Edw Clemons, Goleta
   For Clemons see ONT 268   30 Dec 1914 @42/4; SM cem
    obit Jan 2 1915 p. 1
    F: Martin G Clemons 1845-1916
    M: Josephine M Scull 1845-

  =Gladys Lenore   b. Martin dist 15 Nov 1895 (*Times*)
   SMUHS 1913   d. SM 9 Aug 1972; SM cem; obit Thu
   LA Normal School; teacher   Aug10 p.2
    m.1 Howard G Arbuckle 1898-1924; obit Feb 26 1924 p. 5
    m.2 Leslie Andrew Peterson 1892-1948
    4 sons 5 dau; see ONT 268-271
  =Paul Woodard   b. nr Garey 9 Dec 1900 (*Times*)
    d. 4 June 1905; SM cem
  =Philip Livingston   b. 8 Dec 1905
    d. Goleta 28 Dec 1914; SM cem; obit
 g. m.2 San Luis Obispo 22 Apr 1918 by Wm Mallagh JP    Jan 2 1915
   (Local News Notes *SLO Daily Telegram* Apr 22)
  Rosina T Fischl Beutel   b. Bavaria 1880; m. of SM
   1920: Santa Maria   d. 26 Sep 1956 @76/6/7; SM cem
   1940-1 Dir: RR1 Bradley Cyn   no obit found
    her son: Francis J Beutel b. NY 1903

  =George Henry   b. 22 Oct 1919; living La Crescenta 1972
   m.1 Mildred M Young   d. SM 13 Oct 1995; wife Arlene
   m.2 Jean Armstrong   obit Tue Oct 17 A-5
  =Helen/Ellen Rosalin   b. 28 May 1922; living in Stockton 1972
   m. 1944 Courtland Broughton Long    & 1995
 h. Howell Pratt   b. Ossian IA 14 Apr 1872 (AF)
  1920: Winneshiek co IA   d. IA 22 Aug 1955 (AF) (in Decorah 1949)

| | |
|---|---|
| m. 19 Oct 1892 (AF) | |
| Margaret Harvey | b. IA 1872 |
| 4. Melford Pratt | b. Springboro PA 23 Aug 1833 (AF) |
|   1860: Winneshiek co IA Military tp #539 | d. Santa Maria valley 7 May 1888 @54/8/14 SM cem, obit Wed May 9 |
|   1870: Guadalupe |   Patron T/W; to CA 1868; to SMv 1869 |
|   1879 GR: 48 PA f SM |   SBco Probate Index #1554 |
|   m. c1854 | |
|   Samantha L Howard | b. NY 15 June 1826 (cem) or 1833 (AF) |
| | d. Santa Maria 26 May 1898 @71/11/11; SM cem death notice May 28 |
| | F: VT  M: NH |
|   a. Lorenzo J | b. Winneshiek co IA 1855 |
| | d. Santa Maria 14 July 1877 @22/3/11; SM cem |
|   b. Nellie F | b. OR 1865 |

5. Mrs Curtis
    1889: Fresh bread, cakes and pies at Mrs Curtis', near the Methodist Church. –April 27
        *Note*: the only Curtis family found in local records is the following; on 1880 and 1900 censuses Mrs Curtis' father's birthplace is MA, her mother's NY, which does not comport with the Nicholsons'.

| | |
|---|---|
| William Warren Curtis | b. MA/CAN 1825; F: MA  M: VT |
|   1879 GR: 54 MA f La Graciosa | |
|   1880: Los Alamos | |
| Eliza S/P | b. OH June 1836 |

    1889: Los Alamos Locals. Mrs E Curtis had a young horse badly cut on a wire fence. Under the care of Mr Whitney, it is doing as well as can be expected.    -April 20
    1900: Los Alamos, divorced
    1906 Dir: Mrs Eliza, suburban Los Alamos

## THE WELL AT MAIN & BROADWAY

Ellis H Nicholson died in Sacramento after a twenty-one year residence, but was brought to Santa Maria to be buried next to his wife. So it was that the *Santa Maria Times*, Thursday, June 24, 1937, published a lengthy obituary, starting on the front page. Information provided by Mr McCoy of the Santa Maria Inn stated "…it was an uncle of deceased, M P Nicholson, who, with the late father of Edward Craig, made the first attempt to get oil in this area when they drilled a well near Fugler's point in the '80's. The well was started after Nicholson had drilled a well in the center of the then town of Central City, where the Santa Maria flagpole now stands, in an attempt to secure artesian water. The water well failed and Nicholson and Craig took the rig to Fugler's point to drill for oil. Nicholson was fatally injured by the kick of a horse, the well casing stuck, and the work was abandoned." That information was written fifty years after the fact, and was fairly accurate.

Last year, well over one hundred years after Nicholson's efforts, the *Santa Maria Times* began a series of articles on the local oil industry with these words: "Dawn Of a New Day. Giants slip as industry dries up….From the first attempt to drill in 1887, at the corner of what is now Broadway and Main streets, oil has given the Santa Maria area jobs…"
                                                                                                   -Monday Dec 26, 1994 front page

It had been Broadway and Main streets for well over a decade when the famed drilling took place smack-dab in the middle of the intersection, but it was not oil they were after. An epitome of the origins of the project appeared in the Santa Maria Valley Edition of the *San Francisco Journal of Commerce*, April 14, 1887; "Another important matter of interest not only to the resident of to-day, but the immigrant and future settler, is the digging of an artesian well in the heart of the town near the junction of Broadway and Main streets. The contract has been signed at a cost of $2400 - the contractor to insure bringing water. It is thought that a good flow will be reached at a depth of the wide margin in calculation of from 260 feet to 1200 feet. The present supply of water for the town for fires and domestic purposes is ample, and comes from private wells and tanks, the wells being from 80 to 100 feet deep…"

Santa Maria was not an incorporated city at that time, but was governed on a town-hall sort of system; it was a consensus of the more prominent townsmen that instituted and promulgated the idea of well digging, arranging financing by subscription, or likely, arm-twisting. Their serious intent to find water, though they should have to dig clear to China, surprising the "celestials" (a nickname for Chinese), is reiterated in the reporting in the *SM Times*, a principal instigator.

Later county histories give little or no mention to this enterprise which led to the birth of the oil industry in this valley; following the adventure through the pages of the *SM Times* gives a glimpse of small-town workings, local pride, and 19$^{th}$ century writing style chronicling human aspirations and failures.

## THE TEST ARTESIAN WELL

The artesian well project for which the *SM Times* has labored for the past two or three years, has come to the front again, and this time promises to be put through. About three weeks ago Mr M P Nicholson was sitting in the office of Mr Kaiser when a reporter of the *SM Times* entered and the conversation drifted to the subject of the proposed well. All thought the project only needed to be pushed to make it a success, and then and there a subscription list was prepared and within two hours Mr Nicholson secured $700. Mr Kaiser then took the list and secured signatures for several hundred more. A meeting of citizens was convened on Tuesday evening and the reading of the list showed that about $1,300 had been subscribed. All present exhibited the utmost confidence in the scheme and one of the liveliest meetings ever held in town was the result. Organization was affected (sic) by electing C W Merritt, Chairman, and A W Cox, Secretary. A proposal to donate six acres of land for a park, contingent upon the boring of the well upon it, was received, but the sense was to have the well in the center of Main and Broadway streets. It was decided not to incorporate until the well had been sunk and flowing water obtained. Messrs Nicholson, Hart and Morton were selected as an executive committee with power to contract for the boring of the well as soon as the subscription list reached the sum of $2,000. The meeting then adjourned to next Thursday evening when it is expected the full amount will have been raised. It is useless for us to repeat the arguments in favor of the sinking of a test artesian well. All realize its vital importance to this valley. The project has the right men in charge of it now and it will certainly be put down.

-*SM Times* Jan 22 1887

## OUR ARTESIAN WELL
$2,035 Subscribed for the Purpose and its Success Assured

…..the meeting of citizens interested in boring a test artesian well convened at the office of Jos Kaiser on Thursday evening…The committee on correspondence reported that they had received a letter from Mr Craig, Superintendent of the Pacific Oil Co, in regard to contracting for the boring…It was also decided that a petition be signed by the citizens in this vicinity asking the Board of Supervisors for the privilege of boring an artesian well at the junction of Main and Broadway streets...The success of the project is now assured. Several large land owners who have signified their intention of aiding are yet to hear from and the subscription will undoubtedly be raised to $2,500 or $3,000. We consider this the most important project ever undertaken by our citizens, for flowing water once struck, hundreds of other wells will be sunk and in time our valley will be freed from the fear of a drought. The subscribers should pay in the amount of their subscription promptly and let the work begin immediately. -Jan 29

Nothing new has transpired...Before our next issue it is hoped that the contract will be let...We must not falter in the undertaking this time, but must have water if we have to go through to China. The best judges estimate that flowing well water will be obtained inside of 500 feet, and some estimate even as low as 300 feet. -Feb 5

$2,400 has been subscribed for artesian well water at Santa Maria. Exchanges are requested to direct deep well borers wishing a contract to correspond with either of the following citizens committee: R Hart, L R Morton, M P Nicholson. –Feb 19 and 26

## FLOWING WATER OR NO PAY
Contract for the Test Well Let for $2,400

Committee...received a proposal from Walker, Adams & Nichols that was favorable and they telegraphed them to come over immediately...terms are that they are to receive $2,400 upon turning over to the committee a flowing well, the citizens only advancing the money to purchase the pipe. The drilling machinery now operated by Mr Walker in boring for oil near Port Harford will be sent over and the work is expected to commence within two weeks. –March 5

## BOOMING THE WELL!
Enthusiastic Citizen's Meeting Tuesday Night

The Sinking Machinery all upon the Ground and the Work Commenced    On Monday last the machinery for sinking the artesian well at the junction of Main and Broadway streets arrived and active operations have been commenced. The outfit contains all the tools necessary for boring for oil using steam power. The contractors are in dead earnest and they will punch a hole clear through to China or secure flowing water. On Tuesday evening the enterprise was inaugurated by a very enthusiastic public meeting at which free cigars and other luxuries were passed out without stint. Messrs. Crow, Ayres and Lucas were called upon and responded with ringing speeches, detailing the inception of the enterprise and prophesying immense results from its success. Liberal contributions are still coming in and the financial part of the enterprise is more than a success.
-March 26

Work on the artesian well at the intersection of Main and Broadway streets, is progressing as favorable as circumstances will permit. Last evening the bore had reached a depth of about 65 feet, where they encountered a gravel bed and water, which necessitates cautious work.
-April 2

The artesian well was down 93 feet yesterday noon at which time they had just finished drilling through a huge boulder. Mr Walker is making haste slowly, preferring to get through the gravel and rocks without damaging the casing. As soon as the original formation is reached they will drive ahead faster. –April 9. The artesian well is going down rather slowly, the workmen having a boulder to contend with. –May 21. The crew of workmen on the artesian well have been taking a rest this week and in general the work is progressing rather slowly. –May 28

There's many a slip 'twixt the cup and the lip, or, in this case, 'twixt the borer and the water. Exuberant optimism was significantly modified by circumstance, but the work went on - to success?

## PART II

California was booming in 1887 and Santa Maria received its share of the raging prosperity. Water has always been a vital question in the southern part of the state, and the movers and shakers of Santa Maria were well aware of the need. In but two months the local citizenry had raised enough money to hire a contractor to sink a test artesian well in the middle of the intersection of Main and Broadway; the equipment was steam-driven oil-well boring machinery, which may account for the confusion about the subject of the quest.

M P Nicholson had but recently returned to the Santa Maria valley after some years as superintendent of the Newhall ranch; the Suey ranch, owned by the Newhall family, was under the oversight of Nicholson's nephew, Ellis H Nicholson. This explains the involvement of William Newhall.

Continuing the story as reported in the *SM Times*, we read a sarcastic semi-rhymed piece printed July 23, 1887:

Oh, the well the artesian well. Commences at the surface and runs down to _____, Newhall to secure machinery that can penetrate the inclined excuse for discontinuing the work by the company that said "we will bore you a hole from the center of Broadway through to China," or cause artesian water to come to the surface. Oh! Adams, Oh! Nichols can you ever atone, to the Santa Maria people for striking a stone, whose inclined surface compelled you to go home. But it shall not stop, the money subscribed and soon a force will take charge of the well who will develop artesian water this side of China.

M P Nicholson has had machinery and artesian well fixtures placed on the ground ready for re-commencement of work on the artesian well, in the centre of town, deserted by Messrs. Adams & Nichols some weeks ago. –Aug 10. Mr M P Nicholson informs us that work on the artesian well will be recommenced next week. Mr Stein, the artesian well man, of San Jose, arrived on Monday last and with a crew of workmen is putting things in ship shape for the renewal of the work. The derrick has been erected some 80 feet in height and the machine is being set up in proper position and all bodes fair for the drilling to commence the middle of the week. –Sep 17. Mr Nicholson returned from San Jose on Wednesday noon train. Mr N went to San Jose to secure the balance of machinery needed in boring the artesian well, all of which will arrive today. –Oct 1. The contractor of the artesian well, Mr M P Nicholson, says he will soon have a fine flow of artesian water if it is to be found anywhere this side of China. –Oct 1. The oil boring outfit, secured by M P Nicholson…is the boss. The big boulder talked of and which the former workmen said that they could not penetrate proved to be no boulder at all. The first time this powerful machinery was set in motion Mr N. tells us that the drill went 17 feet into what was termed a boulder by the former company. Knowledge is power and the two combined is most powerful. Mr Stein, the superintendent, has everything in good style for running day and night and has now settled down to the actual work of drilling and piping. –Oct 15. The work on the artesian well was delayed for several days on account of a little bad luck in the way of the pipe breaking at a depth of 270 feet…the threads of the pipe had been cut in too deep, the cause of its giving way. However, this makes bad work of the affair, as the workmen had to move their derrick about four feet west and start in anew. Mr Nicholson is now using 8 inch pipe instead of seven, and we are satisfied the work will move right along this time without any hindrance.

–Nov 12

We again hear the rumbling of the artesian well machinery, and if the celestials (Chinamen) of the kingdom below only knew what was coming they evidently would keep their craniums clear of where the pipe will eventually punch through into their country. However, after much hindrance and delay, Mr Nicholson states that he is satisfied that everything is now free for clear sailing, the long delayed pipe and donkeys having arrived. Work will go right ahead until they strike artesian water, gas or oil. –Jan 14 1888

Gibes from San Luis Obispo county newspapers: "The project of boring for water at Santa Maria has again proven a failure, which it was claimed was caused by the drill coming in contact with nigger head (stones) which turned the drill from its straight and narrow way making further boring impossible." -*SLO Daily Republic*. Not so, Mr Republic, Mr Nicholson is not the man to give up on account of a few nigger heads, he is going for Chinamen's heads on the other side, if he does not strike artesian water beforehand. However, the work goes on. –Jan 14 "Work on the artesian well at Santa Maria has been suspended on account of the drill being turned from its course by the small rock and pebbles." -*Nipomo News*. You are rather a close neighbor, Johnnie, but seem totally ignorant of what is going on in our town only eight miles from your door. Work on the artesian well in Santa Maria is progressing and continues both day and night. Put that down Johnnie. -Jan 21

We have been informed that Wm Newhall while down from San Francisco on his trip this week, donated wood from the Suey Rancho to keep the artesian well machinery going…and also paid $100 in cash. –Feb 4 M P Nicholson seems to be of the opinion that his experience in the artesian well project is fully equal to his time, labor and money expended on the same. –Mar 10

## THE ARTESIAN WELL MACHINERY LEVELED AND MOVED TO FUGLER'S POINT

For nearly one year the artesian well machinery has occupied the centre of Main and Broadway streets. First Messrs. Adams, Nichols & Walker of San Luis Obispo placed their machinery on the ground and when at a depth of some 210 feet came in contact with a gravelly bed where their tools failed to penetrate any deeper, they abandoned the work and moved the machinery to San Luis Obispo. M P Nicholson, one of our public spirited citizens, not being content to let the project go by the board, ordered a new outfit, costing some $3,500. As soon as it arrived he had workmen on the spot and work was again commenced with energy and good faith. The work being entirely new to Mr Nicholson as supervisor, he of course made many mistakes. First came a collapse of the pipe at a depth of some 270 feet, all of which had to be removed; the 80 foot derrick moved some four feet west and a new boring commenced, which was followed by many little difficulties, not usually happening with an experienced workman. Yet Mr N would back out and then take a new start with more vigor than ever, when at last he found that the business had cost him $6,000, and no water as yet though only a depth of 320 feet had been reached he concluded to change his location. Consequently he has planted the machinery at Fugler's Point in the upper edge of the Suey Rancho in this valley, where he will again try his luck and we most sincerely hope that his place will not prove a failure at the Point. –March 24

M P Nicholson was in town yesterday and gave us a report of their progress on the artesian well at Fugler's Point. He said that they had gone down to a depth of 140 feet and as yet perfectly dry…struck an asphaltum bed and gone 15 feet into the same and not yet through. He is under the impression that they will strike oil on getting through this bank of asphaltum. –April 28

A week later Nicholson was dead, dispatched by the "playful" kick of one of his prized horses, but the oil industry was born, and rest is history, in more ways than one.

An abbreviated version of this story appeared in the *Santa Maria Times*, Sunday, Feb 5, 1995, in the Santa Maria Valley Historical Society's column, The Good Years. It was accompanied by a photograph of the derrick with workers and onlookers, and a pile of firewood for the steam-driven machinery. The same picture is reproduced in *This is Our Valley*.

## DEATH OF M P NICHOLSON
### The Kick of a Horse Ends the Life of a Good and Useful Citizen

Mr Nicholson spent a part of last Saturday afternoon in town, returning to his farm residence, about three miles southeast, between 5 and 6 pm and went immediately to work to assist his hired hand in the usual bee of choring. While on his way, with milk bucket in hand, to the cow corral, his attention was attracted by the fine appearance of the horses, which his hostler had just turned out into the barn yard. He stopped to look at them roll and compliment his hostler on the fine care he had taken of them when one of the horses jumped up and in a playful manner kicked toward Mr Nicholson striking him a full force in the left groin, knocking him headlong and landing him in the barn several steps away, thus leaving him in an unconscious state for several minutes.

Drs Lucas and Bagby were at once called to his aid. In looking at Mr Nicholson's watch which he carried about his person it had stopped a few minutes after 6, which designated the exact time of the accident. The injured man seemed to know that he was fatally hurt. For a time he appeared quite bright while Dr Bagby was preparing a poultice. Mr Nicholson was taken with a chill and from that grew suddenly worse and Monday morning at 2 o'clock breathed his last.

When his good old mother, now in her 93$^{rd}$ year and who resides west of town, was informed of the death of her son, she arose and went about her morning work as usual and after breakfast and the hour of prayer was over, she announced that she was ready to go and see her boy. When she entered the room and gazed upon his lifeless form she turned to his wife who was crying and sobbing as if her heart would break, and said, in a perfectly calm and composed manner, "Samantha, don't take on, there is no use."

Today there is a real sorrow at his demise amongst all who have known him. He was a good and enterprising citizen, always taking an active part if not the lead in any new enterprise that he thought would be of any practical value to our town and valley. Twenty years ago he brought his first agricultural machine into this valley, and for a great number of seasons was engaged in running a threshing machine. For a time he was Superintendent of the large Newhall ranch, near the town of Newhall. Shortly after his return to this valley, a short time ago, he purchased an oil boring outfit at the cost of some $3000 or $4000 and went to work developing artesian wells, believing that if he could strike a good flow of artesian water that it would prove a great boon to this section. He was also firm in the belief that oil could be found in the upper part of the valley and just a few days before he died, in boring the well at Fugler's Point he had reached a depth of 250 feet and had bored into an asphaltum bed some 15 or 20 feet which still increased his faith in the oil question.

## HIS FUNERAL

It was tribute to the memory of a genial, intelligent, whole-souled gentleman. At 2 pm on Tuesday he was followed from his family residence to his last resting place by the largest funeral procession ever seen in this valley being composed of 106 vehicles all well filled with relatives, friends and acquaintances. It was a worthy tribute to the memory of a worthy man. The sad and untimely death, in the very flower of his manhood, of a humane and enterprising and progressive citizen is a public calamity.  At the grave the impressive services of the Masonic rites took place, the deceased having been a member of that fraternity. —Wed May 9

    Card of Thanks…Mrs M P Nicholson -Sat May 12

Vol. XXVII, No. 3, Fall 1995, p. 17

**Corrections and Additions**     [Page numbers refer to those in Quarterly]

p.5.     Joyce Westmyer, 922 W Bell Ave, Santa Ana CA 92707-3828, is working on the Howard family.  She has clarified the relationships of Samantha Howard Nicholson and Elias Howard of Santa Maria: Elias was a son of Samantha's brother, John Rhodes Howard.  Other clarifications follow.

p.7     Mercy Thorne was 90 last Monday … son-in-law Samuel Conner .. widowed 4 years ago; husband died @97.  She has five living children, two in Iowa, three in Santa Maria: Mrs S Conner, Mrs Curtis, M P Nicholson. —July 23 1887

    Marilla Nicholson's first husband was Lorenzo Howard, probably older brother of Samantha, above.  Joyce found them on the 1850 census of Crawford Co PA.  Marilla married Samuel Conner in 1852, Fayette Co IA, and Samantha named her son, born in 1855, Lorenzo; it may be that Lorenzo had died, and Samantha saw fit to memorialize him.

p.8.     Among the guests at the China anniversary party for Mr and Mrs Wm Smith were Messrs-dames M P Nicholson, E Nicholson, D M Connor, S Connor, Mrs H Bryant and Mr Joe Ramage. —Jan 15 1887

    Mr and Mrs Samual Connor, Delos Connor and Mrs E H Nicholson left to visit in Iowa, Indiana and Pennsylvania. —Apr 2 1887

    D M Connor and wife, who left Santa Maria 20 years ago, here visiting her sister Mrs R Dodge.  Now of Nebraska, accompanied by his sister Mrs Joe Ramage. —1911

p.10.     George Henry Nicholson died in Santa Maria 13 Oct 1995.  Survivors: wife Arlene, SM; sons Michael J Franco, Milwaukee, WI; Richard E Franco, Pompano Beach, FL; John W Nicholson, Santa Barbara; Mark A Nicholson, Palm Desert; daughter Terry Branas, Hartselle, AL; sister Helen Long, Stockton; 3 gch. —Oct 16 1995

p.11     Samantha Howard Nicholson's parents were Adolphus Howard[7] 1790-1865 (Solomon Hayward[6] James[5] Jonathan[4,3] William[2,1]) and Chloe Rhodes.  Her sisters were Sarah C Hatfield and Lavina Abigail Mattocks.  See Doane chart.

Vol. XXX, No. 1, Spring 1998, p.4

# NIELSEN
## ANOTHER DANISH STORY

Andrew Nielsen (1850-1922), the Danish great-grandfather of Ye Ed., emigrated as a young single man with his brother, Paul. The only oral tradition surviving was their getting off the train in Omaha, and going by foot to a Danish settlement in Iowa, walking up the hills and running down.

Several years ago a grandson located a story complete with photograph, printed in the *Atlantic News-Telegram*, Atlantic, Iowa, Monday, Dec. 9, 1929, entitled "Story of a Pioneer". It was told by Paul P. Nelson (he changed the spelling from Nielsen), "a pioneer of the Elkhorn-Kimballton territory," in response to a request for a narrative of the early days suitable for the golden anniversary of the newspaper.

Conditions had changed markedly in the 15 years since Mrs Kesner's Danish ancestors arrived; there is no comparison to be made in the two accounts, but this one is included to keep the Danish theme.

"On May 10, 1869, together with my brother, Andrew, and my cousin, J. P. Carlson, I arrived in Omaha over the CB&Q (Chicago, Burlington & Quincy) railroad. Our destination was Elk Horn, IA, then a young Danish settlement in the middle-west…we would have to walk, as there was no railroad to that point… We met a man in Omaha by the name of G. E. Hansen… He had been in this country a year or two and we had just come from Denmark. He could talk English so as to make himself understood, and we appointed him our leader.

"We left Omaha at 9 o'clock in the morning…on the ferry boat to Iowa, and struck out for Elk Horn…as we were in the prime of life, all of us from 19 to 23 years old, we made fast time. We ran down almost every hill and by dark we had arrived at a grove twelve miles west of Elk Horn…

"There were a few settlers in the grove and we went to one of them and got a breakfast of fried eggs and coffee and started on the twelve miles left… We all had blisters…so it took us until 3 o'clock …before we reached the house of our cousin, Christian Johnson…the first Dane to settle near Elk Horn, having come in a covered wagon from Moline, Ill., in 1867.

"…there was less than a dozen settlers… All of them lived in log houses, some 16 by 16 and some only 12 by 16. My cousin had two of these log houses on his place…they had some shelves up for a cupboard with a calico curtain in front.

"There were quite a few deer on the prairie…and the wolves howled every evening… rattlesnakes galore… I often have wondered that there were no more people bitten than there were. In the summer time the men-folk nearly all went barefooted and some of the women, too… Our footwear for winter was cowhide boots…would get so stiff…that we had to warm them by the fire before we could get them on. I was several years in this country before I saw a pair of overshoes.

"…I got married…and in 1876 built… My first house was 12 by 16 with a 6 foot shanty along the west side. I am the father of six children…all were born in this house…never had a doctor…some neighbor would…render assistance… I think the people were healthier then… We lived on coarser food… Corn meal mush and milk was one of our principal articles of diet.

"… In the latter part of the seventies the town of Elk Horn was started…grocery store, hardware store…blacksmith shop…people coming in fast, so a church was built and the college established…"

*Ed. Note:* A copy of the article was sent to the Danish Immigrant Museum, An International Cultural Center, 2212 Washington St., PO Box 178, Elk Horn, IA 51531. A friendly response was written by a volunteer, who explained their museum and genealogical collection. There is a Wall of Honor, listing about 3500 names, inscribed thereupon after receipt of $200 and some family history. Uncle Paul's name appears there, paid for by a California granddaughter, grandfather Andrew's few remaining descendants are less generous. The Danish genealogical collection might prove a valuable source for anyone with that interest.

## Andrew Nielsen's Family

Andrew (Anders) Nielsen was born in Mesinge, Odense, Denmark 8 April 1850, 6$^{th}$ child of Niels Madsen 1813-1891, whose father was (parents were) Mads Nielsen, and Eva Christian Jensen, daughter of Jens Andersen. The older children were Dorthe 1835, Mads 1841, Frederik 1843, Maren 1846 and Paul Peder 1847. Andrew married in Omaha NB, 18 Nov 1872 Kiersti (Kjarsti) Andersdotter, a Swede from Glimakra, Skane; the witnesses to the ceremony were Niels and Yngri Madsen of Omaha. This union produced five children: Eva Amanda 1873, Frederick August 1876, Paul Oscar, Nell Christina 1881, and Anna Carolina 1883. Kjarsti died and was buried during the Blizzard of '88, apparently quite an experience for the family, and Eva became mother to her younger siblings. She and Fred died as a result of injuries sustained in a train wreck at Logan IA, northeast of Omaha, in 1896. It was an excursion for employees of the Union Pacific Railroad, for which Andrew worked as a carpenter. It is said that some passengers were beheaded in the telescoped cars, smaller children escaped that fate, protected by the seat backs. Eva's demise, some days after the accident and apparently on the mend, inspired quite a eulogy in the Omaha WORLD-HERALD, praising her efforts at mothering the family as well as having worked as a substitute teacher upon graduating from high school.

Paul left Omaha for Chicago and lost contact with his little sisters, as not much is known about him. Nellie married in Omaha in 1905 John Augustus Bruce, born Johann August Bruse in Dalarne, Sweden, in 1874. He was a civil engineer, city engineer for Omaha twenty years, then worked at Boulder Dam, and, in late '30's, in Ogallala, NE, on the construction of what was, at the time, "the second-largest earth-filled dam in the world." They had two sons, now deceased, and four granddaughters, of whom Ye Ed. is the eldest. Annie married in Omaha in 1913 Roby Franklin Maxwell; they had two boys and a girl, the younger two of whom still reside in Omaha, with three grandsons and one granddaughter.

# NIXON
## UNEXPECTED CLUES IN REGIONAL QUARTERLIES
## -or- DON'T TELL ME THEY ACTUALLY LIVED HERE!

When we started to investigate the history of the Cole family, in 1976, our starting point was the belief that the family had come from Iowa to Cambria about 1876, and that the patriarch, Laurentine Sweet Cole, had died in San Miguel in 1894 within a few days of the birth of his grandson, Linden Shirley Cole, in Santa Barbara. We had no inkling of the peripatetic tendencies of the family, and certainly none that they might have dwelt for any time at all in our adopted town of Santa Maria. We joined the Santa Maria Valley Genealogical Society not because of interest in the area but for the educational advantages of the membership.

We routinely read the Quarterly and when, in the regularly featured newspaper extracts, we saw the name of our patriarch, we discounted it as a coincidence. Later the Quarterly published baptism records from the Methodist Church of Santa Maria, and therein appeared the name of Laura P. Nixon, a daughter of L.S. Cole. By then we had identified all the Coles between here and San Miguel for the era, so determined to check out our family in local information. I chanced upon two references to Nixons in the *Santa Maria Times* for 1890, but made no concerted effort due to lack of time and interest. Last year at the Bancroft Library I read through their collection of filmed newspapers of the 1880's and '90's for this area, of which there are but few scattered examples, finding interesting references to Nixon; since then I have made careful search in The *Santa Maria Times*, gathering additional material. So, since this family did indeed sojourn in this fair city in its glorious youth, it is suitable to recount the story in this publication. And to think that our first hints were in these very pages!

Little is known about the origins of Edward Francis Nixon, called Frank. There is no consistency on the records as to his age, but taking the information found on voter registrations and his pre-emption claim affidavit as coming from him, rather than from wife or children, as on census, it may be stated that he was a native of Massachusetts, born about 1848. The 1875 Directory of Santa Clara, San Benito, Santa Cruz, Monterey, and San Mateo Counties lists E.F. Nixon in Felton, Santa Cruz county, Felton Shingle Mill, Nixon & Colby, Proprietors. It is not certain that this is "our" Frank, although in later years he had an affinity for that part of the state.

Coles lived in Cambria for a couple of years, then moved to the vicinity of San Simeon, from which place they were run off in 1879 by the land-hungry Senator Hearst. They ran all the way to Junction City, Oregon, and it was there in 1880 that Laura Phidelia Cole, not quite 15, married E.F. Nixon, twice her age. Nine months later their first child, Rosella, was born in Salinas City, California, but the family soon moved to Santa Cruz. Frank said he was 33 when he registered to vote in Santa Cruz in October 1882. The 1884-5 directory shows him working for Grover & Co., Centennial Mill, a company in Soquel which sold lumber, principally redwood, up and down the coast.

Soquel   On the Santa Cruz RR 116 mi. from S.F., 5 mi. e. Santa Cruz. Very pleasant place in which to spend a few months. Post, express, and telegraph offices, stores, hotels, and substantial residences are found there. It is a manufacturing town with a pop. of 450. –Coast Counties Directory, McKinney, 1884-5

Their second child, named for grandfather Cole, was born in Soquel in 1885, in which year another of Cole's sons-in-law took up a pre-emption claim in Hames valley, a booming area in southern Monterey county. Cole followed, and later, Nixon; it took Frank three days to build a redwood –what else!– house 12x16 in February 1886. By the next year he had enlarged the house to 24x26, had planted 130 fruit trees, plowed 30-35 acres, and was in possession of 3 horses, 2 goats, 8 dozen chickens, and 3 hogs. Nixon was a mechanic, which is to say, an artisan, as opposed to farmer; his voter registrations call him, also, carpenter and lumberman. Farming was not his calling, and the fact that 1887 was a dry year probably accelerated the termination of his agrarian career. In May 1888 he transferred title to the 160 acres in Hames valley to his wife, and in January 1888 it was sold for $1000.

      The 1889 Coast Counties Directory lists Frank Nixon, carpenter, in Salinas. This may be "our" Frank, but if so, it is the only time he failed to use his correct name.

      There were two newspapers in Santa Maria in 1890. The Santa Maria Public Library's microfilm collection of the *SM Times* lacks an issue here and there; The *Santa Maria Graphic*, at Bancroft, is hit or miss through October. Since Nixon seems to have favored the *Graphic* for his advertising, his departure from Santa Maria may have been noted in that paper; nothing was found in the *SM Times*. Note that Mr Marshall/Marshal was shorted one "l" as often as not.

## 1890   SANTA MARIA   1890

*SM Times* Jan. 18 – Hotel Arrivals. Hart House…E.F. Nixon…; American House…E.F. Nixon & family…; E.F. Nixon … (?)

*SM Graphic* Jan. 30 – Matters Personal: E.F. Nixon, a gentleman lately from the northern portion of the state has been sojourning in Santa Maria for a few days and has determined to remain here. He likes the town, the people, and the climate. He is a blacksmith by trade and will open a shop about next Monday in Mr Marshall's building. He will hang out his "shingle" in the next issue of The *Graphic*.

*SM Times* Feb. 1 – A New Firm—Mr E.A. Nixon, a woodworkman, wagonmaker, etc., from Santa Cruz has gone in partnership with J.L. Marshall blacksmith. An addition has been built to the shop which will be occupied by Mr N. in executing woodwork while Mr M. will hold the iron works level in the other department. Look for new ad. and further information in our next issue.

*SM Times* Feb. 8 is Marshall's last ad. A November 1889 ad located his shop on Main Street opposite Jones and Lucas new building.

*SM Times* Feb. 15 – A New Advertisement – In another column will be found the advertisement of the firm of Marshall & Nixon, who have formed a co-partnership for the purpose of carrying on a general blacksmithing and wagonmaking business. Mr Marshall, as a blacksmith, needs no introduction to our readers, as he has been kept quite busy for the past year in this town at this work. Mr Nixon comes well recommended as a fine mechanic; consequently we feel satisfied that this new firm will give satisfaction in any kind of work they may undertake to do.

MARSHALL & NIXON<br>
Main Street  Santa Maria Cal.<br>
Wagonmaking and Blacksmithing<br>
ALL Kinds of Farm Machinery Repaired<br>
And Done to Order<br>
GIVE US A CALL

*SM Graphic* Feb 27       NIXON & MARSHALL
Wagonmaking, Blacksmithing, and Horseshoeing,
All Kinds of Machinery Repaired and Put in Order
All Work Entrusted to Our Care Will Receive Prompt
Attention, Satisfaction Guaranteed.  Shop on
Main  Street

*SM Times* Mar. 22 – Mr Nixon, of the blacksmith firm of Marshall & Nixon, having bought a couple of lots of J.H. Barry will soon begin erection of a dwelling house.

*SM Times* Apr. 19 – Report of Primary Department of Central School . . . C Grade: Lillian Fleisher, 98; Warren McNeil, 96; Rosella Nixon, 96; Minnie Nelson, 95; Ruby Bryant, 90; Leo Smith, 83; Allie Blosser, 78.     Emma R. Child, Teacher

*SM Times* May 10 – It is said that there is nothing new under the sun, but this is a mistake, for in our stroll the other day we visited Marshall & Nixon's blacksmith shop and there found a brand new wagon, out and out, just finished by the above gentlemen, ready for the paint brush. We examined it thoroughly and found the workmanship first-class. It was built for Mr L. Morris, residing some distance east of Santa Maria. These gentlemen are mechanics that we can heartily recommend to our readers who may desire any work in their line.

Central School Report – Primary Department . . . C Grade: Lillian Fleisher, 96; Warren McNeil, 95; Minnie Nelson, 95; Rosella Nixon, 93; Leo Smith, 89; Ruby Bryant, 85; Allie Blosser, 76.     Emma R. Child, Teacher

*SM Times* June 14 – J.L. Marshall has bought his partners interest in the firm of Marshall & Nixon, Blacksmith and Wagon Makers. Mr M. will continue the business at the same shop where he is ready to meet his customers of old. He understands his business thoroughly and never fails to please his numerous customers. Give him a call.

*Note*:     June 14 is the last Marshall & Nixon ad in the *Times*. Marshall inserted a new ad. In July he reported that two families from his home section in Iowa would be leaving for Santa Maria in a few days. November 15 it was reported that Mr Way, father-in-law of Prof. Denton, a late arrival from Iowa, a blacksmith, had located in Nipomo; the next week Mr Way, of Nipomo, had bought ½ interest in Mr Marshall's blacksmith business and removed to Santa Maria. What influence this had on Nixon is a question.

*SM Times* June 21 – Mrs Nixon was called away suddenly on Monday morning to attend the bedside of her father, at Bradley, who was reported being dangerously ill.

*SM Times* June 28 – Mrs Nixon returned from Hames valley, Monterey county, on Wednesday evening, accompanied by her father, who came down for the benefit of his health.

*SM Times* July 26 – Mr Cole, father of Mrs Nixon, who recently came to Santa Maria for the improvement of his health says that he has improved rapidly, therefore has fallen in love with our climate and talks of disposing of his farm in Hames valley and investing in Santa Maria.

*SM Graphic* July 17; Aug. 14, 21; Sept. 4; Oct. 2; possibly more in missing issues

E. F. NIXON
WAGON-MAKER
Manufacturing and Repairing
All Kinds of Machinery Repaired
And Put in Order
Good Work! Reasonable Charges!
Shop on Main Street
Santa Maria Cal.

Nixons' third child, William, was born in November, but his advent was not published in The *SM Times*. The family may have moved already; the 1891-2 San Luis Obispo County Tax Assessment book shows E.F. Nixon in Road District 7, Arroyo Grande School District, which seems to have been Nipomo at that time. He had no real estate; he was taxed on a $15 sewing machine, and "blacksmith shop, etc." $50. In October 1892 Frank registered to vote in Soquel; he was 45, 5'10", with dark complexion, and brown hair and eyes. Their fourth child, Hope, was born in Soquel in 1894, but by 1896 they were in Pasadena where Rosella married Charles Epperson that year. The 1897 Pasadena directory lists E.F. Nixon, carpenter, at 416 South Pasadena Avenue, the address of Mrs Thomas C Epperson. In 1900 the census-taker found them in San Fernando; it must have been later that year that, as the story goes, 15-year-old Laurentine came home from school to find his father trying to slit his mother's throat. Frank ran from the house and the family never heard of him again.

Billie married Alice Yoder in 1910; he was a house-painter and father of two small children when stirred by the war fever he joined the merchant marine. He shipped out of San Diego during the Great War, and, like his father, was heard of no more. His mother made efforts to locate him, even traveling to San Francisco to try to identify a body, to no avail.

Laurentine, known as "Nick", on the other hand, was something of a celebrity, if only briefly. After a trip to the Alaskan goldfields in 1908-9, he came back to the Los Angeles area and worked as a fireman for the Southern Pacific; by 1911 he was one of those daring young men in the flying machines piloting primitive Curtis Pushers for the amazement of the public around Los Angeles as well as in New Mexico and Arizona. In November 1913 he flew at the Territorial Fair at Phoenix, and was the subject of a front page article in The *Arizona Republican*. (Another interesting write-up appeared in The *Santa Cruz Sentinel*, March 21, 1974, in Wally Trabing's "Mostly about People" column.) He married in 1914, and his son, Ed, the source of some of these stories, was born in 1915 in San Fernando. Some time in the twenties Nick went to work as a mechanic for the Southern California Gas Company, from which he retired in September 1950. He returned to the place of his birth where he spent the remainder of his ninety-one years.

Such is the story that has grown from the clues first noted in the Quarterly of the Santa Maria Valley Genealogical Society.

Postscript to Nixon story . . .

March 13, 1890, John Barry sold to Laura Nixon Lots 9 & 10, block 8, Fesler's Division of Santa Maria, per Geo. W. Lewis survey of Santa Maria of 1875; February 17, 1893, Mrs Laura Nixon of Soquel sold the same to Walter Elliott of Santa Maria. These are 25' lots, and most addresses encompass two of them, although the house next to Nixons' sits on four. Nixons' street address would now be 217 West Mill, and the house on that property might just be the one Frank built. On the other hand, the house that J.L. Marshall built in 1889 at 200 West Mill is long gone.
–Santa Barbara Deed Books 26, Page 627, and 41, Page 93

Mrs Nixon continued to be 'a property owner, having title to two cottages which she rents' in the village of Fernando. 'Mr Paine married for his second wife Mrs Laura Nixon, and they have one child, Faith Paine. Politically Mr Paine is a strong Prohibitionist, and religiously both he and his wife are members of the Methodist Episcopal Church.'
-*A History of California and an extended History of Its Southern Coast Counties also containing biographies of well-known citizens*, Guinn, 1907, Vol. 1, page 994, 'Charles W. Paine'.

Edward Francis Nixon          b. Feb c1848 MA
                                       d. after 1900
                     m. 27 March 1880, Junction City, OR by B.R. Baxter, M.G., at the house of
                         L.S. Cole; divorced

Laura Phidelia Cole b. April 10 1865 Jackson County IA
d. August 31 1940 Newport Beach CA
m.2. 1 August 1904, Fernando, CA, by
Rev A. Hardie, Charles W. Paine, 1860-1944
baptized, adult, June 1 1890, Methodist-Episcopal
Church Santa Maria, CA
F: Laurentine Sweet Cole 1828-1894
M: Laura Anne[7] Culver, 1829-1913 widow of
Riley Williams (Oliver[6] Francis[5] Asher[4] Daniel[3] Edward[2,1])

1. Rosella b. January 11 1881 Salinas City CA
d. August 19 1922 San Bernardino County CA
    m.1. 1896 Pasadena CA.? Charles Epperson; divorced
    m.2. Unknown
    m.3. Guy N. Smith c1914
  a. Laura Louise Epperson (Lola) b. 1897 Pasadena CA
    m.1. 12 August 1914 San Fernando, by Geo. R. Graff, ME min.
Clifford Andrew Gebhart, 21; divorced c1947
    m.2. Clyde Wilkins
    m.3. Joseph M. Shelton, d. June 3 1970 Los Angeles

2. Laurentine Francis b. August 27 1885 Soquel CA
d. October 14 1976 Soquel CA. bur. IOOF cem.
    m.1. January 1914 Alice Leota Lambright 1888-1968 separated 1934
    m.2.
    m.3.
  a. Henry Edward Nixon (Ed) b. May 9 1915 San Fernando CA
    m.1. 1937 Eva Edwards
    m.2. 1947 Mary Robinson
    m.3. December 14 1957 San Jose CA
Helen Ruth Gundo/Moodie, 36
  b. Fred (twin) b. January 1923
    married
  c. Ernie (twin) b. January 1923
d. February 7 1981 Redondo Beach CA
    m.3. Dorothy I.

3. William J. b. November 1890 (or 1889?)
d. date unknown
    m. February 2 1910 Los Angeles by J.W. Summerfield, J.P., Alice Yoder,
daughter of Daniel S. Yoder and Almira Miller
  a. Lois b.
    m. Fowler
  b. Robert b.
    m.

4. Hope b. July 7 1894 Soquel CA
d. April 21 1910 San Fernando CA.
bur. Morningside Cemetery San Fernando

# NORRIS
## SANTA MARIA VALLEY PIONEERS

"Father Norris" was a fixture in the Pine Grove District for well over thirty years. Eight of his ten children grew up in the valley and married into other pioneer families; their histories are intermingled in the biographies collected by Morrison & Haydon, as well as in obituaries.

John R. Norris came to California in 1849, a single man recently discharged from the Missouri White Horse Mounted Volunteers as a 1st Lieutenant in the Mexican War. His marriage took place in Sonoma County in 1854, but he moved to Mariposa County to engage in mining for some years. Thompson & West, of whose Santa Barbara County History he was a Patron, says he came to Santa Barbara County in 1865; however, he was still in Mariposa at that time, as will be seen, and the 1870 census-taker found him in Castroville. Be that as it may, once he came to Santa Maria Valley, he put down roots. As father to ten children, eight of whom lived to adulthood, he was interested in schooling, and served as trustee at the elementary level, and also represented the Pine Grove District on the Santa Maria Union High School Board from its establishment in 1891 until his death in 1909, being replaced only in 1895-1897 by Cash Glines.

By 1882 (T/W) he was farming 360 acres, but a squib in the *SM Times* for Dec. 22, 1894, said he and his sons had moved their teams to their Los Alamos grain ranch where they were putting in 400 acres of grain. In the same paper it was said that Bob Norris had gone into partnership with Mr Coffee for the season at Los Alamos. "They are planning for a 300-acre harvest. So Bob will have 'Coffee' for the season." Earlier that year the Pine Grove Items had included the news that J. R. Norris was grafting his peach orchard to prunes, presumably the "large orchard" he had planted early in 1892, to which he added two years later by clearing more land, "getting his farm in good shape." - *SM Times* Apr 6, 1894; Dec. 26, 1891; Dec. 30, 1893.

### A Valuable Relic

J. F. Norris, of Pine Grove, was looking through the rubbish that naturally accumulates about the premises in the course of a lifetime, some days ago, and came across a copy of the Mariposa Free Press, bearing the date of April 22, 1865, and containing a full account of the assassination of Abraham Lincoln and much western editorial comment. The paper is in mourning and makes some sarcastic remarks concerning the war and points to France as wisely spending her wealth and forces in the direction of the Suez Canal. We prize the relic of by-gone days very highly and have placed it alongside the first pair of balance scales ever used in weighing Mariposa gold dust. The scales were also presented us by Mr Norris.   – *SM Times* Oct. 13, 1894
See also *SM Daily Times*, Tues. Oct. 10, 1944, p.4, "50 Years Ago"

The first issue of The *Santa Maria Times*, April 22, 1882, published school reports, and in that of Pine Grove School, John Coates, teacher, were listed three Norris children with their grades for Deportment and Proficiency. Mattie: 91 and 78; Eddie: 98 and 78; Lida: 98 and 80. They were polite if not brilliant.

Norris' wife, Mary Thomas Mattingly, appears to have been related to the B. H. Drumm family, as both she and they are said to have come to California in 1852, and a girl named Mary Thomas was listed in the Drumm household on the 1850 census of Jackson County, MO. B. H. Drumm's obituary appeared in the same issue of the *SM Times* as that of J. R. Norris, saying that Drumms lived in Monterey County from 1867 to 1875, having come south from near Healdsburg. Since both the Drumm and Norris families were in Castroville in 1870, it could be that they came together to the Santa Maria Valley in 1875, in which case the 1865 date in Thompson & West may be a misprint.

What the relationship of Mary Mattingly to the Drumms was is up in the air; it could be that consulting the Mattingly data presented in Kentucky Ancestors, Vol. 5 #3, pp. 130-132, and #4, pp. 175-181, January and April 1970, would explain the problem. Since her daughter, Mary Bell Norris, married Calvin Rice Drumm, one would hope that the relationship was not too close, although first-cousin marriages were not uncommon in the 19th century. This couple had ten children, so possible genetic anomaly did not result in early death for any of the children; in fact, they were up and around: "C.R. Drumm and family spent Sunday with Father Norris of Pine Grove."
- T June 16, 1894

Of the eight Norris children, one was single; three married until death did them part; one widowed and remarried; one separated or divorced but not remarried; one divorced and remarried; and Mattie, the notorious one, married and divorced three times, apparently coming to her end alone. Ye Ed. has not searched court records for these activities.

The eldest son, the aforementioned Bob, married Nancy Scott, who died two years later. Hers is the only marker in the large Scott plot in the Santa Maria Cemetery. Five years later, on a trip to Missouri, Bob met a German girl, Anna Pfiitzner, married her, and brought her back to the valley. One or other of her brothers followed, and the family is still represented in these parts.

We will leave Mary Bell Drumm for the Drumm family article, and Nettie Earl has already appeared in these pages. (See Drumm and Earl chart)

Lida married George Klink, a native of New York. His family had lived in Los Alamos, but after his marriage he had a farm in the Pine Grove District, contiguous to Norris'. The 1906 Directory shows them there, but the 1909 Directory gives indication of their having separated. A squib from the *Santa Maria Vidette* in 1915 says that he had lived in Lompoc some time before that. He outlived his wife by two years, but ill health and despondency brought on suicide by gunshot.

Klinks' eldest son, William, moved to San Luis Obispo, and his sister Madge, did the same; there she met and married Leo J. Kieran in 1912, who, on their honeymoon in San Francisco, took sick and died after five months of married life. It must be that the Leo J. Kieran in Santa Maria in 1940 was the fruit of that brief marriage. Madge remarried but moved to San Jose in 1943, and further information has not been sought.

Ed Norris was married for about twenty years to Frankie Logan. Their parting of the ways may have taken place in Mariposa County, where he moved about 1909. There were Hopper, Logan, Scott, Foster, and Phillips relatives there, all members of Santa Maria Valley families who had gone to Mariposa after the turn of the century, many of whom stayed there, for which reason information is less readily available.

The notorious Mattie and her three husbands have presented research difficulties, so the data on the chart is the best we could do with the resources and time available. The baby, John M., spent his life in the Orcutt area, and is still represented by his son as well as a street named for the family.

John Richard Norris  b. VA Oct 1827
  Mexican War; to CA 1849  d. 10 May 1909 @82/7/19; Pine Grove cem,
  1850, 1860: Mariposa, miner  parents VA; obit May 15 p.1; Mason.  See M/H p.869
  1870: Castroville, farmer
  1880: Santa Maria valley
  1890 GR: 63 VA f La Graciosa
  1892 GR: 64 5'9½ light complexion grey eyes grey hair b. VA res La Graciosa PO Santa Maria
  1892: Deed 44-72: John R Norris to Edward Maynard S13 T9 NR 34W
      m. Sonoma co CA 5 Feb 1854 by Jas Prewitt, A24
Mary Thomas Mattingly  b. KY Feb 1838
   d. 4 Oct 1910 @71/7/25; Pine Grove cem, parents KY
  1850: Jackson co MO, Sniabar tp w/B H Drumm  obit Oct 8
to CA 1852
    10 births, 8 living 1900, 1909
1. Robert Brent  b. CA Oct 1854; m.1 @25
  1890 GR: 35 CA f SM #1  d. at home nr SM 7 May 1919 @64/6/11, Pine Grove
    cem, obit May 10
  1892 GR: 37 5'8 light complexion blue eyes brown hair b. CA. res La Graciosa PO SM
    m.1 La Graciosa 1 Jan 1880 by Lewis Featherstone, min, B438
      wit: J R Norris, Mack Foster
Anna/Nancy E Scott  b. (Sonoma co) CA 1862; m. @18
   d. 7 Mar 1882 @20/2/15; Santa Maria cem
   F: Benjamin Welcome Scott 1830-1909
   M: Eliza Jane Freshour 1838-1909
  a. Clara Catherine  b. 13 Feb 1882 (obit) or Dec 1881 (cen)
    1900: w/Norris gpar  d. 28 Feb 1962 @80; Santa Maria cem
    lifetime res Orcutt
      m. Pine Grove Sunday 26 Aug 1900 (*Times*)
    Joseph Martin Garrett  b. CA 1871
    1906 Dir: f 6m SE  d. SM 14 June 1942 @70; SM cem
    1910: Tp 10 Orcutt  obit June 15 p.1
    teamster oil  F: Martin Garrett 1825-before 1880?
    1920: Los Alamos  M: Martha 1841-1909
    1940 Dir: rodent cntrl Box 194 Orcutt
    1942: 12y Co Horticultural Dept rodent exterminator
  = Lester J  b. Pine Grove 8 July 1901 (*Times*)
  = Thomas Lee  b. 12 Aug 1904 (*Times*); d. 24 May 1952, obit Sat May 24 p.1, accident
      m.1 Norma Dille; divorced
    +James B sports ed. *SM Times*
    +Donald
      m.2 Catherine I Millburn
      her dau: Doris (Witmer)  Thanks, Doris!
  = Joseph Robert  b. 14 Dec 1908 (*Times*); d. 25 Apr 1955 @46, obit Tue Apr 26 p.6
      m. Susan C Ohler  b. England; d. 6-9-43
    +Charlotte (Gastineau), Robert
1.    m.2 Heritage MO 21/22 Dec 1887 (*Times*)
  Anna Bertha Pfiitzner  b. GER 20 Dec 1871; imm. 1882
  110 Norris st Orcutt  d. Santa Maria 9 March 1960 @88 PG cem
   obit read; date not noted
   F: Herman P Pfiitzner 1845-1913
   M: Minnie Schilda 1841-1912

5 births, 5 living 1910; 4 living 1960; 6 gch; 8 ggch; 1 gggch
  b. Ida Bell      b. nr SM 11 May 1889 (*Times*); m. @19 of SM
         d.
       m.1 San Luis Obispo 12 Jan 1909 by Geo Willett MG, H340
         wit: Wm Calvert, Orcutt; Mrs Minnie Calvert, Orcutt
     Phillip B Pettit      b. IA 1886; m. @ 22 of Orcutt (*Times*)
       1910: Tp 9 oilfields      d.
       1920: 119 S Madrona, Brea, parents OH;    1945: Whittier
   = Phyllis b. 1910
       m.2 Ernst in Whittier 1984
   c. Thomas William      b. Pine Grove 6 Dec 1892 (*Times*)
     SMUHS 1911      d. 3 Feb 1945; electrocuted on the job
     1913: f Orcutt;    1919: Lompoc      obit Mon Feb 5 p.1
     1920: Careaga;   1940 Dir: 605 Union, Orcutt; carpenter; PO Box 3
       m.
     Esther L      b. NE 1899 (cen)
       1951 Dir: Wd Ths 605 Union      d.
   = Vivian (Vann Brickey)
     +Esther Jeannette
   d. John <u>Robert</u>      b. nr SM 9 Sep 1899 (*Times*)
       1920: w/mother      d. Houston TX June 1967; SSDI
         Legal ad Mon March 28 1994 *SM Times*: S13 T9N R34W NE cor S13 John R
         Norris to Edward Maynard May 3 1892, Bk44 p.72. Cor Geo Klink. Deed 1964
         June 10 Bk 2054 p.43 by John Robert Norris Jr & Barbara Joan Norris Aug 31 1978
   e. Dresden D      b. Orcutt 2 Dec 1902
       1940 Dir: 110 Norris st      d. SM 31 July 1981; SM cem; @78
       1951 Dir: bldg contr
         m.1 1924; divorced
     Luella Moody      b. 1907; d. 1987
     See Manfrina      F: Dan Moody 1874-1956
         M: Edna Huyck 1884-1956
         m.2 1926 Bernard Lawson
         m.3 1933 Henry Tuning
   = Nadine Emma      b. 1924 (Lawrence R Bivins) in Thousand Oaks 1978
         m.2 1938
     Pearl C Jennings      b. SM 14 June 1908
       1938-9 Dir: wtrs      d. at home 2 Sep 1978 @70/2/18; SM cem
         Beacon Coffee Shops      obit Tue Sep 5 p.8
       1947, 1951 Dir: 855 Union, Orcutt    her son: Earl Jennings, Orcutt
   f. Clarence Oscar      b. 3 Aug 1905 (*Times*)
     SMUHS 1925 star sprinter      d. 28 July 1984 @78/11/25; SM cem
       – T 4 May p.1      obit Mon July 30 p.11
     1931 ph bk: Norris Sign Shop 215 W Main SM
     1937: Orcutt Notes: Joan & Margie, daus of Clarence Norris visiting grandmother Anna
       Norris & Miss Velma      –*Times* Aug 5
     1940 Dir: C O Norris Signs & Banners 221 E Church US Army Air Force WWII
     1951-2 Dir: Signs; h110 Norris
       m.
   = Joan (Gardner) Orcutt
   = Marjorie (William Stokes) Santa Maria
   g. Alma <u>Velma</u>      b. 7 April 1912

        m.  
   Edward W Black jr  
    43 years Union Oil  
2. Alexander W  
3. Mary Bell  

     m. Guadalupe 7 Dec 1876 by W J Leach, B244  
   Calvin Rice Drumm  

   10 children  
    see Drumm chart  

4. Emma Jane  
   Single  
   1920: w/John M Norris  
5. Nettie Moore  

   m. La Graciosa 15 Nov 1882 by W D King min, C10  
    wit: Nicholas Klink, Mary Winters  
   Robert Wesley Earl  

   5 children  
   See Earl chart  
6. Lida/Eliza Ann  
   1909 Dir: Mrs L A  
    drsmkr 213 W Cook  
   1910: Lida A, divorced, same; 2 lodgers  
   1920: 217 W Cook; 4 lodgers  
   1922 Dir: 227 W Cook  

   m. La Graciosa 15 Nov 1882 by W D King, C11  
    wit: Robert Norris, Margaret Klink. Divorced 1909?  
   George E Klink  
    1880: Santa Maria  
    1890 GR: 32 NY f La Graciosa  
    1892 GR: 34 5'10½ light  
     complexion, grey eyes,  
     brown hair b.NY  
     res La Graciosa PO SM  
    1900: Santa Maria  
    1920: 615 E Church, alone  
    1927: 210 S Curryer st  
   6 births, 5 living 1900; 8 births, 7 living 1910  
 a. William R  
   1910: SLO  
   1912 Dir: SLO, RE & Ins;  
    also San Luis Furn co; h 138 Villa SLO  
   1922: Sacramento;    1925, 1927: Los Angeles/Fontana  
   Josephine E Ferry  

d. at home 12 Oct 1976 @64/6/5; SM cem
  obit Thu Oct 14 p.5  
b. Santa Margarita 17 Oct 1911  
d. SM 7 Feb 1976; obit Mon Feb 9 p.2  
b. CA 1856; d. @16  
b. Mariposa CA 6 June 1858  
d. Santa Maria 28 Dec 1929 @71; SM cem
  obit Mon Dec 30 p.5  

b. Jackson co MO 30 Dec 1848  
d. Santa Maria 26 June 1926 @77; SM cem
  obit Mon June 28 p.1  
F: Benjamin Howard Drumm 1816-1900  
M: Jan M Smith 1820/2-1902  

b. CA 23 Sep 1860  
d. 5 Oct 1927 @67; Pine Grove cem  

b. Mariposa CA 4 Dec 1863  
d. Santa Maria 19 Apr 1935 @72; SM cem  

b. Montreal CAN 19 Dec 1859; imm. 1861  
d. Los Angeles 13 Aug 1920 @59; SM cem  
F: Duncan Earl 1823-1908  
M: Esther Reilly 1835-1910  
b. CA Feb 1865/6; m. @17 of La Graciosa  
d. Santa Maria 22 May 1925 @60; SM cem
  obit Sat May 23; card of thanks May 26  

b. NY Aug 1858; m. @24 of Los Alamos  
d. SM 4 Dec 1927 @69; suicide; SM cem
  obit Mon Dec 5 p.1  
F: Stephen Klink 1821-  
M: Margaret J 1827- (Vallejo 1860 cen) or
  Samantha B 1823- (SM 1880 cen)  

1906 Dir: Geo, Mrs, Wm, Madge 8m S  
1922 Dir: N Bwy & City Limits, handyman  

b. Aug 1883  
d. (San Bernardino co 4-29-35 @51)
  (spouse initial D)  

b. WI 1886  
d.

    = Thelma L                        b. before 1910
    = Dorothy Georgina            b. SLO co 19 May 1911; 4-98 #87
  b. Maggie M/Madge             b. Martin dist 20 Feb 1888 (*Times*)
                                          d.
       1909 Dir: bkpr Pac Tel  213 W Cook
       1910: w/mother         1912: clk The Arcade; r 667 Monterey, SLO
           m.1 Old Mission, San Luis Obispo 11 May 1912 by Andrew Gariga, priest I418
               wit: John Fitzpatrick, Glen Smith, SLO
    Leo John Kieran                  b. San Luis Obispo Jan 1889
       1900: lodger w/Maggie           d. San Francisco 28 Sep 1912 @23
          Williamson, SLO (also bro Charles)       (buried SLO?)
       1912: grocer, Duff Co SLO           F: Andrew Kieran 1856-1916
                                          M: L
    = Leo John        b. 1913
       1920: Leo J @7 step-son w/Moses A Morrison, 5$^{th}$ St, Fowler
         (Fresno co) census 22-47-3-7
       1938/9 Dir: J Leo (Viola) Adv mgr *SM Times* h111 W Pershing
         Viola, sec SM Gas, r111 W Pershing
       1940 Dir: Adv mgr *SM Times* r123 E Cook (Madge Horn h123 E Cook)
       1943: Robert Kieran, grandson, moved to San Jose with Madge Horn  (she sold 123 E
         Cook)                                                 –*Times* Fri Oct 29
b.       m. (3) before 1925
    Ernest E Horn                     b. CA 1893
                                         d.
       1920: Ernie E, lodger  w/Mary E Trott, S Bwy SM
       1922 Dir: Emil E slsmn (genl delivery)
       1930 Dir: E E 217 W Cook
    = Barbara, in SMUHS Class of 1944½ , per SMUHS *Review* 1941 in school in
       San Jose                                       –*Times* Fri Oct 29, 1943
  c. Grace Lovilla                    b. Pine Grove 30 July 1892 (*T*) m. @18 of SM
                                     d. Los Angeles 28 Apr 1927 @33; SM cem
       1909 Dir: bkpr Pac Tel r 213 W Cook
       1910: w/mother
             m. Santa Maria 2 April 1911
    George <u>Ray</u> Jenkins              b. SM 16 May 1890 (*T*) m. @20 of SM
       1910: w/mother                        d. 12? Aug 1946 @56/2/27; SM cem
       1920: 115 W Fesler slsmn           F: Geo W Jenkins 1855-1903
       1938/9 Dir: buyer                    M: Alice Mabel McGuire 1860-1950
         Holser & Bailey; 117 W Fesler       bio O'Neill p.394
    = Elmo R      b. c1916    1938/9 Dir: stu 117 W Fesler
    = Gordon        (b. 9 May 1922, SSDI; d. SB June 1979)
  d. Bernard M                       b. Pine Grove 23 Dec 1895 (*Times*)
       1909 Dir: stu 213 W Cook            d. (Gilroy) 6-23-1972; SSDI
       1910: w/mother
       1920: 244 Walnut, Pacific Grove
       1922: Aromas
       1927: Watsonville
  Thelma F/C                           b. CA 1898
                                       d.
    = Dorothy F   b. c1915
    = Madge T   b. c1916

e. Barbara E    b. Pine Grove 25 Oct 1898 (*Times*)
    1909 Dir: stu 213 W Cook    d. at mother's home 217 W Cook
    1910: w/mother        29? Dec 1922 @24; SM cem; long illness
    1914: Barbara Klink has position at Gardner-Wheaton Co for the holidays
           -*Times* Local Paragraphs Dec 14
   James T Hayes of San Luis Obispo
f. Alma P/S    b. 1902
    1910, 1920: w/mother    d.
    1921: Alma Klink resumed her position at State Mining Bur. after a
        vacation of several months.       -*Times* Jan 4
   E A Coston (in Los Angeles 1927)
g. Norris L    b. 23 Nov 1906 (*Times*)
    1910,1920: w/mother    d. (Modesto) 6 Sep 1988; SSDI
    1922 Dir: stu 217 W Cook
    1927: freshman at U of Oregon
7. Edward Thomas    b. (Mariposa) June 1866; m. @18 of SM
   1890 GR: 23 CA f La Graciosa    d. 8 Nov 1918 @51; Pine Grove cem
   1892 GR: 25 5'11½ light complexion gray eyes brown hair, b. CA res. Santa Maria #2
     lived in Maricopa 9 years before his death, obit read; date lost
   1900: Tp 8 farm laborer
       m. at Washington schoolhouse by Rev Amon (*Times*) 31 May 1885, C221
         wit: H Baker, Elizabeth Baker. Divorced
Mary <u>Frances</u> Logan    b. CA Jan 1867; m. @16 of Santa Maria
    Frankie    d. (Los Angeles co 9-11-52)?
       F: Samuel Hays Hulet Logan 1838-1914
       M: Sarah Jane Hopper 1849-1925
       m.2 J E Geddes (Jos E d. LA 3-2-24 @40)
       1920: Joe Geddes 40 MA 867 Wall st LA
   6 births, 6 living 1900    Mary F 52 CA (in LA 1925, Bellflower 1935)
a. Mortimer Eugene    b. SM 14 Aug 1886 (*Times*); m. @21 of SM
    1906 Dir: lab SM Transfer Co    d. Bakersfield 3-10-1972, SSDI
    1910: tp 10 Orcutt, teamster oil
    1920: Pacific av Orcutt
       m. San Luis Obispo 21 May 1906 by Jas Blackledge MG, G305
         wit: Mrs Geo Walker, SLO; Mrs E T Norris, SM
   Lillie L Dover    b. CA 1885; m. @21 of Paso Robles
       d. Ventura 1-29-1949
       F: Geo T Dover 1862-(1906)
       M: Mary Molissa Labriskie 1865-
         (Lizzie Robinson; in SM 1943)
    1941: Mrs Norris from Ventura visiting her mother Lizzie Robinson    –*SM Times*
   2 births, 2 living 1910
   = Elmer M b. 29 Jan 1907 (*Times*); d. Spokane WA Oct 1967; SSDI
   = Florence Isabel b. Orcutt 12 Oct 1908 (*Times*)
   = Raymond E b. c1914
b. Kenneth E    b. 2 Nov 1888; SSDI
    1906 Dir: lab SM    d. Kern co 8-23-1966; SS benefits to Mariposa
      M A
c. Everett B    b. Apr 1891
    1920: Union av Orcutt    d. (Merced co 11-15-1941; SSDI)?
   Pearl G    b. Utah 1896; d.

    d. Marcia M                                    b. Oct 1894; d.
        Robert M Piles (Pyles)
    e. Eliza <u>Frances</u>                              b. Dec 1896; d.
        Elmer R Queen                       b. TN 1883
           1920: 603 E Bwy, Anaheim        d.
   f. Claud L                                      b. 3 June 1899; SSDI
        rancher, Mariposa                   d. Bakersfield 9-6-1967
  g. son                                            b. nr SM 25 June 1903 (*Times*)
7.     m.2
   (Edith                                      b. OR 1881
                                                  d.
        1920: hired, w/Bert Houk, Careaga    her son: Alvin R   b. CA 1907)

8. Mattie                                   b. Sep 1872; m.1 @20 of SM; m.3 @38 of SLO
                                                   d. Ventura 1-22-1956
       m.1 Pine Grove 14 Oct 1891 by Rev R H Amon at res of J R Norris (*Times*)
    Elmer M Hall                           b. IA Apr 1871
                                             d. Yolo co 1 Nov 1918 "former res SM" (D-H)
                                                 or Sacramento co 1 Nov 1918 @47 (CDI)
      1900: divorced; boarder w/Geo W Cheadle tp8
      1910: Guadalupe              F: SCT     M: WI/CAN
                                 m.2 1903 Maud IA 1879
                                 Issue: Gladys b. 1906; 1920: in SB w/Thomas E Hodges
    a. Edna Bell (Frank Campbell)     b. Oct 1892
       in Los Angeles 1918
       1893: News items from South Side . . Mr and Mrs Elmer Hall former residents of
         South Side drove over from their ranch to spend Christmas with friends here.      -Dec 30
       1894: Pine Grove: Mrs Elmer Hall has gone to Lompoc to reside.            – July 28
        m.2 at res of the ladies (sic) parents, Mr/Mrs J R Norris, Pine Grove 22 Dec 1895
          by Rev Jos Hemphill (*Times*); Div. 1917
    Andrew Jackson Downs            b. Yuba co CA 12 Jan 1874
       1900: tp 4 (Buellton)               d. SB co 3-6-1950
          bio O'Neill p.389                F: Wm Taylor Downs 1848-1943
                                      M: Maggie Miller 1853-
                                      m.2 Gertrude Squires

    b. Perry/Harry                         b. Mar 1898; in Los Angeles 1939
    c. Odessa (Harry Cannon)           b. Nov 1899; in Seattle 1939
    d. Madge M (Nippert)                b. 1903; in Salinas 1939

8.      m.3 San Luis Obispo 27 Oct 1917 by Wm Mallagh JP, '284
        wit: Mrs J Thomas, SLO; Eliza A Klink, Santa Maria
    Manuel I Luis                         b. San Luis Obispo 4 July 1883
      1920, 1921: Leff st SLO           d. San Luis Obispo 12 March 1945; parents Azores;
      1931 Dir: Prop Delux              obit: wife Alice
        Barber Shop 1129 Garden st,     m.1 1908 Clara M Pires b. May 1890
        r 2321 Broad, SLO (Mattie)       M: Rosa Pires 1862-1935
      1910: barber, W Cypress,          Issue: Margaret Pauline b. 1908; m. @18 of SLO,
        Santa Maria (Clara)               17 Oct 1925 Q191 John Ward Carter b. KY
                                      m. @24 of Lompoc

9. Jesse                                         d. @4

10. John McNeil                       b. (La Graciosa) 20 May 1878
    1906 Dir: 7m SE               d. 30 May 1942; obit June 1 p.1
      1931: Bicknell;     1940 Dir: 805 Union, Orcutt
        m. San Francisco Oct 1902 (*Times*)
  Mary Harp                       b. Hanford CA 1 Jan 1882
                                d. Orcutt 28 June 1953; obit Mon June 29
                                F: Ausborn Miller Harp 1830-1923
  2 births, 2 living 1910       M: Endamile      1842-1937
    a. Naomi Frances             b. 1905
        m.1 Griffin; m.2 Natale; res Ventura
    b. Chester Eugene           b. 1908
       1940 Dir: Union Oil. r 555 Union, Orcutt
       1947 Dir: Key Constr co, r 350 Park, Orcutt;    1951 Dir: Union Oil
        m. 1930
     Bonna M                       b. Rock Lake ND; d. @83
       1951/2 Dir: clk US PO          d. SM 12 Nov 1992; obit Nov 15
     = John (twin)
     = Joseph (twin) 1951; both stu; 1955: both USN

## OTHER RELATIVES

1912:    Kieran-Klink wedding attended by M/M Geo Klink, M/M W R Klink, Mrs Ray Jenkins, M/M Smith, Miss Irene Smith, Mrs Elizabeth Fitzpatrick (Leo's aunt), Andrew Kieran
                                                                                  -*SLO Daily Telegram* May 11

1912:    Leo Kieran survived by father Andrew; sisters Mrs J D Francis, Pacific Grove; Mrs Arthur Pidgeon, San Francisco; Mrs Walter Sadler, Oakland; brother Chas K Kieran, San Francisco.                                                     -Ibid Sep 30 p.18

1943:    Mrs Madge Horn and grandson, Robert Kieran, are leaving Tue for San Jose, where she has purchased a home to be near her daughter, Barbara . . . sold home at 123 E Cook to Mrs Catherine Murphy, secretary in county offices . . . formerly residence of Superior Judge and Mrs A B Bigler . . . 9 rooms . . . to be painted white.        -*SM Times* Fri Oct 29

1955:    Joseph R Garrett survived by step-daughters Mrs Dorothy (EH) Stanfield, Orcutt; Sarah Bivins, Santa Maria; Mrs Beatrice Grimes, Coalinga; Mrs Nellie Wells, OR
                                                                                    -*SM Times* Tue Apr 26 p.6

1960:    Anna Norris survived by brothers Fred Fitzner(sic),Logan NM; Emil Pfiitzner, Los Alamos.

1976:    Ed Black jr survived by sisters Edwina Johnson, Sebastopol; Kathryn Williamson, Walnut Creek; Evalita Bitner, Santa Maria

1978:    Pearl Jennings Norris survived by sister Alsia Barnes, Portland.

Vol. XXVI, No. 3, Fall 1994, p.12

**Corrections and Additions**        [Page numbers refer to those in Quarterly]

p.6.     Joseph Robert Garrett's wife Susan C Ohler 1900-1943 was survived by children Beatrice Donaldson Grimes, Nellie Wells, Sarah Bivins and Dorothy J Stanfield.

p.7.     John Robert Norris 1899-1967 died in Houston TX; survivors: wife Stella, Houston; son John R jr, Dallas; sisters, Mrs Eda (sic) Ernst, Long Beach CA; Mrs Velma Black, Orcutt; brothers Dresden and Clarence, Orcutt; 4 gch.      –*Santa Barbara News-Press* June 19 1967 p.2

p.8.     Engagement of Joan Norris, daughter of Clarence, to Bill Gardner, son of Mr & Mrs Al Gardner. She grad SMUHS 1950, he 1947.                                 –Aug 15 1950

Vol. XXX, No. 1, Spring 1998, p.7, 8

p.9. Marriage: Madge Klink Kieran m.2 @28 of Santa Maria in Santa Maria 8 Jan 1914 Moses Alexander Morrison b. GA m. @52 of Fowler, Fresno Co.

Mrs Eliza Klink returned Sunday from a month's visit with her daughter near Fresno ... also visited relatives in Stockton. —July 24 1915

Divorce: Madge Morrison vs Moses Morrison in San Luis Obispo. Extreme cruelty. She demanded first husband's name and received the amount of money requested. (SLO Co M35 14 Mar 1923) —*SLO Morning Tribune* in *SM Times* Fri Mar 17 1922

Leo Kieran grad SMUHS 1932

Divorce: Interlocutory divorce granted by Judge Crow Monday morning to G E Klink from Eliza A ... Mr Klink and Madge Klink testified for him. Mrs Klink did not appear to contest the action. —Dec 25 1909

p.10. Norris Klink married Doris Kribs, birthday Oct 19. Her father, George Kribs died in Colorado Springs, CO on a visit in 1958. He was a resident of Orcutt, buried SM cem. Born in Portland OR 1896, came to Santa Maria valley 1917. Survivors: Mrs Klink, Modesto; Harold Kribs, Arco ID; Keith Kribs, Coquille OR; 4 gch. —Wed Oct 1 1958 p.2

Norris' daughter Carol Jean Klink 4th birthday party Dec 1935

Mr & Mrs Norris Klink and two children of Arroyo Grande and Mrs Wm Klink and son Billy of Fontana were guests of the John Norris home. —Wed Dec 2 1936

p.11. Eddie Norris, youngest son of Mr & Mrs Ed Norris, died in Paso Robles Thursday. —Feb 5 1909

Lillie Dover's mother was Mary Molissa (Lizza) Zabriskie, NOT Labriskie – it was misread in San Luis Obispo county records. Her second husband was Edward Esra Robinson 1853-1940.

Notice of Insolvency: Elmer M Hall. —Oct 12 1895

p. 12. Divorce: Nippert Glen V vs Madge L. SLO Co S429 Dec 24 1934

Divorce: Luis Mattie vs Manuel, SLO Co T488 June 7 1937

Notice: I have purchased the barber shop & cigar store of Manuel Lewis (sic) ... Sisquoc ... BF Quick. —Nov 10 1915

M Luis victim in auto accident at Pismo about one week ago is convalescent at San Luis sanitorium ... will be able to go home to Santa Maria next few days. —*SLO Tribune* Fri Aug 25 1916 from Tuesday's daily

Naomi Norris m.1 Harry Griffin, living in Ventura 1936. In 1961 her surname was Puliafico.

Marriage: Norris-Stanley Marriage in Taft ... Sep 11 1930 Bonna Stanley of Taft, daughter of Mrs Joseph A Blos, married Chester Norris, Rev F S Benedict officiating. Matron of honor, her sister, Mrs Spencer Lighthall; best man, his cousin, Cal Norris. Ushers Fred Kincaid and Mark Blos. Attending from Santa Maria: Mr & Mrs John Norris, Bicknell; Louis Tapscott, Santa Maria; W Wiley and Mrs L H McKenzie, Orcutt. Also Mr & Mrs Harry Griffin, brother-in-law and sister of groom, Ventura. The couple at home 13 Taylor st, Ford City. —Sat Sep 27 1930 p.5

Chester Norris died Santa Maria 19 Apr 1997; Pine Grove cem. Survivors: twin sons John of Orcutt and Joe of Kernville; 6 gch, 9 ggch. Predeceased by sister Naomi Puliafico. —Tue Apr 22 1997 A-5

Joseph Eugene Norris died at home, Kernville, 1 Nov 1997, buried Wofford Heights. Born Santa Maria 19 Jan 1933; Navy, Korean conflict. Survivors: wife of 24 years Diana; twin brother John; daughters Paige Norris, Kristen Norris, Sherri Harvey; son Russell Harvey; 5 gch —Wed Nov 5 1997 A-7

# O R A N D
## NIPOMO VALLEY PIONEERS

Gideon Clark Orand     b. TN July 1839 (cen)
    1860: Clay co IL     d. Nipomo CA 21 Aug 1913 @74/1/5; SM cem
    T3 R7E PO Clay City     F: NC
    1880: Cowley co KS     M: Elizabeth M b. TN 1821
      Walnut tp        (m.2 Isham B Gilham; 1860; Clay co IL)?
    1892 GR: 53 5'9 fair complexion grey eyes grey hair; carpenter TN Nipomo, reg. Aug 25
    m. IL c1861
Lydia Grimes     b. IL Aug 1856 (cen)
    d. at home of dau Mrs Earl east of Santa Maria
      21 Dec 1922 @66/4/3; SM cem
      Christian Science service
      m.2 George Zimmerman
      1892 GR: George Henry Zimmerman 41 5'7
      fair complexion blue eyes grey hair butcher IL
        Nipomo, reg Aug 24

1. John     b. IL 1862
2. Theodore     b. IL 1864     first five children not listed as
3. Erastus     b. IL 1870     survivors of parents
4. Effie     b. IL 1872
5. Stella     b. IL 1876
6. Nellie     b. (Cowley co) KS July 1878 (cen); m. @25 of Nipomo
    d. Salinas CA 25 Feb 1934 @55; of King City; SM cem
    m. Nipomo 21 Sep 1904
    Frederick E Earl 1883-1935; See Earl chart
7. Charles S     b. (Cowley co) KS 1880 (cen)
    m.     d. San Francisco 13 Dec 1936 @56
      Klea
        -San Francisco Directories-
        1910: Chas S clk G & J Tire Co r 722 Golden Gate av
        1912: Chas S salesmn r 40 Fulton
        1924: Chas S (Klea) dept mgr Keaton Tire & Rubber Co r 735 O'Farrell
        1935: Chas S (Claire) off mgr Motor Rim & Wheel Svc h 1327 39th av
        1937: Klea Mrs wid C S bkpr r 2364 32nd av
8. Linder Nathaniel     b. (New) Salem KS 19 Feb 1882
    1900 cen: w/parents     d. Santa Maria 10 Dec 1957 @75; SM cem
    1910 cen: w/Fred & Nellie, wid
    1910: Nipomo Notes. L Orand, recently of Santa Maria is now making his home
       with his parents.     *–SM Times* July 16
    1912: farmer, Nipomo     1920 cen: Nipomo     1940 Dir: Nipomo, lab
    1951 Dir: O'Rand Linder (Irene) Jntr Guad sch r 126 E Cypress SM
      O'Rand Irene O'Rand's Rest Home r 126 E Cypress SM
    1952: retired from Guadalupe schools
    1957, 1968: 215 N Vine SM
      m.1 Lottie Mary Leoni 1881-1909; SM Cem "Wife"; see next page
    a.    Eldon Douglas     b. Nipomo 3 Aug 1906
       1910 cen: w/grandparents     d. Vandenberg AFB 9 Aug 1968 @62/0/6;
          SM cem

1926: joined US Navy; WWII, Korea; 15 years submarine service; 8 years in Japan
1956: retired, Commander   1968: 114 S Concepcion, SM
    m. probably Japan
      Aiko
        No issue

8.    m.2
  Irene B                         b. San Francisco 24 March 1890
                                      d. Santa Maria 17 July 1968 @78; SM cem
                                        St. Mary's Catholic Church
                                        mother's maiden name Netto

  b.  (Gerald Charles)            d. 10-19-1917 @3 days; SM cem)
  c.  Virginia (Campbell)        b. 1919
      (Crawford)                1957: La Mirada; 1968: Fullerton
  d.  Myrtle I                     b. 19 Nov 1922/3 (headstone: 1922; worn?)
                                  d. 29 Dec 1924 @1/2/10; SM cem
  e.  Jane (Jas Harrington)     1957: Los Angeles     1968: Ventura
  f.  Mae/Marie (Ruffoni)       1957: Santa Maria      1968: Ogden UT
      (Stone)

## SCRAPBOOK

1910 Nipomo. Mr Orand's barn, etc. are being improved by a coat of paint.      – *SM Times* Dec 17

1913 Nipomo Pioneer Called to Rest
    Gideon Clark Orand, respected citizen of Nipomo passed away at that place Thursday at the advanced age of 64 years. The funeral was conducted from the residence yesterday at 10 o'clock proceeding to the F & AM and IOOF Cemetery of Santa Maria, where interment was made. He leaves two sons, C S and L N Orand, who reside in Los Angeles and Mrs Fred Earl of this city, besides a widow to mourn his loss.
    The deceased passed away from heart failure after an illness of several months. He was one of the pioneers of Nipomo valley and his demise will be learned with sincere regret by the numerous friends of the family.      – Ibid Aug

The other obituaries have been summarized in the outline.

Additions:
Lottie Mary Leoni     b. Guadalupe 7 Nov 1881
                  d. 19 Aug 1909 @27/9/12
1890 GR: Leoni Jeremiah 40 Switzerland Dairyman Guadalupe naturalized Sept 26, 1876
        Santa Cruz, Cal County court reg. Aug 20. (died Nipomo 27 May 1923)
1860 cen: Clay co IL PO Clay City 24 July
1891 (GR): Isham? B Gilham 55 f 200  600 IL
    Elizabeth M 39 TN
    Orand Gideon 21 Helen 19 James P 18 Geo W 13 Wm 11 all TN
    Caroline N? Gilham 15 IL

Addition: Giovanna (Jennie) Leoni   d. Nipomo 23 Nov 1927 @81; b. Switz. wid. of Jerry Leoni; sons Americo, Guadalupe; Amarbet, Nipomo; grandson Eldon Orand, US army (sic); nc Mrs Severino Ferrari, Guad; sis Mrs V Tomasini, San Jose. Guadalupe cem. -*SM Times* Fri Nov 25 1927

**Corrections and Additions**     [Page numbers refer to those in Quarterly]

p.22.     Marriage: Stella Orand of Nipomo m. SLO 1 Jan 1898 by R W Summers, Epis,     E259; wit: E P Rogers, SLO; Emma Miller, Oso Flaco.    William J Miles of Oso Flaco. F: b. ME; M: b. IN

1892 GR: Wm J 21 6' lt haz br f CA Oso Flaco P O Guadalup, reg. Aug 6
    William James Miles 1871-1912 IOOF cem SLO
Died: M Waldren, grandfather of W J Miles of this city, @79, at Sacramento, Mar 25, 1895
–Mar 30

p.23.     Marriage: Linder Nathaniel Orand b. KS m. @34 of Nipomo m. SLO 20 Nov 1916    by P M O'Flynn, Cath, K33; wit: Dephine Matthias, Nipomo; Annie Muller, SLO.    Irene Broderick b. CA m. @26 of Nipomo
    Nipomo. Mr Orand, confined by La Grippe, is out and about.        –March 25 1911
    News from Nipomo. Mr & Mrs Eldon Orand of Vallejo spend the weekend with Mr & Mrs Linder Orand on route to San Diego … Navy submarine "Swordfish".
–Arroyo Grand Herald-Recorder 1940

# PARNELL
## SANTA MARIA BUSINESSMAN

Henry (Harry) Parnell     b. Devonshire ENG 28 Oct 1873; imm. 1888
   1920: 213 S Lincoln     d. Santa Maria 1 Jan 1936 @62/2/4; SM cem
   1926 Dir: Same, Studebaker dlr.     F: Stephen H Parnell
   bio M/H p. 940     M: Helen Ewens
     m. (OH) 4 July 1896
Lucy Rebecca Waldon     b. London ENG 15 Aug 1875
   r 1107 S Broadway     interred SM cem 25 Aug 1950 @75/0/8
     obit Thu Aug 24 p.1
     F: James L Waldon

1. Helen Lois     b. Mt Vernon OH 20 March 1897
     d. Arroyo Grande 18 Feb 1978 @80/10/19
    m. 17 Mar 1918     obit Mon Feb 20 p.8; r Pismo Beach
   Henry Leroy Tilley 1890-1958; see Tilley chart
    1950 Dir: r 1107 S Broadway

2. Florence Patrea     b. OH 1900
     d. (SM) 1 May 1955 @55/4/2; SM cem;
     no obit located
   1940 Dir: sec Auto Club So Cal   r 1107 S Bwy
   1951 Dir: same
    m. c1918
   Matthew P Hammond     b. MI c1892
    1920: 406 W Chapel; 1922 Dir: slsmn Hammond Bros
    1940: bkpr Coca Cola Co r 1107 S Broadway
   a. Matthew P (Dorothy)     b. 30 July 1919
     d. Pismo Beach 3 June 1973 @53/10/3
     obit: heart attack, clamming
     1950 Dir: trk dvr Kirk Lbr & Bldg r 829 S Smith
     1973: r 295 N Broadway, Orcutt
    = Helen (Brady) (in Santa Barbara 1973)
    = Ann (Blackwell) (in Santa Maria 1973)
   b. Harry S (MaryAnn)
     1951 Dir: 913 N Thornburg, PG&E (in Santa Maria 1973)

Hammond Bros (A J & R D) Hudson & Essex cor Chapel & Broadway (1922)
   Albert J Hammond     b. MI c1889
   Aimee M     b. CA c1894
   Wesley P     b. 1917
    1920: 402 W Chapel; 1922 Dir: 425 S Bwy; 1926 Dir: 211 E Park, auto dlr
    1930 Dir: Hudson Essex 201 N Bwy (A J Hammond)
   Reason D Hammond     b. MI c1886
   Lulu Jane(t)     b. KS c1889
    1920: 205 W Cypress; 1922 Dir: 428 S McClelland; 1930 Dir: 211 E Park
    1940 Dir: slsmn Buick Agency h 112B W Camino Colegio

# PHILLIPS
## PIONEERS OF THE CALIFORNIA CENTRAL COAST

Huston Phillips     b. TN June 1845 (cen)
  1870 cen: SLO co Santa Rosa     d. at home Caliente ck, Bakersfield CA 27 Jan 1922
    tp w/parents        @75; Union cem; obit *Californian* Sat Jan 28
  1880 cen: SLO co San Simeon tp        p.2, Jan 30; no survivors listed
  1882. Home school (Cambria)     F: Reuben Phillips c1821-c1890
    report May 19. 37 pupils     M: Juliann (Bunch?) 1920- (1820?)
    Roll of honor for the month…Michael Wilkinson, Newton Phillips.     –T/W 263
  1882. Mammoth Rock school (nr Santa Rosa ck) report Sep 22. 21 pupils. Not absent for the
    month…Reuben Phillips, Bell Phillips, Alfa Phillips…     -T/W 264
  1882. Deed: Wm Pierce & Anita Pierce to Heuston (sic) Phillips 20 June 1882 SLO co $2800.
    NE4 N2SE4 S26 T27S R9E. Wit: P M Bingham, Thomas Bingham NP. Bk O p403
  1890 GR: SLO co: 43 TN stock raiser Cambria reg Nov 1 1887
  1890 GR: SB co: 39 TN livry Santa Maria #1 reg Aug 4 1890
  1890. A surprise party was tendered George and Willie Miller last Thursday evening at the
    residence of M/M Isaac Miller…present…Bell Phillips, Alfie Phillips…   -(*Times*) Nov 15
  1892 GR: SB co: 45 5'10½ dark complexion blue eyes dark hair TN rSanta Rita PO Stuart
  1892. Los Olivos Items. Mr Phillips of Santa Rita has traded for town property here and expects
    to be one of us within a few weeks. He intends to open a butcher shop here. –(*Times*) Nov 5
  1990 cen: Arroyo Grande tp w/ 2nd wife, m/11y
    m.1 Cambria 30 Aug 1871 by John W Allen, A131. Written consent of parents filed.
Georgiana Music     b. (Salem) OR 23 Nov 1854
  1910 cen: 14 births 8 living     d. Salinas CA 16 Nov 1937; buried Gonzales
       obit *Salinas Index-Journal* Nov 19 p.1; *SLO*
       *Daily Telegram* Mon Nov 22 p.7. 8ch

1.     Newton Jasper Phillips     b. (Santa Barbara—obit) July 1872
  1896 GR: 25 5'9½ dk blu dk     d. Mariposa CA 30 June 1944 @72; Mariposa cem
    CA Santa Rita     obit *Merced Sun-Star* Sat July 1 p.1; 45y Mariposa
  1900 cen: Mariposa co     2 dau 6 sons bro
  1910 cen: Mariposa co Indian Peak tp
  1920 cen: Mariposa co; 1937: Mariposa
    m. Cambria 16 May 1893 by R S Symington, D280
      wit: Mrs Elizabeth J Scott, Mrs M M Scott
Jeannette A Scott     b. (Sonoma co) 25 Sep 1876 (1875?)
  "Nettie"     d. Mariposa 23 May 1959
       F: Benjamin Welcome Scott 1830-1909
  1894. Cambria…M/M N     M: Eliza Jane Freshour 1838-1909 See Scott chart
    Phillips have changed their place of residence and now reside in town. –*Trib* Fri Nov 16
  a.    William Lloyd Phillips     b. (Cambria) 14 Apr 1894
      1920 cen: Mariposa     d. Merced 17 Oct 1969 @75
      1944, 1959 in Merced
      m.
      Katherine W
  b.    Reuben Carl Phillips     b. (Santa Barbara county - obit) 10 Mar 1896
       d. Yosemite 15 July 1959 @63
         obit *Mariposa Gazette* July 16 p.1; 59y
      m.     Mariposa 28y foreman Yosemite Natl Park
      Aileen Wass
      = Helen (Sutton) in Mariposa 1959

|   |   | = Mildred Lodin Phillips (White) | b. Mariposa co 5 July 1928 in Merced 1959 |
|---|---|---|---|
|   |   | = Constance Alair Phillips (Hull) | b. Mariposa co 20 May 1937 in Yosemite 1959 |
|   |   | = Leroy Carl Phillips | b. 25 Oct 1943; drowned 21 May 1955 Mariposa ck |
|   | c. | Lester Newton Phillips<br>1944 in Yosemite | b. 25 Apr 1898; SSDI<br>d. Madera 2 Sep 1985 |
|   | d. | Myrtle Clair Phillips<br>Myrtle Branson in Mariposa<br>1944; Myrtle Nelin in Hawthorne 1959 | b. 11 Jan 1901<br>d. Los Angeles co 21 Jan 1994; surname Nelin |
|   | e. | Robert B Phillips<br>1944 in Vallejo<br>1959 in Walnut Creek | b. 1904 |
|   | f. | David Jasper Phillips<br>1944 in Mariposa<br>1959 in Jamestown | b. 8 May 1906<br>d. San Joaquin co 18 Jan 1997 |
|   | g. | Dorothy J Phillips<br>Dorothy Lake in<br>Yosemite 1944; 1959 in Foresthill | b. 6 Feb 1913<br>d. San Joaquin co 27 Jan 1989; surname Lake |
|   | h. | Donald M Phillips<br>1944, 1959 in Mariposa | b. c1919 |
| 2. | | Reuben Finis Phillips<br>1900 cen: bo w/John R Evans<br>1902 GR: 28 Cambria<br>1937 in SLO co<br>m. 1903<br>Minnie L Williams | b. (Cambria) 2 April 1874<br>d. San Luis Obispo 9 May 1950 @76; IOOF cem obit<br>*SLO Telegram-Tribune* Wed May 10 p.5; May 11 p.7<br>10y Cayucos; realtor; wife dau 3 sis ½bro<br><br>b. Cambria 6 Oct 1882<br>d. San Luis Obispo 17 May 1969 @86; IOOF cem obit<br>*SLO Telegram-Tribune* May 20; 50y SLO co; dau<br>F: Juan Pereira 1839-1906<br>M: Florinda (Silva?) Ruiz 1836-1917 |

1905. Mrs R F Phillips and Minnie Williams of Cambria witnesses to the marriage of Manuel Williams and Neva Bright.

1934. Cayucos Apr 26. Mrs Roy Genardini and daughter Shirley Jean and Mrs R F Phillips were in San Jose last week. —*SLO Daily Telegram* Thu Apr 26

1938. News Notes from Cambria. M/M R Phillips and Mrs Alfie Sayler of Cayucos spent several days last week in the mountains with M/M Manuel Williams.
—*SLO Daily Telegram* Wed Sep 14

|   | a. | Minnabel Phillips<br><br><br>m.<br>Dee F Fitzhugh | b. Cambria 5 June 1904<br>d. Atascadero 25 Oct 1980 obit *SLO Telegram Tribune* Tue Oct 28; 40y cattle ranch: 7X Ranch; husband, cousin Jesse Castillo<br>b. (Cayucos) 13 Mar 1901<br>d. SLO co 30 Jan 1986<br>F: William Thomas Fitzhugh 1863-1951<br>M: Caroline E Hale 1873-1968 |
|---|---|---|---|

1928. Cayucos Aug 7. Elmer and Dee Fitzhugh are over at their mountain ranch on a hunting trip. —SLO Daily Telegram Aug

1932. Locals. Mr D Fitzhugh left Monday for a few days. Mr Manuel Williams and Mr J D Campbell are taking care of Mr Fitzhugh's ranch during his absence.
-The *Cambrian* Jan 28 p.2

1932. Locals. Mr D Fitzhugh returned Friday evening from San Francisco where he spent a few days the past week with friends. —Ibid Feb 4

1946. Dee Fitzhugh Loses Thumb in Roping Accident. While helping with the branding of cattle at the Bonheim ranch in the Adelaida district last Sunday, Dee Fitzhugh had the misfortune of accidentally twisting his thumb in the rope with which he was roping a calf. When the rope tightened, it very neatly amputated part of his thumb. He was taken to a hospital in San Luis Obispo by Archie Soto who was also helping with the branding. Dee has had to remain in the hospital for several days to have some skin grafting done to repair the damage. —Ibid May 23 p.1

1968. Obituaries. Caroline Fitzhugh…mother of Elmer, Cayucos; Dee, Paso Robles; Abbott, Lodge Hill. 2gch. Born Lake co CA Mar 22 1873; died @95. Resident of Old Creek 11 years… —Ibid Mar 28

3. Ruth Isabelle Phillips b. (Cambria) 27 Sep 1875
"Bell(e)" d. Lompoc 27 May 1894 @18/8; Evergreen cem Lompoc; obit *Lompoc Record* June 2; Santa Cruz *Surf* June 6; *Santa Cruz Sentinel*

m. Los Alamos 30 Sep 1893 by Rev Stephen Gascoigne —*Lompoc Record* Oct 7

Edwin Forest Hecox b. Santa Cruz 1874
1896 GR: 22 5'7 fair grey d. Reno NV 28 June 1952 @78
brown CA Lompoc obit *Nevada State Journal* Sun June 29 p.19
stage driver, RR eng SPRR *Reno Evening Gazette* June 30 p.9, 12
F: Oscar Theodore Hecox 1839-1903
M: Emma Arrelia Smith 1854-
m.2 Walter W Oney 1852-1926

m.2 1895 Mary Meyers 1875-c1949; 3ch 5gch 6ggch

No issue

4. Elsie Alpha Phillips b. Cambria 18 Dec 1876; m.2 @33 of Lockwood
1906 to Pleito d. Salinas 25 March 1956 @79; rCayucos; Lockwood
40y Lockwood, thence cem; obit SLO Mon Mar 26 p.2: lived 5 mos w/gdau
Cayucos Mrs Leslie Tankersley, Soledad. 2 sis bro gson 7ggch
1910 cen: cook w/B F Patterson

m. Cambria 23 April 1898 by A D Campbell JP, E296;
wit: C F Mayfield, Cambria; J S Bright, Cambria

James Michael Wilkinson b. (Cambria) Dec 1869
"Mike" d. Pleyto 20 May 1909; Cambria cem obit *SLO*
1902 GR: Los Berros miner 32 *Tribune* May 26; Druids
1904 GR: Cambria 34 F: James L Wilkinson 1840-1876
M: Mary Ann Pilkey 1842-1912

1912. Mrs M A Wilkinson died Cambria @70/9/14; dau of Michael and Catherine Pilkey, born IN. Married 1862, 7 ch: 3 dead, John, Michael, Mary; living, Mrs Rosa Harris, Paso Robles; Mrs Francis (sic) Mayfield, San Luis Obispo; William Wilkinson, Cambria; Mrs Birdie Allen, Orange. 2 sis: Mrs M E Rogers, Cambria; Mrs B C Whitney, Milwaukee, WI. —*SLO Daily Telegram* Dec 16 p.7

a. Barbara Elsie Wilkinson b. Cambria 25 Oct 1903
d. Paso Robles 16 May 1953; Lockwood cem obit *Bakersfield Californian* Mon May 18 p.9; hus son dau

m. (Lockwood) 4 Sep 1921; Monterey co 11-457
Floyd Lester Patterson b. Lockwood 8 Jan 1892

d. King City 29 June 1967 @75

              obit *Rustler* Thu July 6 p.1; wid son dau
              11gch News Notes from Hesperia –Ibid
              F: Benjamin Franklin Patterson 1864-1931
              M: Viola May Sayler 1872-1909
    m.2 Ella Taft
  = Leslie Patterson (Drury Tankersley)
  = Floyd <u>Lester</u> Patterson (1926-1990) (Jessie Lee Wolff)

4.   m.2 San Luis Obispo 8 Nov 1910 by H E Smith JP, I86;
    wit: Fela Serrano, SLO; Mrs Irene Carpenter, SLO. - *Trib* Fri Nov 11. p.2

 Ory Elden Sayler      b. Coesse IN 1868; m. @42 of Lockwood
  1900 cen: Monterey co    d. Cayucos 10 May 1938 @69; Lockwood cem
   San Antonio tp alone     obit *Rustler* Thu May 12 p.1; wife bro 2 sis
  1910 cen: w/ B F Patterson  F: Joseph B Sayler 1846-1921
   single          M: Elizabeth Jett Mossman 1849-c1882

  1916. New from Around the County. Lockwood. Charles and Floyd Patterson and uncle,
    O Sayler, viewed a C L Best traction engine at work near Paso Robles and they say
    it gives satisfactory work.            –*Rustler* Fri Apr 28

  1934. Lockwood News. Members of the Hames valley grange will give a public dance
    Saturday night in Lockwood hall. The home economics division will serve the
    midnight supper. Local ladies who will aid in the supper include: Mrs Floyd
    Patterson, Mrs Orrie (sic) Sayler, Mrs Enos Tucker and Mrs George Walker.
                          -Ibid Dec 6

  1935. Christmas shoppers in Paso Robles…Mrs Floyd Patterson and children, Leslie and
    Lester…             -*Paso Robles Press* Dec 19
    Hames Grange Elects Heads…Pomona, Mrs Floyd Patterson… -Ibid Dec 12

  1939. Cayucos News. Mrs E O (sic) Sayler returned from a two-weeks' visit in Monterey
    county. –The *Cambrian* Thu Jan 5 p.2

 b. Jettie Josphine Sayler    b. Lockwood 1917
                d. San Luis Obispo 22 Nov 1937 @20; long
                 illness; obit *Ruster-Herald* Thu Nov 25, p.1
                 *SLO Daily Telegram* Nov 23. Lockwood cem

5. Franklin Phillips      b. (Cambria) May 1877
  1900 cen: Arroyo Grande tp  d. (after 1944)
   Huasna pct; 1 birth 1 living
  1937 in Bakersfield
    m. Arroyo Grande 24 Dec 1897 by J L Eddy JP, E253; wit: John D Campbell,
      Arroyo Grande; Jennie Campbell, Arroyo Grande. Both being minors the
      consent of their parents is first duly obtained. Divorced 1907.

 Rosanel Mankins      b. Lompoc Apr 1882
  "Nellie"          d. Pismo Beach 1919
               F: Walter Mankins 1834-1908
               M: Sarah E Watson 1843-1902
    m.2 1910 Emory Leon McConnell 1875-1942

 a. Sarah M Phillips      b. Feb 1899
               d.

6. Elden H Phillips       b. Santa Maria 7 Jan 1881 per obit
  1900 cen: Huasna w/     d. Woodlake (Tulare co) 18 Aug 1965 @84; Woodlake
   Dennis Wilkinson      cem; obit *Visalia Times-Delta* Thu Aug 19 p.2,
               13; 12 gch 2ggch

  1901. Items from Avenales. Jan 10. Mr Eldon Phillips and Mr Will Hurst from the Porter
    ranch came in Saturday night, Jan 5th, got to Mr Wilcox' ranch about 8 o'clock

looking for that stray filly without any brand. They started back to the Huasna Sunday in the hardest of the storm. If they got there they were quite damp.

-Semi-weekly *Breeze* Jan 18 p.6

    to Bakersfield @16; to Tulare co 1910. Rancher, cattle foreman; retired 1950
    1937 Bakersfield
        m.
    ??? Owen
      a.   Eldon Theodore Phillips       b. Tulare co 5 Jan 1943
          1965 in Tulare
        step children: Jack Kimberling in Merced 1965
                     Lucile Carter in Visalia 1965
                     Patricia Margaret Kimberling (Shelton) b. Los Angeles co
                        18 July 1933; in Burney (Shasta co) 1965
                 Mary Sweeney in Hacienda Heights (Los Angeles co) 1965

7.   Miles S Phillips                 b. c1883
      1910 cen: St John WA        d. (before 1937?)
      prop confectionary store
        m. (Whitman co) WA c1908
      Nora E Holst                 b. WI 14 Jan 1884; parents Norwegian
      1920 cen: 335 W Oak        d. Alameda co CA 9 March 1958; mother Jensen
        Glendale CA
      1936. Social & Personal. Mrs Georgana (sic) Genardini of Tacoma is here on a visit at the
        home of her brother, U L Music. She is accompanied by her daughter-in-law, Mrs
        Mills (sic) Phillips.             –The *Cambrian* Jan 9 p.8
      a.   Berdette E Phillips            b. WA c1909
      b.   Lorene Phillips                b. WA c1911
      c.   Helen M Phillips (May)      b. WA 30 March 1913
                                        d. Alameda co CA 19 May 1983
      d.   Hazel Phillips                  b. WA c1916

8.   Grant Phillips                    b. Sep 1884
      1900 cen: Huasna w/         d.
        Dennis Wilkinson
      1937 in Greenfield

9.   Grace G Phillips                b. Cambria 8 Feb 1886; m. @18 of Edna
      1937 in San Jose                d. Woodland (Yolo co) 14 Apr 1964 @76; bur Los
      1950 in Campbell               Gatos; obit The *Daily Democrat* Wed Apr 15;
      1956, 1960 in Sacramento      12y Yolo co r1920 Merkeley av W Sacramento;
                                             2 dau son ½ sis
        m. Edna (SLO co) 14 July by Arthur E Johnson ME ch SLO, F634
          wit: Lawrence Tucker, Edna; Lulu Tucker, Edna
      Francis Martin Tucker         b. AR 8 July 1880; m. @24 of Betteravia (SB co)
      "Frank"                              d. Campbell CA 24 Mar 1952 @72/6/6; bur Los Gatos
      1909 Dir: blacksmith             obit *San Jose Mercury-News* Sun Mar 16 (sic)
        r114 W Mill SM; Mrs G       p.8 wife son 2 dau 2gch
      1910 cen: SB co tp8 Garey     F: Louis M Tucker 1849-1930
        Garey st; blksm-wgnmkr    M: Obedience Louderdale 1856-1933
      a.   Frank Milton Tucker          b. Betteravia 4 Oct 1905 (*Times*)
          1952 in Sacramento          d. Sacramento co 19 June 1966
          1964 in No Highland
      b.   Helen Mildred Tucker        b. 21 Apr 1907
          1952 in Sacramento          d. Sacramento co 28 Sep 1991

    1964 in W Sacramento
    m.
    Dewey Craner         b. 9 May 1898; SSDI
                 d. W Sacramento 29 Nov 1984
  c. Winifred M Tucker      b. (San Jose) 20 May 1924
    1952 in Campbell
    1964 in Clarksburg (Yolo co)
    m.
    James Fraser

Huston Phillips
    m.2 Santa Maria 7 Aug 1889 by H W Baker JP, D41
Emma Josephine Logan       b. (Mendocino co) Sep 1865
 1900 cen: Arroyo Grande      d. Santa Cruz 29 Jan 1933
  3 births 3 living         F: Samuel Hayes Hulet Logan 1839-1914
                M: Sarah Jane Hopper 1840-1925 See Hopper chart
                  m.2 Wm F Dutton 1827-1896
     m.1 1885 Edwin J Colby 1848-1888
      m.3 Harry Crosby; in San Francisco 1925
10. Sadie B Phillips        b. Santa Maria 26 July 1890
  1950, 1956, 1964 in       d. Santa Rosa 5 June 1978 @87; obit *Press-*
  San Leandro          *Democrat* June 9 p.15A; June 11 p.13A
                2 dau 4gch 10ggch 2gggch. Personnel mgr Stokeley
  m. (2?)           Canning co Oakland 35y; to Sonoma co 1968
  Joseph T Remington       b. Providence RI 27 July 1893
                d. Hayward CA 8 Dec 1960
                 obit *Hayward Review* Dec 10 p.7; r580 Haas av
                 26y San Leandro; wf 2 dau 2 sis 6gch
                 sis: Mrs Phoebe Hall, Santa Cruz; Mrs Amy Parker,
                 Oakland
                F: Henry L Remington 1859-1939
                M: Martha B Thurber 1871-1938
  a. Garna Verdin McAdoo     b. 7 Jan 1907; SSDI
    Garna Campodonico      d. Santa Rosa 8 Sep 1982; surname
    1960 in San Francisco       Campodonico
    1978 in Santa Rosa
  b. Velva Nadyne Remington    b. Santa Cruz 24 Jan 1924
    Velva N Quinliven in      d. Alameda co 9 Jan 1993; surname
     Oakland 1960         Quinlivan (sic)
    Nadyne Boxley in Oakland 1978
  = grandchildren 1978: Michael Quelliva (sic) San Jose
           Jack Campodonico, Texas
           Andrie Boggs, Sebastopol
           Donna Gunn, Santa Rosa
  = great grands: Steve Petrucci, Ruth Watford, Susan Thorp, Kenneth Boggs,
    Brian and Patrick Campodonico, Eddie and Robbie Lambert, Emily and Joanna
    Quelliva (sic)
  = great-greats: Nike (sic) and Juning Thorp

Colby-Logan girls: Edna B Colby    b. Santa Maria valley 19 Oct 1886
                 d. Santa Clara co 29 Nov 1961; surname Marquart
      Elsie Colby       b. Santa Maria valley 19 Apr 1888 (*Times*

# PRELL
## PIONEER PROFILES – SANTA MARIA VALLEY AREA

John G. Prell, one of the early settlers in the Santa Maria Valley was born near Leipsie, Germany in 1837. When fifteen he was apprenticed, for three years, to learn the cooper trade. Then in 1855, his widowed mother and family immigrated to the United States and settled in South Bend, Indiana. There he worked at brick-molding until 1860, when he decided to try mining in Colorado in the area of Pikes Peak. After a short time there he paid the last of his money for the privilege of accompanying a wagon train on to California where he then tried the mines of El Dorado County. He finally settled in San Jose for the winter.

He spent the summer in Los Angeles but returned again to the Santa Clara Valley at first finding a job of brick-molding. He later took up farming until 1866 when he returned to Indiana. Not liking the cold weather anymore he went to Missouri for a few months before returning again to California and the Santa Clara Valley where he had done so well before.

Before returning he met and married Miss Eliza Ann Bowers (a native of Ohio) at Rolla, Missouri. Mr Prell came to Santa Maria Valley in 1868 and is said to be among the first to buy land in the valley and to have built the first house in November 1868. He then moved his family here.

He then purchased 320 acres of land nearby, where he raised grain and only enough stock for ranch purposes. He had four acres in orchard, with a variety of fruit.

They raised four children, a son and three daughters: John S., who was born in May of 1869 just before he moved the family to Santa Maria, the three girls being born in Santa Maria Valley. Blanche (Mrs Francis Osmond Vincent), Lillian (Mrs W S Cook), and Laura who died when only six years old.

Submitted by Kathryn Brown

Bibliography

*A Memorial and Biographical History of the Counties of Santa Barbara, San Luis Obispo, and Ventura, California*, by Yda Addis Storke, 1891.

*This is Our Valley*, compiled by the Santa Maria Valley Historical Society, written by Vada F. Carlson, Ethel-May Dorsey, Editor in Chief. 1959

# R O S E N B L U M
## GUADALUPE   SANTA MARIA   SAN FRANCISCO

Willie Rosenblum's was a well known face in his more than thirty years behind the counter in his Guadalupe store. Though he has been gone exactly sixty years at this writing, his memory lingers in the minds of some Guadalupe natives, and his residence and business building are still in use.

Bert too, was a well known young man in his dozen or so years as a grocer in Santa Maria. Many are the long-time locals who remember him favorably. The business buildings he occupied have fallen to the wrecking ball of "progress", but the house he and his architecturally talented wife, Miriam, built stand—to their credit and as impetus for the writing of this story of an early Santa Maria valley family.

### Family Lore

There were six brothers and one sister who left their native land, Germany; whether singly or together, with or without parents, is fact lost in the mists of time. Max was a banker in San Salvador; Morris, wife Haidee, and daughters Alice and Gladys lived in Boston; one or other lived in Israel and Havana; one lived in Carpinteria or Paso Robles or San Luis Obispo, likely Sam who later lived in San Francisco with his wife Madeline and daughter Ruth.

### Local Records

The *Paso Robles Leader* carried an ad for Littmann & Rosenblum, fancy goods, for some months in 1887. The identity of these merchants has not come to light.

Samuel Rosenblum was naturalized in the San Luis Obispo county Superior Court 31 July 1890; his sponsors were E Lasar and A W Steinhart, and he renounced his allegiance to Emperor William of Germany. The same day Samuel Rosenblum, presumably the same man, registered to vote in San Miguel; he was 21, a native of Germany, and a clerk. A few weeks later, 13 September 1890, Samuel Rosenblum registered to vote in San Francisco; he was 21, a salesman, and native of California. This is probably another individual, unless he thought that naturalization made him a native. Samuel Rosenblum died in San Francisco 1 November 1943 leaving a wife, Madelon W Rosenblum, and daughter, Mrs Marion H Marks, as found in the *San Francisco Chronicle*, 3 November 1943, page 9.

Dan Rosenblum filed a Declaration of Intention to apply for citizenship 31 January 1894 in San Luis Obispo county. There is not record of his having fulfilled it.

William Rosenblum was granted a certificate of U S citizenship by V A Gregg, Honorable Judge of the Superior Court of San Luis Obispo county on 4$^{th}$ September 1894. He, like Sam, renounced his allegiance to the Emperor of Germany. His witnesses were I Lazar and A W Steinhart. Emanuel Lasar (the spelling is not consistent), a German Jew, had been naturalized in San Francisco in 1855, and by 1894 was a long-time San Luis Obispo merchant, with his California-born sons, Isaac and Marcus, who did business as The Lasar Bros. It may well be that the Rosenblum brothers got their start in business among the Jewish community in San Luis Obispo, where the papers regularly announced the closing of their stores for the High Holy Days.

## Guadalupe

William Rosenblum entered the United States in 1888, according to the date supplied to the census-taker in 1900 and 1910; thus his obituary errs in stating that he came at age 27—that may be a typographical error for 17, which age he attained to in December 1888. Though naturalized in San Luis Obispo county, he registered to vote in Santa Barbara county, Guadalupe precinct, 13 July 1896. The register shows that he was 24, 5'6", dark complexion, dark eyes, black hair; he was a merchant, native of Germany and naturalized. It must have been because it was thought to apply to him that this item was gleaned from the *Nipomo News* for the *Guadalupe Gazette* under date of December 13 1928: "Forty Years Ago in Nipomo…Willie Rosenbulm (sic), a promising young man of 16 summers is counter jumping at Gollober's Farmers Produce Exchange." He must have been but recently arrived.

He was single in 1900 and living in a rented house, according to the census. He bought a piece of property in August 1902 from Mrs Assunta Grisingher for $225; someone acquainted with prices of that era will have to decide if that price indicates a vacant lot or includes a house. The block had been Grisingher property; Mrs G. had a house on a lot to the back, and others fronting on North Main, later called Guadalupe street, were related. In July 1926, reported the *Gazette*, a concrete sidewalk was built on the west side of Guadalupe street "between Second and Third (now 11$^{th}$ and 10$^{th}$), fronting the residences of Wm Bassi, A R Grisingher, Wm Rosenblum and F W Grisingher." F Waldo, Assunta's son, was cousin to Al, of Grisingher & Souza, whose wife was Virginia Bassi.

Rosenblum must have opened a store soon upon his arrival, for he is always recorded as "merchant" rather than clerk or salesman, which would have been the correct appellation had he been in the employ of another. In an article headlined "Daring Thieves Ransack Guadalupe", in the *Santa Maria Times*, September 25 1909, the day Bert was born, there is mention of someone standing in front of Rosenblum's store. Though he had a stroke early in the '20's, he maintained the business, assisted by his wife and Lou Freire, clerk, until his death in 1929. Nadine Grisingher Ferini, Al's daughter, who lived next door, recalls that Lou lived with the Rosenblums.

In the pages of the *Guadalupe Gazette*, which began publication in April 1925, are found many references to the Rosenblums, as well as the weekly advertisements for Wm Rosenblum's, general merchandise store, which appeared throughout 1925 and stopped in September 1926. Outings and business trips were reported, and the visits of Mrs Rosenblum's brother, Dr Arnold Peters, dentist, and sister, Miss Rae Peters, of San Francisco, and of Mr Rosenblum's sister and husband, Mr and Mrs Dave Cohen of Los Angeles were recorded. Cohens brought their daughters, Dorothy and Ruby, to the family gathering in commemoration of Harold's 21$^{st}$ birthday anniversary and the girls bunked with a neighbor, Mrs Edith Abernethy, a few doors up the street. Under the headline "Sneak Thief Steals Watch, Sapphire Ring", the lifting of Ruby's "valuable sapphire ring studded with chip diamonds" was described: the thief simply reached in the open window. "The sapphire had belonged to Mrs Cohen's mother and had been specially set. It was not only valuable intrinsically but as an heirloom." Mrs Abernethy's house was robbed again the next week, the thief making off with $350, a ring, and, of all things, a safety razor.

William Rosenblum was a member of the Masonic lodge. For the November 1910 election the polling place for the Guadalupe Precinct was at the Masonic Hall, and the men involved, as reported in the *Santa Barbara Morning Press*, November 2, page 7, were:

Inspectors: Cremon Lafontaine and A V Wooley; Judges: Wm Rosenblum and Elmer Hall; Clerks: Henry Dolcini and E J Pessoni; Ballot Clerks: Wm McPhaul and Antone Souza.

Mrs Rosenblum's social activities were connected with the Guadalupe Welfare Club, a women's club, of which she was a sometime officer, as was Mrs A W Reum, the druggist's wife. These ladies, their husbands, and several others, attended the concerts given by the Harmony Club in Santa Maria. Mrs Reum was a violinist, and Mrs Rosenblum also a musician; Irene Giacomini Johnson, who lived with her grandmother, Mrs Grisingher, thought that Mrs Rosenblum might have been a piano teacher, although she got no corroboration on that thought from her sister Olga Giacomini Weldon; Nadine Grisingher Ferini, who lived next door, couldn't verify that, either, but did recall Mrs Rosenblum's operatic soprano carrying from one house to the other.

## Other Reminiscences

Rosenblums had the first radio in Guadalupe, according to Irene Johnson, who lived around the corner and went to school with the Rosenblum boys. They liked trying to get China or Japan on the radio, but heard mostly static.

Atilio DeGasparis, in his mid-teens when Rosenblum died, remembered watching him climb the ladder in the store to retrieve merchandise from upper shelves, and several "Guadalupeans" recalled the calendar plates that Rosenblum's as well as the other stores handed out as Christmas-end-of-the-year favors.

"W Rosenblum's General Merchandise"—what does that entail? As agent for U S Royal tires, he carried other U S Rubber products: hose, boots, storm rubbers, rain suites, "University Kotes for the schoolboy", Nap-a-Tan shoes for men, Kewpie Twins shoes for children; Post Toasties, O'Cedar polish; trunks, steamer trunks, suit cases, handbags; flowered violes and jersey broadcloths; Allen A ladies' silk hosiery; sugar, milk, canned pineapple…; Men's negligee shirts (look that up in an old dictionary); gent's furnishings…slip overs, shirts, cravats…; suits to measure; Munsing Wear—women's union suits, vests, bloomers, step-in chemise; Guard Roofing with nails and cement included; flannel shirts; electric percolators, toasters, heaters, hair curlers, irons, lamps; Thanksgiving delicacies—fresh fruits, fruit cake, plum pudding, brandied mince meat, fine candies; toys—express wagons, scooters, "Buzzy Andy", Alabama Coon Jigger, games, mechanical toys, blocks, drawing and painting sets; spring hats; "Lady Sealpax" dainty athletic underwear; auto trunks; 42-piece dinner ware; and, Rah!Rah!Rah! What's the news? Latest craze—College Blues.

In 1927 Leo P Scaroni, an officer of the Bank of Santa Maria, advertised a subdivision on the west side of Guadalupe street for residential and business sites; it extended from Main street, the road to Santa Maria, on the south, to the curve in Guadalupe street just south of the main business section. The north-south street west of Guadalupe street was named Campodonico; the east-west cross streets, from south, bordering the cemetery, to north, were named Holt, Grisingher, Souza and Rosenblum. Four were local merchants; Henry Holt was a landowner with properties in Guadalupe and Foxen Canyon, a bachelor/hermit/miser who was reputed to carry his money around in a gunnysack, according to Mrs Johnson, whose father, Paul Giacomini, rented grazing lands from him. (To be sure, she doesn't impute absolute truth to the reputation.) The street names were changed after World War II to numbers; Rosenblum is now Sixth.

## Good-bye, Guadalupe

October 3 1929 the *Guadalupe Gazette* reported that the Rosenblums had gone to Soledad to meet Dr and Miss Peters who drove down from San Francisco for a picnic; four weeks later it reported his death in San Francisco, where he had gone only the week before. On December 13 Lou Freire conducted a quitting business, selling out sale of "groceries, hardware, men's and ladies' furnishings, household ware, boots, shoes, caps, yardage, etc.," plus fixtures, for "this store closes forevermore on or about January 1 1930." Mrs Rosenblum, averred the *Gazette*, was moving to San Francisco "to make a home for her two sons, Harold and Bertram". By January 10 1930, the Rosenblum residence had become the office of Dr Hugh C Bryan, physician and surgeon; in March the store was occupied by A W Reum, who moved The Guadalupe Drug company there from five doors north. How long the drug store remained in the building is not known, but some time in 1931 Lou Freire was in business selling groceries and men's furnishings, possibly in the Rosenblum building for in 1935 his business address was 322 Guadalupe street, the number for Rosenblum's location until the changes made after the war. Lew's General Merchandise was listed in that location, even after opening Lou-Bert's Market in Santa Maria, until 1940; that year he and Bert separated and he kept the Santa Maria store at 200 South Broadway under the name Town Market. In 1938 Lou was listed with wife Sedalia in Guadalupe; by 1942 they had a new house at 200 South Bonita in Santa Maria, but were not listed in the area thereafter. In November 1946 John Roffoni moved his men's clothing store into the "newly renovated" 322 address, and it has been called the Roffoni Building since.

### Property

Elizabeth Soares Taylor said it was rumored that Mr Rosenblum acquired much property during the First World War as creditor to a number of Guadalupe farmers. That was a common enough phenomenon before the days of cash-and-carry, when merchants put purchases "on account" and their customers couldn't always come up with cash when the crops were in. Many is the public notice in newspapers of earlier days requesting payment to merchants in need of cash or about to close. Whatever lands Rosenblum may have held temporarily, at his death he was in possession of three lots on Guadalupe street: his store, another in the same block, and a third across the street in the next block south, which was leased July 1929 for 7 years to Mrs K Hamasaki; another holding was 80 acres in the Santa Maria valley, bounded on the south by Prell Road and on the west by what is now Highway 101. This, too, was leased in July 1929; M M Purkiss, Carl McCullers and F J McCoy took it for 20 years for oil exploration.

### Mrs Rosenblum

When Mrs Rosenblum came back to Santa Maria, she lived at the Santa Maria Inn, a fact reinforced by the signature of Frank J McCoy as witness to her will. On June 15 1944 she made a contract of sale for the Guadalupe residence to Thomas P and Antonia L Antunez, which transfer was completed by her heirs in August 1947. The house was still in that family in 1976. Though William Rosenblum's will, dated Guadalupe, 2 May 1928, witnessed by J M and Phoebe J Davis of Santa Maria, was very simple, willing everything to his wife with the proviso that she divide the remainder equally between the boys upon her demise, Dorothy Rosenblum's will, dated 15 July 1944, is specific in itemizing her property, both real and personal, and itemizing bequests of heirloom jewelry to her aunt, Dora Goldstein, sister, Rae C Peters, daughters-in-law, Rietta and Miriam, and grandchildren Linda, Jane, William, and "the first granddaughter born after the date of this will," which was Nancy. She died in Los Angeles, having fallen ill on a trip to Palm Springs in November 1946. Six months later Bert and Miriam left Santa Maria for Atherton, thus ending a half-century of Rosenblum residence in the Santa Maria valley.

Next: Harold the Doctor, Bert the Businessman. Watch This Space

## HAROLD – Part Two

Harold's appearance upon the world scene was heralded far, if not wide, by the notice of his birth in Guadalupe published in the *San Francisco Chronicle*: his parents were known in The City. But why Guadalupe?

Since the first part of this story was composed, additional information has come to hand. As was stated, there was a considerable community of Jews in San Luis Obispo; in fact, the oldest business in that town, according to the *San Luis Obispo Democratic Standard* of March, 1870, was Goldtree Bros, established in 1856 (or 1858, in Patrons' Directory of Thompson & West's 1883 SLO Co History). T & W says they started a branch business in San Miguel in 1877, managed by David Speyer and Isador Schwartz. Later it was run by Marcus Goldtree who "about eight months since started anew in Guadalupe". (Obit. May 29 1895) The drought was severe in 1894, with no relief the next year, and in those days before irrigation the farmers and ranchers had little or no wherewithal with which to pay their bills. Goldtree had personal difficulties as well as business embarrassments, so he opted out by drinking strychnine. Besides his clerk, Dan Rosenblum, those who came to help out were his brother, Nathan, from San Francisco; the Fleishers, Schwabachers, Mrs Coblentz (whose son was a close friend of Bert and Miriam's forty years later), Mrs Harris and Mrs Adams from Santa Maria; I Lasar, A Briegar and A Steinhart from San Luis; and William Rosenblum from Arroyo Grande. It appears that Billy Rosenblum was chosen to pick up the pieces and run the store. No formal notice was found in the Santa Maria newspaper; such may well have been printed in the *Guadalupe Moon*, of which there are no known extant examples. The Guadalupe Items column in the *SM Times* mentions "Billy" Rosenblum in February 1896 and again in April; that paper is not available for April 24 1896 to April 10 1897, but when again Rosenblum is mentioned it is as an established business along with Grisingher's and Campodonico's.

So it was that Harold was born in the village of Guadalupe, population about 350. The Swiss settlers held a celebration every year for Swiss Independence Day, and May Day and the Fourth of July were observed with community activities, including music, dancing, games, readings—a far cry from the banality of television. The Masonic Lodge was active, and McPhaul's Hall was a fine place for such gatherings as Thanksgiving masquerade balls. The schoolhouse built in 1897 had 33 pupils in the grammar grade department that year; there were more, no doubt, by the time Harold entered.

Harold's childhood prepared him well for the larger world of high school, and his record in the yearbook documents his success. The Santa Maria Union high school was small, but the annual, the *Review*, was well done and valuable historically, both to students and to the town.

Harold was president of the freshman class. The group photograph of class presidents on page 14 of the 1919 yearbook shows Harold a mature-looking boy of fourteen. He was an honor student that year, and in succeeding years as well.

As sophomore, he held the student body office of Yell Leader, and began his debating career. In the yearbook section, "Sophomore Briefs," it says, "As Guadalupe was too wild, Harold Rosenblum has moved to Santa Maria." Is that a joke, or did he board in Santa Maria?

Although his senior record says he was in the orchestra for three years, the first notice of his participation is noted in his junior year, where he is pictured with the orchestra on page 61 of the 1921 *Review* as banjo player. That year's report of the Dreadnaught Debating Club states, "The last cup debate was held under the auspices of the Dreadnaught and Athenian clubs. The question for debate was: 'Resolved, That the United States Should Intervene in Mexico.'" Harold won first honors and Rebecca Glines, second. "Mr Rosenblum's name was engraved on the debating cup at the expense of the Student Body." (Photo page 59)

"The Junior Asylum Report for 1920-21 and Summary of Violent Cases…#20, Harold Rosenblum, alias Rosie. Thinks he is an overdue note. Cause, Jazz music."

His varied activities included singing the role of Poo-Bah in The Mikado, filling the position of Business Manager on the Student Body Board of Control, and, with others of the junior class, instituting a school paper called The *Breeze*, the first such organized since the discontinuation of the *Rustler* in 1910. "Santa Maria Union High School has been in great need of a high school paper, but it was not until this year that the spirit of the school was strong enough to support one."

In Harold's senior year the Booster's Club was started; "the only qualification for membership is the ability to get behind a thing and boot it until it reaches success." This was appropriate for Harold's proclivities as he continued in the Dreadnaught Debating Club as business manager (photo page 57); played saxophone in the orchestra; served as Senior Class editor of the yearbook. As such he wrote the class history, the class prophecy ("…saw Harold Rosenblum playing the piano in Angus Hobbs' café in Tia Juana"), and compiled the Last Will and Testament of the Senior Class…"I, Harold Rosenblum, leave my piano playing ability to its greatest admirer, John Doe."

The Class of '22 graduated 27 scholars whose final activities were reported in the *Santa Maria Times*. The commencement was held in the Gaiety theater (first block east Main street), and Harold's name appears as accompanist to the violin duet played by Helen and Wilfred Rutherford on that occasion. (June 10, front page)

In April, 1925, The *Guadalupe Gazette* began publication, and Harold's accomplishments at the University of California often made the front page. He was president of the UC Glee Club, which started out near the end of May, 1925, on a lengthy tour, a page of photographs of which appear in the UC yearbook. The *Gazette* kept the home folks apprised of the progress of the trip: May 21—Today the club is in Chico. From there they start on their trip into British Columbia. June 4—…played at Corvallis to a full house, many students of the Oregon Agricultural College…being present…June 18—"U C Glee Club Dined In Seattle"…June 25—…U C Glee Club had reached Prince George, BC, the gateway to Alaska…July 2 – "Local Boy Bumps Into Black Bear"… in Prince George …July 16—The Post-Intelligencer of Seattle…had the picture of Harold Rosenblum in its columns…July 23—…left Astoria, Oregon…en route home…Aug 6—…arrived home...just returned from a tour of the north and into Alaska…

His academic career continued to be reported in the *Gazette*: Aug 20 - …Harold …returns to resume his studies at the University…Nov 12 – "Guadalupe Boy Again Honored By Classmates"…elected a delegate to the annual meeting of the Kappa Nu fraternity…Guadalupe has reason to feel proud of the distinction bestowed on one of the boys from the "old home town." Nov 26—"U C Glee Club Coming To Santa Maria"…Additional interest is shown in the U C Glee Club this year, as Harold Rosenblum of Guadalupe, popular graduate of the Santa Maria Union High School, is president…

1926: April 22—"Harold Rosenblum Presented With Fraternity Ring"…will graduate in May, and will leave the student body with a high record of achievement.

Besides being president of his fraternal order, he was last year president of the University of California Glee Club, which traveled…April 29—"Harold Rosenblum In Extravaganza At The U Of C"…leading part…in the Greek theatre…May 13—"Guadalupe Boy's Voice Broadcast By Station KPO"…solo…and duet…May 20—"Guadalupe Boy On His Way To The Antipodes"…sailed Tuesday from San Francisco to Australia…with him were two other young musicians…to entertain…with music and song during the round trip of six weeks. The boys get their passage, meals, etc., and a nice little bundle of the long green…Birthday Party in Honor of Harold Rosenblum…22-pound turkey, especially fed and fattened…immense cake with 21 candles…July 15—"300 Inches Of Rain Is Normal At Pago Pago". Harold…who returned last week from a trip to Australia, has many interesting things to relate…July 29—…returned from Salinas, where he has been playing with Dalessi's orchestra during the rodeo week. Aug 12 - …leaving Thursday for Berkeley…there about six months on a special course. Dec 16—"Harold Rosenblum Coming With U C Glee Club"…Those who attended the program last year remember what a splendid evening of talent and merriment they enjoyed, but there was a little disappointment in not being able to have Mr Rosenblum with his Club…Dec 23—"U C Glee Club Concert, Santa Maria Dec 28th"…past president…and one of the star performers…giving the people of his home town, Guadalupe, a chance to hear him sing…Dec 30—"University Glee Club Pleases A Large Audience" …Harold…presented special piano and song numbers…

1927: May 24—Harold…will spend part of his summer vacation at Catalina Island, where he will play in the orchestra at the St. Catalina Hotel.

1929: Jan 3—Harold…has returned to San Francisco…interne at Mt Zion hospital…April 11—Harold…interne…made a member of Alpha Omega Alpha, an honorary medical fraternity, and one of the highest honors that can come to students of medicine. July 25— Harold…elected president of the California chapter of AOA…

Winston Wickenden, a classmate of Harold's at Santa Maria high and fellow *Breeze* reporter, was also a student at Cal. He remembers Harold's typical pre-med pranks, and as a geology student, claims not to have shared the macabre sense of humor displayed by his Guadalupe friend.

Dr Rosenblum's biography appeared in *Who's Who in the West*, 5th ed. 1954. He married in 1929, received his MD in 1930 and entered private practice as a cardiologist in 1932. His credits include being clinical professor of medicine at UC Medical Center, Chief of Staff at Mt Zion hospital, consultant in cardiology at the US Naval hospital and the California Department of Public Health. He was a member of a number of medical associations, contributed articles in the field of cardiovascular disease to medical journals, and belonged to the San Francisco Yacht Club and the Commonwealth Club.

His son, the namesake and only grandson of William Rosenblum, died in 1949, aged 8. Mrs Rosenblum, who graciously helped me with this history, died, sad to say, about the time this work was composed. Their daughter, Linda, and her three children carry on the family line far away, both geographically and socially, from the little town of Guadalupe where it all began.

## BERT

Bert's entrance upon the stage of life was announced in the *Santa Maria Times*: Births—To the wife of M A (sic) Rosenblum, a son September 25, 1909. (The accuracy level of the paper has not risen these 80 years.) A month earlier the *SM Times* had reported that Guadalupe had been refused incorporation, lacking 56 of the necessary 500 population necessary for such action.

Santa Maria had upwards of 3,000 people at that time, the discovery of oil having brought a surge of growth. What was there for growing boys to do in the area? Under Recreation, the 1909 Santa Maria Directory lists Buena Vista Park, a race track, and a base ball ground; "Richard's Theatre and McMillan's Hall frequently present first class attractions and each present a moving picture show every evening. There are other halls in which are often presented entertainments of a less professional nature."

Guadalupe eventually boasted a theater. In Bert's youth, "the Crescent theatre, under the able management of Chas Campodonico is becoming a real show house. Last week there was something doing every night but one, and three nights a week are regularly devoted to the movie business, with high class films." (*Gazette* Nov 5, 1925). Better yet, Guadalupe children could see the likes of Cecil B DeMille, Gary Cooper and other famous names of the day when filming was being done in the Guadalupe dunes, and the *Gazette* made a point of noting the screening of a film made in the vicinity, whether being shown in Guadalupe or Santa Maria.

The ten miles between Guadalupe and Santa Maria were traversed by stage in the early years (robbed at least once, in September 1884, according to the *SLO Weekly Mirror*), then by auto stage, and by 1910, an electric streetcar. The Guadalupe high school students got to Santa Maria high school by that means, and home again, too, unless they missed the car, in which case they may have walked. Bert did, Miriam said. School busses were brought into service in the early thirties; Attilio DeGasparis drove the first one when he was a student at Santa Maria Junior College, adjacent to the high school.

The young people of Guadalupe were entertained at parties and dances, music by victrola, given by families—Campodonicos, Sampsons, Tognazzinis, Mrs Pitts—duly publicized in the paper. There were public dances, too; a front page article in the *Gazette* of February 4, 1926, protested the county ordinance prohibiting public dances after midnight, on the premise that "dances given here are community affairs which are attended by the very best element," unlike "certain particularly unsavory roadhouses." School sports were a source of activity; Sammy McBane was on the high school track team and Bert accompanied him to such places as Lompoc for meets, also going with Willie Sampson and others to San Luis for football games.

Bert's activities in august halls of the Santa Maria Union high school were not unlike his brother's. He was president of his freshman class, as noted in the 1923 *Review*; in 1924 he was vice-president of the Dreadnaughts, was on the *Review* staff, pictured on page 39 of that volume, and played lightweight basketball, team picture on page 77. His third year he again filled the position of vice-president of the Dreadnaughts and was a member of the Spanish Club. Warming up to life's work, he was Business Manager of the Board of Control both semesters of his senior year, class president first semester, and vice-president of the Merit Committee second semester. In the Class Will, "I, Bertram Rosenblum do will my hatred of girls to Jimmie Correll." He must have had a reputation along that line, for the squib adjoining his senior picture is this: "Women were born a plague to men, but somehow he seems to like them."

The Class of 1926 graduated 39 students, and Bert was among those participating in the last dramatic presentation of their career. The *Gazette* was proud of him: "Guadalupe Boy Leads In High School Cast", proclaimed the headline. "A Guadalupe boy, Bertram Rosenblum, played the leading role in the comedy, 'The Torch Bearers', which was staged by the Seniors of the Santa Maria Union High school, last Friday evening, in the High school auditorium. The Seniors faced a crowded hall when the curtain rose on their annual attraction, and they managed to keep the big audience convulsed with laughter from the rise to the drop of the curtain. All of the Seniors played their parts well…" (June 3) The *Gazette* fills us in on Bert's plans: July 8—Mr and Mrs William Rosenblum and son, Bertram, left Sunday morning for San Francisco to welcome Harold, who arrived at the port Monday morning from Australia. All with the exception of Bertram are expected to arrive home tomorrow or next day. The latter, in company of his uncle, Dr A B Peters, will go to Truckee on a fishing expedition and then make a trip into Nevada. Aug 12 – Harold…and…Bertram are leaving Thursday for Berkeley, where they will both enter the university, Bertram enters as a freshmen…

Bert entered as a pre-dental student, influenced by his uncle's offer to start him in his office. However, ultimately he decided to forego the dubious pleasures of the dental profession, and, in 1930, took to himself a wife. "Mr and Mrs Bertram Rosenblum of Sacramento visited here Friday evening. They have just returned from their honeymoon in the south. Mr Rosenblum was a resident here and a member of an old pioneer Guadalupe family." (*Gazette* Oct. 2) Bert's business venture in Sacramento was a victim of the Depression, so they moved to Berkeley, where Miriam's family lived. In 1934 Bert brought his bride to Santa Maria where he and his father's long-time clerk, Lou Freire, opened a grocery store at 200 south Broadway, calling it Lou-Bert's Market. By 1937 Bert and Miriam were sufficiently established to consider building a house, so she put her architecture education to work, and with a few corrections from a cooperative professor, produced plans for an $8,000 house. They chose a lot on south Vine/south Speed street (for discussion of the street-name controversy, see the article on John W Speed in Speed chart), with vacant field south to Stowell Road. The contractor absconded with nearly $2,000, but Bert's mother advanced funds, and completion was noted in the Water Connections column in the *SM Times* in April 1938.

Two years later, April 1940, Bert opened another store, the first "supermarket" in Santa Maria, at 301 south Broadway, in a new building built by Frank J McCoy. A full-page advertisement in the *Santa Maria Advertiser* for April 11 drawn by artist/cartoonist "Ferg" showed the store with its own parking lot, and a train loaded with values, heralding the Grand Opening April 11-12-13. Free ice cream, Coco-cola, balloons, "the human pancake machine" using Sperry's pancake and waffle mix, and Bert's Big Free Barbecue served all day. Miriam has a photograph of the crowded store; everyone in town must have been there. The 1940-41 Santa Maria Directory listing is "Bert's Food Market" (Bert Rosenblum) Complete Food Supply. Meats Groceries Baked Goods Fine Candies Fruits and Vegetables. We Maintain a Delivery Service. 301 S Broadway. Joe Olivera worked for Bert in both markets as a high school boy, and when he wasn't delivering he arranged the fruit and vegetables on the stands at the open front of the store.

Between these important building projects Bert and Miriam became parents. They were able to pasture a pony in the vacant field next to the house, and by the time Jane was old enough to learn to drive her little wicker pony cart, there was a war on and the small-town traffic was diminished even further by gas rationing, so she could drive around the streets without danger. They belonged to the Riding Club and the Santa Maria Club; Miriam was a member of the Minerva Club. Bert's natural popularity was enhanced by his ready access to meat for the Santa Maria barbecue that has become "world-famous"—the neighbors often gathered for such feasting.

In spite of her involvement with local society, Miriam was, after all, a city girl, so in 1947, with the war over and Mrs Rosenblum deceased, they sold the house to Charles E Diehl, manager of the Santa Maria Valley Chamber of Commerce, and, with now two little girls, moved to Atherton, leaving the store in the hands of Fred M Dewey. By 1951 it was obvious that long-distance ownership was not working, so the store was sold to Roy Gallison, butcher, and Charles E Felmlee, grocer; Gallison was happy to have the better building, as his place at 211 south Broadway was less desirable. George Gallison, Roy's nephew and, later, partner, said that in 1951 Bert's store was practically empty. An article detailing the transfer appeared on the front page of the *SM Times* October 10, 1951; the business would be called Gallison's and Felmlee's Cash Market, and would open after extensive redecoration and painting. Their lease was up in 1960, and the building ceased to be a grocery at that time. After a series of occupants, it was demolished in 1988, the property now constituting a part of the West Side Mall parking lot.

The house has fared better. Sold by Diehls to Blake Cauvet, manager of the Santa Maria Country Club, it next belonged to Brinton Turner, civil engineer, and, since 1964, to David L Cole, telephone engineer. It was a showplace in its time, and has attracted many would-be buyers. Santa Maria's recent growth has provided much ostentatious new construction, but Miriam's house remains a classic, and for that reason I dedicate this story to her in appreciation.

William Rosenblum      b. Germany December 1871
     d. San Francisco 29 October 1929; buried Home of Peace Mausoleum, Colma; imm. 1888; naturalized SLO 4 Sep 1894 brother: Samuel Rosenblum b. Ger 1869; imm. 1883; d. SF 1 Nov 1943

m. (San Francisco)
Dorothy Peters      b. California 1881
     d. Los Angeles 25 November 1946; buried Home of Peace Mausoleum, Colma; brother: Arnold B Peters d. SF 29 Sep 1935 @52; sister: Rae C Peters d. SF 5 Nov 1951

1. Harold Herbert      b. Guadalupe 17 May 1905
     d. San Francisco 1 January 1977
     Inurned Emanu-El Mausoleum

     m. (San Francisco) 21 December 1929
     Rietta Wilcek      b. Great Bend Kansas 1904
     d. San Mateo 9 October 1989
     F: Leo Wilcek d. LA 29 June 1959
     M: Elsa E Friend d. LA 7 May 1974

     a. Linda      b. 1936
        Barth A Easton
        = Jennifer (Pfaff)
        = Cynthia
        = Philip
     b. William      d. San Francisco 21 Feb 1949 @8

2. Bertram Leon      b. Guadalupe 25 September 1909
     d. San Francisco 19 Oct 1981

     m. (SF/Berkeley) September 1930
     Miriam Garfinkle      b. Sacramento 1910
     living in San Francisco 1990
     F: Leo Garfinkle b. Russia c1879; imm. 1892
     d. (Berkeley) 24 Sep 1940
     M: Alexandra Shragge b. Odessa Russia 1880; d. SF 18 Feb 1981 @101

     a. Jane      b. SF 18 Feb 1939, delivered by Dr Zach Coblentz, formerly of Santa Maria
     b. Nancy      b. SF 19 Oct 1944
        = Ephriam Learned
        = Leah Maxwell
        = Sarah Maxwell

# RUNELS
## NIPOMO PIONEERS

Vitalis S(tephen) Runels    b. Licking co OH 14 May 1845
- Co.D, 136 OH Vols 1864
- Co.C, 47 OH Vols 1864-5
- 1892 GR: 47 5'8 fair complex, brown eyes grey hair; farmer OH Nipomo; reg Aug 25
- 1900 cen: Nipomo
- 1902 GR: 57 Nipomo
- 1904 GR: 60 Nipomo
- 1910 cen: Los Angeles w/Frederick Elsen
- 1920 cen: 2255 Federal av, Los Angeles, alone

d. Santa Maria 28 Nov 1927 @82; AG cem spouse initial E *
obit *MT* Wed Nov 30 p.1; also T Tue Nov 29 p.5 in CA 43y, Nipomo 40y, 17 gch 10 ggch
F: Stephen[5] Runels d. 1862 @45 (Stephen[4] Stephen[3] Ebenezer[2] Samuel[1])
M: Malinda J Brawler
see *A Genealogy of Runels & Reynolds Families in America* ...Rev M T Runnels AM, Boston 1873
*Eliza Runels d. 2 July 1925, AG cem; no obit found; who is she?

m.1 Union Co OH 8 Apr 1866

Mary Eliza Miller    b. OH 26 Mar 1846

1888. Funeral of Mrs Runels.    d. Nipomo 5 Oct 1888; AG cem

A funeral train came up from Nipomo yesterday bearing the mortal remains of Mrs V S Runels to their last resting place in the Odd Fellows cemetery. The family of Mr Runels and a large number of friends accompanied the encoffined body, all sincere mourners. The deceased was a lady of great accomplishments and of high character, so amiable, good and unselfish as to endear her to her family and to her neighbors. Mrs Runels has been an invalid for a year or more, suffering from an affection of the heart which resulted in death. The inevitable fate has been foreseen for a long time and this consciousness brought forth in their purity and brightness the noblest of human and Christian qualities. In hopes of a change of health Mr Runels has traveled much, but nowhere was his wife as comfortable as at their home in Nipomo and there she desired to remain and patiently await the end, which came on Friday evening last, the 5th of October. Religious ceremonies were conducted at the residence in Nipomo, the whole town being present, and forming a procession followed the remains to the depot where a train was in waiting to bring many to this city. Mr Runels being a member of the GAR, at Arroyo Grande the Grande Army Choir joined the escort and at the grave sang a beautiful hymn written by the deceased in anticipation of the mournful event and by her request to be sung at her burial. A husband and seven children, being three sons and four daughters mourn the loss. Two of the children are married and two are quite young.    -*SLO Daily Republic* Mon Oct 8

1888. Funeral of Mrs Runels of Nipomo.

On Sunday last a funeral car was attached to the excursion train at Nipomo bearing the remains of Mrs V S Runels to their last resting place in the Odd Fellows cemetery at San Luis. There was more than one coach filled with sympathizing friends of Mr Runel's family. She has been an invalid for a year or more, suffering from an affection of the heart, which resulted in her death. Mr Runels being a member of the GAR post at Arroyo Grande, quite a number of gentlemen, bearing the GAR badge, accompanied by their wives, joined the friends of the funeral car. At the grave the Army Choir joined the escort and sang a beautiful hymn written by the deceased in anticipation of her death to be sung at her burial. She leaves a husband and seven children to mourn her loss.    -*SM Times* Wed Oct 10 p.3

m.2 1889

Mary M(organ) Talmadge    b. NY Sep 1839

1900 cen: 4 births 2 living
1902: Mrs M M Runnels of Nipomo was in town today. –Apr 2
1910 cen: Los Angeles; sis w/J E Morgan who d. LA 12-8-1915 @82
1920 cen: 2911 W 8th, Los Angeles, sis-in-law w/Cornelia Morgan

d. Los Angeles 5 Mar 1927 @87
spouse initial V S
Her sons: Harry Talmadge
    Frederick E Talmadge b. CA 1878

7 children by first wife
1. Charles Allen Runels    b. OH 31 Mar 1867
    1890 GR: 23 OH f Sisquoc    d. (Fresno) 26 Sep 1942
    1892 GR: 26 5'7 dk br dk, lvryman OH Paso Robles; reg Aug 10
    1892: Santa Barbara Co Deed Index:
        Runels Chas O & V S by sheriff to Guiseppe Muscio; Bk.33 p.71,74, Feb 4
        Rice L C, Runels Chas A & Stephen P by sheriff to Muscio; Bk.33 p.74, Feb 4
    1920 cen: 1813 Stuart, Berkeley; 1927: In Oakland
        m. before 1888
    Minnie M    b. MA c1867
        d. (Fresno) 25 June 1961
    Issue unknown

2. Philip Stephen Runels    b. OH Nov 1869
    "Steve"    d. Santa Maria 20 Sept 1944 @75; SM cem
    1890 GR: 21 OH f Sisquoc    obit Wed Sep 20 p.1; also *AG Herald-Recorder*
    1892 GR: 23 5' 7½ dk hz dk    Fri Sep 22 p.8 3 gch
      f OH Nipomo; reg Sep 2
    1900 cen: Santa Maria
    1908: Mrs Wm Gage this week sold her cottage at the corner of Mill and Pine to
        Stephen Runnells for $750.     –June 20
    1910 cen: Nipomo Mesa, teaming, 4 births 4 living
    1912 Dir: Nipomo
    1916-17 Voter Reg: Nipomo, Philip S 5'8
    1927: in Santa Maria
    1928 Dir: Runels Philip S (Jennie) teamster 527 W Fesler
    1930 Dir, 1938 Dir, 1940-41 Dir: 527 W Fesler
    1944 pall bearers: Fred J Hobbs, Harry Cheadle, Clifford Dunlap, Ulah D Smith,
        Ed Perry, John Altamirano.     –Sep 22 p.4
        m.1 1895
Estella Alice Morrison 1874-1912; See Ezra Morrison chart
        m.2 @46 of Nipomo, in SLO 31 Mar 1915 by Chas B Allen ME ch, J335
            wit: Julie W(ineman) Bell, SLO; L C Bell, SLO, also *Times* Apr 3
        divorced 19 April 1916; SLO co K138
Mattie E Mills Mrs      m. @45 of Nipomo
    1915: A Pleasant Party. Mr & Mrs P S Runels of Nipomo were given a charivari last Friday evening and also Saturday evening. The time was spent in the enjoyment of music and games. At the close dainty refreshments were served. Those present were Mr & Mrs Hans Mehlschau and family, Mr & Mrs Andrew Mehlschau and family, Mr and Mrs W G Burke, Mr Ralph Burke, Mr Earl Cotter, Mr Cecil Cotter, Mr & Mrs A V Runels, Mr Emmett Mills, Mr Chandler, the Misses Chandler, Helen Jensen, Gladys Cotter, Mattie Mehlschau, Dora and Mary Mehlschau, Mr George Dalessi, Mr Ward Mead, Mr James Jensen, Mr & Mrs W M Cotter and Mr Sam Paulson. –Sat Apr10
        m.3      divorced 15 Apr 1920; SLO co L115
Emma

    m.4 of Santa Maria in San Luis Obispo 9 Oct 1924 by Wm Mallagh JP –MT Oct 10
  Mary E Decker
    m.5 by 1928
  Jennie M           d. (Fresno) 11 Feb 1940

2. Children by first wife
  a.  Mildred Beatrice Runels    b. Dec 1897 (cen) 1896?
     1914: Honor Roll, SMHS,    d. San Francisco 24 Jan 1919 @22; SM cem
       junior class          obit Sat Jan 25 p.1. influenza. In SF
                   studying to be graduate nurse
  b.  Orol Alfred Runels      b. Santa Maria 14 Apr 1898 (*Times*)
     grad Nipomo sch 1914     d. 29 July 1919 @21; SM cem
  c.  Donald Steven Runels     b. 8 July 1904 (*Times*)
     Ensign USN          d. on destroyer Northhampton, Solomon Islands
     m.               30 Nov 1940; first SM casualty
     May  (Mae 1911-1983)?   went down with ship
     = 3 boys
       1943: widow and P S Runels went to Texas to christen a destroyer
         named for Ensign Runels, Sep. –from obit 1944
  d.  Blanche E Runels       b. 27 Aug 1907 (*Times*)
     1944: in Medford OR     living 1997 Medford
     m.
     Ray Frisbee

3.  Mary E. Runels          b. (c1871?)
   "Mame"            d.
    1927: in Los Angeles
    1944: in Monterey Park
     m. before 1888
   Clark              b.
                  d. (Died: Clark. At Nipomo Thu Sep 13 1888
                    Wm Clark @27. NY papers please copy. –Sep 15.
                    Also Wm Clark @25 buried Sep 11
                    1888 SM cem; inf V S Runnels)
   *Note*: Heath, Runels and Clark children attended the new Suey school, organized in
   1879. (ONT)
     1879 GR: Clark Edward 39 IRE lab Sisquoc; nat. 1877 Amador co
     1890 GR: Clark Frank E 30 MA farmer Sisquoc
   Issue unknown

4.  Sylvia Viola Runels       b. Biggs Landing CA 21 Jan 1875 (Butte co)
    to Nipomo 1887        d. Santa Maria 24 Nov 1967 @92; AG cem
    1894 Garey: Miss S Runnels   obit Sat Nov 25 p.4; 9 gch 20 ggch
     is guest of sis Mrs Clark. –July 28
    1940-1 Dir: Cotter Sylvia hmkr Nipomo; in Nipomo 1944, 1961
     m. 1898
   William Cotter          b. Healdsburg CA 11 Nov 1866
    to SLO co 1877; 61y SLO co   d. at home Nipomo 11 July 1938 @71; AG cem
    1880 cen: SLO tp         obit Mon July 11 p.2: "Nipomo Market Man is
    1910 cen: Nipomo 5 births 5 living   Called". 27y meat mkt; also constable 35y
    1916-17 Voter Reg: Nipomo pct    in Nipomo;. bro: Henry Cotter, Pozo; sis: Sara
     Wm Cotter 6' Mrs Sylvia 5'    Murray, San Jose
                   F: Henry Cotter
                   M: Mary A

a. Gladys Elsy Cotter     b. Nipomo 10 May 1899
                                 d. living 1997
     m. 1923
     Frank R Munoz     b. Nipomo 25 May 1898
       1922-3 Dir: opr ser sta,     d. at home Santa Maria 17 Nov 1966 @68/5/22;
         r600 W Cypress (w/parents)     SM cem; obit Fri Nov 18 p.10, 4 bro 4 sis
       1925 Dir: Frank Jr (Gladys E)     7 gch; funeral conducted by nephew Father
         trk drvr UO co r306 E Fesler     Frank Munoz of Danville
       1928 Dir: same. 1930 Dir: same     F: Frank Munoz 1855-1925
       1940-1 Dir: Union Oil ser sta     M: Lydia Smith 1871-1953
         629 S Bwy; h113 W Jones
       1955-6 Dir: Union Oil ser sta
         1226 S Bwy; h517 E Boone
     = Wm F   1940-1 Dir: atndt U serv sta 629 S Bwy; h113 W Jones
         1955-6 Dir: Wm F (Randy) U O Serv Sta h316 S Elizabeth
     = Richard Don   1955-6 Dir: Donald R (Phyllis) serv sta opr h548 DeArmond
     = Rosalie (Ferrell)
         1955-6 Dir: Munoz Rosalie J bkpr Rbt Wooten; r517 E Boone
       1965 ph bk: Ferrell Bookkeeping Serv 115 W Clark Orcutt; 1997: same
       1966 pall bearers: nephews Arthur Kelly, Stanley Munoz, Ronald Munoz, Ray
         Campbell, Dennis Hogle, Anthony Gomes; honorary pall bearers: Kenneth Bianchi,
         Lawrence Lavagnino, Rbt Bienert, Manuel Pimentel, Alfred Pimentel, Joe Silva,
         Fred Knotts, Geo Knotts
b. William Earl Cotter     b. 1901
     wife Selma (he in SM 1938)     d. before 1958
     oil fields, Bellflower
c. Cecil Pearl Cotter     b. 1903
     1931-2 SLO Dir: butcher,     d. 27 March 1958
     Nipomo (Isabel)     notice Sat Mar 29 p.8; mother & 3 sis
       m. SLO co 12 Sep 1930; divorced
     Isabel (1911-1983)?
       1930: Nipomoans Give Charivari Party…to Mr/Mrs Laurence Jensen Jr, East Cook
         st, Santa Maria…Present: Mr/Mrs Laurence Jensen Sr, Mr/Mrs SM Dana,
         Mr/Mrs SA Slater, Mr/Mrs Cecil Cotter, Mr/Mrs Louis Brum, Chris
         Dennerlein, Jack Clayton, Ivan Haltom, Johnnie Bicley, Steve Slater, George
         Wright, Ben Wright, Albert Jensen, Misses Alpha Dirk, Leona Kirk, Mary
         Bamboa (Gamboa?), Hazel Smith, Edna Waugh, Frances Slater, Kathleen
         Slater, Johanna Jensen, Othalia Dana.     –Sat Nov 22 p.8
    For Slater see chart.
d. Hazel L Cotter     b. Donovan's house, Nipomo 1905
     1955-6 Dir: Clk Lucas groc,     d. living in Palo Robles 1997
     Nipomo
     m. 1925
     Arthur B Munoz     b. Nipomo 17 Nov 1899
     "Choppo" (Frank's bro)     d. 21 Apr 1988; r Nipomo
       1922-3 Dir: sheet metal wkr Froom     obit Fri Apr 22 p.18; in sheet metal 31 y;
         Tank Co r same     custodian Lucia Mar sch dist; 2 gch
       1925 Dir: lab r same;   1928 Dir: Arthur (Hazel) sheet metal wkr r 610 W Cypress
       1955-6 Dir: emp Froom Tanks; Box 32 Nipomo
     = Muffy (Hud Banks), Paso Robles

e. Erma L Cotter     b. 1907
m.     d. living in Santa Maria 1997
A W Wahrmund
    1940-1 Dir: actg mgr Union Com'l Co Cottage 8 Betteravia
    1955-6 Dir: whsle mt dlr h 326 S Ranch SM; also 1990 ph bk

5. Arthur Vitalis Runels     b. NE 4 Aug 1877; m.1 @25 of Nipomo
    1895: Southside, w/Bob Earl     d. San Luis Obispo 26 July 1961 @83; AG cem
    1900 cen: Sisquoc, day lab     obit Thu July 27 p.2; 7 gch 11 ggch
      w/Wm Hobson     47 y Arroyo Grande; from Nipomo
    1902 GR: 27 Nipomo; 1904 GR: same; 1910 cen: Nipomo Mesa, farmer; 1912 Dir: same
    1920 cen: Oceano pct. 1931-2 SLO Dir: Arroyo Grande RFD #1
    m.1 Arroyo Grande 3 Aug 1903 by C W F Nelson, F506
      wit: Miss Jennie Bristol, Pueblo MX; Miss Daisy P Runels, Nipomo

Edna May Bristol     b. Stafford KS 20 Aug 1881; m. @21 of Nipomo
    1910 cen: 3 births, 3 living     d. Palo Robles 13 Mar 1953 @71
    1916-17 Voter Reg, Nipomo pct     obit Tue Mar 17 p.8; 7 gch 4 ggch; 60y AG ranch.
      Arthur V Runels 5'7     4 sis 1 bro
      Mrs Edna 5'5     F: Charles E Bristol 1851-1916
        M: Sarah E     1856-1924

1924: W R C Members Attend Funeral in Arroyo Grande…Sarah D Bristol of Arroyo Grande. Those who attended from Santa Maria: Mesdames L J Morris, Jane Morrison, M O Winters, Dodge, Carrie Boyd, John West and daughter Mrs Paul Markling.     –Tue May 27

a. Elmer Arthur Runels     b. Nipomo 18 July 1904
    to AG 1919     d. (SM) 23 Mar 1987 @82; AG cem
    farmer w/father, sons     obit Wed Mar 25 p.17
    m. SLO co 16 Aug 1926
    Mazie Leona Baker     b. Tulare CA 29 Jan 1905
      AGHS     d. SLO co 19 Mar 1982 @77; AG cem
      1931-2 SLO Dir:     obit Mon Mar 22 p.8; 70y AG; 14 gch 6 ggch.
        Elmer A (Mazie) f AG RFD 1;     bro: Kenneth C Baker, SB; sis: Marjorie Gray
        Mazie L hswf     (1911-1992) Long Beach; sis: Doris McIntyre, Norwalk
      F: Charles Baker
      M: Mehitable Palmer

      = Robert E, Redwood City (1955-6 Dir: Oso Flaco)
      = Thomas A, Arroyo Grande
      = John J, Arroyo Grande
      = Mazie Ruth (Morton), Santa Rosa
      = Phyllis Corinne (Ernest E White), Lompoc. UCSBC 1952

b. Erwin O Runels     b. 7 Nov 1907 (*Times*)
    1931-2 SLO Dir: trk drvr RFD 1     d. Red Bluff CA 18 Dec 1982
    1961: in Burbank

c. Helen E Runels     b. 1909
    AGHS     d.
      m. SLO co 17 June 1933
    Christian H Mehlschau     b. 28 Feb 1902; SSDI
    1940-1 Dir: Nipomo     d. (Nipomo) 6 Mar 1989
    1953, 1961, 1987: Los Berros     F: Andrew Mehlschau 1863-1928
      M: Lizzie Lorenson 1872-1951

5.     m.2 24 Sep 1953
       Bessie May Lowry McKain    b. MO 23 Apr 1891
                                  d. San Luis Obispo 27 Jan 1972 @80; res AG obit *SLO Telegram-Tribune* Jan 30; bur Union cem, Bakersfield
                                  10 gch 3 ggch
                                  daus: Fern White, Halcyon;
                                      Patricia Basham, Santa Rosa
                                  sons: Jas McKain (1917-1994) res Portland OR
                                      John McKain (1919-1993) Arroyo Grande
                                      Jack E McKain (1923-1997) Whittier
                                      Rbt L McKain, Texas
                                  bro: Leon Lowry (1894-1983) MO

6. Margaret Jane Runels          b. OH 3 Apr 1880; SSDI
   "Jennie"                      d. Long Beach CA 12 Aug 1969
      1900 cen: w/Steve, SM
         rode a bike to Casmalia to teach school   -Gladys Munoz
      m.1
      Sam Westbrook              boat rentals, Avalon; also 100 cottages
                                 d. early 1920's, Catalina, drowned
      a. Genevieve (died young?)
      m.2 after 1927
      George Herwig              from the East
                                 d. (Los Angeles co 11-20-1942)?
      *Note*: Margaret Herwig living in Avalon 1944, Long Beach 1961, 1967

7. Daisy Pearl Runels            b. NE 30 Apr 1883
      to Nipomo @4               d. Fresno 22 May 1960 @77/0/22; SM cem
      1900 cen: w/father         obit Mon May 23 p.2; 7 gch 4ggch
      1910 cen: Nipomo Mesa      in Fresno 3y w/dau
         1 birth 1 living
         m. at home of bride's father Nipomo 15 Nov 1905 by Rev H W Poerts,
            Christian ch SM; to live in Nipomo (*Times*)
      Herbert Watson Grafft      b. Hall co NE 2 Oct 1881
         bio M/H 911: to CA 1902  d. Fresno 24 Aug 1974 @92/10/21; SM cem
         1911: to Suey ranch from Nipomo  obit Mon Aug 26 p.2; 7 gch 8 ggch; 50y SM &
         1922-3 Dir: f rGary rd   Nipomo to Fresno 1957
         1925 Dir: f SM RFD      bro George, SLO
         1928 Dir: trk drvr      sis: Mrs Tony Freitas, Cambria Pines
            r125 W Morison           Mrs Lois Thompson, Morro Bay
         1940-1 Dir: Mech, same  F: James A Grafft 1855-1934
         1955-6 Dir: ret, same   M: Marietta Foreman 1862-1926
      a. Melvin Eugene Grafft       b. 20 Nov 1906; SSDI
         1925 Dir: Gene, stu, SM RFD   d. May 1980; SS ben to Los Alamitos
         1928 Dir: Eugene (Bessie)       SM Cem: "I'd rather be in Nicaragua"
            lab r rear 711 S Bwy         tractor salesman
         in Managua Nicaragua 1960, 1974
         m.
         Edna Bessie               1907-1989; SM cem
      b. Florence Pearl Grafft    b. c1912; grad 8$^{th}$ grade Suey sch 1925
         1928 Dir: stu 125 W Morrison    (ONT). In Fresno 1957, 1960, 1977
         m.
         General Buck Sitton

    c.   Vernon H Grafft                            b. 5 Apr 1916; SSDI
         1940-1 Dir: Vernon (Barbara)           d. Poway CA 22 Mar 1983
         prtsman Moore Tractor co
         h125 W Morrison
      1960: in San Leandro; 1974: in San Diego
        m.
      Barbara A                                          1924-1994

    The land boom of the 1880's brought many settlers from northern California to the central coast, among whom was V S Runels. In a short time he established himself as a solid citizen in Nipomo, dealing in real estate in addition to farming. What is now the Kaleidoscope Inn on Dana street was Runels' house, built in 1887-88 in the V S Runels & Sons addition to the town of Nipomo by A J & C A Todd, contractors, using a plan selected from the Sears-Roebuck catalog, according to Phyllis White, a great-granddaughter. The house was the scene of social affairs for the family, later passing into the hands of Joseph A G Dana. (1) A photo of the house appeared on the front page of The *Santa Maria Times*, Friday, July 18, 1997, illustrating an article about The Olde Towne Nipomo Association.

    Another social venue was Runels' hall, mentioned in the *Tribune* as hosting a dog show and a meeting in the interests of the coming newspaper, both January 1892, and a reception in December 1896. In November 1893 they refused to allow a circus to perform there. (2)

    In 1888 Runels, E G Dana, H C Fry and A Peterson were selected by the Nipomo Republican Club as delegates to the County Convention. (*Times*) Early in 1893 Runels "returned from an extended trip through Antelope Valley…thinks that country has a glorious future and thinks of investing there the coming season." (*Times*) Later that year his wife was reported as submitting a petition to close the saloons from Saturday at 10pm to Monday at 5am. (2) In November 1894 a creamery was built on the site of Runels' washhouse, interested parties being Sheehy, Mehlschau, Popp, Dana, Cook, Paulsen and Brown. (2) The *Morning Tribune* had quite an encomium on "Miss Jennie Runnell's Brave Deed – She Blocked a Burglar's Purpose at Nipomo on Tuesday Morning." (2) –Dec 15 1896.
*Note* that the name is often misspelled.

    Although V S Runels' obituary credits him with a 40-year residence in Nipomo, he was found in Los Angeles on the 1910 and 1920 censuses; his second marriage, apparently, was not a felicitous union, as the second Mrs Runels was the archetypical step-mother, according to Gladys Munoz. Phyllis White adds that each married with the idea that the other had money.

    Mrs Munoz, a granddaughter of V S Runels, was one of the founders of the Santa Maria Valley Genealogical Society, and graciously provided some information for this issue. Her youth was spent in Nipomo, where she was well acquainted with many of the Danes found in the last issue of this quarterly. She graduated with the first class of the Los Angeles Normal School to fly the flag of UCLA, boarding with her aunt Mame Clark; she taught school for several years, spending summers with her aunt Jennie on Catalina Island. Due to her husband's Hispanic heritage, she did not continue her teaching, but became a homebody, until their sons marched off to fight the foe during World War II, at which time she donned slacks, probably the first in Santa Maria, to help out at their service station, for which she was also bookkeeper. Her cousins, the Grafft boys, being heavy equipment operators, found employment in Nicaragua, thus successfully avoiding the dangers of war. Gene Grafft lived many years in Managua, and, according to the inscription on his gravestone, would rather be there still.

Steve Runels was the marrying kind; widowed at the dangerous age of forty-something, he married again, and again, and again. One wonders if he was running competition with Bern Knotts, also a Nipomo resident, oldest son of the Knotts family whose saloon evolved into Jocko's restaurant. Bern was a few months younger than Steve and died just a few months before Steve did, having, like Steve, tied the "Knott" (2) five times. Bern got an earlier start: his first wife, married in 1891, was Sallie Wood; they were soon divorced and she married John West in 1903, becoming Sadie West, real estate agent and first and only woman to sit on the Santa Maria City Council. (Ye Ed's house sits on property bought of Sadie West, as does the one built by her daughter, Mrs Markling, down the street.) Bern's second wife, married in 1901, was Mary Ellen McBane Terry, who died in 1904, aged 28 (see McBane chart); in 1906 Bern married Pearl Lillian Drumm, of the La Graciosa Drumm clan. Divorced, he married a fourth wife, Mae Josephine Corwin in 1915; after her death in 1930 he married Teena—who divorced him in 1938. Only two divorces were found for Steve in the San Luis Obispo county court index; what became of the fourth wife is not known.

Phyllis White says that V S Runels donated the land for the Nipomo school. A V Runels, her grandfather, farmed in the Nipomo vicinity until 1917, when he moved to Arroyo Grande, where the land he bought had been part of a Mexican land grant, his deed being written partly in Spanish. Her father, Elmer, went to Cal Poly, but having farmed all his youth, didn't think they had much to teach him.

In 1914, in between wives, P S Runels' name showed up on the Tax Sale List; he was delinquent on 120 acres and a lot, both part of Dana's subdivision of Rancho Nipomo. See SLOCGS *Bulletin* No. 20; 3 Fall 1987.

No doubt many interesting anecdotes could be gained by interviewing others of the family still living hereabouts, and we would encourage them to write their memories, if not for us, then for the younger generations.

References

1. *Five Cities Times-Press-Recorder*, Arroyo Grande Wed Oct 5, 1955…
   Official Program of the October Festival, p.14 with photo of the Kaleidoscope Inn/ Runels house
2. Extracts from *SLO Morning Tribune*, Wilmar N Tognazzini, several volumes at The SLO City-County Library
(*T*) Santa Maria Times


Vol. XXIX, No. 2, Summer 1997, pp.16, 17

**Corrections and Additions**  [Page numbers refer to those in Quarterly]

p.14. Bill (Tex) Wahrmund and wife Erma (Cotter) became the first independent operators of what had been the Union Sugar Co's company store in Betteravia, to which they added a butcher shop, along with running the gas station; they lived on the premises, as shown in the 1940-1 City Directory. In 1946 they sold out to Jack Burrow and bought the J&J Market in Guadalupe; the 1947-8 Directory lists them at 816 Campodonico st, and The J&J, Manuel Olivera & A W Wahrmund Groc & Mkt 319 Guadalupe st. (Jack H & Lillian Burrow, Betteravia Grocery. box 31) –See *The Good Years*, Shirley Contreras, *Santa Maria Times* Sun Dec 14 1997.


Vol. XXIX, No. 4, Winter 1997, p. 17

p.16. In the same 1955 issue of the *Five Cities Times-Press-Recorder* featuring the Runels house appeared also an article by Hazel Munoz, page 22, filling in some details otherwise undiscovered. She wrote that her father, William Cotter, was born in Healdsburg to Henry and Mary Jane Cotter; her mother, Sylvia Runels, was born in Britts, Butte co, after which the family moved to Nebraska, then Ohio, later returning to California where they lived in Marysville and Fall Brook before settling down in Nipomo. William and Sylvia met in northern San Luis Obispo county, and, after their marriage, moved to Bakersfield where Gladys, Earl and Cecil were born. William worked on ranches until coming to Nipomo. Hazel was born there and was living in that same house when the article was written. William became a butcher, opening a shop with George Juarez of Guadalupe as partner; after buying him out, he ran the market for about thirty years at the location "now occupied by the Feed Barn". He was constable during that time, making little use of the small jail behind the present barber shop. For his business he bought beef and pork on the hoof; his slaughterhouse was at the east end of Tefft St across from Lorraine Vidal's home. Later his son Cecil took over the shop, followed by Jim Cooper. Sylvia was an old-fashioned homemaker, also working for the Red Cross during World War I, participating in PTA and Women's Improvement Club and the Presbyterian Church Ladies Aid. Hazel had a daughter, two granddaughters and a great-grandson; Gladys had three children, Earl had five, and Erma and Cecil had none. She concluded with happy memories of clamming at the beach and fishing in San Luis Obispo County streams.

p.12. Mary E Runels' husband was <u>Frank</u> Clark.

p.14. Helen Runels was born 21 April 1909 (*SM Times*)

Vol. XXIX, No. 4, Winter 1997, p. 17

p.12. Mary E Runels (Frank Clark), born in Marysville 27 Mar 1870, died in Monterey Park Aug 1960 @90, buried Monterey Park Saturday Aug 6. Son Roy, daughter Ethel Reber.
–obit *SLO Telegraph-Tribune* Mon Aug 8 p.2

Vol. XXX, No. 4, Winter 1998, p.13

p.12. Philip S Runels m.3 in Stockton Sat May 6, 1916, Miss Emma Warner of Freeport IL.
–*SM Times* May 13, 1916

p.13. 1936. Nipomo Home Robbed While Family Is Away…the small cottage of Burnett Knotts, the home of M/M Cecil Cotter, was ransacked while they were at dinner with M/M A J Leoni …about $500 loss. –*SM Times* Thu Feb 26 p.4

Vol. XXXI, No. 3, Fall 1999, p.6

# RUSSELL
## CAMBRIA   SAN LUIS OBISPO   SANTA MARIA

One of the westernmost streets in Santa Maria, California, running originally from Alvin Street to what is now the Santa Maria Valley Railroad right-of-way, the length of the Fairlawn addition, is Russell. Russell Street, Russell Park, and Barrett Street, all 2½ blocks of it are reminders of:

>    REAL ESTATE !!
>    BARRETT & RUSSELL
>    SAN LUIS OBISPO, CAL.          -Ads, 1889, *San Luis Obispo Tribune*

Charles J. Russell was an enterprising Yankee from the Connecticut valley of Vermont who died in the Santa Maria Valley of California, having made his mark wherever he went, more by brain than brawn. His obituaries present a surprisingly accurate view of his life, and are here presented as exemplary historically if not journalistically.

Obituary – C J Russell Laid To Rest. Charles J. Russell, one of our best-known citizens passed peacefully away on Tuesday morning just as the year was drawing to its close. He had been in ill health for some time but his condition was not thought serious until a few weeks ago when he grew gradually worse and beyond the aid of medical science.

Mr Russell has been a resident here since 1895 during which time he dealt in real estate and made many sales, some of which of considerable importance. He was always optimistic of the future of this valley and its resources and his firm conviction in this direction helped him greatly. Although none too well off in his declining years, he at one time was considered extremely wealthy and owned much property. He was a native of Vermont, born Nov. 11, 1837. At the age of 9 years his father died and together with his mother moved to Pennsylvania. A year later he went to New York and entered the employ of a railroad company with the surveyor corps. Later on he engaged in the mercantile business, and remained until the war broke out in '61, when he crossed the plains. Arriving in California he landed in Sacramento, and two years later went to Virginia City, arriving there during the boom days, and engaging in the milk business.

In February 1865 he was married to Isabella M Brewster in Virginia City, where he resided until 1868. Then he moved to San Francisco and engaged in the commission business a year. He then moved to Cambria where he engaged in the stock business and did considerable mining. In 1875 he was elected supervisor from the Cambria District, and filled the office with credit and ability.

From Cambria he moved to San Luis Obispo, and lived there until 1895, when he moved to our city. His children are Mrs F A Dorn, Mrs A J Barclay, both of whom died within the past few years; M A F H, Hazel, Mrs E J McBride and Earl Russell.

The death of his wife in 1905, together with the loss of his two daughters in the succeeding years, was a sad blow to him, and did not fail to have its effect upon him.

In disposition he was kind and friendly. On topics that came up for discussion he had his own views, which were always broad and liberal.

The funeral took place yesterday under the auspices of the Knights of Pythias, of which he was an old member, the local lodge escorting the remains to the depot, from which place they were taken to the family burying ground in San Luis Obispo.

— *Santa Maria Times*, Sat, January 4, 1908

Obituary - PASSED TO GREAT BEYOND. Charles J. Russell, former well-known resident of this city, dies in Santa Maria Tuesday. The sad intelligence has been received in this city of the death of Charles J. Russell, which occurred in Santa Maria Tuesday morning after a lingering illness…The deceased was a former well-known resident of this city, where he was associated for a number of years with his brother-in-law, Ralph J. Brewster, in the conduct of a harness shop. At a later date he engaged in the real estate business, forming a partnership with Thomas Barrett, Sr., in 1889. In the earlier days he was a member of the Board of Supervisors, and before coming to San Luis Obispo made his home in Cambria. Several sons and daughters are left to mourn his loss.

-The Telegram, San Luis Obispo, Thursday, January 2, 1908

The Connecticut River divides Vermont from New Hampshire, and Saxton's River, a tributary, conjoins it at Bellows Falls, Windam county, Vermont. Saxton's River Village is a couple of miles upstream, in the northernmost town, or what farther west is called a township, in the county, Rockingham. Here, December 15, 1836, Hiram K. Russell and Sophia Estabrooks were married by Jos. Hemphill, Minister of the Gospel. Charles Jeduthan Russell was born to them November 11, 1837. Hiram Russell, age 35, died April 25, 1848, and was buried in Saxton's River Cemetery.

The 1840 census shows a Hiram Russell family of four in Rockingham town. The 1850 census taker found Charles Russell in the household of Sylvester Easterbrooks (this name has several spellings) in Jackson township, Susquehanna county, Pennsylvania. This man was old enough to be Charles' grandfather, although minimal investigation has not shed light on this. Also in this household was George M. Cole, 25, another Vermonter, who later became Charlie's stepfather. Sophia Russell, 33, Sarah Esterbrooks, 21, and Mrs Post, 40, also Vermonters, were enumerated last on a page of men's names, all guests in an inn, kept by John B. Schofield in Susquehanna village. Sarah Esterbrooks and George Cole were married that year and moved to Beaver Dam, Wisconsin, where John Esterbrooks, 32, relationship not defined, and wife were living in the household of David Post, 49, Pennsylvania. The Coles had two children, Jennie and Charles who became a merchant in Santa Maria; Sarah died, and George married Sophie Russell January 1, 1857, as recorded in Dodge county, Wisconsin. Charles Russell had a sister at last when Clarissa M. Cole was born in 1861.

Charles Jeduthan Russell bore the name of both his grandfather and great-grandfather; Jeduthan; Clarissa Cole was named for her paternal grandmother. However, they, like many others in California far from traditional roots, eschewed the old-fashioned names; he became Charles Jay, she became Claire.

Charles Jeduthan Russell     b. Nov 11 1837 Saxton's River Village,
                                                    Windham co, VT
                                       d. Dec 31 1907 Santa Maria, CA
                                                    bur IOOF Cemetery, San Luis Obispo, CA
                                       F: Hiram K. Russell 1812-1848
                                       M: Sophia Easterbrooks, c1818-c1898
     m. Feb 5 1865 Virginia City, NV

Isabella C. Brewster
- b. Sept 8 1846 Bristol, Wayne co, OH
- d. April 10 1904 Santa Maria, CA
- bur. IOOF cem, San Luis Obispo, CA
- F: Calvin Brewster, 1787-
- M: Harriet Cramer, 1813-

1. Cora B.
   - b. July 1868 Virginia City, NV
   - d. May 26 1905 San Francisco, CA
   - bur IOOF cem, San Luis Obispo, CA
   - m. Nov 11 1890 San Luis Obispo, CA
   - Frederick A Dorn, 1863-____; Attorney

2. Harriette
   - b. c1872 probably Cambria, San Luis Obispo Co., CA
   - d. c1906 probably Reno, NV
   - m. Nov 11 1897 Santa Maria, CA
   - Alexander J. Barclay, 1869-____; Civil Engineer

3. Sadie
   - b. Nov 8 1873 probably Cambria, CA
   - d. Dec 9 1874 Cambria, CA
   - bur Cambria cem

4. Morris A.
   - b. Oct 1876 probably Cambria, CA
   - Civil Engineer

5. Frank H.
   - b. 188_ probably San Luis Obispo, CA
   - Civil Engineer

6. Hazel
   - b. Nov 14 1884 San Luis Obispo, CA
   - d. Aug 29 1970 Santa Maria, CA
   - bur. Santa Maria cem
   - m. July 21 1912 San Luis Obispo, CA
   - Charles Henry Bidamon, 1886-1937 plumber
   - m. W H Patterson, pharmacist
   - elementary school teacher

7. Ailene
   - b. Jan 1887 San Luis Obispo, CA
   - m. Jan 7 1907 San Francisco, CA
   - Edward J McBride of Chilcout

8. Earle
   - b. June 1888 San Luis Obispo, CA

# SCOTT
## SANTA MARIA VALLEY PIONEERS

The Scotts, like so many of the original settlers in the Santa Maria valley, had been residents of northern California for well over a decade before succumbing to the lure of available land in the south. Once here, B W Scott moved about; he lived for a time in Cambria, where Ye Ed. vainly sought his relationship to Cambria pioneer Greenup Scott. After returning to this vicinity, he spent some time in Santa Rita, in the watershed of the Santa Ynez river, where several related families farmed in the later 1890's.

J C Scott, on the other hand, moved around in climes more northerly than their original California home, spending two years, according to his obituary, in Colorado, which may explain his absence from the 1880 California census. After the untimely death of J C and his wife in 1901, the children scattered, David later going to live in Washington for several years. Did the younger brothers go with him? Only he and Jack are mentioned as surviving nephews of Lucy Scott Price in 1930.

Whereas other families treated in this publication were notable for the number of divorces, the Scott clan is notable for the number of orphans. Nancy died at the age of twenty, leaving a baby, Clara Norris; Ben was killed in an oilfield accident, survived by a six-year-old daughter, Bernice Scott, and wife who died eight years later during the Spanish Influenza epidemic; Gladys Foster Hobbs died a week before the last mentioned, her sister, leaving daughters Bessie and Jane Hobbs, both under ten; Mary Bell is thought to be the Mrs Drumm who died aged about 25, leaving two very young daughters, Mabel and Alphoretta; Parlee Davis died age 23, leaving a two-year-old girl, Ella Scott; Annie M died age 22, leaving a newborn son whose fate is unknown; and Ella, the youngest child of J C, was almost nine when her parents died, and went to live with her Aunt Lucy Price. What happened to some of these has not been discovered.

Research Problem. Ella Cook Scott was said to have been born in Bangor, ME; her mother, also a Maine native, was a charter member of the Rebekah Lodge at Yreka. On the basis of that hint, a search for a likely candidate for paternal honors was made in Siskiyou County, Josiah Moores Cook, born about 1820 in Maine, who registered to vote in Sisson and vicinity, looking promising. The AIS Index, 1850, lists Josiah M Cook in Somerset Co, Maine, p.264 W Vien 2R2. This might answer the question.

Inconsistencies. The most recent addition hereunto with the death date from the California Grand Death List for John V Price: he died in 1909 aged 30, but the 1880 census gave him a birth date of 1871. There are many inconsistencies of that sort; let him who can sort them out. (Later thought: since the numbers are hard to read on the Death List, it might well be 38 or 39 instead of 30.)

Thomas Scott  b. KY 2 Nov 1806
  to CA 1855  d. Santa Rosa CA 3 Nov 1875
  1860: Santa Rosa; 1870: Santa Rosa    Shiloh cem, Windsor
    m. Madison co, IL 28 Nov 1828
Anna M Cowhick  b. nr Urbana OH 14 June 1810
  1900: w/J C Scott, wid.  d. nr Santa Maria 31 Oct 1900 @90/4/17
    Guadalupe tp    obit Nov 3

8 births, 8 living      F: Thomas Andrew Cowhick
M: Lucy Adamson

1. Benjamin Welcome      b. Morgan co IL 8 Jan 1830
d. Santa Maria 11 May 1909 @79/4/3; SM cem
     m. (Healdsburg)? 7 Nov 1858 by W R Brown, reg. A2
Eliza Jane Freshour 1838-1909; see B W Scott chart

2. William T      b. Morgan co IL 30/31 Nov 1831
d. Sonoma co 19 Dec 1876; Shiloh cem

3. Sarah Jane      b. Morgan co IL 1 Dec 1833
d. (after 1875)
     m. Santa Rosa 17 Feb 1856 by T J Means, A62
Robert Irwin      b. IN c1827
d.
     1860: Sonoma co, Russian River, PO Windsor
     1870: Sonoma co, Annaly tp, P O Sebastopol
     a. Elizabeth E      b. CA c1857
     b. William L      b. CA c1859
     c. John M      b. CA c1864
     d. George W      b. CA c1866
     e. Mary J      b. CA c1868
     ?(Mary L Irwin m. 2 Dec 1882 Santa Rosa, A F Roux, by A D Laughlin, I 1)?

4. Mary Elizabeth      b. Winchester IL 2 March 1837
d. Sonoma 27 Nov 1862; Shiloh cem
     m. Healdsburg 26 Oct 1857 by Rev F M Marion, A110
John Marion Price      b. IL Nov 1830
d. Fresno/Sanger June 1905
m.2 Lucy A Scott; see #8
     a. Thomas S      b. CA c1859
       m. Sallie      d. Fresno 1897
       Asst cashier S&L of Fresno
     b. son      d. 26 Nov 1862; Shiloh cem

5. John Cowhick      b. Winchester IL 17 March 1839
d. nr Santa Maria 6 Jan 1901 @61/9/20
     m. Santa Rosa 1869
Ella Elizabeth Cook      1848-1901; see J C Scott chart

6. David Patrick Henry      b. Winchester IL 17 June 1841
     1860: w/parents      d.
     1870: w/parents
     1880: Santa Rosa
     m.1 Healdsburg 9 Sep 1866 by D B Austin, B430 or Mark West Church, Santa Rosa
Barbara Ellen Rader      b. Birmingham IA 7 Apr 1850
     1920: MEN co w/son      d. San Mateo 23 March 1931 @80
       Jas M Thornton      F: John Charles Rader 1815-(d. Shasta co)
M: Elizabeth Workman 1818-
       see *Potter Valley History* p. 310
       m.2 1868 (*PV*) or 1870 (cen)
       Joseph Thornton 1829-1911
       1900: Potter Valley; 10 births, 10 living
     a. Oliver      b. CA 1867
       (called Thornton)      d.
         m. Pomo, MEN co 1 May 1887

    Harriet Blake                               b. 1867
                                        d. 1943; for Blake see *Potter Valley History*
      =Jessie 1888-1969                     p. 197
      =Lester 1889-1975
      =Anita 1894-1960
6.     m.2 Santa Rosa 29 March 1874 by G O Birnett, D158
   Elizabeth Power                     b. AR 1853
                                        d. (after 1880)
   b. James D                           b. Santa Rosa 20 Dec 1874
   c. Florence E                       b. Santa Rosa 13 Dec 1875
   d. Nora J                             b. (Santa Rosa) 1879
7. Osee Eleanor                  b. Winchester IL 1 Sep 1843
     1860: w/parents                d. 10/30 Oct 1875; Shiloh cem
     1870: w/parents
8. Lucy Ann                      b. Big Creek tp Henry co MO 9 Feb 1846
     1860: w/parents                d. Fresno CA 2 May 1930 @84
     1910: 1354 P st Fresno       obit *Fresno Bee* Sat May 3 p. 5
        m. Healdsburg 3 Sep 1865 by B Lewis, B183
   John Marion Price             b. IL Nov 1830
     to Fancher Creek 1872     d. Fresno/Sanger June 1905
     1880: Fresno 4th ward
     1900: Fresno 7th ward
     5 births, l living 1910
     a. Mary C (single)             b. c1867; d. c1890
     b. Martha (single)             b. c1868; d. before 1890
     c. John V                       b. Oct 1871; in Gilroy 1907, oil fields
                                       d. Fresno 1-7-1909 @30 (or 38?39?)
     d. Joe Dodd                   b. Academy, Fresno co 12 Mar 1875
        constable, Sanger           killed Fresno co 13 Mar 1907 @32
        deputy sheriff, Fresno      obit *Fresno Morning Republican*
        single                         Fri Mar 15 p. 10, et seq.
     e. Maud E (single)            b. April 1885
        1910: w/mother, tchr       d. Fresno 11 Nov 1924 @39
9. Hardin                          b. Henry co MO 23 Jan 1849; d. 7 Feb 1849
10. Josephine Strong           b. Big Creek tp Henry co MO 2 Feb 1850
     1860: w/parents                d. Soledad CA 9 Feb 1925 @75
        m. Healdsburg 9 Sep 1866 by D B Austin, B424
   Isaiah Rader                     b. Salem tp Highland co OH 29 May 1843
     1870: MEN co Calpella tp    d. Ukiah 16 Nov 1926 @83; Soledad cem
        PO Ukiah                  F: John Charles Rader 1817-(d. Shasta co)
     1900: Siskiyou co, Edgewood tp   M: Elizabeth Workman 1818-
                                          see *Potter Valley History* p. 310
     a. Mary Elizabeth             b. Potter Valley CA 5 June 1867
                                          d. Gazelle, Sisk co
          m.1 Dillard OR 28 Sep 1884
     John W Bell                   b. KY c1849
     =2 sons                         d. Gazelle 1891
          m.2
     Marion Spangle                 d. Tehama co 3-17-1926 @52
                                          spouse initial SM

b. Sarah E     b. Potter Valley CA 30 Dec 1869
    d. Sacramento 6 May 1948

      m.1 Big Springs, Sisk co 2 Sep 1887
   Charles Madison Rader     b. Austin TX 20 Feb 1860
    d. Hornbrook, Sisk co 30 Mar 1931
    F: Abraham S Rader
   =10 children     M: Matilda Ann Dye
      m.2 Weed CA 1 Apr 1934
   Edward A Smith     d. Siskiyou co 7 May 1937 @69

c. Charles Thomas     b. Santa Rosa 15 Mar 1872
    d. Santa Rosa 27 Nov 1876

d. Albert Theodore     b. Santa Rosa 19 May 1874
    d. Weed CA 19 Nov 1945

      m. Yreka CA 10 May 1911
   Clara Agnes Hafner     b. Siskiyou co 13 Jul 1884
   =6 children     d. Mt Shasta 24 Oct 1968

e. Minnie Eva     b. Santa Rosa 18 Nov 1876
    d. Willets 26 Sep 1949

      m. Yreka 17 Jan 1895
   William Stover Spangle     b. OR 1866
   =8 children     d. Willits 11 June 1941

f. Anna Belle     b. Myrtle Creek OR 1 Oct 1879
    d. Fresno CA 24 Mar 1969

      m. Berkeley CA 7 Sep 1902
   Ergo Alexander Majors     b. Santa Cruz 2 June 1877
   =3 children     d. Scottsdale AZ 20 Oct 1962

g. Jessie Henrietta     b. Myrtle Creek OR 14 May 1882
    d. Soledad CA 4 Aug 1973

      m. Sisson CA 2 Sep 1900
   Alan Leonidas Roddick     b. Volcano CA 13 Nov 1879
    d. Soledad 25 Sep 1960
    F: Robert Roddick 1833-1907
   =5 children     M: Christina McKenzie 1843-1915

h. Arthur Leroy     b. Little Shasta, Sisk co 28 Nov 1884
    d. Greenfield CA 26 Nov 1949

      m. Salinas CA c1911
   Vernie Hazel Handley     b. nr Greenfield 28 May 1893
   =2 children     d. Carmel CA 20 Jan 1975

i. Ira Adelbert     b. Big Springs, Sisk co 30 Jul 1887
    West Point     d. Asheville NC 14 Sep 1958
    Arlington National Cemetery

      m. East Orange NJ c1916
   Alice Kent     b. Brooklyn NY 25 Apr 1888
    d. San Diego CA 28 Jan 1988
    Arlington National Cemetery
   =3 children

j. Frank Solomon     b. Edgewood Sisk co 10 Nov 1889
    d. Fresno 21 June 1960

      m. Salinas c1911
   Hattie E Handley     b. nr Greenfield c1891 (Roddick) or
    23 Sep 1884; SSDI

|  | d. San Joaquin co 1 Jan 1972 |
|---|---|
| =4 children | (SS benefits to Los Angeles) |

*Citizens of Sonoma County Entitled to do Military Duty, 1859*, G H Drum, Geo Foster, Alex Scott, B W Scott, Wm T Scott, James Price, J D Price, 4 Irwins…
*The Sonoma Searcher*, Sonoma Co Genealogical Society
   *Ed. Note*: The above is a fine and useful publication.


Benjamin Welcome Scott     b. Morgan co IL 8 Jan 1830
  1860: Santa Rosa next to F     d. Santa Maria 11 May 1909 @79/4/3
  1870: SON co MEN tp              Santa Maria cem; inf: Edward Scott
     PO Healdsburg               obit May 15 p.1
  1879 GR: 49 IL f Santa Maria
  1880: Santa Maria
  1882 GR: 52 f IL Santa Maria, reg Aug 17
  1883: Notice of Intention N2NW4 T9N R34. Wit: W F Johnson, T D Raper,
     Wm Haslam, Santa Maria; H J Laughlin, Guadalupe
  1890 GR: 60 IL f La Graciosa; reg Aug 25
  1892 GR: 62 6'½ light complexion, blue eyes, light hair, f IL Cambria
  1896 GR: 6' fair, blue, brown, IL rSanta Rita; PO Lompoc
  1900: Santa Maria; 10 births, 7 living
  1906 Dir: Scott B W retired rPine st; Scott B M Mrs rPine st
     m. Sonoma co 7 Nov 1858 by W T Brown, reg. A2
Eliza Jane Freshour     b. MO 31 May 1838
                            d. Santa Maria 29 Jan 1909 @70/7/29
                            SM cem, obit Feb 6
                            F: Andrew Freshour
                            M: Jane Marchan
1. George Winfield     b. Santa Rosa Feb 1860; m. @30
  1888 GR: 28 CA f SM     d. Santa Maria 1 Mar 1933 @73/0/29; SM cem
  1890 GR: 30 CA f SM #1     obit Thu Mar 2 p.2
  1892 GR: 32 6'2½ light, black, brown, lab CA Cambria (San Luis Obispo co)
  1898 GR: 38 6'2½ light, black, brown, 2$^{nd}$ finger lh stiff CA SM #1
  1900: w/parents; m/10, no wife
  1910: Santa Ynez
  1920: (59 CA Independence, Inyo co w/Manning E Payson)
     m. Santa Maria at home of bride's parents 19 Oct 1890 by Rev Mr Platt (*Times*)
  Cora Bell Yelkin     b. KS 1873; m.1 @17; m.2 @30
                           d. San Luis Obispo 21 Mar 1951; IOOF cem obit *SLO*
                              *Telegram-Tribune* Thu Mar 22
                           F: Riner Yelkin 1843-1890
                           M: Suffonia Counsel 1843-1890
                              m.2 1903 Mark Miller Evans 1864-1942
   a. Henry William     b. Apr 1891
     1900: w/g'parents     d. (LA co Feb 1982; SSDI)?
     1909 Dir: Scott H W teamster 617 S Lincoln
     1933, 1937: in Hynes (LA co);    1942: in Bellflower

    b. James A                                             b. May 1892
        1900: w/g'parents                        d. Ventura 19 Nov 1937 @45
        1937 Dir: Jas A (Nora M)              obit *Star-Free Press* Mon Nov 22 p.1
            oilwkr h359 Santa Cruz, Ventura
        No issue
    c. Georgie Pearl                        b. SM 7 Apr 1893; m. @17 of SLO
        1900: w/g'parents                        d. SLO 14 Sep 1953 @60; IOOF cem obit *SLO*
        1910: w/Mark Evans, SLO                *Telegram-Tribune* Sep 15 p. 2
        1942: Long Beach
        m. SLO 1 Sep 1910 by Henry Selah Munger, min. I34. Wit: R G Bagley, SLO;
            Cora L Eastman, SLO; Consent of mother Cora Bell Evans first had and filed
    Charles Frederick Godfrey           b. San Bernardino 21 Oct 1885
        bio Davis' *Commercial*                 m. @25 of SLO
        *Encyclopedia of Pacific SW*         d. SLO 5 June 1962 @76; IOOF cem obit *SLO*
        *1915*, p. 277                           *Telegram-Tribune* Wed June 6 p. 2
        laundry business                       F: Wm Mollock Godfrey 1825-1900
                                                   M: Lucia P Huntington 1850-1935
                                                   bio Ingersoll's *Century Annals of*
                                                   *San Bernardino co 1769-1904* p. 701
        =Charles F Jr (Audrey) 1917-1966; obit *SLO Telegram-Tribune* Tue Sep 27
2. Anna C (Nancy)                        b. (Sonoma co) 1862; m. @18
                                           d. SM 7 Mar 1882 @20/2/15; SM cem
    m. La Graciosa 1 Jan 1880 by Lewis B Featherstone, min, B438
        wit: J R Norris, Mack Foster
Robert Brent Norris                       b. (Mariposa co) CA Oct 1854; m.1 @25
   See Norris chart                         d. SM 7 May 1919 @64/6/22; Pine Grove cem
                                           F: John Richard Norris 1827-1909
                                           M: Mary Thomas Mattingly 1838-1910
  a. Clara Catherine                     b. SM valley 13 Feb 1882 (obit)
     1900: w/Norris g'parents                or Dec 1881 (cen) d. SM 28 Sep 1962
        m. Pine Grove Sunday 26 Aug 1900 (*Times*)
    Joseph Martin Garrett 1872-1942
    =3 sons
3. Mary Ellen (Mollie)                   b. Healdsburg 27 Dec 1863
    1922 GR: 5'4 Arroyo Grande          d. Oceano CA 23 Apr 1942 @79, (SLO co
                                         record) or 24 Apr 1942 @78, stone, AG cem obit *SLO*
    1938 Dir: Oceano                       *Telegram-Tribune* Sat Apr 24 p. 3; T Mon Apr 27 p. 2
    m. Santa Rosa 15 Apr 1883 by G O Burnett, min, H80
   George Alonzo Foster                  b. Roseburg OR June 1861
      (Lonnie)                             d. Oceano 27 Oct 1932 @71; AG cem; obit *SLO*
                                           *Daily Telegram* Fri Oct 28 p. 5
                                           F: George W Foster c1823-1906
                                           M: Martha Jane Sawyer c1822-1896
   1892 GR: 32 5'11 light, blue, brown, scar under rt eye, teamster,
        Cambria (SLO co), reg. Aug 27
   1900: Santa Maria
   1910: Indian Peak tp, Mariposa co
   1914 Dir: lab 608 S Pine, Santa Maria
   1920: Arroyo Grande;       1922 GR: 5'10 Arroyo Grande
   1931-2 Dir: lab Oceano

10 births, 8 living, 1910; 8 born in Santa Maria (obit)
   a. Myrtle Fay        b. SM Sep 1884; m. @21 of SM
                         d. Arroyo Grande 30 Oct 1918 @34
                         AG cem  obit Nov 2
                         m.2 Monroe Nell
             m.1 San Luis Obispo 11 Sep 1905 by Geo Willett, min, G191
               wit: Mary Cathryn Egan, SLO; Rbt D Fuller, SLO
    Benjamin Wirt Scott              b. Siskiyou co May 1882; m. @24 of SM
      1906 Dir: Scott Wirt               d. nr McKittrick CA 30 Jan 1912 @30
         lab r Chapel st SM              obit *Californian* Wed Jan 31 p. 2
      1910 Dir: Santa Maria            F: John Cowhick Scott
                         M: Ella Elizabeth Cook
      =Bernice P  b. SM 25 Nov 1905 (*Times*)
        1920: @18 (!) w/Jack & Lottie Scott, Kern co
   b. Raymond Elmer              b. SM 14 Aug 1886 (*Times*)
      1910, 1920: w/parents             d. (Oceano) 1 Sep 1947; no obit found
      1931-2 Dir,1938 Dir: Oceano; 1942: living w/mother
   c. Lottie Hazel                    b. Sisquoc 3 Dec 1888
                         d. Taft CA 14 Sep 1928 @39
                         obit *Californian* Mon Sep 17 p. 10
           m. 1906                 Union cem, Bakersfield
     Marion Jackson Braiden Scott 1885-1961; see J C Scott chart
   d. Gladys Ellen                   b. (Cambria) 20 Feb 1891
      1910: w/parents                  d. Arroyo Grande 24 Oct 1918 @26
      m.                               AG cem; obit Nov 2
    Fred D Hobbs                    b. SM valley 4 Dec 1888
      1914 Dir: Fred S & Gladys, lab,      d. (Oceano) 14 Apr 1959 @70; AG cem obit
        W end Grover, SM               *SLO Telegram-Tribune* Thu Apr 16 p. 2
        (now Boone st)                  F: Joseph Lane Hobbs 1863-1936
      1920: Careaga                    M: Nancy Elnora Stubblefield 1867-1909
                         m.2 Larena.  See Hobbs chart
      =Elizabeth (Bessie) Ellen (Roads)        b. 5 Feb 1910
                         d. Napa 27 Oct 1988
      =Virginia Geraldine (Jane)          b. c1915
        m. Albert LaBorde              b. (Huasna, SLO co) 1908
                         F: Pierre/Peter LaBorde 1862-1935
                         M: Martha Olive Mahurin 1880-1958
   e. Ernest E                         b. (SM) 4 Apr 1898
      FBI                               d. Huntington Park CA 13 Aug 1981
           m.1 Pauline Miller; 2 children
           m.2 Gertie Wideman
   f. Frances Ruby                    b. SM Feb 1900
                         d. Los Angeles 16 Nov 1938 @38
      m.                               AG cem; obit Fri Nov 18 p. 3
    Edward B Annis                  (b. ME; d. SCz co 6-3-1921 @44)?
      1934 Dir: Frances E Annis (wid EB)  r 3809 Brunswick av Los Angeles
      1938 Dir: same
   g. George Alfred                    b. SM 28 Dec 1903
                         d. SLO 25 Feb 1983; AG cem obit *SLO*
      m.                               *Telegram-Tribune* Mon Feb 26 p. 2
    Florence Carr                     living San Luis Obispo 1994

No Issue
- h. Lucile N — b. (Santa Maria) 1907/8
  - 1920: w/parents — d. Cedarville CA 1961
  - m.
  - Walter R Sugden, whose mother died in WA 1935 — *–SLO Daily Telegram* Jan 18
    - ?(Walter F Sugden b. 23 May 1902; d. Placer co 11-18-1986; SSDI; benefits to Roseville)?

4. Elzina <u>Jane</u> — b. Santa Rosa Sep 1866; m. @19
   - d. Bakersfield 3 Sep 1946 @79
   - m. Santa Maria 13 Apr 1886 by M C McCann, ME ch, C301
   - Greenberry Madison Logan 1863-1935   See Logan chart
     - a. Minnie (Thatcher) 1887-1993(!)
     - b. Benjamin H 1892-(1961?)
     - c. Alma J (Hunt) 1898-1968
     - d. Lena P (Melton)
     - e. Harry H/W 1901-
     - f. Ora M (Stubblefield) 1909-1980

5. Thomas <u>Edward</u> — b. CA 1869; m. @38 of Santa Maria
   - 1890 GR: 21 CA f La Graciosa — d. SLO co 28 Mar 1925 @56; Arroyo
   - 1896 GR: 27 6'1½ fair, — Grande cem; no obit found
     - brown, brown, CA rSanta Rita PO Lompoc
   - 1906 Dir: Scott Edward lab rPine st
     - Scott T E lab (no address)
   - m. San Luis Obispo 4 June 1907 by H E Smith JP, H4
     - wit: Cora Evans, SLO; Georgie Scott, SLO
   - Mary B Stewart — b. c1876; m. @31 (3<sup>rd</sup> marriage)
     - 1910: nr Orcutt — d.
     - 4 births, 2 living
       - her ch: Franklin Day b. CA c1898
       - Eugene Day b. CA c1904

6. Frank A — b. (Sonoma co) c1871 (cen)
   - d. Santa Maria 25 Dec 1897 @ 27/9/1; SM cem
   - obit Jan 1 1898; suicide

7. Ada May — b. (Sonoma co) c1873
   - 1909 Dir: Scott Miss AM — d. (Santa Maria) 2 Apr 1910 @36/11/21; SM cem
   - stenographer & bookkeeper — obit Apr 9 p. 3
   - r309 E Chapel
   - m.
   - William R Drumm — b. Santa Maria valley 19 Jan 1881
     - d. Westminster CA 4 Oct 1970
     - F: James Howard Drumm 1850-1916
     - M: Mary C Stubblefield 1864-1894
       - m.2 Dora Emma Thorner/Tomer d. 1930
       - See Drumm chart

8. Jeannette A (Nettie) — b. (Sonoma co) Sep 1876
   - d. Mariposa CA 23 May 1959
   - m. Cambria CA 16 May 1893 by R S Symington, D280
     - wit: Mrs Elizabeth J Scott, Mrs M M Scott
   - Newton J Phillips — b. Santa Barbara CA July 1872
     - 1900: Mariposa co — d. Mariposa CA 30 June 1944
     - 1910: Mariposa co, Indian — obit *Merced Sun-Star* Sat Jul 1 p. 1
     - Pk tp — F: Huston Phillips 1845-1922

1920: Mariposa co  
    M: Georgiana Music 1854-1937  
      *Note*: Huston Phillips m.2 SM 1889 Emma J (Logan) Colby, sister of G M Logan

  a. William <u>Lloyd</u>    b. 14 Apr 1894 (Cambria)  
    1920: Mariposa    d. Merced 17 Oct 1969; SSDI  
    1944, 1959: Merced  
    m. Katherine W  
  b. Reuben Carl    b. Santa Barbara 10 Mar 1896  
    foreman, Yosemite Natl Park    d. Yosemite 15 July 1959 @63  
        obit *Mariposa Gazette* July 16 p. 1  
    m. Aileen    b. ? (15 June 1907; SSDI)  
        d. ? (23 Aug 1988; zip 92330)  
    =Helen (Sutton) in Mariposa 1959  
    =Mildred (White) in Merced 1959  
    =Constance (Hull) in Yosemite 1959  
    =Leroy drowned 1955  
  c. Lester N    b. 25 Apr 1889; SSDI  
    1944, 1959: Yosemite    d. (Mariposa) Sep 1985  
  d. Myrtle C (Branson) (Nelin)    b. Mariposa 1901  
    1944: Mariposa; 1959: Hawthorne  
  e. Robert B    b. Mariposa 1904  
    1944: Vallejo; 1959: Walnut Creek  
  f. David J    b. Mariposa 1906  
    1944: Mariposa; 1959: Jamestown  
  g. Dorothy (Lake)    b. Mariposa 1914 (6 Feb 1913)?  
    1944: Yosemite; 1959: Forest Hill    d. (Jan 1989; Lodi: SSDI)?  
  h. Donald M    b. Mariposa 1919  
    1944: Mariposa; 1959: Mariposa  
9. William L    b. (Santa Maria?) June 1879  
  1900: w/parents    d.  
  1906 Dir: Scott Wm teamster rPine st  
  1909 Dir: Scott, Will teamster W Orange st  
  1910-11 Dir: Scott Wm L lab S Lincoln  
  1920: Huasna, SLO co, alone  
  1933: Oceano  
10. Benjamin W    b. 1881  
  1910-11 Dir: Scott Benjamin W    d.  
    farmer Lincoln st  

*Note*: Ye Ed. is confused about the identity of this man; since J C Scott had a son of the same name born about the same time, it is unclear whether there are indeed two or that this one is assigned to the wrong family.

John Cowhick Scott    b. Winchester IL 17 March 1839  
  1860: Healdsburg w/Ezekiel    d. nr Santa Maria 6 Jan 1901 @61/9/20; SM cem  
    Reynolds fam    obit Jan 12; typhoid pneumonia  
  1890 GR: 51 IL f La Graciosa  
  1892 GR: 53 6'2 light complexion, blue eyes, brown hair IL La Graciosa  
    PO Santa Maria. Reg Sep 19  
  1896 GR: 57 6'3 lt blu br IL f Santa Maria  
  1900: tp 9 (Guadalupe)

    m. Santa Rosa 11 Jan 1869
Ella Elizabeth Cook b. Bangor ME 1 Jan 1848
    d. nr Santa Maria 6 Jan 1901 @53/0/6; SM cem
      obit Jan 12; typhoid pneumonia
    F: ?(Josiah Moores Cook 1829-)?
    M: Mary E     d. nr Garey 29 May 1894
      obit June 2. Charter member Rebekah
      Lodge, Yreka. To CA 1853

11 births, 9 living 1900, 1901
1. Mary Bell b. (1870)? m. of Santa Maria
    d. 11 Jan 1895 (?)
    m. San Luis Obispo 20 Oct 1891 by J H Barrett JP, D72
      wit: J L Wilson, SLO; Peter S Meyers, SLO
  Henry Clay Drumm b. (Sonoma co) Sep 1856
    1890 GR: 32 CA f La Graciosa     d. Ventura 14 May 1939 @83; "no relatives"
    1892 GR: 35 5'9 lt, blue     obit *Oxnard Daily Courier* Mon May 15 p. 1
      brown CA Santa Maria     F: Benjamin Howard Drumm 1816-1900
      reg Aug 8     M: Jane M Smith 1820-1902
    1900: Ventura, alone     See Drumm chart
    a. Mabel J b. (SM valley) 1892
      1909 Dir: 617 S Lincoln,     d.
        stu, w/H W Scott
      1910: @18, cousin w/B*W Scott, Santa Maria   *(Ben & Fay)
    b. Alphoretta/Alpha J b. SM 6 June 1893 (*Times*); m. @18 of SM
      1909: Miss A, same as     d.
      Miss Mabel, stu
        m. San Luis Obispo 4 Aug 1911 by Wm Mallagh JP, I252
          wit: Regina Hopper, Santa Maria; F J Rodriguez, SLO
    Willis G McMillan b. CA c1888; m. @23 of Santa Maria
      Electrician     d. SM 26 Oct 1943 @55/7/7; SM cem
      1914 Dir: lineman PT&T     obit Wed Oct 27 p. 3; no wife
      120 N Lincoln     F: John McMillan 1850-1910
        bio Phillips Vol II p.199
        M: Ellen C Robertson 1864-1936
    =dau (Marshall Elberson) in Los Angeles 1943
2. John <u>Thomas</u> b. CA Oct 1872; m. of Santa Maria
    1900: tp 6 Kern co wid     d. Santa Maria 11 Aug 1916 @44/9/15; SM cem
      teamster     or @45/10 Dudley Mortuary records
    1910: w/bro Marion/Lottie     obit Aug 12
      m. Newsom's Springs, SLO co 7 Apr 1895 by J L Eddy JP, D531
        wit: Charles Davis, Newsom's Springs; D F Newsom, Newsom's Springs
  Parlee Davis b. IN 1876
    d. Bakersfield 18 May 1900 @23; AG cem; obit May 26
    F: Jacob W Davis 1830-1908
    M: America 1844- ; 1880: Barton co KS
    a. child b. 18 May 1896; d. same
    b. Ella P b. Santa Maria 6 Dec 1897 (*Times*)
      1900: 2 listings: in Kern co w/father; also w/JC Scott, gdau
3. David Silas b. Round Mtn, Shasta co CA 23 Mar 1875
    1907 Dir: driller Gilroy     d. Santa Cruz 18 Sep 1969 @94/5; Soquel cem

    1908-9 Dir: same                       obit *Sentinel* Fri Sep 19 p. 14
    1920: 72 Spruce, Santa Cruz
    1930 Dir: well driller 72 Spruce
        m. (before 15 Mar 1907: he and wife went to J D Price funeral)
          no record Santa Cruz co
   Elizabeth Rose Connor            b. Salinas CA 14 Mar 1885
     (Libbie)                           d. (Soquel) 31 Oct 1936 @51/7/17; Soquel cem
     1906-7 Dir: Conner, Libby,          death cert inf: Helen Rackerby
        miss nurse Gilroy Private      F: John Connor
        Hospital rSanta Cruz             M: Rosanna Henrietty 1856-
                                          1900: 610 Pacific av Santa Cruz widow
    a. Helen M (Garner)                 b. WA 20 June 1907
       divorced                           d. SCz co 5 Jan 1965 @57; Oakwood cem
                                          death cert inf: Edna Hunter
    b. Edna L (Hunter)                  b. WA 1909
       1960, 1969 Dir: nurse supervisor Santa Cruz Gen Hosp. r691 35$^{th}$ av
       ?(Edna L Hunter SSDI           d. 4-28-1987 Santa Clara co)?
    c. Mary E (Perkins)                  b. WA 1911
                                          d. before 1969
    d. Irene D                                b. WA 13 May 1912
                                          d. (Watsonville) 21 Oct 1976; Calvary cem,
             m.                                Santa Rosa; death certificate
      Stephen D Gamble                 b.
        1969 Dir: Watsonville             d. survived wife
          Hdw & Bldg Supply h1055 39$^{th}$ ave
    e. John Connor                       b. WA 30 May 1915
       divorced                           d. Santa Cruz 25 Dec 1982 @67
       1969: prop The Sportsman         death cert inf: Josephine Garland.sis.
          Tavern 3530 Portola Dr Santa Cruz w/Rbt E Humphrey
    f. Josephine R                        b. CA 1919
       1969 Dir: wid, clk Dominican Hospital Santa Cruz, h3511 Floral av
         m.1 (Santa Cruz) 1 Dec 1937
      Clarence Murray Doane jr         b. Santa Maria c1916
                                          d. Capitola 30 Mar 1954 @38; accident
                                          See Doane chart

         m.2 _____ Garland
    g. James Edward                    b. (Santa Cruz) 3 Apr 1920; SSDI
       spouse initial L                   d. Los Angeles co 15 Oct 1960
4. Joe Cowhick                          b. CA May 1877
   1898 GR: 21 lab CA SM #2          d. after 1932
   1900: w/parents
5. Anna Mary                            b. CA Jan 1879
   1900: w/parents                       d. nr Santa Maria 28 Jan 1901 @22/0/8 (*Times*)
      m. nr Santa Maria 19 Aug 1900 (*Times*)
   John R (H)? Walker
    a. son                                     b. 4 Jan 1901 (*Times*)
6. Benjamin Wirt                     b. Siskiyou co May 1882; m. @24 of SM
   1900: Wirt B, w/parents            d. nr McKittrick 30 Jan 1912 @30
      m. San Luis Obispo 11 Sep 1905 by Geo Willett, G191
  Myrtle Fay Foster 1884-1918; see B W Scott chart #3 Mary Ellen

7. Harry Calif      b CA Dec 1883
    1900: w/parents      d.
    1907: in Gilroy
8. Marion Jackson Braiden      b. Modoc co 22 Nov 1885
    (BJ or Jack)      d. at home Taft 2 Sep 1961 @75; West Side cem
    1906 Dir: Scott MJ      bio *History of Kern co*, Morgan, 1914
      Chapel st; also Wirt      Brookshire Oil Co
    1907: Gilroy
    1910: tp 10 oilfields, tool dresser, driller near Orcutt
        m.1 Santa Barbara 21 Sep 1906
     Lottie Hazel Foster      b. (Santa Maria) Dec 1888
                     d. Taft 4 Sep 1928 @39; Union cem, Bakersfield
                         obit *Californian* Mon Sep 17 p. 10
                       F: Geo Alonzo Foster 1861-1932
                       M: Mary Ellen Scott 1863-1942
     a. Marion Joseph/Joe      b. Coalinga 30 Mar 1909; m. of Taft
                       d. Fellows/Taft 15 June 1958 @49
                         obit *Californian* Tue June 17 p. 34
                         Chansler-Western Oil Development Co
          m. Cambria 18 March 1932      West Side cem. Taft
     Alma Nettie McKenzie      b. SM/Lompoc? 14 Aug 1913; m. of Cambria
                       d. Arvin nursing home 26 Nov 1990 @77
                         obit *Californian* Wed Nov 28 E19
                       F: Lee Andrew McKenzie 1890-1940
                       M: Minnie Nina Huyck 1894-1914 (Edgar[4]
                          Andrew L[3] Walter[2] Andries[1])
                       See *Huyck Cousins*, Manfrina, Lompoc
                       Historical Society
     =Nina Lee 1937-1994 (Wm L Wade)
     =Marion Jackson b. & d. 1941
     =David Joseph b. 1947
     =John Charles b. 1950
     b. Mary Elizabeth      b. Shale, Kern co 3 Jan 1912
                       d. 2 Nov 1978
          m.1 c1932
     Clarence Nutting
          m.2 13 Apr 1937
     Carl Henry Smith     living in Redondo 1958
     c. Robert Jackson      b. Shale, Kern co 6 May 1915
                       d. 25 Oct 1935
     d. Emma Hazel      b. Shale, Kern co 24 Jan 1917
                       d. 21 June 1991
          m. c1934
     Jayne Darrell Furness      b. 1913
                       d. Salinas 15 Jan 1988
    =Jayne Allen 1935-1987 (Rosa Lee Rader)
    =Jackson Lance b. 1937 (Yoko Oshiro)
    =Dennis Lynn b. 1939 (Margaret Wigley Hicks)
    =Laurance Darrell b. 1941-1980 (Sherry Lynn Davis)
    =William Timothy b. 1943 (Sharon Patricia Crouch 1942-1980)
    =Lottie Hazel b. 1944 (Jerry Cronin)

    =Molly Ellen b. 1950 (Leroy Glenn Hensely)
    =Dixie Diane b. 1951 (Randall Rust)
    =James Edward b. 1953 (Cindy Louise King)
    =Terrance Robyn b. 1955

  e. Charles Richard        b. Shale, Kern co 20 Feb 1919
                               d. 23 Sep 1937

  f. Anna <u>Laura</u>              b. Shale, Kern co 10 Sep 1921
       m. 29 Nov 1951
    Joseph Howard Seymore      living in West Covina 1958

  g. Arthur Benjamin           b. Shale, Kern co 13 June 1925
                               d. 18 June 1925

  h. Dorothy Ellen             b. Fellows CA 28 Nov 1927
                               d. 25 May 1979
       m.1 c1945
    William Addington
       m.2 19 June 1947
    Grady Whittington     living in Torrence 1958

8.        m.2
  Maude Mae ___             1899-1993; West Side cem
                               her dau: Ethel Mae Peterson in Valley Acres 1958

9. Lucy J                    b. CA Dec 1887
    1900: w/parents           d.

10. Ella Elizabeth             b. CA March 1892 Santa Maria
    Single                      d. Fresno 31 July 1949 @57
    1900: w/parents           obit *Fresno Bee* Aug 1, p. 4-B
    1910: w/Lucy A Price, niece
    1920: Lakeport, boarder w/Eli Harman
    1930: w/Lucy Price

## WEDDINGS

1891     The Drumm-Scott Wedding. Mr H C Drumm an energetic young man of the South Side, and Miss Mary Bell Scott of the same section were married on Tuesday last. In order to economize time, this being the busy season, they concluded to have their infare* and wedding tour on the same day, so they went to San Luis, were married by Justice of the Peace J H Barrett, and immediately returned to settle down to the duties of married life.          –*SM Times* Oct 24
        *Infare: a reception for newly married couple (dial.)

1893     Married: Phillips-Scott—In Cambria, Tuesday May 18, 1893 N J Phillips and Miss Nettie A Scott.                           -The *Reasoner* (SLO)

1894     Cambria, *Ed Tribune*:.. Mr and Mrs N Phillips have changed their place of residence and now reside in town.              -*SLO Tribune* Nov 16

1900     A very pretty wedding occurred at the home of the bride's parents, Mr and Mrs J C Scott about six miles west of Santa Maria. The contracting parties were Mr John R Walker and Miss Mary A Scott, Rev O H Derry officiating. Mr and Mrs Walker have many friends who wish them success and happiness through life.
       La Graciosa News. Last Sunday a pretty wedding ceremony was enacted in Pine Grove school house, the contracting parties were Mr Mart Garrett and Miss Clara K Norris. The bride had on a beautiful white costume, and carried a bouquet of white flowers. The marriage was

performed by Rev S S Sampson of the Santa Maria Methodist church. The school was crowded with friends of the bride and groom. After the ceremony the young couple received the hearty congratulations of their many friends. The best wishes go with the young couple and may their married life be more of sunshine than of shadow. -XYZ

Southside Squibs. Miss Mary Harp came down from San Francisco Saturday to attend the Garrett-Norris wedding. She will visit with her parents for a short time before returning to the city.

The school house at Pine Grove was filled to overflowing last Sunday by people anxious to witness the Garrett-Norris wedding. A description of which appears elsewhere in these columns. Married. Garrett-Norris. In Pine Grove Sunday Aug 26 Joseph M Garrett and Miss Clara K Norris

Walker-Scott- Near Santa Maria Wednesday Aug 29 John R Walker and Miss Mary A Scott. –*SM Times* Sep 1

1905 Married in San Luis. Benjamin W Scott and Miss Fay Foster were joined in marriage in the office of the county clerk at 2 o'clock Tuesday afternoon by the Rev George Willett. Miss Mary Egan and R D Fuller were witnesses to the ceremony.

The couple are from Santa Maria and arrived in this city today. They departed for their future home in Santa Maria this afternoon.  -*SLO Breeze, SM Times* Sep 16

1932 Social & Clubs. Alma McKenzie Weds Joseph Scott in Pretty Ceremony.
….he of Taft…Groom's father and sister and close friend, Miss Elma Hitchcock of Taft were present…bride's parents Mr and Mrs Lee McKenzie…Scott in business in Taft…
 -The *Cambrian* Mar 24 p. 8

1932 Locals. Mr and Mrs Joe Scott returned Saturday from their honeymoon trip to San Francisco and Bay cities on a week-end visit to the home of the bride's parents, Mr and Mrs Lee McKenzie. Mr and Mrs Scott left Monday for Taft where they will reside.
 -The *Cambrian* April 7 p. 4

## DEATHS and TRAGEDIES

1901 David and Joe Scott who were in Bakersfield were sent a telegram Saturday evening stating the serious illness of their parents and the boys left immediately for Santa Maria but were caught in Sunday night's storm near the Porter ranch and were unable to cross the river. They reached Santa Maria Tuesday morning too late to be present at the funeral.  -*SM Times* Jan 12

1902 Dave Scott left Tuesday for Sangor (sic), Fresno Co, where he was called to nurse his uncle who is quite ill.  –Ibid Apr 12
*Note*: probably John M Price

1907 Deputy Sheriff Price Killed By Man Under Arrest
James Richardson, a Wood-Chopper, Arrested For Grand Larceny at Squaw Valley, Did to Death His Captor on the Centerville Road

Assassin Escaped, Taking Officer's Pistol And Watch Price's Dead Body Left in Buggy, Bleeding and Mutilated and Showing Signs of Desperate Struggle - Before His Arrest Richardson Snapped His Pistol Five Times in Officer's Face

Sheriff Chittenden And Possee Search Hills For The Murderer
 -*Fresno Morning Republican* Thur Mar 14

…Something of Joe D Price's Life…Joe Dodd Price was born March 12, in Academy. By a strange coincidence he was killed on his $32^{nd}$ birthday, within 6 miles of the place of his birth. His parents were J M Price and Mrs Lucy Scott Price. Mr Price, who passed away in June, 1905, was among the early rush of miners to this state. He settled in Amador County in 1853, and moved to the Russian river in 1857. He was married there in 1865 to Miss Lucy Scott and the couple moved to the Fancher creek district in 1872, after spending some time in Stockton….

In the neat family home on P street are left the near relatives of the gallant peace officer who was killed in such a brave performance of his duty. Besides his bereaved mother, who is in the evening of life, are his sister, Miss Maud Price, who is a teacher in the Bethel school, and a cousin, Miss Ella Scott, who has lived as one of the family for the last six years. Two sisters, Miss Mary C Price and Miss Martha Price, passed away some years ago, while his brother, Thomas S Price, who died in 1897, will be remembered by many old citizens as the assistant cashier of the now defunct Loan and Savings bank of this city. Another brother, John V Price, is now working in the oil fields near Gilroy…B J Scott, Harry Scott, and D S Scott and wife, cousins of the deceased, came from Gilroy yesterday to attend the funeral.  -Ibid Fri Mar 15 p. 10

Memorial Fund…the intent is to apply the fund for the same purpose for which Price was applying his earnings-the raising of a mortgage on his mother's place…  -Ibid Mar 16 p. 4

1912 Crushed To Death On Belridge Bullwheel Last Honors to Late Ben Scott
…Ben W Scott, a tool dresser, whose death occurred last Tuesday by being caught in a bullwheel on the Beldridge Company's lease north of McKittrick…survived by a wife and one child, six years old, and by a brother, who is ill at a hospital in this city. The deceased was 30 years old and was born in Siskiyou county…well-known in Fresno…
-Bakersfield *Californian* Wed Jan 31 p. 2

1918 Mrs Fay Foster Nells passed away yesterday afternoon in Arroyo Grande of pneumonia superinduced by an attack of influenza. She is believed to have contracted the disease while waiting on her sister, Mrs Hobbs, who passed away about a week ago from the malady. She is survived by a daughter, Bernice Scott, and her husband.  –*Santa Maria Times* Nov 2

1937 James Scott, Driller, Falls Dead As He Finishes Shift
James Scott, 45, today had worked his last shift as an oil-driller for the CCMO oil company.
And B M Whitney, driller, whose friendly smile used to greet Scott "out on the lease" at 4 pm as they traded shifts, will have a new partner.
Saturday afternoon the pair exchanged their greetings promptly at 4 o'clock, for Whitney was always at the well right on schedule.
Scott walked into the dressing room as Whitney took over his post to change his clothes. He slumped to the floor. At 4:05 his prostrate body was found by fellow workers. At the hospital shortly afterwards he was pronounced dead from a heart attack…survived by his widow, Mrs Nora Scott, his mother, Mrs M M Evans, of San Luis Obispo, a brother, Henry Scott, of Hynes, Calif, and a sister, Mrs Fred Godfrey, of Long Beach.
-*Ventura Star-Free Press* Mon Nov 22 p. 1

1942 Real Pioneer of SM Passes   Death Calls Mrs Mary Ellen Foster
…Mary Ellen Scott Foster…born in Healdsburg in 1863, she came to Santa Maria in 1873 with her parents, Benjamin and Eliza Scott, who resided on what is now known as the Freeman place. She attended the old Washington school, which once stood on the Orcutt road…
All of her ten children except two were born in Santa Maria. She was married in Santa Rosa, in 1883, to George Foster.
Only a daughter and three sons survive her. The daughter, Lucile Sugden, was with her at the time of her death. Two sons, Ernest and George, reside in Los Angeles. She had been making

her home with the third son, Ray, in Oceano. Two sisters also survive, Nettie Phillips of Mariposa, and Jane Logan of Bakersfield.

...Charter member of the local Christian church...also member of the Col. Harper post of the Women's Relief Corps in Arroyo Grande.

Mrs Foster remained active until the time of her death, and died sitting in her favorite chair, reading. She had just moved into a new home which her son built for her in Oceano after their old home was burned...  -*SM Times* Mon Apr 27 p. 2

1901 Tom Scott's little daughter had her arm broken this week a few miles south of town at the Foster place, but under Dr Paulding's careful attention she is doing nicely.
-Ibid March 2

AND A SUICIDE  Frank A Scott, on Christmas day, while under the influence of liquor and in a house of ill fame, fired a shot at his mistress and turned the gun on himself, firing two shots, one of which entered the head just above the ear...no hard feelings or high words were heard...the blame attaches to too much liquor.

-Frank Scott, a young farmer of Santa Maria, committed suicide Christmas morning...was but 27 years old, a native of the valley, and generally regarded as a "hard character."  -Ibid Jan 1 1898

## (AN)OTHER JOHN C SCOTT(S)

John C Scott m. SON co 1 Jan 1864 by T E Taylor, MG, Petaluma A401
  L C Bowles                    -Sonoma County Marriages 1847-1902, Son Co Gen Soc 1990

1870 cen MEN co: John C Scott 32 IL musician w/John Fay, Cuffey's cove. No wife

1875 GR: John Clement Scott musician 40 IL Eureka, reg. 1873
John C Scott of Eureka $450 to Solomon Cooper house & improvements on lot in Eureka.
    Deed 30 Oct 1877

1880 cen Humboldt co Petrolia pct: John C Scot 41 f OH; Louise 30 IL KY OH; Louise 14, Octavia 12, Joseph 3, John A* 9/12 Sept

1912 Precinct Reg, Upper Matole: John Albert* Scott 33 Rep. rancher, Alder Pt.
The last four items come from the *Redwood Researcher*, Redwood Gen Soc, P O Box 645, Fortuna, CA 95540

Vol. XXVII, No. 2, Summer 1995, pp.22, 23

**Corrections and Additions** (from Marcia Lasher)          [Page numbers refer to those in Quarterly]

p. 11    Parents of Eliza Jane Freshour were Andrew Freshour and Jane Marcum, not Marchan, who were married in Johnson co, MO 5 March 1837. 1840 census: Washington tp, Lafayette co MO: 1850 census: Madison tp, Johnson co, MO.

p. 16.   Mabel J Drumm was born in Santa Maria 25 Dec 1891, died in Los Angeles Jan 1969, married name Sickafoose. She had one child, Richard, 1911-1977. More below.

Alphoretta Drumm and Willis Gladstone McMillan, married in 1911, divorced, then remarried in Los Angeles 22 Apr 1926. Divorced again, Alpha married Carl A Weise, and died in Boise, Idaho, 14 May 1965. Alpha and Willis' only child, Emma, was born in Santa Maria 1 Jan 1913 and lived with her paternal grandmother, Ellen Craig Robertson McMillan. In 1934 Emma married George Marshall Elberson; after their divorce she married Ralph D Siebert. Emma died in Laguna Beach 14 Dec 1977. Marcia Lasher is the eldest of four Elberson children, and it is she who

Vol. XXVII, No. 4, Winter 1995, p. 14

supplied both marriage and death certificates for Alpha, which list as her parents Clay Drumm and Addie Scott, which leads us to Mary Bell Scott, the fictitious daughter of J C Scott.

The lack of the 1880 census record for the family of J C Scott has left a number of unanswered questions; however, Marcia, and Dixie Rust as well, has personal knowledge of the Scott family (whereas Ye Ed. was merely postulating), and their conclusion is that Ma(r)y Bell Scott and Addie May Scott are one and the same. The use of the name Ma(r)y Bell is found nowhere beyond the marriage certificate and the newspaper article about the marriage.

Marcia and Dixie each have the story of Addie Scott's having children by Ed Montgomery, who had married Nora Forrester in 1894-see Forrester chart. Ed's oldest son, Frank, was born 31 Oct 1899 and died in Grover City 18 June 1965; his mother was May Scott, according to his death certificate, and Mabel Sickafoose was a sister, according to his obituary.

Further evidence that Henry Clay Drumm's wife was a daughter of B W Scott, not J C Scott, is that, on the marriage certificate, the bride's parents were natives of Missouri, whereas J C's wife was born in Maine; another clue is that the newspaper notice of the marriage calls both Mr Drumm and Miss Scott residents of the South Side, where B W Scott's farm was. J C Scott's ranch was 6 miles west of Santa Maria, near Guadalupe. Capping the climax is the fact that the Santa Maria cemetery burial record lists Addie May, who died in 1910, under Montgomery as well as Drumm, and she is buried in grave 12, plot 58, Old Section, near B W Scott, who died in 1909, and rests in grave 10, plot 58. (It is no help that the Scotts have no markers.)

Conclusion: strike out the fictitious Mary Bell Scott from page 16; remove H C Drumm and his daughters to page 14 where they belong with Addie May. We will figure out Wm R Drumm later.

Vol. XXVII, No. 4, Winter 1995, p. 14

p.14. Ada May Scott did NOT marry Wm R Drumm.

# S N O W

| | |
|---|---|
| Richard B Snow | b. MO Dec 1853 |
| | d. Laton CA 10 Nov 1910 @56 |
| 1900: Alila tp Tulare co |   obit *Fresno Morning Republican* Thu Nov 10 |
| 1910: Fresno #13 | Parents: TN |
| m. 1886 | |
| Mary Elizabeth Burum | b. TN Feb 1860 |
|   3 ch. | d. Ivanhoe CA 28 Mar 1938 @78 |
| |   obit *Visalia Times-Delta* Tue Mar 29 p.2 |
| | Parents: TN |
| 1.  Mabel I | b. Delano CA 17 Nov 1888 |
| | d. Grover City 1 Oct 1974 |
| |   obit *San Luis Obispo Telegram-Tribune* |
|   m. |   Oct 2 p.1 |
|   John A Salyers | b. |
| | d. SLO co 25 Aug 1958 |
| 2.  Lucia E | 1890-1981 |
|   m.1 B W Stowell; m.2 John Wiegand | |
| 3.  Richard Burum | b. Delano Feb 1899 |
| | d. 7 Aug 1980; SM cem |

Vol. XXIV, No. 1-4, 1992, p.25

**Corrections and Additions**     [Page numbers refer to those in Quarterly]

p.25.    Sudden Death of Laton Vineyardist. R B Snow died at home from an attack of heart failure…inquest necessary. Age 56, had lived at Laton several years. No funeral arrangements made. (none found in later papers)      - *Fresno Morning Republican* Thu Nov 10 1910

    Services Set for Visalia Woman. Mrs Mary Elizabeth Snow, 78, died Monday at her Ivanhoe home; Delano cemetery. Survived by two daughters, Mrs J A Salyers, Ivanhoe; Mrs Lucia Stowell, Fresno; son R B Snow, Santa Maria; grandson Glen Salyers, Ivanhoe; two brothers, William H Burum, Dinuba; Hugh P Burum, Richgrove; two sisters, Miss Alberta Burum, Richgrove; Mrs Minnie Slayton, Manteca; 22 nephews and nieces. Pall bearers: Ernest Burum, Arthur Wynn, Tom Floyd, Percy Burum, James Burum, Warren Ragle.     –*Visalia Times-Delta* Tue Mar 29 1938 p.2 *Note*: the mother, Nancy B Burum, a widow in 1900, is listed on the census with Hugh P Burum in Alila tp, Tulare co; she died in Kern co 16 May 1911 @78.

    Mabel Salyers of Grover City died in Arroyo Grande @85; Arroyo Grande Cem. 21 years in Grover City; survivors: son Robert Salyers, Salinas; brother, Richard Snow, Santa Maria; sister Lucia (Stowell) Wiegand, Pacific Grove; 5 gch.     – *SLO Telegram-Tribune* Oct 2 1974 p.1

    Richard Burum Snow died in Santa Maria 7 Aug 1980 @81/7/6; SM cem. Lived in Santa Maria since 1971; worked for the Will Oakley ranch, drove trucks for Paul Bradley, operated R B Snow Trucking 25 years. Survived by widow Babe, and sister Lucia Stowell Wiegand, Pacific Grove.     – Fri Aug 8 1980

    1930 Dir: R B Snow 314 N Elizabeth
    1939 Phbk: 218 E Alvin
    1940-1 Dir: R B (Floy) dump trucks h 218 E Alvin
    1947-8 Dir: R B (Elgie) oil trucking h 312 S East; 1955-6 Dir: same
    1976 Dir: Richd & Babe h 1701 S Thornburg #76

Vol. XXX, No. 2, Summer 1998, p.20

# SPEED FAMILY
CAVEAT LECTOR
ANOTHER EPISODE IN THE SAGA OF IDENTIFYING TRUTHFUL HISTORY or
I READ IT IN THE PAPER; IT MUST BE SO

When, in 1964, we bought our house on Speed Street, once THE fashionable section of Santa Maria, we suffered the whips and scorns of snide comments from our out-of-town relatives and friends about the supposed velocity of the vehicular traffic past our front door. We would respond flatly that the street was named for Josiah P. Speed, an early settler. We made that up—but of such is "History" concocted.

As time went on, we found that speed is indeed a surname and that there was actually an early settler named John W. Speed. Further, we learned that Speed is an honorable Colonial Virginia name which spread with the westward expansion into Kentucky, Illinois and Missouri, as well as southern states and that it still surfaces in England. A Mr Speed being mentioned as one of her Majesty's functionaries during the Falkland Islands "War."

Our house, built by Bert Rosenblum in 1938, was a showplace in its time, and having been informed that some of the neighboring edifices had been written up in the local newspaper, we essayed to find if our domicile had been so honored. Nothing of the sort was found in the paper, but this four-column advertisement, published in the *Santa Maria Times*, December 19, 1938, was hard to miss:

Let's Keep The Name "Speed Street" In Santa Maria

A Short History of the Speed Family: John W. Speed, pioneer resident of Santa Maria, was a direct descendant of the Joshua Fry Speed who was Abraham Lincoln's most intimate personal friend. Citywide discussion of the naming of Speed Street in Santa Maria, named for Mr and Mrs Speed, makes the following historical data of more than passing interest. (There followed nine paragraphs consisting principally of Speed's own account of his first encounter with Lincoln in Springfield—a patriotic tale if ever there was one!)

"Speed Street" was named in honor of Mr and Mrs John W. Speed, pioneer residents of Santa Maria, and descendants of Joshua Fry Speed…    and so we leave the name Speed Street in the hands of the mighty…praying that the name Speed Lives on Forever! Let's keep the names of these old respected families.    -Leone P. Haslam, owner of Haslam Park Santa Maria's Newest Subdivision. (Mrs Haslam's enthusiasm overlooked the facts)

James Speed, 1679-1719, who immigrated to Virginia in 1695, is said to be the common ancestor of all Virginia Speeds. His second son was John, whose second son, James, betook self and family to Kentucky in 1782, settling in the vicinity of Louisville. James' second son, John, became a judge; his second wife was Jucy Gilmer Fry, daughter of Joshua Fry, and to this union Joshua Fry Speed was born in 1814. After his sojourn in Springfield during which his lifelong friendship with Lincoln was born, he went back to Kentucky, married Fannie Henning in 1842, and died in Louisville in 1882 <u>without</u> offspring.

John Wesley Speed, of Santa Maria, was born in 1849, so, age wise, he could have been a "direct descendant"—a son—of Joshua Fry Speed, IF he had any. John was born in Morgan County, Missouri, 12$^{th}$ child, according to the 1850 census, of James H. and Lucy Speed, natives of Virginia who moved to Missouri after 1840 by way of North Carolina.

"Direct descendants"? Josh and John of James. Period.

Speed's biography in Guinn's history is not flawless, but checks out well enough. Speed came to this area to stay in 1879, registering to vote that year in Oso Flaco, San Luis Obispo County. The 1880 census-taker found him in Guadalupe, where he had lived several years earlier, probably with or near his brother, William, who died in 1878. John had returned to Missouri for a time, but once back, ranched near Guadalupe, married in 1884, and had two sons before buying 160 acres east of Santa Maria, south of what is now Betteravia Road in 1890; a sketch of that farm decorates the lower left corner of the bird's eye view map of Santa Maria published by the *Santa Maria Times* in the 1890's. In 1898 he bought the forty acres now bounded by Broadway, Jones, Miller and the easement just north of Camino Colegio, some of which became Speed's Addition to the town of Santa Maria in 1908. He sold lots to some well-known names: R E Easton, J R Wickenden, and Arthur Froom, among others. In 1921 Speed's 2nd Addition was recorded, and the street now called Speed was named Calle Durazno-Peach Street. It should have been Albaricoque—Apricot—for Speed and many others raised that fruit in this valley in the early days; that would have been a mouthful! However, as the street is a lineal continuation of Vine Street, when the area developed, so did the controversy on the name of the street. Holmes B. Tabb built his house just north of ours in 1937 on what he called Vine Street, and when he died in 1940, his address was still 1115 Vine. It was people like him whose attitude occasioned Mrs Haslam's advertisement in the paper.

Speed's sons by his wife, Fannie Herndon, were James Herndon and John W Jr. Mrs Speed died of "the Grippe" in 1891; John married again in 1893 in San Francisco, and brought his wife back to Santa Maria. They built a large house on the corner of Broadway and Jones – no railroad there then. James died in Columbus, Ohio, in 1910, and John Jr. died in 1918 of the Spanish flu at Camp Fremont just as his outfit was shipping out, so after Mr Speed's death in 1926, Mrs Speed was without local family, making her home with Fred and Leone Haslam the eight years she outlived her husband.

"Haslam Park, Santa Maria's newest subdivision" was the remainder of Speed's 40 acres. We may credit Mrs Haslam's loyalty to her friends for her spirited defense of the respected name of Speed, but must admit the error in her ardor.

James H. Speed            b. c1805 Mecklenburg Co? VA; d. Morgan Co MO
Lucy A. Maroni/           b. c1813 Mecklenburg Co? VA; d. c1863 Morgan Co MO
  Maroney/Malone
Children: from 1850 Census, Richland tp, Morgan County, Missouri
1. Mary E.       b. 1830 VA
2. Emily         b. 1832 VA
3. Susan         b. 1834 VA
4. William H.    b. 1836 Mecklenburg co? VA, d. May 19, 1878 Santa Barbara Co CA
     Landowner Guadalupe, California 1873, Teamster, Pt. Sal, CA 1875 Directory
5. James         b. 1838 VA
6. Thomas        b. 1840 NC
7. Sally         b. 1841 MO
8. Harriett      b. 1843 MO
9. Virginia      b. 1845 MO
10. Rosalina     b. 1846 MO
11. Lolly        b. 1848 MO

12. John Wesley  b. Aug 4 1849 Morgan County, MO; d. Aug 19 1926, Santa Maria CA
    m.1 1884
    Fannie Herndon b. Jan 14 1854 Carrollton MO; d. Feb 22 1891, Santa Maria CA
    a. James Herndon, b. Apr 30 1887 Laguna Ranch, Santa Barbara co CA; d. July 13 1910, Columbus, OH
    b. John Wesley, Jr, b. Jan 25, 1890, Speed's Ranch, Santa Maria CA
    m.2 1893 San Francisco
    Mary Boquet, b. Oct 9, 1859 London, England; d. Jan 26, 1934 Santa Maria, home of Mr & Mrs Fred Haslam

Sources:
*Biographical Cyclopedia of The Commonwealth of Kentucky,* Gresham Co, Chicago  1896
*Historical Encyclopedia of Illinois and History of Sangamon Co*  Vol. 1
*A History of California and an Extended History of Its Southern Coast Counties,* J M Guinn 1907
Santa Barbara County Records; *Santa Maria Times*; Santa Maria Cemetery; SMVGS *Quarterly* 'Extracts'

# STEPHENS
## PIONEERS OF THE CENTRAL COAST

Martin Henry Stephens      b. Darke co OH 3 July 1836; parents PA
  Patron T/W: to CA 1865      d. at home of dau Mrs Thompson, Santa Maria 24 Dec 1910
  to SBco 1869; 160a corner      @74/5; Stephens Mausoleum, Arroyo Grande cem, obit T
  Blosser & Guadalupe rds      Dec 31 p.1; 4 dau 3 sons
1870 cen: SBco tp #3 PO Arroyo Grande
1870 Graciosa Sch dist parents:...M H Stephens      *-This is Our Valley* 98
1875 Paulson Dir: farmer Santa Maria
1875 co-op store founded by John Thornburgh with R D Cook, Samuel Lockwood, M H
    Stephens, SW corner Main & Bwy, also PO.      *-This is Our Valley* 46; ONT 463
1879 GR: 42 OH f SM reg May 24
1880 cen: SM
1882 GR: 45 OH f SM reg Aug 17
1887 Mr M H Stephens is taking a little rest this season from the heading business to say that
    for the past fifteen years he has been engaging in running a header in Santa Maria
    valley during the harvest season. We think Mr S is entitled to a rest, he is a well to do
    farmer, and we do not see why he cannot afford to rest for a season or two.
         *–SM Times* July 23
1890 GR: 54 OH f SM #2 reg Oct 4
1892 GR: 56 5'9 dark complexion brown eyes black hair OH SM #2 reg Sep 24
1894    Land Notice. San Francisco Apr 23, 1894. Martin Stephens. timber cert. #841 lots
    3,4,5 S31 T12N R26W. Wit: Geo L Stephens, F W Black, B McPherson, W H
    McPherson, all SM PO      (SE Corner SLOco - Soda Lake rd)
1895    Mr Wilkinson, a cousin of M C (sic) Stephens arrived from Indiana this week for his
    health.      *–SM Times* May 25
1898 GR: 62 5'9 fair hazel grey OH AG #1
1900 cen: Arroyo Grande; m/39
1900    Petition in Bankruptcy. M H Stevens (sic) of Oak Park, Under Heavy Liabilities with
    Assets Small...Farmer Oak Park District...liabilities 10,692.19, assets 3,155. These
    liabilities are for judgements of years' standing and his assets were accrued since the
    judgements were made. His creditors hopped onto him with both feet as soon as they
    learned of his present holdings. Adcock & Remick of Los Angeles, and A J Monihan
    of San Luis Obispo, attorneys...heard next Thursday.      *–SLO Breeze* Mon Sep 3
1902 GR: 67 AG #1
1904 GR: 68 AG #1
1912 Dir: farmer AG (or is this jr?)
1912    Estate of M H Stephens...      *-SLO Daily Telegram* Mar 6 or 8
    m.. (remarried) Arroyo Grande 1 Aug 1894 by A M Ozborn, ME ch, D445
        wit: Emily M Bishop, AG; Lee Bishop Balaam, AG; groom of AG, bride of SM;
    his 2nd marriage, her 3rd

Mary Ellen Looker      b. Fairfield co OH 7 Aug 1835; parents VA
  see O'Neill 349; grad      d. San Luis Obispo 31 Jan 1907 @72/5/22; Stephens
  Antioch College, Xenia OH      Mausoleum, obit from *SLO Tribune* in T Feb 9; former res
  8 ch, 2 in SBco      SM; 7 ch
1885. Mrs Stephens and daughters have opened the Millinery store in Nance's building
    adjoining the Jasper house and invite their old friends to give them a call. They have an
    excellent stock of millinery, ladies' and children's furnishing goods, Christmas candies,
    novelties, etc. Mrs Stephens is one of the oldest settlers in this valley and her many
    friends will no doubt give her a liberal support.      *-Times* Nov 14

1886. Miss Jennie Stephens is back from the city and will have charge of the millinery Store. -Sep 11

1887 Selling Out At Cost. I am now offering my entire stock of Millinery goods at cost, either by wholesale or retail. Any lady wanting to get into the millinery business can do well by buying my stock and continuing the business. Otherwise I will retail at cost prices. Miss Jennie Stephens -*Times* July 23

Mrs M H Stephens left on Wednesday for Mineral Springs (sic) NV to visit her daughter and son-in-law, Mr and Mrs Thompson. -Sep 10

Miss Jennie Stephens will go to San Francisco on Monday next for a few days visit. -*Times* Sep 17

Personal Mention. The Misses Stephens, Jennie and Mamie left Tuesday to join their mother and sister in San Francisco. -Oct 1

Misses Jennie and Mamie Stephens returned from the city Thursday. -Nov 12

1890 Mrs M A Stephens presented the *SM Times* with a basket of new potatoes and a fine variety of radishes, all grown on her rich farm west of town. -50 Years Ago, *Times* Jan 19 1940

1891 Mrs Stephens offers for rent one of the finest farms in the valley. For particulars see ad. in this issue. Mrs Stephens has moved one of her small dwelling houses from town to her ranch west of town. -Sep 20

1893 To Let-A work horse to let cheap. Inquire of Mrs M A (sic) Stephens three doors west of Presbyterian church. -Dec 20

1894 Mrs Stephens is having a great deal of wood chopped on her ranch and expects to have 500 cords to sell this spring. -Jan 6

Mrs M A (sic) Stephens' yard on Chapel street was considered to have some of the most plentiful and luxuriant flowers and vegetables to be seen in Santa Maria. She has converted into the garden a common used for staking cows. -50 Years Ago, *Times* Oct 5 1944 p.4

1897 Mrs M A (sic) Stephens is visiting her daughter, Mrs O S Sellers, at Pozo. -June 5

In our issue of Oct 23, in reference to ME church committee organization, we omitted committee on visiting the sick, as follows: Mrs John Elliott, Mrs M E Stephens, Mrs E N McGuire, Mrs Geo Stowell and Mrs Tunnell. -Nov 6

Mrs M E Stephens is planning a trip back to her old home in Ohio. She has been away for forty years and anticipates a pleasant time with friends with whom she has been in constant communication. Early in the coming Spring has been chosen as the time to start. -Nov 27

1902 Mrs M E Stephens returned to Verde after several days visiting with friends. -Jan 18

1905 Local & Business Items. Mrs M E Stephens stopped in the valley this week on her return trip from Los Angeles where she visited her daughter who is very ill and not expected to recover. -Jan 22

1907 7 children surviving: G L Stephens, Verde; Lizzie Thompson, AZ; Jennie E Stephens, Redding; S C Stephens, Seattle; Ada Sellers, Pozo; M H Stephens jr, San Luis Obispo; Mamie Moore, Orcutt. -Feb 9

1908 Estate of Mary E Stephens. Lots 8,9,10 Block 5 Miller's subdivision of Santa Maria. Martin H Stephens and Ada C Sellers, Admin of estate. -Jan 4

1. George Lytle Stephens          b. Washington co IA Feb 1862
   1890 GR: 26 IA f Huasna        d. San Luis Obispo 21 March 1930 @67; Stephens
      reg Sep 7 1888                 Mausoleum, obit T Fri Mar 21 p.1; sis Mrs Thompson,
   1892 GR: 30 5'10¾ med br          SM; Mrs Moore, SM; Mrs Sellers, Los Angeles; bro
      US f res Huasna; pct AG;       Sherman, Seattle; M H, San Luis Obispo
      PO AG; reg Sep 21              *Note*: Lytle Stephens Feb 25 1872-July 16, 1908, son
   1900 cen: w/parents, single         of L A & S E Stephens, buried near Stephens

    1902 GR: AG #1, 40                    Mausoleum, Arroyo Grande cemetery
    1904 GR: AG #1, 42
    1907 in Verde; father lived with him after mother died
2. Elizabeth Charlotte Stephens      b. Washington co IA 5 Feb 1863
    across Panama 1869; to          d. at home 25 Oct 1943 @80; Stephens
    SF, to Sonoma co, to SM           Mausoleum, obit Mon Oct 25 p.1; 2 sis 1 bro
    Father gave land for               son dau 3gch
    Agricola school                      74y SM (sic) but see below
    Reunion Pleasant Valley school group photo including Lizzie Thompson      -*Valley* 262
    1907 in AZ
    1910 cen: Santa Margarita: Eliz C 45 m/23 2 births 2 lvg: Hallie E 21 NV, Sherman K
        12 CA
    1912 For sale 21 acres rich first-class land opposite Verdi (sic) station San Luis Obispo
        Co 3 miles from Arroyo Grande, planted to bearing fruit trees, nuts and berries.
        $100 to $150 per acre. -Mrs S S Thompson 207 Chapel St Santa Maria, Cal.
        -May 18
    1914 Dir: Elizabeth C Mrs h209 E Chapel
    1920 cen: SM Samuel S & Elizabeth C
    1922-3 Dir: Mrs E C r209 E Chapel; J Frank Thompson embalmer AA Dudley, r same
    1925 Dir: S S (Eliza C) lab r209 E Chapel
    1928 Dir: Elizabeth Apt house r209 E Chapel
      --not responsible for debts contracted for by anyone but myself. Signed: Mrs
      S S Thompson.                                                      -Wed Dec 15 p.5
    1938-9 Dir: Mrs Elizabeth landlady h217 E Chapel; Wesley Wood r same
    1940-1 Dir: same;  1943 phbk: same
      m. at residence of M H Stephens west of town 10 Aug 1886 by Rev Chas Leach,
        C329; wit: S E Crow, H C Adams. To live in NV; Jennie Stephens
        accompanied them to San Francisco.                    (*Times*)
Samuel Summers Thompson        b. San Francisco 1865; m. @21 of Mineral Hill NV (*T*)
                                        d. at home 209 E Chapel 3 July 1931 @66; AG cem
                                          near Stephens Mausoleum; obit Mon July 6 p.3;
                                          wife, dau, son
                                          to SM 1893 some years after marriage to
                                          Elizabeth Stevens (sic)
    1887 Mr S Thompson of Mineral Hill NV arrived Friday evening of last week and
        intends to go into business in Santa Maria. Mrs Thompson, former Lizzie
        Stephens, will arrive in a week or so.                           -Oct 1
      Mrs Stephens has returned from Minerall Hill NV accompanied by her daughter
      Mrs S S Thompson…Thompsons to make their home in Santa Maria.      –Nov 12
      Mrs Stephens has disposed of her millinery store to Mrs Thompson, who will
      continue in the same building, and will dispose of this fashionable stock, at cost,
      until sold. Ladies are invited to call and examine the goods.          -Dec 17
    *Note*: Mrs T's obituary says her husband was in charge of the grocery department
        of M Fleischer & Co.
  a. Hallie E Thompson                  b. Mineral Hill NV 13 July 1887 (*Times*); 1890 (cen)
                                          (21 on 1910 census); CA 15 Jul 1891 (death record)
                                          d. Santa Monica 3 Sep 1960 @69; Stephens Mausoleum
      m.1 Kostering                    obit Mon Sep 5 p.2; hus, dau, son, bro 5gch
    1931 Mrs F R Kostering returned to Burlingame after a week's visit with her parents,
        M/M S S Thompson. Also guests were M/M Sherman K Thompson & children.
        -July 10

1943 in Santa Maria
=Muriel E Kostering (Dover) b. San Francisco 22 June 1921
   1960 in Enon OH
  1943. Here from Oakland. Miss Muriel Kostering, student nurse, Highland hospital, Oakland, is here for the funeral of her aunt (sic) Mrs Elizabeth Thompson. Her mother, Mrs H E Kostering, is an employee of Hancock College of Aeronautics. -Oct 26

> California Death Index: Kostering
> Charles d. San Francisco 3-19-1912 @76
> Henry F d. Alameda co 10-22-1918 @34; spouse S E
> Evelyn L d. San Francisco 3-1-1937 @25
> Frederich b. 6 Nov 1876; d. Oakland Mar 1970; SSDI

    m.2 c 1944
Jack Pritchard          b. Pineola NC 21 Aug 1907; SSDI
  to Bicknell 1921       d. Nipomo 5 Jan 1994 @86; SM cem
  1945-6 Dir: Jack (Hollie)     obit Jan 7; 9 gch 24 ggch
  emp Union Oil         F: George K Pritchard 1881-1961
  rBicknell               M: Stewart
  1947-8 Dir: Jack (Hallie)     m.1 Violet Brewer
  r250 S Pacific          m.3 Earleen (Moore)
  Orcutt
  1950 phbk: Jack Los Alamos; also 213 E Chapel
  1951-2 Dir: Jack Los Alamos
  1955-6 Dir: Jack (Hallie E) Los Alamos
  1961 in Santa Monica
  1970 to Nipomo
  =Jack Christian Pritchard 1938-1994 reared by Jack and Hallie in Los Alamos
  See Pritchard chart
 b. Sherman Kingdon Thompson    b. CA 5 Dec 1896: SSDI AR
    1931 in Watsonville         d. Oroville CA 2 Nov 1980 @83
    1943, 1954 in Santa Maria
    1945-6 Dir: Sherman K (Ruth) emp Air Base h217 E Chapel
        Ruth C wtrs Burnett's Café r217 E Chapel
    1947-8 Dir: Sherman K h217 E Chapel
    1960 in Downeyville
    ?(Ruth Cathryn Thompson     b. TX 27 Nov 1908; d. Santa Barbara 26 Jul 1982 @74
                                F: Farquhar; M: Watson)
    ?(Ruth A. Thompson         b. CA 20 Jan 1908; d. Chico CA 8 Nov 1977 @69; SSDI)
    =Benjamin Thompson pvt Army Air Corps 1943
    =Ruth Thompson in Santa Maria 1943
3. Jennie Effie Stephens       b. (Washington co) IA c1864 (cen); m. of Verde
  (Effie Jane)              d. Santa Maria 20 Mar 1919 @50; Stephens Mausoleum
  1907 in Redding           obit Mar 22; hopeless invalid
    m. at home of bride's parents, Verde, 8 Aug 1897 by Rev T C Miller      *-Times*
Frank N. Martin Dr          b.     m. of SLO
                               d
  1887 Miss Jennie Stephens lost a walking jacket some three weeks ago between Santa Maria and Laguna lake, the finder will please leave same at Miss Stephens'

        Millinery store in Santa Maria.    -July 23
- 1888. Land Notice. San Francisco Oct 1 1888. Miss Effie J Stephens pre-emption D S #21767 lot 5 SW4NE4 E4NE4 S7 T11N R23W Wit: E S Emerson, J Block, Frank Enis, Geo Nelson all SM PO (land in Kern co)
- 1897. Miss Jennie Stephens from Arroyo Grande to visit parents.    -Aug 1
  Dr Martin and wife (nee Miss Stephens) have separated and San Luis papers are trying to make no accusation. Drinking and abusive language are the grounds on which Mrs Martin decided to leave the doctor.    -Oct 30
  See story and Dr Martin's ad on separate pages.

4. Sherman C. Stephens     b. Sonoma co CA 10 June 1865; m. @26
                                     d. Seattle 3 Mar 1940 @69 (cem) Stephens Mausoleum obit Tue Mar 5 p.2; Thu Mar 7 p.6; body sent to Dudley accompanied by Mrs Mamie Moore; ill several mos, 3 sis 1 bro 8 neph/niece

- 1888 Polk Gazetteer: Santa Maria: Stephens Misses (Ada, Jennie, Mamie) millinery
  Stephens Sherman C cigars
- 1890 GR: 25 CA mcht SM #2
- 1890 ad. Holiday Goods! A Fine Assortment and Presents for All at Sherman Stephen's Store. Here we are again for the Holidays with a bigger and more complete Stock of Holiday Goods, Confections, Apples, etc. than ever before. Presents Suitable for Young and Old. I only rise to repeat the promise that I have so often made: That at my Store you will be able to buy Holiday Goods for less money than at any other place in town. Don't be Tardy, for the Best will Surely be Picked First. Call To-Day Without Further Delay.
     -Dec 13
  A Pleasure Boat. Messrs Sherman Stephens and S M Blosser have just finished the building of a boat for the Laguna. It is well built, about 16 feet long and will carry ten or twelve passengers. Mr George Brown has been busy for the day or two beautifying the new boat with his paint brush. The proprietors propose to launch the boat soon and christen it "The Santa Maria." It is intended for a pleasure boat. A house will be built near the lake to house the boat when not in use. It will be kept in first class order and let out to parties at reasonable rates. Boating on the Laguna is a fine pastime as a run of six miles or more can be made in a single direction. Mr R D Cook will run his bus to the lake, whenever a party of Santa Marians desire to go down and spend the day. -Dec 13
  Note: other boaters. Notice All persons are forbidden to use my boat on the Laguna without permission. A A Fox    -Jan 7, 1888
  Messrs Cole, Moore, and others had a way up time a few days since sailing on Laguna Lake a few miles below town.    -June 11 1887
- 1892 GR: 26 5'9 dk brn dk scar on left thumb stockraiser CA Huasna Huasna SM; reg Oct 8
- 1893 Polk Gazetteer: variety store Santa Maria
  Sherman Stephens has finally succeeded in getting a hearing with the fish commissioners and as a result he expects 10,000 Black Bass spawn in a few days for the purpose of stocking the Laguna. It will be fine sport fishing on the lake when it is full of choice bass and future anglers will thank Mr Stephens for his persistence and finally successful efforts. -Sep 16
- 1898 To Klondike with Addison Powell, Joe Miller, Joe Morrison, Jim Saulsbury, Jim Elliott, W F Jasper, J M Jasper.    *–This is Our Valley* 221
- 1907 in Seattle

1940 Mrs Mamie E Moore Left for Seattle…brother Sherman Stephens is ill…   -date lost
Card of Thanks…to Rev C E Ruckman, Mrs C W Hatch. Mrs Elizabeth
Thompson, Mrs Ada Sellers, Mrs Mamie Moore, M H Stephens.   -Mon Mar 11
   m. Santa Maria 2 Dec 1891 by F L Platt

Florence G Fesler     b. KY    m. @18; parents KY
    d.

5. Ada C Stephens     b. (Sonoma co) CA Sep 1866; m.1 of Santa Maria
    bap ME ch SM Nov 1885     d. Santa Cruz co 20 Jun 1957 @90
    1887 Miss Ada Stephens left for Santa Barbara Friday morning to attend school.   -Aug 27
    1888 Miss Ada Stephens, who has been spending the past few months in Santa Barbara,
        attending school, returned home recently for a few weeks vacation.   -Jan 7
    1907 in Pozo
    1930 in Los Angeles
    1940 in Mt Hermon, Santa Cruz co surname Woodward; also 1943, 1948
    1946 NDGW ceremonies Agricola school Santa Maria. Program to honor teachers and
        former students. Visitors…Ada Stephens Woodward of Mt Hermon, Santa Cruz
        co, her sister Mamie Moore, Santa Maria, brother M H Stephens and wife..   -Sep 20
       m.1 Santa Maria 5 July 1894 by Rev Lawrence; double wedding w/brother Martin.
       see also *SLO Tribune*

Oliver S Sellers     b. OH 9 Aug 1865; m. of Pozo
   1890 GR: 25 of OH f La Panza     d. San Diego co 12 Feb 1957 @91
     reg Oct 6     F. William Sellers
   1892 GR: 27 5'9½ lt blu     M: Elizabeth G Allen 1832-1902
     brn f OH La Panza; reg Oct 18
   1900 cen: SLO co San Jose tp 2 births 2 living
   1902 GR: 37 Pozo
   1902 A Sad Accident at Pozo. Aged Mother of O S Sellers Instantly Killed While Sitting
      at the Table. A Rifle Bullett (sic) Passes Entirely Through her Head. Hired Man Cause
      of Accident. Was Handling a Loaded Gun Just Outside Door…early Sunday
      Morning….Mrs Elizabeth G Sellers…6 miles east of Pozo…advanced age of 69
      years …rifle in the hands of Charles Priest, employee of son, O S Sellers…born E
      Tennessee, married Clay co MO; to CA c1892, shortly after death of husband. Lived
      with son…Husband Rev Wm Sellers, ME minister, chaplain 16th Kansas Vol
      Infantry, Civil War…3 sons 1 dau…Priest born Leavenworth KS, @24, Spanish-
      American war.   –*SLO Tribune* Tue Feb 4
   1910 cen: Santa Margarita retail mcht gnl; 3 births 3 living; also cousin Harriet E
      Clevenger 30 TX MO2 single
   1913 Mgr Santa Margarita Land Co
   1914 Dir: PM & gen mdse Santa Margarita
   1916 former PM Santa Margarita
   1920-21 VR: SLO #8 Mrs Ada C 5'4 CA; Oliver S 5'9½ OH

a. Lelia E Sellers     b. on the Suey ranch 27 Dec 1895   -*Times*
    d.

b. Elmo Martie Sellers     b. 22 Feb 1897; SSDI
   1954 in Los Angeles     d. Los Angeles Apr 1976 @79; Stephens Mausoleum,
       "nephew"

    m. SLO co 22 June 1922
Florence Mae Rostad     b. Grand Forks ND 19 Apr 1899; SSDI
    d. at home Los Osos 21 June 1991 @92 obit *SLO
       Telegram-Tribune* Sat June 22 C7; to Los Osos Nov
       1977

              M: Halvorsen; bro Ralph Rostad, Modesto; 1 bro
              1 sis deceased.  4 gch 1 ggch
   =Florence <u>Elaine</u> Sellers (Caramelli) b. Los Angeles 17 May 1926
     in Los Osos 1991
  c. Marigold G Sellers    b. c1903
5.    m.2
  Frederick A Woodward   b. Canada 14 Aug 1875
           d. Santa Cruz co 23 Oct 1943; AG cem
           notice Oct 26

6. Martin Henry Stephens jr  b. San Luis Obispo 8 Sep 1867; m.1 @26 of Santa Maria
  1890 GR: 21 CA f Huasna  d. San Luis Obispo 5 March 1954 @86; Stephens Mausoleum
   reg Sep 27 1888     obit *SLO Telegram-Tribune* Tue Mar 9; lived in SM, hotel &
  1890 Martie Stephens    store in AG, cattle ranch Huasna; bldg contr San Jose &
   proved up on his pre-emp-  SLO; wife, s/d, s/s, 3 neph 5 nc
   tion claim on Sat last before
   the County Clk of SLOco. -Dec 6
  1892 GR: 24 5'10 dk br blk stockraiser CA Huasna; reg Sep 5
  1894 During the early 1890's, Martin Stevens (sic) came from Santa Maria to manage the
   Union Hotel.  He brought his bride here, and I have heard…what a noisy charivari
   was given the newlyweds & how very indignant Stevens was at the pranks played.
   *According to Madge, Early Times in South San Luis Obispo County and the*
    *Arroyo Grande Valley,* Ditman, 1983
   Wanted: 500 men wanted at Mort (sic) Stephens to eat roasted peanuts. -Mar 10
  1895 We received a letter from Mart Stephens, who is now at Summerland a few days
   since. In speaking of the oil well business, he says oil is all right, lots of it. We
   have a well, already with 60 feet of oil standing in the pipe and good prospects for
   another good well along side. Everything looks quite favorable for a continuation
   of the oil boom.                -Dec 28
  1897 Union Hotel Arroyo Grande Cal. Mart. Stephens Prop.  First Class meals
   First class bar  Rates reasonable.     -ad *Santa Maria Times* Apr 12 &c
   Mart Stephens is in town resting. He concluded hotel life in Arroyo Grande was not
   a rapid road to wealth, and so he quit, and the house is now closed.  -Oct 9
   Mart Stephens and wife came down from San Luis Thursday night and will make
   Santa Maria their home.              -Nov 13
   M Stephens, of San Luis Obispo, a former proprietor of the Union Hotel in Arroyo
   Grande, was in town this week looking for a location. *-Lompoc Journal*.  And
   not finding one he returned to Santa Maria, and decided to remain with our people.
   There is no place to compare to this valley, and sensible men see it and settle.
                   -*Santa Maria Times* Nov 20
  1898 M H Stephens of Santa Maria Notice of Intention…  -*SM Graphic* May 6
  1900 cen: Santa Maria butcher
  1907 Arroyo Grande News. Martie Stephens was a visitor in town yesterday from San
   Luis.                    *Times* June 1
  1908 M H Stephens contr & blDr -*Times* Oct 31
   M H Stephens jr, well-known carpenter, built a handsome 3-room cottage for his
   sister Mrs Harvey Moore opposite the city park.  M/M Harvey Moore moved to
   Santa Maria to occupy it.        -25 Years Ago *Times* Aug 15 1933
  1911 M H Stephens Gen Contr 511 High st SLO  -ad *SLO Morning Tribune* June

1913 Card of Thanks…appreciate good will and honest work done by all parties connected in any way with the building and fixtures of my bungalow. Everything is perfect… "honor where honor is due" and to Mr M H Stephens the contractor and builder, belong the praise and glory of it all…The Owner, Mrs Jane R Forbes, 1804 Osos St. The Optimistic Store. —*SLO Daily Telegraph* Sat July (?)

1914 Dir: Stephens Martin H (Sadie) bldg contr h511 High st SLO
M H Stephens General Contractor Modern Cottages and Designs Special Plans Furnished Residence 511 High st

1918 Local News Notes. M H Stephens is in from Huasna…former resident of San Luis Obispo… - *SLO Daily Telegraph* Apr 24

1954 Pall bearers: Elmo M Sellers, Fred W Jones, K G Schoening, Chas Goforth, O R Johnson, Chas Mallory

    m.1 Santa Maria 5 July 1894 by C H Lawrence, min —*SM Times*

Sadie Eleanor Hampton
    b. (Napa co) CA Aug 1868
    d. San Luis Obispo 18 Jan 1930 @61; IOOF cem SLO
    F: George Washington Hampton 1832-1921
    M: Julia A Hudson 1848-1928

1930. Manslaughter Charges Filed Mrs Stephens Is Killed by Delivery Car William Cattaneo Is Held Following Auto Death…Cattaneo 21…delivering for the United Meat Market…Stephens pioneer resident of San Luis Obispo…He was a candidate for City Council at the last election…she…survived by four sisters, Mrs Blanche Martin, Glendale; Mrs W D Murray, SLO; Bertha M Hampton, SLO; Mrs Ethel Coryns, London, England; brother, Wert Hampton, SLO.
    -*SLO Daily Telegraph* Mon Jan 20 p. 1

Death Trial on Tuesday…manslaughter…pleaded not guilty…free on $1000 bond.
    -*SLO Daily Telegraph* Mon Mar 10

No issue. See Hampton chart
m.2

Sadie Bam(b)sberger
    b. Americus KS 12 Aug 1883; SSDI
    d. San Luis Obispo 28 Nov 1974 @91; AG cem obit *SLO Telegram-Tribune* Nov 29; 3 gch 7ggch; 45y SLO

Her children:
Violet Lovina Carswell (Goforth) b. WA 4 May 1903; SSDI
    in SLO 1954, 1974     d. SLO 20 Apr 1995 @91; notice *SLO Telegram-Tribune* Fri Apr 21 B10

Edwin B Carswell in Hollywood 1954, Burbank 1974
    ?(Edwin Carswell d. 6-10-1904 @21 AG cem)

7. Mary Elizabeth Stephens      b. Santa Maria valley 3 June 1871
    "Mamie"      d. at home 219 W Morrison 5 July 1948 @77; long illness
    bio O'Neill 349; husband      obit Tue July 6 p.1; 2$^{nd}$ girl b. SMv. hus, son, 3 dau
    driller w/Union Oil, Corona      bro, sis; Stephens Mausoleum

1st steno in SM; Stockton Bus Sch. see *SM Vidette* Thu Mar 28 1935; also Pioneer Edition *SM Times*: First Business Woman in Santa Maria Still Living Here. -*Vidette*

Three Sisters First Business Women in S M. Two Stephens Girls Opened Millinery Store, Dressmaking Establishment. Sister Was First Stenographer Here. Parents Were Pioneers On Guadalupe Road on 160-Acre Farm Plot… -*SM Times*

1894. Santa Maria Dressmakers: The Misses Stephens-Residence near the Presbyterian church, Chapel st. Will do sewing at your homes at reasonable rates. Satisfaction guaranteed. Give us a call. (2 others on the list) -June 9

1897. Miss Mamie Stephens and Miss Jennie Lincoln returned Wednesday from attendance at Christian Endeavor convention in San Francisco. -July 17

m. 24 Dec 1892; lived in Suisun City to 1894, according to O'Neill, but this does not comport with the rest of her bio

Harvey Allison Moore     b. SLO co 17 Nov 1873
  1880 cen: SLO co San Jose tp    d. Riverside 24 Dec 1952 @79
                            F: William C Moore 1848-1925
                            M: Anna Cook
  1904. M/M Harvey Moore of San Luis are visiting old friends here the past week. Mrs Moore was formerly Miss Mamie Stephens.     -June 24
  1906 Dir: oil man Pinal Co, Orcutt
  1907 in Orcutt
  1908 to SM: house built; See #6 above
  1909 Dir: driller r E Morrison (sic); Mrs M E
  1910 cen: E Morrison 3 births 3 living
  1914 Dir: Harvey A (Mamie) driller h215 W Morrison
  1920 cen: AG #2 driller oil wells, wife no occ; 4 ch
  1928 Dir: Mrs H A hskpr r205 E Chapel; Harvey S stu; Alberta stu
  1930 Dir: Mamie E 225 W Morrison
  1947-8 Dir: Moore Harvey (Mary) h219 W Morrison; Mary E h219 W Morrison

  a. Anna Elizabeth Moore     b. San Luis Obispo 12 July 1905; SSDI (*Times*)
     "Betty"                   d. (Wildomar) 13 Aug 1994
    1946. Mrs Mamie Moore and daughter Mrs Vic Christenson went to Long Beach and Wildomar to see Mrs Moore's older daughter Mrs Wyman Turner who is ill. Mrs Christenson's son returned with them.     -Mon Apr 15
    1948 in Wildomar
    1993 in Riverside
    m.
    Wyman E Turner          b. CA 27 July 1901; SSDI
      1940-1 Dir: whsmn SMVRR    d. Wildomar June 1967 @65
        h816 S Pine SM           M: Coombs
      =David Turner

  b. Alberta Moore              b. San Luis Obispo 12 July 1907 (O'Neill)
                                    d.
    1929. Alberta and Harvey Moore are visiting Corona and Los Angeles to visit relatives. Mother Mrs H A Moore is in San Luis Obispo with her brother and sister-in-law M/M M H Stephens.     -Oct 1
    1930. Mrs Mamie Moore is visiting in Los Angeles and Long Beach with daughters Mrs Wyman Turner and Mrs Carl Cedarholm.     -Sep 20
    1940-1 Dir: Denner Herman G (Alberta M) Fly Instr Hancock C of A h425A E Church
        Herman G Denner    b. 8 Jan 1905; d. Los Angeles 28 Apr 1974 @69, SSDI
    1948. Alberta Denner in Long Beach

  c. Naomi Alma Moore          b. Santa Maria 16 Apr 1909 (*Times*)
     "Nonie"                      d.
      m.
    Victor T Christenson           b. Chicago IL 15 Jul 1902; SSDI
      1921 to SM from Fresno       d. Santa Maria 10 Sep 1992 @90
                                        obit Fri Sep 11; wife son 4 gch 4ggch; 48y BPOE
                                        M: Johnson
    1940-1 Dir: Victor T (Naomi) frmn G W Shippers h804 E Orange
        Naomi kitchen help Our Lady of Perp Help Hos r804 E Orange

```
       1947-8 Dir: Naomi ofc mgr SMVy Credit Bur r227 W Jones
               Victor T ( Naomi) br mgr Arrowhead & Puritas Waters h804 E Orange
               Donald W emp Sears r227 W Jones
       1955-6 Dir: Donald V (Dixie) Chevron Svc 410 N Bwy h313A E Alvin
         Naomi ofc mgr Cr Bur of SM & Lompoc r227 W Jones
         Victor T (Naomi) br mgr Arrowhead & Puritas wtrs h227 W Jones
       1957 phbk: Vic's Drive-In Liquors 1010 W Main
         Christenson Don Chevron Serv 401 N Bwy
         Donald 213 Agnes
         V T 210 S Western
       1971 retired from 15y liquor store
       1972 Dir: Christenson Victor T (Naomi) ret h933 W Church
       1982 Dir: same
       1992:  bro Fred Christenson, Oceanside; sister Martha Footman, Fresno
      =Donald V Christenson   in Hendersen NV 1992
   d.  Harvey Stephens Moore           b. 26 Dec 1912; SSDI
                                       d. Santa Maria 23 Feb 1993 @80
                                          obit Feb 26
            m. 1935
         Margaret E                    ? b. (NY 23 Mar 1914; SSDI)
                                       d. (Ventura co 29 Nov 1994 @80)
       1940-1 Dir: Harvey S (Marg) emp Acme Serv h319 N Oakley
       1948 in Stoneham CO
       1955-56 Dir: Harvey S mgr Smith Trans h1006 Barbara
       1972 Dir: Harvey S (Mgt E) v-pres Smith Trans Co h1006 N Barbara st
            Margaret E Mrs acct Smith Trans Co r1006 N Barbara
       1982 Dir: same ret
8.  Annie Stephens                     b. 27 Dec 1873
                                       d. 24 Sep 1989 (sic); Stephens Mausoleum "Daughter of M E and
                                          M H Stephens"
```

Vol. XXXIII, No. 1, Spring 2001, p. 13


DR MARTIN IS ANSWERED
His Wife Tells Her Reasons For Leaving His Roof
The Magnificent Wardrobe Said to Have Consisted of Only Three Dresses

For several days past a *Tribune* representative has been aware of an opportunity for a sensational story which embraced a sojourning member of the medical fraternity and his wife. It was a case of desertion and the scribe refrained from giving the facts, thinking that the difficulty might terminate satisfactorily to the interested parties.

That calm may settle upon the household of Dr Frank M. Martin is now far from a possibility. His wife, of a little less than three months, has left him. Her departure was made on last Saturday and the fact was first known to the *Tribune* of the press of this city. Mrs Martin left the following note when she bade good bye to her home:
  "Good bye, I am gone. Get some one who will suit you. Yours,"


Vol. XXXIII, No. 1, Spring 2001, p.16

The following notice to the public appears and explains the possibilities of the future in the case: "The public will herewith take notice that on and after this date I will not be responsible for the payment of any debts contracted by my wife, Mrs Jennie Martin, she having left my home without cause and having refused to return upon my solicitations. Dr F. N. Martin. Oct 27, 1897."

A paper last evening published a statement from Dr Martin and in view of what it contained, the *Tribune* representative visited the residence of Mrs Roberts in the rear of the Methodist parsonage, where Mrs Martin is stopping at present. She volunteered to the writer the following story:

"I deny as totally untrue much of whet (sic) Dr Martin is quoted as having said in reference to our difficulty. He claims not to know why I left him, and yet he is fully aware of the cause. I left him on account of abusive language and drunkenness. He frequently came home drunk and finally brought liquor to the house and took a drink when ever he desired. I pleaded with him to stop drinking and told him that when whiskey came to the house, I left.

"Now, in regard to the $100 worth of dresses which he claims to have purchased for me, I think it is fair to estimate their value at $4 each, for two dresses, and a tea gown valued at $10 at the most. Of these three dresses I have two, and the doctor has kept one.

"The gold watch and chain is nothing more than a gold plated watch warranted for five years, and the chain is a ribbon one. Other wearing apparel, which he gave me, would probably be valued at $10." The reporter was shown the above described articles.

Continuing, Mrs Martin said: "I do not know anything of the buggy, but frequently heard the doctor say that he intended to get one for his traveling. He never told me that it was to be a present to me.

"When I married the doctor he was in debt, but since that time he has paid all of his debts and has $200 in the bank. I did a great deal of securing business for him among my large list of acquaintances.

"I know that the doctor has had two former wives, and I found a paper which told the circumstances of how one of his former wives had left him on account of abusive language.

"My father denies what appeared in the evening paper, that he had told the doctor that I was suffering from mental troubles. Eight years ago I was very sick and delirious, but that is all of that. The doctor told me that he had at one time been confined in an insane asylum. I regret this trouble, but it could not be avoided," said Mrs Martin as she concluded.

Mrs Martin leaves for Pozo this morning with her sister, Mrs O. S. Sellers.

-*SLO Tribune* Thursday Morning October 28, 1897

## DR FRANK N. MARTIN
### The Wonderful Diagnoser Of All Diseases A Lock Of Hair

I wish to announce to the public that I am permanently located in your city. I also which (sic) to say that I am not a spiritualist as some see fit to call me, but I do claim and assert that I am gifted with a superhuman power of reading and accurately diagnosing any case that may be brought to me, or to which my attention may be called. If you cannot come yourself send a lock of your hair by your friend or some one, and I will diagnose your case. I ask no questions of a person, nor does it make any difference whether I see them or not, but will give a true diagnose (sic) in every case.

While I know that I am gifted with a superhuman power, I make no claim whatever as some may do, but I can safely say that it comes from good sources for there has been great good done through the instrumentality of this wonderful power. In my office may by found for sale remedies to suit all diseases, to which man or woman is heir. These remedies are compounded by me, from pure herbs and oils and if taken accordingly as directed do all they claim.

I have special remedies for all forms of female trouble.

My tapeworm remedy will remove the worm in from one to three hours-no starving, no pain. My worm wafers will remove all forms of stomach or pin worms in from one to three days, always alive no bad results from treatment.

My ointment will surely cure any sore in from one to three weeks no matter of how long standing. My pile remedies will cure any case of piles in from one to two applications. If you are troubled with stricture or bladder troubles there is a sure cure for you. Remedies special for all lung troubles.

Information on all diseases gladly given to all who seek it. Diagnosing and consultation always free.

My office will be for a time in the Commercial Hotel parlors, Private Office, room 4.

Office hours 9 a.m. to 12m, 1-5 p.m., 7-9 p.m.

If you wish to test my powers, also the merits of my remedies, call and see me.

Dr Frank N. Martin

Proprietor of the Herb and Oil Remedy Co.

-*San Luis Obispo Tribune* Sun Aug 8, 1897; also Aug 10 (and probably more)

# STOKES
## GUADALUPE PIONEERS

Walter Stokes, of Bowers & Stokes, a Santa Maria Businessman, was a son of a Guadalupe pioneer, and unique among the businessmen treated in this issue in being not only a native Californian himself, but also son of a native, his grandfather, an Englishman, having come, as did others of his compatriots, to live in California during the halcyon days of Mexican rule, marrying a local girl and enjoying the Mexican idyll for a decade or more before the American onslaught.

William C Stokes, next to the youngest of "Santiago" Stokes' ten children enumerated on the 1850 California census, was born in Monterey, and had some adventures driving cattle east before coming to the Guadalupe area as one of the earliest settlers. He operated a dairy about eight miles south of Guadalupe, in the Casmalia district, and most of the children were born there, only the last two being born in Guadalupe, according to the autobiography of W W Stokes. William Stokes purchased property in Guadalupe including the Arrellanes adobes in 1888, and during his lengthy tenure as justice of the peace held court in the large room in the big adobe. After he retired and moved to Orange County, the properties were sold, and one by one the adobes were plowed under, the two-story lasting until 1958. The Guadalupe Veterans' Memorial building occupies that site now. The Rancho Guadalupe Historical Society has reproduced, in post card form, a photograph of the adobe; another view is shown in the Noticias article (see below). W C Stokes was on the Board of Trustees of the Santa Maria Union High School in 1893-4 and 1909-1910; The *Review* for 1910 (yearbook) contains a photograph of him with the other trustees. In passing, it should be noted that The *Review* of the early years is a good source of Santa Maria history, with valuable photographs.

See the autobiography of W W Stokes in files of the Santa Maria Valley Historical Society; also Noticias, Santa Maria issue, Santa Barbara Historical Society, Vol. 11 #4, Autumn 1965.

The Stokes children received their elementary education in Guadalupe, and went on to high school in Santa Maria. Walter and Evelyn were in the graduating class of '02. Evelyn wrote the class history, saying that 43 freshmen started out, 20 returned as sophomores, 12 came back as juniors, and as one renegade returned, 13 graduated. And they worry about drop-outs today! The entire student body was under the tutelage of three – count 'em – three teachers, who taught well enough that most of the graduates could go into the working world without further education. The obvious exception being aspiring teachers. Walter hired on at Union Sugar; he was styled Engineer in the 1906 Santa Maria Valley Directory, office worker on the 1910 census, and when he left in 1918 he had been manager of the company store, whose advertisement in The *Review* called it a "city store in the country."

Evelyn had been writing seriously during her high school years. After graduation she became a regular contributor to The Overland Monthly, a San Francisco magazine. No wonder this comment appeared in The *Santa Maria Times*, Jan 7, 1904: "Miss Evelyn Stokes has purchased the *Guadalupe Moon* and in the future will guide the destinies of the paper. Miss Stokes is a graduate of our high school and is quite a writer. We bid her welcome to the journalistic ranks and may success attend her ambitions." At the age of 20!

The *Guadalupe Telegraph* had been founded in 1875 but was defunct by 1882, when its press was brought to Santa Maria for the *Santa Maria Times*. There were newspapers in other small communities in northern Santa Barbara county in the 1890's, but they were, for the most part, short-lived; thus, Kenneth C Hopper and his cousin, William B Keeney (related to the Hoppers and

Logans of Santa Maria and the Hoques of San Luis Obispo) bought "the outfit of the *Los Alamos Central*" in April 1900 and began anew the newspaper business in Guadalupe. The 1900 census, taken in June, shows Hopper, Keeney, and Keeney's sister, Gertrude enumerated next to the Stokes family; relatively newly arrived, they may have been renting rooms. Surely their influence was felt by Evelyn, even though in July Hopper married Gertrude, and, according to her memoires, was soon thereafter offered a position in Honolulu with the *Honolulu Advertiser*, which, needless to say, he accepted and was thus occupied for thirty years. What happened to the *Moon* until 1904 is a subject for research. Miss Stokes is recorded in the Alumni Notes in later *Review*s as being editor of The *Moon*; nothing can be found therein of her younger sister, Nellie, who is called "compositor" in the 1906 Directory. As Nellie died of Phthisis (a tuberculosis-like disease) in 1909, it may be that she was considered too frail to go to school, and sitting in an office composing type was a suitable occupation for her. In 1908 this ad appeared in The *Review*: "Wherever you are and whatever your business you should patronize the *Moon* Guadalupe's only paper. Honest and fearless it is worthy of your patronage." Evelyn was still at it in 1911, but by 1912 was the Guadalupe postmaster, a fact mentioned in the item in the *SM Times* about her quick trip to Los Angeles to marry Fred Bertrand in 1914; there was no reference to the *Moon*. It did state, however, that her brother Lee was substituting as postmaster in her absence.

The *SM Times*, April 18, 1918, reported that Walter Stokes had quit his position as store manager for Union Sugar in Betteravia to join his father-in-law, F J Bowers, in the Santa Maria Garage. He had been managing a store and went into the automobile business; Bowers' first partner, Harry Parnell, had quit Union Sugar to go into the automobile business, leaving that to run a grocery store – musical chairs? After Bowers' death in 1945, Stokes was president and general manager of the company – see the article on F J Bowers – with Henry LaFranchi, another son-in-law, as sales manager. Stokes retired in 1950, leaving Henry to manage, apparently, but soon sold the business to Allen C. Patterson, who by 1955 had moved the concern to 809 North Broadway. When Ye Ed. came to Santa Maria in 1961, Bowers & Stokes' new Ford Agency building at 210 South Broadway was a ten-cent store. We hate to mention the uprooting of the entire old downtown for the Town Center Mall.

The pioneer Stokes family was given recognition at last in the 1970's with a street in the northeast section named in their honor.

*Note*: When Wm C Stokes died in 1925, he had but two sisters surviving: Louisa Gonzales and Katherine Atherton of San Francisco. Coincidentally, Matilda Stokes, who died in 1937, was also survived by two sisters: Minnie Luedke of Garden Grove and Cora Sheakley of Santa Barbara, who is listed in the 1937 telephone book as Cora B Sheakley, 325 W Los Olivos St.

William Carl Stokes     b. Monterey CA 1 Aug 1846; m. @21 (27?)
   1882 GR: 35 CA F Guad     d. Garden Grove CA 28 Nov 1925 @79 Guad cem
   1890 GR: 45 CA Dairy Guad     F: James Stokes, English physician
   1900: f Guad     M: Josephine/Josefa Soto; obit Mon Nov 30 p.1
   1906 Dir: f Guad         bio M/H p. 323; photo of Mr/Mrs Stokes
   1910: Guadalupe St. Guad
      m. La Graciosa 21 April 1874 by Chas H South JP, B57
Matilda Virginia Fisher     b. nr Zanesville OH Dec 1856
         d. Garden Grove CA 26 Nov 1937 @81 Guad cem
   12 births, 10 living 1900     F: Abraham Fisher b. OH; d. IL
   9 living 1910     M: Rhoda Rogers 1836-1919; IOOF cem SLO
         m.2 Jacob Henry Orcutt; obit Sat Nov 27 p.1

1. Josephine B.      b. Casmalia 1875
    1906 Dir: Miss, Guad      d. Berkeley CA 12 Jan 1919 @43 Guad cem
        m.      notice Jan 18
    (James S)? Colbath      d. (Berkeley 9-19-1937 @65 spouse ED)
    (a. Pearl I Anderson 1910-1970; Guad cem stone says "Colbath-Stokes", "Adopted dau"
        (in Los Angeles 1937)      (1937 obit) Is she Josephine's dau?)
        (in La Puente 1959)
        = Lloyd
2. Ronald D.      b. Casmalia 22 April 1877
    Single      d. Santa Maria 15 June 1939 @62 Guad cem
    Roofing contr Reno NV 30 years      obit Fri June 16 p.1
3. Clinton      d. 1870; Guad cem
4. Walter William      b. nr Guadalupe 10 Aug 1880
    1906 Dir: Eng. Guad      m. @32 of Betteravia
    1910: offc. wkr Union Sgr      d. Santa Maria 12 June 1967 @86; SM cem
    1920: 407 S. Lincoln SM      obit Tue June 13 p.1; photo
         bio Phillips Vol. 1, p.268

    m. Santa Maria 15 March 1913
    Lauretta Katherine Bowers      b. Rome NY 5 Feb 1887/8; m. @25 of Betteravia
    1962: 407 S. Lincoln SM      d. Santa Maria 2 Feb 1962 @73; SM cem
         obit Sat Feb 3 p.1
         F: Francis Joseph Bowers 1864-1945
         M: Katherine Hellen Baulig 1866-1943

    a. Katherine Inez      b. Santa Maria 20 Apr 1916
        1937: at UC; teacher      d. SM 5 Dec 1966 @50/7/15 SM cem.
        1940 Dir: cashier-clk      obit Wed Dec 7 p.4; res 419 S Lincoln
        SM Gas Co. r w/parents
            m.
        Ivan "Hap" Worsham      F: Robert Pearl Worsham 1873-1964
            in SM 1980      M: Gladys Iva Dell 1890-1980
        = William Ivan (in SM 1980)
5. Mary Evelyn      b. Casmalia Nov 1883/4
    1906 Dir: Miss, Guad. Ed      d. Humboldt Co 18 Nov 1955
    1910: same; 1911: same*; 1912: Postmaster, Guad*
    1915: Los Angeles*; 1921: Eureka*; 1925, 1937; Samoa
    *Alumni Notes The *Review* SMUHS
        m. Pico Heights, Los Angeles Tue Aug 25 1914 by Rev Bernard Notice Aug 29
    Frederick G. Bertrand      d. Humboldt Co 25 Dec 1960
    a. Patsy (in Samoa 1927)
6. Nellie      b. Casmalia Oct 1885 (cen)
    1906 Dir: Miss, Guad      d. Santa Barbara 10 Aug 1909 @24; Guad cem
    Compositor      obit Aug 14 p.1; nurse; Phthisis Pulmonalis
7. Eloise B      b. Casmalia 5 June 1887
    1906 Dir: Miss, Guad, stu      d. San Jose 31 May 1977
    (in Inglewood 1925; Hollywood 1937)
        m. 1910
    Willard W. Livingston      b. CA c1886 (cen)
    1910: tool dresser Cat Canyon      d.
         parents English

- a. Willard (in Taft 1937)
- b. Donald (in Berkeley 1937)

8. Juanita   b. Casmalia
   d. 17 June 1890 @10m4d (*Times*) Guad cem Meningitis

9. Alfred Claude   b. Guadalupe 30 Apr 1891/2
   1910: teamster   d. SM 18 Oct 1968; obit Sat Oct 19 p.4
   WWI bio Phillips Vol. 2 p.115
   1930: plumber, Main St. Guad;  1940: plumber 635 Pinal, Orcutt
   1968: 127 N 1st Orcutt
   m. 1921
   Hazel Eames   b. Pine Grove 15 Nov 1895 (*Times*)
   d. at home 17 Dec 1972; obit Tue Dec 19 p.2
   F: Abraham Lincon Eames 1865-1934
   M: Emma Brookshire 1870-1935
   - a. Virginia (Jones) (1937: Guad; in La Crescenta 1968, 1972)
   - b. Clyde H (in Guad 1937; Santa Maria 1968, 1972)

10. Leland F (Lee)   b. Guadalupe 28 Feb 1894; 14 lbs (*Times*)
    WWI   d. SM 17 July 1976 @82; Guad cem
    1925: in Klamath Falls OR; 1930: Electric shop, Guad
    1940: The Electric Shop 213 E. Main; r 206 E Camino Colegio SM
    1959: in Ferndale, CA;  1967: in Arroyo Grande
    1976: in Orcutt
    Ruth
       No issue

11. Paul Winfield   b. Guadalupe 30 Apr 1896
    WWI   d. SM 1 Feb 1959 @62; Guad cem
    1925: in San Francisco   obit Tue Feb 3 p.2; Thu Feb 5 p.2
    1937: in MN   Upholsterer 25y in Chicago

12. Carl   b. (Guadalupe) 12 July 1899
    1925: in Taft   d. (Ventura) 17 Apr 1959; spouse initial "V"
    1937: in Ventura
      m.1 by 1921 (Alumni Notes, The *Review* SMUHS) living in Taft
    Ina M Davis   b. SM 18 March 1900 (*Times*)
    F: Clarence L. Davis
    M: Emma Standt
    - a. Jimmie (in Ventura 1937)

Vol. XXVI, No.1, Spring 1994, pp.18, 19

**Corrections and Additions**     [Page numbers refer to those in Quarterly]

p.17. Guadalupe News. Miss Josephine Stokes arrived here from the South Sunday and after a couple of days visit at home went to Paso Robles for the summer.      –May 29 1909

p.18. Paso Robles Sep 21. Miss Nellie Stokes, who has been lying sick at the Alexander Hotel for the past two weeks, has recovered sufficiently to be removed to her home. Miss Evelyn Stokes, her sister, who is editor of the *Guadalupe Moon*, came here and took her to her home in Guadalupe.

Vol. XXX, No. 1, Spring 1998, p.9

W C Stokes of Guadalupe has been here on a visit to his daughter, Miss Nellie Stokes.
—*SLO Daily Telegram* Mon Sep 21 1908

MARRIAGE: Eloise B Stokes @22 of Guadalupe m. in San Luis Obispo 19 Oct 1910 by H E Smith JP, H487; wit: Mrs May Blosser, SM; G L Blosser, SM. Wallace W Livingston b. CA m. @24 of SM

Willard C Livingston, 87, died in Auberry CA 17 Aug 1997. Born in Santa Monica 30 June 1910. Survived by daughters Donna Wall, Cuyama; Pattie Bell, Huntington Beach; brother Donald Karl Livingston, Reno NV; 4 step-children; 22 gch 27 ggch. —Sat Sep 16 1997 A-3

p.19. Ina M Davis grad SMUHS 1918; at Heald's Business College 1920 –1920 *Review*

# S T O W E L L
## SANTA MARIA VALLEY PIONEERS

Ralph Stowell          b. Hartford CT 1799
                                 d. Santa Maria CA 9 Aug 1872 @73
                                      Thornburgh Cem; reinterred SM cem 11 Jan 1884
                                 F: Seth – Ephraim – Nathaniel – David – Samuel
                                 M: Mary Bancroft
    m. Ohio
Barbara Haines               b. NY
                                 d. Hampshire, Kane co. IL 9 Mar 1849

   1830: Ashtabula co. OH Ashtabula next to Walter Stowell
   1840: Kane co. IL
   1850: Big Grove, Kendall co. IL w/Walter Stowell
   1860:
   1870: San Luis Obispo co. Morro tp, P.O. Old Creek w/George Stowell

1. Lester                     b. Lake co OH; d. @ c4 yr
2. Henry                     b. Denmark, Ashtabula co. OH 24 May 1829
                               d. Santa Maria, 10 Nov 1905 @78/5/17; SM cem

    1870: Genoa, Douglas co. NV, making butter; to SM 1871
    1880: Santa Maria
    1890: 62 OH f SM 1 Aug 4
    1892: @64 5'11 dark complexion, hazel eyes, grey hair, "H" on right wrist OH
       res SM reg Aug 8
          m. Chicago IL 2 March 1853; left immed. for CA

Susan M Stowell            b. DuPage co IL 16 Jan 1833 (census)
   (1st cousins)                 or 1837 (Stowell Gen.)
                               d. Santa Maria 18 Aug 1891 @54 or 58/4
                               F: Walter Stowell b. CT 1789-1876
                                   (brother of Ralph)
                               M: Susan Shay Butler b. NY 1791-1846

   a. Arthur                  b. Placerville, CA
   b. Edgar Henry          b. Placerville, CA 12 July 1856; m.1 @22
                                 d. Santa Maria 31 May 1926 @70
                                   (spouse initial L S)

      1886: Trustee, Tepusquet school
      1890: @33 CA f SM Aug. 25
      1892: @36 5'11½" light complexion, hazel eyes, brown hair.
         CA res Santa Maria, reg. Aug 22
      1900: Santa Maria
      1910: Kings Co.
      1920: S McClelland St., Santa Maria
         m.1 Santa Maria 27 Aug 1878 by H R Stevens, B330

Emma Carey Oakley           b. (American Town) Sacramento Co.
                                   CA 13 Oct 1861 m. @21
    6 births, 6 living 1900;         d. Laton, Kings co. CA
    5 living 1910                    13 May 1910 @48/7; SM cem
                                   F: Cary Calvin Oakley 1829-1890
                                   M: Elizabeth Whaley 1838-1880

      =Arthur D                  b. July 1879; d. Kings co. 7 Jan 1957

=Walter Calvin                          b. 23 Oct 1882
                                        d. Guernsey, CA @20; bur 15 Feb 1903;
                                           SM cem
=Lora May                               b. Santa Maria 29 Jan 1886 (*Times*)
                                        d. SM 20 May 1944 @58; SM cem

    m. Laton, CA 25 Dec 1906
Harry R Saulsbury                       b. CA 3 Aug 1877
                                        d. SM 26 June 1941
  1910: Laton                  F: Thomas Saulsbury 1830-1911
  No issue                     M: Isabelle Randall 1843-1920
=Benjamin Warren                        b. SM 9 Apr 1888
                                        d. SM 16 Jul 1939; SM cem

    m. Fresno, 2 Dec 1911
Lucia G Snow                            b. Delano CA 21 May 1890
                                        d. Pacific Grove 4 Feb 1981;
                                           El Carmelo cem
                                        m. 2 John Wiegand
  1900: Tulare                 F: Richard B Snow 1858-1910
                                        M: Mary Elizabeth Burum 1860-1938

+Oakley Burum 1912-1934; SM Cem
+Frances Evelyn 1915-1922; SM Cem
=Edgar Raymond                          b. June 1889
                                        d. Laton 28 May 1910; SM cem
=Henry Oakley                           b. SM 25 Oct 1891
                                        d. Los Gatos 30 Dec 1969

    m. Riverdale CA
Gladys M Smith                          b. Emmetsburg, IA 1892
                                        d. Hanford 7 Jan 1960 @68
  1920: Fresno                 F: C A Smith
                                        M: _____ Retsloff

  + Raymond C (Frances J) b. 1915
  + William H (Bernice E) b. after 1920
b.  Edgar H    m.2 Santa Ana, CA 21 Dec 1911
    Laura Scott (Mrs)         b. WV 1869 (or 1886)
c.  Katie                               b. Genoa, NV; d. young
d.  Frank Leon                          b. Genoa NV 1 Feb 1865/6
                                        d. Santa Barbara 20 Sep 1904 @38/8; SM cem
  1890: @26 NV music dealer SB #3
  1892: @26 5'7" dark complexion brown hair brown eyes NV SB #5 painter reg Aug 4
  1900: Frank, Santa Paula, woman, 3 ch; Mary J, Santa Maria, 2 ch.
    m. c1890
Mary J Hopper                           b. Mendocino co. CA Oct 1867
                                        d. San Anselmo 24 Apr 1957 @90;
                                           IOOF cem Modesto, CA
                                        m. 2 c1929 John Metzler
                                        F: Greenberry Barton Hopper 1843-1918
                                        M: Sarah E Vann 1848-1935
=Floyd C                                b. Gilroy Dec 1890
                                        d. Stockton 15 Feb 1940 @58/2/13
    m. Mabel J    Issue: Jeanne (Dixon)

      = Mildred E        b. 1896
                                  d. Los Gatos 14 Mar 1928 @32 Single
- e. Frances — b. & d. Placerville
- f. Grace Alberta — b. Santa Barbara (?) 28 Nov 1875
                                    d. Santa Barbara co 23 Oct 1931 @55; SM cem
          m. San Jose 18 Oct 1900
        William Washington Trumbull      b. San Francisco c1867
          1930: Plumber, Santa Maria        d. San Francisco 21 Oct 1946 @82; SM cem
                                      F: Charles W Trumbull (1870, 1880: Benicia)
                                      M: Maria Julia 1833-1917 (Wid. 1900)
       =Henry Wm                 b. SM 15 Sep 1901
          Res. Sherman Oaks           d. 7 Nov 1967 @67; SM cem

3. George                     b. Jefferson, Ashtabula co. OH 25 May 1830
                                      d. Santa Maria 3 Jan 1910 @79/7/9; SM cem
    1850: Lake co. OH, Painesville dist. w/Judson Lazelle fam
    1860: El Dorado co. CA, Incl. C A Stowell, 7, b. Utah terr.
    1870: Morro tp. SLO co. P.O. Old Creek, Incl. Almond C Stowell, 17, b. NV
    1873: Patent 25 June San Luis Obispo co, A715: E2NE4 SW4NE4 S20 NW4NW4 S21
        T28S R10E (Cayucos)
    1880: Salinas tp, SLO co
    1890: @60 OH farmer SM #2 reg Aug 4
    1892: @62 6' dark complexion hazel eyes grey hair; OH; SM. Reg Sep 12
          m. Placerville CA 17 Feb 1856
Lydia Ann Minerva Smith        b. MI 12 Nov 1835
                                      d. Santa Maria 11 May 1903 @67/5/29
                                      F: Edwin Hurlburt Smith
                                      M: Lydia Minerva Hart
                              1860: Upper Placerville
- a. Edwin Ralph              b. Placerville 27 Nov 1856
                                    d. Paso Robles, shot 7 July 1885,
                                        @28/8/10; bur Estrella cem; reinterred
                                        SM cem 17 Oct 1887
         1884: Patent 17 Nov San Luis Obispo co #C60 W2NE4 NW4SE4 S18 T26S R13E
         120a (Estrella) Homestead cert. #2994, recorded at request of George Stowell
         Oct 1885
            m. Paso Robles at res of Mr J Rector 3/23 July 1881 by Rev H E Adams, A435
              wit: Geo Stowell, Paso Robles; John Rector, Paso Robles   (*SLO Tribune* 6 Aug)
    Charlotte Grigsby b. Napa co CA 7 July 1865; m.1 @17 of PR; m.2 @21 of SM
       d. Santa Maria 28 Oct 1908 @43 SM cem; Parents: b. MO (Rector was her uncle)
       m.2, SLO 6 Sep 1887 by R W Summers, Prot. Epis. ch, B245
          wit: J A E Summers, Templeton; Mabel Dunbar, SLO
Edward Fesler                    1864-1937; m. @27
                                      F: Isaac Fesler 1818-1891
                                      M: Nancy Barnes 1822-1895
                                      Issue: Cecil 1890-
                                             Eugene 1893-
      =Charles Ralph              b. Paso Robles 2 Feb 1883
                                      d. SM 28 Nov 1963; SM cem
        m. Santa Maria Feb 1910
       Elizabeth Dudley Robison        b. San Jacinto CA 17 Dec 1888
                                      d. SM @88 bur 12 Aug 1977; SM cem
                                      F: b. KY; M: b. IA

```
                    +Lottie M (Ernest E Munoz) b. 1911
                    +Edwin R b. 1914
                    +Helen A (Feiock) b. 1916
                    +Warren (Katherine)
                1940: (Ray Stowell at same address as Warren)
              =Nellie Maud                         b. Paso Robles 13 Sep 1884
                                                  d. (San Bernardino co Oct 20 1932
                                                     @48)*
                    m. Los Angeles 17 Sep 1908 by Rev B F Cotter (SM Times)
              Ray W Davisson                      b. 7 Sep 1884; Los Angeles
                                                  d. (So. Pasadena) 24 Sep 1970
                                                  F: J I Davisson
                                                  M: Louisa S 1851-1931 (wid 1910)
                    + Pearl A b. 1905? (1910: Los Angeles)
              =Edith Kate                         b. Santa Maria 5 Dec 1885
                    m. Los Angeles June 1908
              Frank Crowley                       d. (Ventura co 9-19-47)*
```
* dates in parentheses not verified
```
      b.   Minerva Jane                    b. Placerville 13 Feb 1861
                                           d. Placerville 23 Oct 1868 (Stowell Gen)
                                              or d. 23 Oct 1866 @5/10/8 SM cem

      c.   George                          b. Placerville; lived one day
      d.   Susan Arminta                   b. Cayucos (Old Creek) 3 Mar 1869
                                           d. Santa Maria 3 Mar 1926 @57; SM cem
              m. Santa Maria 26 Jan 1887 @17
           Duskin Ernest Hobbs 1861-1952; See Farlon Hobbs chart
      e.   Fannie Emma                     b. Cayucos (Old Creek) 4 July 1874
                                           d. 13 Apr 1957 @82; SM cem
              m. Santa Maria 18 Nov 1908
           Henry Clay Tunnell              b. Ukiah CA 5 Sep 1868
              No issue                     d. Santa Maria 29 June 1933 @65; SM cem
                                           F: Martin Luther Tunnell 1824-1903
                                           M: Salina Haskins 1829-1903
              1890: @22 CA farmer SM #1 reg Aug 25
              1892: @24 5'1 (?) light complexion, blue eyes, brown hair; CA; SM reg Aug 15
      f.   Guy Jay                         b. Cayucos 18 July 1876
                                           d. Santa Maria 13 Dec 1896 @20/4/25; SM cem
4.    William Layard                       b. Perry IL 24 Sep 1835
                                           d. Painesville OH 5 Mar 1902
         m. Canada 20 Aug 18__ (Stowell Gen)
      Harriet Elizabeth Huling             b. Canada 20 May 1835
                                           d. Geneva OH 23 Feb 1900 @66
         5 children; see Stowell Genealogy (one named Beda)
5.    Beda Amanda                          b. Elgin IL 14 Aug 1837
         Single                            d. Santa Maria 12 Sep 1915 @78
         1850: Lake co OH, Madison dist w/John Patchen fam.
         1909: Miss A B Stowell, boarding house, 503 W Church St, SM
6.    Mary                                 b. Medina IL 29 July 1842
                                           d.
         m. Hannibal MO 25 June 1868
      William Clark                        (In Stockton CA 1910)
```

## STOWELL ANCESTORS

| | | |
|---|---|---|
| I. | Samuel Stowell | b. England; died Hingham MA 1683 |
| | blacksmith   m. Hingham 1649 | |
| | Mary Farrow 1633-1708, dau of John & Frances Farrow | |
| II. | David | b. MA 1660; d. 1724 |
| | m.2  Cambridge MA 1692 | |
| | Mary Stedman | d. 1724, dau of Nathaniel & Temperance (Willis?) |
| III. | Nathaniel | b. c1703; d. Pomfret CT 11 Mar 1757** |
| | **Pomfret VR 1/66 married *Pomfret 21 Oct 1734 | |
| | *(Pomfret VR 1/2) | |
| | Margaret Trowbridge | b. 1709; d. Pomfret 3 Nov 1794** |
| | **(VR 1/66) dau of James & Hannah (Bacon) | |
| IV. | Ephraim | b. 2 Oct 1732 Pomfret 1/65 |
| | | d. 1805 |
| | m. Pomfret 9 Mar 1758 (VR 1/107) | |
| | Elizabeth Cutler | b. 1735; d. 1823; dau of Seth & Elizabeth (Babcock) |
| V. | Seth | b. Pomfret 15 Oct 1769 (VR 1/65) |
| | | d. North Plato IL |
| | m. | |
| | Mary Bancroft | b. 1767; d. North Plato; dau of Isaac & Mary (Barrett) |

*The Stowell Genealogy. A Record of the Descendants of Samuel Stowell of Hingham, Mass.* Wm Henry Harrison Stowell, Tuttle, 1922. A copy in the Santa Maria Valley Historical Society New England Marriages, Torrey Barbour Records (Connecticut Vitals) located at LDS FHC Los Angeles (film)

From Hobbs to Stowell is a natural step; it has been interesting to investigate the family whose name I have invoked for 28 years every time I give directions to my house: "Take the Stowell Road exit . . . ". Chance found me a copy of the Stowell Genealogy (published in 1922) which, although not without its flaws, was a fine aid.

Henry and George Stowell, the Santa Maria Valley Pioneer brothers, were born in the northeast corner of Ohio, populated largely by erstwhile New Englanders, like the Stowells. The 1830 census-taker found R Stowell in Ashtabula with a wife and two small boys, next to W Stowell with a family of nine; this is the family from which Henry selected his wife, and his first cousin. By 1840 the family had followed the westward surge to Kane County, Illinois. The family seems to have broken up in the 1840's, George's biography implying that it was due to the death of his parents; however, the mother died in 1849, according to the Stowell Genealogy, and the father lasted until 1872. At any rate, George was back in Ohio by 1850 (I haven't found Henry), and ready to go to California in 1853 with his newly-married brother from Illinois. By 1860 any mining inclinations they may have had were abandoned in favor of more steady work, George being listed as "Packer". Teaming was steady work to and from the mines; that must have been what took Henry to Nevada, where he lived in Genoa for a number of years. The *Santa Barbara News-Press* of Sunday, November 15, 1992, Section G, has an article on the Carson Valley of Nevada, and says that Genoa was a stage stop in the 1860's, became the county seat in 1864, but was overshadowed by the boom in Virginia City. The 1870 census shows Henry in Genoa "making butter" but he left for California the next year. Interestingly, George had taken up dairying in the Old Creek section of San Luis Obispo County by that time, and the father was listed in his household, although he joined Henry in

Santa Maria by 1872 when he died in this valley, where Henry had taken up farming. George foresook the coast for the warmer plains near Paso Robles to raise wheat, but moved to Santa Maria in the early 1880's.

The Stowells were not so prolific as some families, and they lost a large percentage of their children at early ages; three boys died at the age of twenty. The most tragic was the shooting of George's firstborn, named after his grandfathers, Edwin Smith and Ralph Stowell, whose death at 28 on his wife's 20$^{th}$ birthday left her with two small children and another on the way. George brought her from San Luis Obispo County to Santa Maria; two years later she married Ed Fesler, son of another pioneer family. She dropped dead at the age of 43 on the day Feslers were transferring their household to Oceano.

George Stowell Hobbs, Jr., our illustrious mayor, is not the only member of this family to make news: the above-mentioned shooting brought reproach upon San Luis Obispo County from all around, and another scion, Ben Stowell, police chief in Santa Maria in the late thirties, "received statewide notoriety" when he was a kidnap victim while on duty. Details on these stories are in the Scrapbook Section.

## STOWELL SCRAPBOOK

1885 Deplorable Shooting Battle at the Estrella—Two Men Killed, and four wounded.

Early in the day of Tuesday last, the telegraph reported a desperate affray on the Estrella Plains, in which a number of men had been shot. We immediately telegraphed our San Miguel correspondent for particulars, and received the following:

San Miguel, July 7$^{th}$

Editor *Tribune*: About 9 o'clock am Tuesday, a fatal shooting affray occurred on the Estrella Plains, about a quarter of a mile from the Estrella School house, which resulted in the immediate death of Ed Stowell and Clinton Brooks, and the fatal wounding of Henry Huston, and slight wounding of Wm Pepper and Johnny McAdams. It seems that Henry Huston has been running a header near the above mentioned school-house, where Mr Joe Sanders is teaching, and Mr Sanders claims that Huston's men used bad language towards him, calling him (Sanders) a s-of a b-, etc. On the morning of the shooting Joe Sanders, Ed Stowell, Francis Rhyne, Clinton Brooks, James Booker, Byron Fortney, and the Ballard boys were seen going from the schoolhouse over to the header, armed with Winchester rifles, pistols, etc., when they arrived on the ground of Mr Brookshire. He (Brookshire) warned them off, but it seemed that they wanted to black snake one of the header crew, and after some words passed firing commenced which resulted as above stated. The header crew, as near as your reporter can ascertain was Henry Huston, Geo Huston, Mr McKenna, Mr Congdon and Martin Heenan. It seems that the main cause of the shooting was an old feud existing there for a year or so. There were about twenty five shots fired. Brooks and Stowell were well known in this vicinity and their death is much lamented. Huston may recover, but it is doubtful at present writing. Sheriff McLeod, District Attorney Patton, and Coroner Tullman are on their way here and arrests will soon be made. S.A.

Little more need be said after the terse and succinct statement of our correspondent. The affray was indeed most deplorable: sad for the promising young men who were its victims; very sad for the surviving parents, families and friends, and an ineffacable (sic) stain upon the section where it occurred, and the county. Sad is the result of unrestrained passion; of the unrestrained conduct of boys and young men; of that exceeding hilarity coarsely indulged in, that degenerates into brutal and destructive exhibitions of so-called fun, inevitably arousing enmities and resulting in quarrels and bloodshed. Here is a community of respectable, christian (sic), church-going, temperance-keeping farmers, their locality disgraced with frivolous broils and their fair fields stained with blood;

families in mourning for the dead, young men in agony of wounds, distress and mortification to follow all, and all the consequences of the neglect of neighborly duties. A proper restraint upon the mischievous proclivities which most boys possess would have kept them within bounds of reputable conduct. Our correspondent says a feud has existed for a year or more. We do not think it amounts to such a serious feud that it cannot be settled by the calm reasoning of individuals and the community resume their course of peace and prosperity in friendship. This terrible tragedy should not inflame the passions, but it should be a lesson for future conciliation and gentlemanly behaviour. He who now attempts to create divisions and continue the conflict does a grievous wrong to himself and the public. The clans of "Owls" and "Vigilantes", and the terms "hoodlums" and "bummers" are unworthy of the community, and should be hushed forever.

    The unfortunate victims, Stowell and Brooks, were buried in the churchyard at the Estrella on Wednesday pm, the funeral being largely attended. Their full names are Edwin B Stowell (sic) and Dewitt Clinton Brooks, both born in California, Stowell being 28 years of age, and Brooks 25. The first leaves a wife and two children. James Henry Huston was reported fatally wounded, but at latest dates there are hopes of his recovery. He is also a native of the State, and 26 years of age. Members of both parties have come into town to surrender themselves. Melville Condon was arrested as the one firing the first gun, killing Brooks. He is a young man, about 19 years of age, and a native of Michigan, and but a short time in California. The latest reports say he was standing in the header wagon and seeing the assault on Huston fired with fatal effect. Huston then fired upon Stowell, killing him, and mounting the header wagon with Condon fled, receiving three shots from the assailing party, one in the small of the back, one in the leg, and one in the heel. The assailing party were called "Vigilantes" and the others "Hoodlumns."(sic). Of the latter Huston and Condon were the only ones armed. Several, if not all of the Vigilantes, carried revolvers. John McAdam (sic) was slightly wounded by some one unknown, subsequent to the affray while fleeing from the ground.

    Wm Pepper received a shot through his clothes. No other casualties. J H Sanders, Horn Bardin, Charles Ballard, James Bucher, Francis Rhyne and Byron Fortney, of the Vigilantes came in on Wednesday to surrender to the authorities.
    –*San Luis Obispo Tribune* July 10 (Quoted verbatim in the *Salinas Weekly Index*)

*Ed. Note*: Affray—In law, a public fight between two or more persons, to the terror of others. A private fight is not an affray in the legal sense.     –*Webster's Unabridged Dictionary*

Shooting Affair
A Long Standing Feud Results in the Death of Interested Parties

    San Luis Obispo. Cal. July 8—A sanguinary shooting affair took place on the Estrella Plains, about 40 miles north of this place. A long standing feud between residents culminated in a fierce encounter, in which Ed Brooks and E Stowall (sic) were killed, and Steve Moody, H Huston, John McAdams and Wm Pepper, were mortally wounded. The portion of the gang known as "The Owls" were at work as header crew on a ranch of a man named Brookshire, when a party of vigilantes rode up and demanded the surrender of H Huston, which was refused. Clifton Brooks, one of the vigilantes, then shot Huston in the back. The header crew being all armed with Winchester rifles the firing became general. Sheriff McLeod and posse have gone to the scene of action.
    –*Santa Barbara Daily Independent* Wed July 8 p.1

Particulars of the Fight

San Luis Obispo, July 9—Particulars of the fight on Estrella plains, 40 miles from here, learned today, prove to be as stated previously. Edward Stowell and Clinton Brooks were killed, Henry Huston fatally wounded. Wm Pepper, M Condon and John McAdams wounded. Condon fired the first shot and killed Brooks. He is in jail and six of the other party have arrived in town and given themselves up. –Ibid July 9 p.1

*Ed. Note*: I am including all the material on this event for a number of reasons: the writing style is interesting and comments indicative of the times and above all, the garbled mess of dates presented shows that news reporting hasn't changed in a century of practice.

War on the Estrella

Our town was thrown into tremendous excitement on Tuesday last by the receipt of a telegram announcing the death of Ed Stowell by violence near the Estrella school house, San Luis Obispo county. The murdered man is the son of our esteemed townsman, Mr Geo Stowell who together with his family immediately started for the Estrella. Exciting rumors were soon current and they grew and magnified until it was generally understood that six or seven men had been killed and twice that many badly wounded. The following report from the *Mirror* is believed to be correct:

Tuesday morning last news reached this place of a tragic affray which occurred in the Estrella district near San Miguel, and which resulted in the killing of two men and mortally wounding of another. Accounts concerning the affair are conflicting and at the lastest (sic) hour no reliable reports were current. We give the version of one side, the other side not yet having been heard from. The cause of the trouble is said to have been of long standing and gradually deepened until it culminated in a fatal collision. Some twelve or fifteen were present during the affray although not all were concerned in it. As near as could be learned, the tragedy came about as follows: It seems that Geo. Huston with a party of men was heading in a field adjacent to the Estrella school house. This was on Monday last. The teacher of the school Joe Sanders, it is affirmed was not liked by Huston, who, during the day, abused Saunders (sic) whenever an opportunity occurred and applied offensive epithets to him. This aroused Sanders and in the evening he secured the company of two or three of his friends and went out into the field for the purpose of having an interview with Huston. Before the approach of the party, Huston and his companions left the field. He was accompanied this time by several of his friends among the number Ed Stowell, Clinton Brooks, Charley Ballard, Jim Bucher, Francis Rhyne, Byron Fortney, and H Barden, who attended to see fair play should any difficulty arise. The two parties met, and Sanders asked Huston to take back what he had said the day previous. At this juncture Brooks went to Henry Huston and asked him to let him have his gun, stating at the same time that it would be best to settle the matter amicably if possible. Brooks had barely spoken when Mell Condon, one of Huston's men, arose in a header wagon and fired on Brooks with a shot gun charged with buckshot. The load took effect in Brooks' head, inflicting a wound from which he died in about a half hour. Huston then seized his gun, also a shotgun, charged with buckshot, and opened fire on Stowell, shooting him through the heart and killing him instantly. At this Sanders and the survivors of his party opened on Huston, wounding him five times. Huston fell, but regained his feet and ran to the wagon in which was Condon and as he was climbing into it he was shot three times more with a Henry rifle. He succeeded in getting into the wagon and was driven off by Condon. These are the most reliable facts to be obtained at the present writing. They may prove correct in the main or later investigations may upset them. Later news are to the effect that Huston has since died, also that three others, Wm Pepper, Mel Condon and John McAdam (sic), were wounded. So many rumors are afloat concerning the unfortunate affair that it is impossible as yet to arrive at a correct version. Sanders and the five survivors of his party came into San Luis yesterday for the purpose of giving themselves up. Warrants will be served on them this morning and will be taken in charge.

Later information states that Huston was only wounded three times and that he was still alive, with the chances for his recovery or death about even.

Mr H Stowell returned from the Estrella last evening. He states that Huston's wounds are not serious. The two murdered men were buried by the Good Templars. The row occurred over an attempt made by the hoodlums element to secure the school houses (sic) for a dance but were refused by the teacher and trustees. They then abused the teacher whenever they met him, and on the day previous to the row they were heading near the school house and took occasion to pester the teacher all they could. Finally the teacher went to Ed Stowell, who was a trustee and told him that he would have to stop the school unless the hoodlums desisted. Ed Stowell went with the teacher and others to try and stop the trouble, with the result above stated. It is Mr Stowell's opinion that the trouble is not yet over. –*Santa Maria Times* Sat July 11

## Terrible Tragedy
### Particulars of the Shooting Mill Near San Miguel

The *San Luis Obispo Republic* of last Thursday contains the following account of the terrible affair that occurred last Monday in the Estrella District near San Miguel. "The statements regarding the terrible tragedy near San Miguel on Tuesday, published in yesterday's issue, were incorrect in some respects, dependent as we were upon rumor for most of the details. From later reports it appears that the shooting was not commenced by Brooks, who was unarmed and was killed by Congdon, who fired the first shot. Following are the latest details we have been able to secure. Robert Parsons, Gus Kingery and Frank Kester, three young men who were present during the latter part of the fighting, arrived in San Luis on Tuesday evening and carried out two coffins for the deceased. They state that the first shot was fired by a man named Congdon who used a shot gun loaded with buckshot at such short range that he literally blew the top of young Brooks' head off. They say the crowd on the header consisted of the Huston Brothers, Stephen Moody, Pepper, Congdon, and others to the number of ten or eleven. Congdon worked on Rude's farm. The hoodlum crowd has always opposed the school element and better class of the community, and have vented their animosity on the teacher, Joe Sanders, by perpetrating various outrages on the school house. On the evening before the fighting a number of them assembled, led by Henry Huston, and insulted Sanders. Next day Sanders and his friends followed them and demanded satisfaction from Henry Huston, when the fighting commenced.

Edwin R Stowell, who was shot and instantly killed in the fracus on Tuesday, was a young man of about 27 years of age, a nephew of O C King, Deputy Assessor, and connected by marriage with the Graves family. He was a married man and leaves a wife and two young children. His father, Geo Stowell, who resides at Santa Maria, arrived here on Tuesday evening, and early Wednesday morning went to the scene of the tragedy. The greatest commisseration (sic) is felt for the family of Stowell. D C Brooks, who was the first man killed in the encounter, was about 24 years of age, unmarried, and bearing a very high reputation in San Luis where he was well known.

The wildest excitement prevails in the entire neighborhood of the "seat of war." The people of the Estrella are determined to wipe out the disgrace these outrages have entailed on their fair name, and assist by every possible means the course of justice.

Messrs Joe Sanders, Chas Ballard, Horn Bardin, J Bucher, Byron Fortney and Burt Rhyne, all of whom were present at the time of the shooting came to San Luis yesterday afternoon to give themselves up to the authorities. From them we learn that three header crews were in the field, consisting of two Huston brothers, two Pepper brothers, McAdams, Moody, Congdon, and others. Congdon was arrested and is in the hands of the Sheriff.

–*Santa Barbara Daily Independent* July 11

## The Estrella Tragedy

The comments of many papers of the State upon the late tragedy on the Estrella have not been complimentary to this county. Some remark upon it as if San Luis Obispo were degenerating into the murdering and law defying ways that have so disgraced Kentucky and some other Southern States. The affair was indeed unfortunate, and it is to be hoped that nothing of the kind will ever again occur in our county or State. A neighborhood feud or vendetta, is disgraceful to the community indulging in it, and casts a shadow of shame over the entire section bearing the common name. One of two evil spirits, or soured, unneighborly, unhappy, selfish dispositions may keep a district in turmoil, but a few strong, upright, honorable men, without taking sides, can show and express their discountenance of the disturbers as to suppress and nullify their evil intentions. The habit of going armed in a farming region anywhere in California seems an insult to law and order, a constant expression of cowardly fears or design to do wrong. There can be no necessity of going armed to the wheat fields of such a section as the Estrella. The presence of arms engenders strife, and the quick, unjustifiable use of them on that fatal 7$^{th}$ of July has caused parents to mourn for their sons, wives for their husbands, and children to bear the punishment and sad memory through their lives. We have heard it said "the end is not yet." To continue the strife would be unfortunate. Peace and forgiveness should be declared at once. The sacrifice has been enough. If peace is made there will be greater lenience shown towards those who participated in the tragedy. As stated last week, a number of the participants came to the city and surrendered to the authorities. Upon examination before the Justice of the Peace, Wayland Brooks, Stephen Moody, George Huston, Francis Rhyne, H Bardin and Byron Fortney were held in $2,000 bonds each, and Joseph H Sanders in $4,000, to appear for trial. Melville Condon, who fired the first gun, killing D C Brooks, was held in $7,500, in default of which he remains in jail.

County Correspondence.    Oak Flat

Ed. *Tribune*:-Our usually quiet neighborhood was thrown into quite a confusion Tuesday last by the intelligence from the Estrella Plains that E R Stowell and D C Brooks had been killed. This entire community laments the loss of two such good citizens, and extends its condolences to the bereaved ones. –Oak Flat July 13          -*San Luis Obispo Tribune* Fri July 17

*Ed. Note*: The list of men who surrendered was repeated in the *Santa Maria Times* July 23.

## Resolutions of Respect
### Adopted by the Estrella Lodge No. 249, IOGT

WHEREAS, The Almighty Ruler of the universe has seen fit, in his inscrutable way, to permit the transmission of our late brothers Edwin R Stowell and Dewitt Clinton Brooks, by the hand of the cruel assassin, from this imperfect to that Great Lodge above, therefore, be it

RESOLVED That in the death of our late brothers the community has lost two good, peaceful, honest and upright citizens, and the Good Templars Lodge has lost exemplary members and ardent workers and supporters of its principles.

While we offer our sympathy to the bereaved widow and helpless orphans and mourning father and mothers and brothers and sisters, we know that they rest where kind and tender hands hold them, and that their epitaphs may well be, "An honest man, the noblest work of God."

RESOLVED, That these resolutions be spread upon the minutes of the Lodge, and a copy thereof be forward to the families of the deceased, and other copies to each of the county papers for publication.
Committee: P T Waggener, Jess Parsons, H W Rhyne, Estrella  July 18 1885
*-SLO Tribune; SLO Weekly Mirror* July 30

Personal Mention: Mr and Mrs Geo Stowell went to the Estrella on a visit and we understand that Mrs E L Stowell and family will return with them.  *–Santa Maria Times* Aug 8

Held to Answer: The preliminary examination into the Estrella shooting affair was held at San Luis last week. Melvin Congdon for the killing of Brooks, was held in the sum of $7,500, and Henry Huston for the killing of Ed Stowell has held in the sum of $7,500. The defendants both gave bonds and was released from jail. The examination of the others who took part in the row is still occupying the attention of the court.  –Ibid Aug 15
*Ed. Note*: something in every issue of the SLO paper in court notes.

Personal Mention: H Stowell has returned from an extended trip through Los Angeles and San Bernardino counties.  –Ibid Sep 12

1885  The trial of Melville Congdon for the killing of Brooks has occupied the attention of the Superior Court for the past four days. The arguments of the respective attorneys were concluded yesterday morning, and the case given to the jury. Up to the hour of going to press no verdict had been agreed upon.  *–SLO Tribune* Sep 24

The trial of Melville Congdon for the killing of Brooks was concluded at San Luis on Wednesday, and a verdict of murder in the second degree was the result. He was sentenced to 25 years.  *–SM Times* Sep 26

Melville Congdon, who was convicted of murder in the second degree for the killing of Clinton Brooks, was sentenced Friday last to 25 years imprisonment at Folsom.  *-SLO Tribune* Oct 1

Henry Huston's case was called in the Superior Court, Wednesday morning at 10 o'clock. The jury was postponed until Oct 15th at 10 am  *– SLO Tribune* Oct 2
*Ed Note*: it dragged on . . .

Mr Geo Stowell brought to our office a few days since a watermelon that weighed thirty-three pounds. It had an excellent flavor and was only a fair specimen of what he can raise on his place. May the shadow of the man never grow less that remembereth the editor in watermelon time.
*–SM Times* Oct 24

Born. Stowell  At Santa Maria, Dec 5th, 1885, to Mrs Lottie Stowell, relict of the late E R Stowell, a daughter.  –Ibid Dec 12

1886  In the Superior Court Feb 4th in the case of People vs Henry Huston, the defendant, by his counsel, P K Woodside, moved the Court that a writ be issued requesting the Warden of the State Penitentiary at Folsom to produce the bodies of Melvin Congdon, Stephen Moody and William Pepper at Court room of the Superior Court of this county on the 16th day of March, 1886, to testify in behalf of the defendant in the above cause. The motion was overruled by the Court, to which ruling defendant, by his attorney, excepted.  *-SLO Tribune*

People vs Henry Huston, charged with murder. State ready..defendant moved for continuance on grounds that important witnesses were now confined in state prison. Motion overruled... –Ibid Mar 22

State vs Henry Huston...progressing slowly... –Ibid Mar 23

The jury in the Henry Huston case returned a verdict of not guilty about 7 o'clock last evening. We understand that on the first ballot they stood 11 for acquittal and 1 for conviction, and on the second...all 12 for acquittal. –Ibid Mar 27

*Ed. Note*: The Stowells in Santa Maria had their thoughts about that, no doubt. The other men were tried for assault with a deadly weapon, dragging on and on through the weeks, mentioned in almost every issue of the paper.

1888 Town and Valley. H Stowell wishes to inform his Dew Drop patrons that his horse has fully recovered from his recent and slight injury and is now ready for service.
–*SM Times* Wed Apr 25

*Ed. Note*: At first blush one thinks Henry is running a saloon, but it must be stud service.

A new wagon and carriage paint shop will be operated in a few days by Ed Crosby and Frank Stowell in the Jones & Lucas Bldg.

Thornburg & Stowell will hold forth in the Hart building, in their new real estate office, after the 1st of next month. –Ibid May 26

Geo Stowell, residing a mile south of town, has about recovered from an attack of pneumonia.

Ed Crosby & Frank Stowell are busy fitting up their new paint shop in Jones & Lucas' building.

Thornburg & Stowell removed to their new real estate quarters in the Hart building, yesterday. –Ibid June 21

*Ed. Note*: Frank Stowell presents something of a mystery. He was in Santa Maria in 1888, as above noted; voter registrations show him in Santa Barbara in 1890 and 1892. The obituary for his son, Floyd, says Floyd was born in Gilroy, date figured to about December 1890. The daughter was born in 1896, place unknown. The 1900 census lists Mary Stowell and her two children in Santa Maria, but Frank is shown in Santa Paula with another woman and three children. Unfortunately the census page is murky and smeared, so the entries are not clear. He died in Santa Barbara in 1904, rating only a passing mention in the *Santa Maria Times*; when his father died the next year, Floyd and Mildred, as Franks' (sic) heirs of the estate, were living in Los Gatos, where they stayed for over twenty years.

1891 Passed On Beyond

Mrs S M Stowell...born Dupage County, Ill...married Henry Stowell March 2, 1853, started at once for California...lived in Placerville, then Nevada for 12 years...to Santa Maria valley 1873...survived by husband and three children... –Ibid Sep 19

Mr Geo Stowell, residing just south of town informs us that his poorest land turned out this season 19 sacks per acre.

Card Of Thanks

Mr Henry Stowell and children desire to publicly express their heartfelt thanks and gratitude to their many friends and neighbors who so kindly assisted them during the sickness, death, and burial of Mrs S M Stowell. –Ibid Sep 26

1896    Delegates elected to attend the Democratic County Convention were Caleb Sherman, Charles Rice, J C Martin, H H Jesse, Henry Stowell and T J Williams.

    —50 Years Ago *SM Times* Sep 28 1946

1903                 The Death of Mrs Lydia Stowell

… Mrs Lydia Stowell, prior to her marriage to Geo Stowell…was Miss Lydia Smith…native of Michigan and came to California with her parents, crossing the plains…two children…Miss Fannie and Mrs Duskin Hobbs,…Methodist church…largely attended…

-Ibid Fri May 15 p.3

1905    Local & Business Items. Miss Fannie Stowell is visiting at Gilroy    –*SM Times* Aug 26

1905                 Henry Stowell Very Low

Henry Stowell is lying at the point of death at his home in this city, and it is not expected that he will survive many hours. He has been unconscious for two days. His son Edgar from Laton and his daughter, Mrs Trumbull from Los Angeles, arrived this week.

Later

As we go to press a telephone message informs us that the late Mr Stowell has just passed away. His funeral will occur on Sunday at 1 pm from the M E church. Obituary will appear next week.    –*SM Times* Nov 11, page 1

Henry Stowell Answers Final Summons

After four years or more of patient suffering, Henry Stowell, a pioneer of Santa Maria and one of the best known residents of this section, died at his home in this city on Friday, Nov 10$^{th}$, 1905. The news of his death was the occasion for expressions of deep and profound regret on every hand, for if ever there was a man who commanded the honor and respect of every man, woman and child who knew him, that man was Henry Stowell. His passing leaves an aching void in every heart, and in their darkest hour of affliction the loved ones who are left to mourn are extended the sympathy of the entire community.

The funeral took place on Sunday afternoon from the M E church, under the direction of the Masonic brethren of deceased and the outpouring of people, gathered to pay their last sad respects, was probably the greatest ever seen in Santa Maria. A touching sermon was delivered by Rev Snudden, pastor of the church, and prayer was offered by Rev Chapman, of the Presbyterian church. Interment in the Santa Maria cemetery followed, with all the solemnity and impressiveness of Masonic rites. Human hands and hearts had paid their final tribute, and in after years the memory of Henry Stowell will be associated with all that is characteristic of persons holding high and lofty ideals and whose attitude toward their fellowmen is that of honesty and kindly mein.

Mr Stowell was born in Denmark, Ashtabula county, Ohio, in the year 1828, and at the time of his death was nearly 77 years of age. He spent his early years in various parts of Ohio and when 26 years old the gold excitement in California induced him to come to this state. He crossed the plains in 1853 and landed at Placerville, where he remained a few years. He later moved to Nevada, and then to Santa Maria in 1871, where he resided until his death. He followed ranching and fruit raising here, a model farm and orchard a mile east of town, sold some time since, being a shining example of the care and attention he was accustomed to give everything with which he was in any way connected. He was prominent in various affairs having for their object the furthering of Santa Maria's interest and was ever ready to aid in any worthy object or to assist his more unfortunate brethren financially or otherwise. His friends were legion and all are as one in voicing the sentiment that Mr Stowell was a man among men.

Vol. XXIV, No. 1-4, 1992, pp.20, 21

## Card Of Thanks
... Geo Stowell, Beda Stowell, Edgar Stowell, Grace Trumbull  —*SM Times* Nov 18

### Henry Stowell Estate

The petition of T C Nance for appointment as executor under the will of the late Henry Stowell of Santa Maria was filed Saturday, together with the will. Under the terms of the will the estate is divided between Edgar H Stowell, a son, residing in Fresno county; Frank Stowell, a son, since deceased; Grace Trumbull, a daughter, residing in Los Angeles and a sister of Mr Stowell, B A Stowell. The children of the deceased Frank, are Floyd and Mildred Stowell, and reside at Los Gatos, Calif. The estate is valued at $5800.  —*Santa Barbara Press* —*SM Times* Nov 25 p.1

*Ed. Note*: Too bad the obituary didn't have more history and less filler; it is included as typical.

### 1908 — Mrs E L Fesler Dies Most Suddenly

The community was shocked on Wednesday morning with the announcement of the sudden death of Mrs E L Fesler, who died between half past eight and nine o'clock from heart disease.

Mr and Mrs Fesler were getting ready to move to Oceano and Mr Fesler was already on his way, with a load of furniture when he was intercepted with the sad intelligence that his beloved wife had been stricken dead.

Mrs Fesler was up and around in apparent good health and was just arranging to attend to a few details before departing for Oceano, when Mrs Ott Fesler, her sister-in-law, heard her fall. Quickly entering the room she picked up the prostrate form and thinking that she had fainted tried to revive her with water. It soon became apparent however that life had taken wings and accordingly a coroner's jury was empaneled, which brought in verdict in accordance with the facts.

The deceased was 43 years of age and leaves a husband and five children to mourn her untimely death. The funeral took place yesterday morning from the Christian church of which she was a devout member, and was attended by many sorrowing friends who knew the deceased as a kind and loving woman.  —Ibid Oct 31

### Card Of Thanks...E L Fesler

*Ed. Note*: Despite much searching, I did not turn up the parents of Charlotte Grigsby. There was a large clan by that name in Napa county in the 1860's and '70's but Lottie doesn't appear with them. In 1880 she was listed with her uncle, John Rector, in northern San Luis Obispo county, and it was in his house that she married Ed Stowell. She may have been orphaned early by the same indisposition that cut her own life short.

### 1910 — George Stowell, Pioneer of Valley Passes Away

On Monday last, George Stowell, one of our most venerable and exemplary citizens, passed away. Although close on to four score of years he clung to life remarkably and withstood the grim reaper long after a man with a less robust constitution would have long ago succumbed.

He had been seriously ill during the year just closed, but his vitality and determination pulled him through several times. This last attack, however, was too much for him and he gradually sank to his end.

George Stowell was a native of Ohio and was born in the city of Ashtabula in 1830. His own home being broke up by the death of his parents, he lived with relatives until he was 17 years of age. He then went to Lake county in the same state, where he learned the trade of carpentering, which he followed until 1853, when with his brother Henry (late deceased) they crossed the plains for California, ending in Hangtown, now Placerville, in August of 1853.

After following mining with varying success for several years, in company with two others they began teaming across these mountains. They brought back the first load of quartz from the famous Comstock mines in Nevada, which they carried to Folsom from which place it was shipped to England.

Mr Stowell followed freighting very successfully until 1867, when he came to San Luis Obispo county and settled near Cayucos. There he followed dairying until 1878, when he sold his interest and moved to Paso Robles where he began raising wheat. In 1882 he moved to Santa Maria and purchased 160 acres one mile south of town, where he has been residing ever since.

Mr Stowell was married in 1855 in Placerville to Miss Lydia Smith, a native of Michigan. His wife died about seven years ago. To this union were born five children, two sons and three daughters, of which two daughters are living, Mrs D Hobbs and Mrs Henry Tunnell. He also leaves two sisters, Mrs Mary Clark, residing in Stockton, and Miss Beda Stowell of this city.

Besides being a devoted member of the Methodist church, Mr Stowell was an Odd Fellow for more than fifty years, having joined the order in Placerville.

The funeral took place on Tuesday afternoon and was conducted under the direction of Santa Maria Lodge No. 302, IOOF, whose worthy chaplain he has been for many years.

Services were held at the Methodist church, with Rev John E Hall presiding, after which interment took place with all the honor and reverence his lodge could bestow. That he was esteemed and beloved was amply attested by the large attendance when his remains were laid in the final resting place.  —*SM Times* Jan 8 p.1

Card of Thanks

We wish to thank one and all who so kindly assisted us in the recent sickness, death and burial of our dear father, grandfather, and brothers, and helped us to bear our great sorrow. We especially thank those who furnished the sweet music and beautiful flowers.

| | |
|---|---|
| Mr and Mrs D Hobbs | Mrs Frank Crowley |
| Mr and Mrs H C Tunnell | Mrs Ray Davidson (sic) |
| Beda Stowell | L A Hobbs |
| Charles R Stowell | George S Hobbs |

Personals. Mrs Frank Newlove and Rev Sampson, of Arroyo Grande were here Tuesday to attend the funeral of the late George Stowell.  —Ibid

*Ed. Note*: The obituary is almost word for word from the biography of George Stowell, *A Memorial and Biographical History of Santa Barbara, San Luis Obispo & Ventura Counties,* Storke, 1891, p. 412

1910     A Marriage license was issued in San Luis Obispo on Thursday to Charles R Stowell and Miss Eliza D Robison of this city.  —Ibid Feb 12

*Ed. Note*: L D Robison, waitress, was listed in the 1909 Santa Maria Directory, 408 W Cypress. Her obituary in The Times Aug 10, 1977, p.3, says she was a member of the Culinary Union, Local 703.

1918     From Mondays daily. L Trumbull, manager of the pipe line and pumping station department of the Associated Oil Company was in town Saturday visiting his brother, Will Trumbull.  —*SM Times* Sat Dec 21

1919     Mr and Mrs Will Trumbull returned last week from San Francisco where they passed New Year's.  —Ibid Jan 11

*Ed. Note*: On the 1900 census, L T Trumbull and wife are listed in Township 8 (south of Santa Maria which is Township 7). In the vicinity were Arthur Bell, superintendent of an asphalt mine, with wife Ellen (Trumbull), two children, and mother-in-law, Marie Trumbull, a native of Switzerland, and mother of four children. When Will Trumbull died in 1946, he was survived by his son, Henry, and brother, Louis of St. Helena, Calif.

1926      Edgar H Stowell Called By Death

  Edgar H Stowell, 70, a native of California and a resident of the Santa Maria Valley for the past 45 years*, passed away late yesterday at the home of Mr and Mrs H R Saulsbury on West Chapel Street. Mrs Saulsbury is a daughter of the deceased.

  Mr Stowell was engaged in ranching and stock raising in this valley for a number of years and enjoyed a wide acquaintance. He had been in ill health for a number of months and had been confined at the home of his daughter for some time following an attack of illness.

  Three sons, Arthur of Maricopa, Henry of Hollywood, Ben of Santa Maria, and one daughter, Mrs Saulsbury, survive. One sister, Mrs Wm Trumbull, also survives.

  Funeral services will be held Wednesday morning at 10 o'clock at the Albert A Dudley Funeral Home. Rev W F S Nelson will be in charge of the service. Interment will be in the Santa Maria Cemetery.      –*SM Daily Times* Tue June 1 p.1

* Not so; he farmed in Kings county and Fresno county for years. (See biog. Henry Stowell, 1969). The death record gives spouse initials L S; 1920 census shows wife Nora J, in Santa Maria. Neither is mentioned above.

1933      Henry Tunnel Succumbs of Bullet Wound

Pioneer Valley Rancher Dies on Tepusquet Ranch Thursday Night Body Discovered By Men In Barn Rifle Kept Handy for Crows is Fatal Weapon in Tragic Case

  Henry C Tunnell, 65, wealthy pioneer rancher of Santa Maria valley, died instantly of a presumably self-inflicted gunshot wound at his ranch in Tepusquet canyon, 14 miles from this city, shortly before 6 o'clock last night.

  Tunnell had been superintending the storage of hay in the barn of the ranch late yesterday afternoon. Ranch hands who were loading a wagon in a nearby field heard the report of a rifle, but continued at their work, thinking that their employer merely fired at a crow while waiting for the arrival of another wagonload of hay.

  A short time later they found his body, shot through the head, in a corner of the barn. Close by lay Tunnell's .32 calibre deer rifle, a discharged cartridge in the breech.

  Local authorities were of the opinion that Tunnell had committed suicide, although it is believed no motive for such an action has been definitely determined.

  Tunnell was born in Ukiah, California, but had lived here for the past 47 years. He leaves his widow, Mrs Fanny Tunnell; one sister, Mrs Charles Shattuck of San Francisco, and two brothers, Frank of Los Olivos, and Martin L Tunnell, Santa Maria.

  Funeral services will be held Monday afternoon at 2 o'clock in the chapel of the Scott B Pyle Funeral home with Rev Glenn C Phillips of Hollywood, former Methodist pastor here, officiating.      –*SM Daily Times* June 30 p.1; See also p.6

1934 Injury Causes Stowell Death

  Former High School Athlete Passes Away from Auto Hurts Month Ago

  Oakley Burum Stowell died yesterday morning…age 22…son of Mr and Mrs Benjamin W Stowell…born Riverdale…20 years in Santa Maria…accident on the Cuyama highway one year ago … graduated June 1930 from Santa Maria high school…Pall bearers: Purvis Glines, Roy Stanley, H Worsham, Wilfred Saunders, Jack McNeil and Edward Kabel.

  …great grandson of Henry Stowell who came to California in 1847* …settled in 1869* on what is now Rosemary Farm.

...Survivors: maternal grandmother Mrs M E Snow. Uncles and aunts: Mr and Mrs R B Snow, Mr and Mrs Harry B Saulsbury, Santa Maria; Mr and Mrs H O Stowell of Monterey, Mr and Mrs J A Salyears of Visalia, uncle A D Stowell, Bakersfield...  –Ibid Mon Nov 19
* Incorrect dates

1939  Capt. Stowell Is Victim of Heart Attack   Native Son Won Notoriety in Kidnapping Episode

Funeral services will be held at 2 pm tomorrow in the chapel of the Dudley Mortuary for Ben Warren Stowell, 51, lifelong resident* of Santa Maria and captain on the city police force. Stowell died unexpectedly yesterday at noon after a two-day illness. Dilatation of the heart was the immediate cause of death...Capt Stowell was taken ill Friday evening...The Rev W D Painter, acting pastor of the Presbyterian church and officers of the local Elks' lodge will be in charge... Fellow officers on the police force will serve as pall bearers and officers of the California Highway Patrol will provide an escort...born Santa Maria April 9, 1888...local high school ...Formerly engaged in farming and cattle ranching, Stowell joined the city police force six and one half years ago. He was promoted to the rank of captain on January 18, 1937.
*not so...

Capt Stowell received statewide notoriety last December 10, when he was the victim of a kidnapping while on duty. Three armed men, whom he was attempting to arrest on a Buellton call, kidnapped Capt Stowell on South Broadway and released him unharmed near the junction of the Cuyama and Maricopa highways, 70 miles northeast of here, after a hectic dash over mountain roads.

For months Capt Stowell endeavored to track down the kidnappers. He assisted in the arrest of two men in Los Angeles and Long Beach, but they were released without filing of charges.

However, information secured from the suspects enabled police to implicate Colorado suspects in the case. Definitely identified as the kidnapers, three men arrested in Denver on postal charges are serving long federal sentences. Two are in McNeil Island penitentiary and the third in Leavenworth.

For the past seven years, Stowell had made his home in the Bradley Hotel.

Surviving relatives include two brothers and a sister, Mrs Harry R Saulsbury and Arthur D Stowell, both of Santa Maria, and Henry Oakley Stowell of Laton, California; two aunts, Mrs D R Daniels of the Tepusquet, and Mrs Geo L Cook of Santa Maria, and an uncle, Aca (sic) Oakley of the Alamo. There are numerous more distant relatives in this vicinity. Stowell was preceded in death by a daughter and a son.  –SM Times July 17 p.1

1944  Mrs Saulsbury Passes Away

Mrs Lora May Saulsbury, widow of the late Harry R Saulsbury, one-time postmaster and member of the high school board, who died three years ago, passed away Saturday night in a local hospital after a long illness.

Mrs Saulsbury was born Jan 29, 1886, in Santa Maria...308 W Mill...she owned a residential court. For many years she was x-ray technician for Drs Lucas and Coblentz of the Santa Maria Clinic. ...daughter of California pioneers Edgar and Emma Oakley Stowell...Stowell road, bounding the southern city limits, is named for the family.

Brothers are Arthur D Stowell of Santa Maria, and Henry O Stowell of Laton...aunt of Raymond C Stowell of Santa Barbara and William H Stowell of Laton, niece of Mrs D R Daniels and A J (Ace) Oakley, all of Santa Maria or Orcutt.

Mizpah chapter, Order of Eastern Star...pall bearers: Elmer and Owen T Rice, Councilman Alfred Roemer, Chas Gardner, John Fesler, W W Stokes.  –Ibid May 29 (?)

1960   Gladys M Stowell, 68, of Laton…native Emmetsburg, Iowa…in the Laton area 48 years . . husband Henry Stowell, Laton; two sons, Raymond Stowell, Los Gatos, William Stowell, Saratoga; sister, Mrs Ruth Morgan, Hanford, three grandchildren…Oak Grove cemetery…
–*Hanford Sentinel* Jan 8 p.2

1963   … Charles Ralph Stowell born Feb 2, 1883 Paso Robles…wife Elizabeth Dudley Stowel… 312 E Fesler…survivors: Edwin Ralph Stowell, Sacramento; Warren Stowell, Orcutt; Lottie Munoz, Helen Feiock, Santa Maria…13 grandchildren, 20 great grandchildren; niece Mary Manning, Whittier; nephew James Crowley . . .   –Ibid Nov 29 (?)

1969   Henry Stowell, 78, of 6384 Murphy St., Laton, died Tuesday in a Los Gatos Hospital. A native of Santa Maria, he had lived in the Laton area for over 60 years.
   Stowell was a cattle raiser and was active in the Laton Rodeo Association having served as president for many years. …sons, Raymond and William, both of Los Gatos, six grandsons and two great grandchildren…Oak Grove cemetery…   –Ibid Dec 31 p.2
   …Honorary pallbearers were Fred Blanchard, Romie Garneau, Ray McGuire, and Ed Smith. Active pallbearers were Kenneth Hurlbut, Bill Blanchard, Joe Cornelius, Howard Evans, Fred Godley and Paul Routh…   –Ibid Jan 5 1970 p.2
   Henry Oakley Stowell was born in Santa Maria Oct. 25, 1891, son of E H Stowell and Emma Oakley…E H born Placerville, Emma born near Sacramento…married Santa Maria… four brothers, 1 sister, four living…at age 11 went to Guernsey, King Co a year at Lemoore, 6 years at Laton, 3 in Riverdale, 2 in Red Bluff…married in Riverdale Gladys Smith, daughter of C A Smith, cashier of First National Bank, Laton…Son Raymond C Stowell…
   -*History of Fresno County California with Biographical Sketches*, Vandor, 1919
   City Directories show Ray C Stowell, tchr, Campbell HS, res Los Gatos, 1956; 1960 he was with Northridge Store Fixtures in San Jose, still living in Los Gatos. 1956, 1960, 1961 William was a telephone co employee; his wife worked for Wells Fargo American Trust co, teller, in San Jose. 1956 Wm was living with Ray, apparently not married yet.

1977   Eliza D Stowell…ch: Edwin, Warren, Helen, Lottie, halfsister Peggy Trunell, Hemet… 13 grandchildren, 20 great grandchildren, 4 great great grandchildren…   –*SM Times* Aug 10 p.3

1981   Lucia E Wiegand, 90, a Pacific Grove resident for 24 years…last resided at Forest Hill Manor and was a member of the First Methodist Church of Pacific Grove, the Forest Hill Manor Methodist Church and the Pacific Grove Civic Club…husband John died in 1976…survived by sister-in-law, Babe Snow, Santa Maria (see Snow chart); daughter-in-law, Vivian Krumbholz of Pacific Grove; step-daughter, Mary E Bates of Santa Cru…   -*Monterey Peninsula Herald* Feb 6 p.4

Vol. XXIV, No. 1-4, 1992, p.25


**Corrections and Additions**   [Page numbers refer to those in Quarterly]

Henry Stowell family
p.9.   Mrs E H Stowell Victim of Poison Placed in Well at Los Berros. Seven-paragraph article: she was in critical condition from drinking water from their well into the pump of which had been placed strychnine and arsenic – a strychnine bottle was found near the well. The couple had returned from spending the evening with Mr & Mrs George Risk when Mrs Stowell drank some freshly drawn water, complaining that it tasted bitter; a short time later she became violently ill. Mr Stowell gave her an emetic, and called the nearest neighbor, Mrs E Cesmat, and Dr L B Coblentz of

Santa Maria, as well as their daughter, Mrs H R Saulsbury and husband. Mrs Stowell had convulsions for a time, but was thought to be out of immediate danger. Stowells had moved to the Berros section from Santa Maria the previous September, and about Christmas time had begun receiving threatening letters, some mailed, some slipped under the door, notifying them to vacate their home and leave Berros. An investigation had been in progress for six weeks, and there were several arrests. About three weeks past, a mob of about 20 persons called on them at night, stating they had been sent by the district attorney, but Mr Stowell drove them out at gunpoint. The District Attorney, M R Van Wormer, denied having sent the mob. It was thought that the mob was organized, and the poisoning was the outcome of the threat to dispose of the Stowells when they refused to leave. The Stowells were old residents of Santa Maria and had many friends; Mr Stowell was reared in Santa Maria. Their children, Mrs Harry Saulsbury and Ben Stowell live in Santa Maria. –May 1 1922 p.1

*Note*: Nothing else was found in the next week's papers, so we can't give the rest of the story, though they must have taken the hint, for Mrs Harry Saulsbury and B W Stowell later brought Edgar Stowell to Santa Maria from Hanford to convalesce. –Feb 22 1924

Frank Stowell died in Santa Barbara in 1904 of kidney disease and syphilis, according to the county death records. A daughter was born to him and his wife in Santa Maria 23 Feb 1895
–*SM Times*
Later that year Mrs Frank Stowell came from Los Angeles to visit her parents, Mr & Mrs G B Hopper. –Dec 28 1895. This family was given to peregrinating; Mrs G B Hopper has returned from Mendocino co accompanied by her father, Mr P W Vann also a nephew, Fred Buckwell, and a friend, Eugene Craven, who have come to Santa Maria to remain for an indefinite time.
-*SM Graphic* Fri Jan 5 1900

p.10. Talk of the Town. Mr & Mrs W W Trumbull arrived from San Francisco where they had been on their wedding tour. They were on their way to their home in the Sisquoc where Mr Trumbull is interested in asphalt mines. –*SM Graphic* Fri Jan 5 1900

Talk of the Town. W W Trumbull has resigned as superintendent of Sisquoc Asphaltum mine plant, and with family will leave for San Francisco. –Jan 3 1903

1922-3 Dir: Trumbull Wm W (Grace A) plumbing & heating r503 W Church; Henri W Student P&S College, SF, r 503 W Church.

W W Trumbull provided the steam heating for the fine new Rubel building, corner Broadway and Cypress, which was designed and built by the Doane Bldg Co, all subcontractors being local. See special section, *SM Times* Fri Mar 10 1922

Local Briefs. Henri Trumball (sic) left Saturday for San Francisco…to England for 3 months' vacation. The recent account saying he joined the U S Navy is in error. His parents accompanied him to San Francisco. –May 3 1922

Local News. Mrs Grace Trumbull returned after spending several days with son Henri Trumbull of Hollywood; he is a prominent actor in the movie colony. –Aug 6 1925

Wm W Trumbull, 501 W Church, was run over by Vincent Faliz (sic) @28 of 204 W Chapel … Trumbull was crossing the intersection of Smith and Main streets…one wheel passed over his right leg, breaking it below the knee…Faliz took Trumbull home, from there he was taken by ambulance to the hospital…the driver was jailed for reckless driving. –Nov 30 1928 p.1

Mrs Trumbull's bio is in O'Neill, *History of Santa Barbara County* 1939 p.450.

George Stowell family

p.9. Raymond Carl Stowell, born 6 Dec 1914 in Red Bluff, died in Los Gatos 22 Feb 1998; the memorial was held at the home of his brother and sister-in-law, William and Bernice Stowell, Los Gatos. He had lived in Santa Maria with his aunt, Mrs Harry Saulsbury, and attended Santa Maria High School. He had a cabinet shop in Dr Albert Missal's garage on Pine St. In 1940 he married Frances Jane Miller, a teacher at El Camino school, who survives, as well as sons Edgar Oakley Stowell, Eric Raymond Stowell, and Mahlon Miller Stowell, 4 gch, 4 ggch, his brother and 3 nephews. –Tue Mar 17 1998 A-7   The 1940-1 Dir shows Frances Jane Miller, tchr 217 W Chapel, and Ray Stowell, cabinet mkr h808 W El Camino, also Warren (Kath) Stowell emp Sadler's Blksmith r808 W El Camino. H R Saulsbury (Lora) subdivider h308 W Mill.

p.10. List of members of the Paso Robles ME Church, Estrella, 1878: Stowell, G & Lydia.
-SLOCGS *Bulletin*

Rural Reports. Cayucos. There was a nice social party the other night ... Miss Susan Stowell, L Stoveall (sic) ...   -*SLO Tribune* Oct 29 1881

p.11. Lottie M (Charlotte Mae) Stowell Munoz b. 1911, d. Oregon City OR Dec 1983 @82 (sic); survived by daughters Margaret Huckaby, Salinas; Juanita Trindade, Casmalia; Selma Morris, Santa Maria; Jacqueline Santos, Arroyo Grande; son Robert Munoz, San Jose; 20 gch, 17 ggch. Husband Ernest Edward Munoz d. 15 Oct 1965 @68/9/6; (son) Jack d. 1968.
-Thu Dec 29 1983 p.16

1976 Dir: Feiock Harold H & Helen A mtr rdr PG&E h618 W Lemon SM
Leslie D mgr W U Tel r618 W Lemon

25th Wedding Anniversary. Warren Stowell and Katherine Alley, now of 130 S Pacific, Orcutt, were married in Reno 23 Oct 1938. Her mother, Mrs Florence Alley, 125 Park st, Orcutt; children Warren E Stowell, Dorene K Biggs with son Alan, and Frances Stowell.
-Thu Nov 21 1963 p.3

Warren M Stowell, 76 died at home, Orcutt, 26 Sep 1994; b. SM 24 Oct 1917. Survivors: Wife Katherine; son Warren E Stowell, SM; daughters Doreen Biggs, SM; Frances Dunn, Hona HI; brother Edwin R Stowell, Sacramento; 8 gch 7 ggch.   –Tue Sep 27 1994 A-5

Guy Stowell died by drowning at E H Nicholson's Suey ranch 1896.

p.13. H Stowell is back from the East accompanied by his sister (Beda), Mr John Patchen, and a granddaughter. Patchen has lived in Ohio all his life but likes California.   –March 14 1885
*Note:* the 1910 census lists Beda A Stowell, 71, in Santa Maria, and with her James M Patchin, cousin, 70, b. OH, and Addie A Patchin, cousin, 58, b. NY.

# STURGEON
## FROM MAINE TO CALIFORNIA

Edward L Sturgeon came to California in steps, living for a time, possibly, in Pennsylvania, marrying an Ohio girl, and sojourning in Michigan before undertaking the trek to California in 1852 with a young family. He lived in Amador, Contra Costa, and Merced counties before his final home in Santa Cruz county. It is his elder son, M M Sturgeon, who represented the name in our locality, though he spent decades in Pleyto, a place now under Lake San Antonio. (Note that Pleyto and Pleito are interchangeable spellings for the Spanish word meaning lawsuit or dispute; Gringos sometimes spelled it Playto or Plato!)

It is noteworthy that the Sturgeon grandchildren, Gene, J J, and Janice, plus June Severns, were members of CSF at Santa Maria Union High School. Maintaining a certain high grade average for most semesters qualified the student for the California Scholarship Federation, the most prestigious of high school honor societies. Helen Sturgeon, pictured next to her cousin Janice in the 1944 *Review*, had come to Santa Maria for her senior year from Mississippi, where she lived with her mother and step-father, so lacked opportunity to qualify.

A telephone interview with Helen, now Mrs Murray, in Templeton, was the source of some of the remarks about her cousins. Her anecdotes provided some otherwise unknown data, and we are grateful for her input.

## OTHER STURGEONS

Nothing is known about M M Sturgeon's younger brother, William. One wonders if the Sturgeons of San Luis Obispo county are his progeny. *Who's Who in the West* for 1963-4 lists one Sturgeon: Vernon Lewis Sturgeon, mayor of Paso Robles. Born in Chandler, AZ, 1915, he was the son of George Howard Sturgeon and Josephine Morris. The 1912 SLO co Directory shows a George H Sturgeon, a farmer, in Creston. The reading of the IOOF cemetery in San Luis Obispo, published by the SLO Co Gen Soc, lists Gent Sturgeon 1897-19-9 (sic) and Margorie (sic) Sturgeon 1890-1946. This couple is on the 1920 soundex for Ventura co, Sespe, he 43, she 30, with Marion, 6, and Jean, 4, all born California.

Another teaser is the family of Ella E Sturgeon, born in Maine 1849, household 19, Merced county township 3, in which Edward L Sturgeon is household 22. Her children were Edward L Ingram, born CA 1876, and Ester B Ingram, b. NV 1880, plus J Clifton Sturgeon born CA 1886, and Leslie D, born 1888. Fathers born IA.

Speaking of Leslie, in the Santa Maria cemetery repose Leslie Cletus Sturgeon 1918-1986, and wife Eldeen, 1920-1978. He was born in Star, Idaho, and after serving in the Army Air Corps in World War II came to Santa Maria, where he lived for 33 years, working as a machinist for Sinton & Brown Cattle and Feed Yards, near Betteravia. The 1955-6 Directory lists him and Eldeen and brother Elmer and wife Nellie in Nipomo. Leslie retired in 1980, moving to Citrus Heights, his last residence. At that time Elmer was in Colorado Springs, and another brother, Alfred, was in Santa Maria. His sisters were Irene Daniels and Ruth Poropat of Nipomo and Gladys Ray of Mesa, AZ. His sons were Leslie D, in Meridian, ID, and Darrell D, in Fairfield, CA. A step-daughter, Carol M Rogers, was living in Templeton. -obit *SM Times* Sunday Dec 14, 1986 p. 30

When Eldeen Sturgeon died in 1978, Carol was living in Santa Maria, Leslie was in Boise, and Darrell in Santa Maria. She had two brothers, Thomas W Connor, Shoshone, ID and Jack Connor, Foster City, CA; there were also six grandchildren. -obit *SM Times* Fri Oct 13 1978 p.13

Edward L. Sturgeon          b. ME Apr 1828 (cen)
   1860 cen: Contra Costa co     d. (Soquel) Santa Cruz co 28 March 1920 @91
     tp 2  PO Lafayette/Alamo; farmer PA; 2ch
   1900 cen: Merced co tp 3 wid
   1910 cen: Santa Cruz co 113-132-1000
   1920 cen: Capitola St, Soquel
     m.
Abigail (Mendenhall)?           b. OH 1825 (cen)
                                            d. before 1900
     (1860 cen next to Sturgeons: Martin Mendenhall 32 OH, Melvina D 26 NY,
         Clara 5 CA, Julia 4 CA 2 lab)
     (IGI: Abigail Mendenhall   b. Greene co OH c1829
          Martin Mendenhall    b. Greene co OH c1830
          F: William Mendenhall;    M: Sarah Peterson)
Known children
1. Martin Meriette Sturgeon       b. MI May 1848 (cen); m. @34
    "Meriette Martin"               d. at home of son Homer, SM, 21 Oct 1926 @77/5/2;
      to CA 1852 Amador co           SM cem. obit Fri Oct 22 p.5; 5gch
      to Contra Costa co               sis Mrs Abby Marlin in SF 1926
    to Merced co, to Hanford 1880; to Pleyto sometime after marriage; back to SM 1924
    1884. Los Alamos Letter…M M Sturgeon moved this week into his new house
       in Cat Canyon.                                                  -Nov 15
    1900 cen: Monterey co San Antonio tp (Pleyto)
    1910 cen: same; mail carrier, 6 births 5 living (Clarence died young—per Murray)
    1920 cen: same
        m. Los Alamos 28 Aug 1883 See Ezra Waite chart 3.a
Nellie May Waite   1865-1927
 a. Homer Lindsey Sturgeon          b. Los Alamos 26 Aug 1884; m. @32 of
    WOW                                  Los Alamos
     K of P: 1929 mechanic SM         d. at home 728 E Cook SM 20 Jan 1964
     1910 cen: w/parents, eng              @79/4/24; SM cem; obit Tue Jan 21 p.8
     1920 cen: Wasioja, no ch;   1938 phbk: 728 E Cook; later same
        m. San Luis Obispo 30 Apr 1917 by Edw Lytten Spaulding MG, K144
          wit: John D Glines, Los Alamos; Earl Stater, Los Alamos
    Charlotte Hinton Holloway          b. SMv 17 June 1885; m. @31 of Los Alamos
                                                        d. 728 E Cook 12 July 1970 @ 85/0/25; SM cem
                                                          obit Tue July 14 p.2, bro Frank Holloway
                                                           North Sacramento 1970
                                                           F: John James Holloway 1839-1918
                                                             (John[5] John[4] George[3] John[2] John[1])
                                                            M: Sarah Elizabeth Miller 1850-1899
                                                               (widow of James Linebaugh)
  =J J Holloway Sturgeon  1920-1992 SMUHS 1936; Outstanding grad SMJC 1939
     (T June); m. 1945 Winifred D Ellis; r El Cerrito. See *Descendants of John and*
     *Mary (Pharo) Holloway…1704-1991* by Doris Holloway Sleath, Nipomo, 1991.
 b. Estelle M Sturgeon                    b. (Pleyto) 16 Dec 1888; m.1 @18 of Pleito
    "Stella"                                     d. San Bernardino co 30 June 1970; SSDI
                                                    SS benefits to Glendora
       m.1 San Luis Obispo 18 March 1907 by Carl M Ross MG, G472
          wit: G L Smith, SLO; Miss Fannie V Ryan, SLO

  Martin Coyne    b. PA   m. @26 of Pleito
               d. (before 1926?)
   m.2 Hills;   living in Los Angeles 1926, 1927, 1931; living in Glendora 1964, 1970
 c. Walter Rey/Ray Sturgeon   b. Pleyto 2 Jan 1893
  to SMv @20 oil wkr    d. Merced 10 Feb 1970 result of auto crash
  1920 cen: Sisquoc no ch     @77/0/18; SM cem; obit Wed Feb 11 p.1
  1922-3 Dir: W R (Fern) pumper Sisquoc & Dist
  1930 K of P: foreman Sisquoc; suspended 1940 @47
  1938-9 Dir: Walter Rey oilman Rural Rte
  1940-1 Dir: Ray R R&G Lease; also W R, oil man Cat Cyn Rd Box 215
  1955-6 Dir: Ray emp G&O Prod h318 Capitol Dr SM;
    living in Ripon 1964, in Nipomo 1966
     m.1 before 1920
  Fern Frances      b. Watsonville 1893
   sch tchr       d. Modesto 13 Feb 1965 @71/11/4; SM cem
            obit Mon Feb 15 p.8. 2gch
  =Robert Eugene SMUHS 1939
   1940-1 Dir: Rbt E bkpr Bank of America   Box 215 RR1
   1945 SMUHS *Review* Honor Roll: Army/killed in Italy last day of WWII (Murray)
    @24/3/10; SM cem
  =Janice (Hollis) SMUHS 1944. 1926-1994; living in Ripon 1965, 1970
   Stanford research biologist (Murray)
   Gene & Janice in Blochman sch; see ONT 322, 324
 c.   m.2
  Ora Vivian       b. England 30 May 1907
             d. SM 15 July 1966 @59/1/15; SM cem
             obit Sat July 16 p.2; rNipomo, 46y in
             local area. sis Mrs Kathleen Olsen,
             San Mateo
             m.1 Ralph Wilson   1885-1961
              1940-1 Dir: Ralph (Ora V) oilwkr Orcutt Hwy
             =Robert Wilson, Port Hueneme 1966
             =Kathleen Jeanne Wilson (Alexander Roman
              Ontiveros) Santa Maria (SMUHS 1944)
 d. Charlotte Etta Sturgeon   b. (Pleyto) Nov 1898 (cen)
             d. SM 1 Apr 1931 @32/4/12; SM cem
             obit Fri Apr 3, p.5   1931 pall bearers:
             Wm Breen, Jas Collins, Harry Takken,
             Lawrence McCandless, Fred Michael, Denzil
             Glines; Honorary pall bearers: members of
             Women's Benefit Assn, Mrs Nettie E Brandt,
             Mrs Bessie Weathers, Mrs Ynez Lukeman,
             Mrs May Hartnell, Mrs Hattie Scott,
             Mrs Gertrude Lowell
  m.1
  Charles Severns   living in Sisquoc 1926, SM 1927
   (1928 Dir: Chas Severns lab r111 N Vine)?
  =June Margaret SMUHS 1935
  =Edith M adopted by Aunt Stella (per Murray)

    d.       m.2 c1928
      Royden (Sy) Bradley  1892-1971  see Waite chart, 3.d.
      =Richard Royden   living in Sacramento 1996 (Murray)
    e. Chester M Sturgeon                      b. Pleyto 20 Dec 1905
      1929 K of P trk drvr SM             d. Los Alamos 12 Sep 1985 @79; suicide
      in SM 1927, 1931, 1945              Los Alamos cem; obit Sun Sep 15 p.6
      1955-6 Dir: opr eng h1022 N Bwy; Operating Engs Union Local 12
        in Long Beach 1964;  in Los Alamos 1970
          m.1 (Whittier) Aug 1924
        Grace Gertrude Farmer            b. TN 22 Sep 1909; SSDI
                                            d. Oakland CA Dec 1977
                                              m.2 c1942 W R McLane
      =Helen L (Murray)  b. SM 1925; SMUHS 1944; built house in Templeton 1975
        still there 1996
      =Joyce (Andrus)      b. SM 1927; living in Alaska 1984, 1985, 1996
  (e.)     m.2 c1937
      Carmel Anita Caligari            b. San Luis Obispo 21 Feb 1908
        "Honey"                                  d. Goleta 28 June 1984 @76
        to Los Alamos from                 obit Mon July 2 p.17; 15gch 11ggch
        Long Beach 1969                     F: Esilio Caligari
                                              M: Rita Catherine Canet 1870-1945 obit *SLO*
        For Canet see SLOCGS          *Telegram-Tribune* Sat Aug 4 1945 p.1
          *Bulletin* 12-2 1979                m.1 Ernest F Gramespacher 1901-1958
                                            =Ernest F 1927-1992
                                            =Donald 1928-1969

2. William Sturgeon                       b. MI 1850
                                      d. (before 1926)

3. Abigail C Sturgeon                  b. CA Apr 1868 (cen)
    1910 cen: w/father                   d. Alameda co 12-15-1939 @72
    1920 cen: same                        living in San Francisco 1926
      m. 1894
    Abe L Marlin                            b. WA May 1864 (cen)
    1900 cen: w/E L Sturgeon          d. (before 1910)
    2 births 2 living                    F: PA;  M: OH
    a. Evan S                                 b. CA Oct 1896
    b. Kenneth                             b. CA Dec 1899

Vol. XXVIII, No.4, Winter 1996, pp. 17, 18

**Corrections and Additions**       [Page numbers refer to those in Quarterly]

p. 15   Other Sturgeons.  1910 census soundex, SLO co. Geo H Sturgeon 29 IN; Josie 27 CA; Gladys 1 6 CA; Francis A 4 CA; Willard L 2 CA.  Benjamin F. Morris, bro/law 31 CA
Templeton Cemetery: Thelma P Sturgeon 1909-1962; Willard Dale Sturgeon 1908-1976

    The Paso Robles Area Pioneer Museum has George Sturgeon's milk truck on exhibit, with some historical data appended.

p. 18   Sisquoc-Garey.  Mr and Mrs Ralph Wilson and family, Lawrence M Abeloe and Janice Sturgeon guests of Mrs Molly Smith, SLO.  Wilsons of Palmer Union lease guests of Mrs Fern Sturgeon and family of Santa Maria.                          -Thu Nov 14 1940

Vol. XXIX, No. 4, Winter 1997, p. 18

# STURGEON
## FROM MAINE TO CALIFORNIA

Sturgeon – an uncommon name; yet there were two pioneer families with that appellation in this out-of-the-way area. Were they related? Not closely, as no connection has been found, although in depth research, for a year inhibited by the unavailability of the SMVGS collection, might show otherwise. The previous chart is for Edward L Sturgeon. We now follow up with Samuel Robert Ines Sturgeon.

Samuel Sturgeon was prominent in Santa Barbara county, having been the first district attorney, so he rated a fairly thorough biography in Thompson & West, much of which was repeated 55 years later in the 1938 Pioneer Edition of The *Santa Maria Times*. He left Maine as a young man to attend Lafayette College in Pennsylvania, presumably the one in Easton, and later went to Sidney, Ohio, to continue his law studies with Joseph S. Updegraff. He enlisted for the Mexican war, and fought as a non-commissioned officer with Taylor and Scott in Mexico, thereafter coming to California in 1849 with the U S Mounted Rifles. From here he went to Oregon with the First Dragoons to fight Indians, both once and again, and upon discharge, went to Los Angeles, where he lived from 1857 to 1861. From there he came to Santa Barbara, and is shown by Thompson & West as victor in the 1863 election for district attorney, a post he held for some time. In 1866 he faced dismissal by the Board of Supervisors, but he prevailed. He was "a forcible writer …under the *nom de plume* of 'El Cabo' worried the politicians and hungry land sharks …" See Thompson & West 445-6,123,130,180.

After his tenure as district attorney he settled down to the pastoral life of a California ranchero in Canada Gato, or Cat Canyon, post office Sisquoc, where he owned 160 acres. His wife sprang from an old Spanish Colonial family, and his children married into others of the same background-Flores, Mendoza, Ontiveros, Ruiz, Yorba-all are well documented in the opus magnum of long time SMVGS member Erlinda Ontiveros, *San Ramon Chapel Pioneers*.

The Pioneer Edition of the *Santa Maria Times* listed the grandchildren who still resided locally, and detailed the relics in their possession: Mrs Tomasini had his medals, Ernest Flores was keeper of the "sabre with which the lawyer-soldier slit the heads of redmen", and Mrs Fouts held the parchment on which was written his commission contacts as First Sergeant of a troop in the First Dragoons, 1856.

It is interesting to see that several of the sibling grandchildren shared domiciles, as shown in the city directories, and that the F H Gates Co, later the S P Milling Co, sand and gravel purveyors in Sisquoc, provided employment for some of the men.

Samuel Robert Ines Sturgeon     b. Eastport ME 1821
  1860 cen: Los Angeles     d. Sisquoc 20 Apr 1885; San Ramon cem
  1867 Pacific Coast Bus Dir:     obit Apr 25; SB probate file #978
    RSI Sturgeon atty-at-law, SB
  1871-3 same: RSJ Sturgeon, atty-at-law SB
  1880 cen: 58 f Sisquoc
  bio T/W 445-6; also *SM Times'* Pioneer Edition Apr 30 1936, see also ONT 134, 160a Sisquoc
    m. Santa Barbara 10 May 1862 (ONT) 10 Aug 1862 (*Ancestors West*)
Ramona Valenzuela     b. CA 1836
    d. (after 1880); San Ramon cem
    F: Jose Maria Trinidad Valenzuela

                                    M: Maria Josefa Cota 1803, see *Spanish Mexican Families of Early California II* 64

1.     Susana Josephine Sturgeon         b. Santa Barbara July 1863; m. @21 of SM
        to SMv 1877                            d. at home 210 S Vine SM 25 Nov 1926 @63/4/20;
        1922-3 Dir: Mrs Susana hskpr         SM cem; obit Fri Nov 26 p.5. 6 gch
          Sisquoc
      m. Santa Maria 1 Apr 1884 by S F Crow, C114, wit: Chas Clarey, S Kalmyer
    Abram J Flores                         b. CA 1860; m. @23 of SM
      1900 cen: tp 8, 5 births 5 living       d. SM 29 Mar 1940 @80/0/16; SM cem
      1910 cen: tp 8 Garey rd                 obit Fri Mar 29 p.1; 7 gch 6 ggch, in Sisquoc 70y
      1928 Dir: lab Sisquoc                     F: Juan Flores 1831-
      1940-1 Dir: RR2 at home               M: Josefa Isodora Valenzuela
                                          (See Flores gen ONT 134-6)

    a.    Anita Lugarda Flores             b. Sisquoc 6 Aug 1884
         or Anna Loretta                    d. at home of dau El Centro 28 Jan 1966
                                                @81/5/22; SM cem obit Mon Jan 31 p.8 4 gch

        m.1
        Chester George Calvert            b. CA Oct 1883
          1900 cen: Nipomo w/mother    d.
            Mrs Johnson, widow              F:
                                             M: Mary ____ 1860-1932
                                               m.2 c1890 (Thos Kearney Johnson 1852-1893)
                                               m.3 1900 Joel M Harris 1852-1933
       = Bert H Calvert in Gardena 1962, 1966; in Lancaster (ONT)
          1940-1 Dir: Bert H (Lou) gdnr r431 E Main
       = Lillian Calvert b. SM 1907; d. Seattle 1990
          m.1 August A Rey. "Sisquoc Girl Weds Resident of Oakland." In SLO Sat,
            Lillian Calvert, dau of M/M Tito Ontiveros and August Rey, son of M/M
            A Rey of Oakland. Attended by Miss Addie Clark of SM & Jack Rogers of
            Oakland.                                                       -Oct 17 1924
          1925 Dir: Mrs Lillian Rey hswf Sisquoc; A A Rey trk drvr Sisquoc
          1928 Dir: A A Rey (Lillian) trk drvr Sisquoc
        m.2: Charles Schlee
    a.   m.2 San Luis Obispo mission 12 May 1915
       Tito Ontiveros                         b. Tepesquet 4 Jan 1887
         1940-1 Dir: Tito (Anna)               d. SM 1 Nov 1962 @75/9/27; SM cem
           gdnr HiSch h 431 E Main (pictured     obit Fri Nov 2, p.2; r429 N Curryer
           in yrbk); also Anna L Ontiveros,      F: Alejandro Miguel Ontiveros 1863-1939
           jan Mesquit's r431 E Main              M: Viviana Antonia Ruiz 1863-1939, see
         1947-8 Dir: (Anna) gdnr SMUHi         Ontiveros gen ONT 65-66
       Dist, h429 N Curryer; also Anna L emp Mesquit's
      = Tita Henrietta Ontiveros b. 1917; m.1 Lawson
         1940-1 Dir: Lawson B K (Henrietta) emp S P Milling co h630A E Main
              Lawson Henrietta opr Tel co rsame
         m.2 1945 Hans Merklein; rEl Centro
    b.   Rosa F Flores                           b. Sisquoc May 1886; m. @20 of Garey
                                            d. 13 Jan 1919 @32/8/4 (flu); SM cem;
                                               no obit found
      m. San Luis Obispo 6 May 1907 by Geo Willett (also *SLO Daily Telegram*), G506
        wit: M/M Geo A Miller, SLO
    Arthur Wm Tunnell                     b. SMv Aug 1883; m. @23 of Garey

    1900 cen: w/parents      d. SM 29 Jan 1919 @35/5/18 (flu); SM cem;
    1910 cen: tp 8 Gary rd      no obit found
    see Tunnell gen ONT 162      F: Thos Jasper Tunnell 1846-1924
                          M: Mary Jane Bradley 1859-1942
  = Wm Ernest Tunnell b. SM 1908 (Dora Olga Sorenson 1909-1991)
    1940-1 Dir: plastering contr hEl Camino (Wm E & Dora)
    1938-9 Dir: plstr Joe Perry h407G E Chapel (W E & Dora)
  = Clarence Arthur Tunnell 1909 (Eunice C Cochran)

 c. Clorinda (Dela?) S Flores      b. July 1889
                       d. (in Long Beach 1926, 1936, 1938, 1966)
   m.
   James K Cooper         b. (Las Tablas, SLO co or SM)? Nov 1896
    in Taft 1919           d. Long Beach 2 Feb 1962; bur Our Lady of
                         Sorrows cem, obit Wed Feb 7 p.2, bro Carl in
                         Bakersfield 1962 (in Lompoc 1919) wife
                         Dela. M/M Tito Ontiveros and M/M Wm
                         Tunnell attended the services
                         F: Charles Richard Cooper 1853-1919
                         M: Sarah Ann Walker 1857-1940
   = James K Cooper jr        see *The Story of Adelaida, MacGillivray*,
                         1992 (SLO co)

 d. Ernest(o) Silveresto Flores     b. Dec 1890
    in Sisquoc 1926         d. 10 June 1939 @49/4/9; SM cem
    1928 Dir: lab Sisquoc       obit Tue June 13; 2 sis 1 bro 1 aunt
    1938-9 Dir: E S Flores tmstr
     Gates Inc Rural Rt; also Ernest S (Frances) lab RR Box 482
    1939 pall bearers: W L Fischer, Ramon Ontiveros, Jas Keegan, Herman Bertinoia,
     J S Calderon, Wm Sumner; directed by Dustin Webber, Moose dictator
      m.
   Frances Muriel Arias of Los Alamos. Grad SMUHS Winter 1925
    1940-1 Dir: Frances M hmkr rSisquoc RR #1
    No issue

 e. Oresto C Flores (Mabel)      b. 30 Oct 1893; SSDI
    1936,1938: Long Beach      d. Long Beach May 1966
    1966: Compton

2. Samuel R jr Sturgeon         b. (Santa Barbara) Apr 1866
                         d. buried San Ramon cem (ONT)

3. Olivia Elena Sturgeon         b. Santa Barbara 15 June 1867; m.2 @25 of Garey
  1900 cen: 3 births 3 lvg        d. at home S Lincoln st SM 24 Jul 1925 @58
  1910 cen: 9 births 6 lvg         obit Fri July 24 p.1 Sat July 25 p.5
                       7 ch, sis Mrs Flores, bro W J Sturgeon

  m.1 (ONT)
  Juan David Ruiz           b. Juan Bautista adobe 26 Nov 1860
                        d. at parents' home 8 July 1908 @47/7/8 suicide; San
                        Ramon cem. obit Sat July 11 "David Ruiz Commits
                        Suicide At the home of His Parents"…single…totally
                        deaf
                        F: Juan Bautista Ruiz 1837-1914
                        M: Maria Rita Ontiveros 1842-1925, see ONT 116

 a. Adelina Ruiz            b. Santa Barbara 1885
                        d. (died young?)

    b.    Dolores Ruiz                               b. Santa Barbara 24 May 1890
        in Anaheim 1938, 1973                  d. Yorba Linda 2 Feb 1976
        m. 11 Jan 1910 (ONT)
        Ernesto Yorba (no data ONT)        F: Jose Antonio Prudencio Yorba 1832-1885
        = 8 ch                                    M: Maria de los Dolores Gertrudis Ontiveros
        See *Saddleback Ancestors* 112f          1833-1894; see ONT 285-6

3.    m. 2 Santa Ynez mission 15 Nov 1893 by Fr Lack
    Meinardo Antonio Ruiz           b. Sisquoc (cen and obit) or Carpinteria (ONT)
      1900 cen: tp 8                          25 May 1869
      1910 cen: tp 8                          d. at home 22 Feb 1942 @72; SM cem; obit Mon Feb 23
      1938-9 Dir: M A Ruiz h309 S Pine        p.1, 8 gch
      1940-1 Dir: same (w/Rbt)             F: Juan de la Cruz Ruiz 1821-1895
                                           M: Martina Ayala 1827 (ONT) (1833 cen) -1915

    c.    Francisco Cruz Ruiz               b. Garey 14 Sep 1893 (ONT) 1892 (cen)
        "Frank"                                 (is he a son of first marriage?)
        1925 in Long Beach                 d. Compton 16 Feb 1936; accident
        m.
        Hannah Tokuda Mendoza of Hawaii
          1955-6 Dir: hmkr h309 S Pine         m.1 c1913 Jose Norberto Mendoza 1880-1954
                                          F: Francisco Mendoza 1855-1944
                                          M: Prudencia Rivera 1856-1908
                                             (see Mendoza gen ONT 149)

    d.    Martina Silvana Ruiz               b. Garey 12 Sep 1895 (ONT) 1894 (cen)
                                           d. 12 Dec 1900; San Ramon cem

    e.    Robert Usbalde Ruiz                b. Garey 7 July 1898
        1938-9 Dir: water well drlr          d. 27 May 1977 @78; SM cem
          r309 S Pine                           obit Sat May 28 p.11; 3 sis; wter wel drlr
        1940-1 Dir: lab r309 S Pine
        1955-6 Dir: 724 S Smith (w/Rojas)
        1961 Dir: lab U Sugar r724 S Smith
        Single

    f.    Samuel Elijio Ruiz                  b. Garey 11 Mar 1901
        1938 in Santa Maria                 d. 24 Nov 1944; SM cem. no obit
        1940-1 Dir: (Saml A Ruiz lab r1143 W Cypress)?
        married briefly; divorced.

    g.    Emelia Facunda Ruiz               b. Garey 12 June 1903
        "Millie"                                 d. Garden Grove, rSanta Ana 24 Mar 1991;
          in SM 1973                          SM cem, obit Tue Mar 26 A-6, to Santa Ana
          in Bedford OR 1984               w/son 1985; 7 gch 5 ggch
          in Santa Ana 1986
        m.1 (?)
    = her son Earl (ONT); called Fouts; in Mountain View 1991
        m.2 12 Sep 1924
        Wilburn Arthur Fouts               b. Thayer co NE (in Chester pct 1900 cen)
        "Bill"                                     6 Apr 1899; SSDI
          1930: in Los Olivos                 d. 24 Oct 1966 (SM)? no record SM cem
          (no Fouts in 1930 phbk SM)
          1938-9 Dir: Fouts: Fred r315 E Main    F: Frederick Fouts 1875-(1928)?
            Millie A maid Calif Hotel            M: Cora C Shutts (?) 1878-1957
            r315 E Main                             obit Fri Dec 20 1957 p.4 to SM 1919
            W A (Nellie) lab h315 E Main

    Wilbur (Mildred) chnmn 315 E Main
  1938 phbk: Fred 617 W Cypress
  1940-1 Dir: Fred r617 W Cypress
   Mildred A maid Calif Hotel r617 W Cypress
   Millie R maid Hotel Calif r617 W Cypress
   Wilbur (Mildred) chainman h617 W Cypress
  1947-8 Dir: Millie R clk Greyhound Lines r617 W Cypress
   Wilbur (Mildred) U Oil Co h617 W Cypress
   Dart Richd (Shirley) emp U Sugar Co h212 E Chapel Apt 1
  1950 phbk: Millie 617 W Cypress
   W A 322 N Benwiley
   Dart Richard E 216 E Chapel
  1955-6 Dir: Cora C hmkr h617A W Cypress
   Millie R Slsldy Swing's h617 W Cypress
   Swing's Men's Wear 114 E Main
   Wilbur A (Josephine) rte slsmn Santry Lndy h212 E Chapel Apt 5
   Josephine clk r212 E Chapel Apt 5
  1961 Dir: Josephine S Mrs 312 S East
   Russell A surveyor Finley Engs r609 N Lincoln
   Wilbur A (Millie A) eng Tuttle Engs h609 N Lincoln
  1969 Dir: Josephine Mrs 312 S East
   Millie R (wd Wilburn A) agt Western Greyhnd Lines h706 W Hermosa
  1976 Dir: Millie R agt Greyhound Lines West r238 E Bunny
   Johnston Barbara E civil serv wkr h238 E Bunny
  = Barbara Fouts b. 1928 (George L Johnston) SMUHS 1947; in Oxnard 1991
   1961 Dir: Johnston Geo L (Barbara E) constr wkr Madonna Cons h238 E Bunny
   1974 Dir: Johnston Barbara E (Barbara's Beauty Shop) h238 E Bunny
  = Russell Fouts b. 1930 (Jeanne Smith) SMUHS 1949; in Santa Ana 1991
*Note:* Charles and Betty Feliz helped explain the confusion engendered by the directory
  listings: Millie and Bill divorced: he married Josephine Dart but went back to Millie who
  cared for him until his death. Josephine died in Sacramento age 82 survived only by
  daughter Shirley Reynolds of Sacramento.    –obit Fri Nov 13, 1981 p11

  h. Silvana Saturnina Ruiz    b. Garey 29 Nov 1905
    "Sylvia"        d. SM 11 Oct 1984 @78; SM cem
    1925 in SM       obit Sun Oct 14 p.22; 5gch 5ggch floral
    1969 Dir: h407D E Chapel   designer
    m. Santa Ynez mission 28 Nov 1925
    Plenio Frank Tomasini    b. SM 2 Sep 1897 or 3 Sep 1898 (obit)
     SMUHS 1923; also bus drv  d. SM 7 Feb 1962 @64; obit Thu Feb 8 p.2
               r510 W Mill, Hanson Equip, 5 gch
    1938-9 Dir: Plenio (Sylvia)
     jan HSch r218 E Mill    F: Camilo Tomasini 1867-1938
    1940-1 Dir: same      M: Guiditta Barca 1864-1921
    1947-8 Dir: emp Hanson Equipt Co h218 E Mill; Plenio jr; Yvonne ofc clk
     Gerrard Co.
    1955-6 Dir: jntr Hanson Equip h510 W Mill; 1961 Dir: same
    1984 pall bearers: Ben & Chas Feliz, Casey Kyle, Harry Weise, Dick Beal, Allen
     Claycamp
   = Plenio F Tomasini jr b. 1927; SMUHS 1945 (Dorothy Vance)
    1961 Dir: sup Martin (VAFB) h518 E. Mariposa; in San Jose 1962; in Beaverton OR
     1984

= Yvonne Beverly Tomasini b. 1929; SMUHS 1947 (Jas Wm Biliardi SMUHS 1947)
    1969 Dir: Jas W (Yvonne B) slsmn Coor's Beer h331 N Valerie; in SM 1962 & 1984

i.  Marta Martina Ruiz                  b. Garey 14 Nov 1908
   "Martha"                                d. 12 June 1986 @77; SM cem
    in Guadalupe 1938,1940              obit Sun June 15 p.20; tel op 25y;
    1928 Dir: Martha Ruiz tel opr            gch: Cheryle McDuffee, Rudy Bondietti jr,
      r411 W Lemon                         Wayne R. Bondietti, SM
    1938-9 Dir: Wm B (Martha)
      emp U Sugar Box 274 Guad
    1940-1 Dir: Mrs Martha hswfe Guad
    1947-8 Dir: Martha R emp Assoc Tel Co Ltd r617 W Cypress (w/Fouts)
    1955-6 Dir: Martha tel opr h215A W Cook SM
    1961 Dir: Martha R sup GTel h311½ W Mill; ret 1964 (obit)
    1969 Dir: Martha r706 W Hermosa (w/Millie)
    in SM 1973,1984
    1986 pall bearers: Jimmie Biliardi, Geo Johnston, Chas & Benj Felez (sic), Bobby Jones, Scoop Nunes
  m. SLO mission Thu 12 Sep 1929 by Fr Buckly; matron of honor, Mrs W A Fouts; best man W A Fouts. To live in Guad…Dance last night for 200 friends and relatives.
                                                                  -Mon Sept 16 1929

    William Bondietti                  b. Guadalupe 12 Oct 1904; SSDI
      1928 Dir: clk, Guad also 1925          d. SM 22 Sep 1970 @65; Guad cem
      1947-8 Dir: Wm jntr Guad sch           obit Wed Sep 23 p.2. r4496 12th st
      1955-6 Dir: Wm "Bill" cust               bros: Bert, Americo; 3gch 2ggch
        also listed under Bill               F: Cesare Bondietti 1864-1949
                                             M: Josephine 1867-1930
      1961 Dir: hd cust Guad Jt U Sch h4495 12th Guad
      1969 Dir: Bill B cust as above
      1970 pall bearers: Bradford Caligari, Dalton Caligari, Abe Juarez, Kermit McKenzie, Frank Rojas, James Parr
    = Rudy W Bondietti 1930-1975
      1955-6 Dir: Rudy (Velma) emp PG&E h113 E Bunny SM
        Velma emp Safeway r113 E Bunny
      1961, 1969 Dir: Rudy W (Velma L) drvr PG&E h1116 N Lincoln SM

j.  Maria Antonia Eulalia Ruiz             b. Garey 12 Feb 1911
    in SM 1936, 1938                       d. at home 724 S Smith, SM, 8 Feb 1973
    1938-9 Dir: Mrs Mary Feliz             @61/11/26; SM cem; obit Sat Feb 10 p.2;
      hskpr r315 E Main w/Fouts          6gch
    1973 pall bearers: Pete Salazar, Clay Brown, Jim Adams, Bobby Jones, Frank Caligarey (sic), Russell Futs (sic), Rudy Bondietti
  m.1 23 July 1927
    Benjamin Feliz                        b. 1903 (Pozo, SLO co?)
      1928 Dir: Benny (Mary) packer       d. at home 306 E Main 31 Mar 1934 @30
        r204 E chapel                          buried Santa Margarita. In SM 10 y,
                                            obit Sat Mar 31 p.4
                                            F: Vicente J. Feliz 1867 –
                                            M: Florinda Garcia 1876-1967
                                               m.2 John E. Domingues 1879-1961
    = Benjamin Jesse Feliz b. 1928, SMUHS 1947 (Dolores Jean Dalporto)
      in Lompoc 1973

     = Charles F Feliz b. 1930, SMUHS 1950 (?) (Betty Munoz)
      1969 Dir: Chas (Betty) equip opr VAFB h125 N Pacific, Orcutt; same 1997
      in Orcutt 1973

  j.  m.2 c1946

| | |
|---|---|
| Frank J Rojas | b. Los Angeles 24 June 1915; SSDI |
| 1938-9 Dir: F Rojas lab | d. Santa Maria 7 Aug 1982 @67/1/13; SM cem |
|  Gates Inc, RRt |  obit Mon Aug 9 p.12 |
| 1940-1 Dir: lab | F: Rafael J. Rojas 1893-1986 |
|  F H Gates rSisquoc | M: Maria Trinidad 1887-1971 |

    1947-8 Dir: Frank J (Mary) mech Moore & Jullien Orcutt h724 S Smith SM
     Moore & Jullien Gar (John F Moore, J E Jullien) W Clark Orcutt
    1951-2 Dir: Frank J (Mary) mech Jack Julian (sic) h724 S Smith
    1955-6 Dir: Frank J (Mary) mech Roemer & Elliott h724 S Smith
     Mary ofc emp Jordano Bros Inc, h724 S Smith
    1961 Dir: Frank J (Mary E) Frank's Mobile scv h724 S Smith
    1963, 1966, 1970 and 1972 Dir: same
    1974 Dir: Frank (Jennie) Bwy Mobil Gas h619 S Pine
    1976 Dir: Frank & Jenny; mach Argrow h619 S Pine
    1978 Dir: Frank J & Jennie F mach J&S Equip h619 S Pine
    1982 Dir: Frank J & Jennie F mech R F Donovan Farms h619 S Pine
    1984 Dir: Jennie F Mrs wd h619 S Pine
    1982 obit: worked for R F Donovan heavy equipment, also Mobile service station,
     Broadway at Tunnell. Survivors: widow Jennie, SM: son Francis, San Jose; daus
     Carol Rincon, Nipomo; Rita Rojas, Reno; Joan Hopkins, SM; stepdaus Margaret
     Mays, Arroyo Grande; Pauline Fain, Orville (sic); Patricia Spears, Pam Gorell,
     Priscilla Greene, all SM; Cindy Greene, San Gabriel; stepsons Victor Dela
     Fuente, Santa Cruz; Donnie Greene, John Saenz, SM; father Ralph, brothers
     Fernando and Pete, SM.

4. Edward I Sturgeon  b. CA 1870
  1906 Dir: E Sturgeon P.O.Garey d.
  1910 cen: San Joaquin co. 103-120-255: Edward Sturgeon 44 CA, w/Lafayette Ward

5. William John Sturgeon  b. Santa Barbara 1873
  1906 Dir: W J Sturgeon  d. Santa Maria 17 Nov 1938 @65/10/15 SM cem
  P.O. Garey     obit Thu Nov 17 p.1, rBuellton. "Son of First
  1925,1926: Garey    Prosecutor in County Passes", 11 nieces &
           nephews named

Who is this? James/Jim Sturgeon d. 28 Aug 1906 @25; San Ramon cem

*Note*: Apparent divorces may be inferred from directory listings.

Vol. XXIX, No. 3, Fall 1997, pp.8, 9

**Corrections and Additions**  [Page numbers refer to those in Quarterly]

p.7 Plenio "Tom" Tomasini jr died in Casper WY 30 Oct 1997 @70. Born in Santa Maria 27 1927; served in US Navy WWII and Korea. Married Dorothy Vance 21 Aug 1949, Los Angeles. Lived in Beaverton OR 23 years, teaching business at Portland Community College. Had been in Casper 17 months. Survived by wife, of Casper; sons Frank, of Casper, and Charles of Aloha, OR; daughter Carol Carrington, London, England; sister, Yvonne Biliardi, Santa Maria; 5 grandchildren.
                              –Mon Nov 3 1997 A-7

Vol. XXIX, No. 4, Winter 1997, p.17

# SWAIN
## CALIFORNIA PIONEERS

Robert Corlin Swain, Capt.      b. (Boston) MA 1815
  to CA 1849      d. at home of dau Mrs Morrison, Santa Maria
  1860 cen: Petaluma      21 Aug 1910 @95; Cayucos cem; obit *SLO*
  to SLO co 1868      *Daily Telegram* Mon Aug 22 p.4; T Sat August 27 p.1
  1870 cen: Morro tp      F: MA; M: Eng
  1874-5 Tax bk: 160a Old Creek
  1880 cen: San Simeon tp
  1892 GR: 77 5'6 fair complexion hazel eyes grey hair dairyman MA rOld Creek, PO Cayucos
  1898 GR: Chorro pct; dairy 83 5'6 fair hazel grey MA
  1902 GR: Cholame pct 87 PO SLO
  1910 pall bearers: J R Anderson, A M Hardie, H Marquart, Wm Fitzhugh, R D Hazard,
        L Pedraita
  m.
Elizabeth A Mansfield (Tripp)      b. Boston MA 1828
     d. Old Creek 13 Feb 1872 @44; consumption
     Cayucos cem; obit SLO Trib

Known children:
1. Andrew Keener Swain      b. CA c1852
     d. Petaluma 8 Oct 1858 @6/6

2. Robert Walter Swain      b. (Petaluma) Dec 1857; m. @24 of Nipomo Mills
  1892 GR: 35 5'11 fair blu auburn      d. SLO 16 Sep 1927 @70; Cayucos cem; obit *SLO*
  rancher CA rLos Berros, PO AG      *Daily Telegram* Sat 17 p.4 60y York grade section
  1902 GR: Josephine pct 45      (=Ascencion). Rancher, road foreman
  PO Templeton
  1920 cen: w/Douglas, SLO
    m.1 at res of bride's father, Old Creek 5 or 15 Dec 1880 by D G Sanders JP, A406
      wit: R J Hazard, Old Creek; Mrs D G Sanders, Cayucos
  Mary Elizabeth Hazard      b. (Tuolumne co) CA Sep 1858; m. @21
     d. 31 Aug 1909 @51; Cayucos cem
     F: Robert Jeremiah Hazard 1826-1914
     M: Elizabeth Fry 1840-1881
    m.2 (after 1920)
  Mabel
    a. Jerry D Swain 1881-1944; Templeton cem; in Hollister 1938
        m. SLO 24 Dec 1906 by Chas P Kaetzel JP, G441
          wit: F J Rodriguez, H H Carpenter, SLO (both courthouse officials)
      Harriet V Kester 1888-1927; Templeton cem
        F: Jesse W Kester (1853-1909); M: Theodosia E Powell 1859-1892
      = 4 boys
    b. Arthur Douglas Swain 1884-1938; Cayucos cem; m. @19 of Templeton
        m. Ascencion 24 Dec 1902 by Jno W Quay, Pres, F424
          wit: Clyde L Anderson, Templeton; Jerry B Swain, Templeton
      Agnes Isabelle Anderson 1879-1940; Cayucos cem; m. @18 of Templeton
      = 3 children
    c. Robert Roy Swain 1887-1961; Cayucos cem; m. @29 of Cayucos
        m. SLO 9 Feb 1921 by Wm Mallagh JP, L506
          wit: John H Swain, Los Angeles; Mrs John H Swain, same
      Alma Louise Pedraita 1902-1963; Cayucos cem; m. @18 of Cayucos

F: Louis G Pedraita 1864-1930; M: Anita Parracini 1867-1944
- d. Guy Thomas Swain 1893- (1986 Idaho?); in Paso Robles 1938
- e. John Henry Swain 1897-1955; Cayucos cem. in Templeton 1938
    - m. SLO 10 Dec 1919 by P M O'Flynn, Cath, L156
        - it: Peter J Tartaglia, Cayucos; Edith Tartaglia, Cayucos
    - Sila L Tartaglia 1901-1983; (Cayucos cem?) in Taft 1945
        - F: Placido Tartaglia 1854-1945; M: Roselia Maria Berguglia 1855-1943
    - = Wanda Mae

3. Charles Henry Swain      b. Petaluma Jan 1858; m. @25 of Cayucos
                                               d. SLO co 6 Jan 1934 @76, auto accident, York Mtn Rd
                                               story *SLO Daily Telegram* Fri Dec 7 p.1 (sic); rPR
    - 1892 GR: 34 5'11 fair grey br f CA Cayucos
    - 1896: sentenced to 7y Folsom st prison for cattle stealing      –*SLO Tribune* Jan 9; also T Jan 4
        - (others involved: Baz Taylor, Irwin Swain, cousin, Rbt Taylor, Chas Beauchamp, Hjalmar Peterson). See below
    - 1900 cen: Prisoner, Folsom
    - 1910 cen: Santa Maria w/W J Wylie
        - m. Adelaida 4 Apr 1883 by J S Jones MG, A542; wit: S P Sitton, Adelaida; E Carpenter, SLO. Consent of bride's father, S B Whitsett, duly obtained. Divorced
    - Nannie C Whitsett      b. CA c1867; m. @16 of Adelaida
                                             d.
    - a. William Swain 1883 (cen) (1884-1969)?; in Adelaida 1934

4. Ellen Frances Swain      b. Petaluma 1859; m. @23
    - 1927, 1938: in Templeton      d. 16 May 1946; IOOF cem SLO; no obit found
        - m. Nipomo Mills 20 Nov 1881 by B F Whittemore, C P ch, A454
            - wit: George Popp, Nipomo Mills; Henry C Findley, Arroyo Grande
    - Robert Francis Fruits      b. IA 23 Aug 1850; m. @30 of Huasna
    - "Frank"      d. at home of nc Mary J Lowe, wid of Dawson Lowe,
    - 1880 cen: Huasna, w/bro Geo      SLO, 24 Mar 1910 @59/7/3; IOOF cem SLO,
    - 1892 GR: 42 5'10¾ fair br br      rTempleton. Bright's disease; obit SLO Daily Tribune
    - scar left wrist f IA Cayucos      Fri Mar 25, Mar 26 p.1; Also *Paso Robles Record*
    - 1900 cen: Morro tp      F: Jacob Fruits (remarried 1859; see *Sonoma*
    - 1902 GR: Cholame pct 52      *Searcher*, Sonoma Gen Soc)
    - PO SLO
    - 1910 pall bearers: Chris Anholm, A Cheda, H N Hansen, A Nelson, H H Carpenter, H Logan
    - a. George Alexander Fruits 1882-1927; Templeton cem; m. @31 of Templeton
        - 1912 Dir: Templeton. Bio M/H 803
            - m. SLO 31 Mar 1915 by Edw J Riordan, Cath, L352
                - wit: Hewett E Schulze, SLO; Will H Schulze, SLO
        - Zella Mae Bierer 1896-1952; Templeton cem; m. @18, of Templeton
            - F: Benjamin B Bierer 1863-1944; M: Mary Cecilia Millman 1875-1957
        - = 2 sons
    - b. Walter Garnet Fruits 1883-
        - 1912 Dir: Morro, dairy; 1917: SM, driller; 1918,1921: Los Alamos
            - m. after 1922
        - Edorina (Dora) M Confaglia (1894-1983); 1922-3 Dir: Los Alamos, single
            - 1937: in Fullerton
            - F: Peter Confaglia 1864-1937; M: Josephine 1873-1935
        - = W G Fruits jr bur SM cem 1926 @5 mos
    - c. Robert Ernest Fruits 1885-1955; IOOF cem SLO; 1912 Dir: Templeton

    d.    Henry Clarence Fruits 1888-1973; IOOF cem SLO; 1917: SM tool dresser,
           1921: Casmalia
           H C Fruits, Def, Myrtle N Fruits, Plntf, case 8025, Feb 20 1928, SLO Bk.P 458
    e.    Mary Elizabeth Fruits d. 16 May 1893 @7m25d; Cayucos cem

5.    Alice Louise Swain                  b. Petaluma Mar 1860; m of Cayucos
                                               d. living in Prosser WA 1927
        m. SLO 2 Apr 1894 by V A Gregg, Judge, D409
           wit: John A Kimball, A M Graves, SLO
    Charles Henry Rock                b. WI Apr 1855; m. of Cayucos
      1900 cen: Morro tp;                 d. Los Angeles 29 May 1927 @72; shot during gas
      6 births 5 living                        station holdup –Hawn
    a.    Morris Rock 1893-1985
    b.    Leland Rock 1894-               A descendant of this family is Ruby Hawn,
    c.    Ferndale Rock 1897-1979       333½ Hawthorn, Kelso WA 98626 (1993)
    d.    Betsy Rock 1898-
    e.    Jessie Ann Rock 1899-

6.    Annie Sarah Swain 1870-1968; see Morrison chart
7.    Mary Anges Swain                  b. 1872
                                               d. 1889 @18; Cayucos cem

A descendant of this family is Ruby Hawn, Kelso WA (1993)

# TILLEY

Justin J Tilley  b. England Nov 1860
  d. Los Angeles 6 May 1937 @77  Henry & Parnell
  1900: 637 E 29th LA  attended the funeral  - T May 10 p.3
  1910: enumerated twice: in LA & w/Alonzo Lapham, San Bernardino
  1920: 612 E 28th LA, brother w/Edith McMurray
  m.
Margaret J Pena  b. CA Sep 1862
  1920: 662½ Burlington av LA  d. Los Angeles Feb 1940; obit Feb 12 p.1
1. Nellie  b. CA June 1884
    m. after 1910
  Charles Graves  b. NY c1887
    a. Helen  b. CA c1913
      1920: w/Margaret
        in Los Angeles 1940, in Inglewood 1958
2. Jesse J  b. CA June 1886
    1920: 720 Clara, LA  d. Los Angeles co 11-18-1955; in LA 1940
  Ruth  b. AZ 1887
    a. Charles  b. CA 1910
    b. Jack  b. CA 1912
    c. Jesslyn  b. CA 1914
3. William W  b. CA Aug 1888
    1920: 1110 Ingraham LA  d. Los Angeles 4 Aug 1941; notice Aug 5
  Mabel A  b. CA 1894
4. Henry Leroy  b. Los Angeles 27 March 1890
    to SM 1915  d. Santa Maria 6 Aug 1958 @68/4/19; SM cem
    1920: Betteravia  obit Thu Aug 7 p.1; photo; bio *Who's Who SM*
      m. 17 March 1918
    Helen Lois Parnell   1897-1978; see Parnell chart
      a. Parnell Waldon  b. 2 Aug 1920
5. Fay  m. after 1920  b. CA 1905
  Harold Yount
    (in Los Angeles 1940; in Hollywood 1958)

# TOY
## SANTA MARIA VALLEY PIONEERS

| | |
|---|---|
| Hugh Daniel Toy | b. Wilmington, DE 5 Apr 1853 |
| | d. Orcutt, CA 3 Oct 1944 @91 SM cem |
| | F. Cornelius 1813-1881(Daniel² Alexander¹) |
| | M. Rebecca Rusk 1823-1886 |
| m. Storm Lake, IA 1877 | |
| Laura A Mudgett | b. nr Bangor, ME 5 Oct 1856 (census: Nov 1854) |
| | d. Orcutt, CA 20 Nov 1946 @91 SM cem |
| | F. Samuel Mudgett 1829-1907 |
| | M. Sarah E 1832-1909 (stone 1910) |
| 1. Zelia Anna | b. Storm Lake, IA 7 Mar 1878 |
| | d. Santa Maria 7 Apr 1979 @101; SM cem |
| m. Arroyo Grande 4 June 1903 | |
| George Christopher Cook | b. Bloomington, IL 9 Dec 1876 |
| | d. Salem, OR 7 Oct 1968 |
| a. Mariellen | b. Nipomo, CA 1904 |
| | d. Gustine, CA 1940 |
| m. Charles Mitchell 1930 | |
| b. George Daniel | b. Orcutt, CA 1907 |
| m. Dessa Tedrow Kehl 1937 | |
| 2. Susan Maud | b. Bodie, CA 22 Jul 1880 |
| | d. Fresno, CA 5 Aug 1975 |
| m. after 1912 | |
| Rex Arnold | d. Fresno, CA 26 Jan 1957 |
| a. Joseph Reginald | b. 1918; killed 1943 |
| b. Marjory Ann | b. 1922 Stockton, CA |
| c. Hugh Augustus | b. 1924 Fresno, CA |
| m. Gerry Park 1948 | |
| 3. Rebecca Blanch | b. Santa Maria Valley 7 Sep 1887 |
| | d. Arroyo Grande, CA 3 Aug 1977 |
| m.1 Santa Maria 22 Jul 1913; divorced | |
| Laman Lorenzo Twyford | b. Sistersville, WV 2 Oct 1880 |
| | d. Orcutt, CA 11 May 1958 |
| a. Harold Loren | b. Santa Maria 1914 |
| m. Maurine Bakeman | |
| b. Paul Reginald | b. Santa Maria 1916 |
| m. Norma L Fagerbourg | |
| m.2 bef 1944 | |
| _____ McGuire | |
| 4. Hugh Daniel, jr | b. Washington dist. 2 Jul 1890 (*SM Times*) |
| | d. Santa Maria 29 Mar 1979; SM cem |
| m. @23 yrs. of Orcutt; 26 Apr 1914; E M Crandall ME ch SM | |
| Alice Beatrice Wylie | b. Santa Maria 21 Aug 1889/90; m. @23 |
| | d. 13 Jan 1970; Santa Maria |
| | F. Richard Columbus Wylie 1867-1945 |
| | M. Joanna Leonard 1865-1935 |
| 5. Fred Cornelius | b. Santa Maria Valley 4 Apr 1893 m. @23 of Betteravia |
| | d. Santa Maria 23 Oct 1988; SM cem |

m.3 Jun 1916, San Luis Obispo, CA, Chas B Allen, ME ch, J554
     wit: Mrs L A Lambert & Mrs H D Toy of SM
  Bessie Irene Lambert            b. Paso Robles, CA 4 Oct 1897; m. @19 of SM
                                        d. Santa Maria 1 Sep 1984 @87; SM cem
                                        F. Louis Lambert 1866-1927
                                        M. Martha Ellen Matney 1875-1918
  a. Pauline Rachel                b. Betteravia 1917
       m. Wm J C Stubblefield 12 Sep 1911-Jun 1971
  b. Helen Elizabeth             b. Santa Maria, CA 1920
       m. Edward Niverth Goodchild 1940
  c. Neil Lambert                 b. Santa Maria 1935
        m.1 Anna Jewel Kelly
        m.2 Yolanda J Acton 1974
6. Carl Samuel                    b. Santa Maria Valley 1 Dec 1898
                                 d. Bakersfield 9 Apr 1988
    m. 18 Sep 1919 Rev A J Hughes; Santa Barbara home of bride's grandmother,
          Mrs E Crist (*SM Times*)
  Alice Georgia Day            b. 9 Feb 1901, Lompoc, CA
                                 d. 23 Jan 1969 Pismo Beach? CA
                                 F. George Warren Day; b. MO
                                 M. Eunice Brown 1880-1963
  a. William Hugh                 b. 1927
       m.1 Anna Mae Phillips 1948
       m.2 Pearl Fuson 1970
7. Paul Palmer                    b. nr Santa Maria 14 Apr 1902 (*SM Times*)
                                 d. Los Angeles, CA 23 May 1927
     m. Hilda Entner

For other members of the Toy clan, see *The Family Tree of Cornelius Toy*, by Elsie Toy Eschbach, 1986, a copy of which was presented to the SMVGS&L by Pauline Stubblefield in 1987, and from which some of the above was gathered.

Biography of Dan Toy in *History of Santa Barbara County*, Storke 1891 p 401. Also see *San Ramon Chapel Pioneers*, Ontiveros; for Goodchild genealogy, and references to Zelia Cook, teacher.

Thanks to Myra Manfrina of Lompoc Historical Society for information on the Day family.

## THE TOY FAMILY SCRAPBOOK

1907    Card Of Thanks. We take this means of expressing our gratitude to the many kind friends who assisted us during the illness and death of our beloved parent. Mrs L A Toy & family.
                                                                                                                                      (*SM Times* Jun 1)
*Ed Note*: Samuel Mudgett was buried in Santa Maria Cem. 5 May.

1909    Dan Toy was caller here from San Luis Obispo this week where his family is now residing, while the children are attending the Polytechnic school.                         -Ibid Nov 7

1918    Well Known Local Woman Passes
Martha Ellen Lambert, beloved wife of Louis A Lambert, passed away most suddenly on Tuesday. Death was due to heart failure, and the news of her demise was a great shock…Mrs Lambert was 42 yrs of age, and besides her husband leaves three daughters, Mrs Mabel Olivers (sic), Mrs Bessie Toy

and Mrs Gladys Grey. She also leaves two sisters and two brothers, being Mrs Myrtle German and Mrs Emma Harrington and J R & Archie Matney, the latter residing in Creston.

The funeral took place on Thursday from the family residence where services were conducted by the Rev J Walter Jordan. -Ibid Sat Jan 26 pg1

1918 CAP: Why is Carl Toy more patriotic in saving light than the rest of us? COON: Search me! CAP: Because he sometimes has a Day at night! -SMUHS *Review* pg 31, "Hits and Misses"

1919 Couple Are Married in Santa Barbara
A romance which was begun in the local high school when the two parties were students together culminated in a wedding last evening at 7 o'clock when Miss Alice Day became the bride of Carl S Toy at the home of Miss Day's grandmother, Mrs E Christ, 623 Castinllo (sic) street, Santa Barbara. Miss Day is the daughter of Mrs W J Brown of Santa Maria. She was one of the popular graduates of the June class of the local high school. Mr Toy is the son of Mr and Mrs Dan Toy, of the Orcutt road. He was prominent in high school athletics and affairs. Only the immediate families of the young couple were present at the wedding. Following a honeymoon in Los Angeles, they will make their home in Orcutt. -*SM Times* Fri Sep 19

Court News: Marriage Certificates: Carl Samuel Toy and Alice Georgia Day in Santa Barbara by Rev A J Hughes. -Ibid Mon Sep 22

1944 Hugh D Toy, 91 Passes Away - Lived in Valley for Past 61 years.
Death came yesterday to Hugh Daniel Toy, 91, known throughout the valley he helped to develop, as "Dan". Sixty-one years ago Toy and his young wife, Laura A Mudgett Toy, came to Santa Maria and settled near Orcutt, where he engaged in farming 160 acres where the Santa Maria Army Airfield is now situated.

Many of the Eucalyptus trees of that area, and the rows of Eucalyptus which line almost all of the road from Santa Maria (then Central City) to Orcutt were planted by this pioneer. A son recalled today that his father had told him of coming into Santa Maria by wagon and team to shop, and on every trip, taking along a load of young plants, to set out along the way.

Here 61 Years
Born in Wilmington, DE Apr 5, 1853, Toy married at the age of 24 in Storm Lake, Iowa. A year later the couple came to Mono County and 61 years ago to Santa Maria Valley.

In 1913, Toy retired from active farming and moved to Los Angeles, where he and his wife lived for ten years. The Toys then purchased farmland near Orcutt and until recently, have spent their time between Los Angeles and their Orcutt home.

Widow, 89, Survives
The widow, now 89, survives. Others surviving are three sons, Hugh D Toy and Fred C Toy of Santa Maria, and Carl S Toy, Bakersfield, and three daughters, Rebecca B McGuire, Los Angeles, Susan M Arnold, Fresno, and Zelia A Cook, Santa Maria. Another son, Paul died in 1927. There are also nine grandchildren and five great grandchildren.

Deceased was a charter member of Santa Maria Lodge #90 Knights of Pythias, becoming a life member last year. The lodge will conduct graveside services and interment will follow in Santa Maria Cemetery. -(*SM Daily Times* Wed Oct 4, pp 1,2)

1946 Death Claims Valley Pioneer – Mrs L A Toy, 91, Came Here in 1883
Death claimed Mrs Laura A Toy, 91, one of Santa Maria Valley's oldest pioneers, in her home west of Orcutt yesterday after a year's illness.

Funeral services will be held in the chapel of the Magner Funeral Home at 2 PM tomorrow with Rev Roy O Yountz officiating. Interment will be in the Santa Maria Cemetery.

Mrs Toy was a resident of Santa Maria Valley for 63 years, having moved here in 1883 with her husband, the late Hugh Daniels (sic) Toy, who died here two years ago at the age of 91.

Mrs Toy was born near Bangor ME, Oct 5, (no yr given) the daughter of the late Mr & Mrs Samuel Mudgett. In 1871 she moved to Iowa with her parents, marrying Toy there in 1877. As a girl she was a district school teacher for a time, and a member of Eastern Star Lodge.

### Settled Near Orcutt

In 1878, the Toys came to California, settling in Mono county, and in 1883 they moved to Santa Maria Valley. They settled on property south of Santa Maria near Mrs Toy's parents, the Mudgetts, who had come in 1880.

She was the mother of seven children, Mrs Zelia Cook of Orcutt, Mrs Susan M Arnold of Fresno, Mrs Rebecca McGuire of Los Angeles, Hugh D Toy jr of Santa Maria, Fred C Toy of Orcutt, Carl S Toy of Avenal and Paul P Toy, deceased. Eight grandchildren and eight great grandchildren survive her. Another grandson, J R Arnold, was killed in service.

Pallbearers at the service tomorrow will be the three surviving sons, Fred, Hugh and Carl Toy, two grandsons, Paul Twyford and Daniel Cook and a son-in-law, Rex Arnold.

*-SM Times* Thu Nov 21 pg1

1888    How Strawberries do in Santa Maria Valley

Mr Editor: - I fully agree with you on the strawberry question that they should not be considered a luxury. As for example, I will give you an idea of the immense yield of a small patch on my place, 4 miles south of Santa Maria. Only one and two years old and no irrigation except as furnished by nature, in the way of rains. My patch consists of 14 rows, 110 feet long. On Saturday last I picked 42 pounds. Many of the berries measure from 3 ½ to 4 ½ inches in circumference. Black berries also do well. I have only a small patch from which I sold several good sized buckets full last season, having plenty for canning and drying for family use. What I have done I know others can do.

D. Toy                                                                             *-SM Times* Sat May 12

*Ed. Note*: It is fitting that some of Toy's acreage, lying between the Orcutt Expressway and the airport, having lain fallow for some years, has recently been planted to strawberries. Much of the acreage southeast of Santa Maria, as viewed from Highway 101, has been producing strawberries for a number of years; one wonders what Messrs Toy and Wiley would say about the method of cultivation.

1992    What We 'Ear

Skaters of the Ice Capades are entertaining audiences in China these days, thanks to Greg Toy of Santa Maria.

Toy is the Ice Capades' "ice maker" according to his aunt, Pauline Stubblefield, of Santa Maria. His father, Neal Toy, also lives in Santa Maria.

Another brother, David Toy, works as an ice maker for the Capades out of Palm Springs.

Greg Toy formerly worked for the company in San Mateo, before leaving in June for the tour in China. He is expected back in California around Sept. 1.      *-SM Times* Aug 18 pg.A-2

**Corrections and Additions** [Page numbers refer to those in Quarterly]

p.14. Quite a serious accident happened to Mrs S Mudgett at her home south of town on Sunday last. While chasing a chicken with the assistance of their large dog he ran against the lady throwing her to the ground which resulted in breaking the bones in her right leg just above the ankle. Dr Bagby was called and gave the limb its proper dressing and at last account the patient was getting along nicely. —Feb 25 1888

Marriage: Zelia Ann Toy @25 of Santa Maria in Arroyo Grande 6 (not 4) June 1903 by Samuel S Sampson, MG, F487; wit: Bertha L Sampson, Arroyo Grande; Stella Arwine, Arroyo Grande.

George C Cook @26 of Nipomo.

Marriage: Paul Reginald Twyford and Norma L Fagerbourg at the home of Harold L Twyford, 520 E El Camino, Santa Maria, by R Banes Anderson, Presbyterian. Her parents, Lyle and Ruth Fagerbourg of rural Santa Maria, sister Louise. —Aug 5 (or 8?) 1941

Paul and Norma's son Thomas L Twyford, born in Santa Maria 2 Oct 1944, grad SMUHS 1962, died in Vietnam. Older brother Ronny, uncle and aunt, Mr & Mrs Clark Willett, Arroyo Grande. —Wed Nov 6 1968 p.2

Louise Fagerbourg Jenkins died in York PA 2 May 1995. Born in Rocky Ford CO, parents Lionel and Ruth Robb Fagerbourg. Raised and educated in Santa Maria. Survived by daughters Cheryl Bahn, Parsippany NJ and Joanne Lynam, Brodbecks PA; 4 gch; brother, Neil Fagerbourg, Santa Maria; sisters Norma Twyford, Grover Beach; Barbara Willett, Arroyo Grande; Marilyn Kies, Cobb Mountain CA. Services were held at Hayshire Church of Christ, Manchester township, PA
—Thu May 11 1995 A-11

Fagerbourgs in Santa Maria cemetery record:
Helen C d. Aug 16 1972 @71/9/10
Blenda buried Jan 16 1943 @79/11/15
Carl Bertil d. Aug 13 1961 @63/7/20
Lionel A d. Mar 31 1955 @65/6/5
Ruth H d. Mar 2 1979 @86/6/26

p.15 Fred Toy and Bessie Lambert, she a linotype operator for the *Santa Maria Times*, took their wedding trip to Los Angeles and San Diego. —June 10 1916

Bessie's mother was Martha Ellen Matney, daughter of Carl/Carrol Sumner Matney, 1850-1912 born in OR after his father, Carl Matney, arrived there from the east, according to the bio of Jackson Rodkey Matney in Morrison & Haydon p.819. Martha's mother was Terah Ellen Patterson 1858-1915, daughter of Joseph Patterson whose 1892 voter registration shows him in Josephine, SLO co @69. C S and Terah had six children; besides Jack 1877-1955 and Martha there were Archie, Emery A 1880-1915, Myrtle 1890-1974 (Andrew German), and Emma (Garth H Harrington).

# TRAVERS
## CANADIANS TO CALIFORNIA

Boyle Travers          b. (ENG)
                                   d. (Milwaukee WI)? 1890s?
    m. (Bay City) Canada c1816
Hannah Laraway         b. Bay City 15 April 1799
                                   d. at home of dau Mrs Rbt Abernethy, Guadalupe
                                           14 Sep 1895 @96/4/29
                                               obit Sep 21; 13 ch 10 grew up; 4 son 2 dau survive
                                               to CA 1892 from Milwaukee & Canada

Survivors:
1.     Charles Travers
        1895 in Milwawkee
2.     Caroline P Travers           b. CAN 6 July 1822
                                     d. Spokane WA 28 June 1912 @90; Guad cem
         m.
     Robert Abernethy 1815-1890; see Abernethy chart
3.     James Travers
        1895 in Milwaukee
4.     William Travers
        1895 in St Louis
        living 1912
5.     Robert Travers                b. CAN 1839 London, Ontario 23 Oct 1840 (?)
        to Milwaukee @3             d. Santa Maria 21 July 1907 @67/8/29; bur San Diego
          1885. Robert Travers, new        obit July 27 p.1; photo; wid, son, neph; plumber,
            hardware store in Bradley        laundry, confectionery. Card of Thanks
            bldg; Louis Mau later              m.2 of SM
            became partner. –*Valley*
        1887 to San Diego
        1890 GR: Robert 51 CAN tinner SM #2 by virtue of na of F; reg Sep 22
        1906 Dir: Robert, Ice Cream Parlor & Confectionery cor Church & Bwy; Charlotte Mrs
           (1906 Dir): Mau L C Hardware, Crockery and plumbing, Main st.
        1909 Dir: Mrs Charlotte, ladies suits r E Chapel
           m.1
       ? Unknown                       d. San Diego
      a.    son in Chicago
          survived father
              m.2 San Francisco 3 Sep 1890 (*Times*)
      Mrs Lottie Zelluff             b.         m. of Ottawa IL
                                     d.
       Zeluff Rae m. of Santa Maria
         m. Hotel Ramona, SLO by Rev Dr Summers 21 Apr 1891 (*Times*)
       Herndon Samuel L m. of Santa Maria d. c37; bur 27 June 1898 SM cem
          1890 GR: Samuel Louis Herndon 27 MO rancher Santa Ynez; reg Oct 6
6.     Harriet Travers Crummery
        1895 in SF

Thomas Francis Travers  b. Avondale NJ 1 Dec 1868
  1922-3 Dir: Thos F frmn mv to  d. Santa Maria 26 Apr 1954 @85/4/25; SM cem
    Orcutt from Sisquoc dist  M: Murphy
  Orcutt: Thos F Prod frmn    obit Tue Apr 27 p.8; to SM 1904
    Union Oil co    Master Mason, Wessington SD 1913
  1925 Dir: Orcutt: Thos foreman    retired from Union Oil 1928; to Buena Park; back to
  1928 Dir: T F dist foreman UO co    SM 1951; wid 2 ch 5gch
    Orcutt
  1954. pall bearers: Robert Bruce, Rodney Rojas, Arthur Howard, Erwin Mitchell, Irwin
    McMillan, Phillip McMillan   gch: Elizabeth & Bruce Travers, San Leandro; Karen &
    Janice Travers, Diane Scott, Buena Park
      m.
Marguerite Emma Ellis  b. Pakenham, Ontario, CAN 19 Oct 1873
  ME ch SM  d. Orange CA 25 Aug 1957 @83/10/6 SM cem
    obit Mon Aug 26 p.8; res Cat Canyon many years
    son, dau 5gch bro Albert B Ellis, Centralia WA
  1957: gch: Elizabeth & Bruce Travers, San Leandro; Karen, Janice & Diane Travers, Buena
    Park

1.    Jean Travers  b. CA 1 Sep 1910
    1940-1 Dir: Jean Travers  d. Santa Maria 30 Apr 1987 @77; SM cem
      tchr grammar sch    obit Sun Dec 20 p.30 (sic); BS Whittier College;
      h416-A W Cook    MS USC; teacher 40y; bro, n/n
        m.
    Yancy Thomas O'Neill  b. Templeton CA 18 Nov 1906
    1927 Cal Poly  d. Santa Maria 30 Apr 1984 @77/5/12; SM cem
    1947-8 Dir: Yancy T (Jean T)  F: Timothy O'Neill d. 1930
      mech USCCA*  M: Lulu York dau of Andrew York; York Mtn
      h829 E Boone    Vineyards; obit Wed May 2 p.21; to SM 1940
      Jean T tchr r829 E Boone    worked for Roemer Hdwr. wid, 3 sis, n/n
    1955-6 Dir: Yancy T (Jean F) fmrn La Brea Gar h801 E Central
      Jean tchr Fairlawn sch r801 E Central
    1972 Dir: O'Neill Yancy T (Jean J) ret h801 E Central
    1984: sisters Marguerite Abbey, SLO; Doris Greenelsh, SM; Helen Peasley, Paso Robles,
      d. 1986
        1982 Dir: Greenelsh Doris K supvr K-Mart h3888 Angeles rd SM
*USC College of Aeronautics (Hancock Field)

2.    Earl R Travers
    1954, 1957, 1987 in Buena Park

Vol. XXXIV, No. 2, Summer 2002, p.13


**Corrections and Additions**     [Page numbers refer to those in Quarterly]

p. 12
1890     Guadalupe Items. Robert Travers of San Diego is visiting his brother-in-law and sister,
       M/M Robert Abernethy.   -May 3
1890     Surprise Party…Robert Travers' birthday…   -Oct 25
1896     R Travers is up from the Summerland oil fields…   -Jan 18


Vol. XXXIV, No. 3, Fall 2002, p.21

1900     ad. Travers and Mau General Hardware etc.

1905     Ice Cream Made Fresh Every Day…Travers' Candy Kitchen…           -ad May 27
Travers stated that she is now ready to take orders for all kinds of fruit trees and plants.

1908     Mrs Travers has the agency for the San Dimas Nursery which took the gold medal at St Louis and Portland fairs. Mrs Travers guarantees all trees sold from this nursery. Mrs Travers stated that she is now ready to take orders for all kinds of fruit trees and plants.

1911     Mrs Lottie Travers married at the residence of Mrs Wm Trumbull, 519 E 4th, Los Angeles Tuesday, William Roberts, of an old Virginia family; they are to live at 3606 C st, San Diego.          –Dec 16

For Trumbull see Stowell chart. Mrs Wm Trumbull = Grace Stowell, dau of Frank Stowell & Mary J Hopper.

## A SURPRISE PARTY
### An Enjoyable Evening Passed at the Residence of Mr Travers

     Another one of those social events that the people of Santa Maria are noted for, took place at the residence of Mr Robert Travers, Thursday evening. It was a surprise party and the occasion was Mr T's birthday; and right royally did he enjoy it - with his comely bride, of a couple of months, sitting on his right and his queenly mother, ninety-one years of age, on his left, who looks to be good for several years yet and no one enjoyed the occasion more than she did.

     At nine o-clock the guests were invited into the dining room and seated at a table loaded with everything good; showing that notwithstanding Mrs Travers being a stranger in Santa Maria she is no stranger to the culinary department. After doing ample justice to the various toothsome dishes the party adjourned to the parlor where they were entertained with music, both vocal and instrumental.

     Miss Zeluff, daughter of the hostess, added greatly to the enjoyment of the occasion; being a fine elocutionist and musician.

     The party broke up at eleven o'clock all feeling that they had enjoyed the surprise party most heartily. The following were present on this occasion.

     M/M Robert Travers, Rev and Mrs Sewell, M/M Caleb Sherman, M/M A H Orr, M/M McNeil, M/M Chas Goodfellow, M/M P W Jones, M/M I N McGuire, Mrs Ketcham, Mrs John McMillan, Grandma Travers, Misses Julia Merritt, Lou Culp, Mille Gwin, Bell Fugler, Miss Fine, and Miss Zeluff. Messrs Thos Sedgwick, Frank Smith and Asbury Cox.          -Oct 25 1890

# TUREK
## TRANSPLANTED CHICAGOANS

| | | |
|---|---|---|
| Charles Alois Turek | b. | Bohemia Apr 1859; imm 1883; na 1889 |
| | d. | Santa Maria CA 28 Oct 1925 @67 |
| | | obit Wed Oct 28 p.1; bur Los Angeles |

Chicago Dir:
1889: Chas A marble 659 Allport
1895: Chas A monuments N 40th Av nr North Branch; h W Ainslie nr N 40th
1897: not found;   1900: Chas A stonecutter h 1372 S Troy; 1900 cen: same
1910: to Santa Maria from Wichita Falls
1915: City Happenings. C A Turek left Wed for Portland where he will erect two large monuments in that city.   -July 17
1918: Epitome of the Week. C A Turek who was severely injured some time ago by a monument falling on his leg...big gash...considerably improved...up again with the aid of a cane.   –Mar 23
1920 cen: 208 W Jones, SM;   1922 Dir: same
1922 Dir: Marble & Granite Wks, W Main St next to Massey Hotel;
   Massey Hotel 221 W Main St
      m.2 c1898

| | | |
|---|---|---|
| Katherine/Katrina T (Dvorak) | b. | Bohemia Dec 1865; imm 1891-2 |
| | d. | (not found in CA Death Index) |

Chicago Dir:
1895: Dvorak Katie wd John  h 285 N Centre Av
1897: Dvorak Catherine wd John  h 859 N Kedzie Av
1937 Dir: Turek Kath wd Chas  r 208 Falcon, Long Beach CA (w/son)
   (not found in 1940 Long Beach Dir)
1900 cen: 10 births, 10 living

By first wife:

| | | |
|---|---|---|
| 1. Mary (Bishop) | b. | (Chicago) IL June 1885 (cen) |
| | d. | (before 1972) (living in Jones, MI 1925) |
| 2. Charles | b. | (Chicago) IL Mar 1886 (cen) |
| | d. | (before 1972) (living in Chicago 1925) |
| 3. Elizabeth (McLaughlin) | b. | (Chicago) IL May 1890 (cen) |
| (Bessie) | d. | (before 1972) (living in Chicago 1925) |
| 4. Louis C | b. | (Chicago) IL Mar 1893; SSDI |
| | d. | Santa Maria 27 Feb 1980; no obit found |

1917: Eight Enlist in Marine Corp (sic)...Chas Howard, Louis Turek, Geo Kemp, Erving Thornberg, Dott Weber, Santa Maria; Ira Murphy, Harvey Lowler, Betteravia; Nanton Silva, Oxnard.   -May 19
1917: City Briefs. Louis Turek & Chas Howard, two of Santa Maria's volunteers, here on brief furlough...hard training since they enlisted...look well hardened. They anticipate their going abroad shortly...in high spirits.   -Aug 11
1918: Louis Turek & Chas Hackett of this city in Galveston, TX...Marine Corps...
   -25 Years Ago, Tue Mar 30 1943
1918: Louis Turek, who is wearing Uncle Sam's uniform in defense of the flag...brief furlough...expects to be sent to France shortly...large number of Santa Maria boys in the Army...all doing nicely...   -June 23
1919: Sgt Louis Turek home from Galveston...   -Mar 19
1920 cen: w/parents, painter;   1922 Dir: same
1939: Louis Turek building house on 100 block Bonita St   -date lost

1926 Dir: r 407 W Lemon; 1928, 1938, 1940: same (1940: w/H E Small, bldg contr)
: *Note:* concrete driveway at 625 E Tunnell stamped H E Small, contr; curb stamped F H Gates, contr. See Gates chart.
1942: built house 625 E Tunnell; sold 1987 to Susan Stever; sold 1988 to Joel and Kathleen Cole Wilson (daughter of Barbara Cole)
1945-6 Dir: Painting contr 625 E Tunnell
: m. c1924

| | |
|---|---|
| Ruby P L | b. Tylertown MS 27 Mar 1901; SSDI |
| 1955-6 Dir: slslady, Mae Moore's Smart Wearing Apparel | d. Hurst TX 23 June 1989 @88; to Hurst Apr 1987 obit Tue July 18; 64 yrs SM |
| a. Vernon L | b. (Santa Maria) c1925 |
| SMUHS 1942; Navy WWII | d. (living in Hurst TX 1986, 1989) |

=dau =son

| | |
|---|---|
| b. David P | b. Santa Maria 6 Oct 1929 |
| SMUHS 1947 | d. Santa Maria 22 Nov 1986 @57 |
| MSgt USAF 20yrs | obit Tue Nov 25 p.10 |

1971 phbk: 615 S Lincoln;  1974 phbk: same Bail Bonds
1982 Dir: Dave Turek bail bondsman h509 E Park Apt 1

| | |
|---|---|
| 5. Eleanor/Ella B | b. Chicago 29 Nov 1895; m. @21 |
| OES | d. Santa Maria 15 June 1972; SSDI obit Sat June 17 p.4; res 227 E Tunnell |

1916: Mrs G S Brown & Miss Eleanor Turek spent the weekend visiting in
: San Luis Obispo.                                                                                          -Sept 23
1917: Ella Turek & sister Mrs Albert Schaffenberg of Chicago…                           -Aug 18
1917 phbk: Miss 208 W Jones
1922 Dir: bkpr Parnell's (groc)
1955-6 Dir: clk Roemer & Rubel (Buick dealer)
1972 survivors: brothers Louis and Jerry Turek, Santa Maria; sisters Mrs Sylvia Averdick, Mrs Zeona Paoli, San Francisco; Mrs Mildred B Coon, Lompoc
: m. San Luis Obispo 26 Sep 1917 by J D Habbick, K255
:: wit: H C Graham, Santa Maria; Mrs J D Habbick, SLO

| | |
|---|---|
| Theodore Joseph Holland | b. Ventura CA 22 Nov 1890; m. @26 of SM |
| 1922 Dir: pntr r310 E Fesler | d. Santa Maria 3 Dec 1959 |
| 1940-1 Dir: not found | obit Dec 4 |
| 1945-6 Dir: Ella T clk | F: Patrick J Holland 1858-1941 |
| WP&RB h227 E Tunnell | M: (Marie S 1873-1915)? |

1951-2 Dir: Theo J (Ella T) pntr h227 E Tunnell;     1955-6 Dir: same
1959: survivors: wife, siblings all in Santa Barbara: C J Holland, Mrs Herbert Franze (sic), Mrs Loretta Williams, Mrs Victor Managan
: WWI, American Legion, NSGW, BPOE, F&AM, Painters Local

By second wife, Katherine (Dvorak)

| | |
|---|---|
| 6. (Bonaslave) | b. (Chicago) IL Apr 1899 (cen) no other data |
| 7. Sylvia Violet | b. (Chicago) IL (not on 1900 cen) m. @18 of SM |
| | d. (living in Honolulu 1925, SF 1972) |

1917: Miss Sylvia Turek accepted a position at SB Tel Co.                              -Mar 24
1917: Miss Sylvia Turek is now ticket seller at Grand Theater.                        -Apr 2
: m.1 San Luis Obispo 23 May 1917 by Wm Mallagh JP, K166
:: wit: R R Hankenson, SLO; H D Becker, SLO. Also *SLO Daily Tribune* May 24

| | |
|---|---|
| Otto Thornton Tulloh | b. (SLO co) 20 May 1891; m. @26 of Casmalia |
|   1922 Dir: candyman, SM | d. (San Mateo) 31 Dec 1968; SSDI |
|     Chocolate Shop |    m.2 Belle C; SS# same   d. San Mateo 1-2-79 |
|     r208 W Jones | F: Wm Anderson Tulloh 1865-1926 |
|   1917: Casmalia Oil fields | M: Margaret Roberts 1863-1930; divorced |
|   a. Thornton |    d. 24 Oct 1918 @14 days; SM cem |
|     m.2 Averdick | |
| 8. Mildred B | b. (Chicago) IL 1902 |
| | d. (living in SM 1925, Lompoc 1972) |

    m.1 Santa Barbara 9 Aug 1919 by Rev W F S Nelson (*Times*)

| | |
|---|---|
| James Woodson Edrington | b. Oso Flaco SLO co 26 Apr 1876 |
|   1900 cen: w/mother Guad | d. Santa Maria 30 Nov 1936 @60; Evergreen |
|   1909-10 SB co Dir: w/A D Pendley |    cem Lompoc; obit Mon Nov 30 p.1 |
|     pubs *Lompoc Journal* | F: Thomas Edrington 1846-18__; 1880 Oso Flaco |
| | M: Mary C   1848-1934; widow 1900 |

  1912: Jas Edrington will return to SM Monday to assume the management of the *SM Times* for a month or more while the editor takes a vacation to Portland and other northern cities.
        -Jun 29

  1919: It was a very pretty home wedding which united…Jas Edrington and Miss Mildred Turek at 8 o'clock Sat eve at the SB res of Rev Nelson…close friend of the young couple… wedding supper at the Arlington…made his home with his sister, Mrs Geo Black… popular manager of the Gaiety Theatre…bride…an unusually pretty young woman of the brunette type…will make their home in an attractive apartment on East Main St…
        -Aug 11, also 25 Years Ago, Aug 9 1944

  1920 cen: 508 E Main;  1922 Dir: musician 508 E Main
  1926 Dir: Jas W (Mildred) prop svc sta r 508 E Main
  1928 Dir: Jas lab r410 E Cook
  1936: Pioneer Editor, Musician, Passes…at *SM Times*, *Vidette*, Lompoc and Guadalupe papers…famous violinist, conducted Gaiety Theatre orchestra c1914-1922…bought Gaiety with Harvey Hite when Hite joined the army, Frank Powell became partner… Clever writer, articles copied and republished. In Garden Valley ensemble…violin repair shop 309 E Main…survived by sisters Nora Fillmore, Lompoc; Mrs Geo Black, San Francisco; brother W T Edrington, San Simeon…        -Nov 30

    m.2 Coon

| | |
|---|---|
| 9. Zeona (Pietropaoli) | b. (Chicago 1903) |
|   1923: Zeona Turek and | d. San Francisco 1-7-1992; SSDI |
|     brother Jerry visiting |    living in San Francisco 1925, 1972 |
|     relatives in Long Beach…–July 23 | |
| 10. Jerry V | b. (Chicago) 14 Feb 1905; SSDI |
|   1922 Dir: lab w/parents | d. San Francisco 20 July 1978 |
|   1925: USS Pennsylvania in Pacific waters;  1972: Santa Maria (?) | |

Children of Katherine Dvorak

| | |
|---|---|
| 1. Rose Dvorak (Klindera) | b. Bohemia Aug 1885; to US 1891 (cen) |
|   1910 Chi Dir: Dvorak Rose M | d. (living in Chicago 1925) |
|     Miss stenog h947 N Centre Av (?) | |
| 2. Ottilia/Tillie Dvorak | b. Bohemia Nov 1889 (cen) |
|   m. before 1917 | d. (living in Chicago 1925; not in Chi Dir) |
|     Albert Schaffenberg (see #5 above) (no Schaffenbergs in any Chi Dir consulted) | |

3. Anna Dvorak                        b. (Chicago) IL Dec 1891 (cen)
    1910 Chicago Dir:               d. (Living in Los Angeles 1925)
      Dvorak Anna Miss tchr h 1542 S Spaulding Av (?)
        m.1 Pickett
        m.2 25 Feb 1923; dau of C A Turek, sis of Mrs J W Edrington (*Times*)
   Stephen Tyrell of Los Angeles

4. James J Dvorak                     b. (Chicago) IL 28 Mar 1895; SSDI
                                         d. Long Beach CA 19 Dec 1966
   1916: Mrs Chas A Turek & son Jas Devorak (sic) expected to return tomorrow
     from extended visit in Chicago…                                     –July 22
   1937 Dir: Jas J (Ernestine G) oil wkr h 208 Falcon, Long Beach
   1945 Dir: JJ&E oil wkr h 1516 E 9<sup>th</sup>, Long Beach; 1966: same

Vol. XXVIII, No. 3, Fall 1996, p.10


**Corrections and Additions**        [Page numbers refer to those in Quarterly]

p.9.      Marriage: Louis Turek and Ruby Pierce of Mississippi were married in Los Angeles
Monday, reception Thursday at Tureks' on Jones St.            -25 Years Ago, Mar 18 1948

p.10.      Marriage: Zeona Turek m. @21 of SM. m. SLO 5 July 1924 by Wm Mallagh JP, N276; wit:
Mrs Jas W Edrington, SM; F P Hays, Orcutt
       Remo Petropaoli (sic) b. Italy, m. @26 of San Francisco

Vol. XXIX, No. 4, Winter 1997, p.19


p.10      Mildred B Turek Edrington m.2 Joaquin Hervie Silveira who died 5 Aug 1980 @83; son Jack in Sunnyvale 1989. Mildred m.3 Mr Conn (not Coon), and died in Lompoc @88; obit 1 Sep 1989 p.2. 5 gch 7ggch. In 1928 she was Mrs Silveira, visiting Santa Barbara with her mother, Mrs K Turek, and sister, Mrs R P Paoli (sic) and son of San Francisco.           -Sep 4

Vol. XXX No. 4, Winter 1998, p.13

# TWITCHELL
## SANTA MARIA VALLEY PIONEERS

The "Red" Twitchells of Santa Maria Valley and the "Black" Twitchells of the Sisquoc-Manzana area: both families descended from a common Puritan ancestor, Benjamin Twitchell of Massachusetts. Fremont Twitchell had auburn hair, hence "Red", but the men of the other family had fair complexions, blue eyes and brown hair, so why "Black"? No explanation is given for the appellation in *San Ramon Chapel Pioneers*, p.357

Sanford Lorenzo Twitchell and bride came to California in 1849 from Iowa; Fremont Twitchell, a single man came in 1877, also from Iowa. Lorenzo lived for many years in San Juan, in the 1880's coming south to San Luis Obispo County to settle in the York Mountain vicinity; some of his offspring numbered among those mountaineering in the Manzana area in the 1890's, scattering to other small communities after the disastrous drought late in that decade. Fremont, on the other hand, came to the Santa Maria Valley and stayed. His youngest son, "Cap", had much to do with water conservation in Santa Barbara County and in this time when water is of great concern, it is appropriate to memorialize Twitchells and their work. See Scrapbook for details

## MARTIN CARR TWITCHELL

| | |
|---|---|
| Martin Carr Twitchell | b. Montville ME 9 June 1822 |
| | d. nr Santa Maria 28 Feb 1913 @90/8/19; SM cem |
| | F: Nicholas 1780-1867 (Jacob$^5$, Moses$^4$, John$^3$, |
| |    Benjamin$^2$, Benjamin$^1$) |
| 1850: Montville, ME | M: Sarah Carr 1785-1866 |
| 1860: Linn to Dallas co, IA, PO Greenvale | |
|    m.1 24 Nov 1848; divorced | |
| Lucy A. Howard | b. (Montville) ME 4 March 1830 |
|    1880: La Graciosa w/Fremont | d. Santa Maria 25 Dec 1891 @61/9/0; Pine Grove cem |
| 1. Mary | b. Montville ME 1850; not on 1860 Census |
| 2. Harriett (Is this Mary's middle name (?): See obit of M C Twitchell) | |
| 3. Ida May | b. ME 11 Apr 1854 |
| | d. Berkeley CA 1 Aug 1931 @77 |
|    m. San Francisco 28 Jan 1888 (*SM Times*) | |
| Lazar Emanuel Blochman | b. San Francisco 1856 |
| | d. San Francisco 1946 @89 |
|    No issue; adopted two boys; see *This is Our Valley* | |
| 4. Fremont Carr | b. Waldo co ME 20 Sep 1856; m. @24 |
|    1880: La Graciosa | d. at home 10 Dec 1929 @73 |
|    1890: @33 ME farmer, La Graciosa | |
|    1892: @35 6' light complexion, blue eyes, auburn hair, ME, res La Graciosa; | |
|    PO Santa Maria | |
| 1906 Dir: 2 miles north of Orcutt | |
|    m.1 La Graciosa 15 Sep 1881 by M. Thornburg, B563 | |
|       wit: John Wilkinson, James Drumm | |
| Martha J Stubblefield | b. Sonoma Co CA 7 Feb 1864 m. @16 |
| | d. 19 May 1887 @22/3/12; Pine Grove cem |
| | F: Absalom Stubblefield 1841-1934 |
| | M: Nancy Jane Harris 1845-1930 |
| a.   May Eva | b. Twitchell Ranch 1 Sep 1882 |
| | d. Santa Barbara 5 Jan 1978; SM cem |

        1910: w/Blochmans, Santa Maria;   1920: w/Blochmans, 2434 Bowditch, Berkeley
           m.1 Charles F Coffin
           m.2 Reginald G Clifford  d. 10 Jun 1960
             No issue

b.     Frederick Martin                 b. (Twitchell ranch) 15 Nov 1884
                                                  d. Arroyo Grande 30 Nov 1973 @89
          m. Rosamond Reed           b. Boston       m. 1920
                                                  d. Sacramento co 5-1-1991 @97
                                                  SSDI, Pine Grove cem
        = Fremont G, Los Angeles co. 9-1-1982; SSDI
        = Glenn R

(4).  m.2 at res of bride's mother in the Martin district 31 Dec 1890 by Rev B F Wolfe, C30
      "Former wife Mattie Stubblefield dec."
     Ida Alice Newlove                  b. Salinas CA 23 Dec 1871; m. @19
                                              d. 1026 E Orange St. SM res of dau Mrs Lee
                                                   19 Dec 1961 @89
                                                 F: John Newlove 1832-1889
                                                 M: Maria Benyon 1838-1913

c.     Lucy Maria                             b. nr Santa Maria 29 Feb 1892 (*SM Times*)
       NDGW Parlor No. 276           d. Santa Maria 14 Nov 1979 @87
       OES Mizpah No. 100
            m. John W Lee                d. (Gilroy) 1953
     = John Ward                           b. Orcutt 14 Jun 1921
            m. Margaret                 d. Santa Maria 11 June 1981 @59/11/27;
            + Lynne (Ehlers)             SM Cem
            + Nicole (Kleinberg)
            + Stephanie (Maier)
            + Laurie

d.     Ward Newlove                       b. 14 June 1894
                                                   d. Anaheim CA 8 Aug 1917 @23/1/25
                                                 Appendicitis; SM cem (*SM Times* 11 Aug)

e.     Glenn Howard                     b. La Graciosa 14 Oct 1895 (*SM Times*)
                                                 d. nr Orcutt 3 Mar 1915 @19/4/12; SM cem
                                                  (*SM Times* 6 Mar)

f.     James Deane                        b. Graciosa dist. 3 May 1899 (*SM Times*)
            m. Merle O                    d. 4619 Orcutt Rd. 30 Dec 1959; SM cem
     = Janice (James L Dugger)
     = John A
     = Myrna L

g.     Theodore Andow "Cap"        b. nr Orcutt 26 Oct 1902
            m. Santa Maria 18 Sep 1926   d. Santa Maria 10 Aug 1955 @52
       Edwina J Zanetti                 b. 16 Dec 1901 (*SM Times*)
                                           d. Santa Maria 8 Nov 1989
     = Maurice Fremont             F: Maurice Zanetti 1867-1937
     = Burton James (Valerie V)    M: Anita C Tonini 1880-1969
     = Dennis Ward
        Marr. Lic: Dennis Ward Twitchell age 26; 157 Palm Ct Dr to Claudia Jean
           Nale age 26, 523 N College Dr *SM Times* June 20 1969

Martin Carr Twitchell    m.2 Amanda Mitchell (Healy) Rose of Thomaston ME
                            m.3 Augusta Carlton Clough 1844-1894

## MARTIN CARR TWITCHELL SCRAPBOOK

1892 Died Twitchell. At Santa Maria, Dec 25, 1892, Mrs Lucy Twitchell, aged 81 years, 9 months.

Card Of Thanks To the kind friends who have so patiently waited on our beloved mother during her recent sickness and death we acknowledge our heartfelt thanks. Ida M Blockman F C Twitchell
-*SM Times* Jan 2

1895 Frank Hall, formerly a resident of this valley is now located at Drum post office, Millard county, Utah. He is prospecting in a mining country and still has hopes of striking it rich almost any time. His old friend and neighbor F C Twitchell, sends him the TIMES for a year to keep him company in camp and to let him know what his old friends are doing. -Ibid Jan 5

1897 La Graciosa Items. F C Twitchell was unanimously elected trustee of La Graciosa school district in place of S B Miller whose term expired and who contemplates moving away this fall. -Ibid June 12

1913 M C Twitchell Passes Away   Martin Carr Twitchell passed away at the home of his son F C Twitchell near Orcutt on Friday, February 28, at the ripe old age of 90 years, 8 months, and 19 days. Notwithstanding his advanced age Mr Twitchell was enjoying excellent health up to within a few weeks ago, when by accident he fell and broke his hip. For several days it looked as if he would recover, but it was deluded hope, for complications set in, and in spite of all that could be done to save him, he passed away.

The deceased was born in Montville, Maine, June 9th 1822. In 1848 he married Lucy Howard, who was the mother of three children: Harriet, who died in infancy, Ida M, now Mrs Blochman, who was for years one of our estimable and capable high school teachers, and Fremont C, one of our substantial citizens and at present a member of the board of supervisors. In 1857 Mr Twitchell moved with his family to Redfield, Iowa, where he lived until 1906, when he joined his children in California. Mr Twitchell was a consistent believer in Spiritualism and died in the full hope that death is but the doorway to the fuller and more perfect life.

Martin Carr Twitchell was a man of excellent habits, fine moral character and one who never forgot the hospitable ways of the Pioneer. The stranger, even though a beggar, never failed to find food and shelter if he sought it at his hands. He was at home by the fireside of the sick and delighted in all kind and neighborly offices. He had plied the various relations of life, as son, husband, father and friend, and filled them well. His life's work was nobly done and the stern Reaper found him "as a shock of corn, fully ripe for the harvest."

The funeral services were held on Sunday afternoon under the auspices of Santa Maria Lodge No. 302, IOOF, Mr Twitchell having been a member in Redfield, Iowa, Odd Fellows Lodge for many years. There was a large attendance of friends at the funeral, who deeply sympathize with the bereaved members of the family. -*SM Times* Sat March 8

1915 Freeman C Twitchell, from the Fifth District of Santa Barbara County, was born in Waldo County, Maine, in 1856, the son of M C Twitchell, who was a school teacher and farmer. The family moved to Dallas county, Iowa, in 1857, where the subject of this sketch received his early education in the public schools, and at the age of sixteen years he entered upon the struggle for an independent livelihood, and his career has been characteristic of the broad, self-made, practical man of the people. Mr Twitchell first came to California in 1876, at which time he spent several months about San Francisco, after which he returned to his eastern home, and in the fall of 1877 he again came to the Pacific Coast, to make California his permanent home. His first business venture was at Oakland, where he purchased an interest in a freight boat plying between the various bay points, but after a few months in this connection he disposed of his interest in the freight boating business, and in 1878 came to Santa Maria, purchasing a quarter section of land south of town, to which he later added and improved it, much of which was devoted to stock raising, but he later disposed of all but about four hundred acres, most of which he now rents.

In September, 1881, Mr Twitchell was united in marriage with Miss Mattie Stubblefield, a native daughter of California, and they became the parents of two children, Eva May and Fred Martin Twitchell, and in May, 1887, Mrs Twitchell died of pneumonia. Mr Twitchell was married the second time, 1890, to Miss Ida A Newlove, and to this union was born one daughter and four sons.

Mr Twitchell has been active in politics for many years, having served as County Road Master, Deputy Sheriff and in 1911, was elected to serve as a member of Santa Barbara's County Board of Supervisors, for the Fifth District, and re-elected in 1914, and his conscientious demonstration of ability and courteous attention to the wants of all has endeared himself to the citizens throughout the entire county, and it is said that not even his most critical opponents have suggested a personal or official wrongdoing against Freeman C Twitchell. His rugged honesty and independence, his fidelity to the interests of his city and county, his unswerving belief in the virtue, integrity and wisdom of the people are the qualities that have caused them to trust him without question in all matters of public moment or politics. ...*Davis' Commercial Encyclopedia of the Pacific Southwest*, Davis, Oakland, p. 308, 1915

1918 ....Lt Fred Twitchell....wounded.... -*SM Times* Nov 16

1918 From Tuesday's Daily. Lt Fredk Twitchell's name appears in today's casualty list among the serverly (sic) wounded. According to letters to his father, Fremont Twitchell, of Orcutt, his son is still in a hospital in France, suffering from a bad wounded (sic) in the leg. -*SM Times* Sat. Dec. 28

1918 The *Review* May 1918 Military Number Dedication  To our former students now in the fighting force of the United States for Democracy Our Honor Roll ...Fred Twitchell...

1919 Miss May Twitchell, daughter of Fremont Twitchell, of Orcutt, has accepted a position as government reconstruction aide and is now stationed at Whipple Barracks, Arizona, working among the returned wounded soldiers. -*SM Times* Jan 11

1919 Deane Twitchell is here, from his ranch in Arizona visiting his parents, Mr and Mrs F C Twitchell of Orcutt Road. -*SM Times* Nov 13

1920 The *Review* May 1920 Football Number The *Review* Staff Edwina Zanetti, Alumni Editor.... Theodore Twitchell, Business Manager p.11

(Photos) Theodore Twitchell: Assistant *Review* Manager (1) Student Body Manager (2) Class President (2) Baseball (3) Track (3) Play Cast (3,4) Football (4) *Review* Manager (4) Edwina Zanetti: Class Secretary (4) Athenians (4) Alumni Editor (4) Play Cast (4)…p. 21

Name: Zanetti - Known as: Eddy - Hobby: Dancing - Ambition: To tame Phoebus - Usually seen with: Blondy - Favorite Song: My Dream Girl .... Name: Twitchell - Known as: Phoebus Hobby: Making eyes - Ambition: To get by easy - Usually seen with: Slim - Favorite Song: We Won't go Home Till Morning

Seniors....On January twelfth we played the Sophomore basketball team. The game was fast and rough. In the first half no field goals were made, but the score was 5-2 in our favor. During the second half our team work improved. As usual, "Ruffemup" Twitchell was disqualified for making the quota of personal fouls. Since there were no substitutes available, the game continued with but four men on our side. Our lineup was: Theodore Twitchell, forward; Daniel Curryer, forward; Kenneth Kennedy, center; Kenneth Adam, guard; Raymond Strong, guard; Ted Sullivan, substitute. p 22

1927 Fred Twitchell enlisted for service in the World War, first joining the Cavalry but was later transferred to a machine gun Battalion. He went overseas in 1918, was made a second lieutenant, and was wounded in the Argonne forest. He was later sent back to a hospital in San Francisco, and on his recovery was honorably discharged. He is now operating his mother's farm in Arizona....

-Philips, *History of SB Co*. pp. 190-1

1929 Fremont C. Twitchell, Pioneer Dies    Resident Of Valley Last Half Century    Death Takes Prominent Valley Citizen at Home Near Orcutt This Morning    Funeral To Be Held Thursday Held High Positions in Fraternal and Business Circles in Santa Maria District. Fremont C Twitchell, 73, for the last 51 years a rancher, later a banker of Santa Maria Valley, passed away early this morning at his home on the state highway north of Orcutt, leaving another vacant chair in the lodge of pioneers and old-timers of the State of California and of this region in particular.

As widely known as any other resident of the central coast area, the deceased had a business and social standing unsurpassed during the half century he made his residence in this valley.

He is survived by his widow, Ida A Twitchell; three sons, Fred M of Peoria, Arizona, James Deane and Theodore A, both of Santa Maria and two daughters, Lucy M Lee of Gilroy and May Coffin of Media, Pennsylvania.

Funeral services will be held at the Masonic hall here Thursday afternoon at 2 o'clock with Rev W P S Nelson officiating, and Hesperian Lodge F and AM rites accompanying.

The well beloved man was held in high esteem by his fellow workers, his position in business and fraternal circles attesting to this. He was a past noble grand for the local order of Odd Fellows, past master of the Hesperian Lodge F and AM, and a trustee of the Benevolent and Protective Order of Elks. He was also a member of the Advisory board of the local branch of the Security First National Bank of Los Angeles.

The news of his death came as something of a shock to the valley, inasmuch as he has not been in ill health, was up and about only a few days ago.

His passing was noticed more than that of the average citizen, for despite his advanced aged, he was still extremely active in business and civic affairs.

Speaking of Fremont C Twitchell and his life in Santa Maria Valley, a history of Santa Barbara county says, "He has led a busy and useful life and stands high in public regard. He comes to the west from the Pine Tree state where he was born in Waldo county, Maine, on the 20th day of September, 1856, and is son of Martin Farr (sic) and Lucy (Howard) Twitchell." Fremont C Twitchell was one year old when the family left Maine. He was reared in Iowa, attending the public schools and spending his boyhood years on his father's farm, while later he rented land on his own account, and also engaged in the meat business, and subsequently in the confectionery business. In January, 1877, he went to San Francisco, California, and until April of the following year was employed on a schooner supplying (sic) the bay. In 1878 he came to Santa Maria and bought 320 acres of land, on which few improvements had been made, the only building being an old shack. He has since sold some of this land, his present farm comprising 200 acres. He is also the owner of 80 acres three miles south of Santa Maria, and a good farm in Arizona. Mr Twitchell has prospered in his business affairs, having exercised sound judgment in all his operations and is a director of the Brooks Oil co and on the advisory board of the Santa Maria branch of the Los Angeles Security First National bank.

"In 1880, Mr Twitchell was married to Miss Mattie Stubblefield, a native of California. Two children were born to this union, May and Fred. The mother died in 1886 at the age of 22 years, and on December 31, 1890, Mr Twitchell was married to Miss Ida Newlove, daughter of John and Mariah Newlove.

"To Mr and Mrs Twitchell have been born five children: Lucy, the wife of John Lee; Ward, who died at the age of 19 years; James; Theodore A, who is a graduate of the law school of the University of California and is now with the law firm of Preisker and Goble.

"Mr Twitchell has always been a strong supporter of the Republican party and has been active in local public affairs. In 1910 he was elected a member of the county board of supervisors, serving four years, and was re-elected in 1914, but resigned the office. He is a member of Hesperian Lodge, #264, Ancient Free and Accepted Masons of Santa Maria of which he is past master; Santa Maria chapter, Royal Arch Masons; the Santa Maria Lodge, IOOF, and the Benevolent and Protective Order of Elks." -*Santa Maria Daily Times* Tue Dec 10 p.1,4; Phillips, *History SB Co* 1927 Vol. II p. 189-91

1955 "Cap" Twitchell Dies    Vaquero Project Leader Stricken by Fatal Stroke (by Bill Sherrill) *Times* Staff Writer (photo) "Cap" Twitchell is dead.

T A (Theodore Antow) "Cap" Twitchell, 52, died at 5:55 pm yesterday in Sisters' hospital after having been hospitalized Sunday afternoon with a coronary illness.

Mr Twitchell was born October 26, 1902, on the Twitchell ranch near Orcutt. His father, the late Fremont C Twitchell, came to the Santa Maria Valley in 1878, from Iowa, after a brief stop in the San Francisco bay region. He married Miss Ida A. Newlove in 1890, and to them were born three children: T. A. Twitchell, Mrs Lucy Twitchell Lee, and James D. Twitchell.

"Cap" Twitchell (the "Cap" being a friendly title with no military significance) grew up on the home ranch and received his first two years of schooling from his grandfather, the late Martin C Twitchell, an Ohio (sic) school Master, who came here after his son, Fremont, had settled in the Santa Maria Valley. Completing his grammar schooling in Orcutt, "Cap" entered Santa Maria Valley Union High School and graduated in June 1920.

He then entered the University of California, graduating cum laude in 1924, winning his Doctor of Jurisprudence degree in 1926. Returning to Santa Maria, Twitchell entered the law offices of Preisker, Preisker and Goble on July 25, 1926, and became a member of the firm on January 1, 1927.

Mr Twitchell married his high school sweetheart, Miss Edwina Zanetti, September 18, 1926, four month (sic) after his graduation from U C Law School.

During his almost thirty years of active community service in Santa Maria and Santa Barbara county, Mr Twitchell has: 1- Led the fight for the Vaquero Dam water conservation and irrigation project (now nearing a vote by the residents of the area). 2- Served as chairman and legal counsel for the Santa Barbara County Water Agency since 1942, guiding their steps in development of water resources throughout the county. 3- Been largely instrumental in the passing of legislation which brought to a successful fruition the Cachuma dam project, with its essential water storage and distribution to the south county, and the recreation area surrounding Lake Cachuma as it is today. 4- Served on the County Board of Supervisors from 1943 to 1950; elected twice without opposition and declining to run for the third term and during which he served as chairman of the Board. 5- Served as Chairman of the county Planning and Public Works Committee. Mr Twitchell was a past master of Hesperian Masonic lodge No. 264; past exalted ruler of BPO Elks Lodge No. 1538; past president of Santa Maria Rotary Club; past president of the Santa Maria County Club; vice-president of the Masonic Hall Association and had been active in the financing of the new Masonic Temple and in many civic posts in the community.

With his assistant, William C Rice, Mr Twitchell moved last year to new law offices which they built at 215 N Lincoln.

Mr Twitchell is survived by his wife, Mrs Edwina Twitchell; three sons, Maurice Fremont, 25; Burton James, 23, and Dennis Ward Twitchell, 13; two brothers, James D Twitchell, Orcutt Road; and Frederick M Twitchell, Valley Springs; two sisters, Mrs Lucy Lee, formerly of Gilroy, now living here, and Mrs May T Coffin of Santa Barbara; his mother, Mrs Ida Twitchell, and many cousins, nieces and nephews.

Masonic rites will be conducted at 2 pm tomorrow in the chapel of the Dudley Mortuary. Graveside services will be conducted by Santa Maria Elks Lodge in the Santa Maria cemetery.

Pallbearers who will serve are: William P Adam, Frank L Roemer, Ellis Rice, C Leo Preisker, Fred J Gobel, William C Rice, Kenneth Trefts and Ernest E Righetti.

Memorial services for Twitchell will be conducted tomorrow morning at 10 am in Superior Court by his fellow attorneys and Superior Court Judge Ernest Wagner. Court will be convened in his memory following the services.  -*SM Times* Thu Aug 11 p. 1, 6

1973 Obituaries. Twitchell, Frederick Martin Twitchell, 89, 295 Alder St, Arroyo Grande died Friday. Funeral services will be conducted at 2 pm, Dudley-Hoffman Mortuary, Santa Maria, with the Masonic Lodge officiating and cremation to follow. Twitchell died Friday at an Arroyo Grande Hospital. He was born Nov 15, 1883, in Orcutt, lived in Arroyo Grande after retirement…veteran of World War I, member of the Military Order of Purple Heart; member Hesperian Masonic Lodge No. 264, Santa Maria, and American Legion.

Twitchell taught at Santa Maria High School and coached football at Santa Maria Junior College 1931-1940…survived by widow, Rosamond, Arroyo Grande; two sons, Fremont of Anaheim and Glenn of Loomis; two sisters, Mrs Reginald Clifford of Santa Barbara and Mrs Lucy Lee of Santa Maria; 7 grandchildren and 5 great-grandchildren.

Dudley-Hoffman will hold visitation hours this afternoon and evening.
-*SLO Telegram-Tribune* Mon Dec. 3

1978 Obituaries Mary Clifford  A funeral service for Mary (May) Twitchell Clifford, 95, Santa Barbara, will be 11 am in the chapel of the Santa Barbara Cemetery. Friends, if they so desire, may make memorial contributions to the L E and Ida M Blochman Scholarship Fund at Allan Hancock College. Mrs Clifford died Thursday in Santa Barbara. She was born Sept 1, 1882, on the Twitchell Ranch near Orcutt. Her parents were Fremont C and Mattie Stubblefield Twitchell. She attended elementary and high school in Santa Maria and the University of California at Berkeley, returning upon graduation to teach at Bonita school in the Santa Maria Valley and in Alaska. She enlisted in the U S Army in World War I and was a member of the occupational therapy Corps at Prescott, Ariz. After the war she taught school in Pennsylvania until 1944 when she retired to Santa Barbara. Survivors include one sister, Lucy Twitchell Lee of Santa Maria; nine nieces and nephews; Fremond (sic) G Twitchell of Anaheim; Glenn R. Twitchell of Sloughhouse; John W Lee of Gilroy; Janice Dugger, Myrna Twitchell, John A Twitchell, Maurice F, Burton J, Dennis W Twitchell, all of Santa Maria. She was preceded in death by her husband Reginald Clifford, who died in 1960.

1989 Edwina Twitchell Rosary 7 pm Friday...died brief illness. Mass 9 am Saturday St Mary of the Assumption ch....born rural Santa Maria...graduated high school 1920. In her early years she worked for Joe Davis Bookkeeping service for 6 years and the original Bank of Santa Maria, which was later acquired by Security Pacific National Bank. She was a member of Minerva Club, Catholic Daughters of America, A to Z Club, Santa Maria Historical Society, Santa Maria Senior Citizens and St. Mary's Catholic Church. Survivors:: Maurice F and Burton J Twitchell, Santa Maria; Dennis W, Myrtle Creek, Oregon; 8 grandchildren, nieces and nephews. Husband T. A. Twitchell died Aug 19, 1955.
-*SM Times* Thu Nov 9 p. 8

The Beloved Blochmans..."If to be remembered is the greatest of all monuments, Ida M Twitchell Blockman well deserves special mention in this story of the development of Santa Maria Valley, for she is remembered with affection respect and gratitude by those pioneers who were so fortunate as to have come under her forceful and stimulating influence during their youth. "She was born in Maine, April 11, 1854, and came to the small community of La Graciosa in 1879 to join her mother, Mrs M C Twitchell, and her brother, Fremont, who had settled on an acreage on what is now known as Orcutt Road.

She was principal of the Santa Maria Grammar school for six years; started teaching at the high school in 1896, acting as vice principal the first year. They moved to Berkeley in 1909, financed by oil found on land of theirs.         -*This is Our Valley*, Chapter XIV p.156 –ff
See also *San Ramon Chapel Pioneers* for other reminiscences.

1981 Obituaries John W Lee John W Lee, 59, died Thursday at his Santa Maria residence. Private graveside services will be held Saturday at 10:30 am in the Santa Maria Cemetery.

Mr Lee was born June 14, 1921, in Orcutt and was raised in Gilroy. He graduated from Gilroy High School, Hartnell College in Salinas, and San Jose State University. He had served as a captain in the U S Army Air Corps and as a pilot during WWII, and was the son of the late John and Lucy Twitchell Lee, early Santa Maria Valley Pioneers.

Survivors include his wife, Margaret Lee of Los Gatos, daughter, Lynne Ehlers of Orinda, Nicole Kleinberg of Woodside, Stephanie Maier of Kingston, Jamaica, and Laurie Lee of Palo Alto; and three grandchildren. Dudley-Hoffman is in charge of arrangements.         -*SM Times* Sat June 13

The Daily Times Saturday May 22, 1937, front page    Death Calls M S Zanetti    S M Pioneer Death Claimed another of Santa Maria's Pioneers when Maurice S Zanetti, 70 next November, passed away yesterday afternoon in a Santa Barbara Hospital after an illness of several months with heart trouble. Deceased was the owner of the Santa Maria Furniture Co, of which his son-in-law, Gordon Miller, is the manager, and had been active in the community almost continuously since first coming here in 1885, except for a few years spent in Santa Paula and Ventura and in Europe. He was the father of Mrs Miller (Ellen Zanetti), Mrs T A (Edwina) Twitchell, and Mrs James (Wilhelmina) Hamill, 737 Bay Street, San Francisco. All survive. Two brothers, S and Plenio, of Santa Maria, and four brothers in Europe - Ferdinand, Giuseppi, Peter and Fidele Zanetti, also survive. Death occurred at 3:30 yesterday afternoon.   Born in Switzerland   Deceased was born in Bellengona, Canton of Tecino, Switzerland, Nov 1 1867, the son of Peter and Louisa Salco Zanetti, and came to America in 1883, at the age of 16. He located first at Duncan's Mills in Sonoma County and for two years worked for an uncle. He came two years later to Santa Maria and first worked for B Pezzoni. He then went into partnership with his brother, S Zanetti, in the dairying and ranching business on the Tognazzini ranch near Betteravia. He sold out and returned to Europe in 1891, where he remained for four years, but returned to California in 1894 and went to work for John Lagomarsino at Ventura and was also in business for himself in that city and Santa Paula for a time. He returned to Santa Maria and entered the wholesale and retail liquor business here, continuing until 1918. During this time he also operated ranches with his brothers, S and Peter Zanetti, near Betteravia.

In 1925, he purchased the furniture business of T A Jones & Son…changed the name to the Santa Maria Furniture Co. and had operated the business since that time. Deceased was married July 8, 1900, to Miss Anita C Tonini, daughter of Mr and Mrs Michael and Elizabeth Tonini of San Luis Obispo. Besides the brothers and children living, deceased was also the uncle of Tilden, Sylvester and Henry Zanetti, Alma Delco, Olympia Thompson, Daisy Bisco and Ancilla Souza. He was grandfather of Maurice and Burton Twitchell, Ronald Miller and Judith and Douglas Hamill. He was a member of the Druids (San Francisco Lodge) and was a charter member of Santa Maria Lodge of Elks. Rosary will be said this evening and tomorrow evening at 8 o'clock in the Dudley Mortuary Chapel, and funeral services will be held Monday morning. A Requiem high mass in St. Mary's Catholic Church at 9:30 will be said by Rev Fr Thos V Murphy. Interment will be in Santa Maria Cemetery. The funeral cortege will leave the Dudley Mortuary at 9 am.   – *Santa Maria Daily Times* Mon May 24, 1937 p.6

Last Rites For Morris Zanetti   Cemetery Walks Lined With Floral Tributes to Pioneer Citizen.   Requiem high mass was said in St. Mary's Catholic Church at 9:30 this morning by the Rev Father Thomas Murphy, for Maurice S Zanetti, Santa Maria Pioneer business man who died in Cottage Hospital, Santa Barbara, Friday afternoon in his 70th year. He had been suffering from a heart ailment for several months. Remains of the pioneer, in a silver-finished metallic casket were laid to rest in Santa Maria Memorial Mausoleum, Santa Maria cemetery. The casket was covered with a large spray of red roses. At rosary services in Dudley Mortuary Chapel, there were many wreaths, basket bouquets, floral pieces on easels and sprays, which surrounded the casket. At the cemetery, the walks to the Mausoleum, and the family crypt were lined with flowers in baskets, wreaths and sprays. Pall bearers were L P Scaroni, M M Purkiss, Wm. MacDonald, J P Hanson, Dan Donavan, F J De Martin, L C Palmtag, Henry Pezzoni. The funeral cortege formed at Dudley Mortuary at 9 o'clock this morning, and a large number of friends and relatives of deceased followed the bier to the church and to the cemetery.

Morris & Hayden – *History of San Luis Obispo County, California & Environs*-Biographies: Maurice Zanetti, p. 1008, Severino Zanetti p. 1006, Tilden E Zanetti p. 1010.

See *Genealogy Of The Twitchell Family, Record of the Descendants of the Puritan Benjamin Twitchell of Dorchester, Lancaster, Medfield and Sherborn, Mass, 1632-1927*, by Ralph Emerson Twitchell. Privately printed 1929 (a copy in Genealogy Dept., Stockton, CA, Library; reprint available from Tuttle).

## CALIFORNIA FORTY-NINERS
### The TWITCHELL Family of Monterey, San Benito, San Luis Obispo and Santa Barbara Counties

The Twitchells arrived at Sutter's Fort early in the summer of 1849, having overwintered in Utah. Joshua and Ursula Twitchell were accompanied by their children: Eunice, the eldest, a widow with three small boys; Jasper, whose wife had died on the Trail, with young son; Lorenzo and bride; and the younger Silas, Julia and Jane. Early in the 1850's they betook themselves to San Juan. (Though the mission is San Juan Bautista, the town was long called simply San Juan, and was in Monterey County until the formation of San Benito County in 1874.)

The Gabilan range separates the Salinas and San Juan Valleys. *East Of The Gabilans*, by Marjorie Pierce, 1976, a history of the area, mentions several times that Jasper Twitchell was a member of the Mormon colony which settled in San Juan Canyon; land records bear out that location. Pierce identifies a nephew, Jasper Henry Lawn, who came west as a small boy, as having been a traveling minister of the Re-organized LDS church for 35 years. William Stowell, oldest son-in-law of Lorenzo, was the son of a couple killed in the Mormon Massacre in Provo Utah in 1856. The other Twitchell brothers lived elsewhere in the valley, and are not specifically called Mormon. Lorenzo lived for a time in Santa Cruz, on August 1, 1864, buying from J T Fitzgerald for $400 the 120 acre Quail Hollow Ranch plus the right "to cut timber, cut hoop poles, and to make shingles on adjoining land belonging to the party of the first part." (Santa Cruz co Bk 7 p. 453) His eldest daughter was married there that year, but the second daughter was married in San Juan in 1866 and later records show him there until his move to Paicines, south of Hollister, and, in 1881, much farther south to San Luis Obispo County. His children also left the San Juan valley; the Stowells moved east into the San Joaquin valley, a natural direction from Llanada and Panoche, their sometime residences which are on what was the main road from Hollister over the mountains to Fresno. Most of Lorenzo's younger children came as far south as the Santa Maria Valley and on up into the Upper Sisquoc-Manzana, 35 miles from the town of Santa Maria, and a difficult 15-20 miles into the mountains from the edge of the valley. When the drought of the late 1890's drove them out, they relocated, for the most part, to other areas of small population. Interesting tidbits on these people in the Manzana setting, along with a goodly number of photographs, may be found in *San Ramon Chapel Pioneers*.

The Twitchell Genealogy, published in 1929, was not much help on the California branch, except to clarify Celesta's husband as Stowell, not Stovall; the Stowell Genealogy, 1922, provided much information and details the longtime connections of William Stowell's progenitors to the Mormon movement. A biography of Jasper Twitchell in *A Memorial And Biographical History Of The Coast Counties Of Central California*, 1893, was apparently accurate, whereas a biography of Jacob S Twitchell in Morrison & Hayden is so faulty that one wonders how it came to be composed. The historical data in the obituaries seems to be relatively accurate; any known errors are noted.

The sources are, for the most part, public record; most of the searching was done in San Luis Obispo County, but happenstance allowed visits to the Monterey, San Benito, and Santa Cruz County courthouses in recent weeks. The numbers in brackets after a death date are the SLO co certificate or book numbers. Other death dates come from the California Grand Death List; those in parenthesis have not been verified, but those which seem uncontestable, though not verified, are set out as given on the Death list: i.e. 4-14-1934, etc. Dates followed by SSDI indicate that index as the source. 1850, 1860, etc. are census years; GR means Great Register of Voters. Some few dates are from cemetery readings, which are the most likely to be wrong. The discrepancies in ages given stem from the inaccuracies of the records (and not too many typographical errors of the present compilers). Much more could be done, but this has gone on longer and has become longer than intended; may it be a boost to someone to take up the cause.

CAVEAT LECTOR

SANFORD LORENZO TWITCHELL SCRAPBOOK

## 1. CELESTA ANN HICKOK 1849-1934
Woman, Born In 1849, Dead

Alameda, May 28. Funeral services will be held Thursday for Mrs Celesta Ann Hickok, who was born in a covered wagon at the gates of Sutter's Fort in 1849. She died Saturday after a short illness, at the home of a daughter, Mrs George A Marshall, 3363 Fernside Boulevard. Mrs Hickok had been here since last October. Her body will be returned to her former home at Lockeford, San Joaquin County for burial.

Mrs Hickok, according to early California history, was born at the west gate of Fort Sutter in a covered wagon just as the vehicle drew up there during the gold rush. The date was July 6, 1849. Her father was Lorenzo Twitchell, a young Iowa farmer, who had brought his bride to the gold fields of California. Her mother was Irene Twitchell. In 1864 Mrs Hickok married William A Stovall.* She made her home for many years in San Benito County. He died in 1915. They had nine children: William A, George D, Henry T, Seth M, Fred B, and Frank A Stovall,* Mrs Ellen L Rarden, Mrs George A Marshall and Mrs Jeanette Wendling. Later she married William Hickok, making her home in Lockeford… She was a member of the "Covered Wagon Babies" and the Women's Relief Corps of the GAR.  *Stowell       – *Oakland Tribune* Mon May 28 1934 p.4D

1937    Funeral is Planned for J G Hoskins, Turlock, May 5. Funeral Services for J G Hoskins, 68, who died Tuesday morning in a Modesto hospital, will be conducted here tomorrow afternoon at 2 o'clock at the O'Hara-Drake Mortuary. Interment will be in the Turlock Cemetery. Hoskins was born in Auberry, Fresno County, and had lived in the Turlock-Mitchell district the last 20 years. He leaves a daughter, Mrs W T Trivelpiece of Stockton, and three brothers, Ernest and Louis Hoskins of Turlock and W J Hoskins of Delhi.        -The *Modesto Bee* May 5-6 1937 p.6

*Ed. Note*: 1920 census Stanislaus Co, Turlock tp, Chatom pct John G Hoskins 51 CA IL AR owns farm; Lilly M 30 CA IL GER; Ruby M 6; Henry G $1^{5/12}$; Stepsons Melvin F Stowell, 12, and Cecil A Stowell, 10.

## 2. MARTHA ELLEN TWITCHELL 1851-1936

1895    Sisquoc Local News… Mr Adkins has taken up a ranch in the Manzana Country.
-*Santa Maria Times* Feb 9

Manzana Items … A Few Interesting Notes From up the River… Mr H. P. Wheat and Mr Adkins are still grubbing and clearing so as to sow more small grain.        Ibid Jan 26

1897    Upper Sisquoc Items…J J Adkins of the valley is spending a few weeks in the mountains for his health.        -Ibid Dec 25

1898    Upper Sisquoc Items…H P Wells and Jake Adkins made a business trip to Santa Maria the forepart of the week.        - Ibid Jan 1

1914    Local News Notes. From Oceano  J W Adkins and mother, Mrs M E Adkins of Oceano, came up last evening on 21 and are attending to local business matters in the city this afternoon.
-*SLO Daily Telegram* Mon June 1

1921    Cambria, March 15. Mrs J A Adkins was a San Luis Obispo visitor Saturday.
-*SLO Daily Telegram* Mar 15

1928    J C Adkins, Centenarian, Resident of County for Seventy Years, is Dead    Last rites for J C Adkins, 99, a resident of Fresno County for 70 years, who died Friday night at a local hospital, will be conducted tomorrow afternoon at 2 o'clock at the chapel of the Westside Undertakers, followed by interment in Mountain View Cemetery. Adkins, a retired farmer, a native of Ohio, would have celebrated his 100$^{th}$ birthday anniversary next Saturday. He is survived by his widow, Mrs Mattie Adkins, and six sons, Bert Adkins of Fresno, T J Adkins of Michigan, J J Adkins of Point Richmond, J L Adkins of Woodland, F W Adkins of Nevada and J W Adkins of Los Angeles. (photo: white beard)                    -*Fresno Bee* Sun March 11 p.5

*Ed. Note*: Mattie d. 2-12-1936 San Joaquin Co; no obit *Stockton Record* or *Fresno Bee*.

1935    Adeline Adkins Taken By Death    Mrs Adeline Adkins, 86, former Chico resident, died at the home of her daughter, Mrs Lillian Dorrett of Doe Mill Ridge, yesterday morning. Funeral services will be held at the Westfall Funeral Home at 1:30 o'clock tomorrow afternoon, Rev Harris Pillsbury will officiate and interment will be in the Chico Cemetery. A native of Wisconsin, Mrs Adkins was a resident of California 70 years. She lived for many years (sic), moving to reside with her daughter about four years ago. In addition to Mrs Dorrett, Mrs Adkins is survived by the following children: Mrs Dorothy Cavell, Paynes Creek; William Roberts and Jess Adkins of Doe Mill Ridge, and George Adkins of Chico; eight grandchildren.
                                -The *Chico Record* Tue morn April 2 p.3

1944    Resident Of Nice Passes On Sunday    Joseph J Adkins, 83, a resident of Nice for the past 11 years, passed away at the County General Hospital in Lakeport on Sunday evening. He had been in the hospital only four days. Mr Adkins, a native of California, had lived for some time at the home of Mrs Perry of Nice. He is survived by two sons who are thought to live near Chico. The sons were not located and the Russell Funeral Home held interment at the Upper Lake Cemetery.
                                -*Lake County Bee* Fri Sep 15 p.8

4. SANFORD MARION TWITCHELL 1854-1924

1924    York Mountain Pioneer Is Dead    Sanford M Twitchell, a pioneer resident of the York Mountain section, died yesterday afternoon at the age of 69 years. Deceased was a native of California, having been born in San Bernardino*, and had been a resident on York Mountain for 43 years. He is survived by a widow, Mary J Twitchell. Funeral services will be held at his late residence at 2 o'clock tomorrow afternoon and burial will take place in the Templeton cemetery.
                                -*Paso Robles Star* Mon Mar 10 p.1

*Ed. Note*: *San Benito, not San Bernardino, was meant; even that would be incorrect, as the county was formed in 1874, 20 years after Sanford's birth.

5. WILLIAM J. TWITCHELL 1857-1937

Deeds: W J Twitchell to R Ashurst July 14, 1884, 1-294 (transcribed from Monterey co to San Benito Co) Wm A Stowell, Lorenzo O Lawn, Wm J Twitchell all of San Benito co. to D F McPhail of San Benito co, 800 acres in T15S R5E Sep 2 1883, 7-344

1897    Upper Sisquoc items…W S (sic) Twitchell made a business trip to Santa Maria the past week.
                                -*Santa Maria Times* Dec 25

1898    Upper Sisquoc Items: W J Twitchell and family (celebrated Christmas) with Mr and Mrs H Wells . . . The balance of the settlement at their homes . . .        -Jan 1

Deed: US Patent 4 Feb 1909 to Mrs Jane A Twitchell, Monterey Co J555

1915    Lucia: Redwood Dell, formerly owned by Riel Dani, now owned by the Gamboas, is for the first time in 15 years in cultivation, and the Gamboas have just completed a flume to the place to take care of a fine crop of alfalfa.    *-King City Rustler* June 18

1915    Notice of Final Proof San Francisco May 15, 1915: Roy Linwood Mitchell, Gorda. NE2NE4 S30 T22 R5E. Wit: E J Dutton, Henry A Gill, Jolon; Henry Von Kilsdonk, John Ingram, Gorda.    -Ibid Fri June 4

1936    Mrs Twitchell Passes Away. Funeral Tomorrow After an illness of two weeks, Mrs Anne Twitchell, 71, passed away at the home of her daughter, Mrs Irene E Ingram, in Greenfield Saturday evening. Deceased had been making her home in Santa Cruz, but had previously lived in this section, being a pioneer of the coast district. She was born July 7, 1865, in Utah, and came to California with her parents ten years later. Mrs Twitchell is survived by four *daughters, Mrs Ingram; Mrs Marjorie (Sam) Avila, of King City; Mrs Mary Holcomb of Korbel, Calif; and two sons, William Twitchell of Santa Cruz, and Sanford L Twitchell of Gorda. There are also 30 grandchildren, and 5 great grandchildren. Funeral services will be held at Foor's Chapel tomorrow at 2 pm, with interment in the IOOF cemetery here. Pallbearers will be C C Avila, J A Carlson, Julius Brunette, George Gamboa, Ed Plaskett, and W P Mansfield    *-The King City Rustler* May 4 p.1
*only three are named

Card Of Thanks    Mrs John Holcomb, Mrs Samuel Avila, Mrs Lloyd Miller, W A Twitchell, S L Twitchell....    -Ibid

1937    Death Calls P R Prospector Paso Robles, Jan 7    William Twitchell, about 80, a native of San Bernardino* County, passed away at the home of Mrs Maggie O'Neill Tuesday Jan 5. Mr Twitchell had lived in and around Paso Robles for many years and had followed prospecting as a vocation.

Survivors    He is survived by a brother, John Twitchell; a sister, Mrs Hannah Welles (sic), of Maricopa; three daughters, Mrs Irene Ingraham of Greenfield, Calif; Mrs Mary Holcomb of Blue Lake, Calif; and Mrs Sam Avila, of King City; and two sons, William Twitchell of South San Francisco and Sanford Twitchell of Pacific Valley; also 32 grandchildren.

Services    Services will be held in the Templeton Cemetery. Interment by the Kuehl Funeral Home with Rev Choate N. Balch officiating.    *-SLO Daily Telegram* Thu Jan 7 p.5
**Ed. note*: A deed for land in the San Juan vicinity to Sanford L Twitchell dated July 13, 1857 (C166), a month before William's birth would contra-indicate the San Bernardino/San Benito confusion.

1960    William Twitchel (sic) Service Today at Ree Grim Chapel Funeral services were to be held at 1:30 this afternoon at Ree C Grim Funeral Chapel for William Alvin Twitchel, who passed away Sunday on the family ranch in Pine Canyon.

Monsignor Martin McHugh, pastor of St John's Catholic Church, will be officiant. Interment will follow in King City Cemetery. A veteran of World War I, Mr Twitchel was born in Templeton but spent most of his life on the coast and in Pine Canyon. He farmed both in Templeton and on the Hearst Ranch near San Simeon. It was in the early 1940's that Mr Twitchel moved to Pine Canyon where he had been living in semi-retirement. His activities had been limited the past few years due to a lingering illness, which led to his death. Besides his wife, Lorraine of Pine Canyon, Mr Twitchel is survived by two daughters, Mrs Jane Gillis of Salinas and Mrs Connie Folks of Priest Valley; a son,

William (Mike) Twitchel of Santa Rose (sic); three sisters, Mrs Marjorie Avila of Pine Canyon, Mrs John Ingram of Pine Canyon and Mrs Mary Holcomb of Eureka; and nine grandchildren.

-*King City Rustler-Herald* Thu Sep 1 p.1

*Ed. note*- Pine Canyon is southwest of King City.

1960 "Mike" Twitchel dies at 52 William Frank (Mike) Twitchel, a former resident of King City, died Jan 16 at the age of 52 at Eskaton Monterey Hospital in Monterey after a long illness. He has been a resident of Carmel since March. Mr Twitchel was a resident of Paso Robles and a graduate of King City elementary school and King City High School. After graduation Mr Twitchel worked at King City Tire Shop. He then worked for Prudential Life Insurance Company, rising to the office of district manager in Sunnyvale after 21 years. In 1969 he moved to Hilo, Hawaii where he became co- owner of Ken's House of Pancakes. He moved to Carmel due to ill health. Mr Twitchel was a veteran of World War II. He is survived by two daughters, Sue Twitchel of Colorado Springs, Colo, and Judith Twitchel Cumming of Friday Harbor, Wash; a son, Thomas Twitchel of Hilo, Hawaii, and one grandchild. Also surviving is Mr Twitchel's mother, Mrs Lorraine Twitchel of King City; two sisters, Mrs Warren Gillis of Salinas and Mrs George Folks Sr. of Priest Valley. Numerous nephews and nieces also survive. Services were held Friday morning at the Ree C Grim Funeral Chapel with Father Salvino Zanon of St. John's Catholic Church officiating. Burial followed in the King City Cemetery. Pallbearers were Thomas Twitchel, Bill Gillis, Mike Gillis, Dennis Folks, George Folks, Jr and Ken Pruit.

-The *Rustler* Jan 24 p. 14

1984 Wedding Feb 25 1984 (Excerpted)
Bride: Gina Mosley, King City; dau of Mr and Mrs Clyde Allen of Hanford. Groom: Dennis Folks of Priest Valley; son of Mr and Mrs Geo. Folks Sr. Maid of Honor: Paula Allen, bride's sister. Bridesmaids: Linda Chambers, Bitterwater, groom's sister; Vanessa Folks, Priest Valley, groom's sister-in-law. Friends: Rosie Camarillo, Lynn Harris, Gerry Ortega, Mary Long, all of King City. Best Man: George Folks, Jr., groom's brother. Ushers: Kelly Koester, Salinas; David Grimes, Hollister, Nessen Schmidt, King City; Mark Coelho, Laton; Ted Barnes, King City; David Gillis, Slack Canyon. Junior Bridesmaid: Buffy Mosley, bride's daughter. Flower girl: Dennalee Folks, groom's daughter. Ring bearer: Jed Folks, groom's nephew

Bride graduated from King City HS 1969; employed by Safeway Stores, King City. Groom graduated from Coalinga HS, attended West Hills College, Coalinga. Works for Koester Construction. Honeymoon: Morro Bay. -Ibid Apr 11 p.5 (Group Photo)

*Ed. Note*: Priest Valley is on the road to Coalinga from San Lucas.

1984 Pioneer Resident Succumbs Funeral services were held Monday at Ree C Grim Funeral Chapel for Irene Elizabeth Ingram, who died April 26. She was 95. A Pioneer of this area, Mrs Ingram spent her early days in the Big Sur area. She married John F. Ingram in 1906 and raised ten children. She later moved to Chowchilla and then to King City where she remained the rest of her life. Said her family, "Many stories of the Old West have been rendered from this great lady, declared as the most beautiful woman on the coast in her early years. When the Salinas Valley was only dusty trails and sage brush, she had to travel many miles from the coast to King City - then known as Hog Town - for supplies before the Valley was cultivated." She is survived by two sons, William of King City and Walter of Arkansas; three daughters, Irene O'Connor of King City; Hanah (sic) P Miller of Cupertino and Saray (sic) O'Connor of King City; Brother-in-law San (sic) Avila of King City; sister-in-law Larraine (sic) Twitchell of King City; 30 grandchildren, 40 great grandchildren, 25 great great grandchildren and numerous nieces, nephews and cousins. Her husband preceded her in death in 1965. Pall bearers were Andy Hill, Tim Hill, Monty Hill, John O'Connor, Robert O'Connor and Galen Hill. Burial at King City Cemetery followed services which were officiated by the Rev Ron Shumaker of Grace Luthern (sic) Church of King City. -Ibid May 2 p.11

6. JACOB SILAS TWITCHELL 1859-1932   The biography of Jacob Twitchell in Morrison & Hayden has as many errors as truths. The marriage date is correct; after that, it says he went to Humboldt County, later coming back to Panoche and in 1903 to Oceano, and to Creston in 1906. The information on his grandfather, whose name is given as Josiah instead of Joshua, is garbled, and does not bear repeating.

Deed: Indenture made Sept 12 1908 between W M Forrester of San Luis Obispo Co*...210 acres in T16S R9E (east of the village of San Benito). San Benito Co. 41-208   *to Jacob Twitchell of SLO Co

1910   WILSON-TWITCHELL   Wednesday at high-noon Mr Edward R Wilson and Miss Maude M Twitchell were united in marriage at the Alexander hotel. Both young people are residents of Creston and have hosts of friends in this section of the county who joins (sic) with the *Record* in congratulations and best wishes.   -*Paso Robles Record* Jan 29

1921   Emil Stemper, son-in-law of Mr and Mrs Jake Twitchell, while acting as Santa Claus, Christmas eve, was badly burned about the face and hands when his Santa Claus costume took fire from the lighted candles on the tree. Mr Twitchell had his hands burned trying to put out the fire on Mr Stemper's clothes and for a time it was feared that the Central hotel would take fire. The injured are getting along nicely.   -*Paso Robles Star* Jan 5

1924   Templeton, Mr and Mrs Jake Twitchell were here Saturday from Oxnard looking after property interests. (From the Advance)   -Ibid Mar 22

1927   Nevada Native Dies In City   Funeral for Mrs Sophia Twitchell to Be Held Tomorrow   Mrs Sophia Twitchell, of 936 Park Avenue, passed away yesterday morning at 5:30 o'clock after a lingering illness. She was the wife of Jacob S Twitchell. She leaves five daughters, Mrs Maude Wilson, of the St. Francis hospital; Mrs W H Hendrick (sic), of Serena Park; Mrs J R Sands, of Santa Barbara; Mrs W F Wickham, of Santa Barbara, and Mrs E P Stemper, of Los Angeles; and a son, E H Woon, of Gilroy.* Mrs Twitchell came to Santa Barbara a year ago to live with her daughter, Mrs Sands, on Park Avenue. Mrs Twitchell was born in Nevada in 1874. The funeral will be held tomorrow morning at 9:30 in the Haider Chapel, followed by cremation in Santa Barbara cemetery.
* Woon was her brother.   -*Santa Barbara Morning Press* Sun Nov 20 p.2

Mrs Twitchell Rites   Funeral Services for Mrs Sophia Twitchell, who died Saturday, took place this morning at the Martin J Haider Chapel, and were followed by committal services in the chapel at the Santa Barbara Cemetery, where cremation occurred.   -*SB Daily News* Mon Nov 21 p. 13

1932   Heart Attack Fatal to Pioneer Rancher   The funeral of Jacob S. Twitchell of Serena Park, Carpinteria Valley, who died of a heart attack Sunday afternoon will be conducted at 2 o'clock this afternoon in the Martin J. Haider Chapel, Rev Tom B Clark, pastor of the First Christian Church, officiating. Interment will be in Santa Barbara cemetery. Mr Twitchell was born in San Juan 73 years ago and had passed his life in this state. He was for many years a successful rancher in the north, having resided in this section only six years. His wife, Mrs Sophia Twitchell, died here in 1927. Surviving are five daughters, Mrs Albert B Christensen and Mrs E P Semper (sic) of Carpinteria; Mrs W H Kendrick and Mrs W F Wickham of Serena Park, and William of Maricopa; and three sisters, Mrs Emma (sic) Hickok of Sacramento, Mrs Martha Atkins (sic) of Fresno and Mrs Anna (sic) Wells of Maricopa.
   -*Santa Barbara Morning Press* Tue June 7 p. 12

Last Rites held for J S Twitchell   Final rites for Jacob S Twitchell of Serena Park, Carpinteria Valley, who died on Sunday, were conducted at 2 pm yesterday in the Martin J Haider Chapel. Rev Tom B Clark, pastor of the First Christian Church, officiating. Interment was in Santa Barbara cemetery.
   -Ibid Wed June 8 p. 12

Vol. XXV, No. 1 & 2, 1993, pp.18, 19

Santa Maria Valley Genealogical Society and Library *Quarterly*, B. Cole Research

1956 Obituaries Maude May Christensen  Mrs Maude May Christensen, 64, died at her home, 438 Toro Canyon Rd, Carpinteria, at 1:30 pm following an illness of several months. She was the former Maude Twitchell, born Dec 18, 1891, in California. She had resided in Carpinteria since she was 18, and married Albert B Christensen there July 28, 1930. Survivors are a daughter, Alice May Cox of Carpinteria; two grandchildren, Georgiemay and Bobbiekay Cox, both Carpinteria, and four sisters, Mrs Carrie Kendrick of Los Angeles, Mrs Mattie Sands of Santa Maria, Mrs Tavie Santens of Grover City and Mrs Bertha Stemper of Avila. Friends may attend services at 2:30 pm Thursday at the graveside at Carpinteria Cemetery. Dr George J Hall of All Saints By-the-Sea Episcopal Church will officiate. Welch-Ryce....   -*SB News-Press* Mon Apr 2 B2

1962 Obituaries Jesse Sands  Funeral services will be conducted at 1 pm Tuesday in the chapel of the Dudley Mortuary for Jesse Sands, 70, who died Thursday in a local hospital. Born Sept 28, 1892 in Greenfield, Calif., Mr Sands had been a barber for the past 50 years. He had resided in Santa Maria for 37 years. He was a member of the Knights of Pythias and a World War I Veteran. Besides his wife, Mrs Martha Sands of 716 S. Pine St, Mr Sands leaves four sons, Marvin J Sands, Delano; Marion F Sands, Madera; Robert L Sands, Albuquerque, New Mexico and Richard L Sands of Arroyo Grande. Also surviving are two brothers, Ezekial (sic) Sands of San Jose, Wren Sands of Greenfield and two sisters, Mrs Ethel Herbert of Greenfield and Mrs Della Brandt of San Diego. He leaves nine grandchildren and 3 great grandchildren. Rev Claire Nesmith will officiate. Interment: Santa Maria Cemetery.   -*SM Times* Fri Nov 23 p.2

1963 Obituaries Mrs Martha Sands  Funeral services will be held at 1 pm Wednesday in the Chapel of Dudley Mortuary for Mrs Martha I Sands, 65, who died Sunday in a local hospital. Born May 1, 1896, in Gilroy, California, Mrs Sands was the widow of the late Jesse R Sands who preceded her in death in Nov 1962. Survivors include four sons, Marvin J Sands of Delano, Marion F Sands of Madera, Robert L Sands of Albuquerque, N Mexico and Richard L Sands of Arroyo Grande. Three sisters, Mrs Octavia Santens and Mrs Carrie Kendrick of Grover City and Mrs Bertha Stemper of Avila, and nine grandchildren and 3 great grandchildren also survive. Rev Michael E Winstead will officiate at the rites. Interment Santa Maria Cemetery.   -Ibid Mon April 8 p. 8

1964 Funeral Notices. Albert B Christensen of 124 Toro Canyon Rd....funeral arrangements will be announced later by Welch-Ryce....   -*Santa Barbara News-Press* Dec 19, 20, on & on

Obituaries   Albert B Christensen, 69, ...Carpinteria Cemetery, Rev Paul Gammons officiating. Born Carpinteria 1895...retired rancher...Survivors: daughter, Mrs Alice Donovan, Carpinteria; two grandchildren, Barbara and Georgiemay Cox, Carpinteria, nieces and nephews...   -Ibid Dec 27 F8 1965

Funeral Notices. Edward R Willson of 690 Palm Ave, Carpinteria.,.wife... Mrs Flora (Lena) Willson...Requiem Mass St Joseph's Catholic Church, Carpinteria...Carpinteria cemetery ...Contributions to St Joseph's school in memory of Mr Willson will be appreciated by the family.   -Ibid Oct 7 Dl

Deaths And Funerals  Edward R Willson  Edward Ray Willson, 83, ranch worker for 44 years, died Wednesday at his home, 690 Palm Ave, Carpinteria. A native of Gilroy, he was born Aug, 1882, son of Henry and Sarah Shepard Willson. He married Flora Evalena (Lena) Tognazzini in Our Lady of Mt. Carmel Church here Nov 17, 1930. He was a resident of the county since 1912. He last was employed by the Carpinteria Lemon Association. Mr Willson is survived in addition to his wife by three sisters: Mrs Edith May Barbara (sic) of Paso Robles, Mrs Winnifred Davis of Creston and Mrs Mabel Brown of Eureka, Nevada, several nieces and nephews. Rosary...mass...Carpinteria cemetery ... Haider Mortuary...memorials to St. Joseph's school, 4698 7th St, Carpinteria...   -Ibid Oct 8 C IO

1936    Sarah Willson called by Death After Brief Illness    Paso Robles Aug 29-Sarah Elizabeth Willson, 82, pioneer resident of Paso Robles, passed away at the home of her daughter, Mrs Hazel Barba at 1728 Spring St. Friday following a brief illness. Mrs Willson was predeceased by her husband Henry S Wilson (sic) in 1921, Her parents crossed the plains by ox team and settled in Hollister* in 1852. In 1877 she was married to Henry Willson and moved with him to the Paso Robles district the following year.    * Hollister was settled in the 1860's

Survivors    She is survived by the following sisters: Mrs Mary Beckwith of Gilroy; Mrs Martha Blackwell of Newman; Mrs Daisy Moody of Stratford; a brother, Eugene N Shepherd, Tucson, Ariz; seven children, Mrs Lilly Willson of Gilroy, Harry L Willson, Shandon; Mrs Edith Barba, Paso Robles; Edward R Willson, Carpinteria; Mrs Hazel Barba, Paso Robles; Mrs Winifred Davis and Mrs Mabel Brown, of Creston. She is also survived by twelve grandchildren. Funeral services will be held Monday morning from the Kuehl Funeral Home at 9:30 o'clock. Following the last rites, the funeral cortege will proceed to Lawn Memorial cemetery in San Luis Obispo where interment will be made.
-*SLO Daily Telegram* (?)

Her sister, Mary Beckwith, is probably the Mary listed on the 1880 census of San Juan precinct, age 20, with children David F, in household of John Beckwith. 30, who must be the son of Eunice Twitchell Lawn, eldest sister of Sanford Lorenzo Twitchell, and her second husband, Silas Beckwith, whom she married upon arrival at Sutter's Fort in 1849. (Another son was also named David.) Mary's mother's birthplace, like Sarah's, is Illinois, but she gave Missouri instead of Kentucky for the father's; many Kentuckians came to California from Missouri. More can be done on this question.

Dan Willson came around the Horn to California, apparently in the early 1850's. He married Vicenta Sanchez, who ran off in 1866 with Dave Hilderbrand, leaving him with several children. The 1870 census of San Juan township shows Dan with another wife, new baby, and additional children (hers); his growing family was still there in 1880, but Henry, the eldest, had married and moved to San Luis Obispo County. Henry, 37, and his full brothers, George S, 34, and Eldridge Douglas, 30, are shown on the Great Register of Voters for 1892 as residents of Creston (town established in 1884). Also on that voter list is John Bolivar Sheperd, 67, resident of San Luis Obispo, native of Kentucky; Sarah Shepherd, 67, resident of San Luis Obispo, native of Kentucky; Sarah Shepherd's father was born in Kentucky—is this he?

Sources: *East of Gabilans*, Marjorie Pierce, 1976; Creston 1884-1984; Centennial. Family Memories 1889-1989, Paso Robles, California

Henry Sanford Willson b. San Juan CA 1855
    d. (SLO co) 1921 IOOF cem SLO
    F: Dan Willson  b. NH c1827
    M: Vicenta Sanchez  b. CA
  1892 GR: @37 5'4 dark complexion, hazel eyes, brown hair, index finger left hand
    amputated at 2$^{nd}$ joint, stockman; res Creston, reg Aug 9
      m. (San Juan) 1877
Sarah Elizabeth Shepherd b. (nr San Juan) 1854
    d. Paso Robles 28 Aug 1936 (16 408) IOOF cem SLO
    F: KY;  M: IL
  1900: Santa Margarita; 9 births, 8 living
1. Lillie
2. Henry Leslie b. June 1880; d. 26 March 1948; (25 248) IOOF cem SLO
3. Edward Ray b. Aug 1882; d. Carpinteria 6 Oct 1965; Carpinteria cem (Maude May Twitchell 1891-1956; divorced) (Flora E Tognazzini)
4. Edith M (twin) b. Aug 1882; (Mike Barba)

5. Hazel Cornelia b. Jan 1885; m. 1907 Ramon Natta Barba b. 1881 F: Refugio Barba; M: Jacinta Sanabria
6. Dan L b. May 1887 d. 1930 (Creston bk) or 1932 IOOF cem SLO
7. Winnifred (Davis) b. Mar 1893
8. Mabel F (Brown) b. May 1898

George S. Willson 1856-1914; IOOF cem SLO 1892 @34 5'6½" Dark hazel, black, farmer, CA Creston, reg Aug 15

1967  Vital Statistics Obituaries  Carrie Ann Kendrick Grover City. A Funeral service for Mrs Carrie Ann Kendrick will be conducted at 2 pm Friday in Grensted Funeral Home Chapel here. The Rev L A Miller of the Arroyo Grande Peace Lutheran Church will officiate. Interment will follow in Arroyo Grande District Cemetery. A Native of California, Mrs Kendrick was born on July 29, 1893 and came to Grover City 10 years ago from Los Angeles. She died Tuesday in Arroyo Grande Hospital. Survivors include the widower, Wm H Kendrick of Grover City, three sons, William Kendrick of Long Beach, Walton Kendrick of West Covina and John Kendrick of Lake Arrowhead; two sisters, Mrs Arcadia Santines* of Grover City and Mrs Bertha Stemper of Avila Beach; 9 grandchildren and two great grandchildren.  -  *SLO Telegram-Tribune* Thu Nov 2
*Octavia (Tavie) Santens

1969  Raymond Henry Santens Grover City  Raymond Henry Santens, 79, died in a San Luis Obispo hospital Thursday…Res. 960 Brighton. Grensted Funeral Home. – SM TIMES Fri June 20…Arroyo Grande Cemetery, Loyal Order of Moose, Pismo Beach, officiating. Born Nov 5, 1889, New York…22 year member of Loyal Order of Moose…Survivors: Widow, Mrs Octavia Santens; one step-son, Don Cupp, Delano; one step-daughter, Mrs Evelyn Pewitt, McFarland; two brothers, Henry Santens, Arroyo Grande; Joseph Santens, Pixley; one sister, Mrs Marie Covert, Long Beach; eight grandchildren, 2 great grandchildren.  – Ibid Sat June 21

1974  Vital Statistics Obituaries William Kendricks (sic) Funeral Services for William Henry Kendricks…Rev Larry Miller of Peace Lutheran Church…Arroyo Grande Cemetery…Kendricks, 86 died Monday in Arroyo Grande Hospital…born April 2, 1887 in Corsicana, Texas…A retired barber, Kendricks has lived in Grover City 15 years…Three sons, William of Lakeview, Walton of Huntington Beach and John of Lake Arrowhead…10 grandchildren, 6 great grandchildren…
– Ibid Thu Mar 28

1918  W A Kendrick, formerly of this city, died at his home, Santa Margarita yesterday morning, as the result of a stroke of paralysis. Mr Kendrick lived here four years ago and two years ago went north to Santa Margarita to reside. The remains are to be sent to Chatfield, Texas for interment. (Wilie A Kendrick d. 27 March 1918; 7-3 #12)  -*SLO Tribune* Fri May 29

1937  Wiley Albert Kendrick, 191 Beebe St, San Luis Obispo died June 11. Survived by widow, Mrs Florence R Kendrick; daughter, Mrs Louis Burton of Bakersfield; sister, Mrs B O Harper, Taft; three brothers, J O Kendrick, Lebec, C H Kendrick, Waco, Texas, and W H Kendrick, Carpinteria.  –*SLO Daily Telegram* Sat June 12 p.6
(1920 census: Wiley Kendrick 39 b. TX, res SLO; Florence R 37 b. VA; Anna Louisa 8 b. CO)

## 7. JOHN JASPER TWITCHELL, 1861-1942

1895  Manzana Notes  We are all feeling good, as we have had 8 inches of rain, Mr John Twitchel (sic) has had several head of horses and cattle stray away of late.  –*SM Times* Jan 12

Manzana Items   John Twitchell is still plowing and sowing grain. He says he will have 36 acres of small grain.

1897   Upper Sisquoc Items   The weather has been uncomfortably warm this past week. At the school election on the 4th, Geo R Tunnell was elected high school director, Wm Tunnell and John Twitchell district director, the latter to fill a vacancy. John Twitchell has about completed a fine barn.
- June 12

Upper Sisquoc   Mr and Mrs John Twitchell are stopping at Mr Wheat's ranch during Mrs Wheat's illness.
-Ibid July 24

Upper Sisquoc   First snow of the season one week ago.   The weather is unusually cold, at least so say the pioneers. ...J J Twitchell and family came up from the valley the forepart of the week. Christmas trees at the school house followed by a dance, is the manner in which we celebrate the eve of the natal day of Christ.
-Ibid Dec 25

1898   Upper Sisquoc   The weather has moderated... The irrepressible Strong Man is going to be absent in the valley for some weeks, the guest of Mr and Mrs John Twitchell; if he survives celebrating the new year in the latter place. Mr and Mrs J Twitchell have returned to their valley ranch. Christmas activities were postponed at the school house on account of inclement weather. Never within the recollection of the oldest inhabitant, has the Manzana and Sisquoc been at so low a state of water as at the present time. There is very little water in the Sisquoc this side of Mr Willman's ranch and it continues to disappear. The continuous dry spell is causing some anxiety among the stockmen. Unless rains come very soon stock will suffer for both feed and water.
-Ibid Jan 1

South Side Notes.   John Twitchell made a business and pleasure trip to the Manzana last week.
-Ibid March 2

1900   Southside Short Stops. By the time these items are in print it is expected John Twitchell and family will be on their way to San Joan (sic). Ellis Willy and Frank Gutherie will accompany them.
-Ibid Apr 28

1910   Mr and Mrs J J Twitchell of Highland drove to this city on Tuesday. They returned in the afternoon, accompanied by their daughter, Miss Nellie, who is attending high school here. She will remain until tomorrow.
-*Paso Robles Record*

Jan 29   *Ed. Note*: There were Highland school districts in Santa Barbara and San Luis Obispo Counties, and Twitchells were associated with both.

1940   Death Claims Mary Twitchell   Mrs Mary Elizabeth Twitchell, resident of Summerland since 1914, died yesterday at a local hospital after a few days' illness. She was 66 years old, and she and her husband John J.Twitchell, celebrated their golden wedding anniversary last April 1. Mrs Twitchell was born in Egan Canyon, NV, March 6, 1874, but moved to California as a child. She and her husband were married in San Luis Obispo in 1890 and moved to Summerland 26 years ago, taking up her residence in a house on Ortega Hill where she lived until her recent illness. She is survived by two sons, John Twitchell, Jr, of Santa Barbara, and Leonard L Twitchell of Summerland; a daughter, Mrs Nellie T Mackie of Montecito; two nieces, Mrs Beverly Snow of Carpinteria and Mrs Cecil Lambert of Summerland; a brother, Hiram P Wells of Maricopa, and four sisters, Mrs Henry Holland and Mrs Bertha Wright of Highland, Mrs E E Forrester of El Centro, and Mrs Will Holland of Paso Robles. Funeral services will be held Thursday at 2 pm with Rev John N Ashley officiating.
– *SB News-Press* Wed Dec 11 p.16

Vol. XXV, No. 1 & 2, 1993, pp.22, 23

Santa Maria Valley Genealogical Society and Library *Quarterly*, B. Cole Research

Funeral Notices    Twitchell, Mrs Mary E    Friends are invited to the services at 2 pm in the chapel of Eppel, Kurtz & Barber, Rev John N. Ashley officiating. Interment Carpenteria Cemetery.
– *Ibid* Thu Dec 12 p.16

News up and Down California    Mrs John J Twitchell, 66, is dead in Santa Barbara. She and her husband celebrated their Golden Wedding anniversary this year. A surviving sister is Mrs Will Holland of Paso Robles.    – *SM Daily Times* Thu Dec 12 4B

1942    Summerland Pioneer Dies    John J. Twitchell, 80, a native of California and a resident of Summerland for the last 25 years, died of a heart attack while chasing a mule. His body was found on Ortega Hill near his home. Deceased was born in 1862 in Monterey County. His parents came to California from New England* by wagon several years before. He spent much of his early life in San Luis Obispo County where he engaged in ranching. In 1890 he was married to Mary Elizabeth Wells. Mrs Twitchell died two years ago shortly after the couple had celebrated their golden wedding anniversary. For many years deceased operated meat stores in Summerland and Carpinteria. Mr Twitchell is survived by two sons, John of Santa Maria, and Leonard of Summerland, and a daughter, Mrs Harold Mackie of Montecito, and John J Twitchell III, Richard Lee Twitchell, Robert Dean Twitchell and Patricia Lou Twitchell, all of Santa Maria.    – *Ibid* Dec 16 p.3
*Early generations of Twitchells were New Englanders; the parents came to California from Iowa or Illinois.

1945    Twitchell Funeral Set for Thursday in Santa Barbara    Funeral services for John J Twitchell, who died yesterday in a local hospital, will be held tomorrow at 2 pm in Eppel & Kurtz Funeral Home, Santa Barbara. Deceased was the son of Pioneer Valley residents, the late Mr and Mrs J. J. Twitchell, and he was born in 1896, in the Upper Sisquoc River region. He lived for a time with the family in Santa Barbara, and graduated from Santa Barbara High School. He was attending Cal Tech, when called to service in the world war as a sergeant.
Here Three Years    The Twitchells have lived in Santa Maria for the past three years. He was engaged here with the U. S. Engineers, in work in Camp Cooke and on the Air Field, and prior to that, was with the Forestry Service. He had been ill for about three weeks. Besides his wife, the former Gladys Doty, member of a well known Santa Barbara family, he is survived by four children, John, 18, now in Navy service, Richard, 16, Robert, 13, and Patricia, 10.
Other Relatives    Other relatives surviving are a sister, Mrs Harold Mackie of Montecito, a brother Leonard, who occupies the family home on Ortega Hill, Summerland, and two cousins with whom he grew up, Mrs Cecil Lambert of Summerland and Mrs Bernard Snow of Santa Barbara.
– *Ibid* Wed May 23 p.8

1955    Obituaries    Mary Twitchell    Funeral services for Mrs Mary Lucia Twitchell, who was burned to death early yesterday while apparently trying to rescue her two children from a fire, will be conducted at 10 am Saturday at the graveside in Carpinteria Cemetery. The family had just returned to Carpinteria two weeks ago from South Dakota, largely because Mrs Twitchell preferred a warmer climate. They lived at 2270 Lilly Ave., the home which was gutted by the fire. Mrs Twitchell was born Dec 5, 1908, in Cartereggio, Italy. Surviving are her husband, Leonard T Twitchell; three sons, Charles L Twitchell, 10, John Tveidt, at present attending Notre Dame University, and M/Sgt Richard Tveidt, USAF in French Morocco, and one daughter, Sandra Lou Twitchell, 9. Also surviving are three sisters, Mrs E R Krauss of Pleasant, Mrs Josephine Trucano of Los Angeles and Mrs Richard Platt of Lead, SD, and a brother, A G Trucano, Deadwood, SD. There is also one grandson, Lawrence Tveidt. Mrs Twitchell was a member of the Forresters of America in Lead. The family moved in 1947 from Carpinteria to Deadwood. At the funeral services, according to Haider Mortuary, the Rev Paul M Gammons, pastor of the El Montecito Presbyterian Church, will officiate.
-*Santa Barbara News-Press* Nov 9 p.2

1960 Private Services Slated for Mackie Harold Herbert Mackie, 32, was one of seven men who were part of a tragic expedition to the Channel Islands last week. His body was recovered in the Santa Barbara channel Friday. .....born Santa Barbara Aug 30, 1927...graduated UCSB 1953....electronics engineer Raytheon; member Delta Tau Delta, El Montecito Presbyterian Church, Santa Barbara Camera Club, Junior Chamber of Commerce...Married Dec 16, 1955 Betty Lou Curtis...sister Mrs James Cumming of Columbia Falls, Montana, parents Mr and Mrs H H Mackie, Santa Barbara... (body found off Port Hueneme; map) Funeral Notices. Harold H Mackie Jr, 26 La Cadena. Private services. Rev Paul M. Gammons. Santa Barbara Cemetery. -Ibid June 21 A8

## 8. CHARLES E. TWITCHELL 1863-1898

1912 Violet and Myrtle Twitchell, attendants, are identified in a group picture of the royalty of the Upper Salinas Valley Fair, with Queen Ursula Bayne et. al., September 28, 1912.
 *-Centennial Family Memories*, Paso Robles, 1989, p.32

1958 Deaths And Funerals Beverly Snow Beverly B. Snow, 67, who was born and lived all his life in Toro Canyon, died yesterday in a local hospital after an illness of two weeks. Born Sept 1, 1890, he attended Montecito and Carpinteria Schools. He married Violet Twitchell at El Montecito Presbyterian Church on December 10, 1915. On August 1 last year he retired after 31 years with the Santa Barbara Road Dept. Surviving besides his wife are two sons, Bernard and Ernest, both of Santa Barbara; a brother, Elmer Snow, Baywood City; three sisters, Mrs Annie Watson, Baywood City, Mrs Ruby Thompson, Santa Barbara, and Mrs Joseph Stewart, Carpinteria, and three grandchildren. He was pre-deceased by another brother, Elmer, (sic). Welch-Ryce will announce funeral services later.
 *-Santa Barbara News-Press* July 1958 A6

1979 Deaths And Funerals Violet L Snow Private graveside services for Violet L Snow, 86, of 57 Warwick Place, Goleta, will be conducted in the Carpinteria Cemetery by Rev Paul M Gammons. Mrs Snow died Tuesday in Goleta Valley Hospital after an extended illness. She was born Nov 1, 1892, in Sacramento, the daughter of Mr and Mrs Charles E Twitchell. She attended school in Paso Robles and moved to Summerland in 1914. Mrs Snow married B B "Ted" Snow in El Montecito Presbyterian Church Dec 10, 1915. They lived in Toro Canyon for many years. Mr Snow died in 1959 (sic) ....(illegible) years at the Carpinteria Mutual Citrus Company. She is survived by a son, Bernard Snow of Goleta, a sister, Mrs Myrtle Lambert of Summerland; four granddaughters and 8 great grandchildren. Friends may remember their favorite charity in memory of Mrs Snow. ...Welch-Ryce...
 -Ibid Thu Aug 9 B4

## S N O W

1930 Ernest Snow Rites Tomorrow Funeral services for Ernest Snow, 78, early resident of Santa Barbara, who died early yesterday morning, will be held tomorrow afternoon at 2 o'clock in the L E Gagnier Chapel, Rev Jerome F Tubbs of Carpinteria officiating. Interment will be in Santa Barbara Cemetery. *-SB Morning Press* Oct 31 p. 4

1937 Mrs Snow, Pioneer, Dies Nancy Ellen Snow, 75, native of Humboldt County, died Wednesday evening at Templeton following a short illness. She was the wife of Ernest Snow, who died in 1930. For the past 60 years Mrs Snow had lived in San Luis Obispo County (!) most of the time being spent in the Adelaida section. She made her home with her son, Carl Snow, in Templeton for the past year. Surviving her are the following children: Carl of Templeton, Elmer Snow and Mrs Josephine Stewart of Carpinteria; Beverly Snow of Montecito, Mrs Annie Watson of San Jose, Mrs Ruby Thompson of Santa Barbara. Ten grandchildren, one great grandchild survive. Three brothers, Robert C Whitsitt and James Whitsitt of Adelaida and Jefferson Whitsitt, whose whereabouts are unknown, also survive. Funeral services will be held Saturday at 11 am at the Kuehl Funeral Home in Paso Robles with Rev Bruce Ellis, pastor of the Paso Robles Methodist Church officiating. Interment will be in the family plot in the Adelaida Cemetery.  -*SLO Daily Telegram* Fri Nov 26 p. 6

Whitsitt deaths, San Luis Obispo Co.:
    James H 18 Dec 1941; 20-358
    Stanton Dale 13 Jan 1965; 49-324
    Robert C 29 March 1968; 55-234
    Samuel Lee 17 July 1913; 7-358 Health

Summons: Callie E Whitsitt vs R C Whitsitt March 17 1909.      – *Paso Robles Leader*

1892    Samuel L Whitsett (sic) @21 5'11, light, grey, auburn, farmer, CA; Adelaida, Las Tablas, Adelaida, reg. Oct 20

Ernest Snow                      b. IL Nov 1853; m. @27 of Santa Barbara
                                     d. Santa Barbara 30 Oct 1930 @78
1880: @25 dairyman b. MO, parents MO, w/Huston Phillips, San Simeon tp SLO Co.
1890: @38 IL farmer Carpinteria
1892: @39 5'8½, light, grey, brown, scar on nose; IL; Carpinteria, Montecito, reg Aug 4
1900: Santa Barbara #1 (Carpinteria/Summerland); 1920: Same
     m. in house of Chadborn Whitsett 18 April 1881 by J L Jones
         wit: Silvester Ramage, Susanah Crane
Nancy E Whitsett                b. Humboldt Co CA Apr 1863; m. @17 of Adelaida
                                     d. Templeton 24 Nov 1937 @75
                                       F: (Samuel B Whitsett)

1. Carroll/Carl                        b. Sep 1882      d. before 1958
2. Elmer E                             b. July 1884
3. Josephine C (Stewart)         b. Aug 1886
4. Beverly Bernard               b. Sep 1890      d. 1958
5. Annie L (Watson)              b. Sep 1893
6. Ruby (Thompson)              b. Sep 1896

## 9. HANNAH IRENE TWITCHELL 1867-1953

1894    South Side Items. Hila* Wells and his family are visiting Mrs Wells' parents at Paso Robles.      - *SM Times* Aug 4
*Nickname, see Ontiveros

1895    Manzana Notes     Messrs C and H Wells finished seeding their large acreage this week.
                                                                                    –*SM Times* Jan 12

1895    Manzana Items     A few interesting notes from up the River. H Wells has concluded to sow more small grain since the last rain.      -Ibid Jan 26

Manazana Items     H Wells' donkey afforded much merriment at the lower ranch house the other day. It was equal to a circus.      –Ibid March 2

1897    Upper Sisquoc Items     Messrs Forrester, Wells and Tunnell Bros drove their cattle to the valley last week. Mr and Mrs Hiram Wells were on a trading venture this week. They disposed of some stock.      -Ibid July 3

1897    Upper Sisquoc Items    Mr and Mrs Hiram Wells made a trip to the valley this week, with a correspondent as ballast.

Mr and Mrs Wheat, Mr and Mrs Hiram Wells and family, and the too-numerous correspondent, with Matt. Story as general roustabout, made a trip to the Upper Sisquoc, the past week. The trip was a very enjoyable but difficult one to accomplish. The pleasure of it was somewhat marred by the discovery that some dastards had been killing fish by means of giant powder.

1900    H P Wells of Garey was a witness for Proof of Claim for G R Tunnell & Henry C Tunnell
-*SM Times* Apr 21

1927    Cambria, Sep 17  Mr and Mrs Wells and small child are the guests of Mr and Mrs Geo Warren. The men went for a hunt in the mountains.    – *SLO Daily Telegram*

1946    Edward Stemper Dies Suddenly    Edward Henry Stemper, 52, dropped dead with a heart attack Friday after he crossed the street in Paso Robles and started to enter Phlum's General Store. He had been in excellent health apparently. He was a native of Creston, having been born there on March 16, 1893. His entire life had been spent in that town. Stemper is survived by two sons, Eugene H, Oceanside, Calif, and Russell, of Creston; two brothers, Emil, Avila; and John, Salinas; a sister, Mrs Kate Schlegel, Creston, and two grandchildren. Funeral services will be held Tuesday at Keuhl's (sic) Funeral Chapel in Paso Robles at 1 pm with Rev Theodore Kaeusner of Paso Robles Lutheran Church officiating. Interment will be made in the Creston Cemetery. Pall bearers will be Henry Schlegel, Hubert Karau, Lin Clinton Brumley, Fred Phlum*, Clarence Wachs and Geo F Davis.    – *SLO Telegram-Tribune* Sat Feb 9
*See 1953 below

*Ed. Note*: Among original settlers of the Huer-Huero were Wells and Stemper families. "Edward Stemper married Hattie Wells of Creston in 1914; after two years they moved to Carissa Plains, and homesteaded near Mr and Mrs Wells."    – Creston 1884-1984

1953    Obituary Notices    Wells, Hannah Irene    Funeral services will be conducted at 10:30 am Monday in the chapel of Ericksen-Brown Funeral Home, Taft, for Mrs Hannah Irene Wells, 86, of 513 Hazelton Street, Maricopa, who died en route to a doctor's office Sept 30. Burial will be in the West Side Cemetery. Mrs Wells was born in Hollister, June 6, 1847* and came to Maricopa from Carissa Plains 14 years ago. Her husband, Hirman (sic) T Wells, survives her as do three daughters, Mrs Hattie Plumm of Creston, Mrs Hazel Woodard, Bakersfield and Mrs Hannah Hill, Maricopa; 10 grandchildren and 13 great-grandchildren.
*1867    – *Bakersfield Californian* Sat Oct 3 p.23

1954    Death Summons Hattie Plumm    Paso Robles, Oct 7  Mrs Hattie A Plumm, a native of California and a resident of Creston, died this morning in the Paso Robles hospital following a short illness. Mrs Plumm was born on March 19, 1895, in San Juan.* Her family came to the Carrisa Plains when she was a baby and later to Creston in 1900. Mrs Plumm's father was an early settler of the Carrisa Plains and Wells' Corner, east of here, was named after him. Mrs Plumm is survived by her father, Hiram P Wells of Winnemucca, Nev., a sister, Mrs Hazel Woodered (sic) of Bakersfield; two sons, Russell Stemper of Creston and Eugene Stemper of Gridley; four grandchildren. Funeral arrangements are under the direction of Kuehl Funeral Home where time and place of service will be announced.    -Ibid Thu Oct 7 p.2
**Ed. Note*: Her father's donkey was affording merriment in the Manzana two weeks before her birth. It is unlikely that her mother had gone to San Juan, but not impossible. The chronology is erroneous. Wells' corner was 7 miles southeast of Creston.

1955   Deaths   Hiram P Wells, 85, 464 Green Street, Maricopa, died yesterday in the West Side District Hospital, Erickson and Brown.   -*Bakersfield Californian* Wed Mar 2 p.42

Obituary Notices   Wells Hiram Presivid (sic)   Funeral services will be conducted at 11 am Friday in the chapel of Erickson-Brown Funeral Home, Taft, for Hiram Presivid Wells, of 564 (sic) Green Street, Maricopa, who died March 1 en-route to a West Side hospital. The Rev Max E Grelee, pastor of the First Presbyterian Church, will officiate. Burial will be in the West Side Cemetery. A retired farmer, Wells was born in Wisconsin, March 14, 1869, and came to the West Side 40 years ago. He is survived by two daughters, Mrs Hazel Woodard, Bakersfield, and Mrs Hannah Hill, Maricopa; 10 grandchildren, 14 great-grandchildren, and three sisters, Mrs Bell Holland, Cayucos; Mrs Charity Warren, Adelaid (sic) and Mrs Bertha Wright, Redlands.   -Ibid Thu March 3

1971   Vital Statistics Obituaries. Amelia R Joslin   Services will be held for Amelia Rebecca Joslin, 77, of Modesto, at 3 pm Friday in the Mausoleum of the Odd Fellows Cemetery. Arrangements are under the direction of the Salas Bros Funeral Chapel in Modesto. Mrs Joslin died Tuesday in a Modesto hospital. She was born in Holbrook, Ariz. She lived in San Luis Obispo from 1903 until about 25 years ago. She was active in Jobs Daughters and in the Order of the Eastern Star in San Luis Obispo. She is survived by a daughter, Helen Kiemele of Modesto; a son, Dan, of San Jose; a brother, Ted Testermon (sic), also of Modesto; 8 grandchildren and 19 great grandchildren.

WELLS-FORRESTER

Catherine Elizabeth Wheat 1845-1918       F: Hiram Preserved Wheat 1822-1903
                                          M: Elizabeth c1828-c1900
    m.1 1865 William Harvey Wells
1. Charles 1865-(1918)?   m. 1894 Annie St Clair
2. Emma Linda 1866-1947   m. 1883 Edward E Forrester 1860-1936
3. Hiram Preserved 1869-1955   m. 1891 Hannah I Twitchell 1867-1953
4. Mary Elizabeth 1874-1940   m. 1890 John J Twitchell 1861-1942

(Catherine)   m.2 William Merchant Forrester 1856-1912
5. Evalyn 1878-1940   m. c1895 Henry Holland 1873-1957
6. Isabelle E 1882-1969   m. 1903 Wm David Holland 1882-1971
7. Charity E 1885-1957   m. 1911 Geo Walter Warren 1879-1982
8. Bertha 1887-   (Wright) See *San Ramon Chapel Pioneers*, Ontiveros for photos and text.

STEMPER

1909   Creston, July 29   Peter Stemper left last Monday for a trip to Germany to be gone at least six months. The community wish Mr Stemper a most enjoyable trip but a speedy return into their midst.   -*Paso Robles Record* July 31

1914   Creston Pioneer Dies   Peter Stemper, a former rancher of the Creston section who in latter years had conducted a hotel in that section, died suddenly last evening of heart disease. Coroner Palmer held an inquest today. Burial will be held in Creston tomorrow (Tuesday).
   -*SLO Daily Telegram* Mon June 1

Peter Stemper           b. LUX (Ger) 27 Apr 1851;   imm 1872
                        d. 31 May 1914; Creston cem, m. c1882; to Tulare CA 1888
Mary Goutschy (Gautschy b. Switz Nov 1858; imm 1879
   or Giger)            d. 17 Dec 1936; Creston cem.1900; Santa Margarita tp

7 births, 5 living
Known:
1. Rosa (Kitchell)      b. NE Apr 1886; d. 1939
2. Katherine Elizabeth (Kate)      b. Tulare 15 July 1890; d. 23 May 1972
     m. (2nd wife) Joseph Schlegel Jr 1875-1964
3. Edward Henry      b. Creston 16 Mar 1893; d. Paso Robles 8 Feb 1946
     m. 1915 Hattie Adelia Wells 1895-1954 (divorced)
4. Emil Peter      b. Creston 8 Nov 1896; d. Arroyo Grande 2 Apr 1980
     m. 1919 Bertha Twitchell 1900-
5. John Adolph      b. Creston 20 Apr 1899; d. Paso Robles 8 Feb 1962
     m. Beverly Helena ____      d. 26 March 1972

## SCHLEGEL

Joseph Schlegel      b. GER Aug 1844; imm 1877; d.__
     m. c1870 Rosa ____      b. GER Dec 1845; imm 1876; d. 1 Jan 1932
     1900: Salinas tp SLO Co
     8 births, 7 living
1. (Henry)
2. Joseph      b. SLO co (nr Edna) 11 Sep 1875; d. 22 Feb 1964
     m.1 1900 Violet Brumley 1883-1909
     m.2 Katherine E Stemper 1890-1972
3. Amelia
4. Louisa
5. Lena I      b. July 1883
6. Mary
7. Minnie R      b. Nov 1886
8. Henry Howard      b. Mar 1893
     m. 1922 Laura M Adkins 1903-1984

See Creston 1884-1984; also Morrison & Haydon, *History of SLO Co and Environs*, 1917, p.809, Joseph Schlegel Jr.

# JOSHUA TWITCHELL JR.

Joshua Twitchell Jr      b. VT c1786
     1816: Tax list Meigs co OH      d. 24 Aug 1867 @62/11/12; San Juan cem
     1830: Salisbury tp Meigs co OH      F: Joshua$^5$, Thomas$^4$, Ephraim$^3$, Joseph$^2$, Benjamin$^1$
     1840: McDonough co IL
     1850: Sacramento, "eating house"; 1860: San Juan
     m. (Meigs co OH)?
Eunice Ursula Knight      b. MA c1797 (census) or 1807 (Tombstone)
     1970: Silas w/her      d. 1903; San Juan cem
     1880: w/Silas      F: (Silas Knight; Miegs co 1816)?
1. Eunice Corinthia      b. Rutland, Meigs co OH 27 Apr 1817 (IGI)
     d. 25 July 1881; San Juan cem
     "Mother of 12 children including J H Lawn" (Tombstone)
     m.1 (IL)
     ____ Lawn      b. Scotland; d. before 1848
     m.2 Sutter's Fort June 1849
     Samuel B Beckwith      b. NY c1820
     1850: Sacramento

|  |  |
|---|---|
| m.3 c1854 | |
| Benjamin H Hollowell | b. PA 1 Apr 1821 |
| 1870: San Benito tp | d. 8 Nov 1886; San Juan cem (Hallowell on stone) |
| 1880: San Juan pct | "In memory of daughter Sarah C Baker" on stone |
| 2. Jasper Harrison | b. Meigs co OH 1 Sep 1820 (bio) or 28 Oct 1821 (IGI) |
|  | d. San Juan 26 Oct 1894 @74; dropsy; San Juan cem |
| m.1 Macomb IL 8 Dec 1841 (IGI) | |
| Sarah Rutledge | d. On Oregon Trail Chimney Rock 1848 |
|  | F: (Andrew Rutledge; McDonough co 1840)? |
| m.2 Sutter's Fort? 1849 | |
| Emeline E Hopper | b. nr Quincy IL 2 Apr 1832 (IGI) |
| 1850: Sacramento | d. San Francisco 19 March 1912 @79; San Juan cem |
| 1860-80: San Juan | F: William Stephens/Stevens Hopper |
|  | M: Hannah Moore |
| 1900, 1910: she w/son Harrison, San Juan | |
| 3. Sanford Lorenzo | b. (Meigs co) OH c1825 |
|  | d. 6 April 1900 @77; Templeton cem |
| m. (KY; Twitchel Gen) | |
| Irene C Hopper | b. Adair co KY Dec 1827 (IGI) |
| 1850: Sacramento | d. 11 Nov 1905 @79; Templeton cem |
| 1860, 1870: San Juan | F: William Stevens Hopper c1803-after 1874 |
| 1880: Paicines | M: Hannah Moore c1802-before 1870; |
| 1900: she w/son Marion, | 1840: (Warren co IL); 1850: Sacramento |
| Morro tp SLO co | |
| 4. Silas Willis | b. OH c1830 |
| 1860-1880: San Juan | d. Fresno co 4-14-1911 @80 |
| m. San Juan 4 July 1874 by John W Whitney, 1-6 | |
| Elizabeth Bonner | died or divorced by 1880; he w/mother, no wife |
| 5. Julia Malissa | b. (McDonough) co IL 1832 (census) or Meigs OH |
|  | 20 Feb 1833 (IGI) |
| m. c1851 | d. Fresno co 4-1-1910 @77 |
| Alonzo Woodworth | b. NY 1825-30 |
| 1870: San Juan | |
| 6. Jane Electa | b. (McDonough co) IL c1838 |
| m. c1854 | d. Monterey co 7-19-1922 @88 |
| William P Ball | b. Culpeper co VA c1829 |
| 1870, 1880: San Juan | d. Carmel 19 June 1915 @88 |

The biography of Jasper Twitchell says his parents moved from Meigs co OH to McDonough co IL in 1830

# SANFORD LORENZO TWITCHELL

Sanford Lorenzo Twitchell        b. (Meigs co) OH 1823/5
                                                     d. 6 Apr 1900 @77; Templeton cem

    1874 GR: farmer San Juan, reg. May 5
    1875 Dir: farmer res 16 m S of Hollister; PO Paicines
    1889: Patent SLO co D203: Nov 4. Lot 1 W2SW4 S20 T27S R11E 156.86 acres
        (7 miles west of Templeton, near York Mtn)
    1892 GR: @67 5'5 fair complexion, blue eyes, grey hair, farmer, OH, res & precinct
        Josephine; PO Templeton

    m. (KY)
Irene C Hopper        b. Adair co KY Dec 1827 (IGI)
             d. 11 Nov 1905 @79; Templeton cem
1. Celesta Ann         b. Sutter's Fort 6 July 1849; m. @15 of Santa Cruz
  1900: Stockton w/George    d. Oakland CA 26 May 1934; bur Lockeford,
    8 births, 7 living        San Joaquin co
      m.1 Santa Cruz 27 July 1864 by J D Hyde JP, Santa Cruz tp (Old bk 1-124)
  William Augustus Stowell     b. Erie PA 19 April 1841; m. @19 of Syante Valley
    1874 GR: San Juan farmer     Consent by D I Harland, Co Clk
    1880: Paicines          d. Monterey co 20 May 1915 @77
    1884-5 Dir: Paicines Teamster    F: Dan$^6$, Augustus Oliver Artemis$^5$, Oliver$^4$,
    1900: Tuolumne co w/Seth;      Nathaniel$^3$, David$^2$, Samuel$^1$
     blacksmith           M: Louisa Barnum. Killed by Indians, Massacre of
    1910: Yolo co. bo, w/Herman     Mormons, Provo, UT 16 Mar 1856
    Waldeck (See Stowell Gen pp. 220, 419, 663)
  a. William Lorenzo        b. San Juan 22 Sep 1865
    1900: Mariposa co tp #1     d.
    1910: San Francisco
    1920: Cedar av Fresno, mechanic
      m. Llanada, San Benito co 1 June 1892 by Stephen H Langford, (2-308)
  Mary Eliza Strohn        b. CA July 1865
  = Hazel Louisa b. Llanada 25 Sep 1894; 1920: Cedar av Fresno
    m. Chas B McLaughlin b. CA c1894
   + Charles LeRoy b. CA 1919
  = Willeta May b. Llanada CA 8 March 1898
  b. George Daniel         b. San Juan 19 June 1867
    1900: Tuolumne co #3, (Livery stable) d. (Fresno co 12-2-1940)
    1910: Stockton
     m. Big Oak Flat (Tuolumne co) 13 Oct 1900
  Adelia Frances Van Geen      b. CA 1876
    1910: San Francisco (w/mother)   d. (Fresno co 1-23-1942)
                  M: Fanny
  = Leona May b. 24 Nov 1903
  = Thelma Maxine b. 1 Mar 1908
    1910: these girls w/father, Stockton
  c. Ellen Louise          b. San Juan 2 Nov 1869
                  d. (Washington)?
     m. Hollister 3 Apr 1889 by Wm G Lee; (2-118)
  James Bucanan Rardin/Reardin    b. OH 1 Feb 1857
    1882 GR: @25 OH farmer      d. (Washington)?
     Mulberry, reg Apr 29       F: Daniel Rardin
     (San Benito co)         M: ____ Pierrott
  = Anna Maude b. Hollister 15 March 1890
    m. Tecino CA 25 May 1907 Clifton Turvey; F: E N Turvey; M: Flora Angles
  +: Evelyn Louise
    Clifton Norman (Cliff Turvey b. 6 July 1912
                  d. Nov 1964; SSDI)
  = Jessie Louise  b. Hollister 26 Nov 1891
  = Lottie Estella   b. Oakland OR 30 Oct 1893
  = George Lewis  b. Oakland OR 4 Feb 1896
  = William James  b. Oakland OR 1 Sep 1899

|   |   |   |
|---|---|---|
|   | = Wilford Augustus | b. Bucoda WA 6 Sep 1904 |
|   | = Roland Eugene | b. Bucoda WA 17 Mar 1910 |
| d. | Franklin Augustus | b. Markleeville CA 31 Dec 1871 |
|   | 1900: Tuolumne co #3 teamster | d. Alameda CA 8 Apr 1910 @38 |
|   | m.1 Sacramento CA 2 Jan 1906 |   |
|   | Lilly May Washburn | b. CA 1890 |
|   | 1910: wid w/Hiram P Wells, niece | d. |
|   |   | F: IL  M: Germany |

m.2 Turlock 30 Aug 1911, John G Hoskins 1869-1937
Issue: Ruby M (W T Trivelpiece) b. 1914
Henry G b. 1918
1920: 2 listings: Turlock w/Hoskins
French Camp w/children
= Annie May died 1 Jan 1907 (SF 1 mo. 12-30-06 Grand death list)
= Melvin Franklin b. 21 Oct 1907
= Cecil Augustus b. 12 June 1909

|   |   |   |
|---|---|---|
| e. | Seth Marion | b. Markleeville CA 10 March 1873 |
|   |   | d. (Yolo co 7-24-1939 @65; spouse initial M O) |
|   | 1900: Tuolumne co w/father; machinist |   |
|   | 1910: 2 listings: Dorris, Siskiyou co w/family; Redding w/John Quistini |   |
|   | 1920: Alameda |   |
|   | m. San Francisco 19 Jan 1908 |   |
|   | Matilda Opie | b. CA July 1886 |
|   | 1900: svt w/Wm L Stowell | d. (Santa Clara co 4-27-1961; SSDI) |
|   | = Edith Elizabeth | b. Oct 1908 |
|   | = Bertha Frances | b. Feb 1910 |
|   | = Paul | b. c1913 |
|   | = Dorothy | b. c1915 |
|   | = Marian | b. c1917 |
|   | = Mildred | b. c1918 (1920: $1^{10/12}$) |
| f. | Henry Tilden | b. Paicines CA 2 Oct 1876 |
|   |   | d. Sonoma co 10-1-1965 |
|   | 1900: Tuolumne co w/Frank, blacksmith |   |
|   | 1910: Siskiyou co w/Seth;  1920: Electric av, Auburn CA |   |
|   | m.1 Coulterville CA 1 Jan 1901 (Mariposa co) |   |
|   | Pauline Mary Garbarino | d. before 1910? |
|   | = Phyllis Irene | b. 28 Dec 1901 |
|   | m.2 Marie L | b. MN c1879 |
| g. | Frederick Barnum | b. Paicines 2 June 1878 |
|   | 1900: Bakersfield, alone | d. |
|   | 1910: (68-61-323 county?);  1920: 1126 American av Stockton, real est |   |
|   | m. Oakland CA 15 Dec 1903 |   |
|   | Charlotte May Garbarino | b. Coulterville 17 Mar 1881 |
|   |   | d. |
|   |   | F: Angelo Garbarino |
|   |   | M: Theresa Ferretti |
|   | = Bernice May  b. Stockton 29 March 1905 |   |
| h. | Harriette Irene (Hattie) | b. Cienega CA 23 Oct 1882/3 |
|   | 1900: w/George | d. Sonora CA Dec 1972; SSDI |
|   | m. San Francisco 30 Aug 1905 |   |
|   | George Alexander Marshall | b. Hornitos CA 12 Mar 1881 (Mariposa co) |

        US Customs, Oakland         d. Yountville CA Apr 1975; SSDI
        No issue         F: Thomas Edwin Marshall
        M: Charlotte Sophonia Scott
  i.  Mary Ann Jeannette (Nettie)     b. Vallecitos CA 8 Feb 1884/6
      1900: w/George         d.
        m.1 Oakland CA 5 Jan 1907
      Henry Wadsworth Jones         b. MN 3 May 1880; SSDI
        1910: Oakland         d. Santa Clara March 1973
      = Violet Ann  b. 17 June 1908
      = Freda Mignon  b. 30 May 1910
        m.2 _____ Wendling
(1.)  m.2 William Hickok      b. PA c1847
    1920: French Camp, San Joaquin co    d. San Joaquin co 5-20-1930 @84; spouse initial "C"
2.  Martha Ellen         b. CA 1851; m. @16 of San Juan
        d. (San Joaquin co 2-17-1936 @75) no obit found
        *Stockton Record* or *Fresno Bee*
      1910: Oceano SLO co divorced; cook
      8 births, 6 living
      1920: SLO hskpr w/Easton Mills
        m. San Juan 15 March 1866
    Jacob C Adkins         b. OH 17 Mar 1828 (obit) or 1835* (census)
      1860, 1870: San Juan         d. Fresno 10 Mar 1929 @99 (Hype!)
      1880: Paicines         F: ME;  M: PA
        *m. @36 of Monterey co; could be 30 – writing not clear
      1892 GR: @56 5'10 fair complexion blue eyes grey hair laborer OH res Paso Robles
      1900: Madera
  a.  Joseph J         b. CA July 1866/7
      1900: Arroyo Grande         d. Lakeport CA 10 Sep 1944 @83
        m. San Luis Obispo 26 May 1891 by J H Barrett JP, D16
          wit: Hiram Wells, Santa Maria; Hannah Wells, Santa Maria
    Adelina Wheat Roberts         b. WI June 1851
      5 births, 5 living 1900         d. Doe Mill Ridge, Butte co 1 Apr 1935 @86
        F: Hiram Preserved Wheat 1822-1903
        M: Elizabeth _____ c1828-c1900
        m.1 Harry/Henry E Roberts b. France c1849
          = Elizabeth m.#8 C E Twitchell
          = Irvine Wm b. 1882
          = Dorothy (Cavell)
      = Jesse b. March 1893 (1910: @18 alone San Benito 74-24-161)
      = George Dewey b. March 1899
  b.  Anna Martha         b. CA 1869; d. before 1910
  c.  Jacob L         b. CA 1871
        d. (Fresno co 12-12-1931 @60)
      1910: Cholame w/Adriano R Gonzales, cattle ranch; Edw Willson #6a here also
  d.  Thomas J         b. CA 8 July 1875
      1900: Madera         d. Shoreham MI June 1968; SSDI
  e.  Nathaniel         b. CA 1880; died young?
  f.  Bert         b. CA 1881
      1920: Cholame         d.
        m.
    Mary         b. (7 Nov 1881; SSDI

```
                                                    d. Reedley March 1974)
              = Laura Marguerite      b. CA 14 Nov 1903; m. @18 of Annette, Kern co
                                      d. Paso Robles May 1984; SSDI
                 m. San Luis Obispo 27 Nov 1922 by Wm Mallagh JP, M421
                     Wit: Joseph Schlegel, Creston; Mrs Kate Schlegel, Creston
              Henry Howard Schlegel b. CA Mar 1893; m. @29 of San Luis Obispo
                                      d.
                                      F: Joseph Schlegel 1844-
                                      M: Rosa 1845-1932
                  1940: constable 218 Guadalupe St. Guadalupe, CA
              = Lawrence              b. c1909
              = Lucile                b. c1911
              = Vernal                b. c1913
              = Mirian                b. c1916
              = Noel                  b. c1918
      g.  F W                         b. (In Nevada 1928)
      h.  Jesse Wilburn               b. CA 1890; m. @21 of Paso Robles
          1910: Oceano w/mother       d. (San Mateo co 7-10-1940) ?
          1914: Oceano
              m. San Luis Obispo 1 Nov 1910 (I 83)
                  wit: Mrs V Testerman, Paso Robles; Mrs M E Adkins, Paso Robles
                  Consent of Mother of Amelia Rebecca Testerman…
              Amelia Rebecca Testerman    b. Holbrook AZ 10 Feb 1894
                                          m.1 @16; m.2 @21
                                          d. 16 Nov 1971; IOOF cem SLO
                                          F: Chas Games Testerman d. 1928
                                          M: Victoria 1871-1943
                                          m.2 SLO 25 Sep 1915 by Rev C B Allen, (J429)
                                              wit: Mrs Jose Y Villa, Mrs W B Weathers,
                                                  SLO; John L Joslin
                                          b. CA 13 Feb 1892
                                          m. @23 of Coalinga
                                          d. 29 Oct 1961; IOOF cem SLO
                                          F: John L Joslin 1851-1923
                                          M: Mary E 1852-1925
                                              1920: Avila, SLO co
                                          Issue: Helen Alberta b. 1920
              = Charles Dan           b. c1913
              = Elmer Ray             b. c1914   d. before 1971
                  These boys adopted by Joslin
              = Helen (Kiemele)
  3.  Lorenzo Philetus                b. CA 1853
                                      d. 25 Nov 1913 @60; Templeton cem
      1874 GR: 21 CA farmer Paicines, reg. Mar 25
      1880: Paicines w/Benj H Hollowell (uncle?)
          m. Hollister 20 July 1880 by B B McCroskey, 1-204
      Elisa Theodora Rosas            b. Salinas c1865; Feb 1864 (census)
      1900: San Juan, div             d. (in San Juan Bautista 1942)
      a.  Maggie Frances              b. Paso Robles 30 Aug 1881; Delayed Birth in
                                          SLO official records 322-281 Recorded 23
                                          Oct 1942 at req of Mrs Maggie Espinoza
```

        1900: w/Isabella Pico, Salinas          d. 1957; San Juan cem
           m. Hollister 13 Dec 1914 by G Agnew, 6-75
        Louis A Espinoza
    Others unknown. See end of chart for additions.

4.   Sanford Marion                  b. San Juan Sep 1854; m. @25 of Cambria
                               d. York Mtn SLO co 9 Mar 1924 @69
                                    Templeton cem; (6-164 Health or 10-79A)
      1877: @23 CA farmer Paicines, reg Sep 3
      1900: Morro tp SLO co
      1892 GR: @36 5'8 fair blue brown CA Josephine PO Templeton; 1902: same
      1920: SLO co
         m. Josephine 3 July 1881 by F J Dunn JP, A431; wit: James Miller, Cambria;
            Jacob Twitchell, Josephine. Written consent of parents of bride.
            "Mother married 3 times; 1. Butler; 2. Miller; 3. Griffith; don't know if dead
            or alive." (this on license)
      Mary Jane Miller                 b. CA Aug 1864; m. @16 of Cambria
        No Issue                        d.            F: TX      M: TX

5.   William Joshua                  b. (San Juan) Aug 1857; m. @28 of San Antonio
                                 d. Paso Robles 5 Jan 1937 @80; 17-27 Templeton cem
      1877 GR: @21 CA farmer Paicines, reg Sep 3
      1900: Tuolumne co #3; 1902 GR: @46 res Josephine, PO Templeton
      1912 Dir: farmer Creston
         m. San Lucas (lic. 1 Nov 1887) by Wilson Whitlock, San Lucas; Bk. B
      Jane Anne Dani                  b. Utah 7 July 1865; m. @22 of San Antonio
                                 d. Greenfield CA at home of dau Mrs Ingram
                                    2 May 1936 @71; King City cem
                                    F: (Gabriel Dani; 1884-5 Dir: 160a Jolon)
                                       (d. Monterey co 6-2-1908 @76)
      1920: 2 listings: Monterey co w/son Sanford; (Felton) Santa Cruz co w/daughters;
            divorced or separated
         5 births, 5 living 1900
        a.   Irene Elizabeth                b. CA 28 July 1888; m. @18 of Lucia
                                          d. King City 26 Apr 1984 @94; King City cem
            m. on Sunday afternoon 21 Oct 1906 at the Hubbel res, on the East Side (SCruz)
                by Rev E R Bennett of the Baptist ch, SCruz (old bk 12-113)
                wit: Joel Ingram, res nr SCruz; Mrs Sarah Ingram, SCruz.
                Consent of father of John F Ingram obtained (*Santa Cruz Surf* 23 Oct p.2)
            John F Ingram                   b. CA; m. @18 res nr Santa Cruz
            10 children; known:             d. 1965
            = William        b. 8 Oct 1909; SSDI; SS benefits to a Salinas address
            = Walter
            =Irene (O'Connor)
            =Hannah P (Miller)
            = Sarah (O'Connor)
        b.   William Alvin                  b. Templeton CA 14 Nov 1889; m. @30
             WWI                                of Lucia
                                          d. Pine Cyn Monterey co. 28 Aug 1960
            1920: farmhand w/Aaron W Harlan, Monterey Co
              m. San Luis Obispo 3 Jan 1925 by Wm Mallagh, N430
                  wit: John A. Mallagh, Mrs Wm Neal, SLO
            Lorraine Madeleine Garner        b. CA; m. @18 of Lucia
                                                   d. (King City) 9-4-1990

```
          = Jane Lorraine              b. SLO co 3 Nov 1925; (12 480)
             (Warren Gillis)           in 8th grade, Washington sch Cambria, 1930
          = William Frank              b. SLO co 26 May 1927 (13 403)
             WWII                      d. Monterey CA 16 Jan 1980 @52
          + Sue, Judith (Cumming), Thomas
          = Connie (George Folks)
     c.   Mary I/J                     b. CA 12 Jan 1892; m. @18 of King City
                                       d. San Jose Apr 1980; SSDI
          m.1 Santa Cruz 4 Nov 1909 by E R Bennett, Clgy (Old Bk 14-107)
             wit: Mrs E R Bennett, Santa Cruz
          Richard Dogherra             b. CA; m. @21, res nr Santa Cruz
                                       d. Santa Cruz co 2-8-1908 @66
                                       F: Felix Dogherra b. IT
             m.2                       M: Mary Pettijohn b. FR
          John Holcomb
     d.   Hannah C                     b. Jan 1895; m. @27 of Santa Cruz
          m. Santa Cruz 15 Sep 1922 by C W Hawkins, min, Santa Cruz (old bk 22-189)
             Wit: Albert H Quick, SCruz; Mrs F E Rodriguez, SCruz
          Landel A Bueb  aka Leland    b.       m. @35, of Santa Cruz
                                       F: (Landel Bueb 1846-1892; Holy Cross cem,SCz
                                       M: ? (Pauline b. SW 1845-17 Feb 1922) (or
                                           Zenobia Jane b. MS d 20 Oct 1938 @88
                                           IOOF cem SCz)?
     e.   Sanford L                    b. CA Jun 1897; m. @26
             1920: Monterey co ice truck driver   d. Sonoma co 5-11-1939 @41
          m. 1923 by C W Hawkins, MG of San Jose (1-309)
             wit: Hannah C Bueb, Jane A Twitchell, Santa Cruz
          Ida Wayne Milligan           b. CA m. @22; bookkeeper
                                       F: William Milligan b. ME
                                       M: Susi (Cooney)? b. CA
          = Sanford Edward     b. SCruz co 5-22-1924
          = Ida Geraldine      b. SCruz co 6-8-1925
          = Donald Lorenzo     b. SCruz co 9-3-1926
          = Shirley Ellen      b. SCruz co 12-26-1927
          = Marilyn Joyce      b. SCruz co 8-29-1931
     f.   Marjorie Ellen               b. CA 1901; m. @19 of SCruz
                                       d. before 1984
          m. Santa Cruz 8 June 1920 by Harry J Bias, JP, Santa Cruz (old bk. 20-262)
             wit: Mrs Jane A Twitchel, Hannah C Twitchel, Santa Cruz
          Samuel R Avila               b. CA; m. @22 of King City; rancher
                                       F: C C Avila, b. CA
                                       M: Florence Green b. CA
     g.   Bessie Inez                  b. CA 1905 m. @20 of Santa Cruz
                                       d. Santa Cruz co 5-3-1938 @33
          m. 1925 by L A Smith, min (3-287)
             Wit: Mrs Jane A Twitchell, Santa Cruz; Virgil E Miller, Watsonville
          Lloyd C Miller               b. CA; m. @21 of Corralitos
(These two girls listed twice with mother   F: James Frank Miller b. CA
          in 1920 census)              M: Fannie Horn b. CA
6.   Jacob Silas                       b. San Juan 15 May 1859
                                       d. Serena Park, Carpinteria valley 5 June 1932 @73
```

1892 GR: @30 5'7½ fair complexion blue eyes brown hair farmer Josephine
    PO Templeton
1900: Panoche tp San Benito co
1912 Dir: farmer, Creston
1920: Creston; to Carpinteria 1926
    m. SLO 17 Dec 1889 by J H Barrett JP, C17
        wit: Hiram Wells, Santa Maria; Carrie Woon, Garey. Consent of father…
Sophia E Woon                       b. NV April 1874
                                    d. Santa Barbara 19 Nov 1927 @53
                                    F: George Albert Woon 1846-1910
                                    M: Minerva Wheat 1846-c1885
  a. Maude May                       b. 18 Dec 1891; m. @18 of Creston
                                    d. Carpinteria 1 Apr 1956 @64; Carp cem
        m.1 Alexander Hotel, Paso Robles 26 Jan 1910 by B F Bonell, min, H551
            wit: Jacob Twitchell, Creston; Ramon Barba, Creston
        (See *Paso Robles Record*)
        Edward Ray Willson               b. Gilroy CA 9 Aug 1882
                                      d. Carpinteria 6 Oct 1965 @83
                                      F: Henry Sanford Willson
                                      M: Sarah Elizabeth Shepherd 1854-1936
                                        m.2 Santa Barbara 17 Nov 1930
                                                Flora Evalena Tognazzini
    1910: Cholame, w/Adriano L Gonzales, cattle ranch
    1920: Santa Barbara
    No issue
        m.2 Carpinteria 28 July 1930
        Albert B Christensen              b. Carpinteria 11 Aug 1895
                                        d. Carpinteria 18 Dec 1964; @69; Carp cem
      = Alice May (Cox) (Donovan)
      + Georgiemay, Bobbiekay Cox
  b. Carrie Ann                        b. 29 July 1893; m. @20 of Creston
                                    d. Arroyo Grande 31 Oct 1967 @74; (54-420)
        m. SLO 23 Apr 1913 by H H Hocker ME ch, I 594
            wit: B Y Harper, SLO; W A Kendrick, SLO
        William H Kendrick                b. Corsicana TX 2 Apr 1887;
                                         m. @26 of Santa Margarita
        1910: SLO co w/Wm Groundwater    d. Arroyo Grande 25 Mar 1974 @86
        1920: Fresno                            F: Wilie A Kendrick d. 1918
        = William       b. c1914
        = Walton O    b. c1918
        = John          b. after 1920
  c. Martha Irene                     b. Gilroy May 1895; m. @19 of Creston
                                    d. Santa Maria 7 Apr 1963 @65; SM cem
        m.1 SLO 19 Aug 1914 by Harvey H Hocker ME ch J224
            wit: Mrs Sophie Twitchell, Creston; Wm H Kendrick, Santa Margarita
        Miles E Sutfin                       b. CO 1893; m. @21 of SLO
                                        d. WWI? (no record CA death list)
        = Marvin J     b. c1915 (adopted) by step-father; called Sands
        = Marion F     b. c1916    These boys w/grandparents in 1920
        m.2. after 1920
        Jesse R Sands                       b. Greenfield CA 28 Sep 1892

      barber                                      d. Santa Maria 22 Nov 1962 @70; SM cem
      1920: Bassett st King City w/H Frank Brandt, brother-in-law
      =Robert L
      =Richard L
  d.  Octavia                          b. Jan 1897
        1920: w/Willsons             d.
          m.1 after 1920
      W F Wickham
          m.2
      Raymond Henry Santens         b. 5 Nov 1889
                                             d. 19 June 1969 (100-211) SSDI
                                               res Grover City
  e.  Bertha                           b. (Panoche) March 1900; m. @19 of Maricopa
                                        d.
          m. SLO 11 June 1919 by Gustav E Kirchner, Ev-Luth Ch, L10
              wit: Chas Robert Lawson, Maricopa; Octavia Twitchell, Maricopa
      Peter Emil Stemper             b. Creston 8 Nov 1896 (1-169 Delayed)
                                        d. Arroyo Grande 2 Apr 1980 @83; burial at sea
        1922 Dir: Los Alamos, cigar/tobacco    *SM Times* 3 Apr
        1942: to Avila                      F: Peter Stemper 1851-1914
      = Emil Jr                          M: Mary Gautschy 1858-1936
      + daughter, granddaughter
7.  John Jasper                       b. (San Juan) 1861; m.1 @22; m.2 of Templeton
     1900: San Juan tp              d. Summerland 14 Dec 1942
     1902 GR: res Josephine, PO Templeton
     1920: Morris Pl, Santa Barbara
        m.1 SLO 20 Feb 1882 by G W Barnes JP, A470
            wit: G W Morss, W D Manley, Arroyo Grande. Consent of parents for minor
    Terah E Morss                    b. CA 1865; m. @16, of Arroyo Grande
                                      d.
                                      F: George W Morss 1840-1919
                                      M: Elizabeth M _____ 1849-
                                        (m.2 John R. Drum)
      Deed, San Benito co 9-101: J J Twitchell to Terrah E Twitchell 29 May 1887. ½ int.
      SE4 S19 T15S R1OE (near Panoche)
        m.2 SLO 1 Apr 1890 by John H Barrett JP, B425
            wit: H. Laughery, Elizabeth E Laughery, SLO. Consent of mother for bride
    Mary Elizabeth Wells           b. Egan Cyn NV 6 Mar 1874
                                      d. Santa Barbara 10 Dec 1940
        1910 Highland Dist SLO co;       F: Wm Harvey Wells
          to Summerland 1914          M: Catherine Elizabeth Wheat 1845-1918
                                      m.2 W M Forrester
  a.  Nellie M(ary)                    b. Sep 1893; in Paso Robles HS 1910
        m.                                  d.
      Harold Herbert Mackie
      = dau (Mrs James Cumming)
      = Harold Herbert Jr              b. Santa Barbara 30 Aug 1927
        m. 16 Dec 1955 Betty Lou Curtis     d. drowned Santa Barbara Channel 10 June 1960
  b.  John Jasper Jr                   b. Upper Sisquoc 14 Feb 1897
        m.                                  d. Santa Maria 22 May 1945; Carpinteria cem
      Gladys R Doty                     b. Santa Barbara c1903
                                      F: Charles J Doty

              M: Annie L
  = John Jasper III (Betty L) b. 1927
  = Richard Lee (Patricia A) b. 1929
  = Robert Dean     b. 1932
  = Patricia Lou      b. 1935
 c. Leonard L        b. 29 Oct 1899
              d. Oroville 30 June 1980; SSDI
   m.1          (spouse initial J F)
  Mary Lucia Trucano Tveidt   b. 5 Dec 1908 Cartereggio, Italy
              d. Carpinteria 8 Nov 1955; Carp cem
               Her sons: John Tveidt, Richard Tveidt

  = Charles L       b. 1945
  = Sandra Lou      b. 1946
8. Charles E        b. (San Juan) 1863; m. of Santa Maria
              d. 5 Apr 1898 @35; Templeton cem
  Patent, SLO co F529, 22 June 1891: #15284. Lots 1,2,3 SE4NW4 S19 T27S R11,
   161.27 acres (Josephine/York Mtn area)
  m. SLO 27 Aug 1890 by John H Barrett JP, B460
   wit: Hiram Wells, Santa Maria; Hannah Twitchell, Santa Maria
   Consent of mother of Elizabeth Roberts, a minor, first obtained and filed
 Elizabeth Roberts      b. WI Feb 1877; m. of Santa Maria
  1900: Arroyo Grande tp widow d.
  3 births, 3 living       F: Henry/Harry E Roberts b. France c1849
              M: Adeline Wheat 1851-1935
               (m.2 J J Adkins)
 a. Rose Elizabeth       b. Paso Robles Apr 1891; m. @18 of
               Santa Margarita
              d.
  m. SLO 31 Oct 1908 by H E Smith JP, H283
   wit: May Twitchell, John Jasper Twitchell, Santa Margarita
  James Earl Clark      b. KS c1883; m. @25, of Creston
              d. (Merced 12-27-1934 @50 spouse initials RS)?
  = Violet Pearl    b. Creston 27 Aug 1909; (SLO co Delayed Birth 5-58)
   m. SLO co 23 Dec 1926 @17
   Charles W Shoemaker b. (11 Dec 1905)
      d. (Rio Dell CA Feb 1974) (SSDI)?
   1940, 1950, 1951 Dir: Los Alamos
 b. Violet L         b. (Sacramento) 1 Nov 1892
              d. Goleta 7 Aug 1979; Carp cem
  1910: w/J J Twitchell; to Summerland w/him
   m. El Montecito Pres Ch 10 Dec 1915
  Beverly Bernard Snow    b. Santa Barbara 1 Sep 1890
   1900: SB pct #1      d. Santa Barbara 12 Jul 1958 @67
              F: Ernest Snow 1853-1930
              M: Nancy Whitsett 1863-1937

  = Ernest
  = Bernard Elden   b. Santa Barbara 7 Mar 1923
    m. Jackie    d. Goleta 5 Nov 1981 @58; Carp cem (spouse initial E M)
   + Becky (Kent); Donna (Yaeger); Dee
 c. Myrtle Agnes        b. Paso Robles 25 Oct 1896* or
   1910: w/J J Twitchell      Dec 1895 (census)
              *See Summerland book by May Lambert

     m. Montecito 1 Nov 1915
    Cecil Edwin Lambert    b. Summerland 18 Oct 1896
               d. Summerland March 1977
               F: Fred Lambert 1872-1928
               M: Ella May Croop
    = William Edwin    b. Summerland 13 June 1916
    = Gwilda Lorraine (Loyd) b. Redlands 17 Jan 1919
9. Hannah Irene      b. (Hollister) 6 June 1867; m. of Templeton
              d. Maricopa 30 Sep 1952 @86
  m. Templeton 25 Feb 1891 by Wm Donelson JP, C31
    wit: Marion Twitchell, Lydia Twitchell, Templeton
  Hiram Preserved Wells    b. WI 14 Mar 1869; m. of Santa Maria
              d. Maricopa 1 Mar 1955 @85
              F: Wm Harvey Wells
              M: Catherine Elizabeth Wheat 1845-1918
  1890 GR: @21 WI Sisquoc  (m.2 W M Forrester)
  1892 GR: @23 5'4 dark complexion black eyes black hair WI res Sisquoc PO Garey
  1910: Creston, 6 births, 4 living; 1920: Maricopa
    (called Joe Hiram Wells on marriage license)
  a. Harvey L      b. 1892; 1920: w/parents
   (single)       d. (Kern co 5-17-1938 @46)
  b. Hiram P       b. 1893; 1920: w/parents
             d. (Kern co 11-19-1946) (spouse init L W)
  c. Hattie Adelia     b. (Manzana) 19 Mar 1895; m.1 @20
               of Santa Margarita
             d. Paso Robles 7 Oct 1954
    m.1 SLO 21 Apr 1915 by Gustave E Kirchner Ev-Luth ch, J343
     wit: Jos S Schlegel, SLO; Hazel Wells, Santa Margarita
    Edward Henry Stemper    b. Creston 16 Mar 1893; m. @22, of Creston
               d. Paso Robles 8 Feb 1946 @52
               F: Peter Stemper 1851-1914
               M: Mary Gautschy 1858-1936
    = Eugene Henry   b. SLO co 1916
    = Russell E     b. Taft 21 Oct 1917
            d. Paso Robles 13 Mar 1983
     m. 1939 Helen D Perry (Helen Marie on birth record of children)
      + Leon Russell   b. SLO co 1941 (Jan Alexandra Myers)
      + Gary Eldon    b. SLO co 1942
      + Gene Raymond  b. SLO co 1946 (Nanci Ann Jordan)
      +*Jerry Alan    b. SLO co 1955 *Leslie
      + Paul Wayne   b. SLO co 1960
    = Lois Aileen   b. SLO co 1920 d. 1924; Creston cem
     m.2 _____ Plumm
  d. Hazel E (Woodard)    b. 1898
  e. _____
  f. Bessie        b. Sisquoc 3 Aug 1902 (*SM Times*)
             d Oct; bur. Manzana
  g. Hannah L (Hill)     b. 1912

Addition to #3 Lorenzo Philetus from 1900 census, San Juan
    Twitchell Eliza b. Feb 1864; div; CA, parents CA; laundress
        Maggie dau Aug 1881 (listed again w/Isabella Pico, Salinas)
        Lily dau June 1884
        Joseph son Oct 1888
        Ida dau Nov? 1889

San Benito County marriages:
    Twitchell Joseph to Josie Joseph Nov 7 1906 by G Agnew, Hollister, 4-87
    Twitchell Josie J to Joe Frazier Sep 27 1914 by E A Pearce, San Juan, 6-47

Vol. XXV, No. 1 & 2, 1993, p.41


**Corrections and Additions**       [Page numbers refer to those in Quarterly]

Martin Carr Twitchell family
p.7.     Biography of Lazar Emanuel Blockman in the *Berkeley Gazette* on his birthday Nov 1939. Obit *Santa Maria Times* Tue Mar 19 1946 p.1

p.8.     John Wm Lee died in Santa Barbara, NOT Gilroy, 7 Jan 1953. Born Dunkirk NY 16 July 1886; came to Santa Maria 1918 to work in oil fields. Owned and operated a ranch near Phoenix AZ 1920-24; operated a service station in Gilroy where he lived the last 24 years. Survived by wife and son John W Lee; South Gate; 3 gch. Pall bearers: Glenn Twitchell, Jack Jullien, Fred L May, Cerfee Luis, Gordon Miller, Edward Reed.     –Fri Jan 9 1953

Sanford Lorenzo Twitchell family
p.33.     Adkins-Wheat data updated in Hiram P Wheat chart.

p.34.     Bert Nathaniel Adkins is one person; in Fresno 1931
    F W Adkins seems to be Ernest W Adkins
    Divorce: Jesse Wilburn Adkins vs Amelia R Adkins SLO co K63 Sep 24 1915
    Mrs Della Adkins of San Francisco visiting friends in Cambria; former resident of San Luis Obispo and Cambria.     –*SLO Morning Tribune* Oct 24 1924

p.38.     Woon-Wheat data updated in Hiram P Wheat chart as above p.7
    Octavia Twitchell Santens an accomplished artist, survived by her sister Bertha Stemper of Paso Robles, six nephews, a niece, and grand nieces and nephews.     –Sun Jan 9 1994 A-4

p.40.     Wells-Twitchell data updated in Wheat chart as above p.6
    Violet Pearl Clark Shoemaker died in Bakersfield 28 Sep 1993 @84; buried Los Alamos cem. Resident of Los Alamos 1929-1976. Survivors include brother (?=son?) Charles M Shoemaker, Redwood Valley; daughter Katharyn I Weston, Bakersfield; sister Lillian Payne, Ballard; 8 gch, 12 ggch, 4 gggch.     –Sat Oct 2 1993 A-5


Vol. XXX, No. 1, Spring 1998, p.13

## OUR TRIP TO CALIFORNIA 1848-1849 by LORENZO TWITCHELL

This account was submitted by Winona Woon Sears, who obtained it from her cousin, Octavia Twitchell Santens, a granddaughter of Lorenzo Twitchell. Octavia's mother, Sophia Woon Twitchell, was a sister of Winona's father, Ernest Woon. It is a valuable addition to the Twitchell story.

Copied from Xerox copy of handwritten journal, as well as could be deciphered, by W W Sears, 5 May 1988. Copy obtained from Octavia Twitchell Santens 13 June 1986, Oceano, CA.

April 8, 1848 our trip to Calif.

we left norvow on a monday morning bound for the calif gold mines  one month on our road we lost the twin boys our trip had been anything but pleasant 2 weeks out we had to garde the wagons at night we could not go over 15 miles a day  Some days only 10 miles as our oxen and cows could not travel fast had 2 cows on the toung 2 oxen on the leed I had 2 Sadle horses these i kept to hunt on as i was one of the hunters for the traine when we had tim 3 weeks out we came up to a train waiting for us  our train was only 75 wagons and they were 50 wagons then we had a very nice little train  father was captan of the train at end of a month we had a hot fight with the indians we lost 2 men but we came out victoras we buried our ded and started on our trip

May 9th 1848

i killed 2 big bufflows bulls when i got to camp irene was very sick.  we moved on the next day we traviled in peace untill the 13th then we had a hot Set to with indians they lost 2 and we lost 1 horse  when we got to plat river Sarah died here we layed over for 3 days She died right in the hotiest of a fight with the indians on Sweetwater we had a hot fight.  then all was peace and in oct 2 1848 we arrived in Salt lake here they told us we could not cross the mountains  So we wintered in Salt lake in april 2 1849 on a monday morning we left or fixt to leave but was detained.

April 2 1849

When the mormans found we intened to leave they preached out on the front end of a wagon and old preacher _masaliman said the men and boys can go and go to hell but wimon and stock will remain here we then got 5 mountaineers and they got 500 Sue indains to escort us and on tuesday april 4 we pulled out for california 4 days on our trip we was met by the distroying angels old port rockwell and his men there were 60 of them our train stoped and the out laws were 30 on each side of the train now it keep the mountaineers buisy to keep the indains from attacking them the captain of out laws told the train they were the distroying angles and that they wanted 2 little boys that the train had picked up out in the hills they had ben taken there by these 60 men one child was 5 years the other 10 they were brothers they had told him they had seen thire father mother and 2 smaller brothers killed by these men and how they had thrown them out for the wolves to eat i had the 5 year old boy father had the 10 year old one our 300 indians came to the california line then they went back and we came on we arrived at the old Sutters fort on the 4 day of july 1849

when we left Salt lake we were only 4 wagons of our train the others stayed in Salt lake

July 4 1849 here in California thank god and safe pitched camp at the west gate of the fort things was very high eggs was $100 each flour a dollar lb meat was cheap as elk deer and other game was plentiful iren was taken sick and on the 6th of July at 2:10 p m annie was born She being the firs white child born there we could hardly keep the miners out of the wagon they all wanted to see the first birth as soon as mother hopper could dress her I took her out to the miners to see. they near killed her or crushed her with gold dust my baby was very small only 3 lbs but she was the pet of the old fort  when she was 18 month old in 51 i moved to San Juan then monterey co.  there were 2 other children born there 5 weeks later at Sutters fort.  and in San Juan my girl was raised we had 8 other children after her 3 girls 6 boys annie was maried there to Wm Stowell

     i want each one of the children to have thire history from birth it is all here on difrent pages and my trip to the gold fields i there father Loranzo Twitchell

# WAITE
## LOS ALAMOS PIONEERS

Ezra Waite     b. Cambridge, Washington co NY 9 June 1800 (IGI)
   1850 cen: Huron co OH     d.
     Norwalk tp f     F: William Wait
           M: Alice Gilman
      m. Bethany, Genesee co NY 25 Feb 1829 (IGI)
Experience Keep Felt     b. Cavendish, Windsor co VT 19 July 1807 (IGI)
           d.

1. Mary Janett Waite     b. NY 1833 (cen)
           d.
      m. Huron co OH 7 Dec 1858 (IGI)
   Lanson Smith     b. OH c1826 (IGI)
           d.

2. William Felt Waite     b. OH 16 Nov 1834 (IGI)
           d.
      m. Huron co OH 10 Feb 1862 (IGI)
   Mary Elizabeth Prouty

3. Ezra Alonzo Waite     b. OH 1841 (cen)
   1870 cen: Labette co KS     d. (Los Alamos) 21 Dec 1880 @40/4/27
     Mt Pleasant tp       Los Alamos cem
     PO Ralston f
   1879 GR: 30 OH eng Los Alamos
   1880 cen: Los Alamos blacksmith
     First blacksmith in Los Alamos valley; Waite street named for him
      m. Huron co OH 26 Nov 1861 (IGI)
   Harriet Maria Prouty     b. Norwalk OH 22 Jan 1842; m.2 @42 of Los Alamos
     1884-5 Dir: Wait Mrs HM     d. at home of dau, Pleyto, Monterey co 26 Sep 1921
       proprietress of blksm       @79; in that place 6 mos
       & Wagon shop       obit Mon Sep 26 p.3
     1900 cen: Centennial st,     F: NY; M: MA (cen). F: MA; M: NY (2nd mar lic)
       Los Alamos; also w/Sturgeons, Pleyto
     1906 Dir: Centennial st
     1910 cen: tp 6 Los Alamos 6 births, 3 living
     1920 cen: w/Seth

   a. Nellie May Waite     b. IN June 1865 (cen) m. @18 of Los Alamos
           d. at home of son Homer 510 N Lincoln, SM,
              visiting from Los Angeles 5 Aug 1927
              @62/1/10; SM cem. obit Fri Aug 5 p.4   6gch
        m. Los Alamos 28 Aug 1883 by Rev Whitman, C67
          wit: Mrs H M Wait, Mr & Mrs George Stater
   Meriette Martin Sturgeon 1848-1926    See Sturgeon chart
     1887: Los Alamos Items. Mrs M Sturgeon of Merced is visiting her mother
       Mrs L Gates of this place.        -Nov 15

   b. Frederick A Waite     b. IN 1867
           d. (Los Alamos) 3 Mar 1879 @11/7/17
             Los Alamos cem. "Freddie son of EA & HM"

   c. Jennie Estelle Waite     b. KS Sep 1870; m. @18 of Los Alamos
           d. Los Angeles co 2-26-1931 @60

m.1 Los Alamos 6 Oct 1888 by W O Askins, C541
   wit: Seth Waite and Nancy W Askins

Frank Carson Hathaway     b. Sanilac co MI Mar 1863; m. @25 of
  1880 cen: River st,              Los Alamos
    Alpena MI                    d.
  1890 GR: 26 MI f Los Alamos     F: Frank Hathaway 1816
  1893. Los Alamos Items:          M: Susan 1837-     wd 1900 Los Alamos)
    Frank Hathaway leased the Hutt place… –date lost
    The mother and youngest brother of Frank Hathaway have come from Michigan to locate
      here. -June 24
    (Wm W Hathaway 1877-1966 Los Alamos cem. He and family went to Mariposa co
      before 1910 with Logans, Strongs, and Fosters) See Logan chart
  1900 cen: Shaw st Los Alamos
    bio Storke, 370: to CO @18; to CA 1885; to Los Alamos 1887, manager Los Alamos
=Harry B  b. Nov 1889                                        rancho
    1920 cen: 317 C st Eureka (24-44-11-8) @30 Lucile 27, Helen 5, Jean 1, all born Eureka
(c.)    m.2
 F Cunningham     living in Los Angeles 1927
d. Seth Richard Waite            b. Merced CA 6 July 1874; m. @25 of
  1890: Highland sch dist            Los Alamos
  see ONT                       d. 21 Nov 1958 @83; Los Alamos cem
                                obit Sat Nov 22 p.1; r Cat Canyon
                                Dominion Lease-Palmer Lease
  1893. The Los Alamos Fire    The chief business portion of the town reduced to ashes.
    On last Thursday morning a fire broke out about 4 am, in the paint shop a few doors east
    of the Alamo Hotel in Los Alamos. An east wind soon drove the flames westward the
    direction of the Alamo Hotel. In a very short time the buildings were reduced to ashes:
    Paint Shop and Barber Shop, owned by Seth Waite and valued at $1,000; The Alamo
    Hotel Block, valued at $20,000; the Laughlin Block, valued at about $10,000…supposed
    to be the result of an incendiary…                       –Sat Feb 23
  1900 cen: w/mother
  1906 Dir: rancher, Garey PO
  1906 Dir: also in Los Alamos D E Waite, barber, Mrs & Earl, stu.
  1905 Orcutt News: Earl Waite got work in the Union Oil mech shop. -June
    Daniel E Waite d. in Los Angeles co 12-3-1906 @40; is he one of the
    deceased-by-1910 children of Ezra and Harriet?
  1910 cen: Sisquoc, Bradley tract (also 1914 & 1922 Dirs)
  1932. Los Alamos Notes. One of the oldest buildings and landmarks of the town was razed
    on the James Eddy property during the week…one of the first barns built in the valley and
    was used many years ago by B F Whitney as a blacksmith shop and later by Seth Waite…
      m. Lompoc 15 Nov 1899 by J E Elliott, ME ch            –June 25
        wit: J S Graham, Esther Graham, Lompoc
Nellie/Helen/Ellen Bradley        b. (Sisquoc) 29 July 1873; m. @25 of Garey
  1900 cen: 1 birth 1 living           d. close to birthplace 26 Oct 1938 @65
  1910 cen: 1 birth 0 living             Los Alamos cem. obit Thu Oct 27 p.1
                                F: Paul Bradley 1820-1890
                                M: Elizabeth (wd of Spencer) 1825-1914
                                see Elvidge chart
=her son Royden Bradley           b. 9 Apr 1892; SSDI
  1900 cen: w/gm "adopted"           d. July 1971
  Apr 1906 7th grade Suey sch

Aug 1907 Suey sch, step-son of Seth Waite. See ONT 387-8
1910 cen: w/Seth "brother-in-law"; 1920 cen: Sisquoc bunkhouse w/Roy Tulles
1922-3 Dir: oil wkr     1928 Dir: rotary helper Palmer Union Rt A
1955-6 Dir: Rt 1 Box 199A; 1961 Dir: same
    m. c1928
Charlotte Etta Sturgeon Severns 1898-1931; see E L Sturgeon chart 1.d.
+Richard Royden SMUHS 1947
    1955-6 Dir: Richard R (Janet) Bradley's Norwalk Svc Sta; h 736 E Central SM
      Bradley Norwalk Ser Sta (Dick Bradley) auto svc, trlr rental 619 N Bwy
    1961 Dir: Bradley Rchd R (Janet) Dick Bradley's Norwalk Svc, h 1022 N Thornburg SM
      Bradley's Dick Norwalk Svc Tires Batteries & Accessories. Trailer Rentals. Agents
      Natl Tlr Rental Assn. S&H Green Stamps. 619 N Bwy
   e. Fannie J Waite     b. CA 1 Dec 1876
      d. 3 Mar 1882; Los Alamos cem
4. Albert Henry Waite     b. OH 1843 (cen)    d.
    m. Norwalk OH 2 Feb 1869 (IGI)
Harriet Rosanne Wooden
5. Homer Hosea Waite     b. Norwalk OH 21 Nov 1845 (IGI)
    blacksmith Los Alamos (T/W)     d. San Luis Obispo CA 23 Dec 1909 @64/1/3 buried
      Los Angeles. obit *SLO Daily Tribune* Dec 23 p.1
    1883-4 McKenney Dir:     also Dec 28 p.1
      H H Waite blksm Los Alamos.     1884-5 Dir: Wait Hamer H Carp (sic)
    1892 GR: 47 6' wht hz gry mach OH SLO #4
    1893: About the Country. Business Affairs in San Luis Obispo…Mssrs Waite & Ryan
      are doing an immense business in their planing mill and foundry. G B Hopper,
      formerly in business in Santa Maria, is helping in their foundry and he says he has
      a good position and is going to stay with it. (See Hopper chart) .     -March 11
    1900 cen: San Luis Obispo "single" millwright
    1909. Prominent Business Man…to Merced CA @30; planing mill in Oakland, burned,
      no insurance; to Los Alamos for 3 years; then to San Luis Obispo, planing mill
      & machine shop with Ryan; kept it after Ryan died, until too ill…pall bearers:
      J A Renetzky, D C McMillan, D W Ford, Jas Wilkinson, H H Carpenter, T A
      Greenleaf. Funeral from family residence.
      m.
Sabrina L     d. Los Angeles co 1-10-1925 @68
    1912 Dir: Waite Iron Wks (F A Faulkner) 246 Higuera SLO
      Faulkner Forrest A (Waite Iron Wks) h 1130 Pacific SLO

Vol. XXVIII, No. 4, Winter 1996, p. 10, 11

**Corrections and Additions**     [Page numbers refer to those in Quarterly]

p.10. Two Men Injured in Road Crash. Car Rams Truck. Vehicles Suffer. Royden Bradley was cited for failure to observe "Boulevard Stop" at Rosemary road and Stowell; his car rammed a heavily laden grain truck. Seth R Waite suffered a brain concussion; Bradley, his son-in-law (sic), had minor injuries. They were residents of Bradley Canyon. Martin Serna, the truck driver, was cited for having an expired chauffeur's license.     -Thu Nov 14 1940 p.1

p.11. Marriage: Homer Hosea Waite m. @54 of SLO. m. SLO 29 Sep 1901 by Rev Geo H Bigelow, F149; wit: Mary Renetzky, SLO; Mrs J Wilkinson, SLO
    Bina L Ryan b. NY m. @42 of SLO, apparently widow of Waite's former partner.

Vol. XXIX, No. 4, Winter 1997, p.18

# WHEAT
## PIONEERS OF THE CALIFORNIA CENTRAL COAST

Hiram Preserved Wheat (Wheet)
  1850: Wayne co MI, Greenfield
  1885: to Manzana
  1890 GR: 70 NH Sisquoc; reg Aug 16
  1892 GR: 66 (!) 5'10 light complexion
    blue eyes grey hair NH Sisquoc
    PO Garey; reg Aug 27
  1896 GR: f 74 5'9 lt blu gry NH Sisquoc
  1900 GR: 81 Arroyo Grande #2 PO Arroyo Grande
  1900 cen: Arroyo Grande tp (Oceano) w/J J Adkins
  1902 GR: 84 Arroyo Grande #2 PO Oceano
  1902: Deed H P Wheat from Wm M Forrester Mar 8 SLO co 50-446
  1903: Deed H P Wheat to Adeline Adkins Apr 11 SLO co 55-617; block 3
    Warner's add'n to town of Oceano, 3 acres. Also Strattons
    subdivision...signed by mark H P Wheat.
    b. NH Apr 1822 (cen)
    d. Oceano CA 14 May 1903 @85; Wood-Voakes records. Funeral ordered by J J Adkins
    parents born VT
  m.
Catherine Elizabeth
    b. Canada c1828
    d. at home of daughter near Templeton CA 1897     -*Times* Sep 4

1. Catherine Elizabeth
  1900: tp #8 (Casmalia)
  8 births, 8 living
    m.1 22 Feb 1865
  William Harvey Wells
    b. (Greenfield) MI 5 Nov 1845
    d. Los Angeles co 2 Sep 1918 @75 (W)
    b. RI/VT
    d. (1897)

  a. Charles A Wells
    1890 GR: 26 WI f Sisquoc
      reg Aug 16
    1892 GR: 27 5'6¾ lt br
      br WI La Graciosa PO Santa Maria; reg Sep 1
    1892: Deed Chas Wells of SLO co to J H Logan of SM; NE4SE4, SE4NW4
      N2SE4 S17 T32 R17E 160a, SLO co 35-279, Oct 20
    1893: Letter list *SM Times* Mar 11: Chas Wells
      m. San Luis Obispo 31 July 1894 by M Egan JP, D496
        wit: Hiram Wells, SM; Mrs Hannah Wells, SM
    b. WI 17 May 1866; m. of SM
    d. Maricopa/Cuyama 16 Aug 1918 @52 Midway cem, Taft. Notice in *Bakersfield Californian* 17 Aug
    Annie M St Clair
    =No issue in his obit
      b. NV 1877; m. of SM
      d.
      F: L W St Clair (1880: StarValley, Elko co NV)
      M: Helen R Forrester

  b. EmmaLinda Wells
    b. WI July 1866; m. @16
    d. Yolo co CA 3-12-1947 (EE)
    m. Santa Maria 17 May 1883 by D G Wright, B615
      wit: L L Forrester, Mary E Wright, G A Woon
    Edward Everett Forrester 1860-1936; see Forrester chart

  c. Hiram Preserved Wells
    1890 GR: 21 WI f Sisquoc
      reg Aug 4
    b. WI 14 March 1869; m. of SM
    d. Maricopa 1 Mar 1955 @85; obit *Bakersfield Californian* Thu Mar 3

1892 GR: 23 5'4 dk blk blk WI Sisquoc PO Garey; reg Aug 22
1896 GR: Hiram Purified (!) f 26 5'5 lt br br WI Sisquoc
1900 GR: 28 Arroyo Grande #2 PO Oceano
1904 GR: 37 Arroyo Grande #2 PO Oceano
1910: Creston
1912 GR: rancher Santa Margarita, dem
1919: Patent SLO co June 2
1920: Pozo
1938: Carissa Plains
    m. Templeton 25 Feb 1891 by Wm Donelson JP, C31
        wit: Marion Twitchell, Templeton; Lydia Twitchell, Templeton
Hannah Irene Twitchell 1867-1953: see Twitchell chart
    1892: Patent SLO co Mar 26 Hannah Twitchell
    1912 GR: housewife Santa Margarita, dem

| =Harvey Lorenzo | b. Sisquoc 13 Dec 1891 |
|---|---|
|   1920: Patent | d. Taft 17 May 1938 @46; appendicitis |
|     SLO co Apr 21 |   West Side cem, obit *Taft Daily Midway* |
|     rancher; single |     *Driller* May 17 |
| =Hiram Preserved | b. Sisquoc 3 June 1893 |
|   1920: Patent | d. Taft 19 Nov 1946 @53; thrown from horse |
|     SLO co Apr 21 |   West Side cem, obit *Midway Driller* Nov 19 |
|   m. | |
|   Laura Stubblefield | b. (Cuyama valley) 1907 |
| | d. (living 1995) |
| | F: Wm Riley Stubblefield 1870-1934 |
| | M: Sadie Pearl Jobe 1884-1956 |
| | See *Cuyama Valley*...Albright 1990 |
|   +Rosalie (Norris) | |
| =Hattie Adelia | b. (Manzana) 19 Mar 1895; m.1 @20 of Santa Margarita |
| | d. Paso Robles 7 Oct 1954 |
| |   obit *Bakersfield Californian* Thu Oct 7 p. 2 |

    m.1 San Luis Obispo 21 Apr 1915 by Gustave E Kirchner, Ev-Lutheran ch, J343
        wit: Jos S Schlegel, SLO; Hazel Wells, Santa Margarita
Edward Henry Stemper 1893-1946; see Twitchell chart
    (Hattie Stemper vs Edw Stemper Oct 7 1934; judgement #10257 SLO Bk S p. 379)
  +Eugene Henry    b. SLO co 1916
  +Russell Edward b. Taft 21 Oct 1917; m. @21 of Paso Robles
        d. Paso Robles 13 Mar 1983
    m. SLO 10 Feb 1939 by A E Mallagh, W415
        wit: Johnny Perry, Paso Robles; Madelon McKim, SLO
    Marie Helen Perry b. CA m. @18 of Paso Robles
        F: Manuel M Perry;  M: Mary Areia
  +Lois Aileen b. SLO co 1920; d. 1924; Creston cem
=Hattie m.2 before 1938

| Ralph R Plumm | b. (Lompoc) 1903 |
|---|---|
| | d. SLO jail 3 Sep 1946; suicide |
| |   story: see Scrapbook |
| | F: Charles F Plumm c1850-1925 |
| | M: Nettie A Ball 1873-1965 |

    (Hattie A Plumm vs Ralph Plumm case #12966, c1942; no data in index)

  =Hazel E          b. 1898
   m.1           d. Kern co 12-15-1964 (MB)
   Homer Q Bradfield     b. CA c1895; d. Kern co 11-8-1946 (HE)
    1920: Fresno
    1938, 1946: Bakersfield
   +Iris and +Barbara Bradfield
    m.2 by 1953
   Michael Woodard  1953, 54, 55: Bakersfield
  =_____
  =Bessie          b. Sisquoc/Manzana 3 Aug 1902 (*Times*)
              d. Oct 1902; bur Manzana

  =Hannah L         b. 1912; d. Kern co 1-24-1959 (WS)
   m.
  William Smith Hill 1938: Carissa Plains; 1946, 1955: Maricopa
   ? (Wm Hill SSDI    d. 12-6-1955 Kern co)?
  d. Mary Elizabeth Wells     b. Egan Canyon NV 6 March 1874
               d. Santa Barbara 10 Dec 1940
                obit *SB News-Press* Wed Dec 11 p. 16
   m. San Luis Obispo 1 Apr 1890 by John H Barrett JP, B425
    wit: H Laughery, SLO; Elizabeth Laughery, SLO. Consent
     of mother for bride
   John Jasper Twitchell 1860-1942; see Twitchell chart
    1896 GR: f 32 5'10 dk br br CA Summerland
    1900: 2 census listings: San Juan tp, Monterey co; also Salinas
     in a hotel w/Geo W Morss, his first father-in-law
    1902 GR: 39 Josephine PO Templeton
    1904 GR: 39 Arroyo Grande #2 PO Oceano
    1910: Santa Margarita
    (*Note*: Jacob Twitchell, a brother, went to Oceano in 1903 and
     operated a livery for three years. -M/H)
  =additional notes on the children to augment Twitchell chart
   Nellie M graduated from what became Santa Barbara State Normal
    School. 1924 Alumni Notes: Mrs H H Mackie, Summerland
   John J Jr graduated from Santa Barbara High School 1916, transferred
    from Paso Robles High School
(1.) m.2 c1876
  William Merchant Forrester 1856-1912; see Forrester chart
2. Minerva           b. (Greenfield) MI c1846
              d. Santa Barbara c1885
   m. c1873
  George Albert Woon      b. Canada 1845
   1882: blksm/wgnmakr   d. San Luis Obispo co 11-16-1910 @65
   w/ L L Forrester,       no obit found
   Central City-Santa Ynez rd, ½ mi from Juan Flores. -T/W p. 307
  1888 GR: 42 CAN blksm Sisquoc
  1888 Polk Dir: blksm Santa Maria
  1890 GR: 44 CAN blksm Sisquoc
  1892 GR: 46 5'9 lt blu br CAN nat Sep 12 1886 SB Sisquoc PO Garey reg Sep 1
   a. Sophia E Woon       b. NV Apr 1874
              d. Santa Barbara 19 Nov 1927
              obit *SB Morning Press* Sun Nov 20 p. 2

m. San Luis Obispo 17 Dec 1889 by J H Barrett JP, C17
   wit: Hiram Wells, SM; Carrie Woon, Garey. Consent of father...
Jacob Silas Twitchell 1859-1932; see Twitchell chart
=Maud M 1891-1956 m.1 1910 Edward Ray Willson 1882-1965
             m.2 1930 Albert B Christensen 1895-1964
  +Alice May (Cox) (Donovan) b. 1935
=Carrie Ann 1893-1967 m. 1913 Wm Henry Kendrick 1887-1974
  +Wm Albert 1914-1980
  +Walton Oliver 1917-
  +John Jacob 1921-
=Martha Irene 1895-1963 m.1 1914 Miles Sutfin
    (Mattie I Sutfin vs Miles F Sutfin July 22, 1920; judgement #5898 SLO bk L p. 156)
        m.2. Jesse Robert Sands 1892-1962

| | |
|---|---|
| =Octavia | b. Panoche, San Benito co 19 Feb 1898 |
|   1920: Santa Barbara | d. Arroyo Grande 6 Jan 1994; AG cem |
|   w/Willsons |   obit Sun Jan 9 A-4 |
|   m.1 after 1920 | |
|   Wilder Frank Wickham | b. MI 28 Jul 1896; SSDI |
|     1920: Fresno w/Wm C Reeder | d. Reno NV Feb 1971 |
|   m.2 | |
|   Raymond Henry Santens 1889-1969 | |

=Bertha 1900-living 1995; m. 1919 Peter Emil Stemper 1896-1980

| | |
|---|---|
| b. Caroline/Carrie J Woon | b. CA 1875 |
| | d. Monterey co 13 Mar 1893 @16; Strych- |
| |   nine. Inf: S B Gordon, coroner, Bradley |
| c. Ernest Hiram Woon | b. CA 1879; m. @32 of Carpinteria |
|   1910: SLO alone | d. Santa Cruz co 18 Aug 1965 (ME) |
| |   res Gilroy; dairyman |
|     m.1 Santa Barbara 23 Dec 1911 by Rev Warren D More | |
|   Katherine Mabel Sanders | b. SLO Oct 1889; m. @21 of SLO |
|     Teacher | d. San Jose 12 May 1948 |
| |   obits *Gilroy Dispatch*; see scrapbook |
| |   F: Joseph Sanders |
| |   M: Sadie |

  =Winona Sara 1913-1995 (David R Sears MD d. 1993)
  =Barbara Minerva 1915-  (Ivan Chester Buckner)
  =Rosalie Katherine 1922-  (Samuel David Stephens)
  =Ernest B 1925-1963
 (c.)  m.2
  (Mary E Hautow d. Santa Cruz co 4-25-1969)

| | |
|---|---|
| 3. Lucy F | b. Greenfield MI July 1850 |
| |   died young or ran away... |
| 4. Adeline | b. WI June 1851 |
|   1900: Arroyo Grande tp | d. at home of dau Lillian Dorrett, Doe Mill |
|   5 births 5 living |   Ridge, Butte co 1 Apr 1935 @86; Chico cem |
| |   obit *Chico Record* Tue Apr 2 p. 3 |
|   m.1 WI | |
|   Henry E Roberts | b. France c1849 |
|    (Harry) | d. (Alaska?) |

  1888 GR: 38 cook SM nat Oct 1887 SB Sup CT, reg July 6
  1892 GR: 42 5'5 dk br br FR SM nat 1 Oct 1887 SB Sup Ct, reg Sep 19

1891: Letter List *SM Times* April –(Mr) Roberts
   a. Elizabeth Adeline Roberts        b. WI Feb 1877
     (Libby/Lily)                     d. (Carmel?) (Married several times;
    1900: Arroyo Grande tp             surnames unknown)
    3 births 3 living
       m.1 San Luis Obispo 27 Aug 1890 by John H Barrett JP, B460
          wit: Hiram Wells, SM; Hannah Twitchell, SM. Consent of mother for bride
   Charles E Twitchell 1863-1898; see Twitchell chart
    =Rose Elizabeth            b. Twitchell ranch nr Templeton Apr 1891
                               d. Santa Maria 25 July 1955 @64/3/0; SM cem
                                   obit Tue July 26 p. 6
      m.1 San Luis Obispo 31 Oct 1908 by H E Smith JP, H283
         wit: John Jasper Twitchell, Santa Margarita; May Twitchell,
         Santa Margarita. Divorced c1922
      James Carl Clark          b. KS; m. @25 of Creston (worked for H P Wells)
       1920: Sisquoc                 d. 27 Dec 1934; buried Los Banos
       1922 Dir: Jas Clark rancher w/Fugler & Purkiss
        +Violet <u>Pearl</u>               b. Creston 27 Aug 1909; 5-58 Delayed SLO co
                                  d. Bakersfield 28 Sep 1993 @84; Los Alamos
                                    cem, obit Sat Oct 2 A-5, m. @17
           m. SLO co 23 Dec 1926
         Charles Walter Shoemaker      b. Joplin MO 11 Dec 1905
                                       d. Bakersfield 12 Feb 1974 @68; Los Alamos
                                       cem, obit Thu Feb 14 p. 2, rLos Alamos
                                       1914-60
                                       F: Chas Isaac Shoemaker 1854-1922
                                       M: Lily Annette Cooper 1868-1957
      ~Marvel A (W A Taylor) d. Santa Cruz co 1-14-1930 @18
      ~Charles J Clark 1914-1977
      ~Lillian Blanche 1917-   (Donald A Payne 1914-1983)
      ~Harry W Clark USN 1921-1990
   (=)Rose Elizabeth Twitchell Clark m.2 Castroville CA 19 Nov 1928; 17-326
      Earl Raymond Saulsbury       b. KS Dec 1888 (cen) 20 Dec 1889 (Hawley)
                                       d. Santa Maria (3) Jan 1944 @55/0/11; SM cem
                                       obit Mon Jan 3 p. 3
                                       F: Joseph Saulsbury 1854-1921
                                       M: Annie E (in Berkeley 1944)
    =Violet L 1892-1969 (Beverly Bernard Snow 1890-1958)
    =Myrtle Agnes 1896-19__   (Cecil Edwin Lambert 1896-1977)
      see Twitchell chart          Rose, Violet, and Myrtle lived in the Odd Fellows
      Orphanage in Vallejo until c1907, when their uncle, H P Wells, brought them to
      Creston.        -Lillian Payne
   b. Irvine Wm Roberts               b. CA Feb 1882
      1900: w/J J Adkins                d.
      ?1908 GR: Erwin H Roberts 26 lab SLO #2?
      ?1910: rArcher st SLO, Cook Hotel w/Richard Pierce family?
        m. ?1907
      ?Nettie L                          b. Cayucos 21 June 1882
                                       d. 721 Monterey st SLO 3 Sep 1951; OM cem
                                       obit *SLO Telegram-Tribune* Mon Sep 3 p. 8
                                       sis Mrs Rafael Mora, SLO

*Note*: Lillian Payne thinks Uncle Irvine was single; IF this is the man in question, he could have been divorced by the time she knew him. Her niece, Yvonne Hawley, added data.

    c. Dorothy Helen (Roberts?)      b. CA 1891
        1920: w/mother Chico      d.
        m.1
          Barton
    =Opal R      b. TX c1914 (1920: w/gm Chico)
        m.2 after 1920
      Todd Carvell

(4.) "Miss Adeline Wheat" m.2 San Luis Obispo 26 May 1891 by J H Barrett JP, D16
    wit: Hiram Wells, SM; Hannah Wells, SM also (*Times*)
    Divorced 1904?

| | |
|---|---|
| Joseph J Adkins | b. CA July 1866; m. of Santa Maria |
|   1896 GR: Sisquoc f 29 | d. Lakeport CA 10 Sep 1944 (AA) |
|   5' 9½ lt blu br CA | obit *Lake Co Bee* Fri Sep 15 p. 8. 2 sons |
|   1900 GR: 33 AG #1 | F: Jacob C Adkins 1835-1928 |
|     PO Oceano | M: Martha Ellen Twitchell 1851-1936 |
|   1900 cen: Arroyo Grande tp (Oceano) | |
| d. Jesse W | b. CA Mar 1893 (cen) |
|   1900: w/J J Adkins | d. |
|   1910: (@18 Panoche, mine yard?) | |
|   1920: w/mother Chico @22! | |
| e. George Dewey/Geo N | b. CA March 1899 (cen) |
|   1920: w/mother @19! | d. (Butte co 9-23-1963; SSDI)? |

Chico Directories
1920    Adkins Adeline (wid Jos) r4235 5<sup>th</sup>
        Geo N opr Lyric Theater b4235 5<sup>th</sup>
        Jesse W emp DMco (Diamond Match co) b4235 5<sup>th</sup>
        Barton Dorothy wtrs Federal rest b4235 5<sup>th</sup>
1927-8  Adkins J W w/DMco r1417 S Bwy
        Jess lab h1930 S Normal Av
      Carvell Dorothy H (wid Todd) h1417 S Bwy
1929-30 Carvell Dorothy H (wid Todd) h4527 1<sup>st</sup> Av CV (Chico Vecino)

Vol. XXVII, No. 4, Winter 1995, p. 9

**Corrections and Additions**     [Page numbers refer to those in Quarterly]

p.5.    Land Notice. Hiram P Wheat #20663 (20668?) S2NE4 NW4NE4 NE4NW4 S26 T9N R30W. Wit: Henry Roberts, L L Forrester, Albert Woon, Edward Forrester, all Santa Maria PO.
                                                                                                       –April 1888

p.5.    Joyce Preuitt of Taft has submitted data on the Charles Wells-Annie St Clair family. They were in Elko co NV, Star Valley precinct on the 1900 and 1910 censuses; Annie was there in 1920, a widow. They had seven children: Harvey Leonidas b. NV Dec 1894; Lottie E b. CA June 1897; Charles jr b. NV 1901; Lloyd E b. NV 1902; Lois B b. NV 1904; Ida M b. NV 1907; and last boy, Clair, b. NV 1908.

Vol. XXIX, No. 4, Winter 1997, p.21

p.8.   Marriage: Elizabeth (Roberts) Twitchell of Paso Robles, former husband dead.
m. SLO co 24 Mar 1899 by J Lambert Clay, E379; wit: J J Adkins, SLO; Mrs Adkins, Paso Robles, Wm Waiters.

    Silas W Waiters b. GA, of Paso Robles
      1892 GR: 21 5'11 lt blu lt lab GA Paso Robles; reg Aug 18
      1892 GR: Wm Amos Waiters 52 carp GA Paso Robles; reg Aug 18

*Note:* Elizabeth is listed as Twitchell on the 1900 census. Short marriage?

p.10.   South Side Items. Mr Adkins and wife went to Paso Robles to visit parents.
    –June 24 1893

p.10.   1894. Garey News. Come to life – it was reported that Charlie Wells and wife were drowned in the cloud burst "but I guess not" as they have come back safe and sound.   –Sep 15

    Upper Sisquoc. Chas Wells and bride returned from their wedding tour to the head of the river the first of the week. They were caught in a thunderstorm in the mountains and Chas got his thumb mashed. They were thought to be lost and Hiram Wells was hunting for them five days before they returned home.   Ed Forrester is digging a well and struck solid rock. He says he will blast through to China or strike water.   –Sep 15

    Upper Sisquoc.   Father Wheat Is Preparing for a Big Bear Hunt   H P Wheat is preparing for a big bear hunt at the head of the river. He has his cattle up there and bruin is having a feast.   L L Forrester spent the week in the valley on business. John Twitchell is hauling grapes to Lompoc peddling them there at 2¢ per pound. He gets them from H P Wheat and pays $1.50 license fee in Lompoc. See what Santa Maria could make on peddlers were she incorporated.   Chas Wells and bride are stopping for the present at the Hiram Wells place.   –Sep 29

p.11.   South Side Items. Hiram Wells and family have moved back up the Sisquoc. Oceano did not seem to have many charms for him after all.   –Feb 24 1900

p.11.   Creston. Hiram Wells was brought home from Veterans' Hospital, Sawtelle, as far as Maricopa Sunday; rest of the journey on Monday.
    –*SLO Telegram-Tribune* Sat May 25 Sec.2 p.1 1940

p.12.   Land Notice. Henry Irving Roberts. Homestead #8238. Lot 3 S33 T9N R29W; NE4SW4 N2SE4 S25 T9N R30W. Wit: G A Woon, Santa Barbara PO; Ed Forrester, Santa Maria PO; Wm Forrester, Santa Maria PO; H P Wheat, Santa Maria PO. Oct 15 1887.
*Note:* this land is in the Manzana district.

# WHEAT-WELLS-WOON-FORRESTER-ROBERTS-ADKINS
PIONEERS OF THE SANTA MARIA VALLEY
The Upper Sisquoc-Manzana District

"The pioneers in the south end of the valley, Upper Sisquoc, were Alvis Davis, Forresters, Roberts, Wheat, Hirum (sic) Wells, William, George and Henry Tunnell, Adolph Willman, Edward Montgomery and his father Josiah T Montgomery," according to a speech by Robert Easton, long associated with the Sisquoc ranch, at the annual Pioneer Association picnic in Waller Park, May 1955
*-Santa Maria Times*

From the sandy flatlands of the Santa Maria valley, not much above sea level, to the settlement in the Upper Sisquoc, where the highest peaks tower above 4000 feet, is a distance of about 35 miles. To reach that location, now in Los Padres National Forest, one traversed a variety of terrain. From the Sisquoc ranch the route followed the river-the river was, in fact, the route, for the most part-which often enough was fordable, but subject to flash floods, at which time the wayfarer had no recourse but to wait for the water to subside. A selection of articles and reminiscences on the Manzana settlement and its people was published in *San Ramon Chapel Pioneers*, by Erlinda Ontiveros, 1990; it has also a fine collection of photographs. Another source is the news articles from outlying localities in the valley to be found in the *Santa Maria Times*. Much of what was pertinent from Upper Sisquoc and Manzana has been presented in the Twitchell family chart; however, additional information has been gleaned, and the emphasis shifted to Wheat and Wells. Of the above-mentioned families, all but Willmans were related somehow. Tunnells are detailed in Mrs Ontiveros' book; Davises and Forresters were often mentioned but not specifically chronicled. Of these latter Ye Ed. has much data from the *SM Times*, and, it is hoped, will be able to publish it some time. Until then, anyone interested may make request for it.

The vagaries of the weather, the varieties of wildlife, the hunting, the crops, the visits, the births and deaths, the joys and sorrows are to be found in the newspaper columns. The unnamed writer(s) had something of a sense of humor, and their submissions are interesting as well as providing vital data not elsewhere available.

Wheat – Wells – Woon     S C R A P B O O K     Forrester – Roberts – Adkins

1891   Judge Woon of Garey was in town this week.    –Dec 26

1892   Long Valley Items. Judge Woon returned from Paso Robles last Tuesday. Mr Woon is talking of locating somewhere in that country. Mr P Wheat and wife who have been visiting near San Jose returned Sunday. Their granddaughter and husband, Mr and Mrs Twitchell, accompanied them home, and will visit among friends for a few days.    -Oct 22

Gary (sic) Brieflets. The town now appears to be on the up grade. A first-class blacksmith shop…is just finished…Mr Steve Niverth is the owner. Now we have two good shops, the people of this section need not go without sharp plow points. Mr A H Davis has succeeded to the ownership of the shop originally owned by Mr Woon. Mr Davis and family are of the first residents of Garey…they lived in Cuyama…    -Dec 24

1893   Christmas Eve Party. On Chirstmas Eve, Mr and Mrs William Forrester gave their neighbors a pleasant reception at their home in Orange Vale. The event was one long to be remembered by all present. Music, dancing and popping corn was the order of entertainment until 1 o'clock in the morning. The favored ones were Mr and Mrs Chas More, Mr and Mrs Forrester, Mrs Adkins, Misses Maud More, Madge More, Hopel (sic) Adkins, Eva Forrester, Mr Fred Baker, M Beeson, Mr Adkins, Wells, Liston, Perry More.    -Dec 30

*Ed. Note*: The More family is shown on the 1880 census in the Sisquoc area; in 1894 Chas O More was operating a dairy on the South Side. He, Baker, and Beeson are listed in Sisquoc precinct on the 1890 Great Register of Voters, which is reproduced in the SMVGS *Quarterly*, 1993.

1894 South Side Items. Rumor says Chas Wells and Miss Anna St Clair were married in San Luis Obispo the first of the week and are honeymooning near Templeton. Hila Wells and his family are visiting Mrs Wells' parents at Paso Robles. -Aug 4

The Sisquoc river got up and came down all at once the first of the week. The stories concerning its actions are somewhat conflicting, but not more so than the endless mass of debris strewn the full length of the valley, to the sea. The bold front presented at first, indicated a cloud burst. Wood haulers will have a picnic. -Dec 15

1895 Manzana Notes. Messrs C and H Wells finished seeding their large acreage this week. -Jan 12

Manzana Items. A Few Interesting Notes From Up the River. H Wells has concluded to sow more small grain since the last rain. Grant Cockran had the bad luck to lose the roof of his house in last week's storm. It was carried by the storm 200 yards away. Mr C Wells and wife have been visiting at Ed Forrester's the past week. -Jan 26

Sisquoc Local News. Grant Cobran (sic) is in the hills again, repairing his mountain ranch dwelling and otherwise improving the place. Mrs St Clair of Nevada is visiting her brother, E E Forrester. -Feb 9

Manzana Notes. Mr J Adkins is putting up a large barn to store his crop of hay and barley in. A lion killed one of John Twitchell's fine colts one day last week. M Spitler and H Wells returned from Santa Barbara last week. Mr Spitler has proved up on his mountain ranch and now feels very much at home. Wm Tunnell was elected high school trustee and A E Davis for Manzana school district. The Manzana people are glad to learn that an electric road is to run up the valley as far as Foxen canyon. We hope that it may be extended into our neighborhood. -June 22

1896 J J Adkins of Manzana has been spending the week in town on business of importance. -Jan 18

1897 Real Estate Transactions: Wm H Spittler to Hiram P Wells $400 S33 S34 T9 R29... -May 22 (?)

1897 Upper Sisquoc Notes   Chas Wells has purchased the Cochran ranch and went to the valley the forepart of the week on business connected with the transfer -June 12

Messrs Forrester, Wells and Tunnell Bros drove their cattle to the valley last week. Mr and Mrs Hiram Wells were on a trading venture this week. They disposed of some stock. -July 3

Mr and Mrs John Twitchell are stopping at Mr Wheat's ranch during Mrs Wheat's illness. -Jul 24

Mr and Mrs Will Forrester, and family, of Santa Barbara, are visiting friends in the Canyon.

Mrs Jos Adkins, of Paso Robles, is visiting at the home of her parents, Mr and Mrs H P Wheat.

Mrs H P Wheat is very ill. All of her relatives living in the State have been with her during the past week. Mr and Mrs Charles Twitchell, of Templeton, with their family-all girls-were visiting relatives the past week, and returned to their home the fore part of the week. Mr J S Twitchell has a narrow escape with his life, last week. Riding near a pine tree that was being sawed down and was about ready to fall, the wind threw it in a different line than was anticipated, and before he could get out of the way, the tree fell across the horse, striking the horn of the saddle, crushing both horse and rider. In some unaccountable manner, by which so many people escape instant death-neither was seriously injured. –EX.  -Aug 7

John Twitchell is engaged hauling logs to the sawmill. He intends building a residence on his ranch. Mrs H P Wheat, who has been seriously ill, was taken on a trip north this week. Mrs J J Adkins has returned to her home in Templeton. Mr and Mrs Wm Forrester and family have returned to their home in Santa Barbara. Ed Forrester's apricot crop is about ready for market. They are of very fine quality. The sawmill has been running for several days, and is turning out several thousand feet per day. J J Twitchell and Messrs Davis and Sturgeon were hunting on the Zaca this week. They killed one buck that dressed 160 pounds. Fat? Oh, no; -only 1½ inches on the back.  -Aug 14

"All's quiet" on the upper Sisquoc. L L Forrester will spend some time in the valley the coming week. John Miller passed down the creek en route to the ranch of E E Forrester where he will engage in cutting peaches for drying. The mesas of the upper Sisquoc contain fine elements for the green gage plum. I never saw finer grown anywhere, and seldom as good. H H Welch, of Hanford, is camping here. He spent some months with Mr Wheat a year and a half ago, being treated for Bright's disease. He says he is cured. Mr and Mrs H P Wells accompanied Mr and Mrs H Wheat to the home of their daughter near Templeton. They report Mrs Wheat as much improved when they departed for home.  -Aug 21

The hot wave overcame us. Joe Montgomery and son made a trip to the valley this week. As I write the reverberations of heaven's artillery is heard in the distant mountains. In com-com parlance, it is thunderin' like thunder. F L Twitchell, brother of John, is here, direct from Randsburg. He says most of the newspaper reports are exaggerated, and it is no place for a miner without capital. He has interest there, and will return after the fall rains set in.  -Aug 28

Weather much cooler. Jerome Forrester killed two more deer this past week with a thirty-two Winchester. Mrs H P Wheat died suddenly at the home of her daughter near Templeton. We have no details of the sad affliction. Mr and Mrs Twitchell and Mr and Mrs Wells have gone to attend the funeral.  -Sep 4

Mr and Mrs Chas Wells escorted A C Doane to his home in Summerland. They formerly resided there.     (end of Upper Sisquoc items)  -Nov 6

1914    Local News Notes. Married Last Evening—At Sutfin home 654 Monterey st. Miles F Sutfin and Mattie Twitchell of Creston, by Rev H H Hocker…relatives: Mrs Sophia Twitchell, mother; Miss Bertha Twitchell, Octavia Twitchell, Miss Hattie Wells and Miss Hazel Wells of Creston; Mrs W H Kendrick, Wm H Kendrick and Master William Kendrick of Santa Margarita; and Mrs E R Wilson of Carpinteria…  -*SLO Daily Telegram* Thu Aug 20

1918    Local News Notes. Back from Colorado. Wm Kendrick of Santa Margarita returned last night from a trip to Arizona, Colorado and Utah. He left several weeks ago for Houston, Texas, with the remains of his father, who died in Santa Margarita. He later visited a sister in Colorado Springs, Col, and returned via Salt Lake City and Los Angeles. Mr Kendrick says when he left Colorado Springs there was 3 inches of snow on the ground there the weather was very cold. He is glad to be back in California and is satisfied to stay here.  -Ibid April 23

Santa Margarita Apr 23. Will Kendricks (sic) is back home from his trip to Texas. He reports everything fine there since the rain.  -Ibid

1925    Los Alamos Locals. Mr and Mrs E P Stemper…moving…into the J M Kirkpatrick home which they have leased.    -June 7

1938    Harvey L Wells Called Beyond…..rancher of Carrisa Plains died early this morning, following an emergency appendectomy…was in critical condition when he entered the hospital, having ridden 40 miles on horseback…    -*Taft Daily Midway Driller* May 17

1941    Creston. Mr and Mrs Hi Wells left for San Francisco on Monday on business…returned Wednesday. Rosalie Wells…guest of Mrs H Swaze during absence.
    Mr and Mrs Hi Wells motored to Cuyama valley Saturday staying overnight with parents of Mrs Wells.    -*Paso Robles Journal* Mar 26
    Mrs Laura Wells and daughter Rosalie attended Glee Club festival Paso Robles Tuesday evening.    -Ibid May 7
    Mrs Sadie Stubblefield and son Bill visiting Mr and Mrs Hiram Wells.    -May 14
    Mr and Mrs Hiram Wells and daughter Rosalie spent weekend near Maricopa…    -May 21

1945    Two Jail Suicides Within A Week    -*Paso Robles Record* Thu Sep 6 p. 6
    Rancher Kills Self In Jail    -*SLO Telegram-Tribune* Tue Sep 4 p. 1
    Ralph Plumm, Creston rancher, in jail on drunk charges, dived from the top of the cell block onto his head. When arrested, said he'd been drunk for two months, and now would get sobered up. He was playing cards with other prisoners in the bullpen, when he suddenly climbed the 8 ft steel bars and dived off, never regaining consciousness.

1946    Hiram P Wells Dies from Injuries…of Maricopa, in hospital six weeks after being thrown from a horse…Employed as foreman at Russell Brothers ranch in Cuyama valley; recently resigned as State Cattle Brand Inspector. Veteran of World War I, member Cuyama post 656, American Legion.    -*Taft Daily Midway Driller* Nov 19

1948    Principal of Rucker School Succumbs. Mrs Ernest Woon Funeral Services Here Saturday. Rucker school district three years, principal the last year…Unity Rebekah lodge of Gilroy…lived in Gilroy 23 years…husband, well-known dairyman of Pacheco Pass Highway…teacher at Prunedale and Rucker schools for some years..husband, three daughters, son, sister, Mrs Alma Pierce of Avenal, brother, Davis Sanders of San Francisco…
    -*Gilroy Dispatch* Wed May 12 p. 1, Thu May 13 p. 1, 6

1955    Rose Saulsbury died in Santa Maria…born Templeton…daughter Pearl Shoemaker, Los Alamos; Lillian Payne, Santa Inez; sons Charles Clark, Torrence; Harry Clark, USN, San Francisco; sisters Violet Snow, Carpinteria and Myrtle Lambert, Summerland.
    -Ibid Tue July 26 p. 6

1956    Sadie Stubblefield died in Santa Maria 15 July @72; buried Bakersfield….living with daughter Mrs Laura Wells 309 S Miller, Santa Maria…    -*SM Times*

## ROBERTS' RESTAURANTS

1887    Mr Joe Montgomery, of the Pioneer harness shop has bought Mr Roberts' ranch east of town in the mountains. Mr Roberts will open up a restaurant on Broadway and move to town.    -Dec 10

1888    Our town is now well supplied with restaurants, yet they all seem to be doing a thriving business. We notice a sign, painted by J R Weeks, hoisted in front of Mr Roberts' new restaurant on Broadway street, in the Weber building. This new restaurant was formally opened to the public on Sunday last. At this new eating establishment the public will find home cooking, as it is superintended by Mrs Roberts who has the reputation of being hard to beat in the culinary department. -Jan 7

In this issue will be found an ad of the Santa Maria house or restaurant, opened on the 1st instant by Mr and Mrs H I Roberts in the Weber building. They have fitted this restaurant up in first-class order and Mrs Roberts presides over the cooking department and we hear the boarders of this new restaurant speak highly of the cooking and the manner in which the tables are furnished.
-Jan 14

Santa Maria House—H I Roberts, Prop. –Single meals 25 cents   Board week $4.50
On Broadway north of M Fleisher & Co's store   –Ibid

1888   Polk Directory: Henry E Roberts Propr Santa Maria House, Andrew B Crosby, restaurant

1888   Town & Valley   Mr and Mrs Roberts, formerly keeping the Santa Maria House, in the Weber building, has rented the Crosby Dining Palace and recently taken charge of the same.
--May 5

Wm F Dutton has taken charge of the Crosby Dining Palace.   -Oct 24

1890   The Crosby Dining Palace has been reopened by Mrs Roberts whose advertisement will be found elsewhere in the columns of the *SM Times*. Mrs Roberts promises as good a meal for 25 cents as the town ever furnished. No trouble to call around at the Dining Palace when hungry and be convinced that the best meals are served for little money.   -Dec 6

The Dining Palace - reopened by Mrs I Roberts - Main St Santa Maria - Meals only 25 cents –The tables supplied with the best the market affords. Call around and get a good Square meal.   -Dec 6

Letter From Winona Woon Sears, Kapaa, Hawaii 4 Feb 1995

Hiram Preserved Wheat, my great-grandfather came with a party in covered wagons from Pottawatomie County, Kansas, and settled in the Sisquoc. He was the "patriarch" of the group… H P Wheat's oldest daughter, Catherine Elizabeth married (1) William Harvey Wells in Wisconsin 22 Feb 1865, and (2) William Merchant Forrester. I have had some luck in tracing the Forrester cousins, and found at least one line of Wells.

H P Wheat's second daughter was my grandmother, Minerva, who married my grandfather some time before they came to California from Kansas, since my aunt Sophia was born on the way in Nevada. A third daughter, Lucy, has "disappeared." I do not know if she died early, or if the rumor that she "ran away" is true. The fourth daughter was Adeline (Addie) who married (1) Henry (Harry) Roberts and (2) Joseph J Adkins…I know, of course, my own line, but have had no luck with the Roberts or Adkins. I might add that the family in California has been plagued with fires and floods…

Forrester cousins' tradition is that H P Wheat was New England Puritan (WASP), who was caught up in the new religions springing up in the 1830-1840's, married a French Canadian, who was Catholic, and both families promptly disinherited them. So far I have had no luck finding a maiden name for Elizabeth Catherine (the first daughter was named for her, and the names seem to be in either order) and her parents, and parents for H P. We have searched in N H where he said he was born Aug 1822. We also tried the Canadian-American research library, where they said they could only help if I have a maiden name for her!!!!!!!

# WISE
## GUADALUPE PIONEERS

Edward Hale Wise     b. MA 1837; parents b. MA
    1890 GR: 53 MA f Guad     d. Guadalupe 13 Jan 1916 @78/11/5
    1906 Dir: well driller Guad       buried Monterey, obit Jan 15 p.1
    1910: 2nd St Guad       Justice of the Peace, Guadalupe
    1895 ad: Artesian Wells bored. E H Wise, Guadalupe. 50¢ per foot.     –Sept 28
    m. c1876
Margaret     b. CA 1859
    (called Catherine Cox     d. at home Guadalupe 3 May 1918 @60
    on confirmation records)       buried Monterey, obit May 4
      F: ENG; M: CA.    sister Mrs Kate Morrison
                            in Los Angeles 1918

1910: 3 births, 3 living

1. Carlotta/Charlotte/Lottie     b. 1881
        d. (Lottie S Wise d. LA co 4-19-1959)
    Confirmed St Pat's Ch AG 3 June 1894 @13; sponsor Mary Fox
    1906 Dir: Lottie Miss sch tchr Los Alamos r suburban single
2. Edith C     b. Monterey 12 Sep 1886
    Confirmed St Pat's Ch     d. 20 Sep 1961 @75; Guad cem
      AG 7 Oct 1901; no age;       obit Fri Dec 22 p.2. 60y Guad
      sponsor Lottie Wise       40y tchr, 6 gch 3ggch, retired 1957
    1906 Dir: Miss stu Guad
    1922 Dir: hskpr Guad
    1926 Dir: sch tchr Guad
    1940-1 Dir: tchr rGuadalupe St Guad
    1955-6 Dir: tchr Box 163 Guad
    1961 pall bearers: Raymond Lopez, Kermit McKenzie, Thos P Weldon, Fred Gracia,
      Leo Acquistapace, Albert Cicero
        m. c1911
    Roy Frederick Abernethy     b. Guadalupe Apr 1883
      1900: w/parents Guad     d. Guadalupe 14 Nov 1918 @36; Guad cem
        poultry dealer       influenza;. notice Fri Nov 15 p.3
      1910: w/parents Guad S     F: Frederick Wilbur Abernethy 1857-1939
      1906 Dir: eng, Guad     M: Mary Eudora Abbott 1861-1934
    a. Raymond F     b. (Guad) 10 July 1912; SSDI
        m.     d. Santa Maria 12 Jan 1986 @73; Guad cem
      Betty J       obit Tue Jan 14 p.19; 20y w/Smith
                           Transportation 14 gch, 24 foster ch
      SMHS 1931; San Jose State 1935
      1940-1 Dir: emp Golden St Ltd r114 Guadalupe St Guad
      1955-6 Dir: Laundromat, constable h 4605 2nd Guad
      =JoAnn (Lopez)
      =Serena (Frazier)
      =Rayma (Brayton)
      =Raedine
      =Barbara
      =Danny

      =Ray Jr
      =Anthony
3.   Edward Henry                      b.   Guadalupe 24 Nov 1892 (*Times*)
    1922 Dir: bkpr Guad

Vol. XXVIII, No. 2, Summer 1996, p.17

**Corrections and Additions**      [Page numbers refer to those in Quarterly]

p.17.   E H Wise bored a fine artesian well in Pat Moore's place on Oso Flaco, largest flow of water obtainable in that neighborhood.  See Moore chart.            –Apr 9 1887

p.17.   Charlotte Wise d. 5-14-1923 @42, buried Monterey, per Dudley-Hoffman Mortuary records.

      Edward Wise Victim of An Accident. Gets Caught at Bromella Station in the Hoisting Gear … (sugar) beet dump … tending hoisting machine. While working at the rope on the drum, he was caught and whirled thrice around before the engine could be stopped, suffering terrible injuries on the right arm and right leg … right arm fractured below elbow, right leg badly crushed … necessary to amputate arm at elbow … has, owing to his healthy condition, all hope of a speedy recovery.
                                          -*Guadalupe Sun*, in *SM Times* Sat Dec 17 1913 p.1

# YOUNG
## SANTA MARIA RESIDENTS

Lewis Wiggins Young     b. Horseheads* Chemung co NY 1835
    schoolteacher NY; in NE 30y     d. Santa Barbara 12 Dec 1919 @ "almost 84"; SM cem
    State senator 1892-3, 1899     obit Dec 13 p.7. 18 gch
    1910 cen: w/Floyd, wid; parents NY

       *Horseheads, formerly Fairport, a post village in Elmira tp, Chemung co. on the
         Chemung canal, and on the Chemung branch of the New York and Erie rr, 6 mi N from
         Elmira. Here Gen Sullivan, during his expedition against the Indians, killed his
         pack-horses, the heads of which were piled up; hence the name.
                       -*A New & Complete Gazetteer of the US*, Baldwin & Thomas, 1854

    m. (NY)

Sarah Elizabeth Langdon     b. (Elmira) NY
    Said to be a sister of Mark Twain's     d. Wilsonville NE c1900, poison
    wife, Lydia Langdon. If so, her parents were Jervis Langdon c1811-1871 and Olivia Lewis. See
    Langdon note at end of chart.

1.    Wilmot Lewis Young     b. Horseheads NY 1864; m.2 of SM
      1890 GR: 26 NY carp Lompoc     d. Santa Maria 28 Nov 1918 @54/9/17; SM cem
      1906 Dir: W L Young, prop,     obit Fri Nov 29 p.3; 25y SM; Eagles
        The Jesse Moore, rChurch st; Mrs also Henry C, John R
      1909 Dir: W L Young, Knotts & Young r205 W Cypress; Mrs E
      1910 cen: 205 W Cypress; emp retail liquor
      1918: Card of Thanks for son and brother: L W Young, Louise V Whitney, F C Young,
        A H Young
         m.2 San Luis Obispo 2 July 1898 by Louis Lamy JP, E313
           wit: Chas Pedraita, Miss Theresa Pedraita
    Rosetta Modesta Blosser     b. Willitts CA 17 Nov 1871
      "Etta"     d. Pasadena (15) Jan 1947 @75/1/28; SM cem
      to Santa Maria 1879; in Stockton     obit Thu Jan 16 p.8. 2 gch
      1926, in Fresno 1928,     F: Samuel Martin Blosser 1839-1926
      Pasadena 12 y     M: Harriett E Whitcomb 1851-1928
    a.    Floyd W Young     b. Orcutt 15 Feb 1907 (*Times*)
         in Pasadena 1947     d. San Francisco 8 May 1985; SSDI
         Spouse RC. W L Young's grandchildren in Colorado

2.    Harry Young     b. Horseheads NY 6 Oct 1865
                       d. Apr 1868

3.    Louise V Young Whitney     b. Horseheads NY
                       d. (living in Yonkers 1919)

4.    Floyd Clarendon Young     b. Creston IL 5 July 1872
      1900 cen: Furnas co NE,     d. Santa Maria 5 July 1959 @87; SM cem
        Sherman pct; to SM 1908     obit Mon July 6 p.2; 9 gch 22 ggch
      1910 cen: tp 10 (Orcutt) farmer
      1922 Dir: slsmn Holser & Bailey r523 W Orange; Bert stu; Edna steno UO Plant
        Lucreice (sic) stu
      1925 Dir: slsmn H & B r512 E (sic) Orange; Miss Lucretia A stu; Bert L clk
      1928 Dir: Floyd C (Mary A) slsmn r512 W Orange; Bert clk
      1930 Dir: same. Jan 1930: Mary Whitney's letter said he had an operation
      1940-1 Dir: SB Co Far Mut Fire Ins h512 W Orange; 1947-8, 1955-6: same
      1959: 15y Holser & Bailey, then Farmers Mutual Insurance
      m. Wilsonville NE 7 Oct 1893

Mary Bell Anderson     b. Washington, Adams co IA 28 Oct 1876
   to SM 7 Oct 1908     d. at home 512 W Orange 6 Apr 1947 @70/5/8
   1910 cen: 5 births 5 living     SM cem; obit Mon Apr 7; 9 gch 5 ggch
   1940-1 Dir: cook SM sch dist     F. William Anderson
   1947: 4 dau 1 son; cook Miller     M: Roxanna DelPeretta Cherry d. c1887
     sch 12y; president Womens Club, niece Roberta Anderson in Cuba. Pall bearers: Elmer Rice, O F Glenn, Charles V Gardner, Robert Bruce, Ralph Sharer, True Myers

a.    Edith Gertrude Young     b. Wilsonville NE 8 Jan 1894
      d. Santa Barbara 11 Apr 1975 @81/3/3; SM cem; obit Mon Apr 14 p.2. 3 sisters surviving
   m. at home of bride's parents nr Orcutt (Glines ranch) Thu 31 Oct 1914 by Rev Crandall, ME ch; to live in Kingsburg (*Times*)
   Harry Sigurd Nelson     b. Wilsonville NE 30 Dec 1888;
      m. of Kingsburg
    to SM 1929, garage to 1952     d. at home 322 E El Camino 2 Feb 1968
    1930 Dir: 322 El Camino.     @79/1/1; SM cem; obit Sat Feb 3 p.4
    1940-1 Dir: same; auto repr 517     F: F Olaf Nelson
    N Miller. 1955-6 Dir: same     M: Augusta Samuelson Wickstrom
   = Arthur Wayne Nelson b. Kingsburg 1928; m. Pacific Palisades 1954
     Martha Alice Patterson rSanta Barbara. 1 dau 1 gch
      1990: Arthur helped officiate at Aunt Edna's funeral

b.    Ruth Margaret Young     b. sod house Wilsonville NE 24 May 1896
    1955-6 Dir: emp Miller sch     d. living SM 1998
    r715 N Miller
     m. at home of bride's parents Cypress st Sat 30 Sep 1916 by J Walter Jordan DD (*Times*); divorced
   Horace Hazard Chaffin     b. OH 30 March 1891
    1947-8 Dir: Horace H (Ruth M)     d. disappeared; no further data
    Variety Store Guad h715 N Miller     F: Wm John Worth Chaffin 1846-1919
      (Shadrach[4] Reuben[3] Francis[2] Robert[1])
      M: Nancy Call 1855-1937
   = Georgina Frances Chaffin b. SM 1920; m. 1947
     Willard Bacon Utley Jr 1897-1970; 5 ch
   = Mary Jean Chaffin b. SM 1923; m.1 Wichita, Gordon W Collier, 1 son
     m.2 Salina KS 1943 James Francis Lyman, 2 dau
     m.3 Guilford CT 1954 Richard Joseph Langley, 3 ch
      1932: Mary Jean won piano competition San Francisco
     See Chaffin chart

c.    Edna Louise Young 1900-1990; m. SM 1922
   Mark Holgate Whitney 1886-1949; see Whitney chart

d.    Bert Lewis Young     b. Wilsonville NE 14 June 1904
    1926: clk SM, Knights of Pythias     d. nr Portland OR on vacation 1 Aug 1962
     records     @68/1/17; SM cem. obit Wed Aug 2
    1940-1 Dir: Bert (Doris) meat mkt Guad;
     h319 W Church
    1947-8 Dir: mt ctr Bwy Mkt r319 W Church; 1955-6 Dir: same
     m. Santa Maria 12 Feb 1929
   Doris Elizabeth Glenn     b. Henry co IL 29 July 1907
    1976 Dir: wid h217 E Hermosa     d. living SM 1998
      F: Oscar Franklin Glenn 1873-1960
      M: Maude Amelia Chamberlain 1878-1961

    = Grace Glynne Young b. SM 1932; m. 1950. 5 births
     Wm Alan Kyle b. MT 1926   F: Charles Larrabee Kyle 1889-1973
                  M: Marguerite Pearl Stephens 1886-1996
  e. Lucretia Ann Young     b. Wilsonville NE 25 Feb 1908
                  d.
    m.1
   Howard Samuel Wines     b.
                  d.
    1928: Mrs Howard Wines (Lucretia Young) here from Jackson for a stay of the
     summer months with parents M/M F C Young. Mrs Wines is attending the
     summer session at Oregon Agricultural College.   -Wed June 13 p.5
   = Floyd Howard Wines b. SM 1928; m. San Rafael 1954
    Margaret Lucille Douthit b. Walla WA 1936; 3 dau
   = Robert Wm Wines b. Patterson CA 1933; single
    m.2
   John Slaugh        b. 5 Feb 1916
                 d. Fairfield CA June 1967
                 F: John Detreich Slaugh
                 M: Anna Bizalski
   = Marianna Slaugh b. San Francisco 1951; m.1 _____ Powell
    m.2 Mendocino co CA 1989 Larry Connor b. 1941
   Lucretia Slaugh in Alhambra 1947, Fairfield 1959-1975
5. Albert Huron Young    b. Wilsonville NE 2 Aug 1879
  to SM 1908. 1909 Dir: A H Eng d. Santa Maria 31 Oct 1966 @87
  r cor Cypress/Lincoln; Mrs   obit Wed Nov 2; 10 gch 18 ggch
   T S (sic), rode on the first steam plow in Santa Maria Valley. –Gordon Emerson
  1916: Bert Young's family moved into town from oil fields, res. Marriott Apts. –June 17
  1925 Dir: Albert H (Flora) rancher rE Main; Miss Marion stu; Arthur stu
  1928 Dir: A H (Flora) gas plant opr Palmer U rOrcutt; 1930 Dir: A H, Orcutt
  1947-8 Dir: Albert H (Flora S) carp pntr h625 Union, Orcutt; also Arthur Gordon
   Emerson stu and Ralph Stanton Emerson opr eng
  1955-6 Dir: A H lab canry rOrcutt Hotel. 1966: r310 S Concepcion
   m. Wilsonville 4 Feb 1903
  Flora Sparks        b. Meadeville (obit) or Avalon (Anc File) MO
                 27 July 1883
                d. Santa Maria 19 Jan 1948 @64/5/22; SM cem
                 obit Tue Jan 20 p.5; 8 gch 1 sis 2 bro in OR
                F: James Clayton Sparks (LDS Ancestor File)
                M: Helen Beecher Arnold
  a. Lois Sparks Young     b. Orchards WA 22 Mar 1904
    (Lois E)         d. Bakersfield CA 29 Mar 1936 @32
    m. 1 Sep 1923
   Ralph Waldo Emerson    b. Chelam WA 8 Apr 1900
                d. Tacoma WA 11 Aug 1941
   = Ralph Stanton Emerson 1925-1995
   = Arthur Gordon Emerson living in Las Vegas; see below
    Marjean Maughan     F: Parley Baxter Maughan 1907-1997
     SMUHS 1946      M: Janet Beattie 1903-1990
    1947 Dir: Maughan PB (Janet) mgr Bwy Bootery h606 E El Camino
     Janet B clk Ames & Harris r606 E El Camino

The Maughan family came to Santa Maria in the 1940's from Salt Lake City; they are from a long-time LDS clan.

- b. Arthur C Young — b. Wilsonville NE 19 Mar 1907
    1928 Dir: A C Rotary hlpr — d. at home 28 May 1981; cremated
    Palmer Union, rOrcutt
    1940-1 Dir: Arthur C (Virginia F) supt Casmite, rCasmalia; 1947-8 Dir: same
    1955-6 Dir: sls agt h310 S Concepcion; Virginia slsldy Conrad's Drugs
    m.
    Virginia F Wyse — b.
    SMUHS 1931 "Jenny" — d. predeceased her husband
    1928 Dir: Casmalia, Wyse, Boyd C, postmaster; Frances A, at home;
        Lucille E, stu (SMUHS 1928); Virginia F stu
    = Arthur C Jr, in Salinas 1981
    = Karyl Ortega in SM 1981
- c. Marion Young — b. Santa Maria 2 Nov 1908
    1928 Dir: Marion Young bkpr — d. Long Beach 23 Dec 1945
    r630 S Lincoln — obit Mon Dec 24 p.1
    m. 1938
    Paul A Stevens — lived in Whittier, then Long Beach
- d. Mary Louise Young — b. Santa Maria 24 May 1915
    — d. Los Gatos 27 July 1997 @82; SM cem
       obit Thu Sep 25 A-7; 6 gch 4 ggch
       2 neph 1 nc; rSaratoga (?)
    m.1 (div)
    Philip I Elder living 1998  (Louise Elder in SM 1948)
    = Philip I Elder Jr
    = David M Elder
    = Linda F Elder Bell
    m.2 (div)
    Richard L Kurtz living in Hayward 1998
    1955-6 Dir: Richd L (Mary L) h220 Pinal, Orcutt; Mary secy Van Wyk
    Louise Kurtz in Whittier 1981
- e. Frances E Young — b. Santa Maria 25 July 1916
    in Montebello 1948 — d. (Whittier) 5 Oct 1985
    in Whittier 1966, 1981
    m.
    Paul Cox of Montebello

Unidentified: James Lewis Young buried SM cem 4 Jan 1926 @0/0/0

Langdon Note: Samuel Langhorne Clemens (Mark Twain) (1835-1910), was married in Elmira NY in 1870 to Olivia Langdon, daughter of Jervis Langdon (c1811-1871) and Olivia Lewis. 1850 census, Chemung co NY, shows them as family 431, Elmira; Jervis 42, lumberman; Olivia 49, a girl O L (Olivia Lydia?) 4, and Charles J 1, plus Susan 14. Among others in the household was Mary Lewis 18. Family 1106 was Amos Langdon 71, Mary 60, Joseph 20, Sarah J 16, and Mary J 7, all New York natives.

The LDS Ancestor File avers that Olivia Langdon, daughter of Jervis, married Samuel L Clemens; only she rated listing in the Ancestor File, apparently.

Mark Twain's biographies report that on his trip to the Holy Land, which became the basis for The Innocents Abroad, in 1869, he met Charles Langdon who carried a miniature portrait of his sister, with whom Clemens fell in love and subsequently married. His style mellowed considerably under the genteel influence of his in-laws, it is said.

## Notes and Remembrances

Mary Belle Anderson's mother died when Mary was 11, so she went to live with her aunt Molly and uncle John Cherry, later to Wilsonville to live with her father. After their marriage, she and Floyd lived in an apartment across from the post office, and then moved to the Youngs' farm, where they lived with the parents in the "big" house until their sod house was built. Ruth was born in that sod house, but when she was five, in 1900, the family moved back to Creston, IL for 14 months, on the way visiting her mother's family in Washington, IA, the family consisting of aunt Molly, uncle John, and great-grandmother Cherry, about 84 years of age. Floyd's mother's death prompted the return of the Youngs to Wilsonville to take care of the father. Lewis Young had moved from Creston to Wilsonville years earlier, and, along with farming, had been a representative to the state legislature.

Ruth remembered her "grandmother Young as being very beautiful, and she felt very sorry when she died. Mrs Young had taken poison, and as she laid in her casket you could see the burn marks around her mouth."

In 1908 Floyd and Mary, with the five children, came out to Santa Maria where hauling for the oil fields would be more profitable than farming the Nebraska prairie. Floyd and Bert tended the mule team and Sanko, the pony, in the box car in which they traveled. Once here, they found a house on the Glines ranch, near what is now Patterson Road and the Orcutt Road and the children rode Sanko from there to the Pine Grove school. Sanko was eventually retired to live out his days in a pasture in Sisquoc.

This story is excerpted from the family history of the Floyd Young family provided by Shirley Van Stone of Santa Rosa. Martha Nelson of Santa Barbara, and Gordon Emerson, 6716 Cabra St., Las Vegas, NV 89107, also contributed generously to this compilation.

# ZABRISKIE
## PIONEERS OF THE CALIFORNIA CENTRAL COAST

Bolivar Zabriskie     b. Niagara co NY Nov 1832 (cen) (1836 AF)
  1860 cen: Watsonville @26 IA     d. San Luis Obispo 19 Aug 1914 or 12-1-1913
  1880 cen: SLO co Salinas tp     no obit found
         parents Ger/Russia

  1882. Fair View School    We visited Fair View school in company with G A Freeman and Mr Zabrieska (sic) Trustees of the district. This is one of the "new districts" and for the short time that it has been in existence it has really accomplished wonders. Miss Mary L McKennon is the fortunate teacher who dispenses the benedictions. The school house and some other improvements have been secured by subscriptions, and the school census was taken free of charge last year by Mr G A Freeman. A lively contest is anticipated tomorrow over the school election.     -T/W 263

  1890 GR: 55 NY farmer Cayucos; reg Oct 25 1887
  1890. Mrs C H Clark, Pt Sal, sold dairy ranch to Mr B Zabriskie of Cayucos who lived 8 years on Beebe Rancho.     –*SM Times* Nov 1
  1893. C H Clark again at Pt Sal – prepared to accommodate a limited number of guests – perfect climate and beach.    (Is this when Zabriskie left?)     –Dec 2
  1900 cen: SLO co San Jose tp PO Pozo m/44 3 births 3 living (?)
  1910 cen: San Miguel tp, Las Tablas & Adelaida rd m/54; 7 births 5 living

         m. (San Bernardino)? 1856

Sarah A Bickmore     b. OH/IL Mar 1833
         d. SLO co 20 April 1918 @85; no obit found
         F: ME (Samuel David Bickmore c1794- )
         M: PA (Sarah Jane Hamilton c 1804- )

1.    Sarah Jane Zabriskie     b. Los Angeles May 1857
         d. at the home of dau Mrs Beavers, Adelaida 29 Oct 1928 @72; obit *PR Press* Oct 31; IOOF cem PR 2 sons, 1 dau; r many years Willow Creek

     m. San Bernardino 5 Dec 1877 by E G Brown JP, C127
       wit: Clarence Stewart, Riverside co; J A Calkins, Riverside co

   John Wesley Casteel     b. Los Angeles (or San Berdo?) Apr 1859; m. @19 of
     1890 GR: 29 CA f Arroyo     Riverside co; parents IL/IA
     Grande; reg Aug 30 1888
     1900 cen: SLO co Salinas tp     d. SLO co 6 June 1928 @69; IOOF cem Paso Robles
     1902 GR: 43 Templeton PO     obit *SLO Daily Tribune* Thu June 7; *Paso Robles Press*
     Paso Robles     June 13 p.4 45y SLO co, rancher Oakdale sch dis; 2
     1904 GR: 45, same     sons 1 dau 5 gch 6 sis
     1910 cen: SLO co Salinas tp     F: James Nowlin Casteel
     Templeton 3 births 3 living     M: Marinda
     1914 Dir: PR RFD box 45
     1920 cen: Templeton own income

     a.    Clarence Wesley Casteel     b. Riverside 14 Mar 1879
        1902 GR: 23 PR #3     d. at home Willow Ck 17 Jan 1953 @73 obit
        1904 GR: 25 Templeton PO PR     *SLO Telegram-Tribune* Mon Jan 19 p.5; 40y
        1912 Dir: C W Casteel RFD #1     Willow Creek district; to Arroyo Grande 1892,
        Paso Robles; also Clarence W     then Josephine wf, 3 sons, dau, bro
        farmer Templeton
        1920 cen: PR

    1928. in PR/Willow Creek
    m.
    Ethel (Leona?) Heaton     b. IN c1882; F: IA; M: IN
        d.
        F: Phineas Albert Heaton
        M: Louisa
    = Leslie Evin Casteel     b. 1909-18 July 1922 @13
    = Clarence Harlan Casteel     b. 20 Apr 1911; SSDI
        d. 28 Aug 1990, San Miguel
    = Elvin Morris Casteel (twin)     b. 19 May 1914; SSDI
        d. 31 Aug 1993, Atascadero
    = Melvin Norris Casteel (twin)     b. 20 May 1914; SSDI
        d. 23 Apr 1980, Paso Robles
    = Louisa Casteel (Scott)     b. 1917 in So Carolina 1965

b. Mattie J(ane) Casteel     b. Cayucos Mar 1879
    1922-3 VR: Mrs Mattie Beavers     d. at home Templeton 7 Nov 1945 @63; PR cem
    5' CA Las Tablas     obit *SLO Telegram-Tribune* Nov 8 p.6; to PR
    1928. in Adelaida     area as a child, school in Templeton and
        Willow Ck; hus, son, 2 bro
    m. SLO 1 June 1903 by J L Eddy JP, F478; wit: Clarence Casteel, PR;
        Sadie Bickmore, Edna –*PR Record*, to reside Kentucky ranch     –June 13
    Obe Beavers     b. Sonoma co CA 28 June 1874; SSDI
    1900 cen: San Miguel tp     d. SLO/Atascadero 28 Nov 1971 @97; of Pismo
    1904 GR: Las Tablas     obit *SLO Telegram-Tribune* Nov 30 p.2; 89y
    1910 cen: Las Tablas & Adelaida     Paso Robles area; bro Jerome, Paso Robles
    rd 1/1     F: John C Beavers 1847-
    1911. son in Lincoln sch     M: Artilda 1852-1924
    1922-3 VR: 5'9½ CA Las Tablas
    = Gordon Beavers     b. CA 1904

c. Albert O Casteel     b. Kentucky ranch 28 Nov 1895
    "Bert"     d. Paso Robles 2 Jan 1965 @89 obit *SLO*
    1920 cen: Templeton     *Telegram-Tribune* Jan 4 r2130? Vine st; PR
    1920-1 VR: 5'11¾ CA Templeton;     cem 3 neph 1 nc
    Mrs Mae 5'10 SD
    1928. in PR/Templeton; in Santa Maria 1945; in Paso Robles 1953
        m.1 (before 1920)
    Ada Mae Fowler     b. ND/SD/MI 23 Mar 1888
        d. Arroyo Grande 7 Feb 1987 @98; Templeton
        cem obit *SLO Telegram-Tribune* Feb 10 p.7B;
        dau, 3gch 3ggch,2gggch; mother's maiden
        name Bunting Templeton cem: Charles A
        Fowler 1865-1939; Annie Eliza Fowler 1860-
    1931. Templeton Aug 27. Mrs May Casteel visiting Truckee –*PR Press*     1949
    1934 to AG from Templeton (div?)
    1938 phbk: Mrs Mae, Arroyo Grande
    = Thelma (Ashton) and son in AG 1939; Thelma (Hopkins) AG 1987
        1964 Dir: Casteel Mae A Mrs 351 Alder AG
        Ashton Chas D (Ralph & Duane's Tavern) h351 Alder AG
        Hopkins Ralph E (Thelma) (Ralph & Duane's Tavern) h947 Cypress ct AG

```
            1976 Dir: Ashton same
               Hopkins Ralph E & Thelma M (Ralph & Duane's Tavern) h942
                  Sandalwood AG
            1999 phbk: Ralph & Duane's 108 W Branch AG
               Ashton Duane 351 Alder AG
               Hopkins Ralph 942 Sandalwood av AG
      c. m2
            Daisy Velma                      b. OK 17 Apr 1906; SSDI
                                             d. (Paso Robles) 17 June 1962 @56
                                                mother's maiden name Hooper
               1940-1 Dir: Casteel Bert (Daisy) lab 618 W Chapel, Santa Maria
                          Casteel E C (Lucille) leadingman St Hgy Mant h508 E Fesler, SM
                     (is this Elvin?)
2.    Samuel H Zabriskie                     b. CA Nov 1858; m. @36 of SLO
         1890 GR: 29 CA dairyman              d. 1920; IOOF cem SLO
            Cayucos; reg Sep 7 1888
         1900 cen: w/parents, single
         1910 cen: Salinas tp Templeton pct m/7; she m/2 2 births 2 living
               m. SLO 8 Sep 1903 by J L Eddy JP, F514
                  wit: Frank Fletcher, SLO; Miss Bessie Cole, SLO
         Amelia A Clausen                    b. San Luis Obispo 1 Dec 1870
            "Minnie"                          d. Atascadero at home of dau Mrs Minetti 6 Mar 1954
         1920-1 VR: Mrs Minnie 5'5 CA           @83 IOOF cem SLO; obit SLO Telegram-Tribune Sat
            Templeton                           Mar 6 p.2, Mon Mar 8 p.2; dau, 2 gdau, 2 ggch
                                                res Arroyo Grande
                                             F: Rasmus Clausen 1837-1912
                                             M: (Anna) Katarina 1833-1903
         Note: Minnie's two oldest siblings were born in Australia
            her ch: Mamie C Peterson b. CA 1891; in SLO 1941, Atascadero 1954
                     m. Barney Minetti b. (Cayucos) 26 Mar 1889; SSDI; June 1975 SLO
                        F: Secondo Minetti 1863-1927
                    Ellis G Peterson b. CA 1894; d. (before 1954)
         Note: Minnie E Clausen of Pozo m. SLO 16 Dec 1890 by R A Loomis JP, B476
               wit: Charles Lauritzen (her bro-in-law) SLO; S M Corrick, SLO
               F: DK; M: GER
            John Peterson of SLO; parents DK (1856-1919 IOOF cem SLO)
               1890 GR: 33 DK dairy Corral de Peidra; nat Aug 2 1886 SLO Sup Ct; reg Aug
                  22 1890
               1892 GR: 35 5'3 dk blu dk stock raiser DK Cor de Ped PO SLO; reg July 30
               Apparently Minnie m.3 her brother-in-law, J W Zabriskie
                  Surviving    gdau:   Mrs Eleanor Washburn, Santa Ana 1954
                                       Mrs Gordon Curtis, San Mateo 1954
                               ggch:   Carrol Bayer, Dennis Bayer, Santa Ana 1954
3.    Mary Molissa Zabriskie               b. CA 26 May 1865; m.1 @18 of Cayucos
         "Lizzie"                            m.2 of San Miguel
         in Orcutt 1939; 1941,              d. Ventura 14 Nov 1951 @86
            Santa Maria 1943
               m.1 San Luis Obispo 30 Oct 1883 by M M Dodson, A570
                  wit: D M Hulett, SLO; Wm Rose, Adelaida
         George T Dover                     b. NV 1862; m. @22 of Josephine
            1890 GR: 25 CA rancher Las       d. (Sacramento co 12-6-1906 @46)?
```

Tablas; reg Sep 29 1887  F: James Madison Dover 1836-1913
M: Margaret Elizabeth (Humphreys) 1844-1931

1892. Complaint for divorce 31 March SLO Sup Ct: Mary M Dover vs George T Dover
on ground of cruel treatment. *–SLO Tribune* Apr 1

   a.  Lillie L Dover                   b. CA Nov 1885; m. @21 of Paso Robles
                                        d. Ventura 1-29-1949

     m. San Luis Obispo 12 May 1906 by Jas Blackledge MG, G305
        wit: Mrs Geo Walker, SLO; Mrs E T Norris, Santa Maria

    Mortimer Eugene Norris       b. Santa Maria 14 Aug 1886; m. @21
     1922-3 Dir: Mortie E Norris    d. Bakersfield 3-10-1972
      oil wkr Orcutt                 F: Edward Thomas Norris 1867-1918
     *Note*: This directory lists Lillie   M: Mary Frances Logan
      with Mort's brother Everett

    1941. Orcutt. M/M M Morris (sic) of Ventura visiting her mother Mrs Lizzie
      Robinson.      -Aug 8
    See Norris chart
    See Logan chart

   b.  Stella A Dover                 b. CA Oct 1887; m. @19 of Paso Robles
                                        d. (before 1940)

     m. San Luis Obispo 4 Mar 1907 by H E Smith JP, G470
        wit: Mrs Jessie Rule (sic), Paso Robles; W A Clark, Shandon

    Roy J Handley                  b. CA Apr 1889; m. @21 of Templeton
                                          d.
                                          F: James L Handley
                                          M: Ida M

    1900 cen: SLO co Salinas tp w/parents (Templeton?)
    1909 Dir: Handley R, slaughterer rWest Main st Santa Maria; Mrs Stella, same
    1914 Dir: Hanley (sic) Roy (Stella) butcher h507 W Main Santa Maria
    1914: Local Paragraphs. Roy Hanley (sic) of this city a caller in SLO Wed    -Sep 5

   c.  Jessie Dover                      b. CA June 1890; m. @18 of Paso Robles
                                          d.

     m.1 San Luis Obispo 7 Jan 1907 by H E Smith JP, G445
        wit: W G Johnson, SLO; Geo Evans, SLO
     (m.2 Clark)

    John G Rude                       b. CA 10 Jan 1885; m. @21 of Paso Robles
     1910 cen: PR nightwatchman    d. 6 Apr 1965
      No issue                        F: William Loyd Rude 1847-
     constable, police chf           M: Emma Anna Kearney 1867-1942
     see PR book; M/H              (d. @75; PR Pio Queen 1941)

    1910. John G Rude vs Jessie Rude Dec 6 1910; dismissed
    1912 Dir: John G Rude police ofr Riverside av, Palo Robles
    1932. John G Rude vs Jessie A Rude Aug 27 1932; 9506 R414
    1938 phbk: John Rude r1413 Riverside, PR

3.      m.2 Paso Robles 21 Aug 1898 by L Dahlgren JP, E326
        wit: Felix Liss, PR; Christine Liss, PR

Ezra Edward Robinson         b. Ontario CAN 15 Mar 1858; m. of San Miguel;
                                         imm 1880; F: IRE; M: ENG
  1902 GR: Ezra 42 Estrella      d. Santa Maria 23 Oct 1940 @82/7/8; SM cem
    PO San Miguel                 obit Thu Oct 24 p.6; wid, 2 s/dau, 5 gch; 2 sis

1900 cen: Monterey co, Cholame tp (Parkfield) "Ed C" b. ENG
Mrs Mary Thompson, Mrs Eliza Jackson, Ontario CAN, 3y Orcutt 33y SM

1914 Dir: Ed C (Lizzie) h510 W Main SM  not in later directories

1936. Mrs Ed Robinson of Pismo and dau, Mrs Jessie Rude of Long Beach guests of friends here. —Orcutt column, T Dec 2

1940. Mrs Lillie Norris, Bakersfield; Mrs Jessie Clark, Taft

1941. Lizzie Robinson, Orcutt, b. May 26 1865, wit to affidavit of birth of Henry Jacob Morss (nephew) —SLO co 296-100 OR

4. John William Zabriskie
  Wm J
  1902 GR: Wm J 33 Shandon PO Pozo
  1900 cen: w/parents Single
  1910 cen: same
  1920-1 VR: Wm M (sic) 5'8 CA Templeton
  1922-3 VR: John W 5'8 CA; Mrs Minnie 5'6 CA Almond pct

  b. CA Aug 1869
  d. Paso Robles Tue 3 June 1941 @71
  obit *PR Press* June 5; wf, dau, 2gch, 1ggch, 1 sis
  35y PR, from Cayucos
  Card of Thanks: Mrs Amelia Zabriskie, M/M Barney Minetti

5. Alva Lenzo Zabriskie
  1900 cen: w/parents
  1910 cen: same
  1938 phbk: A L r1228 Mill SLO
  Single

  b. San Bernardino July 1872
  d. San Luis Obispo 5 July 1939 @66; PR cem obit *SLO Telegram-Tribune* Thu July 6 p.5; bro, sis
  to Paso Robles @6; 60y Paso Robles

# ZERFING
## PIONEERS OF THE CALIFORNIA CENTRAL COAST

Amos Zerfing      b. PA Aug 1833 (cen) 1834 (cem); parents PA
  1890 GR: 56 PA rancher Corral de      d. 1916; Morro Bay/Cayucos cem
    Piedra; reg Sep 28 1888
  1892 GR: 60 6' light complexion blue eyes grey hair 1st joint 3d finger lh off;
    farmer PA; reg Pilitas pct Pilitas PO Santa Margarita; reg Sep 20
  1900 cen: SLO co San Jose tp m/39 6 births 5 living
  1902 GR: 70 Simmler PO Simmler
  1910 cen: Morro tp dairy m/48 6 births 5 living
    m. (1861)
Charlotte Dolan      b. OH Feb 1843 (cen) 1844 (cem); parents OH
         d. Fri 21 Aug 1931 @87; home on Old Creek above
            Cayucos; obit *SLO Daily Tribune* Mon Aug 24 p.4; 3
            sons 2 dau
  1931. Pall bearers: Paul Ratcliff, S A Hubbard, Wm Ganouing (sic), Jim Maggetti, Pablo
    Montano, W M Duff

1.     Nathan C Zerfing      b. IA Jan 1863; m. of Santa Margarita
    1890 GR: 24 IA blksm SLO #1      d. Los Angeles co 11-4-36 @73 (N)
      reg Jan 26 1888
    1892 GR: 28 5'10½" lt blu lt scar on left wrist blacksmith IA; res Pilitas pct Pilitas PO
      Santa Margarita; reg Aug 17
    1900 cen: Arroyo Grande blacksmith rents
    1910 cen: Ide st AG blacksmith rents m/17 @43
    1931 in Los Angeles
        m. Paso Robles 28 Feb 1892 by T C Miller MG, D137
           wit: Sarah A Miller, Paso Robles; E H Miller, Paso Robles
    Nancy C/J Davis      b. TN June 1866; m.2 of Santa Margarita; parents TN
      1900 cen: 5 births 4 living      d.
      1910 cen: @49(!) 4 births 3 living

    a.    Lottie A Zerfing      b. CA June 1893
                                   d.

    b.    Mary Jane Zerfing      b. rural Arroyo Grande 6 June 1895;
        1954 in SM            m. @19 of Orcutt SLO co
                                 d. Santa Maria 5 Feb 1988 @92; SM cem
        m. San Luis Obispo 22 Sep 1914 by H H Hocker ME ch, J240
           wit: Mrs B Mae Hocker, SLO; Mrs D Beth Williams, SLO
       William Henry Ganoung      b. SLO 29 Nov 1887; m. @26 of AG
                                      d. Santa Maria 15 Oct 1964 @76/10/16;
                                        SM cem
        See Ganoung chart      F: Edwin Ganoung 1868-
                                     M: Priscilla Whiteley 1847-1926; m.1 Smith

    c.    Henry A Zerfing      b. (AG) Feb 1898
       1910: w/parents      d.
      (Florence A Zerfing d. Los Angeles co 3-6-1931 @31 spouse A H)?

    d.    May Zerfing      b. (AG) May 1900
                                 d. 16 June 1900 @6 wks (Woods-Voakes
                                    records)

2. Anna Lee Zerfing     b. IA 11 July 1871
    Single     d. San Luis Obispo 4 Nov 1954 @83; MB/C cem obit *SLO Telegram-Tribune* Mon Nov 15 p.2; 27y SLO; 1 sis, 4 nc, 1 neph; svl gnc/gnph including Mrs Steven Pavitt, SLO

3. Julia Zerfing     b. IA Jan 1873
    1931 in Fresno     d.
    in Taft 1952, 1954
         m. Santa Margarita 1 Nov 1893, D346
    William A Fairbanks     b. CA Feb 1871; parents IN
       1900 cen: SLO co San Jose tp     d.
         next to Amos Zerfing     F: Augustus D Fairbanks 1826-1883
       4 births 4 living     M: Lucy A 1934-1914
    a. A M Fairbanks (dau)     b. Sep 1894
        (Mrs Alfred Ash, in Long Beach 1954)?
    b. W L Fairbanks (dau)     b. July 1896
        (Mrs Verne Detar, in Taft 1954)?
    c. H S Fairbanks (dau)     b. Feb 1898
        (Mrs George Butlin, in Taft 1954)?
    d. W Z Fairbanks (son)     b. Jan 1900
        William Fairbanks, in Honolulu 1954

4. Arthur L Zerfing     b. IA 13 Jan 1876
    Single     d. San Luis Obispo Sun 30 Oct 1955 @79; MB/C cem obit *SLO Telegram-Tribune* Tue Nov 1 p.2; retired dairy; res SLO
    1902 GR: 26 Simmler
    1910 cen: w/parents
    1914 Dir: dairy Cayucos

5. Louzanis Franklin Zerfing     b. Fresno 21 Oct 1879
    "Lute"     d. San Luis Obispo 6 May 1952 @72; MB/C cem obit *SLO Telegram-Tribune* Wed May 7 p.8; 50y SLO co; left Old Creek ranch for SLO in 1937; r1228 Mill st; 1 bro 2 sis
    Single
    1902 GR: 22 Simmler
    1910 cen: w/parents
    1914 Dir: dairy Cayucos

# REFERENCES

All obituaries from *Santa Maria Times* unless otherwise attributed

1906 Santa Maria Valley Directory, including Orcutt, Los Alamos, Betteravia, Casmalia, Guadalupe and Garey Post Offices

1909 Santa Maria Directory, Santa Maria and Betteravia only

Ancestral File, Church of Jesus Christ of Latter Day Saints

*Arroyo Grande Cemetery,* published by San Luis Obispo Genealogical Society

*Breeze,* San Luis Obispo newspaper

*Californian,* Bakersfield newspaper

Carlson, Vada, *This Is Our Valley,* 1959 (SM Valley Historical Soc)

*Daily Telegram,* San Luis Obispo newspaper

Death date thus: 3-12-1946 (EE) is from California Death List, not corroborated by obituary or other verification. The parenthetical initials are those of the spouse

Ditmas, Madge C.: *According to Madge, Early Times in South San Luis Obispo County and the Arroyo Grande Valley,* South County Historical Soc, AG 1983

*Evergreen Cemetery,* Lompoc Historical Society

*Graphic,* Santa Maria newspaper

Great Register 1892-98: age, height, color of complexion, color of eyes, color of hair; scars or marks, if any; voting precinct and post office. If foreign-born, place and court of naturalization.

Guinn, *History of California and Extended History of Southern Coast Counties,* 1907

*History of Fayette Co Iowa, 1878, bio of M M Doane* p.723

International Genealogical Index (IGI), LDS

Manfrina, Myra, *Houk-Huyck Cousins,* Lompoc, CA

*McKenney's Coast Counties Directory,* 1884-5

*Morning Tribune,* San Luis Obispo newspaper

Morrison & Haydon, *History of San Luis Obispo County & Environs,* 1917

*Old Mission Cemetery,* published by San Luis Obispo Genealogical Society

O'Neill, *History of Santa Barbara County,* 1939

Ontiveros, Erlinda P., *San Ramon Chapel Pioneers,* 1990

*Polk's California State Gazetteer,* 1888

Phillips, Michael J., *History of Santa Barbara County,* 2 vol, 1927

*Saddleback Ancestors: Rancho Families of Orange County, California,* Orange County California Genealogical Society, c1998

Shelton, *From Acorns to Oaks, A Potter Valley History--1855 to 1985*

Sleath, *Descendants of John and Mary (Pharo) Holloway from New Jersey to California 1704-1991.* Privately printed; copies in Santa Maria Public Library and Santa Maria Valley Historical Society

SMUHS *Review,* the year book of the Santa Maria Union High School

Sonoma County Marriages, 1847-1902, Sonoma Co Gen Soc 1990

*Spanish-Mexican Families of Early California, 1769-1850,* So Cal Gen Soc. 2 vols.

Stephens, *Who's Who in Santa Maria,* 1931

Storke, *A Memorial & Biographical History of the Counties of Santa Barbara, San Luis Obispo & Ventura,* 1891

Tesene, May, Novo, *The Story of the Pioneer Picnics,* 2002

*The Salinas City Index 1873-1882.* Newspaper Abstracts. Monterey Co. Gen. Soc., n.d.

*Telegram-Tribune,* San Luis Obispo newspaper

Thompson & West, *History of Santa Barbara & Ventura Counties,* 1883

*Times,* Santa Maria newspaper

*Tribune,* San Luis Obispo newspaper

*Vidette,* Santa Maria newspaper

*Yesterday Today Tomorrow,* South County Historical Society 1989, San Luis Obispo

Santa Maria Valley Genealogical Society and Library *Quarterly*, B. Cole Research

# INDEX

Abbey .................................. 524
Abbott .... 11, 12, 13, 24, 584
Abeloe 14, 15, 16, 17, 18, 19, 20, 165, 312, 313, 314, 316, 319, 506
Abels .................................... 96
Abernathy ........................ 226
Abernethy 12, 21, 23, 24, 25, 424, 523, 524, 584
Ables ...................... 182, 201
Acquistapace .... 24, 226, 584
Acton ................................ 519
Adam. 26, 27, 28, 29, 30, 31, 32, 33, 34, 35, 36, 49, 50, 60, 66, 74, 111, 148, 177, 211, 220, 266, 270, 281, 337, 534, 536
Adams 22, 35, 51, 55, 63, 68, 69, 224, 269, 313, 320, 337, 390, 391, 392, 427, 468, 485, 512
Adamson ......................... 446
Adcock ............................. 466
Addington ....................... 457
Adkins ... 368, 540, 541, 554, 558, 559, 564, 566, 572, 576, 577, 578, 579, 580, 581, 583
Agnew .................... 560, 566
Aguilera ................... 99, 360
Aguirre ............................ 202
Ainscough .................. 33, 36
Albee ............................... 140
Albright ........................... 178
Aldrich ............................ 153
Alexander ...... 22, 26, 33, 34, 180, 315
Alford .............................. 301
Allen .... 52, 68, 69, 133, 243, 258, 307, 308, 320, 416, 418, 434, 471, 519, 543
Alley ................................ 502
Allgar .............................. 138
Allinie ............................. 238
Allison ................... 153, 221
Allott ................................. 70
Altamirano ..................... 434
Alvin ............................... 315
Ambler ............................ 265
Ames ............................... 314
Amon .................... 408, 409
Amstutz .......................... 234
Andersen ........................ 110

Anderson 47, 50, 52, 84, 106, 184, 193, 214, 218, 227, 235, 274, 363, 480, 514, 522, 587
Andrade .......................... 211
Andrus ............................. 506
Angell .............................. 180
Anholm ........................... 515
Annice ............................... 67
Annis ............. 251, 252, 451
Anthony .......................... 197
Antognazzi ............. 301, 338
Antunez .......................... 426
Anzalone .................... 68, 69
Apgar ............................... 378
Apger ............................... 378
Applegate 305, 327, 331, 335
Arata ................................ 263
Araujo ..................... 161, 171
Arbuckle ................. 119, 387
Arellanes ..... 31, 98, 99, 255, 360
Argrow ............................ 513
Arias ................................ 509
Armstrong ..... 101, 102, 103, 279, 302, 305, 384, 387
Arneson .......................... 225
Arnold .... 518, 520, 521, 588
Arrellanes ...................... 478
Arwine ............................ 522
Ash ......................... 196, 597
Ashley .................... 548, 549
Ashton .................... 592, 593
Ashurst ........................... 541
Ashworth ....................... 250
Atherton ......................... 479
Atkins ............................. 544
Atkinson ................. 227, 236
Atwater ........................... 134
Aubert ............................... 51
Aughe .............................. 210
Austin. 50, 99, 446, 447, 448
Avegeno ............................ 51
Averdick ................. 527, 528
Avila.. 95, 99, 542, 543, 545, 547, 552, 559, 561, 563
Ayala ............................... 510
Ayers ............................... 379
Ayres ...................... 186, 390
Azbell ............. 160, 161, 171
Azbill .............. 160, 161, 171
Baber ....................... 22, 293
Babigan ........................... 271

Backus .................... 134, 135
Bacon .............................. 487
Bagby 65, 126, 230, 393, 522
Bahn ................................ 522
Bailey ............... 19, 334, 586
Baird ................................ 346
Bakeman ........................ 518
Baker. 16, 17, 18, 37, 38, 39, 40, 41, 42, 43, 44, 45, 59, 60, 61, 62, 64, 65, 115, 147, 157, 163, 191, 201, 236, 285, 288, 290, 300, 303, 304, 310, 313, 329, 330, 334, 368, 370, 408, 421, 437, 555, 579, 580
Balaam ............................ 466
Balch ............................... 542
Baldwin .......................... 147
Ball ......... 150, 248, 555, 573
Ballagh ........................... 341
Ballard .... 488, 489, 490, 492
Bam(b)sberger ............... 473
Bamboa .......................... 436
Bancroft .......... 299, 483, 487
Banks .............................. 436
Banner ............................ 191
Banta ............................... 133
Barba ............. 546, 547, 562
Barbarino ....................... 557
Barber .................... 306, 549
Barbour .......................... 487
Barca ...... 17, 18, 20, 57, 511
Barclay ..... 75, 127, 442, 444
Barden ............................ 490
Bardin ............. 62, 489, 492
Bardrick ........................... 73
Barker ............. 12, 188, 215
Barkley ................... 314, 317
Barling ........................... 192
Barnard .......................... 356
Barnes 50, 96, 144, 171, 254, 324, 410, 485, 543, 563
Barnett .................... 234, 309
Barnold .................... 84, 89
Barnum ................. 556, 557
Barr ....................... 152, 153
Barrett ..... 89, 190, 359, 360, 361, 443, 454, 457, 487, 558, 562, 563, 564, 574, 575, 576, 577
Barry ....................... 29, 46
Bartel ............................... 32
Bartleson ....................... 299

| | | |
|---|---|---|
| Bartlet............... 55, 352 | Betts .......................... 361 | Bolen ........................... 216 |
| Bartlett .............. 60, 169 | Beutel ........................ 387 | Bolls ........................... 297 |
| Barton............... 68, 577 | Bevans....................... 305 | Bond............................. 32 |
| Bartron .... 46, 47, 50, 51, 52, 53, 113 | Beve .......................... 320 | Bondietti.................... 512 |
| Basham......................... 438 | Beyer.......................... 207 | Bonell.......................... 562 |
| Bashfield ..................... 138 | Bianchi..... 49, 149, 208, 436 | Bonetti...... 93, 177, 205, 210, 330 |
| Bassi............................ 424 | Bias ............................. 561 | Bonham ....................... 237 |
| Bastanchury.................. 17 | Bickett........................ 271 | Bonilla............ 52, 53, 68, 69 |
| Bates............................ 500 | Bickmore........... 90, 591, 592 | Bonner.......................... 555 |
| Battelle ................... 16, 20 | Bicknell.. 328, 331, 410, 411 | Bontadelli .................... 338 |
| Battles ..... 32, 54, 55, 56, 57, 178, 200, 352, 353 | Bicley ......................... 436 | Booker.......................... 488 |
| Bauer......................... 47, 48 | Bidamon........ 78, 84, 86, 444 | Boosinger ....................... 99 |
| Baulig.............. 72, 181, 480 | Bidwell................. 160, 299 | Booth............................ 357 |
| Bausher ...................... 151 | Bienert........................ 436 | Boothe.......................... 292 |
| Baxter......................... 400 | Bierer.......................... 515 | Boquet ......................... 465 |
| Bayer........................... 593 | Bigelow ............ 39, 249, 571 | Borland........................... 99 |
| Beach ..... 133, 134, 135, 136 | Biggs .......................... 502 | Boronda....................... 246 |
| Beal ....................... 17, 511 | Bigler........................... 410 | Botiller ........... 277, 339, 340 |
| Beard.. 78, 79, 82, 83, 85, 94 | Biliardi................. 512, 513 | Bott............................. 270 |
| Beattie .... 167, 169, 171, 588 | Billington ....................... 57 | Bouton..................... 68, 257 |
| Beatty ......................... 238 | Bingham ...................... 416 | Bowden ......................... 361 |
| Beauchamp................... 515 | Birdsall........................ 135 | Bowers .. 70, 71, 72, 73, 180, 181, 248, 422, 478, 479, 480 |
| Beavers................. 591, 592 | Birnett ........................ 447 | |
| Beck . 14, 304, 305, 312, 347 | Bisco........................... 538 | Bowman ................ 123, 339 |
| Becker ......................... 527 | Bishop .... 158, 159, 466, 526 | Boxley........................... 330 |
| Beckett .................. 64, 104 | Bitner.......................... 410 | Boyd 66, 74, 78, 81, 86, 167, 170, 171, 175, 200, 201, 204, 210, 211, 266, 437 |
| Beckstrom .................... 110 | Bittick.......................... 158 | |
| Beckwith .............. 546, 554 | Bivins................... 405, 410 | |
| Bedwell ....................... 355 | Bizalski ........................ 588 | Boydstun ...................... 218 |
| Beeson............ 368, 579, 580 | Black ... 47, 78, 81, 175, 176, 235, 239, 341, 357, 360, 406, 410, 466, 470, 528 | Boynton........................ 379 |
| Belk ............................. 320 | | Brackett........................ 144 |
| Bell.. 80, 314, 317, 434, 445, 447, 450, 454, 457, 461, 482, 498 | | Bradfield ...................... 574 |
| | Blackledge..... 183, 353, 361, 408, 594 | Bradford......................... 88 |
| Bellamy........................ 378 | Blackwell ............... 415, 546 | Bradley...... 35, 74, 201, 202, 209, 219, 292, 296, 356, 357, 462, 506, 509, 570, 571 |
| Bellew ......................... 297 | Blake ........................... 447 | |
| Bello ...................... 17, 49 | Blanchard 133, 134, 136, 500 | |
| Benedict ...................... 411 | Blochman 148, 530, 532, 537 | |
| Benge ............................ 34 | Block .................... 467, 470 | Brady........................... 415 |
| Benham .......... 134, 135, 136 | Blockman ........ 532, 537, 566 | Braem .......................... 146 |
| Bennett.. 152, 236, 307, 560, 561 | Blodgett....................... 63, 92 | Bramlett........ 84, 89, 91, 106 |
| | Blomquist .................... 194 | Branas .......................... 394 |
| Benning........................ 156 | Bloomer................... 58, 180 | Brandt............ 505, 545, 563 |
| Benny .......................... 156 | Blos ............................. 411 | Brannagan ............. 152, 153 |
| Benson ................... 171, 289 | Blosser 28, 33, 34, 44, 59, 60, 61, 62, 63, 64, 65, 66, 67, 104, 112, 114, 124, 147, 201, 285, 360, 399, 466, 470, 482, 586 | Branson ................. 417, 453 |
| Benyon ........................ 531 | | Brant................... 183, 210 |
| Berger.......................... 320 | | Brass..................... 17, 95 |
| Berguglia..................... 515 | | Braun................... 46, 230 |
| Berry .............. 117, 144, 243 | | Brawler........................ 433 |
| Bertinoia...................... 509 | Blower.......................... 113 | Brayton........................ 584 |
| Bertrand .............. 479, 480 | Blumberg................ 314, 317 | Brazell......................... 215 |
| Bess............................. 243 | Blumhorst.................... 215 | Brazil........................... 297 |
| Bettancourt.................... 48 | Boardman.................... 134 | Breckinridge................. 128 |
| Bettiga ........................ 161 | Boat............................ 237 | Breen .......... 57, 71, 181, 505 |
| | Boehringer..................... 57 | Breilein................. 236, 237 |
| | Boggs .......................... 421 | |

Breneiser ............... 88, 285
Brenneman ..................... 96
Brenton ......................... 369
Bresette ............... 132, 276
Brewer ........................... 469
Brewster ...... 75, 76, 77, 442, 443, 444
Brians ............. 144, 145, 308
Brickey ............. 19, 334, 405
Bridge ............................ 331
Briegar ......................... 427
Bright .... 127, 132, 248, 276, 277, 417, 418
Brinton ......................... 243
Briscow ............................ 93
Bristol ........................... 437
Brkovich ....................... 313
Brock .............................. 53
Broderick ...................... 414
Bronson ........................ 135
Brooks ... 262, 294, 488, 489, 490, 491, 492, 493
Brookshire ..... 208, 248, 297, 481, 488, 489
Brophy ............................ 71
Broughton .................... 197
Brower ......................... 305
Brown 38, 51, 55, 57, 62, 66, 72, 73, 78, 79, 80, 81, 82, 83, 84, 85, 86, 87, 88, 89, 90, 91, 92, 93, 94, 99, 100, 105, 106, 121, 122, 123, 143, 174, 193, 195, 196, 197, 203, 212, 234, 235, 244, 253, 256, 265, 266, 267, 268, 274, 297, 298, 305, 311, 313, 330, 335, 348, 373, 422, 439, 446, 449, 470, 503, 512, 519, 520, 527, 545, 546, 547, 552, 553, 591
Browning ...................... 166
Bruce ............. 132, 524, 587
Brum ............................ 436
Brumana ...................... 315
Brumley ....................... 554
Brune ........................... 277
Brunette ...................... 542
Brush ........................... 133
Bryan ............. 307, 330, 426
Bryant .... 192, 383, 385, 394, 399
Buchanan ............... 129, 130
Bucher ............ 489, 490, 492
Buck ............................. 135
Buckner ....................... 575

Buckwell ...................... 501
Bueb ............................ 561
Buell ............. 230, 307, 310
Buffington ................... 233
Bullock ............... 186, 257
Bunce ... 95, 98, 99, 100, 172
Bunch ............ 297, 329, 416
Bunds ........................... 49
Bundy ......................... 238
Bunker ........................ 285
Bunting ....................... 592
Burchardi ............. 268, 270
Burd ............................ 166
Burke ...... 246, 250, 358, 434
Burleson ..................... 369
Burnett ........... 251, 309, 469
Burnham ..................... 294
Burns ................... 277, 314
Burola ......................... 266
Burritt ........................ 320
Burrow ........................ 440
Burton ... 126, 303, 536, 537, 538
Burum ............ 462, 484, 498
Butler ............. 171, 483, 560
Butlin .......................... 597
Cadwell ............... 167, 171
Caile ........................... 349
Calderon ............... 81, 509
Caldwell .................. 16, 20
Caligari ........... 338, 506, 512
Calkins ................. 217, 591
Call ..................... 103, 587
Callaway ....................... 25
Callender .................... 316
Calloway ...................... 97
Calvert .... 306, 358, 405, 508
Camarillo .................... 543
Camozzi ..................... 146
Campbell 164, 167, 169, 210, 324, 378, 381, 409, 413, 417, 418, 419, 420, 436
Campodonico 177, 181, 226, 330, 421, 425, 427, 430, 440
Canet .......................... 506
Canfield .................. 68, 69
Cannon ................. 335, 409
Capitani ....................... 32
Capson ....................... 110
Caramelli .................... 472
Cardoza ....................... 48
Careaga . 16, 18, 19, 20, 186, 312, 319, 320, 321, 409
Carlson ...... 83, 90, 349, 395, 422, 542

Carman ................. 376, 377
Carp ............................ 571
Carpenter 132, 135, 163, 328, 360, 419, 514, 515, 571
Carr 203, 253, 358, 451, 530, 531
Carrington .................. 513
Carroll 55, 57, 143, 198, 199
Carrow ........................ 157
Carswell ..................... 473
Carter ...... 160, 347, 409, 420
Cartereggio ................. 549
Carvell ........................ 577
Carver ........................ 384
Casady ....................... 216
Case ...................... 17, 250
Casenini ....................... 92
Cass ............... 250, 326, 327
Cassidy ........................ 18
Cassner ...................... 358
Casteel .... 308, 591, 592, 593
Castro ......... 30, 99, 232, 338
Catherwood ................. 234
Cattaneo ..................... 473
Caughell ............... 220, 221
Cauvet ....................... 432
Cavaletti ..................... 192
Cavell ................... 541, 558
Cedarholm .................. 474
Cesmat ....................... 500
Ceton .......................... 238
Chacon ....................... 210
Chaddick ...................... 49
Chaffin .. 79, 84, 89, 94, 101, 102, 103, 105, 106, 107, 219, 220, 587
Chalmers .................... 163
Chamberlain ........... 57, 297
Chambers ......... 31, 308, 543
Chandler ........... 35, 161, 434
Chapman ............ 22, 86, 495
Charles ................ 134, 135
Chase .......................... 250
Chavez ....................... 199
Cheadle ... 15, 182, 383, 384, 409, 434
Cheda ......................... 515
Cheeseman ................. 384
Cherry .................. 587, 590
Chester .................. 212, 214
Chiesa ........................ 312
Child ........................... 399
Chinello ...................... 381
Chisholm ........ 245, 246, 250
Chittenden .............. 137, 138
Chrisman .................... 210

Christ..............................520
Christensen.... 108, 199, 274, 275, 544, 545, 562, 575
Christenson ............ 474, 475
Christiansen......................49
Church............................238
Churchill ........................209
Cicero........................24, 584
Cipresso .........................215
Clarey.............................508
Clark.. 16, 99, 138, 200, 201, 207, 217, 218, 224, 227, 231, 236, 237, 241, 266, 269, 274, 276, 279, 280, 413, 435, 436, 439, 441, 486, 497, 508, 513, 544, 564, 576, 582, 591, 594, 595
Clarke..............................319
Clausen......................15, 593
Clay.................................578
Claycamp .......................511
Clayton....................312, 436
Clemens .................. 589, 590
Clements ................ 112, 116
Clemons 117, 118, 119, 309, 382, 383, 387
Clevenger 345, 350, 375, 471
Cliff.................................197
Clifford................... 531, 536
Cline........................ 105, 330
Clinkscale............... 163, 171
Close ....................... 182, 183
Clough ...................... 47, 531
Clovinger................... 42, 304
Cloward..........................243
Coale ..............................215
Coates.............................402
Coblentz 358, 359, 427, 432, 499
Cochran................... 231, 509
Cockran...........................580
Coe..................................283
Coelho ............................543
Coffee.............................402
Coffey ............................309
Coffin .............. 531, 534, 536
Cohen .............................424
Coiner....................... 66, 263
Colbath ...........................480
Colby..... 229, 300, 329, 397, 421, 453
Cole. 79, 120, 121, 122, 123, 124, 125, 126, 127, 128, 131, 132, 133, 136, 146, 151, 230, 239, 276, 277,

397, 399, 400, 401, 432, 443, 527, 593
Collier ................... 234, 587
Collins..... 98, 141, 196, 254, 505
Collyer.................... 277, 280
Colombo.........................169
Colver.... 132, 133, 134, 135, 136, 137
Conaty ..............................72
Condon........... 489, 490, 492
Confaglia................. 17, 515
Congdon. 488, 491, 492, 493
Coni...................................29
Conn................................529
Connelly ........................254
Conner 28, 35, 182, 382, 384, 385, 394
Connery..........................238
Connor 26, 27, 180, 383, 385, 394, 455, 588
Conrad ..............................91
Conser ............................325
Contreras ........................440
Conway ............. 62, 175, 222
Conwell ..........................285
Cook...... 102, 103, 104, 105, 106, 124, 134, 135, 147, 151, 159, 190, 251, 252, 313, 334, 362, 380, 422, 436, 439, 445, 446, 451, 454, 466, 470, 474, 499, 518, 519, 520, 521, 522
Coon ....... 339, 374, 527, 528
Cooney ...........................561
Cooper 15, 51, 166, 237, 441, 509, 576
Corbett............................299
Cornelius ........................500
Correll ................... 117, 430
Correy ............................150
Corsby ............................153
Corwin.................... 337, 440
Coryns............................473
Costa ..............................291
Coston ............................408
Cota ....................... 246, 508
Cotter..... 434, 435, 436, 437, 440, 441, 486
Cottle ..............................236
Counsel ..........................449
Covarrubias ....................269
Covert.............................547
Cowan ...........................191
Cowhick 445, 446, 451, 453, 455

Cowling..........................235
Cox.. 47, 152, 166, 167, 176, 260, 261, 389, 525, 545, 562, 575, 589
Coyne .............................505
Crabtree. 245, 248, 249, 253, 290
Craig....... 238, 320, 388, 389
Craiton............................308
Crakes ............ 177, 210, 325
Cramer...... 76, 315, 318, 444
Crandall..........................518
Crane ....................... 49, 551
Craner.............................421
Craun..............................340
Craven ............................501
Crawford ........................413
Crewe .............................138
Crews .............................255
Crist.............. 92, 93, 94, 519
Cronin ............................456
Croop ..............................565
Crosby 55, 59, 230, 330, 494, 583
Crouch ................... 132, 456
Crow...... 113, 114, 363, 390, 411, 468
Crowder/Crocker............298
Crowley .......... 486, 497, 500
Crummery ......................523
Cruttenden .....................138
Cuddeback......................206
Cuesta.............................263
Cullen ............... 50, 185, 186
Culp ................................525
Culver.... 121, 122, 123, 128, 129, 132, 133, 136, 139, 401
Cumming 543, 550, 561, 563
Cummings .............. 101, 243
Cunningham .. 79, 83, 90, 91, 93, 94, 570
Curryer .... 37, 44, 45, 46, 47, 48, 50, 51, 52, 144, 331, 337, 406, 508, 534
Curtis..... 384, 388, 394, 550, 563, 593
Cutler..............................487
Dagger..............................16
Dailey ............................165
Dale ................................381
Dalessi.... 148, 149, 380, 434
Dalporto .........................512
Dalton..................... 124, 126
Damm...............................15
Dana 15, 215, 224, 316, 317,

321, 337, 436, 439, 440
Dani .................. 542, 560
Daniel ........... 313, 315, 317
Daniels .. 286, 291, 296, 297, 499
Dappen ........................ 320
DaRin ............................ 72
Dart ............................. 159
Daut ............................ 340
Davenport ............... 40, 381
Davidson .............. 302, 497
Davis 29, 31, 39, 57, 89, 101, 107, 132, 136, 140, 141, 142, 143, 144, 145, 146, 147, 148, 149, 150, 151, 152, 153, 154, 155, 156, 157, 158, 159, 160, 161, 162, 163, 164, 165, 166, 167, 168, 169, 170, 171, 201, 218, 225, 227, 228, 230, 232, 233, 236, 238, 240, 243, 250, 264, 323, 327, 343, 348, 355, 361, 371, 374, 380, 426, 445, 450, 454, 456, 481, 482, 533, 537, 545, 546, 547, 552, 579, 580, 581, 582, 596
Davison ....................... 166
Davisson 172, 173, 382, 386, 486
Dawson ....................... 380
Day .... 78, 80, 81, 83, 86, 87, 90, 92, 93, 292, 452, 519, 520
Dayton .......................... 36
De la Guerra ..... 99, 186, 301
De Martin ..................... 538
DeBoux .......................... 52
Decker .......................... 435
DeGasparis ............ 425, 430
Deguan ........................ 336
Del Monte .................... 306
Dela ............................. 509
Delay ........................... 242
Delco ........................... 538
Deleisseigues ................ 224
Dell ............................. 480
Delnotaro .............. 337, 338
Deming ........................ 218
DeMoss ....................... 276
DeNise ... 174, 175, 176, 222
Denner ......................... 474
Dennerlein ................... 436
Dennis ......................... 337
Dent ............................ 358
Denzil .......................... 505
Derry .................... 381, 457
Desmond ........ 272, 273, 274
DeSolminihac ............... 310
Detar ............................ 597
Detlefsen ....................... 15
Deton ........................... 102
Detro ........................... 241
Devine .................. 142, 143
DeVries ........................ 215
Dewey .......................... 431
Dias ............................. 381
Dickerson ..................... 353
Dickey ......................... 335
Dickinson .............. 220, 221
Dicks ........................... 234
Diehl ............................ 431
Dierlam ........................ 217
Dierlan ......................... 217
Dille ...................... 73, 404
Dillwood ...................... 187
Dimock ........................ 197
Dirk ............................. 436
Dirkes .......................... 315
Dittman .................... 14, 15
Dixon ............. 303, 309, 484
Doak ..................... 210, 324
Doane ..... 58, 71, 72, 74, 155, 177, 178, 179, 180, 181, 200, 351, 352, 382, 394, 455, 581
Dobbins ......................... 12
Dobell .......................... 320
Dodge .. 46, 47, 49, 114, 182, 183, 394, 437
Dodson ........................ 593
Dogherra ..................... 561
Dolan ........................... 596
Dolcini .... 224, 225, 226, 425
Dominguez ................... 301
Donaldson ...... 136, 306, 410
Donavan ...................... 538
Donelson .............. 565, 573
Donnelly ........................ 70
Donnely ........................ 93
Donner ......................... 299
Donovan 29, 33, 36, 57, 255, 270, 380, 436, 513, 545, 562, 575
Dorland .................. 56, 57
Dorn .............. 75, 442, 444
Dorrett .................. 541, 575
Dorsey ................... 66, 422
Doty ..... 34, 36, 57, 549, 563
Doud ............................. 32
Douglas ................. 17, 320
Douglass .............. 292, 296
Douthit ........................ 588
Dover ..... 326, 327, 408, 411, 469, 593, 594
Dowell ......................... 298
*Down* .................. 146, 165
Downs .... 168, 169, 195, 409
Downy .......................... 153
Doyle ..................... 70, 254
Drake ........................... 540
Draper ......................... 313
Drenon ......................... 29
Drum ..... 184, 185, 186, 187, 188, 191, 197, 198, 199, 449, 532, 563
Drumm .... 71, 168, 184, 189, 191, 193, 194, 195, 196, 197, 198, 199, 201, 337, 369, 371, 402, 403, 404, 406, 440, 445, 452, 454, 457, 460, 461, 530
Dryden .................. 320, 370
Dudley ..... 81, 82, 88, 89, 91, 274, 485, 498, 499, 500
Duff ...................... 330, 596
Dugger .................. 531, 537
Dunbar .................. 35, 485
Duncan ...... 68, 84, 115, 199, 315, 386
Dunlap .................. 132, 434
Dunn ...................... 502, 560
Dunstan ................. 174, 176
Dunton ......................... 328
Durley ..................... 34, 36
Durm ........................... 184
Dutard .......... 79, 84, 85, 87
Dutcher ... 203, 323, 324, 325
Dutra ...................... 15, 69
Dutton ... 107, 295, 300, 302, 421, 583
Dvorak .... 526, 527, 528, 529
Dye ............................. 448
Dyer ............... 195, 266, 320
Eakin ........................... 288
Eames ............ 208, 211, 481
Earl .. 30, 49, 53, 75, 98, 104, 150, 154, 156, 170, 171, 172, 173, 186, 187, 197, 200, 201, 202, 203, 204, 205, 206, 207, 208, 209, 210, 211, 262, 269, 276, 290, 320, 324, 325, 334, 337, 403, 405, 406, 412, 413, 434, 436, 437, 441, 442, 504, 510, 524, 564, 570, 576

Easterbrooks .......... 126, 443
Eastman ............... 179, 450
Easton ........... 432, 464, 579
Eddy ............. 159, 592, 593
Edgar ........................... 11
Edgerton ............... 140, 141
Edie ..................... 319, 320
Edmands 212, 213, 214, 216, 217, 218
Edrington ............. 528, 529
Edwards 16, 17, 70, 97, 149, 213, 218, 275, 319, 320, 327, 401
Egan ...... 251, 252, 369, 370, 451, 458, 572, 574
Eggler ........................... 18
Ehlers ............. 236, 531, 537
Eiland .......................... 298
Elberson ......... 190, 454, 460
Elder ............................ 589
Eldred .......................... 386
Eldridge ........................ 243
Elliott 83, 174, 203, 235, 267, 291, 296, 354, 357, 375, 400, 467, 470, 513, 570
Ellis ... 61, 64, 134, 135, 311, 504, 524, 548, 551
Elson ........................... 171
Elvidge .... 74, 105, 219, 220, 221, 270
Emerick ........................ 28
Emerson .. 16, 169, 386, 470, 588, 590
Emmert ................ 213, 214
Emory ..................... 11, 101
Emslie ........................... 32
Engel ........................... 202
Engels .......................... 222
Enis .............................. 470
Entner .......................... 519
Eppel ............................ 549
Epperson ............... 400, 401
Ericksen ....................... 552
Erkens .......................... 170
Erkins ........................... 170
Ernest ........................... 355
Ernst ..................... 405, 410
Esabrooks .................... 127
Eschbach ..................... 519
Escobar ................ 351, 353
Espinoza ............... 559, 560
Estabrooks ............. 126, 443
Evans ..... 226, 245, 417, 449, 450, 452, 459, 500, 594
Eves ............................. 242
Ewald ............................ 17

Ewens ........................... 415
Ewing ........................... 144
Faber ............................ 129
Fagerbourg .......... 518, 522
Fain .............................. 513
Fairbanks ..................... 597
Faliz ............................. 501
Falkenstein ................... 241
Fanny ........................... 380
Faria .............................. 17
Farley ............. 132, 276, 280
Farmer .......................... 506
Farrell .................... 285, 288
Farrow .......................... 487
Faulkner ................ 198, 571
Fauntleroy .................... 360
Fay 451, 454, 455, 458, 459, 460
Featherstone .......... 404, 450
Featherton ..................... 77
Fee ............... 31, 60, 89, 268
Feiock ............ 486, 500, 502
Feliz 337, 338, 511, 512, 513
Felmlee . 95, 96, 97, 431, 432
Felt ........ 187, 262, 263, 569
Fennell .......................... 348
Ferante ......................... 239
Ferguson ................. 16, 235
Ferini .................... 424, 425
Fernandez ..................... 336
Ferrari ................... 78, 413
Ferrell ........................... 436
Ferretti .......................... 557
Ferry ............................. 406
Fesler ..... 124, 400, 471, 485, 488, 496, 499, 500
Fickle ........................... 186
Fife ............................... 225
Filipponi ....................... 266
Filliponini ..................... 311
Fillmore ........................ 528
Findley ..... 12, 205, 210, 515
Fine 175, 176, 222, 223, 525
Finley .................... 308, 511
Firfires ........................... 70
Fischer ......................... 325
Fischl ........................... 387
Fisher ................... 384, 479
Fisk ...................... 102, 241
Fitzgerald ............. 244, 539
Fitzgibbons ................... 311
Fitzhugh ......... 417, 418, 514
Fitzner ......................... 410
Fitzpatrick 92, 336, 407, 410
Fleck ....... 224, 225, 226, 254
Flecks ........................... 224

Fleischer ............. 358, 468
Fleisher ... 125, 126, 172, 399
Fletcher . 137, 138, 225, 325, 593
Flick ...................... 101, 226
Flint ........ 160, 162, 163, 171
Flores ..... 229, 507, 508, 509, 574
Flournoy ....................... 195
Floyd ............................ 462
Flynn .............................. 88
Folks ............... 542, 543, 561
Folsom ......................... 166
Foote ............................ 133
Footman ....................... 475
Forbes .... 163, 195, 199, 296, 357, 473
Ford ..................... 29, 30, 571
Foreman ....................... 438
Forrester 105, 140, 141, 152, 201, 209, 227, 228, 229, 230, 231, 232, 233, 234, 235, 236, 239, 240, 241, 242, 244, 300, 368, 371, 461, 544, 553, 563, 565, 572, 574, 577, 578, 579, 580, 581, 583
Forsythe ....................... 150
Fortney ... 488, 489, 490, 492
Foster ..... 187, 200, 245, 246, 248, 253, 290, 298, 362, 363, 403, 404, 445, 449, 450, 455, 456, 458, 459, 460
Fouts ....... 507, 510, 511, 512
Fowler ......................... 592
Fox .... 31, 92, 176, 225, 227, 235, 236, 254, 255, 256, 470, 584
Foxen ............. 277, 339, 340
Frago ........................... 180
France ............. 56, 83, 90, 94
Francis ......................... 410
Franco ......................... 394
Franklin ....................... 225
Fraser ........................... 421
Frates ........................... 180
Frazier .................. 566, 584
Fredericksen ................ 166
Freeman .......... 177, 312, 591
Freer ............................. 249
Freire ............. 424, 426, 431
Freitas .................... 17, 438
French ............ 208, 211, 291
Freshour 251, 289, 329, 404, 416, 446, 449, 460

Frew ....... 202, 208, 211, 255
Frick ............... 197
Friend ............. 432
Frisbee ............. 435
Fritges ............. 202
Fritts ............... 303
Froom ............ 84, 464
Fruits ............ 515, 516
Fry .............. 51, 439, 463
Fryer ............... 349
Fuente ............. 513
Fuentes ............ 62
Fugler ........... 229, 525, 576
Fuller ...... 251, 252, 451, 458
Fumia ............. 30
Funk ............. 185, 186
Furman ........... 352, 353
Furness ............ 456
Fuson .............. 519
Futs ................ 512
Gable .............. 123
Gage ............... 434
Gagliardo ........... 381
Gale ............ 132, 248, 249
Galewsky ........... 360
Galindo ............ 337
Gallison .......... 97, 431
Gamble ........... 32, 455
Gamboa .......... 436, 542
Gammons ...... 545, 549, 550
Gandaubert ......... 355
Gann 152, 249, 289, 295, 300
Ganoung. 257, 258, 259, 596
Gantz ............... 242
Garbarino .......... 557
Garcia ........... 24, 275, 512
Gardner ... 60, 61, 64, 65, 66, 331, 334, 405, 408, 410, 499, 587
Garey ..... 202, 203, 207, 209, 323
Garfinkle ........... 432
Gariga ............. 407
Garing ............. 220
Garland ............ 455
Garneau ........... 500
Garner ........ 22, 66, 455, 560
Garrett ... 167, 217, 250, 260, 261, 285, 302, 303, 326, 327, 330, 404, 410, 450, 457, 458
Garrison ............ 164
Gascoigne ........... 306, 418
Gastineau ........... 404
Gates 98, 115, 202, 203, 208, 211, 262, 263, 308, 309, 507, 509, 513, 527
Gautschy ......... 553, 563, 565
Gaxiola .......... 47, 51
Gaydos .......... 343, 345, 346
Gebhart ............ 401
Geddes ........... 328, 330, 408
Genardini .......... 417, 420
Gentry .............. 34
Gerard .............. 48
German ............ 520, 522
Gerrard ............. 511
Getman ............ 339, 340
Gewe ............. 22, 23
Giacomini .......... 225, 425
Gibbs .............. 243
Gifford ............. 206
Giger ............... 553
Gilbert .... 227, 234, 240, 374
Gilham ............. 412, 413
Gilkeson ............ 292
Gill ............... 64, 66
Gillespie .......... 156, 380
Gillette ............ 11, 12
Gillilan ............ 371, 372
Gillis ............. 542, 543, 561
Gilman ............. 569
Gilmer ............. 463
Giraud ............. 117
Gisin ............ 246, 249
Gjerdrum ........... 106
Glade ............... 103
Gladhill ............ 160
Glenn ............ 234, 587
Glines .... 144, 145, 155, 173, 201, 294, 363, 371, 380, 386, 402, 428, 498, 504, 505, 587, 590
Gnesa ............. 186, 198, 199
Goatley ............. 291
Gobel .............. 536
Goble .............. 33, 535
Godfrey ............ 450, 459
Godley ............. 500
Goforth ............. 473
Goldtree ............ 427
Gollober ............ 424
Gomes .............. 436
Gonzales ... 12, 479, 558, 562
Goodale ............. 68
Goodchild. 96, 153, 229, 519
Goodfellow ....... 21, 315, 525
Goodman ............ 32
Goodrich .......... 134, 135
Goodwin ........... 229, 375
Gordon ........... 320, 321, 575
Gorell .............. 513
Goutschy ........... 553
Grabil .............. 218
Grable .............. 279
Gracia .............. 584
Grady ...... 144, 322, 324, 325
Graff ............... 401
Grafft ............ 438, 439
Gragg ...... 264, 265, 340, 374
Graham 35, 36, 74, 124, 188, 198, 219, 271, 277, 278, 279, 527, 570
Grainger ........... 218
Gramespacher ....... 506
Granacher .......... 163
Granas .............. 31
Grand ............... 207
Grant ..... 47, 49, 50, 51, 206, 208, 211, 237
Graves 11, 12, 185, 491, 516, 517
Gray... 27, 83, 87, 88, 89, 94, 124, 184, 197, 199, 266, 267, 268, 269, 270, 271, 383, 437
Green ........ 51, 171, 306, 561
Greene ............. 513
Greenelsh .......... 524
Greenleaf ........... 571
Gregg ............ 330, 423, 516
Gregorio ............ 206
Gregory ... 76, 136, 185, 206, 211, 235
Grelee .............. 553
Grey ................ 520
Griffin .... 182, 288, 410, 411
Griffith ... 170, 285, 310, 560
Griffiths ........... 235
Griffitts ............ 304, 310
Grigsby ............ 485, 496
Grim .............. 542, 543
Grimes ............ 410, 412, 543
Griset ............. 19, 29
Grisingher.. 56, 72, 224, 352, 353, 424, 425, 427
Grisson ............. 107
Grottkau ............ 206
Groundwater ........ 562
Grove ...... 145, 158, 165, 308
Groves ............ 292, 293
Grube ............... 95
Grutzmacher ... 147, 227, 236
Gruwell ............. 117
Guichard ........... 225
Guidotti ............ 319
Guinn ...... 299, 376, 377, 378
Gularte ............. 52

| | | |
|---|---|---|
| Gundo............................. 401 | Hargear............................127 | Heaton............................592 |
| Gunn................................421 | Hargrave............................38 | Hebard....................306, 310 |
| Guntle................................32 | Harisen............................110 | Hecox .... 281, 282, 284, 296, 418 |
| Gutherie...........................548 | Harker......................286, 288 | |
| Guthrie.................. 169, 170 | Harlan..............................560 | Hedge.............................132 |
| Guymon...........................153 | Harman............................457 | Hedges.. 87, 88, 89, 266, 267 |
| Gwin................................525 | Harmon............................129 | Hedrick..............................25 |
| Haas ........ 272, 273, 274, 275 | Harp................ 233, 410, 458 | Heenan.............................488 |
| Habbick...........................527 | Harper........................63, 359 | Heimlich..........................356 |
| Haddon..............................49 | Harriman 132, 133, 276, 277, 278, 279, 280 | Heinrick...........................356 |
| Hadley.......................76, 305 | | Heiser...............................269 |
| Hagen..............................220 | Harrington..... 370, 371, 413, 520, 522 | Heitkotter........................320 |
| Hagerty............................147 | | Heller...............................177 |
| Haider............. 544, 545, 549 | Harris .. 18, 19, 20, 298, 354, 357, 358, 362, 369, 418, 427, 530, 541, 543 | Helmquist..........................17 |
| Hails................................310 | | Hemmingway ..................46 |
| Haines .... 210, 237, 238, 483 | | Hemphill .... 60, 83, 244, 409 |
| Halcomb............................53 | Harrison...................208, 209 | Henderson.................49, 215 |
| Hale.........................237, 417 | Hart ... 11, 12, 13, 22, 62, 63, 74, 125, 175, 176, 193, 197, 229, 230, 300, 323, 389, 390, 485, 494 | Hendricks.................171, 544 |
| Hall.... 35, 56, 142, 143, 145, 164, 173, 179, 184, 186, 268, 321, 348, 360, 385, 409, 411, 421, 424, 427, 497, 532, 536, 545 | | Hennessy..........................259 |
| | | Henning...........................463 |
| | | Henrietty.........................455 |
| | | Hensely ...........................457 |
| | Harte................................309 | Hensley ...........................363 |
| | Hartley.............................306 | Herbert.............................545 |
| Halter ..............................209 | Hartnell....................301, 505 | Hernandez........................301 |
| Haltom............................436 | Hartzell............................338 | Herndon...................465, 523 |
| Halvorsen........................472 | Harvard............................174 | Herold..............................278 |
| Hamann..........................359 | Harvey... 328, 388, 411, 472, 474, 475 | Herriman.........................280 |
| Hamasaki........................426 | | Herring............................348 |
| Hamby............................322 | Haskins.. 115, 147, 257, 304, 486 | Herron.............................176 |
| Hames.............................171 | | Hersman..........................312 |
| Hamill.................... 153, 538 | Haslam 19, 74, 81, 463, 464, 465 | Hertz................................313 |
| Hamilton 37, 38, 39, 41, 246, 304, 376, 384, 591 | | Herwig.............................438 |
| | Hastings.............................60 | Herz.................................380 |
| Hammon..........................193 | Hatch.............. 192, 218, 471 | Hess.................................293 |
| Hammond......... 73, 310, 415 | Hatfield.......... 178, 181, 394 | Heyman...........................165 |
| Hammonds......................143 | Hathaway ....... 203, 263, 570 | Hibbard....................179, 297 |
| Hampton..................215, 473 | Haug..................................17 | Hicklin.....................131, 132 |
| Hand........................151, 336 | Hauman...........................192 | Hickman..........................185 |
| Handley....................448, 594 | Hautow............................575 | Hickok............. 540, 544, 558 |
| Hankenson......................527 | Haven..............................349 | Hicks .............357, 358, 456 |
| Hankerson.......................185 | Hawkins . 115, 192, 197, 561 | Higbee.............................328 |
| Hannah............................259 | Hawks ... 121, 122, 123, 132, 133 | Higginbotham..................163 |
| Hanrahan.........................314 | | Hilberg.............................328 |
| Hansen .. 312, 313, 314, 316, 319, 321, 369, 395, 515 | Hawley................... 576, 577 | Hilbish...............................35 |
| | Hawn...............................516 | Hilburg............................328 |
| Hanson ...... 18, 20, 314, 319, 511, 538 | Hayden.................... 539, 544 | Hildebrand.......................345 |
| | Haydon... 201, 203, 382, 402 | Hilderbrand.....................546 |
| Hapgood.. 76, 82, 90, 91, 92, 93, 94 | Hayes...... 193, 194, 196, 340 | Hilford............................344 |
| | Hays.................................529 | Hill 152, 164, 165, 166, 167, 168, 169, 271, 306, 307, 308, 309, 310, 543, 548, 549, 552, 553, 565, 574 |
| Harbin.....................205, 322 | Hayward..........................101 | |
| Harden.............................540 | Hazard.............................514 | |
| Hardenbrook ............35, 296 | Heacock.......... 282, 283, 284 | |
| Hardie......................401, 514 | Headrick..........................293 | |
| Harding.......... 213, 214, 215 | Healy...............................531 | Hillard 83, 84, 105, 185, 186, 187 |
| Hardison.........................307 | Hearn.................................17 | |
| Hardy..............................208 | Heath...............................262 | Hilliard................... 132, 187 |

Hills .................... 505
Hilton .............. 263, 314
Hinds ............... 63, 357
Hines .................... 368
Hingley ................. 308
Hinman .................. 98
Hinton ... 354, 355, 361, 363, 372, 374
Hitchcock ............. 187
Hitchman ............. 207
Hite .................. 218, 528
Hixon .................... 263
Hobbs .... 200, 245, 249, 252, 253, 285, 286, 287, 288, 289, 290, 291, 292, 294, 295, 296, 297, 298, 300, 428, 434, 445, 451, 459, 486, 487, 488, 495, 497
Hobson ........ 304, 326, 437
Hocker ... 210, 259, 324, 562, 581, 596
Hockett ................ 144
Hodges ................. 409
Hoefling ............... 209
Hoey .............. 202, 209, 211
Hoffman ............... 175
Hogle .................... 436
Holcomb ........ 542, 543, 561
Holden ................. 112
Holdridge .. 12, 24, 383, 384, 385
Holdt ............... 312, 321
Holgate ................. 274
Holland .. 145, 228, 240, 279, 527, 548, 549, 553
Hollis .................... 505
Holloway 145, 229, 278, 356, 360, 363, 372, 504
Hollowell ........... 555, 559
Holmes ................ 216
Holser .............. 19, 586
Holshauser ............ 303
Holst .................... 420
Holt ............. 15, 144, 425
Hood ............ 42, 122, 123
Hooker ............ 293, 298
Hooper ................. 593
Hoopes ........ 242, 243, 244
Hopkins ... 31, 113, 287, 327, 334, 513, 592, 593
Hopper 12, 37, 38, 39, 40, 41, 44, 117, 148, 190, 217, 230, 233, 260, 261, 295, 299, 300, 301, 302, 304, 305, 306, 308, 309, 310, 326, 331, 333, 334, 335, 403, 408, 421, 454, 478, 479, 484, 501, 525, 555, 556, 571
Hoque .............. 305, 479
Horn ............ 407, 410, 561
Hoskins ............ 540, 557
Hostler ................ 144
Hough ................. 147
Houghton ............. 97
Houk ....... 201, 292, 296, 409
Hourahane ............. 55
Hourihan ......... 57, 72, 318
Hourihane ............ 336
Houser .................. 69
Howard 16, 17, 20, 181, 315, 380, 382, 387, 388, 394, 524, 526, 530, 532, 534
Howe ............ 129, 294, 326
Howell .................. 219
Howerton 171, 289, 292, 293, 294, 295, 296, 298, 357, 371
Hoy ................. 162, 171
Hubbard ......... 129, 130, 596
Hubbel ................. 560
Huckaby .............. 502
Huddleston .......... 238
Hudgins ............... 238
Hudson ... 105, 107, 219, 473
Huey .................... 160
Huffman .............. 132
Hughes .. 193, 195, 197, 212, 218, 238, 519, 520
Hulet .................... 217
Hulett ............. 213, 593
Huling ................. 486
Hull 137, 138, 139, 417, 453
Humphrey ........... 455
Humphreys ...... 84, 105, 594
Hunnicutt ............. 48
Hunt ............... 329, 452
Hunter ............ 279, 455
Huntington ........... 450
Hurd .................... 335
Hurlbut ................ 500
Hurst ............... 381, 419
Huseman ......... 292, 296
Huston ... 192, 488, 489, 490, 491, 492, 493, 494
Hutchins ................ 47
Hutchison ....... 83, 88, 268
Hutt ............... 282, 370
Huxtable .......... 354, 355
Huyck .... 292, 294, 296, 405, 456
Hyde ................... 237
Hyder ................... 296
Hynes .................. 327
Ilenstine ............ 96, 100
Ingraham .............. 542
Ingram .... 503, 542, 543, 560
Irefeldt ................ 340
Irvine . 78, 79, 82, 83, 84, 86, 87, 88, 89, 90
Irwin .............. 186, 446
Itjen .................... 268
Jackson .... 90, 138, 155, 158, 184, 191, 342, 595
Jacobs ................... 39
Jacobson .............. 218
Jakobsen .............. 275
James ............... 95, 96
Jarboe ................. 345
Jared ................... 191
Jasper ............ 466, 470
Jasperson ......... 14, 313
Jeffrey ................. 148
Jeffreys ................ 160
Jenkins ... 311, 314, 407, 410, 522
Jennings ............ 49, 405
Jensen 14, 15, 16, 17, 49, 70, 110, 111, 312, 313, 314, 315, 316, 318, 319, 320, 321, 420, 434, 436
Jespersen ............. 319
Jesse .................... 495
Jessee ..... 148, 200, 203, 205, 210, 211, 322, 323, 324, 325, 380
Jessen ................. 312
Jeter .................... 300
Jett ..................... 199
Jobe .................... 573
Johnson 15, 31, 84, 111, 148, 154, 157, 178, 219, 220, 270, 285, 288, 309, 317, 358, 360, 386, 395, 410, 420, 425, 473, 474, 508, 594
Johnston .. 30, 121, 122, 123, 132, 202, 209, 356, 511, 512
Jones 99, 125, 175, 275, 285, 297, 358, 360, 375, 381, 473, 475, 481, 512, 515, 525, 538, 558
Jordan. 57, 72, 106, 107, 520
Jordano ................ 513
Jorgensen ............. 110
Jory ............... 293, 298
Joseph .... 298, 309, 541, 545,

547, 550, 554, 558, 559, 566
Joslin .................. 553, 559
Jourdan ........................ 234
Juarez ........................... 512
Jullien ............. 117, 513, 566
Kabel ................ 62, 114, 498
Kacenta ........................ 320
Kaeding ........................ 319
Kaetzel .................... 51, 514
Kaeusner ...................... 552
Kahn ............................. 185
Kaiser .................... 375, 389
Kalin ..................... 293, 298
Kalland .......................... 30
Kalmyer ........................ 508
Karau ............................ 552
Karl ............................... 482
Kaserman ..................... 320
Kaucher ........................ 186
Kays ...................... 246, 250
Kearney ........................ 594
Keegan .......................... 509
Keene ...................... 63, 105
Keeney ..... 12, 299, 305, 478
Keeton .......................... 143
Keffer ............................ 107
Kehew .......................... 293
Kehl .............................. 518
Kelcher ......................... 160
Kellar ............................ 238
Kelley 27, 28, 296, 349, 357, 379
Kellogg .................. 170, 265
Kelly 170, 242, 331, 436, 519
Kelsey ........................... 289
Kemp ............... 92, 260, 526
Kendall ......................... 349
Kendrick. 544, 545, 547, 562, 575, 581
Kennedy .... 81, 82, 225, 246, 383, 534
Kenney ......................... 305
Kennison ...................... 272
Kent ....................... 448, 564
Kerr ............................... 315
Kesner .................... 111, 395
Kessler ............................ 51
Kester ..... 257, 347, 491, 514
Ketcham ................. 288, 525
Kiemele .................. 553, 559
Kieran ..... 403, 407, 410, 411
Kies ............................... 522
Kifer .............................. 345
Kimball .................... 51, 516
Kimberling ................... 420

Kincaid .......................... 411
Kindle ..................... 319, 320
King 57, 135, 144, 163, 202, 207, 208, 263, 324, 406, 457, 491, 500
Kingery ......................... 491
Kinseth ... 84, 89, 91, 94, 106
Kinsey ............................. 57
Kirchner . 220, 563, 565, 573
Kirk ....................... 269, 436
Kirkpatrick ................... 582
Kirner ............................. 47
Kise ................................ 85
Kitchell ......................... 554
Klein ............................. 116
Kleinberg ...................... 531
Klin ............................... 409
Klindera ........................ 528
Kline ..................... 112, 116
Klink ..... 200, 207, 263, 403, 405, 406, 408, 410, 411
Knapp .... 128, 129, 237, 321, 381
Knaus ............................ 314
Knight .... 138, 174, 308, 554
Knighten ....................... 115
Knoles ........................... 193
Knotts 51, 52, 312, 336, 337, 436, 440, 441
Knowles ........................ 171
Koberg ............................ 97
Koester .......................... 543
Kohler ........................... 313
Kohn ............................. 237
Kolding ........ 14, 15, 17, 291
Kolterman .............. 227, 236
Koons ....................... 47, 53
Kostering ............... 468, 469
Krauss ........................... 549
Kreidel .......................... 358
Kribs ............................. 411
Krieger .......................... 271
Krumbholz .................... 500
Kudera .......................... 165
Kuehl ...... 542, 546, 551, 552
Kunkle .......................... 344
Kurtz ............. 210, 549, 589
Kuykendall ............. 146, 147
Kwasigroch ................... 328
Kyle ...................... 511, 588
LaBorde .... 47, 252, 297, 451
Labriskie ....................... 408
Lack .............................. 255
Lackey .......................... 237
Lacy .............................. 349
Laffie ............................... 33

Lafontaine ................ 17, 425
LaFranchi ................ 72, 479
Lagomarsino ................. 538
Lail ............................... 346
Lair ....................... 128, 129
Laird ... 26, 27, 29, 33, 34, 35
Lake ............... 417, 418, 453
Lamb ............................ 362
Lambert . 268, 421, 519, 522, 548, 549, 550, 564, 565, 576, 582
Lamberton .................... 238
Lambeth ....................... 216
Lambright ..................... 401
Lamy .............................. 60
Lane .............................. 321
Lang ............. 166, 319, 321
Langais ........................... 27
Langdon ........... 60, 586, 589
Lange ............................ 321
Langley .................. 106, 587
LaPatera ....................... 310
Lapham ........................ 517
Lapp .................. 32, 98, 216
Laraway ............ 21, 102, 523
Largey ........................... 325
Largo ............................ 210
Largo/Larco ................... 323
Larsen .............. 15, 110, 314
Larson ..................... 91, 185
Lasar ...................... 423, 427
Lasher ........................... 460
Lathrop ......................... 325
Laughery ............... 563, 574
Laughlin 176, 198, 199, 221, 355, 375, 446, 449
Laughter .......................... 31
Launders ....................... 285
Lauritzen ...... 14, 15, 16, 593
Lavagnino ..................... 436
Law .................... 206, 210
Lawn ....... 539, 541, 546, 554
Lawrence 176, 320, 321, 471, 473
Laws ........................ 16, 17
Lawson ... 117, 405, 508, 563
Lawyer ......................... 102
Lazar ............................ 423
Lazelle .......................... 485
Leach ..... 114, 337, 354, 371, 468
Learned ........................ 432
Lee 12, 48, 49, 133, 228, 273, 284, 531, 534, 535, 536, 537, 549, 551, 556, 564, 566

Leffingwell.... 175, 246, 248, 249, 250
Lehrer .............................. 130
Leigh ............................... 302
Leonard ................. 106, 518
Leonare ......................... 297
Leoni ............ 412, 413, 441
Leonidas ................. 227, 577
Leslie .............................. 263
Lester ............................ 308
Letterman ..................... 315
Lewellyn ....................... 293
Lewis ..... 152, 161, 190, 193, 197, 235, 243, 268, 287, 293, 326, 357, 358, 400, 447, 586, 587, 589
Leyva ............................... 34
Lieber .................... 314, 316
Lierly ................... 61, 63, 64
Lighthall ....................... 411
Lillard ........................... 194
Lincoln .................. 379, 473
Lind ............................... 167
Lindbery ....................... 237
Lindsay .......................... 270
Lindsey .......................... 379
Linebaugh .............. 362, 504
Lingwood ...................... 138
Liss ................................. 594
Liston ............................ 368
Littmann ....................... 423
Livingston .............. 480, 482
Ljungmark ..................... 111
Llanada ................. 539, 556
Locarnini ......................... 23
Locey .................... 270, 271
Lockard ......................... 156
Lockwood ...................... 466
Logan .... 176, 216, 217, 230, 231, 233, 260, 261, 300, 302, 326, 327, 334, 335, 403, 408, 410, 421, 452, 453, 460, 479, 572, 594
Logsdon ........................ 386
Lombard ....................... 131
Long .. 47, 48, 51, 56, 60, 64, 84, 89, 102, 103, 106, 141, 145, 148, 149, 167, 172, 187, 194, 197, 198, 199, 208, 210, 215, 219, 231, 232, 238, 267, 275, 288, 298, 310, 312, 315, 320, 322, 325, 339, 340, 347, 350, 352, 356, 384, 385, 386, 387, 394, 410, 437, 438, 450, 459, 474, 489, 499, 506, 509, 510, 526, 528, 529, 543, 547, 579, 589, 595, 597
Longshire ...................... 258
Longwood .................... 138
Looker ........................... 466
Loomis ... 138, 279, 336, 371
Lopes ............................ 320
Lopez .......... 24, 25, 291, 584
Lorenson ...................... 437
Lorentzen ..................... 312
Lorenzen ...................... 312
Lorraine ........................ 237
Louann .......................... 144
Loustalot ........................ 52
Love .............................. 234
Lovier ............................. 52
Lowe ............. 101, 211, 515
Lowell ........................... 505
Lowenza ....................... 215
Lowler .......................... 526
Lownes .. 300, 302, 305, 327, 328, 330, 331, 334, 335
Lowry ........................... 438
Loyd .............................. 565
Lucas ..... 126, 230, 297, 358, 390, 393, 494, 499
Ludi ............................... 123
Luedke .......................... 479
Luft ................................ 209
Luis 319, 320, 321, 323, 324, 325, 403, 406, 407, 408, 409, 411, 530, 538, 539, 540, 544, 546, 547, 548, 549, 550, 551, 553, 558, 559, 560, 566
Lukeman ...... 53, 68, 69, 505
Lund .............................. 348
Lundgren ...................... 153
Lundy ............................ 235
Lusk .............................. 207
Lutnesky ........................ 33
Luttropp ......................... 53
Lux ................................ 329
Lyman ........................... 587
Lynam ........................... 522
Lynch ............. 28, 29, 32, 35
Lynn ...................... 132, 199
Lyon ............... 49, 286, 297
Lyons .............................. 29
Mabray ......................... 338
MacDonald 31, 35, 115, 155, 538
MacGillivray ................. 509
Machado ......................... 48
Mackey ............ 25, 228, 241
Mackie ... 548, 549, 550, 563, 574
Madge ........................... 380
Madigan .................... 68, 69
Madonna ....................... 511
Madsen .......................... 220
Maggard ......................... 13
Maggetti ....................... 596
Maggord ......................... 13
Magner ........................... 90
Maguire ........................ 216
Mahoney ..... 29, 30, 31, 160, 266
Mahurin. 47, 48, 49, 50, 252, 260, 303, 451
Maier ............................ 531
Maines .................. 237, 239
Majors ........................... 448
Malizzia ........................ 226
Mallagh ..... 52, 97, 178, 190, 194, 291, 330, 387, 409, 435, 454, 514, 527, 529, 559, 560, 573
Mallory .. 79, 84, 86, 87, 370, 473
Malloy ............................ 47
Mamejia ........................ 238
Managan ....................... 527
Manahan ......................... 99
Mandell ......................... 381
Manfrina. 167, 281, 294, 519
Mankins ................. 321, 419
Manley .......................... 563
Mann 28, 140, 149, 315, 317
Manomi ........................... 25
Mansfield ........ 380, 514, 542
Marchan ................. 449, 460
Marcia ........................... 298
Marcum ................. 371, 460
Marian ........................... 380
Marino ............................ 50
Marion ........................... 446
Marker/VanMarter ......... 146
Markham ...................... 321
Markling ................ 437, 440
Marks ............................ 423
Marlin .................... 504, 506
Maroney ........................ 464
Maroni ........................... 464
Marquart ........... 14, 421, 514
Marr ............................... 165
Marrion ......................... 380
Marriott ..... 63, 70, 177, 266, 268, 269, 270
Marsh ............................ 230
Marshall .... 27, 35, 187, 219,

235, 269, 360, 398, 399, 400, 540, 557, 558
Marston .......................... 149
Martensen ...................... 338
Martin .... 14, 29, 59, 63, 126, 147, 148, 153, 154, 176, 186, 199, 201, 205, 216, 222, 223, 228, 244, 260, 261, 274, 289, 291, 294, 295, 296, 371, 380, 467, 469, 470, 471, 472, 473, 475, 476, 486, 488, 495, 498
Martindale ...................... 383
Martinelli ......................... 28
Martinez .................. 52, 325
Marvin ................... 135, 136
Masengill ....................... 268
Mason ................... 102, 312
Matheson ....................... 385
Mathew .......................... 325
Mathews ................. 319, 320
Matlock ........................... 40
Matney ... 268, 519, 520, 522
Matthias ........................ 414
Matthis ........................... 117
Mattingly 207, 402, 403, 404, 450
Mattocks. 178, 179, 181, 394
Mau ....................... 523, 525
Maughan ................. 588, 589
Maulsby ......... 141, 200, 201
Maupin ........................... 147
Maxson .................. 204, 210
Maxwell ......................... 432
May 309, 354, 355, 356, 357, 358, 359, 360, 416, 417, 418, 419, 420, 421, 530, 531, 533, 534, 535, 536, 537, 538, 540, 542, 543, 545, 546, 547, 549, 553, 554, 555, 556, 557, 558, 559, 560, 561, 562, 563, 564, 565, 566
Mayfield ........................ 418
Maynard ........... 49, 404, 405
Mays ............................. 513
McAdams 17, 488, 489, 490, 492
McAdams [sic] ............... 490
McAdoo ........................ 421
McAfee ........................... 53
McBane ... 92, 336, 337, 430, 440
McBride ................. 442, 444
McCabe ......................... 363

McCandless ................... 505
McCann ............. 47, 51, 329
McCartney ..... 339, 340, 362, 374
McCaw .......................... 378
McClaine ........................ 62
McCloskey .................... 356
McClure ........................ 308
McCollum ..................... 320
McCom ............................ 75
McConnell .................... 419
McCord ......................... 160
McCorkle ....... 293, 354, 362
McCoy .................. 426, 431
McCrackett .............. 47, 49
McCrakey ..................... 201
McCroskey .... 173, 363, 370, 386, 559
McCullagh .................... 272
McCullers .................... 426
McCullough .................. 166
McDermott ................... 379
McDevitt ........................ 18
McDonald ..................... 301
McDougal ................. 29, 35
McDuffee ..................... 512
McElhaney ............. 361, 362
McEntee ...................... 369
McFadden .................... 308
McFall .......................... 351
McGee .......................... 340
McGerry ........................ 14
McGill ........................... 339
McGinnis .............. 166, 347
McGlashan ........ 68, 313, 318
McGovern ...... 341, 342, 344
McGuire 407, 467, 500, 518, 520, 521, 525
McHenry 172, 322, 369, 386
McHugh ........................ 542
McIntosh ............... 117, 381
McKain ......................... 438
McKee .......................... 305
McKeen ............ 94, 266, 267
McKelvey ....................... 93
McKenna ....................... 488
McKenney .................... 341
McKennon .................... 591
McKenzie 24, 411, 448, 456, 458, 512, 584
McKim .......................... 573
McKinley 120, 122, 123, 132
McKinney .................... 161
McKinnon ................. 49, 81
McLahan ........................ 36
McLanahan .................... 34

McLaughlin ...... 92, 526, 556
McLean ........................ 199
McLeod ................. 488, 489
McMaster ....................... 52
McMichael ..... 205, 210, 211
McMillan 103, 190, 309, 386, 454, 460, 524, 525, 571
McMurray ..................... 517
McNeal .......................... 262
McNeil .... 74, 175, 262, 341, 342, 343, 344, 345, 346, 347, 348, 349, 350, 399, 498, 499, 525
McNulty ........................ 304
McPhail ......................... 541
McPhaul .. 56, 178, 351, 352, 353, 425, 427
McPherson ..... 247, 371, 466
McQuire ........................ 329
Meacham ........ 323, 324, 325
Mead ...... 312, 313, 318, 434
Meade ........................... 254
Mehlschau ... 15, 16, 17, 312, 313, 314, 316, 319, 434, 437, 439
Melchoir ........................ 307
Melfert .......................... 221
Melton .................. 329, 452
Mendenhall ............. 317, 504
Mendoza ................. 507, 510
Menser ........................... 25
Menzie .......................... 216
Meredith ....................... 218
Meritt ............................. 34
Merklein ....................... 508
Merriman ............... 134, 135
Merritt ............ 360, 389, 525
Mesquit .......................... 95
Metcalf ......................... 384
Metraud ........................ 292
Metzler ... 161, 163, 303, 484
Meyers ... 281, 283, 284, 418, 454
Michl .............................. 18
Mickelson ..................... 238
Migele .......................... 288
Miles ........ 14, 243, 337, 414
Millburn ........................ 404
Miller. 31, 71, 105, 122, 124, 141, 147, 168, 227, 229, 231, 232, 233, 234, 236, 237, 252, 288, 297, 301, 329, 354, 355, 356, 357, 358, 359, 360, 361, 362, 363, 371, 372, 409, 410, 414, 416, 433, 449, 451,

467, 469, 470, 502, 508, 532, 538, 542, 543, 547, 560, 561, 566, 581, 582, 596
Milligan .................... 561
Milling ................. 507, 508
Millman ..................... 515
Mills ....... 160, 322, 324, 434
Miner ....................... 56, 57
Minetti .................. 593, 595
Minor ........................ 239
Mirely ........................ 362
Mirley ........................ 362
Miservey ..................... 277
Missal ........................ 502
Missall .................. 198, 199
Mitchell . 149, 162, 255, 263, 518, 524, 540
Mitts ......................... 152
Moffett ....................... 371
Mohler ........................ 153
Monighetti ................. 18, 19
Monihan ...................... 466
Montano ...................... 596
Montgomery.... 33, 227, 232, 233, 236, 299, 461, 579, 581, 582
Monwell ...................... 376
Moodie ....................... 401
Moody 49, 77, 405, 489, 491, 492, 493, 546
Moore .... 15, 60, 66, 92, 126, 190, 196, 256, 266, 267, 292, 310, 336, 368, 372, 467, 469, 470, 471, 472, 474, 475, 513, 555, 585, 586
Mora .......................... 576
More ...... 201, 264, 338, 340, 354, 355, 368, 369, 370, 371, 372, 373, 374, 575, 579, 580
Morford ....................... 147
Morgan .... 67, 239, 259, 434, 500
Morgante ..................... 348
Morgensen ..................... 14
Morisoli ...................... 319
Morrell .................. 352, 353
Morrill ......................... 97
Morris.. 49, 52, 95, 120, 123, 131, 146, 175, 203, 260, 261, 286, 325, 399, 437, 502, 503, 506
Morrison.. 20, 205, 210, 280, 287, 375, 376, 377, 378, 379, 380, 381, 382, 402, 407, 411, 434, 437, 439, 470, 473, 474, 514, 516, 539, 544, 554, 584
Morrow ........................ 71
Morss ...... 185, 249, 563, 574
Morton... 129, 290, 291, 292, 329, 389, 390, 437
Mosier ........................ 127
Mosing ........................ 235
Mosley ........................ 543
Moss ..................... 48, 135
Mossman ...................... 419
Motz ...................... 342, 343
Moyer ......................... 130
Mozier ........................ 183
Mudgett . 248, 518, 519, 520, 521, 522
Muir ............ 37, 38, 39, 263
Mull ........................... 164
Mullen ........................ 255
Muller ........................ 414
Mumford ...................... 282
Muncy ..................... 84, 90
Munger .......... 205, 211, 450
Munoz ... 301, 436, 438, 439, 441, 486, 500, 502, 513
Munro .......................... 349
Murphy.. 146, 153, 216, 249, 262, 410, 524, 526, 538
Murray..... 75, 305, 338, 435, 473, 503, 506
Music ............ 248, 416, 453
Myers ....... 30, 236, 240, 565
Nale ........................... 531
Nance ................... 201, 496
Nash ............................ 23
Natale ........................ 410
Naten ........................... 97
Naylor ................... 233, 234
Neal ........................... 560
Near ........................... 279
Neece .......................... 166
Neel ........................... 373
Nelin ................... 417, 453
Nell ........................... 451
Nelson 14, 15, 16, 17, 18, 64, 81, 85, 163, 171, 207, 209, 211, 216, 269, 274, 275, 315, 317, 349, 360, 362, 395, 399, 437, 470, 498, 515, 528, 534, 587, 590
Nendel ........................ 374
Nesmith ....................... 545
Nettleton ................ 137, 138
Netto .......................... 413
Neville ................... 339, 340
Newark ......................... 31
Newhall .......... 391, 392, 393
Newlove .. 29, 148, 497, 531, 533, 535
Newsom ................. 159, 454
Newton .......... 154, 160, 171
Nicholes ................ 128, 129
Nichols ..... 58, 390, 391, 392
Nicholson ...... 118, 119, 150, 172, 173, 177, 178, 181, 201, 375, 378, 382, 383, 384, 387, 388, 389, 390, 391, 392, 393, 394, 502
Nickson ....................... 218
Nieggemann .................. 225
Nielsen.. 108, 109, 110, 111, 313, 314, 319, 395, 396
Nightengale .................... 71
Nippert ................. 409, 411
Niverth ................. 296, 357
Nixon..... 131, 132, 133, 397, 398, 399, 400, 401
Nohl ...................... 341, 342
Nolan .......................... 372
Noriega ........................ 301
Norman ............ 95, 100, 103
Norris ...... 49, 123, 191, 192, 195, 197, 198, 200, 201, 204, 207, 261, 294, 326, 330, 334, 402, 403, 404, 405, 406, 408, 409, 410, 411, 445, 450, 457, 458, 573, 592, 594, 595
Norton .......................... 157
Norwalk ................. 569, 571
Novo ........................... 331
Noyes .......................... 279
Nunes .......................... 512
Nunn ..................... 117, 309
Nutting ........................ 456
O'Connor 178, 256, 336, 560
O'Flynn .............. 414, 515
O'Hara ........................ 540
O'Leary ........................ 379
O'Neill 57, 70, 72, 192, 228, 255, 407, 409, 501, 524, 542
Oakley ..... 65, 342, 344, 380, 462, 483, 484, 498, 499, 500, 502
Oaks ........................... 371
Obarr ........................... 31
O'Connor ..................... 543
Odenbaugh ..................... 14
Offenbach ..................... 102

| | | |
|---|---|---|
| Ohler .................. 404, 410 | Parsons ................ 491, 493 | Philbrick ............... 68, 341 |
| Ohles ......................... 171 | Pasfield ....................... 138 | Phillips .. 149, 159, 178, 247, |
| Olds ............................ 154 | Patchen ................ 486, 502 | 248, 281, 307, 319, 321, |
| Olinger ......................... 14 | Patchin ........................ 502 | 329, 358, 359, 360, 403, |
| Oliver ..................... 372, 373 | Patterson 268, 277, 326, 418, | 416, 417, 418, 419, 420, |
| Olivera ............ 268, 431, 440 | 419, 444, 479, 522, 587 | 421, 452, 453, 454, 457, |
| Olsen ...... 109, 110, 120, 505 | Patton .................... 354, 488 | 460, 498, 519 |
| Olsen-Wong .................. 226 | Paul ............................... 97 | Phipps .......................... 32 |
| Olson ..................... 164, 218 | Paulding ................ 159, 460 | Phlum ......................... 552 |
| O'Neill ............ 466, 473, 474 | Paulsen .................... 15, 439 | Pickett ........................ 529 |
| Oney .......................... 418 | Paulson ..... 17, 313, 316, 434 | Pickle .......................... 335 |
| Ontiveros ... 70, 98, 192, 200, | Paulus ......................... 306 | Pico ... 17, 95, 186, 187, 198, |
| 209, 294, 299, 300, 301, | Pavitt .......................... 597 | 199, 301, 560, 566 |
| 507, 508, 509, 510, 579 | Payne ..... 264, 374, 380, 381, | Pidgeon ....................... 410 |
| Opie ............................ 557 | 566, 576, 577, 582 | Pierce ..... 152, 347, 348, 416, |
| Orand ..... 207, 412, 413, 414 | Pearce ......................... 566 | 529, 539, 546, 576, 582 |
| Orby .................... 16, 18, 20 | Pearson ....................... 263 | Pietropaoli .................... 528 |
| Orcutt .... 143, 144, 151, 156, | Peasley ........................ 524 | Pilcher .......................... 60 |
| 164, 166, 168 | Peck .................... 146, 242 | Piles ........................... 409 |
| Ore .............................. 160 | Pedersen ..................... 312 | Pilkey .......................... 418 |
| Ormon ......................... 226 | Pedraita .... 60, 514, 515, 586 | Pimentel ...................... 436 |
| Orovada .................. 274, 275 | Pena ........................... 517 | Pine ............................. 14 |
| Orp ............................... 49 | Pendley ....................... 528 | Pinheiro ........................ 17 |
| Orr ............................... 525 | Pennington .................. 158 | Pinick .......................... 235 |
| Orsoline ......................... 85 | Pennock ...................... 243 | Pinnick ... 140, 227, 232, 349 |
| Ortega ............ 543, 549, 589 | Pepper ... 488, 489, 490, 491, | Pires ........................... 409 |
| Orvis ..................... 134, 135 | 492, 493 | Pitts ............................ 430 |
| Osborn ................... 221, 377 | Peppermon .................. 222 | Plaskett .. 146, 152, 228, 240, |
| Osborne . 155, 305, 306, 310, | Perales .................. 224, 225 | 542 |
| 333 | Pereira .................. 381, 417 | Platt ............... 134, 135, 549 |
| Oshiro ......................... 456 | Perkins ............ 129, 130, 455 | Plumm ... 147, 361, 552, 565, |
| Ostendorf ..................... 214 | Perona ......................... 181 | 573, 582 |
| Osterman ..................... 372 | Perrinoni ...................... 311 | Plummer ...................... 227 |
| Otho ............................ 166 | Perry .. 48, 49, 186, 199, 293, | Poerts .......................... 438 |
| Ott ....................... 227, 235 | 434, 509, 541, 565, 573 | Polk ............................ 239 |
| Overby ......................... 381 | Pessoni ........................ 425 | Pollock ........................ 276 |
| Overman ................... 22, 103 | Peters ..... 160, 424, 426, 431, | Poncetta ....................... 32 |
| Ow .............................. 193 | 432 | Poole ........................... 243 |
| Owen ..................... 278, 420 | Petersen ........................ 14 | Pope ........................... 218 |
| Ozborn ........................ 466 | Peterson ... 52, 113, 119, 312, | Popp ..................... 439, 515 |
| Page ............................ 186 | 314, 387, 439, 457, 504, | Porter. 24, 25, 27, 28, 31, 32, |
| Paige .................... 374, 411 | 515, 593 | 35, 36, 135, 136, 225, 227, |
| Paine ....... 132, 276, 400, 401 | Petropaoli .................... 529 | 235, 313, 318 |
| Painter ......................... 499 | Petrucci ....................... 421 | Porters ................. 28, 31, 33 |
| Palmer ............. 66, 166, 437 | Pettijohn ...................... 561 | Post ............................ 224 |
| Palmtag ........................ 538 | Pettit ................. 83, 89, 405 | Potter ..................... 219, 321 |
| Paoli ...................... 527, 529 | Peugh .......................... 87 | Powell ... 187, 198, 274, 470, |
| Park ....................... 17, 518 | Pewitt ......................... 547 | 514, 528, 588 |
| Parker .... 135, 153, 262, 320, | Pezzoni ........................ 538 | Power .......................... 447 |
| 354, 421 | Pfaff ............................ 432 | Powers ........................ 176 |
| Parnell ..... 70, 105, 181, 415, | Pfeiffer ........................ 209 | Pratt ................. 27, 110, 265 |
| 479, 517 | Pfiitzner ..... 16, 49, 403, 404, | Preisker 33, 34, 36, 175, 211, |
| Parr ............................. 512 | 410 | 325, 535, 536 |
| Parracini ...................... 515 | Phelps 79, 82, 83, 84, 85, 86, | Prell ....................... 55, 422 |
| Parshall .................... 83, 90 | 87, 88, 89, 90, 91, 92, 94, | Prentice .... 26, 28, 31, 32, 36 |
| Parslow .................. 286, 288 | 166 | Preston ............ 159, 160, 234 |

| | | |
|---|---|---|
| Preuitt ............................ 577 | Reiman ........................ 194 | Rodriguez ...... 190, 330, 336, 514, 561 |
| Prevost ............................. 34 | Reims ........................... 217 | |
| Prewitt .............. 12, 89, 404 | Reiner ........................... 218 | Roemer .... 17, 314, 316, 499, 513, 524 |
| Price ...... 445, 446, 447, 449, 455, 457, 458, 459 | Rembusch ........... 33, 36, 220 | |
| | Remick .......................... 466 | Roffoni .......................... 426 |
| Priest ............................. 471 | Remington ...... 133, 330, 421 | Rogers ..... 71, 197, 344, 414, 418, 508 |
| Pritchard ....................... 469 | Remschner .................... 321 | |
| Pritchett ......................... 25 | Renetzky ....................... 571 | Rojas ..... 149, 510, 512, 513, 524 |
| Proctor .......................... 160 | Resch ............................. 193 | |
| Prouty .................... 263, 569 | Reum ..................... 425, 426 | Rollins .......................... 212 |
| Pruit .............................. 543 | Rey ................................ 508 | Romero ..................... 68, 69 |
| Pruitt ................ 20, 194, 197 | Reynolds ... 83, 90, 101, 103, 179, 433, 511 | Rosas ............................. 559 |
| Pryor .............................. 218 | | Rose ....................... 531, 593 |
| Puliafico ........................ 411 | Rheams .......................... 217 | Rosebin ......................... 198 |
| Purkiss ............ 426, 538, 576 | Rhodes ................... 178, 394 | Rosenbaum ............ 228, 241 |
| Pyle ............................... 498 | Rhyne .... 488, 489, 490, 492, 493 | Rosenblum .... 285, 423, 424, 425, 426, 427, 428, 429, 430, 431, 432, 463 |
| Pyles ............................. 409 | | |
| Quay .............................. 514 | Rianda ........................... 311 | |
| Queen ............................ 409 | Rice ... 48, 49, 59, 60, 61, 62, 64, 65, 66, 70, 71, 72, 81, 87, 102, 115, 182, 183, 190, 266, 321, 327, 334, 342, 353, 383, 434, 495, 499, 536, 587 | Rosenbrock ..................... 20 |
| Quelliva ......................... 421 | | Ross ............... 193, 337, 504 |
| Quick ............................. 561 | | Rostad .................... 471, 472 |
| Quinliven ............... 330, 421 | | Rotheimer ....................... 57 |
| Quinlon ......................... 341 | | Rougeot ......................... 163 |
| Quistini .......................... 557 | | Routh ............................ 500 |
| Raab ................................ 81 | Rich ....................... 147, 355 | Routzahn ........................ 11 |
| Rackerby ....................... 455 | Richardson .................... 458 | Roux .............................. 446 |
| Rader ...... 446, 447, 448, 456 | Richter ................... 308, 315 | Rowan ...................... 30, 36 |
| Radke ............................ 170 | Rickard ..................... 18, 19 | Rowe ............................. 381 |
| Ragle ............................. 462 | Riddell ........................... 235 | Rowley .................... 95, 215 |
| Raleigh .......................... 243 | Ridgeway ...................... 192 | Royce .................... 134, 135 |
| Ralls ............... 236, 237, 239 | Riffe .............................. 159 | Royden ................... 506, 571 |
| Ramage . 182, 384, 385, 394, 551 | Riggs ............................. 271 | Rubalcava ....................... 23 |
| | Righetti .................. 358, 536 | Rubel ... 17, 79, 91, 311, 373, 501 |
| Ramey .................... 329, 371 | Riley .............. 134, 135, 320 | |
| Ramirez ......................... 378 | Rimell ............................. 48 | Rucker ........................... 188 |
| Ramsey .......................... 376 | Ringo ..................... 182, 183 | Ruckle ............................ 57 |
| Rancher .......................... 61 | Riordan .......................... 515 | Ruckman ....................... 471 |
| Randall ............. 49, 170, 484 | Rippey ........................... 305 | Rude ............... 491, 594, 595 |
| Rardin ............................ 556 | Risk ............................... 500 | Ruffoni .......................... 413 |
| Ratcliff ........................... 596 | Rivera ............................ 510 | Ruggera ......................... 319 |
| Raughilda ...................... 173 | Rivers ............................ 381 | Ruh ................................ 211 |
| Raybourn ....................... 104 | Roach ............................ 313 | Ruiz . 25, 202, 209, 278, 359, 417, 507, 508, 509, 510, 511, 512 |
| Razo .............................. 270 | Roads ............. 252, 297, 451 | |
| Reardin .......................... 556 | Robbins ........ 17, 22, 23, 242 | |
| Reber ............................. 441 | Roberts .. 229, 528, 558, 564, 575, 576, 577, 578, 579, 582, 583 | Rule ............................... 594 |
| Rector .................... 485, 496 | | Runels ... 316, 378, 379, 433, 434, 435, 437, 438, 439, 440, 441 |
| Redmond ........................ 76 | | |
| Redwine .......................... 43 | Robertson ....... 190, 454, 460 | |
| Ree ........................ 542, 543 | Robinson ... 76, 83, 286, 401, 408, 411, 594, 595 | *Runnels* ........... 433, 434, 435 |
| Reed . 97, 101, 306, 531, 566 | | Rupe ............................... 39 |
| Reese ............................. 331 | Robison ..... 14, 15, 218, 485, 497 | Ruperto ........................... 68 |
| Reich ............................... 69 | | Rupp ...................... 236, 240 |
| Reid ..... 83, 88, 89, 146, 267, 268 | Robrecht ................ 354, 359 | Rusk ............................... 518 |
| | Rock .............................. 516 | Russell . 75, 76, 77, 360, 442, 443, 582 |
| Reik .............................. 218 | Roddick ......................... 448 | |
| Reilly ..................... 204, 406 | Rodoni .................... 215, 216 | Russo ............................. 146 |

| | | |
|---|---|---|
| Rust .............. 457, 461 | Schmitt .................. 380 | Shearin .................... 271 |
| Rutherford .............. 428 | Schnebly .................. 30 | Sheehy ......... 28, 31, 36, 439 |
| Rutledge .................. 555 | Schnepple ................ 132 | Sheen ..................... 264 |
| Ryan ........ 16, 175, 504, 571 | Schoening ................ 473 | Shefty .................. 17, 19 |
| Ryce .................. 545, 550 | Schofield ................. 312 | Shelburn .................. 147 |
| Sadler ................ 410, 502 | Schultz .................... 274 | Sheldon ................... 238 |
| Saenz ..................... 513 | Schulze ................ 48, 515 | Shell ...................... 326 |
| Saladin .................... 191 | Schurtz ..................... 52 | Shelley ............... 271, 315 |
| Salas ..................... 553 | Schutt ..................... 239 | Shelly ................ 271, 341 |
| Salazar .................... 512 | Schwab .................... 345 | Shelton .......... 299, 401, 420 |
| Saling ..................... 206 | Schwabacher .............. 359 | Shepard ................... 132 |
| Salladay ................... 101 | Schwartz .................. 427 | Sheperd ................... 546 |
| Salyears ................... 499 | Schwarz ................... 160 | Shepherd ............. 546, 562 |
| Salyers .................... 462 | Scoles ..................... 148 | Sherer ................ 146, 171 |
| Sample .................... 187 | Scott 45, 159, 180, 190, 198, | Sherman 124, 387, 485, 495, 525 |
| Sampson .. 50, 180, 193, 358, 458, 497, 522 | 238, 247, 248, 251, 252, 253, 255, 268, 278, 291, | Sherrill .......... 27, 31, 60, 170 |
| Sanchez ................ 98, 546 | 298, 315, 329, 330, 333, | Sherwood ...... 118, 223, 228, 234, 241 |
| Sander .................... 380 | 335, 358, 403, 404, 416, | Shield ..................... 160 |
| Sandercock ........... 154, 360 | 445, 446, 449, 451, 452, | Shiffrar ..................... 30 |
| Sanders .. 250, 272, 273, 274, | 453, 454, 455, 456, 457, | Shimmin .................. 309 |
| 275, 307, 320, 488, 489, | 458, 459, 460, 461, 484, | Shipman .................. 336 |
| 490, 491, 492, 514, 575, | 498, 505, 507, 524, 558, | Shipsey ................ 29, 30 |
| 582 | 592 | Shoemaker ..... 185, 186, 198, |
| Sands ...... 544, 545, 562, 575 | Scouten .................. 237, 238 | 564, 566, 576, 582 |
| Sanford .................... 238 | Scribner .................... 48 | Sholes ..................... 158 |
| Sanor ...................... 255 | Scull ............... 118, 382, 387 | Short ...................... 240 |
| Sans ....................... 313 | Seals ....................... 239 | Shoup ..................... 381 |
| Santee ..................... 239 | Sears .................. 567, 575 | Showers ................... 145 |
| Santens ... 545, 547, 563, 566, 567, 575 | Sedgwick ... 47, 52, 112, 113, 114, 115, 525 | Shragge ................... 432 |
| Santos ..................... 502 | Sedwick .................... 49 | Shuart ................ 268, 269 |
| Satnam ..................... 45 | Seim ...................... 340 | Shubert .................... 147 |
| Sauders ................... 239 | Seitrich .................... 346 | Shumaker ................. 543 |
| Saulsbury. 64, 169, 170, 185, 198, 298, 470, 484, 498, 499, 501, 502, 576, 582 | Sellers ...... 99, 467, 471, 472, 473, 476 | Shutts ..................... 510 |
| Saunders ................. 197, 255 | Semper .................... 544 | Sibilio ....................... 49 |
| Sawyer ... 133, 253, 321, 450 | Serna ...................... 571 | Sibley ............. 54, 179, 180 |
| Sawyers .......... 194, 197, 358 | Serpa ............... 17, 319, 321 | Sickafoose ............. 460, 461 |
| Sayler .............. 36, 417, 419 | Severns ................ 505, 571 | Siebert .................... 460 |
| Saylor ..................... 361 | Sewell ..................... 525 | Siegel ..................... 303 |
| Scaroni ..... 31, 177, 425, 538 | Seymore .................. 457 | Sierra ...... 248, 315, 339, 374 |
| Schaeffer ................... 49 | Seymour ................... 320 | Silliman ... 33, 128, 129, 130, 132 |
| Schaffenberg .......... 527, 528 | Shaffer ................. 25, 216 | Silva . 98, 353, 417, 436, 526 |
| Scharer ..................... 20 | Shane ...................... 354 | Silveira .................... 529 |
| Schatz .................... 142 | Shannon ................. 267, 268 | Silver ...................... 242 |
| Schelgel ................... 554 | Sharer ...................... 587 | Silverton ................... 307 |
| Schiefferly ................. 324 | Sharp ...................... 383 | Silvia ....................... 53 |
| Schilda .................... 404 | Sharren .................... 271 | Simas ..................... 325 |
| Schilling ................... 215 | Shattuck ................ 116, 498 | Simko ..................... 206 |
| Schlee ..................... 508 | Shaug ..................... 146 | Simmler ................... 362 |
| Schlegel. 552, 554, 559, 565, 573 | Shaw .................. 193, 196 | Simmons .................. 160 |
| Schlinder ................... 68 | Shay .................. 196, 379 | Simon ..................... 294 |
| Schmidt ................... 543 | Shea ...................... 379 | Simons .................... 234 |
| | Sheaffe .................... 138 | Simpson .................. 257 |
| | Sheakley ................... 479 | Sims ...................... 135 |

Sinclair ............... 76, 264
Singleton ........ 292, 293, 298
Sinsheimer............... 52, 360
Sittenfield ...................... 160
Sitton ..................... 438, 515
Slater .............. 331, 334, 436
Slaugh ........................... 588
Slayton .......................... 462
Sleath ............................ 504
Slebeska ........................ 343
Smailes ...................... 63, 64
Small ............................. 127
Smalley .......... 228, 241, 331
Smith. 16, 22, 24, 28, 29, 31,
 48, 83, 94, 99, 112, 114,
 115, 128, 129, 132, 142,
 154, 163, 166, 176, 189,
 192, 195, 201, 216, 218,
 237, 242, 258, 259, 260,
 267, 274, 285, 288, 292,
 306, 307, 315, 328, 348,
 360, 373, 386, 387, 394,
 399, 401, 406, 407, 410,
 418, 419, 434, 436, 448,
 452, 454, 456, 482, 484,
 485, 488, 495, 497, 500,
 501, 504, 506, 510, 511,
 512, 513, 525, 561, 564,
 569, 574, 576, 594
Smithers ......... 154, 174, 175
Smyth ............................... 95
Smythe ............................ 96
Snider ............................ 129
Snively .......................... 304
Snodgrass ..................... 147
Snow . 7, 110, 206, 462, 484,
 499, 500, 548, 549, 550,
 551, 564, 576, 582
Snudden ....................... 495
Snyder ............... 33, 175, 387
Soares ........................... 426
Soper ............................. 344
Sorensen ....................... 293
Sorenson ......... 307, 321, 509
Soria ................................ 99
Soto ............................... 479
South .................... 250, 479
Southwick ..................... 313
Souza 68, 255, 424, 425, 538
Spackman ..................... 244
Spalding ........................ 154
Spangle ................. 447, 448
Sparks ...................... 31, 32, 588
Spaulding ...... 152, 154, 201,
 233, 371, 504
Spears ........................... 513

Spedick .......................... 143
Speed. 92, 93, 142, 148, 463,
 464, 465
Speer ............................. 346
Speers ........................... 130
Spencer ....... 35, 74, 140, 141,
 152, 219, 227, 570
Speyer ................... 160, 427
Spinage .......................... 134
Spinning ................. 134, 135
Spitler ............................ 580
Spittler ................... 232, 580
Squier .............................. 33
Squires .......................... 409
St Clair .. 154, 228, 232, 240,
 241, 572, 577, 580
Stafford ......................... 254
Standt ........................... 481
Stanfield ........................ 410
Stanley ............ 309, 329, 498
Starnes ............................ 17
Stater ..................... 504, 569
Staudt ........................... 156
Steele ....................... 62, 174
Steffensen ..................... 166
Steiert ............................. 72
Stein .............................. 391
Steinhart ................. 423, 427
Stejer ............................. 225
Stemper.. 544, 545, 547, 552,
 553, 554, 563, 565, 566,
 573, 575, 582
Stemple ......................... 242
Stephan ......................... 218
Stephens 137, 138, 320, 466,
 467, 468, 469, 470, 471,
 472, 473, 474, 475, 575,
 588
Stephenson ................... 113
Stepner ........................... 53
Stevens .. 129, 130, 132, 133,
 137, 139, 163, 466, 468,
 472, 589
Stevenson ...... 128, 129, 208,
 355, 357, 370
Stever ........................... 527
Stewart .. 102, 201, 243, 250,
 340, 371, 372, 373, 452,
 550, 551, 591
Stickney ........................ 343
Still ....................... 160, 162
Stillwell ......................... 195
Stiranka ........................ 346
Stoddard ............... 148, 151
Stokes 70, 72, 156, 405, 478,
 479, 480, 481, 482

Stone ............ 138, 214, 413
Stonebarger ................... 166
Stonier ........................... 159
Storke ......... 74, 77, 188, 422
Story .............................. 384
Stotera ............................ 56
Stovall .................... 539, 540
Stover ............................ 219
Stowell .. 285, 288, 289, 300,
 303, 309, 372, 462, 467,
 483, 485, 486, 487, 488,
 489, 490, 491, 492, 493,
 494, 495, 496, 497, 498,
 499, 500, 501, 502, 525,
 539, 540, 541, 556, 557
Stratton ........................... 78
Straub ............................. 97
Streeter ........................... 14
Stringer ................. 212, 213
Strohn ........................... 556
Strong .... 210, 217, 218, 327,
 380, 534
Stuart ............................ 203
Stubblefield ..... 71, 163, 190,
 252, 291, 327, 329, 451,
 452, 519, 521, 530, 531,
 533, 535, 537, 573, 582
Studley ......................... 313
Sturgeon 263, 503, 504, 505,
 506, 507, 509, 513, 569,
 571
Suey 382, 385, 386, 387, 391,
 392
Sugden .... 251, 253, 452, 459
Sulan ............................... 50
Sullivan .... 72, 143, 301, 534
Summerfield .................. 401
Summers . 14, 156, 414, 485,
 523
Sumner ........... 160, 171, 509
Sunday .......................... 206
Surgy ............................ 219
Sutfin .............. 562, 575, 581
Sutter .............................. 94
Sutton ..... 356, 363, 416, 453
Swain ..... 205, 375, 380, 514,
 515, 516
Swan ............................. 215
Swaze ........................... 582
Sween ........................... 158
Sweeney ....................... 420
Sweet ...... 120, 121, 122, 128
Swift .............................. 134
Sydess ........................... 307
Sylvester ....................... 244
Syverson ......................... 42

Tabb ............................. 464
Taft ............... 234, 297, 419
Takken ......................... 505
Talmadge ............... 433, 434
Tankersley ............. 418, 419
Tapscott ....................... 411
Tartaglia ...................... 515
Tausig ........................... 237
Taylor 15, 30, 32, 40, 64, 66, 138, 140, 168, 192, 193, 235, 236, 275, 326, 339, 349, 350, 385, 409, 411, 426, 460, 507, 515, 576
Teague ........................... 76
Teixeira ......................... 48
Temple ......................... 242
Ternes ........................... 100
Terra ............................. 337
Terradell ...................... 268
Terrill ........................... 175
Terry ............... 186, 337, 440
Testerman ............. 553, 559
TeWinkle ....................... 60
Thackrey ...................... 331
Thatcher ................ 329, 452
Thayer ................. 53, 68, 69
Thea ............................. 360
Theobald ....................... 64
Thine ............................ 338
Thomas .... 84, 177, 213, 217, 218, 285, 371, 372, 402, 404, 405, 408, 409
Thomasdatter ................ 312
Thompson 81, 101, 212, 213, 214, 255, 301, 307, 308, 310, 315, 319, 372, 381, 402, 403, 427, 438, 466, 467, 468, 469, 471, 538, 550, 551, 595
Thomsen ....................... 110
Thornberg ..................... 526
Thornburg 31, 32, 33, 42, 60, 68, 87, 97, 201, 211, 357, 362, 363, 369, 372, 415, 462, 494, 530, 571
Thornburgh ..... 60, 124, 143, 247, 293, 466
Thorne ............ 383, 384, 394
Thorner ........................ 452
Thornton ...................... 446
Thorp .................... 225, 421
Thorpe .................. 307, 310
Thrailkill ...................... 168
Thurber ........................ 421
Tico .............................. 293
Tietzen ................... 172, 382

Tilley . 31, 70, 181, 221, 316, 415, 517
Tinker ........................... 356
Tinsley ......................... 219
Tobey .................... 105, 107
Tobin ...................... 57, 303
Todd ............................ 439
Tognazzi ........................ 23
Tognazzini ..... 440, 537, 545, 546, 562
Tognin .......................... 360
Tognini ........................ 360
Tokuda ......................... 510
Tolladay ....................... 255
Tomasini 220, 221, 359, 380, 413, 507, 511, 512, 513
Tomer ........................... 452
Tonascia ........................ 29
Tonini .................... 531, 538
Tooley .......................... 137
Toomire .......................... 97
Toquini ......................... 254
Torchiana ..................... 237
Torgeson ...................... 213
Torrence ................ 307, 310
Townsend ............... 290, 297
Toy .. 83, 88, 90, 91, 94, 106, 107, 268, 518, 519, 520, 521, 522
Trabucco ...................... 199
Travers ..... 21, 523, 524, 525
Treat ............................ 358
Trefts .................... 218, 536
Treloar .................. 228, 240
Trimble ........................ 371
Trindade ...................... 502
Trinidad ............... 507, 513
Triplett ............. 74, 231, 380
Tripp ............ 11, 24, 380, 514
Trivelpiece ............. 540, 557
Tron ............................. 184
Trott .. 65, 74, 175, 192, 193, 201, 286, 297, 383, 385, 407
Trotter .......................... 238
Troup ........................... 165
Trucano ................. 549, 564
True ............................. 206
Truesdale ............... 217, 218
Trujillo ......................... 330
Trumbull 485, 495, 496, 497, 498, 501, 525
Trunell ......................... 500
Trussell .......................... 35
Tubbs ........................... 550
Tucker ... 117, 153, 282, 419,

420, 421
Tulles ........................... 571
Tullman ....................... 488
Tulloh .......................... 528
Tumbleson ..................... 20
Tuning ......................... 405
Tunnell .... 71, 115, 141, 147, 148, 149, 203, 208, 233, 288, 296, 297, 299, 300, 301, 304, 306, 309, 310, 325, 357, 380, 467, 486, 497, 498, 508, 509, 548, 579, 580
Turek ...... 526, 527, 528, 529
Turnage ................. 206, 210
Turner ............. 72, 160, 474
Turvey .......................... 556
Tuso ............................. 348
Tuttle ........ 38, 487, 511, 538
Tveidt ................... 549, 564
Twisselman ................... 237
Twitchell 162, 201, 233, 248, 266, 309, 310, 530, 531, 532, 533, 534, 535, 536, 537, 538, 539, 540, 541, 542, 543, 544, 545, 546, 548, 549, 550, 553, 554, 555, 558, 560, 561, 562, 563, 564, 565, 566, 567, 568, 573, 574, 575, 576, 577, 578, 579, 580, 581
Twyford .......... 518, 521, 522
Tyler ............................ 338
Tyrell ........................... 529
Ulery ............................ 340
Ulmer ........................... 320
Umbro .......................... 339
Unangst .... 51, 193, 196, 330
Unis ............................... 67
Updegraff ..................... 507
Upton ................... 171, 292
Utley ..................... 106, 587
Valentinsen ................... 110
Valenzuela ........ 93, 507, 508
Van Cleve ....................... 62
Van Geen ...................... 556
Van Horn ...................... 376
Van Nelson .................... 16
Van Pelt ....................... 225
Van Reese .................... 356
Van Stone ....... 274, 275, 590
Van Valkenburg .............. 62
Van Wormer ................. 501
Vance ............ 243, 511, 513
Vandyke ...................... 180
Vanina .......................... 205

Vann ............... 302, 484, 501
Vasconcellos .................... 68
Vasquez ...................... 337
Vaughan ........................ 223
Vaughn ........................... 68
Vedder ........................... 132
Veit ................................ 239
Veith ............................... 146
Vernon .......................... 218
Vernor ........................... 319
Vestal ............................. 144
Vidal ......................... 99, 209
*Vidette* .................. 142, 144
Vincent ................... 124, 422
Virgil .............................. 65
Volk .......................... 48, 49
Voshall ............................ 14
Wachs ............................. 552
Wade ............. 160, 316, 456
Wadhams ...................... 134
Wagner .......................... 536
Wahrmund ............. 437, 440
Wait ............... 263, 569, 571
Waite 74, 219, 263, 308, 309, 504, 506, 569, 570, 571
Waiters .................. 311, 578
Walcott .......................... 101
Waldeck ........................ 556
Walden .......................... 320
Waldo ............................ 424
Waldon .......................... 415
Waldren ......................... 414
Waldron ........................ 374
Walker 35, 60, 192, 193, 196, 221, 229, 380, 390, 392, 408, 419, 455, 457, 458, 509, 594
Wall ............................... 482
Wallace ......................... 248
Wallenback .................... 310
Waller ............................ 225
Walsh ............................. 361
Walter ............................ 208
Walters .......................... 198
Walton ........................... 244
Waltrip ...................... 37, 40
Wancke ......................... 114
War ................................ 203
Ward. 36, 138, 205, 207, 358
Waren .............................. 25
Warner .................... 441, 572
Warren .... 34, 205, 228, 240, 306, 543, 553
Warwick ........................ 184
Washburn .............. 557, 593
Wass .............................. 416

Waterbury ....... 101, 102, 103
Watford ......................... 421
Watson .... 13, 112, 114, 115, 301, 419, 469, 550, 551
Watters .......................... 320
Waugh ........................... 436
Wear .............................. 265
Weatherly ........................ 72
Weathers ....................... 505
Weaver ............... 84, 91, 106
Webb .................... 208, 363
Webber .. 185, 234, 237, 244, 325, 509, 526, 582
Webster ......................... 279
Weed ............................... 50
Weeg ............................. 105
Weeks ............... 38, 230, 582
Weid ............................... 15
Weise .................... 460, 511
Welborn .................. 51, 185
Welbourne ..................... 135
Welch .... 203, 340, 545, 550, 581
Weldon ............. 24, 425, 584
Wells ..... 228, 233, 241, 286, 297, 410, 540, 541, 544, 548, 549, 551, 552, 553, 554, 557, 558, 562, 563, 564, 565, 572, 573, 574, 575, 576, 577, 578, 579, 580, 581, 582, 583
Wendling ................ 540, 558
Wenk ............................. 127
Werling ................ 27, 28, 36
Werthman ....................... 25
Wesley ................... 204, 207
West ...... 326, 334, 337, 402, 403, 427, 432, 437, 440
Westbrook ..................... 438
Westermeyer ............. 15, 16
Westfall ......................... 151
Westmyer ...................... 394
Weston .......................... 566
Weyburn ........................ 135
Whaley ........... 143, 360, 483
Whearty ................. 147, 154
Wheat .... 228, 229, 240, 540, 548, 552, 558, 562, 563, 564, 565, 566, 572, 577, 578, 579, 580, 581, 583
Wheaton .................... 65, 66
Wheeland ...................... 240
Wheeler .. 126, 240, 304, 310
Whisman ....................... 257
Whitcher ......................... 22
Whitcomb ........... 59, 61, 586

White 15, 138, 212, 326, 417, 437, 438, 439, 440, 453
Whiteley ................ 258, 596
Whitelock ...................... 152
Whitlock ......... 213, 215, 560
Whitney ... 61, 272, 273, 274, 275, 278, 570, 586
Whitsett .......... 515, 551, 564
Whitsitt ................... 550, 551
Whitson .......................... 187
Whittaker ....................... 250
Whittemore ............ 265, 515
Whitten .......................... 314
Whittington .................... 457
Wichman ....................... 105
Wickenden .... 153, 263, 380, 429, 464
Wickham ......... 544, 563, 575
Wicksom ....................... 240
Wickstrom ..................... 587
Wideman ............... 252, 451
Wiegand ......... 462, 484, 500
Wiilliams ....................... 122
Wilcek ........................... 432
Wilcox ............ 265, 346, 419
Wildings ........................ 289
Wiley ..... 192, 193, 195, 201, 238, 385, 411
Wilkerson ....... 37, 47, 51, 65, 151, 160, 304
Wilkes ........................... 105
Wilkins ... 171, 218, 304, 401
Wilkinson ...... 203, 210, 322, 325, 416, 418, 419, 420, 466, 530, 571
Will . 96, 141, 152, 153, 154, 164
Willard .......................... 240
Willett ... 118, 157, 251, 252, 330, 359, 405, 451, 455, 458, 508, 522
Williams ...... 29, 57, 64, 120, 121, 123, 131, 132, 146, 147, 153, 166, 171, 248, 259, 276, 280, 292, 306, 345, 369, 371, 401, 417, 495, 527, 596
Williamson ...... 83, 161, 279, 407, 410
Willis ............................... 61
Willman ................. 548, 579
Willson .. 545, 546, 547, 558, 562, 575
Willy .............................. 548
Wilson 11, 22, 126, 151, 212, 213, 214, 237, 248, 263,

268, 341, 342, 344, 350, 360, 363, 454, 505, 506, 527, 544, 546, 581
Wimmer ........................... 97
Winans ........................... 292
Winberg .......................... 110
Wineman .................... 15, 17
Wines ............................. 588
Winfield ......................... 481
Winter ............................ 211
Winters .. 200, 201, 203, 204, 207, 209, 210, 324, 371, 406, 437
Wise ......... 24, 256, 584, 585
Wisener ......................... 218
Witmer .......................... 404
Witzen ........................... 201
Wolf ....................... 32, 213
Wolfe ............ 117, 361, 531
Wolff ............................. 419
Wolford ................. 166, 293
Wolverton ...................... 271
Womack ......................... 374
Wood... 17, 28, 68, 135, 337, 468
Woodard 118, 119, 385, 387, 552, 553, 565, 574
Woodcock ............... 12, 224
Wooden .......................... 571
Woodered ....................... 552
Woodmancy ................... 138
Woodmansee ................. 137

Woodmansie ................. 137
Woods ............. 14, 135, 248
Woodside ....................... 493
Woodward ..... 133, 243, 471, 472
Woodworth .................... 555
Wooley .......................... 425
Woon..... 141, 229, 544, 562, 566, 567, 572, 574, 575, 577, 578, 579, 582
Wooten .......................... 436
Word .............................. 218
Workman ............... 446, 447
Worsham ................ 480, 498
Wray .............................. 158
Wright . 15, 36, 65, 212, 213, 228, 243, 291, 436, 548, 553, 572
Wrinn ............................ 271
Wybrandt ....................... 319
Wylie ..... 106, 107, 192, 196, 515, 518
Wynn ............................. 462
Wyrsch .......................... 320
Wyse ....................... 18, 589
Yaeger ........................... 564
Yager ....................... 14, 17
Yarnell ................... 260, 261
Yates ............................... 50
Ybarra ................... 270, 315
Yearsley ........................ 243
Yelkin .................... 266, 449

Yoder ..................... 400, 401
Yorba ..................... 507, 510
York ............... 326, 327, 524
Yost .............................. 146
Young 17, 37, 43, 44, 60, 61, 81, 106, 163, 179, 210, 238, 274, 275, 308, 310, 336, 387, 470, 586, 587, 588, 589, 590
Yount ............................ 517
Yountz .......................... 521
Zabriskie 411, 591, 593, 595
Zach .............................. 432
Zadok ............................ 133
Zahlke ............................. 68
Zanetti ... 531, 533, 535, 537, 538
Zanoli ........................... 349
Zanon ........................... 543
Zaragoza ......................... 25
Zederian ....................... 260
Zelluff ........................... 523
Zeluff .................... 523, 525
Zerfing ............ 259, 596, 597
Zimmerman .............. 63, 412
Zimry .............................. 36
Zin ................................ 242
Zinkand ......................... 116
Zumwalt ........................ 306
Zvolaneck ....................... 96

www.ingramcontent.com/pod-product-compliance
Lightning Source LLC
Chambersburg PA
CBHW080935300426
44115CB00017B/2823